About Pearson

Pearson is the world's learning company, with presence across 70 countries worldwide. Our unique insights and world-class expertise comes from a long history of working closely with renowned teachers, authors and thought leaders, as a result of which, we have emerged as the preferred choice for millions of teachers and learners across the world.

We believe learning opens up opportunities, creates fulfilling careers and hence better lives. We hence collaborate with the best of minds to deliver you class-leading products, spread across the Higher Education and Test Preparation spectrum.

Superior learning experience and improved outcomes are at the heart of everything we do. This product is the result of one such effort.

Your feedback plays a critical role in the evolution of our products and you can contact us – reachus@pearson.com. *We look forward to it.*

Deep Learning

S. Sridhar
Department of Information Science and Technology
College of Engineering
Guindy Campus, Anna University
Chennai

D. Narashiman
Department of Information Science and Technology
College of Engineering
Guindy Campus, Anna University
Chennai

Senior Manager—Product: Neha Goomer
Senior Editor—Production: C. Purushothaman

ISBN 978-93-671-3866-3

First Impression, 2025
Third Impression, 2026
Fourth Impression

Published by Pearson India Education Services Pvt. Ltd, CIN: U72200TN2005PTC057128.

Head Office: 1st Floor, Berger Tower, Plot No. C-001A/2, Sector 16B, Noida - 201 301, Uttar Pradesh, India.
Registered Office: 6th Floor, Tower A, Unit A and B International Tech Park, CapitaLand Chennai, 200 Feet Radial Road, Zamin Pallavaram, Old Pallavaram Chennai – 600 117, Tamil Nadu, India.
Website: in.pearson.com, Email: companysecretary.india@pearson.com

Compositor: MAP Systems, Bengaluru
Printed in India by Gopsons Papers Pvt. Ltd.

This book is dedicated to my father, mother, and my mother-in-law,
Late Shri. P. Sundaramurthy, Late Tmt. S. Parameswari and Late Tmt. Renuka Nagarajan
for their eternal inspiration for writing this book.

Dr S. Sridhar

This book is dedicated to God, the almighty, mother, father, Father-in-law, wife, daughter, and brother,
Late Tmt. Lalitha Chari, Late G. D. Chari, Late Dr P. Balakrishnan, Dr N. Sivagami, Dr N. Ranjana, and Mr. D. P. Sarathy and Family
for their love, support, and unwavering belief in me and their inspiration for writing this book.

Dr D. Narashiman

Table of Contents

Preface

Deep learning is an emerging technology that challenges the limits of human capacity. While machines are excellent in doing numerical computations, humans have always prided themselves on tasks like recognition and creativity. Often, it is thought that creativity and imagination, such as writing a story, composing a poem, or composing music, is an exclusive domain of humans. Till recently, it was thought that machines could not generate stories. But, deep learning technology is challenging that notion.

Artificial Intelligence (AI) systems have always attempted to mimic the capabilities of human beings such as making machines to learn like human beings. Machine learning attempted to solve that issue by developing data-driven systems that learned from the data. Deep learning is a branch of machine learning that uses deep neural networks to generate models that help in prediction and forecasting. Inspired by the human brain, deep learning technology could be able to solve many complex problems in image classification and natural language processing. This deep learning revolution is made possible because of the increased availability of big data such as social media data, computer hardware like GPU (Graphics Processing Units) and TPU (Tensor Processing Units), and powerful deep learning algorithms.

Deep learning algorithms excel in tasks like image recognition. Historically, image recognition marked the beginning of a deep learning revolution. These developments in image recognition influence other domains, such as the medical domain, where deep learning is used to diagnose skin cancers and other diseases. Similarly, there have been huge developments in the field of natural language processing. Its deep impact is felt by the common people now in daily life in the form of voice assistance systems such as Alexa. Language translation systems like Google Translate that can translate languages in a fraction of a second demonstrate the power of deep learning algorithms. Deep learning algorithms, such as AlphaZero, show the power of deep learning in games such as Atari games and GO. Similarly, the impact of recommender systems like Netflix and Amazon is felt by the commoner.

OpenAI introduced ChatGPT **in November 2022.** ChatGPT is a conversational artificial intelligence system that aims to generate humans. ChatGPT is a transformer-based architecture built on deep learning algorithms to generate texts like human beings, making Large Language Models (LLM) versatile and accessible to the commoner. Generative AI is a powerful domain of deep learning where the deep learning algorithms generate not only text but also images, video, and music. In recent times, machines have been put to use for creative tasks like writing stories and composing music.

The knowledge of deep learning is rated as the greatest requirement of any modern IT industry. This book is an attempt to provide a solid foundation of deep learning principles.

About the Book:

Deep Learning is designed to be a textbook for undergraduate and postgraduate students. Many Indian universities have started giving UG courses in Artificial Intelligence, Machine Learning, and Data Science. This book would be helpful for computer science and IT students who specialize in these degrees. The book aims to provide basics like artificial intelligence, machine learning, natural language processing, image processing, and computer vision that are necessary to understand deep learning technologies. The concepts of basic neural networks are discussed along with activation and loss functions. The concept of optimization and regularization are dealt with in this book.

The major deep learning networks like convolutional neural networks and object detection networks like R-CNN family algorithms with YOLO are covered to understand the basics of image classification and object detection. Advanced CNN architectures like AlexNet, VGGNet, InceptionNet, and ResNet are covered along with transfer learning.

The fundamental concepts of Generative AI are introduced in this book. The concepts of Large Language Models with an introduction to how ChatGPT works would help the readers understand modern technologies. The book also covers the Generative Adversarial Model for Image generation as part of Generative AI.

The recurrent neural networks and the recent development of Transformers technology are discussed in this book. The Restricted Boltzmann machine (RBM), Deep Belief Networks (DBN), and Deep Reinforcement learning algorithms are included as part of the book.

The book includes a variety of pedagogical features such as a summary, glossary, conceptual questions, and numerical problems to help the readers understand the concept of deep learning. The crosswords and jumbled words are given to make learning fun and give a thorough review of the fundamentals of deep learning. The appendices provide details of the Anaconda environment and Keras. An online lab manual of Keras is provided to lab experiments for deep learning.

Key Features:

- This book explains deep learning in a light and approachable manner with minimal requirements of mathematics.
- Complete syllabus coverage of most Indian Universities.
- A lab manual of Keras is provided to implement deep learning algorithms.
- Numerical problems to assist the readers in understanding deep learning concepts.
- Special focus on the basics of image processing, computer vision, and natural language processing that are necessary for understanding deep learning.
- A detailed view of artificial neural networks, activation functions, optimization, and regularization provides a solid foundation for deep learning. The details of neural networks for regression and classification are provided as a starter to understand how deep neural networks work.
- Convolution Neural Networks and Advanced CNN architectures like AlexNet, VGGNet, InceptionNet, and ResNet.
- A special focus on Generative AI would help the readers understand the latest developments like ChatGPT. The discussion on Generative Adversarial Networks helps the readers understand the latest developments in image generation.
- Helps by providing summary, glossary, conceptual questions, numerical problems, and multiple-choice questions.
- Rich pedagogy techniques like crossword and jumbled words reinforce the concepts.
- Instructor manual and PowerPoint to assist instructors.

ORGANISATION OF THE BOOK

In this book, there are eighteen chapters.

Chapter 1 deals with the introduction of deep learning. The topic of deep learning is introduced, along with a brief discussion of artificial intelligence and machine learning. The important jargon of deep learning is discussed, and this chapter ends with a brief survey of deep learning applications along with historical notes.

Chapter 2 provides the basics of artificial neural networks. The concept of neurons is introduced. Then the basic concept of perceptron and multilayer perceptron is discussed in this chapter.

Chapter 3 discusses the concepts of activation functions and loss functions. Activation functions are used to bring the non-linearity into the neural networks, and loss functions measure the error between model predictions and actual values. Many numerical problems are given for activation functions and loss functions to understand the basics of deep learning.

Chapter 4 discusses the basics of optimization theory. Optimization is necessary to adjust the weights and biases to get better accuracy. The optimization algorithms like the stochastic gradient descent algorithm and its variants, are discussed in detail. The concept of momentum-based algorithms is introduced as part of this chapter.

Chapter 5 deals with the concept of regularization. Regulation is useful to avoid overfitting in models so that the performance of the model is better for new data. Regularization algorithms are introduced in this chapter.

Chapter 6 introduces the concepts related to dataset preparation. The basics like data preprocessing, noise, and outliers are introduced. The concepts of the evaluation models and their interpretation are the focus of this chapter.

Chapter 7 introduces the concepts of linear regression, logistic regression, and classification algorithms.

Chapter 8 is a refresher on image processing. The basics of image processing and computer vision are introduced here. The basic jargon of image processing, image operations such as convolution, and the neural network way of image classifications are discussed. This chapter provides the starting materials for understanding CNN.

Chapter 9 introduces CNN (Convolutional Neural Networks) for image classification. Image classification takes an image and generates a label for it. The basics of CNN, such as the convolution layer and pooling layer, are introduced along with its parameters. This chapter gives a basic implementation of LeNet.

Chapter 10 introduces the concept of transfer learning. The idea of transferring knowledge from a pretrained network is discussed in this chapter. Transfer learning enables faster training and using only minimal resources for implementing deep neural networks. This chapter discusses many architectures of CNN, such as AlexNet, VGGNet, InceptionNet and ResNet are introduced in this chapter.

Chapter 11 introduces the concept of object detection. Object detection algorithms not only find the label of the input images but also detect the objects that are present in the images. The object detection algorithms such as R-CNN algorithms and YOLO are introduced in this chapter.

Chapter 12 deals with sequential data and Recurrent Neural Networks (RNN). This chapter also introduces Long Short-term Memory (LSTM) and Gated Recurrent Units (GRU).

Chapter 13 focuses on autoencoders. The idea of compressing the input features is discussed with a detailed discussion of the varieties of autoencoders.

Chapter 14 is a refresher on natural language processing (NLP). NLP, as a domain of computer science, deals with the interaction of humans with systems using natural language. The basics of natural language processing (NLP), along with the word embeddings, are the focus of this chapter.

Chapter 15 is about the attention networks and transformers. Transformers are neural network-based architectures to process sequential data such as text. This chapter discusses the encoders and decoders of transformers with attention networks. The concepts of LLM (Large Language Models) are introduced in this chapter with a brief discussion of BERT and ChatGPT. Some basics of prompt engineering are also introduced here.

Chapter 16 deals with Generative Adversarial Networks (GAN). The idea of generating art is called style transfer. The idea of image generation using GAN, Autoencoders, and diffusion models is the focus of this chapter. The different types of GAN are discussed. This chapter, along with the previous chapter, aims to provide ideas for the larger domain of generative AI.

Chapter 17 introduces the concept of Deep Belief Networks (DBN). Boltzmann machines are introduced in this chapter, and then using them to build deep belief networks is the focus of this chapter.

Chapter 18 deals with deep reinforcement learning. This chapter focuses on concepts that enable agents to learn complex environments using rewards. The basic algorithms like Q-learning for simple games and DQN networks are dealt with in this chapter.

Appendix A deals with the basics of the Anaconda environment and installation of Keras.

Appendix B discusses Keras. Keras with Python is a popular environment for implementing deep learning algorithms.

Appendix C is an online lab manual for Deep learning. The lab experiments for deep learning are provided online. See inside cover for steps to access.

Dr S. Sridhar

Dr D. Narashiman

About the Authors

Dr S. Sridhar is presently a Professor at the Department of Information Science and Technology, College of Engineering, Guindy Campus, Anna University, Chennai. He has an active teaching and research experience for more than 30 years. His academic career includes 25 years of teaching and research at Anna University, around four years of teaching and research at the National Institute of Technology (NIT), Tiruchirappalli, and around two years of teaching at SRM University.

He is an approved PhD guide for Anna University. He has published many technical papers in reputed International and Indian Journals. Also, he has conducted, participated in, and served as a resource person for several short-term courses, seminars, and workshops conducted at the national and International level. He has delivered lectures on Design and analysis of algorithms in the EDUSAT television Programme and E-Pathasala for Anna University. He has also served project internship in the Council of Scientific and Industrial Research (CSIR), Chennai, and the Indian Space Research Organization (ISRO), Bengaluru.

He has authored books on Digital Image Processing, Design and Analysis of Algorithms, Machine Learning, and Python Programming.

Dr D. Narashiman is presently a faculty in the Department of Information Science and Technology, College of Engineering, Guindy Campus, Anna University, Chennai. His PhD research work is based on translating Text to Sign Language gestures. He has won the best project and best paper award based on his research work. His areas of Interest include Deep Learning, Natural language Processing, Animation, and Video Analytics.

Acknowledgments

A book of this nature could not have been possible without the help of friends, colleagues, and well-wishers. We thank all the students in our classes who have motivated us to write a book on Deep Learning. All the materials of this book are tested in the class, and we express our gratitude to the students who provided valuable feedback. We express our gratitude to all our colleagues at the Department of Information Science and Technology, College of Engineering, Anna University, for their support and inspiration. Our colleagues at the National Institute of Technology, Thiruchirapalli, Vellore Institute of Technology, Vellore, and SRM University deserve special mention for their constructive suggestions for the betterment of this book.

Dr S. Sridhar acknowledges the support provided by his wife, Dr N. Vasanthy, and daughters, Dr S. Shobika and Dr S. Shreevarshika, for providing constant support and encouragement for writing this book.

Dr D. Narashiman acknowledges the support provided by his wife, Dr N. Sivagami, his daughter, Dr N. Ranjana, and his brother D. P. Sarathy and his family for the support provided for writing this book.

The authors also acknowledge the great support provided by Ms. Neha Goomer and Mr. Purushothaman at various points to improve the contents of this book. We reserve our special thanks to the reviewers of the book for their review to improve the quality of the book. The authors express their gratitude to Pearson Education for its continuous encouragement and support.

Dr S. Sridhar
Dr D. Narashiman

List of Reviewers

Pearson would like to credit the reviewers (mentioned below) for their timely and valuable feedback that helped in enhancing the content:

AMIT KONAR
Department of Electronics and Telecommunication Engineering
Jadavpur University, Kolkata
West Bengal

ASHUTOSH KUMAR
Department of Computer Science and Engineering
Institute of Technology Baun, Uttarkashi
Uttarakhand

RAJIB GHOSH
Department of Computer Science and Engineering
National Institute of Technology Patna
Bihar

SATVIK VATS
Department of Computer Science and Engineering
Graphic Era Hill University, Dehradun
Uttarakhand

Introduction to Deep Learning

CHAPTER 1

> We're living in the age of AI, where technology has the power to augment human intelligence and transform industries. — **Jensen Huang**

Credits: © Jensen Huang

Deep learning is a branch of machine learning that challenges human capability in many tasks, pushing the limits of what machines can do. Deep learning is a transformative technology that radically changed the way of approaching complex problems such as image classification, object detection, machine translation, voice-assisted services, self-driven car systems, and even designing programs for games like chess and GO. The new technology of Generative AI can generate new content. like text, images, and even music. Hence, deep learning, an emerging technology with a wide-reaching impact on human day-to-day of humans is the focus of this chapter. The specific learning objectives of this chapter are:

- Explore the basics of artificial intelligence.
- Introduce machine learning concepts.
- Know about the types of machine learning.
- Provide an overview of deep learning.
- Explore the reasons for the popularity of deep learning.
- Explore the history of deep learning.
- Survey Deep learning applications.

1.1 Overview of Deep Learning

Computers are better than humans in many tasks like computation. If someone asks the square root of a large number, then an average man may blink, but computers can give results in a second. The power of systems has increased with the improvement of hardware and software systems. However, humans can outperform computers in recognition and planning. Now, deep learning systems challenge humans in recognition and activities requiring tremendous intelligence.

Deep learning, a branch of machine learning, has emerged as a powerful tool in modern society. Deep learning systems not only challenge but also extend the boundaries of what we thought was possible. Deep learning algorithms increasingly play an important role in applications like forecasting, decision-making, and recommendations, where high levels of knowledge are required. Therefore, Deep learning is an exciting field of study.

What about creativity? Often, imagination and creativity are exclusive domains of humans. Now, this frontier, too, is challenged by deep learning algorithms. In November 2022, ChatGPT was released and immediately got millions of subscribers. ChatGPT is a deep learning system that can generate text. Now, deep learning systems can generate text, images, and video. The deep learning systems can generate paintings, compose poems and even music.

The relationship between deep learning and its associated fields like Artificial intelligence, machine learning, and Generative AI is illustrated in Figure 1.1.

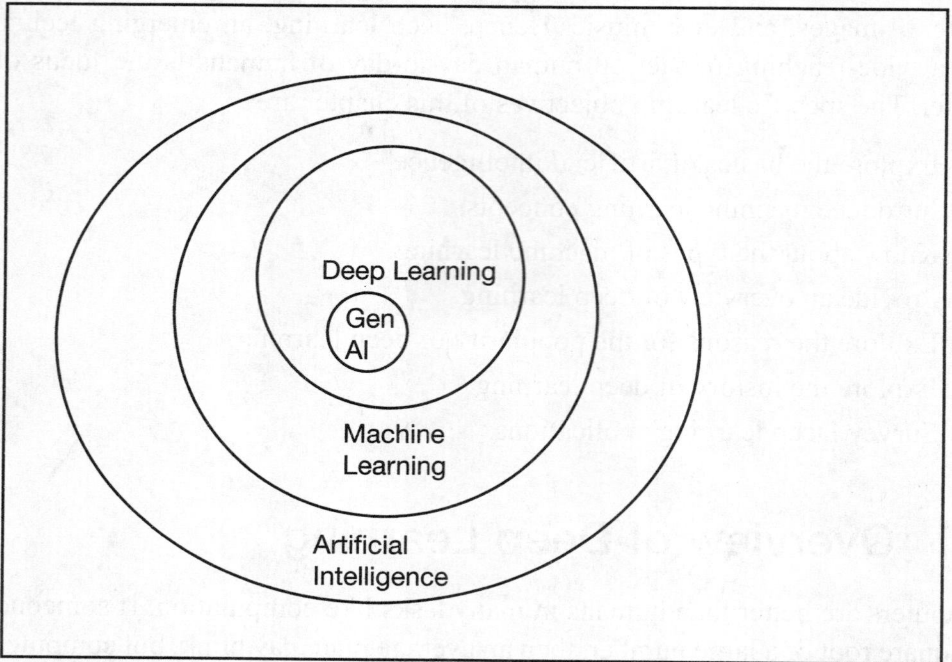

Figure 1.1 Relationship of AI, Machine Learning, Gen AI with Deep Learning

The success of deep learning has brought attention back to Artificial Intelligence (AI) and Artificial Neural Networks (ANN).

1.2 Introduction to Artificial Intelligence

Can machines learn like human beings? This question was raised by many mathematicians, philosophers, and people who have practiced logic over many centuries. The attempt to answer this question marks the beginning of Artificial Intelligence. In 1956, John McCarthy organized a ten-week project conference at Dartmouth University. This conference focused on developing systems that mimic human intelligence in performing intelligent tasks. The enthusiasm led to the branch called Artificial Intelligence.

Artificial Intelligence is an attempt to make machines that mimic the capabilities of humans. Artificial Intelligence problems are different from traditional problems. For example, solving a quadratic equation cannot be an AI problem, as analytical solutions are available. Instead, AI is supposed to develop autonomous and independent systems that require intelligence like human beings, such as learning, planning, reasoning, and understanding.

There is a variety of notions of intelligence. It may mean knowledge and reasoning ability, including wisdom and consciousness. So, defining intelligence is difficult. Also, it takes work to measure intelligence.

1.2.1 Classical Period

For instance, in 1956, Allen Newell and Herbert Simon created General Problem Solver. Another product of this era was the Logical Theorist. Also, this era witnessed some primitive conversational systems like ELZA. Allan Turing proposed the Turing test to measure the intelligence in this period. The details of the Turing test are given in Box 1.1.

Box 1.1 Turing Test

Alan Turing came up with his famous Turing test to measure the intelligence of machines. In a classical parlour game, there is a woman and a man in separate two rooms and assume these two rooms are connected only by exchanging notes in written form. There is an interrogator in another room connected to these two rooms. All communications take place in written notes. Based on the written notes, the interrogator must decide the gender identity between a man and a woman. In addition, the woman tries to help the interrogator, and the man wants to fool the interrogator.

The Turing test is a modified parlour game where a machine replaces the interrogator. The test of intelligence is that the machine must be intelligent such that the interrogator can find it difficult to pick the true gender of one from another. As per the Turing test, many machines are not able to pass this litmus test of intelligence.

1.2.2 Symbolism Period

In this period, intelligence is said to be the manipulation of symbols. Knowledge-based systems and logic-based systems are classic examples of symbolism-based systems. The focus of this era was on developing knowledge representation mechanisms and manipulation in the forms of rules. So, Rule-based systems or expert systems marked the early development. Expert systems take the input, match it with the database, and infer it. In expert systems, the expert's knowledge is encoded as rules. For example, an expert system like MYCIN was designed for medical diagnosis during this period. It took input, matched it with the database, and found all the rules matching it. Expert systems then use an inference engine to infer the conclusions from the formed IF-THEN rules. Therefore, it can be observed that MYCIN is not merely memorizing but uses the prototype of reading, matching, and inferring. Even now, Symbolism-based systems are helpful as AI planning systems. For example, Google Maps still uses heuristic reasoning to locate places on a map. Unfortunately, there was not much progress in that line of thought. John Searle's Chinese room argument conclusively proved the weakness of Symbolism-based systems (Refer Box 1.2).

Box 1.2 John Searle

John Searle made a strong criticism of the symbolism-based system. He created a Chinese room argument. In the Chinese room argument, an English-speaking person is locked in a room where the only outside communication is written notes. The person has a Chinese book, and the floor is filled with Chinese characters. In the adjacent room, there is a native Chinese speaker. Chinese speaker sends a message in the note, and the English speaker uses the book and characters on the floor, prepares a letter, and returns the Chinese speaker's query. It creates an impression in Chinese speakers that the other person knows Chinese, while the reality is the reverse. The inability to properly understand Chinese is the central issue in intelligence. This experiment led to the notions of Strong and weak intelligence.

The weakness of expert systems in achieving "true Intelligence" leads to the review of the fundamentals of AI. This review led to the realization of the classification of AI systems, as shown in Figure 1.2.

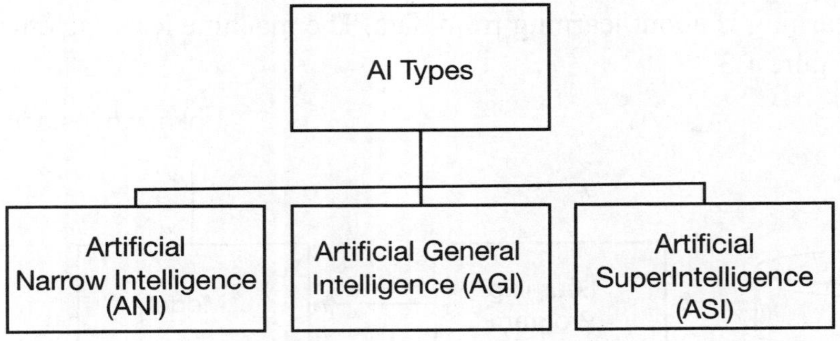

Figure 1.2 Types of AI

(i) Artificial General Intelligence (AGI):

The tasks proved more challenging as systems that aimed for general intelligence were called "Strong AI." All the movies that portray characters who surpass the capability of humans are classic examples of strong AI. However, this approach did not progress much as the programs lacked "real intelligence" as this approach was impractical in many domains. Moreover, the program depended on human expertise and could have been more truly intelligent.

(ii) Artificial Superintelligence (ASI):

This kind of intelligence is yet to be achieved and is under serious research.

(iii) Artificial Narrow Intelligence (ANI):

The focus is to develop systems that can perform a specific task better than humans. Here, the big goal of general intelligence is shelved, and instead, the focus is placed on making systems better than or at least similar to human beings. Slowly, the momentum shifted to machine learning in the form of data-driven systems and machine learning.

1.3 Machine Learning Explained

Machine learning is a branch of Artificial Intelligence that takes data as input and uses a learning program to create models.

Tom Mitchell's definition of machine learning is, "A computer program is said to learn from experience E, concerning task T and some performance measure P, if its performance on T, measured by P, improves with experience E." For example, task T detects an object in the object recognition task.

Machine learning is about learning from data. The machine learning environment is shown in Figure 1.3.

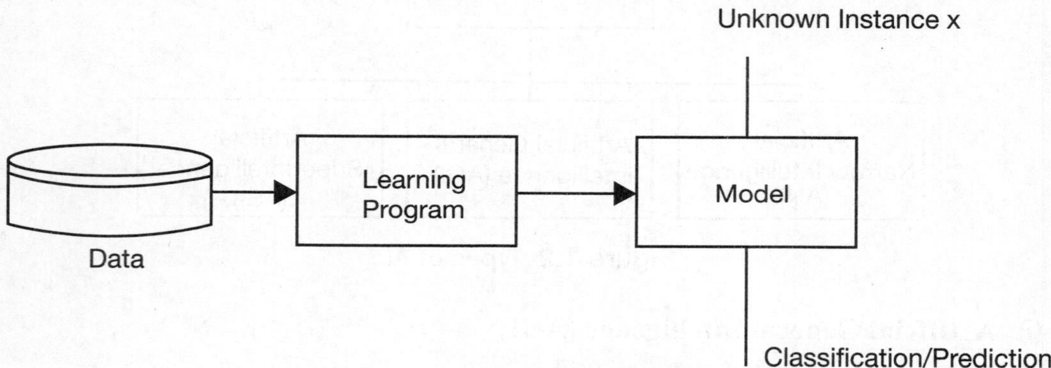

Figure 1.3 Machine Learning Environment

The created model is not by explicit programming. Arthur Samuel quoted, "[Machine learning is the] field of study that gives the computer's ability to learn without explicitly programmed." The caveat is "automatic." There are no explicit attempts to write a program for a task. Instead, the focus is to make systems "learn" concepts using the given data by extracting the patterns and the relationships that are present in the input data. These patterns are stored in the form of a model. A model is a mathematical concept that can explain the patterns.

The training dataset is equivalent to experience E. So, the focus is to use experience E for task T with some performance measures (P) like precision and recall. Course correction can be done based on the performance measures to improve the system's performance. If the performance is increased, then one can see that the machine has learned. To illustrate this definition, let us take a classification program that classifies an input mail as spam/not spam mail. In this case, the tasks, experience, and performance measures can be defined as follows:

- Task T is the classification of emails into spam or not-spam mail.
- Experience E is the training dataset labelled emails where every mail is associated with a predefined label.
- Performance measures P may be the percentage of correctly classified mail, and performance metrics can be sensitivity, specificity, and accuracy.

If the system's performance can be increased to the level of humans, one can suggest that the system is intelligent.

The flow of data in machine learning is shown in Figure 1.4.

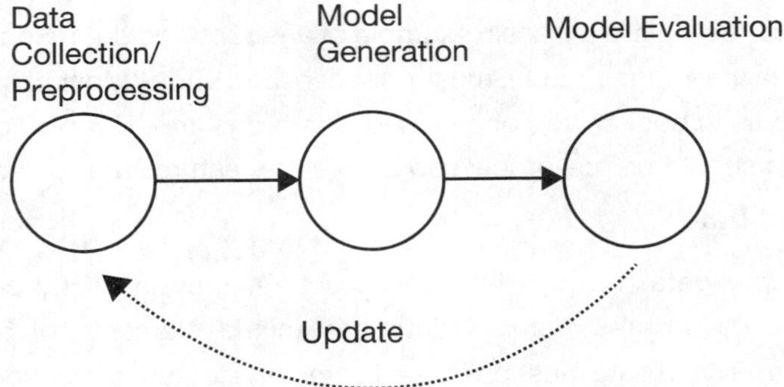

Figure 1.4 Flow of Data

Box 1.3 What is Data?

Data is a raw fact, and the processed data is called information. Data can be classified as structured, unstructured, or semi-structured. The classification of data is shown in Figure. 1.5.

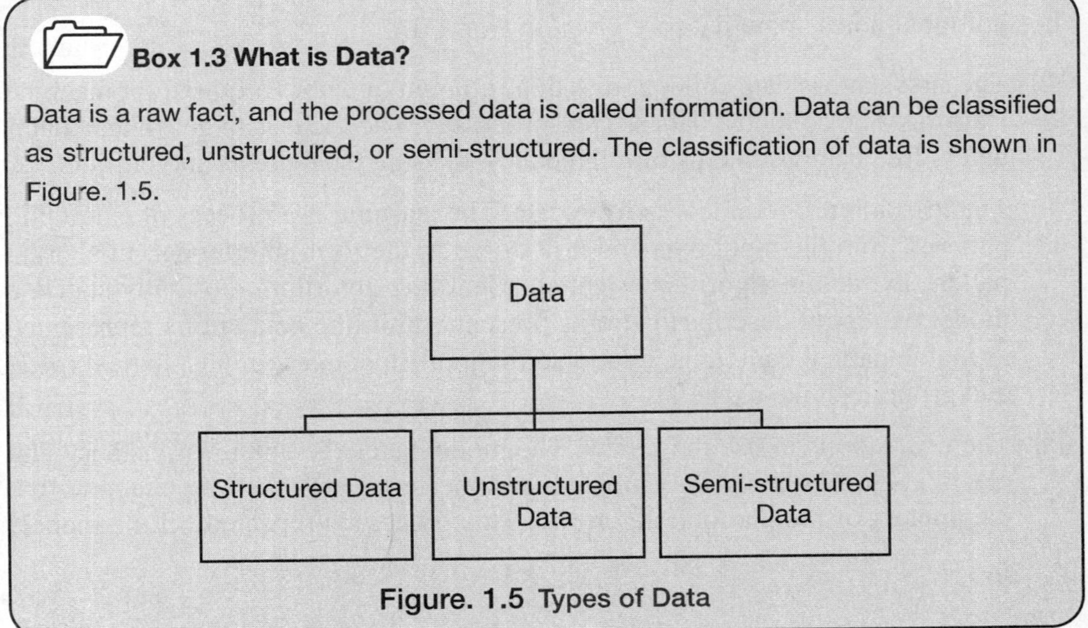

Figure. 1.5 Types of Data

Structured Data

Structured data conforms with data model structures and follows some consistency. Tabular data is one such example of structured data. The data present as tables in relational databases and Excel sheets, spreadsheets, online forms, and log files are examples of structured data. The computer systems can readily process it. Only very little data is available in the form of structured data.

Unstructured Data

Unstructured data is not an organized data. In other words, these data do not have any predefined structures. Text is a classic example of unstructured data. Some examples of unstructured data are Images, video, music, speech, and audio. Most of the data that are available around us in books, web pages, and web blogs are examples of unstructured data. These data should be pre-processed before the features are extracted.

Semi-structured Data

Even though some data have an inherent structure, they lack any conformity with the structured data. Semi-structured data has mixed elements of structured and unstructured data. These data must be parsed before the feature extraction is performed. Some examples of unstructured data include emails, XML, JSON, HTML pages, binary executables, and zipped files.

The additional notes about data are given in Box 1.3.

(i) The first stage is data collection. A huge amount of data is required for machine learning. The collected data are pre-processed. The focus is to get "Clean data" that is free from problems of redundancy, missing data, noise, and outliers.

(ii) The learning program learns from data. The learning is a process of extracting patterns from the input data and it is stored in the form of a model. In short, a pattern extraction algorithm is called a learning algorithm. Formally stated, a model explicitly describes patterns present within the data and is represented as mathematical equations, relational diagrams like trees/graphs, logical rules, and groupings like clusters.

(iii) The next step is to use the model. The model takes the unknown instance and classifies it. The error is computed, and measures are taken by changing the parameters of the learning algorithm. This process is repeated till the models work for all testing data. If the model works fine for training data but not for testing data, it means that the learning is not taking place. This situation is called overfitting.

So, the main elements of the machine learning flow are given in Figure 1.6.

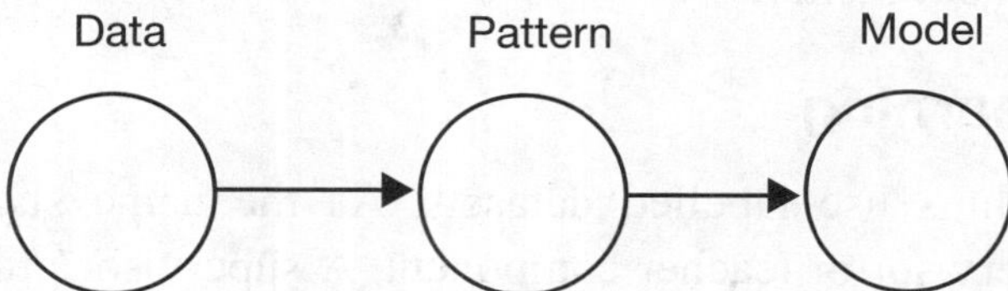

Figure 1.6 Relationships among data, pattern, and Model

(i) **Data:** The primary component is data.

(ii) **Pattern:** A pattern is a regularity of events or elements in the input data. A pattern can be visualized or mathematically that indicates the regularity, trends, or correlations among the input data. A pattern can be a rule that can expressed as a condition. Similarly, the relationship between the output and input, $y = f(x)$, can be a pattern.

(iii) **Model:** A model is the representation of the system that is expressed mathematically, visually, or as a procedure to predict or simulate systems. All patterns are condensed in the form of a model. An example of a model can be a linear regression equation like $y = 14x + 15$, where x is the input data and y is the predicted variable.

The differences between pattern and model are given in the following Table 1.1.

Table 1.1 Differences between Patterns and Models

Patterns	Models
A pattern is a repeating event or element that are in specific context.	A model is a mathematical representation of a system used for prediction.
Patterns are local and are specific to certain observations and context.	It is a representation of the system and, hence, global.
The pattern is local and applicable only to specific attributes.	The model is global and fits the entire dataset.

1.3.1 Types of Machine Learning

Machine learning has four types of learning. They are supervised learning, unsupervised learning, semi-supervised learning and reinforcement learning.

Let us discuss about them now.

Supervised Learning

Supervised algorithms use labelled datasets. As the name suggests, supervised learning has a supervisor or teacher component. A supervisor provides the labelled data to construct the model and gives test data for checking the model. In supervised learning algorithms, learning takes place in two stages.

(i) Training Phase:

The labelled data is given to the learner program during the first stage to generate a model.

(ii) Testing Phase:

In the second stage, the model is tested with unseen data. The learning system aims to categorize by assigning a label to unseen data. The details of labelled and unlabelled data are given in Box 1.4.

Box 1.4 Labelled and Unlabelled Data

The input data of the machine learning algorithm can be either labelled or unlabelled. For example, let us consider the dataset called the Iris dataset. The dataset has details about Iris. The properties or attributes of Iris are called features.

The data set has 150 samples of Iris – with four attributes, as shown in Table 1.2. The four attributes are sepal width, sepal height, petal height and petal width. The classes are Iris setosa, Iris versicolor, and Iris virginia. The classes are encoded as 0, 1 and 2, respectively.

Table 1.2 A Sample Dataset

Sepal Length	Sepal Width	Petal Length	Petal Width	Class
5.11	3.55	7.41	0.22	0
4.88	3.0	4.39	0.21	0

> Each table row is called a data point, and columns are features. The target variable is called class. This kind of data is called labelled data.
> Unlabelled data are those data that are not associated with any target label. Examples of unlabelled data are images and text data that do not have labels.

The machine learning types are shown in Figure 1.7.

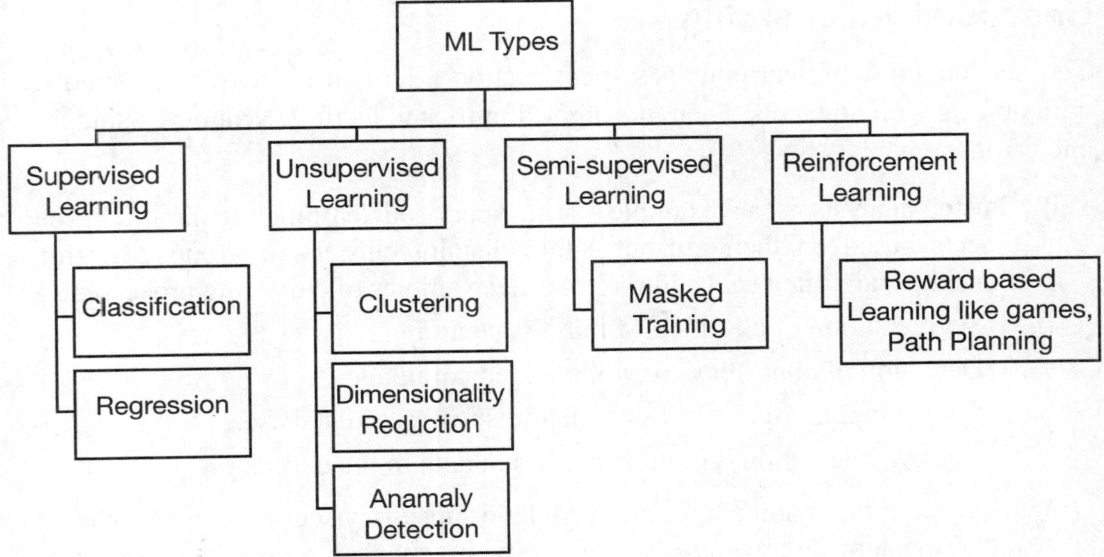

Figure 1.7 Types of Machine Learning Tasks

Supervised learning can solve two machine learning tasks – Classification and Regression.

(i) Classification is the process of assigning a label or predefined category for the input data. Classification is a supervised method that takes the input as independent variables. The target attribute is called a label or dependent variable. Formally stated, the focus is to search for a discrete function f, such that, $y = f(x) \in \{c_1, c_2, \cdots, c_n\}$, where $\{c_1, c_2, \cdots, c_n\}$ a set of all possible classes. The classification focuses on predicting the 'label' that is a discrete form (a value from the set of finite values) by minimizing the error between the actual output and the expected output. Some of the examples of classification are:

- Classifying an email as normal or spam.
- Classify an image as a cat or dog.
- Predicting the brand of the car.

(ii) Regression models, unlike classification models, predict continuous variables such as price. Therefore, the focus is to find a function $y = f(x)$ that takes input x and generates a model. Here, x is an independent variable that may be one or more attributes. y is called a dependent variable. The examples of regression are:

- Predicting the price of the car.
- Sales prediction for a quarter.

Unsupervised Learning

The second kind of learning is self-instruction. Here, the program is supplied with objects with no labels. Then, the algorithm tries to learn by grouping using trial and error.

(i) Cluster analysis is an example of unsupervised learning. It aims to group objects based on their attributes into disjoint clusters or groups. Learning algorithms are often trial and error. Some examples of clustering processes are:

- Segmentation of a Region of Interest in an image
- Detection of abnormal growth in a medical image
- Determination of clusters of signatures in a gene database.
- Anomaly detection – Finding abnormal data in the dataset.

(ii) Dimension reduction is also an example of unsupervised learning. Dimension reduction aims to reduce the dataset with few features without losing the generality. Techniques like principal component analysis (PCA) and linear discriminant analysis (LDA) do dimension reduction only.

The differences between supervised and unsupervised algorithms are listed in the following Table 1.3.

Table 1.3 **Differences between Supervised and Unsupervised Algorithms**

No.	Supervised Learning	Unsupervised Learning
1.	There is a supervisor component.	No supervisor.
2.	Uses labelled data.	Uses unlabelled data.
3.	Assign categories or labels.	Perform a grouping process such that similar objects will be in one cluster.

Semi-supervised Learning

There are circumstances where the dataset has vast collections of unlabelled data and few labelled data. Labelling is a costly process and difficult to perform by humans. Semi-supervised algorithms use unlabelled data by assigning a pseudo-label. Then, the labelled and pseudo-labelled datasets can be combined.

Reinforcement Learning

Reinforcement learning mimics human beings by allowing an agent to interact with the environment for rewards. The reward can be either positive or negative. When the rewards are more, the agent reinforces the actions that lead to that state; in other words, the agent learns. Thus, the reinforcement model focuses on the maximization of rewards. The differences between Reinforcement learning and supervised learning are given in Table 1.4.

Table 1.4 Differences between Reinforcement and Supervised Algorithms

No.	Reinforcement Learning	Supervised Learning
1.	Labelled data are not available readily.	Labelled data are available.
2.	It uses agents to learn from the environment through its interactions.	It uses training phase to learn concepts.

Examples of reinforcement learning are:

1. Planning a path for a robot.
2. Games where the rewards are used.

1.4 Artificial Neural Networks and Deep Learning Explained

Artificial Neural Networks (ANN) is an alternate mechanism for developing intelligent systems. The biological neurons of humans inspire it. The human brain has a network of biological neurons. Biological neurons absorb information, and encountering danger triggers another neuron at a certain point. This process is repeated and finally carried to the human brain, and the brain reacts to danger. Artificial Neural Networks (ANN) create mathematical models equivalent to biological neurons.

Deep learning is the "family of algorithms using ANN structures with two or more hidden layers." By 'Deep' means the depth of the neural networks, defined as the number of levels of the composition of non-linear operations.

Deep learning places hidden layers upon hidden layers, creating "deep" networks. The output of one hidden layer is an input for another hidden layer. Each layer learns a new abstraction and data representation. Learning abstractions leads to learning subtle features automatically. Deep learning systems thus extract features automatically and can form complex features from simple features. The idea of creating complex features from simple features is called representation learning.

The differences between deep learning systems and ANN (Shallow networks) are shown in Table 1.5.

Table 1.5 Differences between Deep Learning and ANN

No	Deep Learning Networks	Shallow Networks
1.	Representation learning	Only one hidden layer
2.	The focus is not on feature engineering	Focus on hand design of features
3.	Learns global and local features	More local structures
4.	Huge datasets	Small datasets

1.4.1 How does Deep Learning Work?

Deep learning is better than machine learning because deep learning algorithms effectively learn data representations called hierarchical learning.

In representation learning, the lower dimensional features are captured first. Then, the higher abstractions are defined and learned in terms of lower-level abstractions. As a result, deep learning systems can learn the hierarchy of features of the input data automatically. This kind of hierarchical learning is necessary for deep learning, where the learned concepts are held by multiple neurons simultaneously. Each neuron represents a local concept. The processed data on multiple neurons and layers represent an abstraction distributed across the layers and multiple layers.

These representations can be useful for handling many tasks like classification clustering. The deep learning models can be classified into two types, as shown in Figure 1.8.

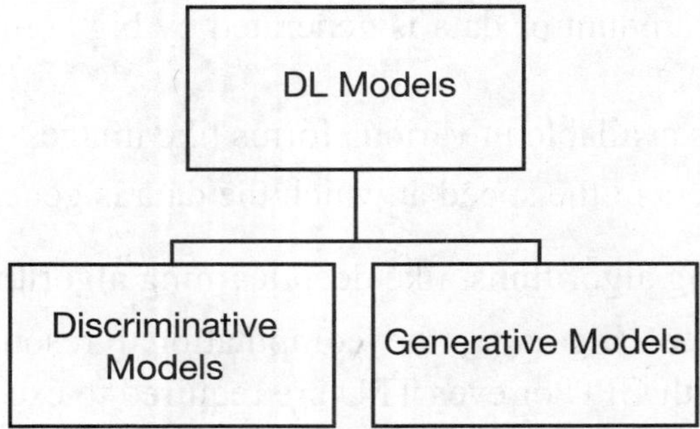

Figure 1.8 Types of Deep Learning Models

So far, the discriminated models dominated the scene. It is often in the form of classification and clustering. In general, the discriminative models are used mostly for analytical tasks. But now, Generative models is emerging as a new area, especially after ChatGPT was released in November 2022. Now computers too can generate text, images, and music.

1.5 Challenges of Deep Learning

The challenges of Deep Learning are shown below in Figure 1.9.

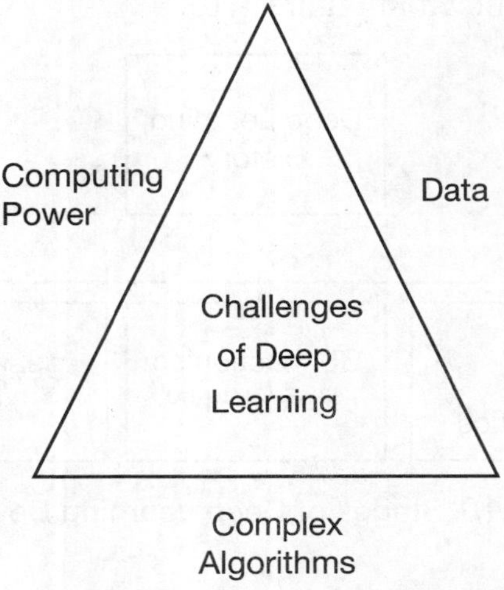

Figure 1.9 Challenges of Deep Learning

Data is one major challenge in deep learning. Big data is a field of data science that deals with data with the following characteristics:

- Volume – Huge amount of data is generated by big companies like Facebook, Twitter, YouTube.
- Variety – Data is available in various forms like images, video, and formats.
- Velocity – It refers to the speed at which the data is generated and processed.

Many machine learning algorithms, like deep learning algorithms, use big data.

With the availability of big data, the computational resource requirement also increased. Systems with GPU or even TPU are required to execute machine learning algorithms. Also, machine learning tasks have become complex; hence, time complexity has increased, which can be solved only with high computing power.

The selection of algorithms, describing the algorithms, application of algorithms to solve machine learning tasks, and comparison of algorithms have become necessary skills for machine learning or data scientists. Therefore, algorithms have become a massive topic of discussion, and it is a challenge for machine learning professionals to design, select, and evaluate optimal algorithms.

1.6 History of Deep Learning

The history of deep learning can be divided into three periods. The stages of deep learning development is shown in Figure 1.10.

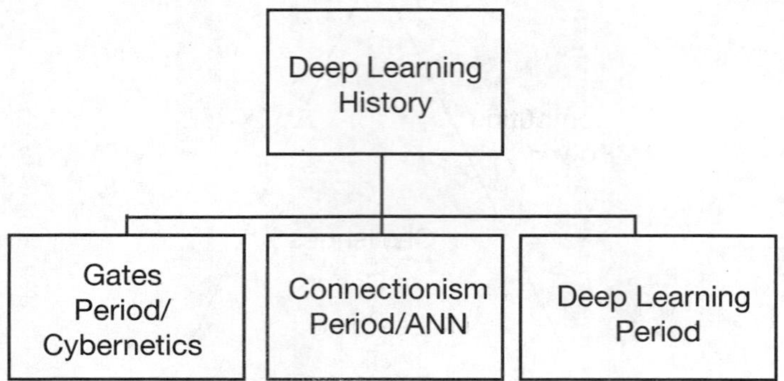

Figure 1.10 Stages of Deep Learning Development

1.6.1 Early Period

The first period is known as the gates period, where gates were developed. At that time, deep learning was known as Cybernetics, and much of this period focused on creating a binary gate using the neuron model. Much of this period was focused on creating a binary gate using the neuron model. Perceptron created binary gates.

1.6.2 Connectionism

The second phase, called the connectionism phase, focuses on Artificial neural networks (ANN). Some of the crucial developments are listed below in Table 1.6.

Table 1.6 Developments in ANN

Year	Persons	Remarkable Achievements
18th Century	-	The 18th Century marked the development of many statistical models for various tasks.
1943	Warren McCulloch and Walter Pitts	The concept of the neural network started, and the first neuron mathematical model was proposed in the classical paper published titled "A Logical Calculus of Ideas Imminent in Neural Activity," later called the McCulloch- Pitts model.
1949	Donald Hebb	In the book titled "Organization of Behavior," Hebb put forth the concept of activations of neurons.
1950	Alan Turing	Alan Turing created the famous Turing test. In addition, he published an influential paper titled "Computing Machinery and Intelligence." as a measure of intelligence.
1950	Arthur Samuel	Arthur Samuel coined the word machine learning. He is considered the founding father of the area of machine learning.
1952	Arthur Samuel	In 1952, he developed a program for playing the checker using the then-AI tool of alpha-beta pruning.

Year	Persons	Remarkable Achievements
1958	Frank Rosenblatt	He published an influential paper titled "The perceptron: A Perceiving and Recognizing Automaton." In Cornell Aeronautical Lab, the perceptron model was designed by combining the ideas of Donald Hebb and Arthur Samuel. Perceptron was used for image recognition and shape recognition. In addition, he published an influential paper titled "A Logical Calculus of Ideas Immanent in Nervous Activity," which pioneered the development of a perceptron that aimed to mimic human thought processes.
1959	David Hubel and Torstein Wiesel	They discovered the concept of simple and complex cells in the primary visual cortex. Both received Nobel prizes for their achievement. This remarkable work influenced ANN and later CNN in a big way.
1969	Minsky and Papert	A Multilayer perceptron was designed. Multilayer perceptrons are also called feed-forward neural networks.
1960	Bernard Widrow and Marcian Hoff	The development of Linear models. Adaptive Linear Element (ADALINE) and MEDALINE are the earliest linear models developed during the period. ADALINE can detect binary patterns. In a binary data stream, ADALINE can predict the next bits. MADALINE can be useful for echo removal in telephone systems. In addition, the concept of the Stochastic Gradient Descent (SGD) algorithm was developed.

Year	Persons	Remarkable Achievements
1970s	The Backpropagation algorithm.	Henry Kelly published an influential "Gradient Theory of Optimal Flight Paths" paper in control Theory. The idea of feedback in that work was implemented as backpropagation in neural networks. The concept of a backpropagation algorithm that distributed error backward through neural network layers was proposed. The error distribution updates the neural network weights and makes learning possible.
1976	Ackley, Hinton and Sejnowski	Boltzmann machine.
1980	Fukushima	The concept of Neocognitron is the forerunner of Convolutional Neural Networks (CNN) and the idea of Rectified Logical Unit (ReLU). Neocognitron was used to recognize visual patterns and to do pattern recognition tasks. Thus, Neocognitron influenced the development of Convolutional Neural Networks (CNN).
1982	John Hopfield	Hopfield created a network that used bidirectional lines just like human neurons. It is a recurrent neural network that aims to create a content-addressable memory system.
1985	Terry Sejnowski	NetTalk was created to pronounce English words using typed text.
1986	Rumelhart, Hinton and Williams	Generalized Delta rule and Backpropagation algorithm.

1.6.3 Deep Neural Networks

The third phase, the historical development, is due to the developments in the core field of Deep Learning and Deep Neural Networks. In 2006, ANN was rebooted as deep learning. Some of the key developments in this area are marked in Table 1.7.

Table 1.7 Developments in Deep Neural Networks

Year	Persons	Remarkable Achievements
1986	Hinton	Distributed representation was introduced where the knowledge is distributed.
1989	Yann LeCun	Yann LeCun combined CNN and Backpropagation nets. This work was to recognize handwritten checks and zip codes in US postal addresses.
1989	Q-Learning	Christopher Watkins created a Q-learning algorithm for reinforcement learning.
1998	Yann LeCun	He published an influential paper titled "A Gradient-Based Learning Applied to Document Recognition."
2000	Geoffrey Hinton	He coined the word deep learning to explain massive neural networks. The term "deep learning" was first used by Igor Aizenberg and his colleagues around 2000.
2001	Geoffrey Hinton, Yoshua Bengio, and Yann LeCun	Canadian Institute for Advanced Research (CIFAR) started researching deep neural networks through its Neural Computation and Adaptive Perceptron (NCAP) program.
2006	Geoffrey Hinton	Deep Belief Networks (DBN) was introduced with its Greedy layer-wise pretraining.
2009	ImageNet	A Stanford student named Fei-Fei Li created ImageNet. It is a vast and free database that has 14 million images that are labelled. Every year, it started conducting contests to evaluate deep learning systems.

Year	Persons	Remarkable Achievements
2011	IBM	IBM Watson won the US Quiz show Jeopardy against two humans.
2012	Google X Lab	It created a program that automatically browsed to recognize the cats in videos. It used 10000000 unlabelled images that were randomly picked from YouTube. It performed 70% better than the earlier designed programs.
2012	Jeff Dean	Google Brain project created neural nets for pattern recognition in images and videos.
2014	DeepFace	Facebook created DeepFace to recognize and verify human faces. It recorded an accuracy of 97.35%.
2014	DeepMind	DeepMind can play basic video games, and DeepGo beats the professional player of the GO game.
2014	Ian Goodfellow	Ian developed Generative Adversarial Networks (GAN) for unsupervised learning.
2015	OpenAI	Elon Musk funded open architecture OpenAI to create AI applications.
2015	Amazon	AWS was designed to help products like the Alexa search service.
2015	AlexNet Generation	The development of many pretrained models like GoogleNet, AlexNet, GoogleNet, and Residual networks marked the advancement of deep learning technology.
2015	U-Net	A biomedical segmentation project. U-net is aimed at extracting anatomical structures from images.
2016	AlphaGO	DeepMind learned to play GO and won four out of five against Lee Sedol.

1.7 Deep Learning Applications

Deep Learning technologies are used widely now in different domains. Machine learning applications are everywhere! Therefore, one encounters many machine learning applications in our day-to-day life!

1.7.1 Natural Language Processing

Natural language processing (NLP) is a computer science domain that deals with the interaction of computer systems and natural language. NLP is an emerging domain that is the intersection of computational linguistics, computer science, Artificial Intelligence, and deep learning.

Some of the applications of deep learning in natural language processing are listed below.

- Sentiment analysis is an application of natural language processing (NLP) where the words of documents are converted to sentiments like happy, sad, and angry, which are captured by emoticons effectively. Sentiment analysis programs can be used for movie and product reviews by attaching stars from five to one.
- Recommendation systems can recommend products or services. Amazon recommends that users find related books or books bought by people with the same taste as our recommendation. Netflix, which shows associated movies and movies of similar like, is an example of a recommendation system.
- Deep learning algorithms can do applications like document classification, text summarization, and document clustering.
- The latest technology is LLMs. Large-scale Language Models (LLM) are Transformer-based architectures that use deep learning algorithms that can generate text. ChatGPT, Co-pilot, and Google BARD are good examples of LLMs. The details of LLMs are given in Box 1.5.

Box 1.5 Large Language Models

Some of the examples of LLMs are:

- Voice assistants - Chatbots are the result of machine learning technologies. Some of the voice-based Chatbots are Amazon Alexa, Microsoft Cortana, Apple Siri, and Google Assistant are all voice assistants. These systems take speech commands and perform tasks.

- Developing Chatbots for customer support, Speech to text, text to Voice. Chatbots to interact with patients, like IBM Watson, use machine learning technologies.
- Google Translate.
- ChatGPT4 is a transformer-based LLM that can generate new content.

1.7.2 Generative AI

Generative AI is a new technology powered by deep learning networks. These generative models can generate new content. For example, the following Figure 1.11 is a generated one.

Figure 1.11 **Realistic, Clear and Cinematic Image of Fruit Basket Kept on a Table With Variety of Fruits**
Credits: AI Image © Pearson Education

Generative models can generate images, music, text, and paintings.

1.7.3 Image Processing and Vision

Deep learning is used immensely in the domain of Image processing and vision. Computer vision involves images and videos. This branch of computer science aims to mimic human vision abilities and helps by interpreting the visual information for computer systems. Some of the greatest applications of deep learning are in Image classification. Deep learning models can take an image and can generate a label.

Deep learning models can also locate the object. The difference between image classification and object detection is that object detection locates the position of the objects in the image in addition to the label.

Some of the other useful applications are in biometrics, where the face can be recognized—biometric projects like the identification of a person from a large image or video database.

The advances in image processing can help applications in medicine also like the prediction of diseases given symptoms such as skin cancer, lesions, or diabetes.

1.7.4 Navigation Systems

Navigation systems deal with tracking the position and movement of objects, say vehicles. Technology like Google Maps and technologies used by Uber are all examples of deep learning algorithms. These deep learning algorithms can offer vehicles to navigate the shortest paths to reduce time.

1.7.5 Business and marketing

Retail sales analysis, Market basket analysis, Product performance analysis, Market segmentation analysis, predicting the bankruptcy of a business firm, prediction of bank loan defaulters, Detecting credit card frauds, and Churn analysis. Detection of Email spam viruses, Personalized web services, Customer personalization as recommendation systems, dynamic pricing systems, and analyzing sales data.

1.7.6 IoT Applications

Now, sensors and smartphones that use sensors generate enormous data. These data can be stored and processed. The IoT revolution led to many monitoring health applications, smart homes, and smart agriculture applications.

1.7.7 Game design

Game design is a domain of computer science that focuses on the creation, design, and implementation of computer games. Deep learning is used in game programs like Chess, GO, and Atari video games. Deep reinforcement learning coupled with games marks tremendous development now. (See Box 1.6)

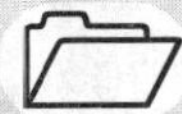

Box 1.6 Deep Learning in Games

In March 2016, a deep learning-based model, AlphaGO, beat the then Champion Lee Sedol. The machine won three games against him, stunning the world, as GO is a more complicated game than even chess.

1.7.8 Web Analysis

Web analysis is a domain of computer science that deals with the collection of web data for analysis using tools and techniques. Search Engines like Google, Promotion of user websites, and Finding customer loyalty for users' loyalty are some of the case studies of web analysis. Google uses deep learning algorithms to refine user queries automatically for better information retrieval.

1.7.9 Security and Surveillance

Security is about the methodologies and technologies that protect systems, networks, and data from unauthorized access and attacks. Some of the deep learning applications are anomaly detection, video surveillance, and biometric authentication systems.

Summary

1. Deep learning is an enabling technology that provides various advancements that impact the life of an ordinary man.
2. Machine learning is about learning concepts from data automatically without being programmed explicitly.
3. The systems that focus on general intelligence are called "Strong AI." On the other hand, soft AI focuses on developing systems that can perform a specific task as good as the humans.
4. Symbolism is the idea of developing intelligent systems using logic and reasoning.
5. Learning is acquiring knowledge and expertise through study, experience, or being taught.
6. In supervised learning, the input is given to the learner, and its generated output is compared with the actual result. This difference is called an error. A supervised learning algorithm tries to minimize errors.

7. In unsupervised learning, the learning program is supplied with objects with no labels. The learning algorithm itself tries to learn by grouping using trial and error.
8. Semi-supervised algorithms use unlabelled data by assigning a pseudo-label. Then, the labelled and pseudo-labelled datasets can be combined.
9. The reinforcement model focuses on the maximization of rewards.
10. Deep learning is a branch of machine learning. Machine learning and deep learning are different because models are constructed using neural network technology. Neural networks are models built based on human neuron models.
11. Deep learning is better than machine learning because deep learning algorithms effectively learn data representations.
12. Representation learning maps the input to an intermediate representation before prediction.
13. Neural networks have multiple-layer setups, and the lower layers serve as input for the higher layers. For example, the first layer may find edges in an image. The next layer combines this information to form intricate details. Another view is the representation view, where deep neural networks learn from data representations.
14. Some of the challenges of deep learning are the requirements of vast training data, overfitting and convergence, and vanishing gradient problems.
15. Deep learning history originates in neural networks, and deep learning has many applications that can impact an ordinary man's life.

Glossary

1. Machine Learning – A branch of AI that involves learning from data.
2. Data – Data is a basic fact or detail.
3. Pattern – A repeating trend in the data is a pattern.
4. Model – The model is an encoded pattern in the data.
5. Deep Learning – A branch of machine learning that involves constructing models using neural networks to extract concepts from data.
6. Learning – Learning is about the pattern and generalizing it in the form of a model.

7. Label – A target attribute.
8. Labelled and Unlabelled data – Structured data associated with a label is called labelled data. Unlabelled data is unstructured data without labels.
9. Supervised Learning – Supervised learning is a type of machine learning where the learning program takes labelled data as input and learns to perform tasks like classification or regression.
10. Classification Program – A supervisory learning method that takes an unknown input and assigns a label or category is called a classification problem.
11. Unsupervised Learning – A machine learning program that uses unlabelled data as input and extracts the pattern in it for tasks like clustering.
12. Semi-supervised learning – Semi-supervised learning is a type of machine learning that takes both limited labelled and extensive unlabelled data as input. It then tries to label unlabelled data using limited labelled data.
13. Reinforcement Learning – Reinforcement learning is a type of machine learning that uses agents to learn from the environment.
14. Well-posed problem – A problem with well-defined specifications is called a well-posed problem. Otherwise, it is called an ill-posed problem.
15. Bias – The inability of machine learning to predict correctly because of error is called bias due to lack of generalization.
16. Variance – This is the model's error for training data.
17. Artificial Neural Network – ANN is a learning model that simulates a human brain by forming a network of neurons.

Short Questions

1. Distinguish between strong and weak AI.
2. What are the challenges of machine learning?
3. Distinguish between shallow and deep neural networks.
4. What are the challenges of deep learning?
5. List out at least five major applications of deep learning.
6. What is hierarchical learning?
7. What is meant by representation learning?
8. What are the pros and cons of deep learning?

Long Questions

1. Why is deep learning more popular than machine learning?
2. Describe the evolution of the deep learning area.

Numerical Problems and Activities

1. Survey and list at least five deep-learning products.

Crossword

Across

1. A tabular datda is a structured data. (yes/no)
3. A label is a __________ attribute
4. Pattern are repetative structures present in the data. (yes/no)
5. DeepFake poses a threat in security. (yes/no)
7. A problem without any specifications is an well-defined problem. (yes/no)
8. Arthur Samuel coined the word "Artificial Intelligence". (yes/no)
11. Dimensionality reduction is an example of __________ learning.
13. Classification is an example of __________ learning.
14. Data is a __________ fact.
16. Patterns are stored in a __________ by the learning program.

Down

1. Machine learning is a data-driven system. (yes/no)
2. A table is an example of __________ data.
5. Google Translate can be called as a large language model. (yes/no)
6. Clustering is an example of __________ learning.
8. A neural network with more than two hidden layers can be called as deep neural networks.
9. Reinforcement learning is based on rewards. (yes/no)
10. Deep learning primarily uses __________ networks to learn from data.
12. The challenges of deep learning are huge __________, computing power and algorithms.
15. Generative AI can not generate a painting. (yes/no)

Jumbled Sentences

R	I	K	N	Z	U	B	Z	S	D	P	N	T	L	D	C	D	R	U	A	D	P	Y	R	N
H	M	F	D	S	T	I	T	E	U	V	K	E	L	C	T	L	D	K	S	O	P	L	E	O
U	D	N	O	N	E	U	R	A	L	E	Q	R	K	D	U	O	X	V	E	V	Q	P	T	S
M	X	S	K	R	F	U	O	N	B	X	F	U	E	N	Q	X	U	P	A	U	N	R	N	R
D	J	Q	K	W	T	P	E	S	J	I	Q	S	N	U	S	F	A	L	W	N	H	J	D	T
Z	M	S	B	C	Q	R	E	V	A	H	I	V	N	S	M	L	L	D	A	B	Q	E	X	M
M	S	I	U	M	S	Y	J	W	Y	V	G	P	R	U	U	A	N	N	G	X	S	S	G	Q
W	A	R	G	E	X	T	X	S	R	J	L	I	X	A	C	P	I	E	J	I	R	C	W	O
C	T	S	Y	C	E	G	U	E	H	P	D	I	X	Y	W	H	E	I	V	G	Q	J	G	M
S	E	R	O	G	K	L	P	G	K	F	C	C	W	P	E	S	E	R	G	E	T	D	X	D
Y	C	A	R	M	D	U	X	L	C	T	R	W	C	Q	E	S	E	S	V	X	L	A	I	I
K	R	A	I	H	S	V	E	E	N	M	S	E	Y	Y	D	P	E	P	S	I	W	R	A	C
X	T	V	W	N	V	D	R	W	Z	Y	U	V	W	Y	U	Y	H	L	F	A	S	O	Z	K
L	G	C	U	C	O	Q	G	P	K	N	L	G	B	S	D	A	Z	M	W	E	T	E	J	Z
M	Q	L	P	M	S	C	Y	Q	B	O	M	L	N	Y	T	W	X	H	X	H	A	K	D	O
T	F	O	J	D	O	A	E	Q	S	M	G	Q	E	A	C	L	K	C	E	U	L	N	U	C
C	C	P	U	M	V	M	S	N	H	S	Y	Q	D	C	H	F	E	J	J	E	V	O	S	M

yes	raw	yes	model	neural
structured	yes	supervised	unsupervised	unsupervised
no	yes	data	yes	yes
yes	target	yes	no	

CHAPTER 2

Introduction to Artificial Neural Networks

> The advent of neural networks marks a new era in artificial intelligence, where machines are increasingly capable of performing tasks that were once thought to require human intelligence. — **Pedro Domingos**

Credits: © Pedro Domingos

The domain of Artificial Neural Networks (ANN) is the foundation of deep learning. Neural networks form an alternative paradigm of computing that mimics brain behaviour and is designed to work like a human brain. Neural networks are effective in solving complex problems that require human intelligence. It is a data-driven system, and it takes a huge amount of data as input and extracts a model from the data that can be used to solve problems that involve forecasting, decision-making, and recommendations that normally require human intelligence. Artificial Neural Networks is already an established area in computer science. Deep learning extends neural networks by using complex and more hidden layers. This chapter gives the basis necessary for understanding deep learning.

The learning objectives of this chapter are as follows:

- Understand biological neurons and artificial neurons.
- Understand McCulloch-Pitts model.
- Know about perceptron.
- Learn to use perceptron as a binary classification model.
- Know about the structure of artificial neural network and its types.
- Understand the single and multilayer neural networks.

2.1 What is a Neuron?

The artificial neural network is an alternate way of doing computations based on the concept of neurons. In traditional programming, one writes explicit rules as a program to solve the problems. In a neural network, it is not so. Neural networks can learn from examples. It is a data-driven system where a huge amount of examples are given as input for the neural network. The neural network learns by extracting the patterns and by constructing a model. For example, if one wants to classify a dog from a tiger, the neural network should be provided with lots of dog and tiger images as input so that the network can learn. Once it is trained, it can predict the class of the unknown images of dogs and tigers.

The basic unit of the human brain and the nervous system is called a neuron. The brain contains approximately 10^{10} (10 thousand million) basic units called neurons. The basic functionality of a neuron is to receive, process, and transmit nerve impulses from one part of the body to another. All the neurons are connected to other neurons. One can visualize the neuron as a tiny messenger and this network of messenger systems carries information in the human body.

A single neuron consists of four parts:

(i) **Soma:** The neuron body is called soma. One can compare the soma to the trunk of a tree.

(ii) **Dendrites:** One can visualize the dendrites as the branches of the tree. They accept the input information from other neurons and process it in the soma.

(iii) **Axon:** The neuron's long arm is called the axon. One can visualize this as the root of a tree. A neuron is connected to around 10,000 neurons through this axon. A neuron usually has only one axon, and through these axons, the processed information is passed from one neuron to another neuron. If the neuron wants to talk with another neuron, it sends an electrical signal called action potential. This action potential travels through the axon and causes the release of neurotransmitters in the synapse.

(iv) **Synapses:** The synapse couples the axon with the dendrite of another neuron. It helps the brain to form complex networks for our thoughts, feelings, actions, and activities. One can visualize this as a connector or junction where actual communication among neurons happens.

The synapse of a neuron is connected to the dendrites of other neurons that cause the communication between the neurons. The communication is through electrical signals and chemical messages. The synapse releases the neurotransmitters when the action potential is high. Some synapses excite or inhibit the other neurons by altering the local potential of the dendrite in positive and negative directions. The transmitted signal can have excitatory or inhibitory effects on the other neurons.

The simple structure of a biological neuron is shown in Figure 2.1.

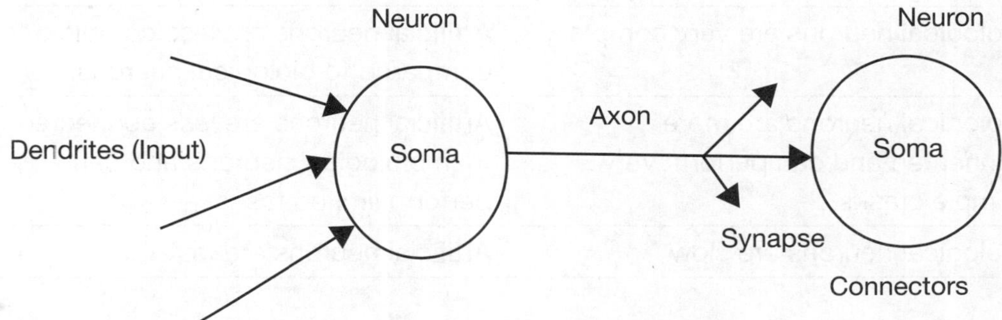

Figure 2.1 Biological Neuron

The structures of the biological neuron can be compared with a tree, and its mapping is given in the following Table 2.1.

Table 2.1 Mapping of Biological Neuron with Mathematical Model

Biological Neuron	Mathematical Model
Neuron	Computational Node
Connections Between the neurons	Weights
Dendrites	The input
Soma	A node or the processing center
Axon	The output
Synapse	A connection or junction that connects the output of a neuron to another neuron's input

Warren McCulloch and Walter Pitts published an influential paper titled "A Logical Calculus of Ideas Immanent in Nervous Activity," where they proposed a mathematical model of a neuron is published. The differences between the biological neuron and the artificial neuron are given in the following Table 2.2.

Table 2.2 Differences between Biological Neuron and Artificial Neuron

Biological Neuron	Artificial Neuron
Biological neurons are the building blocks of the human nervous system.	It is a mathematical model of the biological neuron.
Biological neurons are very complex.	Artificial neurons are less complex compared to biological neurons.
Biological neurons are more connected and can perform very complex tasks.	Artificial neurons are less connected than biological neurons and can perform limited tasks.
Biological neurons are slow.	Artificial neurons are fast.

Let us discuss about McCulloch-Pitts model now.

2.1.1 McCulloch-Pitts (MP) Model of an Artificial Neuron

The biological neuron is modelled as a computing node in this model, as shown below in Figure 2.2.

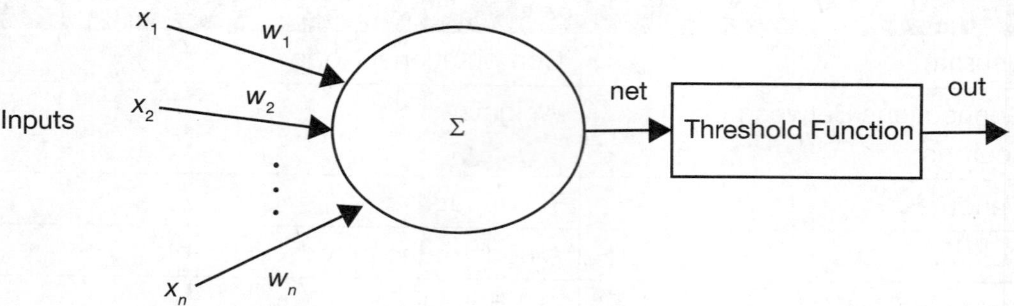

Figure 2.2 A McCulloch-Pitts Model for Three Inputs

1. The artificial neuron receives multiple input signals x_1, x_2, ..., x_n through the dendrites. All inputs to the McCulloch-Pitts models are binary. It indicates

the excitatory or inhibitory nature of the neurons. Excitatory signals have a positive magnitude, represented by +1, and the inhibitory inputs have a negative magnitude, represented by –1. The inputs of the McCulloch-Pitts model can be denoted as a vector as follows:

$$x = \begin{pmatrix} x_1 \\ x_2 \\ \vdots \\ x_n \end{pmatrix}$$

2. The associated synaptic weights in the connection links are w_1, w_2, …., w_n. McCulloch-Pitts model does not learn. So, these weights are fixed. Some even call these weights Pseudoweights. The weights of the MP models are given as follows:

$$w = \begin{pmatrix} w_1 \\ w_2 \\ \vdots \\ w_n \end{pmatrix}$$

The weights are set manually based on the given problem.

3. The received information from neurons is processed in the cell body and transmitted through the axon to multiple other neurons. The node does the summation function (aggregation) on the received input and the weights and computes the linear weighted sum as

$$\text{net} = x_1 \times w_1 + x_2 \times w_2 + \ldots + x_n \times w_n.$$

It can be represented mathematically as

$$\text{net} = \sum_{i=1}^{n} x_i w_i .$$

One can use the dot product to represent the linear combination of inputs and weights. The details are given in Box 2.1.

Box 2.1 Dot Product

The dot product (or scalar product) is a first-level operation in vector algebra. It takes two vectors of the same length and returns a scalar. Suppose, if $x=[x_1,x_2,x_3]$, and $w=[w_1,w_2,w_3]$, then the dot product is given as

$$x \cdot w = x_1w_1 + x_2w_2 + x_3w_3$$

In a neural network, the weighted sum of the input and the weights can be expressed in terms of the dot product to get a single output as a scalar. This dot product is given mathematically as

$$x.w = \sum_{i=1}^{n} x_i w_i$$

For example, x = [1, 2, 3] and w = [1, 1, 1], then the dot product x.w is given as 1 × 1 + 2 × 1 + 3 × 1 = 6. Sometimes, by convention, the weights and inputs are expressed as column vectors as

$$x = \begin{pmatrix} x_1 \\ x_2 \\ \vdots \\ x_n \end{pmatrix} \text{ and } w = \begin{pmatrix} w_1 \\ w_2 \\ \vdots \\ w_n \end{pmatrix}$$

In that case, the dot product can be given as $w^T \cdot x$. Here, x^T is the transpose of x. In short, the dot product is computed by transposing the input vector and performing the matrix multiplication with the weight vector.

4. The activation function mimics the firing of the biological neuron. In McCulloch-Pitts model, this is given as

$$\text{out} = \phi(net).$$

ϕ is called an activation function called a thresholding function. Mathematically, a thresholding function is given as follows:

$$\text{out} = \begin{cases} 1 & \text{if } net \geq T \\ 0 & \text{if } net < T \end{cases}$$

Here, T is the threshold value. This threshold includes the bias of the perceptron.

One can also use a step function as an activation function. If the step function is used as an activation function, the above equation can be rewritten as follows:

$$out = \begin{cases} 1 & if\ net\text{-}T \geq 0 \\ 0 & if\ net\text{-}T < 0 \end{cases}$$

Threshold value T is the only parameter that can be adjusted is the threshold function, and it should be noted that the terms bias and threshold are used interchangeably in this model.

More additional notes on activation functions are given in Box 2.2.

Box 2.2 Additional Notes on Step and Signum Function

Step functions are often used in the McCulloch-Pitts model as well as perceptron for operational convenience. Basically, step and signum functions are activation functions. These functions are required to convert a linear sum of inputs and weights into a discrete output. Usually, it is a continuous number to a discrete number.

The step function takes the input x and outputs a binary value of 0 or 1, depending on whether x is above or below the threshold value. Mathematically, it is given as follows:

$$out(x) = \begin{cases} 1 & if\ x \geq 0 \\ 0 & if\ x < 0 \end{cases}$$

The step function is shown as a plot in Figure 2.3.

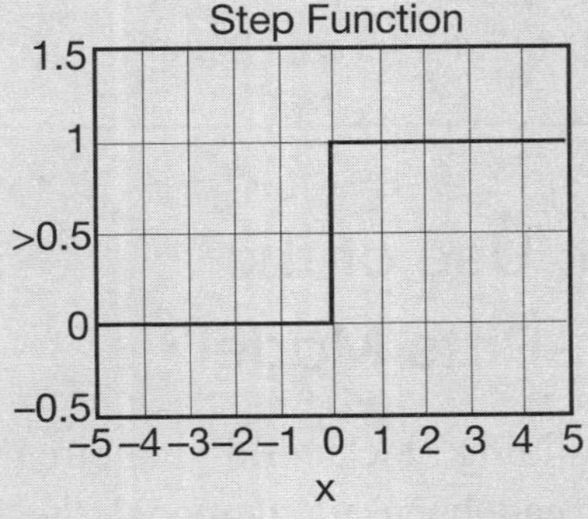

Figure 2.3 Plot of a Step function

The signum function is another useful function and is often used in perceptron. It takes the input x and outputs the response –1, 0 and +1. Mathematically, the signum function is given as

$$out(x) = \begin{cases} 1 & \text{if } x > 0 \\ -1 & \text{if } x < 0 \\ 0 & \text{if } x = 0 \end{cases}$$

Often, it is used in binary classifiers with two classes, –1 and +1. Hence, usually 0 is omitted. The mathematical function of signum is given as

$$out(x) = \begin{cases} 1 & \text{if } x \geq 0 \\ -1 & \text{if } x < 0 \end{cases}$$

The plot of the signum function is given in Figure 2.4.

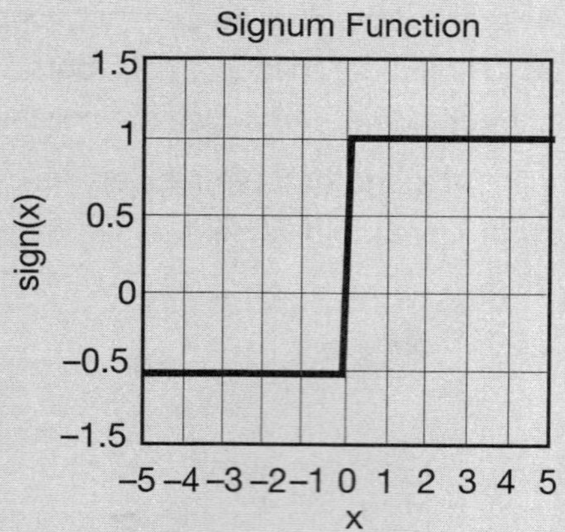

Figure 2.4 Plot of a Signum Function

2.1.2 What is the Use of the McCulloch-Pitts Model?

Logic gates are the basic building blocks of digital circuits. The simple McCulloch-Pitts (MP) Neuron model can be used to model the binary gates. This neuron model can learn a Boolean function with a fixed threshold value *T*; hence, it is called a linear threshold gate model. The following numerical problem explains the implementation of the AND function.

Example 2.1: Let the input be $x = [1, 1, 2]$. Let the weights be $w = [0.5, 0.5, 0.6]$. Let the threshold T be 1. Use the McCulloch-Pitts model and show whether the neuron would fire or not using the thresholding function.

Solution:

The linear sum of the input x and the weights are given as below:

$$net = 1 \times 0.5 + 1 \times 0.5 + 2 \times 0.6 = 2.2$$

Apply the threshold function,

$$\text{out} = \begin{cases} 1 \, if \; net \geq 1 \\ 0 \; if \; net < 1 \end{cases}$$

Therefore, the neuron would fire as the net is ≥ 1.

Example 2.2: AND Boolean function is an electronic circuit that only gives an output (1) if both inputs are 1. The truth table of AND is shown below in Table 2.3.

Table 2.3 AND Truth Table

x_1	x_2	y
0	0	0
0	1	0
1	0	0
1	1	1

Simulate the gate using the MP model, assuming $T = -1$, and assume the activation function used is the step function.

Solution:

It can be observed that the AND gate has two inputs and one output. The perceptron is given as shown in Figure 2.5.

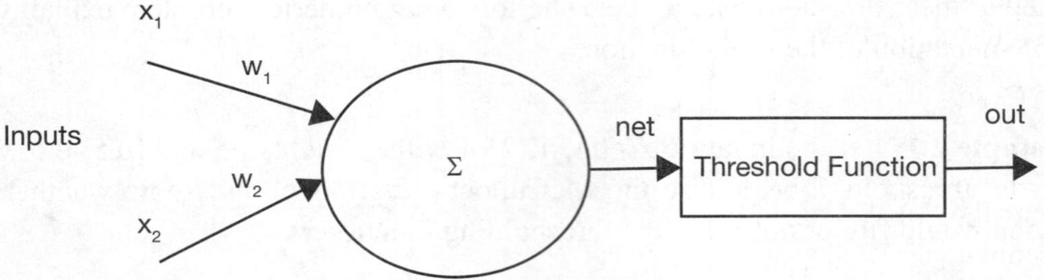

Figure 2.5 McCulloch-Pitts Model for AND Gate

The values of the weights are chosen randomly. Let us assume that the weights are $w_1 = 0.8$, $w_2 = 0.8$, and the threshold value is $T = -1$. Here, the net is given as $\text{net} = \sum_{i=1}^{2} x_i w_i$. Assume the threshold value is –1. Let us check whether this works. The computations are shown in the following Table 2.4.

Table 2.4 Output Calculation

x_1	x_2	w_1 (fixed)	w_2 (fixed)	$\text{net} = \sum_{i=1}^{2} x_i w_i$ Bring T LHS as net – T as a step function is used.	Out = f(net-T) with step function as activation function. $out = \begin{cases} 1 & \text{if } net\text{-}T \geq 0 \\ 0 & \text{if } net\text{-}T < 0 \end{cases}$
0	0	0.8	0.8	$-0.8 \times 0 + 0.8 \times 0 - 1 = -1$	$-1 < 0 = 0$
0	1	0.8	0.8	$0.8 \times 0 + 0.8 \times 1 - 1 = -0.2$	$-0.2 < 0 = 0$
1	0	0.8	0.8	$0.8 \times 1 + 0.8 \times 0 - 1 = -0.2$	$-0.2 < 0 = 0$
1	1	0.8	0.8	$0.8 \times 1 + 0.8 \times 1 - 1 = 0.6$	$0.6 \geq 1 = 1$

It can be checked that for all the input combinations, the results are coming true. Therefore, one can conclude that this acts as an AND gate when the weights $w_1 =$

0.8 and $w_2 = 0.8$. One can check by changing the threshold value to +1, then the above will not work. Hence, the choice of T is very important.

2.2 Perceptron Model

Later, the first neural network model, "Perceptron," was designed by Frank Rosenblatt in 1958. Many attempts have been made to integrate the McCulloch-Pitts model with the learning mechanism of adjusting the weights. The best-known model that succeeded is the Rosenblatt Perceptron model. Rosenblatt modified the fundamental McCulloch-Pitts Neuron model by combining two concepts – The McCulloch-Pitts model and the Hebbian learning rule of adjusting weights.

Donald Hebb published a book titled "The Organization of Behavior," where he postulated memory creation. The significance of the postulate is that the information is stored in the connections between the neurons, and the learning occurs by changing the connections based on the activation patterns and the network weights.

A perceptron is a combination of the McCulloch-Pitts model and the Hebbian rule. The differences between the Perceptron and McCulloch-Pitts models are given below in Table 2.5.

Table 2.5 Differences between Perceptron and McCulloch-Pitts Model

Perceptron	McCulloch-Pitts
It can take a real number as input.	It only take binary input.
Inputs are weights and hence more flexible and can learn.	Inputs are not weighted. In a sense, the weights are fixed and do not vary.
Useful for classification and regression problems.	Useful for modelling the gates.

2.2.1 What are the Advantages and Disadvantages of Perceptron?

The advantages and disadvantages of the perceptron are given below in Table 2.6.

Table 2.6 Advantages and Disadvantages of Perceptron

Advantages	Disadvantages
Perceptron is a binary classifier with supervised learning.	The perceptron output is only a binary number because of the thresholding function.
Automatic weight learning.	Only linear separable problems can be solved by a single perceptron.
Linear separable problems can be solved.	This single perceptron is not useful for non-linear separable problems.

One can consider perceptron as the building block of the artificial neural network. Perceptron can take a non-Boolean value, and as McCulloch-Pitts model, it aggregates it as a linear sum and gives a binary input based on a threshold value.

The perceptron model is shown in Figure 2.6.

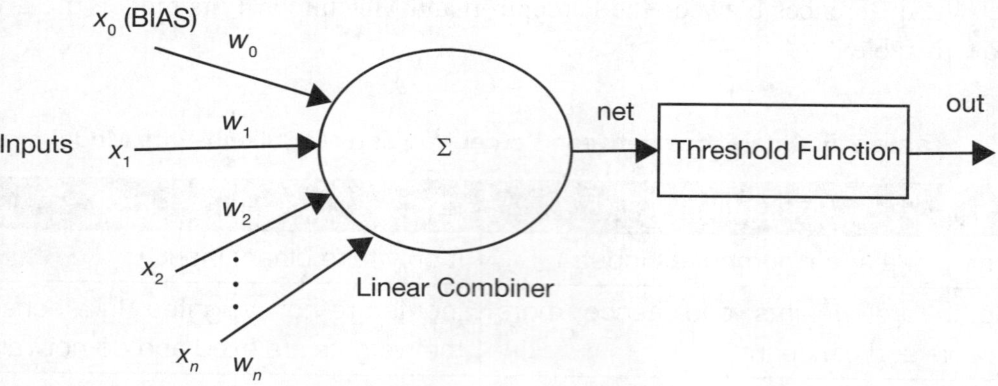

Figure 2.6 Perceptron Model

The following parameters characterize a perceptron:

1. Input signals from other neurons, $[x_1, x_2, ..., x_n]$. The input values are accepted by an input layer of perceptron, whose neurons focus on input data.
2. Weights applied to the input signals $[w_1, w_2, ..., w_n]$. Weight indicates the strength of the neurons. Bias is a special weight and can be considered an intercept. Bias is a constant factor. It is the weight w_0 of an active input x_0. x_0 is always 1.

3. Net sum is the sum of the linear product of input and the associated weight. Net input is the Summation function that computes the sum of the products of the inputs with their weights. The bias is added to the weighted sum as [net = $\sum_{i=1}^{n} x_i w_i + b$], where b is the bias. The purpose of using the bias in the perceptron is to shift the decision boundary away from the origin to interpret the results easily. Bias also can be adjusted like other weights to provide the best fit of the data. To simplify the problem, bias can be added as a weight w_0 and modified in the above net equation as

$$net = \sum_{i=0}^{n} x_i w_i$$

Here x_i is the input w_i is the weights. The bias is with the associated input x_0, which is always.

4. The activation function takes the net sum and produces the output.

   a. If the activation function of the perceptron is a step function.

   $$\text{out} = \phi(\text{net})$$

   Perceptron can use the step function as an activation. The step function can be mathematically given as follows:

   $$\text{out} = \begin{cases} 1 \; if \; net \geq 0 \\ 0 \; if \; net < 0 \end{cases}$$

   The output can be binary 0 or 1.

   b. But for binary classification, where +1 is used for one class and –1 for another class, perceptron can use a non-linear activation function called the signum function. A signum (sgn) function produces a bipolar response that accurately models the neurons.

   Sgn(net) is similar to the binary step function where threshold value $T = 0$. A sgn function returns –1 if the input is negative and 1 if it is positive.

   $$\text{out} = \begin{cases} 1 & if \; net \geq 0 \\ -1 & if \; net < 0 \end{cases}$$

   It can be observed that the activation functions give different responses when the net value is less than zero.

The procedure for the perceptron can be summarized as follows:

1. Select the input be $x = (x_1, x_2, \cdots, x_n)$, and the weights be $w = (w_1, w_2, \cdots, w_n)$
2. Compute the net by element-wise multiplication of the inputs with the weights and add the products.

$$net = w_0 + x_1 w_1 + \cdots + x_n w_n$$

$$net = \sum_{i=0}^{n} x_i w_i$$

   Here, the bias is taken inside the summation, and the bias is added to the weight w_0, With the input $x_0 = 1$ always.

3. Apply the activation function (Sign function) on the net to get the output out of the perceptron.

$$\text{out} = \text{sgn}(net)$$

   Therefore, out = $\begin{cases} 1 & if\ net \geq 0 \\ -1 & if\ net < 0 \end{cases}$

2.2.2 Perceptron Learning Algorithm

The Perceptron learning algorithm, also known as the perceptron rule, was introduced by Frank Rosenblatt in 1958. A learning rule is a formula to adjust the weights and biases of the neural network to minimize the error between the actual and expected output. The purpose of this perceptron rule is to minimize the misclassification errors. The training process is given in Figure 2.7.

Perceptron uses supervised learning. So, the perceptron should be trained with labelled examples. Perceptron can act as a binary classifier. So, the input data has a target label also. Perceptron takes these data as input and makes a prediction. The predicted label or class is compared with the actual or expected output. If the prediction is wrong, the perceptron adjusts its weights and biases to improve the prediction. This process of input-output–comparison–weight adjustment is iteratively done for a predefined number of epochs (Epoch is a complete training cycle) or till the error becomes negligible. By that time, the perceptron would have learned to classify the input data better.

The learning of a perceptron is done in two phases, namely forward propagation and backward propagation.

1. It should be noted that the input for the perceptron input is a set of labelled data that are of the form $\{(x_1,t_1),(x_2,t_2),\cdots,(x_n,t_n)\}$. Here, the input values are $x_1,x_2,\cdots,x_n$ and $t_1,t_2,\cdots,t_n$ are corresponding labels (target values). The goal of the perceptron is to get the inputs and often classify them into two binary classes. $c_1 = +1$ and $c_2 = -1$.
2. The weights are initialized to a small random value.
3. The learning rate (η) is initialized to a value in the range [0 – 1]. The learning rate is a hyperparameter that is manually controlled and is used to control the step size for weight update. The role of the learning rate is crucial for convergence.
4. For each input, (x_i,t_i) do

   4.1 [forward propagation] During forward propagation, a linear sum of the products of input signals and their associated weights are computed as

$$net = w_0 + x_1 w_1 + \cdots + x_n w_n$$

$$net = \sum_{i=0}^{n} x_i w_i$$

   4.2 The activation function signum is used to compute the output (out) as

$$\text{out} = \text{sgn(net)}$$

Here, out is the output of the perceptron.

The training process is given in Figure 2.7.

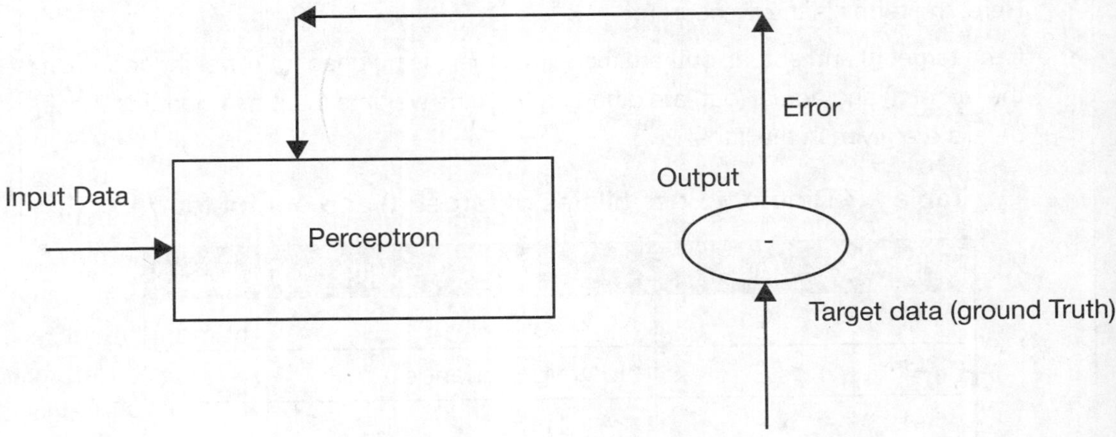

Figure 2.7 Training Process of a Perceptron. The perceptron output is out, and the target is *t*.

4.3 The error between the predicted output target (out) and the actual output of the perceptron (t). Compute the error as

$$\delta = t - out$$

The details of the error are given in Box 2.3. The perceptron aims to minimize the error between the target and actual output.

4.4. [Backward propagation] In backward propagation, the error is propagated backward to update the weight using the perceptron rule as $w_i = w_i + \Delta w_i$

The weights are adjusted based on the error to minimize to minimize the difference between the target and output (out).

5. Repeat the iterative process to adjust the weights such that the magnitude of the error is minimized in every iteration using the perceptron rule. The convergence is checked using the predetermined number of epochs, or the error is tolerable.

Box 2.3 Error Computation for a Binary Classifier

The perceptron rule is used to adjust the weights during the backpropagation of the perceptron. The procedure is as follows:

1. Compute the error as the difference between the target and actual output as

$$\delta_i = (t_i - out_i)$$

   Here, the term i is the ith neuron.

2. If the target (t) and actual (out) are the same, there is no need for a weight update. If the target (t) and actual (out) are different, then the weights must be updated. These details are given in the Table 2.7.

Table 2.7 Different Possibilities of target (t) and output (out)

(t)	(out)	*t* – out
+1	+1	No weight change
–1	–1	No weight change
+1	–1	1 – (–1) = 2
–1	+1	–1 – 1 = –2

The weight update is as follows:

$$\Delta w_i = \eta \times \delta_i \times x_i$$

Here, η is the learning rate, δ_i is the error of the ith neuron indicated by Table 2.7, and x_i is the input.

Therefore, the final weight update is $w_i = w_i + \Delta w_i$. The weight update is continued till it converges, or the process is repeated for a predetermined number of epochs.

2.3 Perceptron as a Binary Classifier

One can recollect that the classifier's job is to assign a label to the input data. If the label is 0 or 1, then the classifier is called a binary classifier. Takes the input data and generates a class label. Perceptron is a primitive classifier. The goal of the perceptron is to get the inputs and classify them into two binary classes. $c_1 = +1$ and $c_2 = -1$.

2.3.1 How does Classification Work in Perceptron?

The basic perceptron for two-dimensional input works as a simple linear function. A linear function is a straight line with a slope and y-intercept. The slope represents the perceptron weight' w' and the y-intercept its bias 'b'. Bias is added as a controlling factor to shift the result of the summation function either toward the positive or negative side. x is the input, and y is the output. The linear function can be shown as

$$y = wx + b$$

The focus is to put a line that separates the input data into classes. Instead of a line, a plane is required to separate the classes in three dimensions. In general, for n-dimensional data, an n-dimensional hyperplane is required to separate the input data.

Perceptron works well for linear separable problems only. The details of the linearly separable is given in Box 2.4.

Box 2.4 Linearly Separable

The two classes are linearly separable if we can draw a single line to separate them. One class falls on one side of the line, and the other class is on the other side of the line. A single line can be easily drawn for linear boolean functions such as AND (Refer to Table 2.8).

Table 2.8 AND Truth Table

x_1	x_2	y
0	0	0
0	1	0
1	0	0
1	1	1

It can be observed that the input line is a decision boundary that splits the input space into two regions that indicate the class, and there is no misclassification of data. Data is linear separable if a single decision line can be drawn to separate the classes perfectly, resulting in no misclassification, as shown in Figure 2.8.

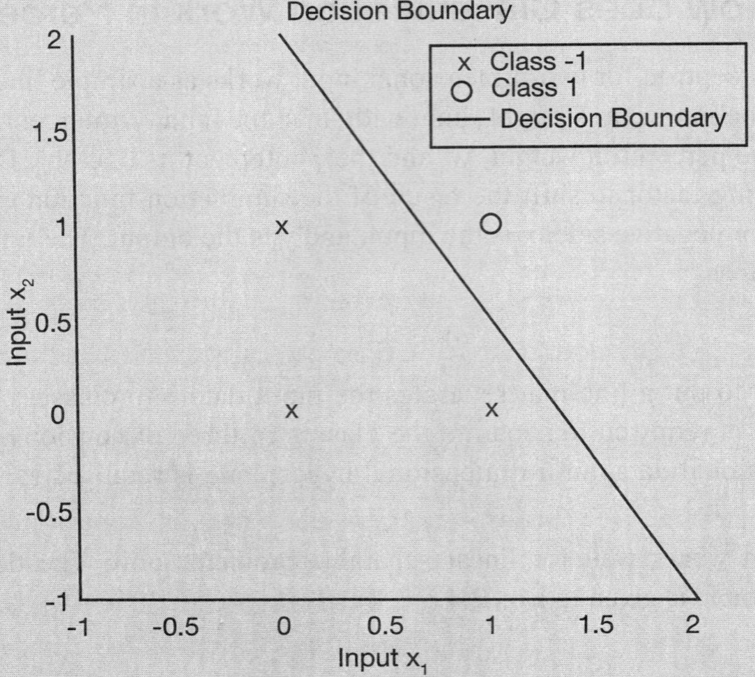

Figure 2.8 The Decision Line Clearly Separates the Data Points

Non-Linear Separable

The problem is called non-linear separable if using a single decision line to separate the classes is impossible. For example, it is impossible to draw a single line to separate the two classes for boolean functions such as XOR. The XOR gate is shown in Table 2.9. Its plot is given in Figure 2.9. It can be observed that no single-line decision function can be drawn to avoid misclassification.

Table 2.9 XOR Gate

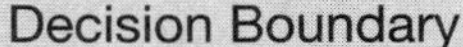

x_1	x_2	y
0	0	0
0	1	1
1	0	1
1	1	0

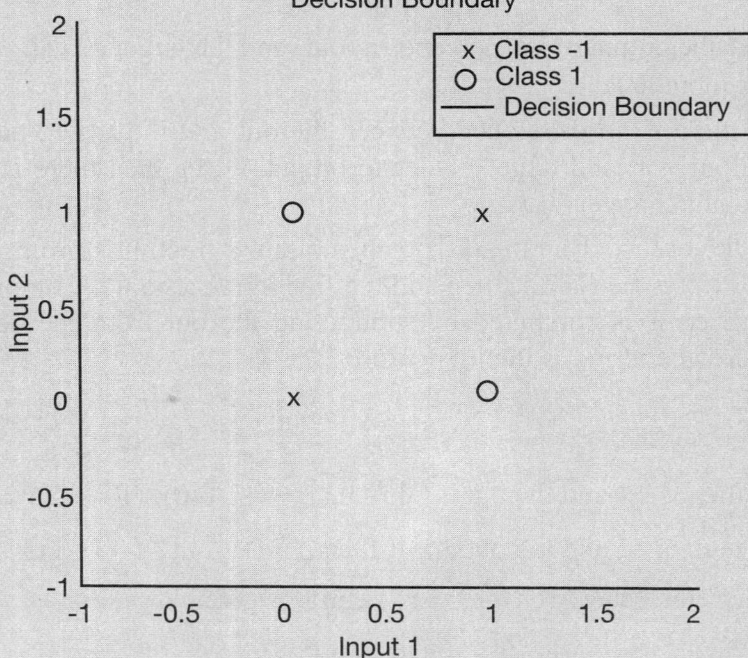

Figure 2.9 Difficulty in Drawing a Single Decision Line to Classify the Data Points

Hence, a single perceptron is not sufficient to model an XOR gate.

2.3.2 Algorithm for Using Perceptron as a Binary Classifier

The complete formal algorithm for Perceptron classification is given as follows:

1. Read the labelled data.
2. Initialize the weights and learning rate η randomly.
3. Compute the linear sum of the products of input signals and their associated weights as the weighted sum of the weights and inputs as

$$\text{net} = w_0 + x_1 w_1 + \cdots + x_n w_n$$

$$\text{net} = \sum_{i=0}^{n} x_i w_i$$

The activation function signum is used to compute the output (out) as

$$\text{out} = \text{sgn(net)}$$

Compare the output of the perceptron (out) and the target (t) value that is given with the input data.

3.1 If there is no difference between the out and the t (i.e., target = 1 and output = 1, and target = –1 and output = –1), then there is no need for weight change.

3.2 If the out is +1 and t = –1, then subtract a fraction x_i from w_i. If the out is –1 and the t is +1, then add the fraction of x_i to w_i. Compute the error. The error is computed by subtracting the out from the desired target. Here, the term i is the ith neuron.

$$\delta_i = (t_i - \text{out}_i)$$

If the t is +1 and the out is –1, then $\delta = (\text{t} - \text{out}) = (1 - (-1)) = +2$

If the t is –1 and the out is +1, then $\delta = (\text{t} - \text{out}) = (-1 - 1) = -2$

Therefore, the error for the ith neuron is given as

$$\delta_i = \begin{cases} 2 & \text{if } t = 1 \text{ and out is } -1 \\ -2 & \text{if } t = -1 \text{ and out is } 1 \end{cases}$$

4. Apply the perceptron learning rule is given as

$$\Delta w_i = \eta \times \delta_i \times x_i$$

where x_i is the input value, δ_i is the error at node i, η is the learning rate, and Δw_i is the difference in weight that has to be added to w_i. Therefore, the change in weight, as the new weight, is given as $w_i = w_i + \Delta w_i$

5. Repeat the above steps for all the samples to get the correct classification. Finally, assign the input c_1 if the out is 1. Otherwise, assign the input to the class c_2 .

Example 2.3: Use perceptron and implement the following problem. Let the training sets consist of the following data as in Table 2.10.

Table 2.10 Sample Data

	F1	F2	Target t
x_1	0	0	–1
x_2	0	4	+1
x_3	1	1	+1
x_4	1	–3	–1

It can be observed that $x_1 = \begin{pmatrix} 0 \\ 0 \end{pmatrix}, x_2 = \begin{pmatrix} 0 \\ 4 \end{pmatrix}, x_3 = \begin{pmatrix} 1 \\ 1 \end{pmatrix}$, and $x_4 = \begin{pmatrix} 1 \\ -3 \end{pmatrix}$ with the targets that are given by $t_1 = -1, t_2 = +1, t_3 = +1$, and $t_4 = -1$. For simplicity, assume all the weights $w_0 = 1, w_1 = 1, w_2 = 1$ and $\eta = 1$.

Classify the above training vectors into two classes given to be $c_1 = -1$ and $c_2 = +1$.

Solution::

Dot products can be used to reduce computations. To facilitate that, the data vectors can be augmented with $w_0 = 1$ a third dimension to get the vector as follows:

$$x_1 = \begin{pmatrix} 1 \\ 0 \\ 0 \end{pmatrix}, x_2 = \begin{pmatrix} 1 \\ 0 \\ 4 \end{pmatrix}, x_3 = \begin{pmatrix} 1 \\ 1 \\ 1 \end{pmatrix}, \text{ and } x_4 = \begin{pmatrix} 1 \\ 1 \\ -3 \end{pmatrix}$$

1. Let us compute the outputs.

Assume all the weights and learning rate 1 as per the problem. Hence,

$$w_0 = 1, w_1 = 1, w_2 = 1 \text{ and } \eta = 1$$

$$\text{So, } w = \begin{pmatrix} w_0 \\ w_1 \\ w_2 \end{pmatrix} = \begin{pmatrix} 1 \\ 1 \\ 1 \end{pmatrix} \text{ and } x = \begin{pmatrix} x_0 \\ x_1 \\ x_2 \end{pmatrix} = \begin{pmatrix} 1 \\ 0 \\ 0 \end{pmatrix}$$

$$\begin{aligned} o_1 &= \text{sgn}(x_0 w_0 + x_1 w_1 + x_2 w_2) \\ &= \text{sgn}(1 \times 1 + 0 \times 1 + 0 \times 1) \\ &= \text{sgn}(1) = +1 \end{aligned}$$

It can be checked that the output of the perceptron does not match the target $t_1 = -1$. This difference between the output and the target needs the weights to be updated per the perceptron rule. It can be recollected when the sgn threshold function is used in perceptron with the output $o_1 = +1$, $t_1 = -1$, $\delta = -2$. So, update the weights as per the perceptron rule.

$$\delta_i = \begin{cases} 2 & \text{if t} = 1 \text{ and out is } -1 \\ -2 & \text{if t} = -1 \text{ and out is } 1 \end{cases}$$

So, the weight updation would be as per the perceptron rule. Therefore, it is new weight = old weight + learning rate X error X input. Note that the learning rate is 1.

$$w = (1 \quad 1 \quad 1)^T + (-2)(1 \quad 0 \quad 0) = (-1 \quad 1 \quad 1)^T$$

Or

$$w = \begin{pmatrix} 1 \\ 1 \\ 1 \end{pmatrix} + (-2) \begin{pmatrix} 1 \\ 0 \\ 0 \end{pmatrix} = \begin{pmatrix} -1 \\ 1 \\ 1 \end{pmatrix}$$

It can be observed that the weights are revised to (–1, 1, 1).

2. This logic is repeated for the next data (1, 0, 4). The computations are similar to the computation of the first point. It can be observed that the second point and the revised weight are as given below:

$$x_2 = \begin{pmatrix} 1 \\ 0 \\ 4 \end{pmatrix} \text{ and the revised weights are } w = \begin{pmatrix} w_0 \\ w_1 \\ w_2 \end{pmatrix} = \begin{pmatrix} -1 \\ 1 \\ 1 \end{pmatrix}$$

Compute,
$$\begin{aligned} o_2 &= \text{sgn}(x_0 w_0 + x_1 w_1 + x_2 w_2) \\ &= \text{sgn}(1 \times -1 + 0 \times 1 + 1 \times 4) \\ &= \text{sgn}(3) = +1 \end{aligned}$$

It can be observed that $o_2 = +1$ and $t_2 = +1$ There is no change in the weights.

3. Let us proceed to the next data point.

$$x_3 = \begin{pmatrix} 1 \\ 1 \\ 1 \end{pmatrix} \text{ and the weights are } w = \begin{pmatrix} w_0 \\ w_1 \\ w_2 \end{pmatrix} = \begin{pmatrix} -1 \\ 1 \\ 1 \end{pmatrix}$$

Compute,
$$\begin{aligned} o_3 &= \text{sgn}(x_0 w_0 + x_1 w_1 + x_2 w_2) \\ &= \text{sgn}(1 \times -1 + 1 \times 1 + 1 \times 1) \\ &= \text{sgn}(1) = +1 \end{aligned}$$

It can be observed that $o_3 = +1$ and $t_3 = +1$ there is no change in the weights.

4. let us proceed to the next data point.

$$x_4 = \begin{pmatrix} 1 \\ 1 \\ -3 \end{pmatrix} \text{ and the weights are } w = \begin{pmatrix} w_0 \\ w_1 \\ w_2 \end{pmatrix} = \begin{pmatrix} -1 \\ 1 \\ 1 \end{pmatrix}$$

Compute,
$$\begin{aligned} o_4 &= \text{sgn}(x_0 w_0 + x_1 w_1 + x_2 w_2) \\ &= \text{sgn}(1 \times -1 + 1 \times 1 + -3 \times 1) \\ &= \text{sgn}(-3) = -1 \end{aligned}$$

whereas and $x = \begin{pmatrix} x_0 \\ x_1 \\ x_2 \end{pmatrix} = \begin{pmatrix} 1 \\ 1 \\ -3 \end{pmatrix}$

It can be observed that $o_4 = -1$ and $t_4 = -1$ there is no change, and the algorithm terminates. One can also go for the next iteration and check that the weights do not change.

One can observe that the final weights are

$$w = \begin{pmatrix} w_0 \\ w_1 \\ w_2 \end{pmatrix} = \begin{pmatrix} -1 \\ 1 \\ 1 \end{pmatrix}$$

So, the first input $x_1 = \begin{pmatrix} 1 \\ 0 \\ 0 \end{pmatrix}$, $w^T.x = 1 \times -1 + 0 \times 1 + 0 \times 1 = -1$, Hence class c_1

Similarly, for input $x_2 = \begin{pmatrix} 1 \\ 0 \\ 4 \end{pmatrix}$, $w^T.x_2 = 1 \times -1 + 0 \times 1 + 4 \times 1 = 3 (3 \geq 0)$, out = 1, Hence class c_2

For $x_3 = \begin{pmatrix} 1 \\ 1 \\ 1 \end{pmatrix}$, $w^T.x_3 = 1 \times -1 + 1 \times 1 + 1 \times 1 = 1 (1 \geq 0)$, out = 0, Hence class c_1

For $x_4 = \begin{pmatrix} 1 \\ 1 \\ -3 \end{pmatrix}$, $w^T.x_4 = 1 \times -1 + 1 \times 1 + -3 \times 1 = -3 (-3 < 0)$, out = 0, Hence class c_1

The decision boundary is shown in Figure 2.10.

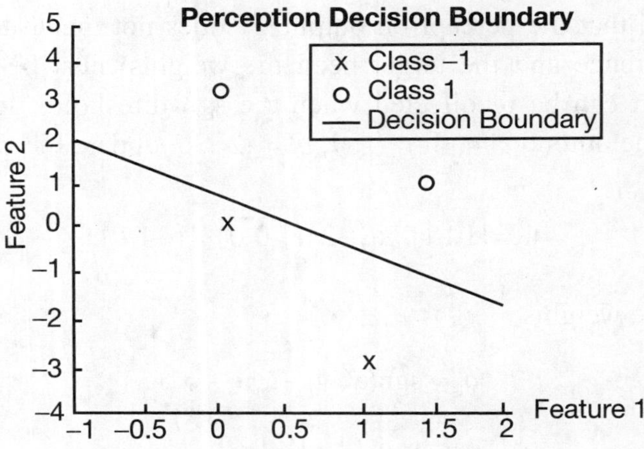

Figure 2.10 The Decision Boundary

Example 2.4: Implement the OR gate using perceptron.

It can be observed that $x_1 = \begin{pmatrix} 0 \\ 0 \end{pmatrix}, x_2 = \begin{pmatrix} 0 \\ 1 \end{pmatrix}, x_3 = \begin{pmatrix} 1 \\ 0 \end{pmatrix}$, and $x_4 = \begin{pmatrix} 1 \\ 1 \end{pmatrix}$ with the targets given by $t_1 = -1, t_2 = +1, t_3 = +1,$ and $t_4 = +1$. Design the Perceptron.

Solution:

Dot products can be used. To facilitate that, the data vectors can be augmented with $w_o = 1$ a third dimension to get the vector as follows:

1. Let us compute the outputs.

So, $w = \begin{pmatrix} w_0 \\ w_1 \\ w_2 \end{pmatrix} = \begin{pmatrix} 1 \\ 1 \\ 1 \end{pmatrix}$ and $x = \begin{pmatrix} x_0 \\ x_1 \\ x_2 \end{pmatrix} = \begin{pmatrix} 1 \\ 0 \\ 0 \end{pmatrix}$

$$\begin{aligned} o_1 &= \text{sgn}(x_0 w_0 + x_1 w_1 + x_2 w_2) \\ &= \text{sgn}(1 \times 1 + 1 \times 0 + 1 \times 0) \\ &= \text{sgn}(1) = +1 \end{aligned}$$

It can be checked that the perceptron output +1 does not match the target $t_1 = -1$. This output difference and the target need the weights must be updated per the perceptron rule. It can be recollected when the sgn threshold function is used in perceptron with the output $o_1 = +1$, $t_1 = -1$, $\delta = -2$. So, update the weights as per the perceptron rule.

$$w = (1\,1\,1)^T + (-2)(1\,0\,0) = (-1\,1\,1)^T$$

After changing the weights

$$\begin{aligned} o_1 &= \text{sgn}(x_0 w_0 + x_1 w_1 + x_2 w_2) \\ &= \text{sgn}(1 \times -1 + 1 \times 0 + 1 \times 0) \\ &= \text{sgn}(-1) = -1 \text{ which is equal to } t_1 = -1. \end{aligned}$$

It can be observed that the weights are revised to $(-1\,1\,1)$.

2. This logic is repeated for the next data $(1, 0, 1)$. The computations are similar to the computation of the first point. It can be observed that the second point and the revised weight are as given below:

$x_2 = \begin{pmatrix} 1 \\ 0 \\ 1 \end{pmatrix}$ and the revised weights are $w = \begin{pmatrix} -1 \\ 1 \\ 1 \end{pmatrix}$.

So,

$$\begin{aligned} o_2 &= \text{sgn}(x_0 w_0 + x_1 w_1 + x_2 w_2) \\ &= \text{sgn}(1 \times -1 + 1 \times 0 + 1 \times 1) \\ &= \text{sgn}(0) = +1 \end{aligned}$$

It can be observed that $o_2 = +1$ and $t_2 = +1$ there is no change in the weights.

3. Let us proceed to the next data point. $x_3 = \begin{pmatrix} 1 \\ 1 \\ 0 \end{pmatrix}$ and the weights are $w = \begin{pmatrix} -1 \\ 1 \\ 1 \end{pmatrix}$ as there is no change in the weights. So, compute the output as

$$o_3 = \text{sgn}(x_0 w_0 + x_1 w_1 + x_2 w_2)$$
$$= \text{sgn}(1 \times -1 + 1 \times 1 + 0 \times 1)$$
$$= \text{sgn}(0) = +1$$

It can be observed that $o_3 = +1$ and $t_3 = +1$ there is no change in the weights.

4. Let us proceed to the next data point. $x_4 = \begin{pmatrix} 1 \\ 1 \\ 1 \end{pmatrix}$ and the weights are $w = \begin{pmatrix} -1 \\ 1 \\ 1 \end{pmatrix}$ as there is no change in the weights. To compute

$$o_4 = \text{sgn}(x_0 w_0 + x_1 w_1 + x_2 w_2)$$
$$= \text{sgn}(1 \times -1 + 1 \times 1 + 1 \times 1)$$
$$= \text{sgn}(1) = +1$$

It can be observed that $o_4 = +1$ and $t_4 = +1$ there is no change, and the algorithm terminates. One can also go for the next iteration and check that the weights do not change.

One can observe that the final weights are

$$w = \begin{pmatrix} w_0 \\ w_1 \\ w_2 \end{pmatrix} = \begin{pmatrix} -1 \\ 1 \\ 1 \end{pmatrix}$$

So, the first input $x_1 = \begin{pmatrix} 1 \\ 0 \\ 0 \end{pmatrix}$, $w^T.x_1 = 1 \times -1 + 0 \times 1 + 0 \times 1 = -1$, Hence class c_1

Similarly, for input $x_2 = \begin{pmatrix} 1 \\ 0 \\ 1 \end{pmatrix}$, $w^T.x_2 = 1 \times -1 + 0 \times 1 + 1 \times 1 = 0$, Hence class c_2

For , $x_3 = \begin{pmatrix} 1 \\ 1 \\ 0 \end{pmatrix}$, $w^T.x_3 = 1 \times -1 + 1 \times 1 + 0 \ \times 1 = 0$, Hence class c_2

For $x_4 = \begin{pmatrix} 1 \\ 1 \\ 1 \end{pmatrix}$, $w^T.x_4 = 1 \times -1 + 1 \times 1 + 1 \times 1 = 1$, Hence class c_2

Therefore, the OR gate is represented by the weights correctly.

2.4 Single and Multilayer Neural Networks

A neural network consists of neuron cells. A neuron may be connected to another neuron. A neural network is capable of learning, recalling and capable of forecasting. There are two types of neural networks, as shown in Figure 2.11.

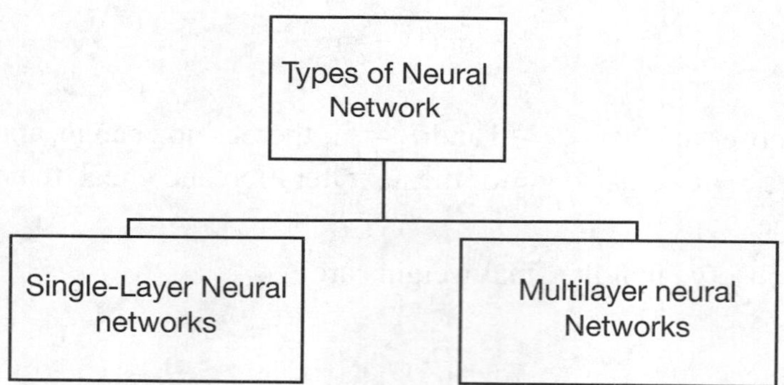

Figure 2.11 Types of Neural Networks

2.4.1 Single-layer Neural Networks

A single-layer neural network is often called a single-layer perceptron or single-layer feedforward networks. The terms single-layer perceptron and single-layer neural network are often used interchangeably in the literature.

The subtle difference is that while perceptron uses only step or signum function, a single-layer network can use all activation functions like ReLU, Sigmoidal, or Tanh. So, a single-layer model can be used for many tasks other than binary classification. The architecture of the single-layer neural network is given as follows:

(i) Input Layer: A set of neurons or nodes organized as the Input layer. Here, every neuron corresponds to an input variable. These input neurons pass the input variable directly to the output layer. It should be observed that there is no processing happening here. There are no hidden layers in the single-layer network. So, there are no computations taking place in a single-layer neural network.

(ii) Output Layer: The output layer again consists of one or more neurons. A single-layer network mostly has a single neuron in the output layer. The single-layer neural network can use any activation function, unlike perceptron, and hence can be used for a variety of classifications.

The advantages and disadvantages of the single-layer neural network are given in Table 2.11.

Table 2.11 Advantages and Disadvantages of Single-Layer Feedforward Neural Network

Advantages	Disadvantages
Single-layer perceptron can solve only linear separable problems.	If the problem is non-linear, the single-layer layer neural network will not converge.
Singe-layer perceptron is one of the simplest neural network.	It cannot solve complex problems.

A sample single-layer neural network is shown in Figure 2.12.

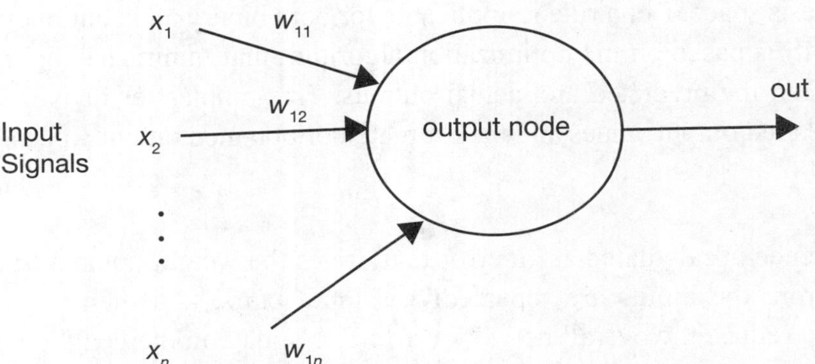

Figure 2.12 A Single-layer Neural Network

Delta rule is the fundamental rule for training single-layer or linear perceptrons. The Delta Rule, also called the Widrow & Hoff Learning rule or the Least Mean

Square (LMS) rule, was named after the inventors Widrow and Hoff in the early 1960s. The differences between the Perceptron and LMS rules are shown in Table 2.12.

Table 2.12 Differences between the Perceptron and LMS Rule

Perceptron Rule	LMS Rule
The Perceptron rule is meant only for binary classification algorithms with either +1 or −1 outcomes. The limitations of the perceptron rule are that it can classify only if the input is linearly separable.	LMS rule is for classification and regression problems. The output is a continuous number.
The perceptron rule will not terminate if the inputs are non-separable. The termination is guaranteed only for linearly separable problems.	The LMS rule will not terminate if the inputs are non-separable. Converge is guaranteed, but the rate of convergence would vary.
The focus is to reduce the misclassification.	The focus is on the minimization of error.
There is a weight update in case of misclassification.	The weight update is based on the error between predicted and actual values.

The Delta Rule is an interesting mechanism that strives to find the best-fitting model in the hypothesis space. Delta rule is applicable for both binary and continuous input and output. LMS is based on the optimization algorithm that minimizes the mean square error between the predicted and actual outputs. The simplest error is the difference between desired output values and the estimated or obtained output values.

$$e_i = t_i - out_i$$

This difference is calculated as an error that drives the weight update. In the context of perceptron, the inputs are repeatedly as input pairs, and then the weights are modified to reduce the overall network error. The update in the weight is given as

$$\Delta w_{ij} = \eta \times e_i \times x_i$$

Here e_i is the error that is the difference between the desired target value, the output for neuron j, and the learning rate. The new weight is given as

$$w_{ij} = w_{ij} + \Delta w_{ij}$$

The procedure for a multilayer neural network is given as follows:

1. Initialize the weights randomly to a smaller value.
2. The data is fed to calculate the predicted data in the forward pass.
3. The error is computed as the difference between the predicted and the target output and is often expressed as a loss function.
4. The weight is updated to minimize the error.
5. The steps 2-4 are repeated for all the inputs
6. The steps 2-5 are done for certain iterations or error convergence.

2.4.2 Multilayer Networks

The multilayer networks are also called multilayer perceptron layer networks. Also, these networks are called feedforward networks if the input moves from the input to the output layer. There are no loops. The difference between multilayer neural networks and single-layer neural networks is that multilayer neural networks have more hidden layers. The differences between the single-layer and multilayer neural networks are given in Table 2.13.

Table 2.13 Differences between Single-layer and Multilayer Neural Networks

Single-layer Neural Network	Multilayer Neural Network
A single-layer neural network has only input and output layers.	A multilayer neural network has many hidden layers.
Only simple problems can be solved.	Complex problems can be solved.

A sample multilayer neural network is shown in the following Figure 2.11. A multilayer neural network is the foundation of modern deep learning. It has been successfully used in many applications like image classification and regression, as multilayer neural networks can solve very complex problems. The multilayer neural network has the same structure as the single-layer model but many hidden layers. The architecture is given as shown in Figure 2.13.

(i) **Input Layer:** As usual input layer consists of many neurons. Each neuron corresponds to an input.

(ii) **Hidden Layer:** There can be one or more hidden layers. Each hidden layer consists of neurons that help to solve complex problems by studying the complex relationships among neural networks. These layers use complex activation functions.

(iii) **Output Layer:** The output layer consists of many neurons that help binary and multi-class classification.

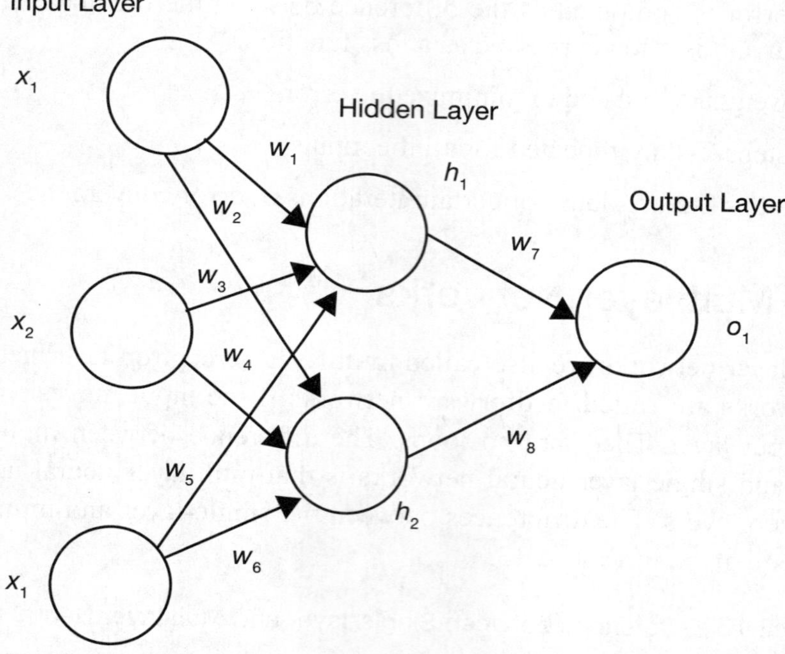

Figure 2.13 Feedforward Network

There are two stages given for the implementation of Feedforward networks as given below:

(i) **Forward Stage:** In this stage, the data starts from the input and terminates with the output.

(ii) **Backward Stage:** In this stage, the weights and biases are modified based on the backpropagation model. MLP also uses many non-linear activation models.

Multilayer neural networks use the Generalized delta rule (GDR) instead of the delta rule. It is a fundamental algorithm for adjusting the weights and biases. The generalized delta rule is the generalization of the delta rule and is essentially used for multilayer feedforward networks.

The differences between the delta and generalized delta rules are given below in Table 2.14.

Table 2.14 **Differences between the Delta Rule (DR) and Generalized Delta Rule (GDR)**

Delta Rule	Generalized Delta Rule
Delta rule is used only for the single-layer perceptrons.	The generalized delta rule is used for single-layer as well as multilayer perceptron.
The error reduction is very simple.	The weight update is complex and uses a chain rule.
There are no variants.	The variants of GDR are backpropagation and other optimization methods.
Perceptron converges only in the case of linear separable problems. Otherwise, the perceptron may not give results.	Convergence is guaranteed, but the rate of convergence would vary.

The steps of multilayer neural networks are given as follows:

1. In the forward pass, the input is passed from the input layer to produce an output.
2. The error is computed as the difference between the prediction and the desired output. This step is the quantification of the error.
3. The error is backpropagated backward as the gradient of the error. The weight update in this case is given as

$$\Delta w_{ij} = \eta \times \delta_i \times x_i$$

   where $\delta_i = \phi'(error)$, Here, ϕ' is the first derivative of the function. Here, the error is the difference between the desired target value, the output for neuron j, and the learning rate. The new weight is given as

$$w_{ij} = w_{ij} + \Delta w_{ij}$$

4. The weight update uses the Generalized delta rule for weights and bias to minimize errors.
5. Steps 1-4 are repeated for multiple iterations until the convergence.

The advantages and disadvantages of multilayer neural networks are given below in Table 2.15.

Table 2.15 Advantages and Disadvantages of Multilayer Neural Networks

Advantages	Disadvantages
It can solve complex non-linear problems.	Training of data is a big challenge in multilayer neural networks.
It can handle small as well as big data.	Computations are very complex.
The accuracy of this model is very high.	The operations of multilayer neural networks are time-consuming.

Summary

1. Artificial Neural Networks (ANN) provide the foundations of deep learning. It mimics the learning mechanism that models a human brain to solve problems.
2. The human nervous system is the learning system that consists of billions of functional units called neurons that artificial neurons model as a computing node or unit.
3. McCulloch-Pitts model is a mathematical model that implements a biological neuron. The summation function receives input signals and their associated weights to compute the linear weighted sum. It has an activation function called threshold function that mimics the firing or non-firing of neurons.
4. Perceptron, designed by Frank Rosenblatt, is a linear binary classifier.
5. Delta Rule is an LMS rule useful for training the single-layer perceptrons.
6. A multilayer perceptron or feedforward network has three layers: an input, hidden, and output layer.

Glossary

1. Artificial Neural Network (ANN) – ANN is an alternative paradigm that mimics the human brain to solve complex problems that require human intelligence.

2. Neurons – Neurons are called nodes or computing nodes.
3. Soma – The neuron body is called soma.
4. Dendrites – The input mechanism of the neurons for input.
5. Axon – The output of the neuron
6. Synapse – A junction that is used to communicate with another neuron.
7. Artificial Neurons – It is a mathematical model to imitate the biological neuron.
8. McCulloch-Pitts model – It is a mathematical model of a biological neuron.
9. Activation function – It is a function that mimics the firing of neurons. If the linear combination of input and weight is greater than the threshold value, the neuron fires.
10. Perceptron – Perceptron is a linear binary classifier that uses supervised learning for classification.
11. Classifier – A classifier is a program that takes an input and generates labels for it.
12. Binary Classifier – A binary classifier has two classes as the output.
13. Hyperplane – Hyperplane is a line or plane drawn to separate the inputs into classes.
14. Linearly separable Problem – A hyperplane construction is possible without any misclassification of samples.
15. Bias – An offset used to move the hyperplane away from the origin for easy interpretation.
16. Perceptron rule – The perceptron rule is a formula that is used to adjust the weights and biases to minimize the misclassification error.
17. Learning rate – A measure of step size.
18. LMS rule – Also called delta rule to train a single-layer neural network.
19. Generalized Delta Rule – It is the generalization of the delta rule that is used primarily for multilayer neural networks.
20. Single-layer neural networks – It consist of only an input layer and an output layer. There is no hidden layer in a single-layer neural network.
21. Multilayer neural networks – It consist of an input layer, one or more hidden layers, and an output layer.

Review Questions

1. What is a neuron?
2. Compare and contrast biological neurons and artificial neurons.
3. Define McCulloch-Pitts' model of an artificial neuron.
4. Use McCulloch-Pitt's mathematical model and implement a NAND gate.
5. How can perceptron implement an AND gate?
6. Why can the XOR problem not be solved by a simple perceptron?

Numerical Problems

1. Let $x = [1, 6, 7]$ and $w = [0.1, 0.1, 0.6]$. Let the threshold be 0.5. Use the McCulloch-Pitts model to find whether the neuron fires or not.
2. Implement an AND gate using a McCulloch-Pitts model.
3. Let the input be (1, 4), (2, 4), (8, 8), and (10, 10). Let the target of these inputs be + 1, +1, –1 and –1, respectively. Use a perceptron and classify the above inputs.
4. Implement the NOT gate using perceptron.

Crossword

Across

4. A group of neurons are organized as a __________
5. In a single-layer neural network, there is a single hidden layer, (yes/no)
6. The learning rate is __________ (hyperparameter/parameter)
9. Multilayer networks use the generalized delta rule, (yes/no)
10. The step size of the weight adjustment is called __________ rate.
12. A classifier assigns a __________ for the input data.
14. The output of the neuron is called __________
16. Artificial Neural networks are different from traditional way of solving the problems (yes/no)
17. One can visualize a neuron as a tiny messager carrying an information (yes/no)
18. The neuron body is called __________

Down

1. Perceptron is a __________ separable classifier.
2. A line that separate input points is in general called __________.
3. The weight of the McCulloch-Pitts model is __________ always.
7. GDR is a variant of the backpropagation algorithm, (yes/no)
8. An artificial neuron is a mathematical __________ of an biological neuron.
11. LMS rule is same as Perceptron rule (yes/no)
13. Perceptron rule adjusts the weights and __________
15. A single-layer perceptron is same as single-layer neural network in all aspects (yes/no)
16. Neural networks mimic the human brain (yes/no)
17. McCulloch-Pitts is the earliest model that explained the biological neuron (yes/no)

Jumbled Sentences

Y O T N D R Q H V V G E O J S G Q R E P L Y D P A

E T L E W E L K Y L X X T C I G Z A I L J Z E G C

S D B M K U T L X P M H F B A N C X U A Z E J S U

D I J Y G M U E U I E F A O I R U O Z Y N V X C P

B U Q N R N H N P D M R I D I N S N R E J L L S G

L S O M A M E U U M M O P X Z H A D M R R R U J M

Q O J I A Q Q G S K P D D A E Y O R V Q U N K N P

V A H N J O V W T R L P A E R D W E Y X Q T Z N O

F U D I O P U U V L A B E L L A U Q K K A Y O K W

P O T N K C B B Q X J J E U C M M Z X K H Q X Q U

E T Y C T J G I J L F E H Y H Y P E R P L A N E C

C D E X N D C Q A I C Y R Q A G D Q T I E C P W E

P H S Y B X V T G S U K O B W D T T A E D Y N Z N

J F O W S C X I L I E F G J D V K L P N R E X W E

W F E E B G H E V Y S S N S X T F E I G J S Y G U

F B Y F Y E S N I Z V F O K N H H J B H T A F G Y

P X S A S H S H F I A U L E A R N I N G R A T E Q

yes	yes	yes	soma	axon
model	yes	fixed	binary	label
hyperplane	biases	hyperparameter	learning rate	layer
no	no	yes	no	yes

Introduction to Activation and Loss Functions

CHAPTER 3

> The neural network is this kind of technology that is not an algorithm; it is a network that has weights on it, and you can adjust the weights so that it learns. You teach it through trials. — **Howard Rheingold**

Credits: © Howard Rheingold

One of the major pillars of deep learning is the concept of activation functions and loss functions. Activation functions mimic firing of biological neurons. There are many activation functions available now. Selecting an activation function is a challenging task. Similarly, loss functions are important. Loss is another name for error and is measured as the difference between actual and predicted values. The goal of the neural network is to minimize errors. The learning objectives of this chapter are as follows:

- Understand why activation functions are required.
- Know the types of activation functions.
- Understand the loss functions.
- Know the types of loss functions.
- Know about feedforward networks.
- Know the basics of backpropagation.

3.1 Overview of Shallow Networks

Humans receive a lot of information from the outside world. However, the brain significantly knows how to remove all the unnecessary information to extract only the necessary information. This ability is one of the greatest mechanisms of the human brain to extract important information and suppress irrelevant information. This important extraction of information requires the usage of activation functions.

Also, a single neuron can do only a limited task. One requires a complex interconnection of the neurons as a neural network to perform complex tasks. As discussed in the last chapter, these are called multilayer neural networks.

A neural network is organized as a set of layers. A layer is a group of neurons. Each layer is connected to the previous layers. One layer serves as the input and presents the data to the subsequent layers, thus making the layer's output the input for the next layer.

There are three layers in multilayer neural networks.

(i) **Input Layer:** The input layer is the collection of grouped neurons that aim to get the input data and send it to the subsequent layers. The input layer consists of many neurons. Each neuron corresponds to an input.

(ii) **Hidden Layers:** There can be one or more hidden layers. Hidden layers distinguish shallow networks from deep learning networks.

Each hidden layer consists of neurons that help to solve complex problems by studying the complex relationships among neural networks. These layers use complex activation functions.

(iii) **Output Layer:** The output layer consists of many neurons that help binary and multiclass classification. This output layer is the final layer and generates the final output. There will be only one output layer for all the networks.

Feedforward neural networks are a type of artificial neural network where the connections between the nodes do not form a cycle.

A fully connected network is also called a dense network. Here, each neuron in the layer is connected to every other neuron in the next layer.

Also, it should be noted that multilayer neural networks and multilayer perceptron (MLP) refer to the same concept. The multilayer neural network is said with respect to the architectures, and MLP is often said in the context that the neural networks have perceptrons as neurons. Both views are correct. The core difference is that multilayer neural networks can use all activation functions compared to multilayer perceptrons.

3.1.1 Shallow vs. Deep Neural Networks

The difference between shallow and deep learning networks is the number of hidden layers. In deep learning, the number of hidden layers is more. The number of layers makes a network deep, as shown in Table 3.1.

Table 3.1 Differences Between Shallow and Deep Learning Networks

Shallow Networks	Deep Neural Networks
Shallow networks have only one or two hidden layers. The main difference between the shallow and deep neural networks is in the number of hidden layers.	Deep networks have more than two layers. These have multiple hidden layers.
These networks learn mostly local features.	These networks learn both global and local features.
These networks characterized by small datasets.	These networks work on large datasets.
These networks are useful for solving simple tasks like binary and multiclass classification only.	These networks are useful for solving complex tasks like image and object recognition.

The computations are illustrated in the following numerical example:

Example 3.1: Consider the neural network as given in Figure 3.1.

A sample neural network is given in Figure 3.1.

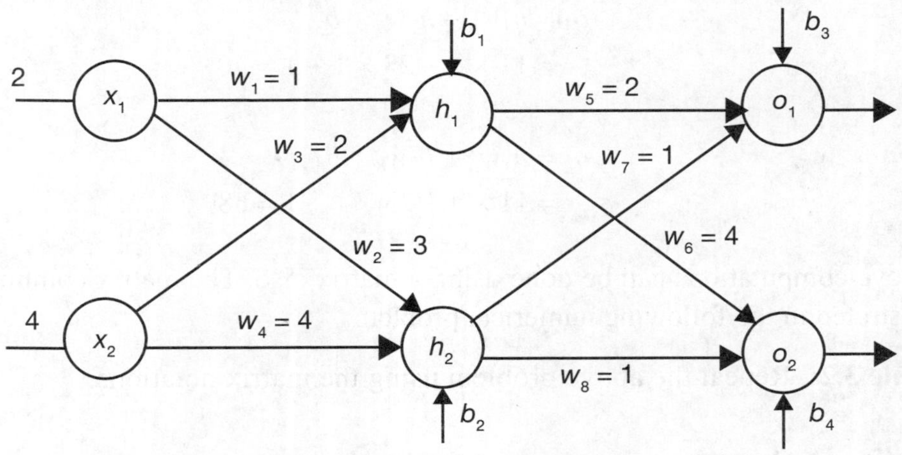

Figure 3.1 A Sample Multilayer Perceptron Model

Assume the inputs $x_1 = 2$ and $x_2 = 4$. The weights are given as

$$w_1 = 1, w_2 = 3, w_3 = 2, w_4 = 4, w_5 = 2, w_6 = 4, w_7 = 1, w_8 = 1$$

Let all the biases $b_1 = b_2 = b_3 = b_4$ be: 1. For simplicity, let us consider the activation function to be a linear function. In other words, the outputs are the same as the input. Show the output of the neural network.

Solution

Let us consider the following neural network. Let the inputs be $x_1 = 2, x_2 = 4$.

Let us compute the values at the hidden node h_1 and node h_2. The computation h_1 can be computed at the weighted sum of the input and its associated weight. It should be observed that the biases $b_1 = b_2 = 1$.

At the node h_1,

$$\begin{aligned} h_1 &= (x_1 w_1 + x_2 w_3) + b_1 \\ &= (2 \times 1 + 4 \times 2) + 1 = 11 \end{aligned}$$

At the node h_2,

$$\begin{aligned} h_2 &= (x_1 w_2 + x_2 w_4) + b_2 \\ &= (2 \times 3 + 4 \times 4) + 1 = 23 \end{aligned}$$

And at node

$$\begin{aligned} o_1 &= h_1 w_5 + h_2 w_7 + b_3 \\ &= 11 \times 2 + 23 \times 1 + 1 = 46 \end{aligned}$$

And

$$\begin{aligned} o_2 &= h_1 w_6 + h_2 w_8 + b_4 \\ &= 11 \times 4 + 23 \times 1 + 1 = 68 \end{aligned}$$

The above computations can be done using a matrix also. The matrix computations are illustrated in the following numerical problem.

Example 3.2: Repeat the above problem using the matrix notations.

Solution

The matrix W can be constructed as

$$\begin{pmatrix} \text{Weights of the first node} \\ \text{Weights of the second node} \\ \vdots \\ \text{Weights of the n}^{\text{th}} \text{ node} \end{pmatrix}$$ and the input and bias as the vectors. Based on this, it can be observed that all the weights of h_1 are listed in the first row, and the second row is all the weights of the neuron h_2. It should be observed that the biases $b_1 = b_2 = 1$. The inputs and biases form a vector in matrix computation. The matrix computation for the neural network of Figure 3.1. is computed as

$$h = \begin{pmatrix} 1 & 2 \\ 3 & 4 \end{pmatrix} \begin{pmatrix} 2 \\ 4 \end{pmatrix} + \begin{pmatrix} 1 \\ 1 \end{pmatrix}$$
$$= \begin{pmatrix} 10 \\ 22 \end{pmatrix} + \begin{pmatrix} 1 \\ 1 \end{pmatrix} = \begin{pmatrix} 11 \\ 23 \end{pmatrix}$$

It can be observed that the resultant is the same as the computed values. The weight at the output units o_1 o_2 can be computed in the same manner using the following matrix form. It can be observed that the weights o_1 form the first row and the weights o_2 form the second row. It should be observed that the biases $b_3 = b_4 = 1$.

$$o = \begin{pmatrix} 2 & 1 \\ 4 & 1 \end{pmatrix} \begin{pmatrix} 11 \\ 23 \end{pmatrix} + \begin{pmatrix} 1 \\ 1 \end{pmatrix}$$
$$= \begin{pmatrix} 45 \\ 67 \end{pmatrix} + \begin{pmatrix} 1 \\ 1 \end{pmatrix} = \begin{pmatrix} 46 \\ 68 \end{pmatrix}$$

It can be observed that o_1 is 46 and o_2 is 68. It matches with the hand calculations. Neural networks learn by supervised learning. The steps are listed below:

1. All the weights and biases are initialized randomly. The labelled inputs are given to the neural network.
2. The linear combination of the weights and inputs, along with the biases, are computed. These computations form the first step of the neural network. It is the linear part of the neural network.
3. The activation function is the non-linear part of the neural network. The subsequent section covers the activation function.
4. The neural network produces the output. This predicted output is compared with the ground truth, and the loss is computed by the loss functions. The loss functions are the focus of section 3.3.

5. Finally, the errors are backpropagated back, and the weights are updated. This weight updation is discussed in section 3.5.
6. The above steps are iteratively done for a predetermined number of steps or till the error becomes acceptable.

The above process constructs the model for the given data.

3.2 The Motivation of Activation Functions

The activation functions are one important pillar of deep learning.

The activation functions are required for the following reasons:

(i) Introduce non-linearity into the computation. (refer to Box 3.1)

(ii) Helps neural networks to learn very complex patterns and behaviours.

(iii) To mimic the behaviour of firing of biological neurons

Not only activation functions mimic the firing of neurons, but it also brings non-linearity in the process. Without the non-linearity, the neural networks can only act as linear regression and collapse the neural network as a single-layer network. The details of the linearity and non-linearity are given in the Box 3.1.

Box 3.1 Linearity Vs Non-Linearity

Linearity is a property of the system or function. Here, the input and output have a proportional relationship. By that, it means that if the input is increased, the output is also increased and vice versa.

Mathematically, a linear function is given as

$$f(x) = ax + b$$

Here, x is the input, $f(x)$ is the output, and a is the slope or coefficient that scales the input, and b is the y-intercept or constant value.

If a linear function is plotted, it produces a linear line in a cartesian coordinate system.

Mathematically, a linear relationship satisfies the property of homogeneity (also called scaling) and additivity (also called superposition). A linear relationship satisfies two properties as given below:

1. Property of additivity: $f(a + b) = f(a) + f(b)$.
2. Property of homogeneity: $f(kx) = k * f(x)$

In non-linearity, the input and output are not proportional to each other and exhibit complex behaviour. It does not satisfy the principle of superposition also. Examples of non-linear functions are exponentials (e.g. ae^x), logarithms (log n), trigonometric functions (cos(x)), and polynomial functions whose degree is greater than 1 (E.g. $ax^2 + bx + x$).

There is no point in having a linearity in neural networks. If the linear activation function is used, no matter how many layers one adds to another, the neural network's capacity to learn will not increase because the composition of multiple layers would still be a linear transformation.

To prove the above statement, let us consider two layers as follows:

1. The first layer is denoted as
$$y_1 = w_1x + b_1$$
2. The second layer takes input from the first layer and is hence denoted as
$$y_2 = w_2y_1 + b_2$$
Substituting the value of y_1 into this equation gives
$$\begin{aligned} y_2 &= w_2y_1 + b_2 \\ &= w_2(w_1x + b_1) + b_2 \\ &= (w_2w_1)x + w_2b_1 + b_2 \end{aligned}$$
The above equation is still linear only and can be expressed as
$$y_2 = wx + b$$
Where, $w = (w_2w_1)$ and $b = w_2b_1 + b_2$

The results are the same. This concept is illustrated through a numerical example given below:

Example 3.3: Let the input be $x = \begin{pmatrix} 2 \\ 4 \end{pmatrix}$. Let the weight of the first layer be given by $w_1 = \begin{pmatrix} 1 & 2 \\ 3 & 4 \end{pmatrix}$ with the bias given as $b_1 = \begin{pmatrix} 1 \\ 1 \end{pmatrix}$. Another linear layer is placed over that with the weights given by $w_2 = \begin{pmatrix} 2 & 1 \\ 4 & 1 \end{pmatrix}$ with the bias $b_2 = \begin{pmatrix} 1 \\ 1 \end{pmatrix}$. Prove that the result of two layers is the same as the first layer and second layer.

Solution

$$y_1 = \begin{pmatrix} 1 & 2 \\ 3 & 4 \end{pmatrix}\begin{pmatrix} 2 \\ 4 \end{pmatrix} + \begin{pmatrix} 1 \\ 1 \end{pmatrix} = \begin{pmatrix} 10 \\ 22 \end{pmatrix} + \begin{pmatrix} 1 \\ 1 \end{pmatrix} = \begin{pmatrix} 11 \\ 23 \end{pmatrix}$$

$$y_2 = w_2 y_1 + b_2$$

$$= \begin{pmatrix} 2 & 1 \\ 4 & 1 \end{pmatrix}\begin{pmatrix} 11 \\ 23 \end{pmatrix} + \begin{pmatrix} 1 \\ 1 \end{pmatrix} = \begin{pmatrix} 45 \\ 67 \end{pmatrix} = \begin{pmatrix} 46 \\ 68 \end{pmatrix}$$

The stacking of linear layers gives the resultant, as discussed before

$$y_2 = wx + b$$

where, $w = (w_2 w_1)$ and $b = w_2 b_1 + b_2$

Substituting the values one gets

$$y_2 = (w_2 w_1)x + w_2 b_1 + b_2$$

$$= \left(\begin{pmatrix} 2 & 1 \\ 4 & 1 \end{pmatrix}\begin{pmatrix} 1 & 2 \\ 3 & 4 \end{pmatrix}\right)\begin{pmatrix} 2 \\ 4 \end{pmatrix} + \begin{pmatrix} 2 & 1 \\ 4 & 1 \end{pmatrix}\begin{pmatrix} 1 \\ 1 \end{pmatrix} + \begin{pmatrix} 1 \\ 1 \end{pmatrix}$$

$$= \begin{pmatrix} 5 & 8 \\ 7 & 12 \end{pmatrix}\begin{pmatrix} 2 \\ 4 \end{pmatrix} + \begin{pmatrix} 3 \\ 5 \end{pmatrix} + \begin{pmatrix} 1 \\ 1 \end{pmatrix}$$

$$= \begin{pmatrix} 42 \\ 62 \end{pmatrix} + \begin{pmatrix} 4 \\ 6 \end{pmatrix} = \begin{pmatrix} 46 \\ 68 \end{pmatrix}$$

It can be observed that the values are the same. Therefore, no matter how many layers are added, the result would be predictable. This linearity makes the network collapsable. This fact is illustrated through the example 3.4.

Example 3.4: Show that the neural network shown in Fig. 3.1 can collapse because of linear activation functions.

Solution

Let us understand that:

$$o = \begin{pmatrix} 2 & 1 \\ 4 & 1 \end{pmatrix}\begin{pmatrix} 11 \\ 23 \end{pmatrix} + \begin{pmatrix} 1 \\ 1 \end{pmatrix}$$

It should be noted that the term $\begin{pmatrix} 11 \\ 23 \end{pmatrix}$ is obtained as the results of previous computation.

So, rewrite the computation of o as follows:

$$=\begin{pmatrix}2 & 1\\4 & 1\end{pmatrix}\left(\begin{pmatrix}1 & 2\\3 & 4\end{pmatrix}\begin{pmatrix}2\\4\end{pmatrix}+\begin{pmatrix}1\\1\end{pmatrix}\right)+\begin{pmatrix}1\\1\end{pmatrix}$$

$$=\left[\begin{pmatrix}2 & 1\\4 & 1\end{pmatrix}\begin{pmatrix}1 & 2\\3 & 4\end{pmatrix}\begin{pmatrix}2\\4\end{pmatrix}\right]+\left[\begin{pmatrix}2 & 1\\4 & 1\end{pmatrix}\begin{pmatrix}1\\1\end{pmatrix}\right]+\begin{pmatrix}1\\1\end{pmatrix}$$

$$=\begin{pmatrix}5 & 8\\7 & 12\end{pmatrix}\begin{pmatrix}2\\4\end{pmatrix}+\begin{pmatrix}4\\6\end{pmatrix}$$

It shows that the original neural network can be collapsed. It can be shown that the neural network given in Figure 3.1 is equivalent to the network given in Figure 3.2.

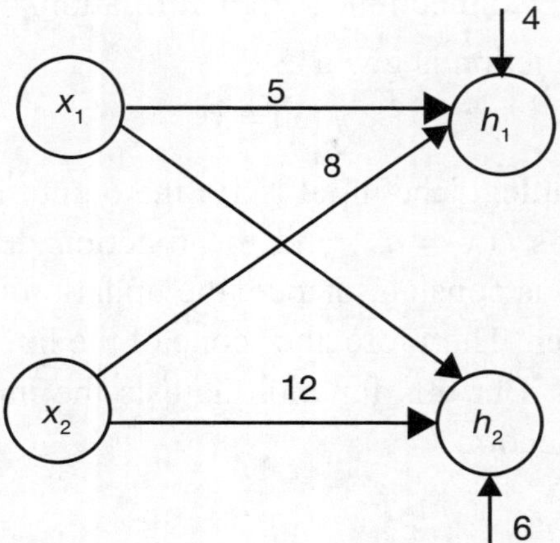

Figure 3.2 The Collapsed Network

One can check the results.

$$=\begin{pmatrix}5 & 8\\7 & 12\end{pmatrix}\begin{pmatrix}2\\4\end{pmatrix}+\begin{pmatrix}4\\6\end{pmatrix}$$

$$=\begin{pmatrix}42\\62\end{pmatrix}+\begin{pmatrix}4\\6\end{pmatrix}=\begin{pmatrix}46\\68\end{pmatrix}$$

The results are still the same.

The above discussion concludes that the importance of non-linear activation functions and hence the subject of discussion in the subsequent sections.

3.3 Types of Activation Functions

The activation functions are of two types:

1. Linear activation function
2. Non-linear activation function

Let us discuss some of the important activation functions.

3.3.1 Identity Activation Function

An example of a linear function is $f(x) = x$ or $f(x) = a$ where the x range is between $-\infty$ to $+\infty$. This function returns the same values that are given to it as input. It is also known as an identity map, connection, or transformation.

The identity activation function is given as

$$f(x) = x$$

where $\forall x \in \mathbb{R}$. For example, if the input is 10, the output is 10. The linear function can generally be given as $f(x) = ax$, and the function derivative is $f'(x) = a$. In other words, the gradient is constant; hence, the updation is the same, so the neural network cannot learn much. Therefore, the scope of the linear functions as activation functions is very limited. But this function adjusts the input so that the input and output have a linear connection.

3.3.2 Binary Step Function

This function is called the Heaviside step function, named after Oliver Heaviside. One can recollect that this function was used in McCulloch-Pitts model. This function returns zero for the negative input and +1 for the positive input. Mathematically, this function is given as

$$\begin{cases} 0 & \textit{for } \mathrm{x} < 0 \\ 1 & \textit{for } \mathrm{x} \geq 0 \end{cases}$$

The plot of the binary step function is shown in Figure 3.3.

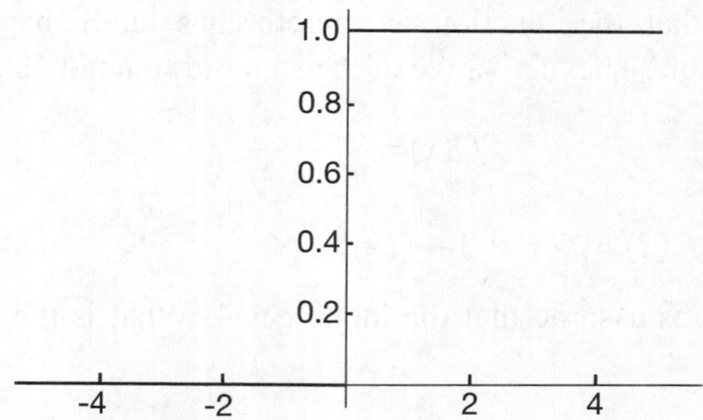

Figure 3.3 Binary Step Function

The binary step function is not useful for multiclass classification problems. One can recollect that the binary step function is the activation function for perceptron. The gradient of the binary step function is zero, that is $f'(x) = 0$, for all x.

3.3.3 Sigmoid Activation Functions

A sigmoid function is an S-shaped curve. The output of the sigmoid function is a probability that ranges between [0 – 1]. The sigmoidal function is given as follows:

$$f(x) = \frac{1}{1 + e^{-x}}$$

The plot of the sigmoidal function is shown in Figure 3.4.

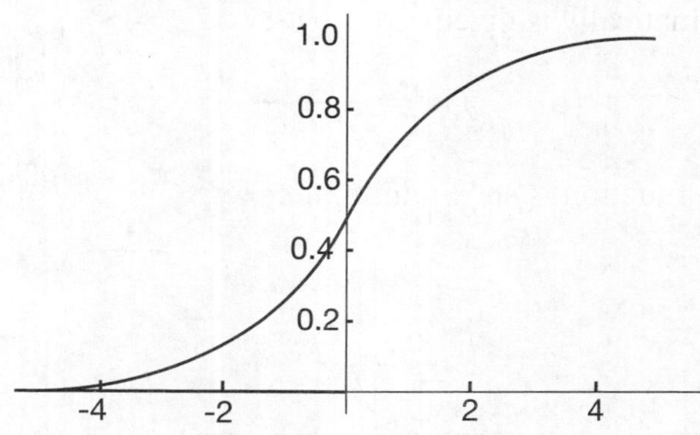

Figure 3.4 Sigmoidal Function

One can observe that the function is smooth, has an S-shaped curve, and is continuously derivable. The derivative of the sigmoid function is given as

$$f'(x) = \frac{e^{-x}}{(1+e^{-x})^2}$$

It can be given as $f'(x) = f(x) - (1 - f(x))$.

Example 3.5: Let us assume that the input x is 4. What is the output of the sigmoidal function?

Solution

The sigmoidal function is given as $f(x) = \frac{1}{1+e^{-x}}$

So, substitute the value $x = 4$ in the above equation, and we get

$$f(x) = \frac{1}{1+e^{-4}} = \frac{1}{1+0.018} \cong 0.982$$

So, for an input of $x = 4$, the sigmoidal function value is approximately 0.982.

3.3.4 Hyperbolic Tangent function (Tanh Function)

Hyperbolic tangent function Tanh is a non-linear function. The output of the tanh function is bipolar. The function is symmetric around the origin. Hence, the output ranges from -1 to $+1$. Therefore, the output does not always have the same sign.

The function mathematically is given as follows:

$$f(x) = \frac{e^x - e^{-x}}{e^x + e^{-x}}$$

The plot of the tanh function is shown in Figure 3.5.

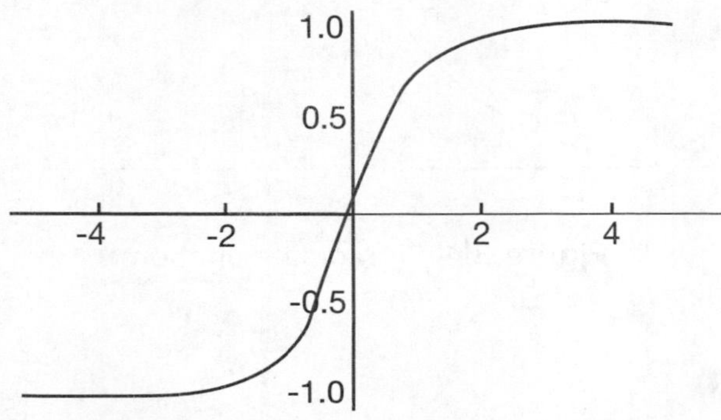

Figure 3.5 Tanh Function

This function crosses zero at $f(0)$, and its asymptotes are −1 and +1. The derivative of the function is given as

$$f'(x) = (1 - f(x))^2$$

3.3.5 ReLU Function

ReLU stands for Rectified Linear Unit. This function is also known as the ramp function. ReLU is a non-linear activation function. It does not activate all neurons at the same time. The output of the ReLU function ranges between 0 to +∞. ReLU provides an improved convergence. The function is mathematically given as

$$f(x) = \max(0, x)$$

The derivative of the ReLU function is given as

$$f'(x) = \begin{cases} 1 & for\ \mathrm{x} \geq 0 \\ 0 & for\ \mathrm{x} < 0 \end{cases}$$

The derivative of ReLU is either 0 or 1.

The advantages and disadvantages of the ReLU function are given in the following Table 3.2.

Table 3.2 Advantages and Disadvantages of ReLU Function

Advantages	Disadvantages
Sparse activation.	Not differentiable at zero but differentiable elsewhere.
Improved gradient propagation algorithm.	The outputs are unbounded.
Fewer vanishing gradient issues.	Dying ReLU problems as it suppresses weak signals, making it zero. These dying neurons reduce the network capacity.

One should observe that if the error is zero when it is backpropagated, it results in no learning. This problem is because of the essential property of ReLU, which suppresses all the weak signals. Therefore, ReLU should be used only in the hidden layer. Since it suppresses all weak signals, ReLU creates more dead neurons. This problem is solved by one of the variants of ReLU called leaky ReLU.

There are many variants of ReLU, as shown in Figure 3.6.

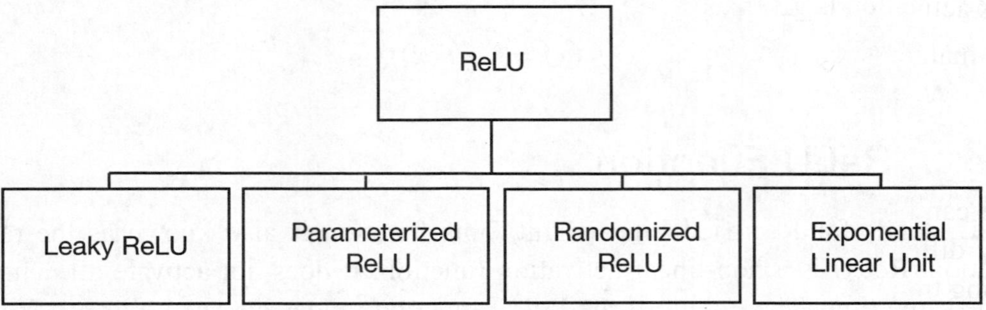

Figure 3.6 Types of ReLU

In the traditional ReLU, the output is zero for negative values. This rapid transition to zero means that some of the information is lost. Leaky ReLU solves this problem.

Example 3.6: Let us assume that the input x is –4 and +17. What is the output of the ReLU function?

Solution

Suppose the input of $x = -4$, substituting this in ReLU equation

$f(-4) = \max(0, -4) = 0$ as –4 is less than 0.

Suppose the input of $x = +17$, substituting this in ReLU equation

$f(17) = \max(0, 17) = 17$ as 17 is greater than 0.

Thus, the positive values are unchanged in ReLU.

Leaky ReLU

Leaky ReLU maintains a parameter called β. The function converges β so that the smoothing process is gradual and not abrupt. The default value β is 0.01. Therefore, the mathematical function of the leaky ReLU is given as follows:

$$f(a,x) = \begin{cases} \beta x & \text{for } x<0 \\ x & \text{for } x \geq 0 \end{cases}$$

The derivative of the Leaky ReLU function is given as below:

$$f'(x) = \begin{cases} 1 & \text{for } x \geq 0 \\ \beta & \text{for } x<0 \end{cases}$$

Parametric ReLU

This activation function is another variant of ReLU.

The mathematical function of the parametric ReLU is given as follows:

$$f(a,x) = \begin{cases} \beta x & for\ \mathrm{x<0} \\ x & for\ \mathrm{x \geq 0} \end{cases}$$

One can observe that the mathematical function is similar to the leaky ReLU. The only difference is that β it is a tuneable parameter in parametric ReLU, learned during training. When $\beta = 0.01$, this activation function reduces to leaky ReLU.

Randomized ReLU

In the randomized ReLU, one can assign the value β randomly to a smaller value. This function can be used as a good regularizer also for preventing overfitting. This kind of regularization is helpful for complex parameters.

Exponential Linear Unit Activation (ELU)

ELU is also another variant of ReLU. The ELU is given as follows:

$$f(a,x) = \begin{cases} \alpha(e^x - 1) & for\ \mathrm{x<0} \\ x & for\ \mathrm{x \geq 0} \end{cases}$$

The range of this function is between $-\infty$ to $+\infty$. Here, α is a constant and is positive. This function modifies the slope of the negative part of the function. It uses a log variant for the negative values of x. In other words, When the inputs are negative, this function gradually smooths until the output reaches α, which α is generally a small number. The advantage of this is that this is smooth, unlike the ReLU function, where the transition is rapid.

The derivative of ELU is given as follows.

$$f'(a,x) = \begin{cases} x & for\ \mathrm{x \geq 0} \\ a(e^x) & if\ \mathrm{x < 0} \end{cases}$$

3.3.6 Swish Function

Swish is a new activation function designed by Google. The swish function is mathematically given as

$$f(x) = x \times \sigma(\beta x)$$

Here β is a tuneable parameter, and σ is the sigmoid function.

The derivative of a swish function is given as, where σ is the sigmoid function. One advantage of the swish function is that it is not monotonic. Also, the function is smooth and differentiable at all times.

3.3.7 Softmax Activation Function

A softmax function transforms a vector of integers to another vector of probability values that range between 0 to 1. One can consider this as an upgraded sigmoid function and can be given mathematically as

$$\text{Given } [x_1, x_2, \cdots, x_n],$$

$$\text{softmax}(\text{x}_i) = \frac{e^{x_i}}{\sum_j e^{x_j}}$$

Softmax is useful for multiclass classification problems. If there are N classes, then softmax can be used. Often, the softmax function is used in association with on-hot encoding.

Example 3.7: Let us assume that the input vector is (4, 2, 1). Calculate the softmax probabilities for each class.

Solution

Let us compute the exponentials for all the elements of the input vector.

$$e^{4.0} = 54.599$$

$$e^{2.0} = 7.389$$

$$e^{1.0} = 2.718$$

The sum of all the exponentials is

$$\sum_i^3 e^{x_i} = 54.599 + 7.389 + 2.718$$

$$= 64.706$$

Now, the softmax probabilities can be computed as follows:

$$p_1 = \frac{e^{4.0}}{64.706} = \frac{54.599}{64.706} \cong 0.844$$

$$p_2 = \frac{e^{2.0}}{64.706} = \frac{7.389}{64.706} \cong 0.114$$

$$p_3 = \frac{e^{1.0}}{64.706} = \frac{2.718}{64.706} \cong 0.042$$

So, for the input vector $x = [4.0, 2.0, 1.0]$, the softmax probabilities are approximately 0.844, 0.114, and 0.042.

3.3.8 Softplus

Softplus is another activation function that was released only in 2001. The function returns the output in the range 0 to $+\infty$. Mathematically, the function is given as follows:

$$f(x) = \log(1+e^x)$$

The derivative of the function is given as

$$f'(x) = \frac{1}{1+e^{-x}}$$

One can observe that this is the same as the softmax function.

The guidelines for choosing activation functions are given in Box 3.2.

Box 3.2 Guidelines of Activation Function

There are four important characteristics of activation functions.

1. The function must be continuous and infinite in the domain
2. Functions are monotonic functions.
3. Good activation functions are non-linear
4. Computing the activation functions and their derivatives should be easy.

The informal guideline is sigmoid functions are good for classifiers. But sigmoid and tanh functions have the problem of vanishing gradients, and ReLU is a more popular choice in deep learning. Because of the dead neuron problem, ReLU is used only in hidden layers. Softmax is for multiclass classification problems.

3.4 Loss Functions

Loss functions are the second pillar of deep learning after activation functions.

The loss functions measure the neural network's performance by computing the error as the difference between the predicted and actual values (or ground truth). The goal is to ensure that the error is as small as possible. In the literature, two terms are used: loss functions and cost functions. Sometimes, they are used interchangeably. But there is a subtle difference. The difference between the loss function and the cost function is that loss functions are for the single training example, and the cost functions are the average loss function of the entire dataset. Suppose y and y' are the actual and predicted values, and if there are m data points in the training dataset, then the loss function is given as

$loss$ function $= L(y, y')$. The cost function is given as

$$\text{cost function} = \frac{1}{m}\sum_{i=1}^{m} L(y, y')$$

The goal of the neural network is to minimize the error of the neural network. The loss functions measure the error. The types of loss functions are shown in Figure 3.7.

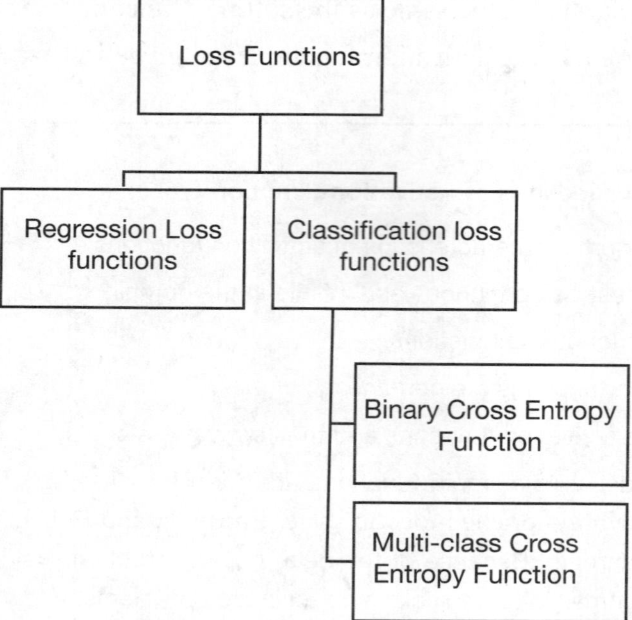

Figure 3.7 Types of Loss Functions

3.4.1 Regression Loss functions

Regression loss functions measure the error for regression problems. Some of the commonly used regression loss functions are listed below:

1. Error

   The regression cost function involves numbers. This regression cost is defined as the difference between the actual and the predicted values. Mathematically, this is given as follows:

   $$\text{Error} = y - y'$$

   Here, y is the output, and y' is the predicted value.

   This error is called distance-based error and forms the basis for all computations. The main problem of the regression cost function is that the positive and negative values are cancelled out, which usually creates a problem in understanding and, hence, is not normally recommended.

2. Mean Error

   The error of the sample is computed using the distance error, and then the mean of all errors is computed.

Example 3.8: Compute the mean error: the actual values y are {5, 6, 8, 10, 12} and the predicted values $y' = \{4, 7, 9, 10, 8\}$.

Solution

The actual values and the predicted values are given in Table 3.3. The error is computed as the difference between the actual and predicted value. The mean error is the average of all the errors of all data N.

Table 3.3 Illustration for Computing Mean Error

y (Actual Value)	y' (Predicted Value)	Error = $y - y'$
5	4	1
6	7	–1
8	9	–1
10	10	0
12	8	4
	Sum	3
	Mean	3/5 = 0.6

It can be seen that the positive and negative values are cancelled out, which usually creates a problem in understanding and, hence, is not normally recommended.

3. Mean Absolute Error (MAE)

The mean absolute error is also known as the L_1 loss. It is the difference between the dataset's actual and predicted value. The mean absolute error is mathematically given as follows:

$$MAE = \frac{\sum_{i=0}^{N} |y - y'|}{N}$$

The advantage and disadvantages of MAE is given in Table 3.4.

Table 3.4 Advantages and Disadvantages of MAE

Advantages	Disadvantages
Intuitive	The graph is not differentiable
Easy to visualize	
Very robust to outlier	

The mean absolute error is computed as the mean of all absolute errors of N data.

Example 3.9: Compute the mean absolute error as the actual values y are {5, 6, 8, 10, 12} and the predicted values $y' = \{4, 7, 9, 10, 8\}$.

Solution

The actual values and the predicted values are given in Table 3.5. The error is computed as the difference between the actual and predicted value. The mean error is the average of all the errors of all data N.

Table 3.5 Illustration of Computing MAE

y (Actual Value)	y' (Predicted Value)	Error = $\lvert y - y \rvert$
5	4	1
6	7	1
8	9	1

y (Actual Value)	y' (Predicted Value)	Error = $\|y - y'\|$
10	10	0
12	8	4
	Sum	7
	Mean	7/5 = 1.4.

It can be seen that the mean absolute error amplifies the error as it removes the concept of positive and negative values. This kind of error amplification is a good aspect of mean absolute error.

4. Mean Square Error (MSE)

   MSE is the square of the difference between the actual and the predicted value. It is then the average sum of squared differences between the predicted and the actual value. MSE is also known as L_2 loss. The formula for MSE is given as follows:

$$MSE = \frac{\sum_{i=0}^{N} (y - y')^2}{N}$$

   The advantages and disadvantages of the MSE are given in Table 3.6.

Table 3.6 Advantages and Disadvantages of MSE

Advantages	Disadvantages
Easy to interpret	Error is always positive because of square making the understanding difficult
Penalizes the error by magnitude, the strength of the error	Less robust
Always differentiable	Not robust to outliers
Only one local minimum	

   It can be observed that the mean square error aims to reduce the negative error by taking the square of it. Therefore, the mean square error is computed as the mean of all squared errors of N data.

$$\text{MSE} = \frac{\textit{Sum} \text{ of the squared errors}}{N}$$

That is, $$MSE = \frac{\sum_{i=0}^{N}(y-y')^2}{N}$$

Example 3.10: Compute the mean squared error: the actual values y are {5, 6, 8, 10, 12} and the predicted values y'= {4, 7, 9, 10, 8}.

Solution

The actual values and the predicted values are given in Table 3.7. The error is computed as the difference between the actual and predicted value. The mean square error is the average of the squared errors of all data N.

Table 3.7 Illustration of Computing Mean Square Error

y (Actual Value)	y' (Predicted Value)	Error = $\sum_{i=0}^{N}(y-y')^2$
5	4	1
6	7	1
8	9	1
10	10	0
12	8	16
	Sum	19
	Mean	19/5 = 3.8

It can be seen that the mean square error amplifies the error as it removes the concept of positive and negative values. This amplification part is a good aspect of mean square error.

5. Huber Loss

Huber loss is very popular in Support vector machines. The function is given as follows:

$$Huber(y, f(x)) = \begin{cases} \frac{1}{2}(y-f(x))^2 & \textit{for } |y-f(x)| \le \delta \\ \delta\left(|y-f(x)| - \frac{1}{2}\delta\right) & \textit{Otherwise} \end{cases}$$

Here, y is the target value, and $f(x)$ is the $\hat{y}$ the predicted value and δ is the hyperparameter. Here δ is the transition point from quadratic to linear function. The advantages and disadvantages of Huber loss are given in Table 3.8.

Table 3.8 Advantages and Disadvantages of Huber Loss

Advantages	Disadvantages
Robust to outliers	Complexity is very high and needs to be optimized
It is in between MAE and MSE	

Example 3.11: Compute the Huber loss: the actual values y are 6, and the predicted value $f(x)$, i.e., $\hat{y}$, is 4. Assume the value δ is 4.

Solution

Compute the difference between the actual and the predicted value $=|y - f(x)|$ $=|6-4|=2$.

This value is $\leq \delta$. So, one should take the quadratic part of the Huber loss. So, Huber's loss is $\frac{1}{2}(y - f(x))^2 = \frac{1}{2}(6-4)^2 = 2$

6. Hinge Loss

Hinge loss is also used in SVM. Its output is +1 or –1, and the hinge loss is given as follows:

$$Hinge(D) = \max(0,\ 1 - y \times h(y))$$

The hinge loss for the entire dataset is computed by summing the hinge loss of all N data points.

Example 3.12: Compute the Hinge loss: the actual values y are $\{1, 1, -1, -1\}$ and the predicted values $y' = \{0.5, 1.5, 0.8, -1.4\}$ as shown in Table 3.9.

Solution

The actual values and the predicted values are given in Table 3.9. The error is computed as the difference between the actual and predicted value. The mean error is the average of all the errors of all data N.

Table 3.9 Illustration of Computing Mean Square Error

y (Actual Value)	*y′* (Predicted Value)	Error = max(0, 1 – *yh*(*y*))
1	0.5	Max(0, 1 – (1 × 0.5) = max(0, 0.5)) = 0.5
1	1.5	Max(0, 1 – (1 × 1.5)) = max(0, –0.5) = 0
–1	0.8	Max(0, 1 – (–1 × 0.8)) = max(0, 1.8) = 1.8
–1	1 – 1.4	Max(0, 1 – (–1 × 1.4)) = max(0, 2.4) = 2.4
Hinge Loss		4.7

It can be observed that the hinge loss is the sum of all hinge loss of the data of the entire dataset.

3.4.2 Classification Based Error Functions

Cross-entropy provides the basis for all classification problems. One can observe that the classification problems give output as labels and not numbers like regression problems. Cross entropy is a measure of Information Theory (refer to Box 3.3).

Box 3.3 Information Theory and Cross-entropy

Information theory deals with the quantification of information. Information theory is useful for areas like communication and data compression. Claude Shannon is the "Father of modern digital communication and Information Theory." His paper in 1948 titled "A Mathematical Theory of Communications" showed how to measure information. Cross-entropy is the measure used for loss functions, and it measures the differences between two probability distributions for random variables or events. In this case, the two distributions are the actual value and the predicted value distributions.

The two types of cross-entropy are binary cross-entropy and categorical cross-entropy.

Binary Cross Entropy

Binary cross entropy is applicable for classification problems. Binary Cross-entropy is also known as log loss. It takes the probability of the predicted and actual labels and measures their dissimilarity, called error. The formula for computing the binary cross entropy for a single data is given below:

$$L(y, \hat{y}) = -(y\log(\hat{y}) + (1-y)\log(1-\hat{y}))$$

It can be noted that y is the actual label, and $\hat{y}$ is the predicted label.

Example 3.13: Compute the binary cross entropy if the actual label is 1 and the predicted value is 0.3.

Solution

As per the problem statement, $y = 1$ and $\hat{y} = 0.3$. Substituting the value in the above formula, one gets

$$\begin{aligned} L(y,\hat{y}) &= -(1\times\log(0.3)+(1-1)\log(1-0.3)) \\ &= -(\log(0.3)) \\ &\cong 0.523 \end{aligned}$$

Like this, the binary cross-entropy is calculated for every data, and the final performance of the classifier is the sum of all binary cross-entropy of all the points. The classifier better fits the given data if the final value is small. One of the biggest advantages of the binary cross entropy function is that it amplifies the error manifold, thereby giving its greatest contribution. Cross-entropy uses base e or natural logarithms. So, the units are called nats and not bits.

Categorical Cross-Entropy for Multiclass Problems

Categorical cross-entropy measures the dissimilarity between the predicted class probabilities and the actual class labels. Therefore, categorical cross-entropy is used for multiclass classification problems. The formula for computing the categorical cross-entropy is given as

$$L(y,\hat{y}) = -\sum_{i=1}^{N} y_i \times \log(\hat{y}_i)$$

Here y_1 is the one-shot vector of the encoded actual class labels and $\hat{y}_i$ the vector of predicted variables. N is the number of classes of the multiclass problem.

Example 3.14: Let the output of three items, red, green, and blue, be, respectively, (1, 0, 0), (0, 1, 0), and (0, 0, 1). Let us assume that the output given the neural network is P(0.5, 0.4, 0.1). What is the cross entropy of the red, green, and blue?

Solution

The cross-entropy of red is given as

Cross entropy(Red, P) =

$$-[1\times\log(0.5)+0\times\log(0.4)+0\times\log(0.1)] = -(\log(0.5) \approx 0.301$$

Similarly, the cross entropy of other items can be computed

Cross entropy(green, P) =

$$-[0\times\log(0.5)+1\times\log(0.4)+0\times\log(0.1)]=-(\log(0.4))\approx 0.398$$

Cross entropy(blue, P) =

$$-[0\times\log(0.5)+0\times\log(0.4)+1\times\log(0.1)]=-(\log(0.1))=+1$$

The above is the categorical cross-entropy of the single data. So, all the cross entropies should be summed to get the overall performance of the multiclass classifier. A multiclass classifier is best when its value is low.

3.5 Mathematics of Backpropagation

The backpropagation is called reverse differentiation. This name is because the gradient of the loss function is computed with respect to each weight using the chain rule and goes in the reverse direction. This computation process is continued till the first hidden layer that is present after the input layer. The movement of the gradients is in reverse form from the output to the input. The main advantage of this approach is that gradients are not computed from scratch. The gradient computed in the intermediate steps is reused. This reuse reduces the computational complexity of the neural networks.

The concept of derivatives and gradients comes directly from Calculus. Some of these details are given in Box 3.4.

Box 3.4 Role of Calculus in Deep Learning

The role of calculus in deep learning is immense. During the training of the neural network, the concepts of calculus are immensely useful. Calculus helps in designing and understanding activation functions, and the derivatives determine how the information flows through the network.

The jargons like derivatives and gradients are required in order to understand deep learning well as gradients are used to update weights and biases during the backpropagation stage.

(i) Derivatives: The derivative of a function is a measure of the change in output of a function with respect to the change in input. It is called the rate of change of a function at a given point.

(ii) Gradient: In deep learning, a gradient is a vector of partial derivatives of the loss function with respect to weights and biases. A gradient is a vector that describes the rate of change of a function at a given point. What is the need? The optimization algorithms use the gradients to update the weights and biases. For example, if the function is $f(x, y)$, then the gradient is given as $\nabla f = \left(\frac{\partial f}{\partial x}, \frac{\partial f}{\partial y}\right)$. This symbol ∇ is called nabla.

Partial derivatives and total derivatives are from the domain of calculus, especially multivariate calculus.

(iii) Total Derivatives: Total derivative (indicated as $\frac{dy}{dx}$, called differentials), on the other hand, indicates the change of function changes with respect to all its variables together. It indicates the changes of all variables simultaneously. For example, if $f(x) = x^3$, then its derivative is given as $f'(x) = 2x^2$. It indicates that, for a change in x, the function would change by the factor of $2x^2$.

(iv) Partial Derivatives: Partial derivatives (denoted as $\frac{\partial y}{\partial x}$, where ∂ indicates the partial derivative and x is the variable with respect to the partial differentiation done) represent a concept where differentiation is made with respect to a single variable while keeping all other variables constant. It indicates the effect of one variable while keeping all other variables constant. In other words, partial derivatives indicate the sensitivity of a function with respect to changes in a specific variable.

3.5.1 Role of Computational Graph and Chain rule

What is a computational graph? A computational graph is an acyclic graph that shows the graphical representation of a mathematical model to illustrate how the derivatives are calculated during the backpropagation process. It is an effective visualization tool for understanding the backpropagation process.

A computational model has nodes (Operations, functions) and edges representing the data flow. There are two types of nodes.

1. Variable nodes – These nodes can represent the variables, say inputs, weights, *W*, and biases, *b*.
2. Operation nodes – These nodes represent the operations (like *, +) and help to transform the input to the next level nodes.

The edges of the computational graph illustrate the data flow between the nodes. Also, these are effective visualizations of the flow of gradients.

Example 3.15: Consider the function $f = xy + zk$ and construct a computational graph.

Solution

Let the variables be x, y, z, and k. Let the intermediate variables be r and s, such that,

$$r = xy$$
$$s = zk$$
$$\text{so}, f = r + s$$

The computation graph for the above expression is given, as shown in Figure 3.8.

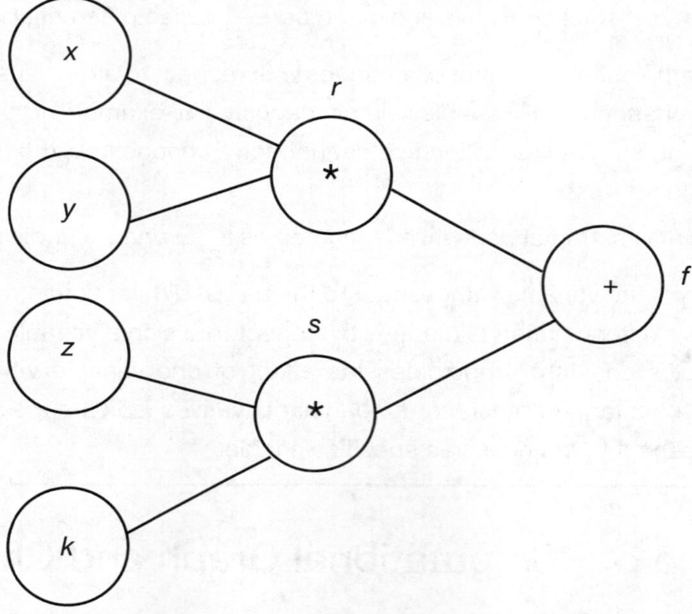

Figure 3.8 A Computational Graph

Chain Rule

The chain rule is fundamental in calculus. It allows us to find the derivative of a composite function. A function can have one or more variables as its arguments like $f(x)$, $g(x, y, m, z, s, r, y)$. The function $f(x)$ is called a univariate function, and the function $g(x)$ is a multivariate function as it is of many variables.

A composite function is a combination of two functions. For example, consider two functions, $f(x)$ and $g(x)$. The composite function is defined as

$$h = g(f(x))$$

The combination of functions is called a chaining process. The derivative of the above composite function is given as $h(x) = u$. Then, the derivative of the composite function $y(u(x))$ with respect to x can be computed as

$$\frac{\partial h}{\partial x} = \frac{\partial h}{\partial u} \times \frac{\partial u}{\partial x}$$

Thus, the partial derivative of the composite function is the product of the partial derivative of h with respect to u and the derivative of h with respect to x.

A neural network can be visualized as a composite function. For example, a neural network can be visualized as

$$F^3(F^2(F^1(F^0(x))))$$

So, the chain rule is applicable in finding derivatives of these neural networks.

Example 3.16: Consider the computational graph as shown in Figure 3.9. Show how the chain rule is applied for backpropagation.

Solution

One simple computational graph is shown below in Figure 3.9.

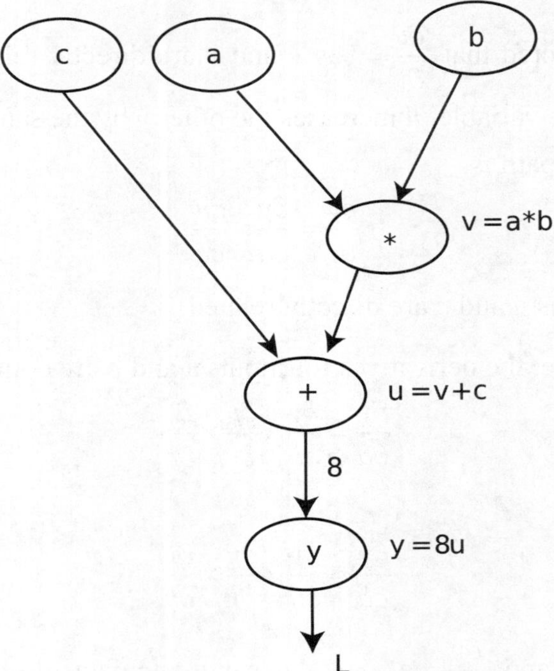

Figure 3.9 A Sample Computational Graph

The function $f(a, b, c)$ is given as: $f(a, b, c) = ab + c$

The computational graph can be created as follows:

Create intermediate variables,

1. $v = ab$ and
2. $u = v + c$
3. $y = 8u$

1. In the first step, for simplicity, L, the loss is assumed as y.
2. In the second step, the derivative of y with respect to the intermediate value u is computed as

$$\frac{\partial y}{\partial u} = 8$$

3. In the third step, the derivative of y with respect to the next intermediate value, v, is computed as

$$\frac{\partial y}{\partial v} = \frac{\partial y}{\partial u} \times \frac{\partial u}{\partial v}$$

It should be noted that $\frac{\partial u}{\partial v} = 1$ as u and v are directly related in the sense the increase in one variable, u increases the other v by the same quantity.

And the other path is

$$\frac{\partial y}{\partial c} = \frac{\partial y}{\partial u} \times \frac{\partial u}{\partial c}$$

Here, $\frac{\partial u}{\partial c} = 1$ as u and c are directly related.

4. In the last stage, the derivatives for inputs a and b are computed as

$$\frac{\partial y}{\partial a} = \frac{\partial y}{\partial u} \times \frac{\partial u}{\partial v} \times \frac{\partial v}{\partial a}$$

And

$$\frac{\partial y}{\partial b} = \frac{\partial y}{\partial u} \times \frac{\partial u}{\partial v} \times \frac{\partial v}{\partial b}$$

Here, $\frac{\partial v}{\partial a} = b$ and $\frac{\partial v}{\partial b} = a$. So, the weight update of the variable is "a" is $8 \times 1 \times b = 8$b. If b is 3, then the weight update of a is 24. In the same manner, the other weights can be computed.

Let us discuss the application of the chain rule in the backpropagation algorithm in the next section.

3.5.2 Backpropagation Algorithm

A sample multilayer neural network is shown in Figure 3.10.

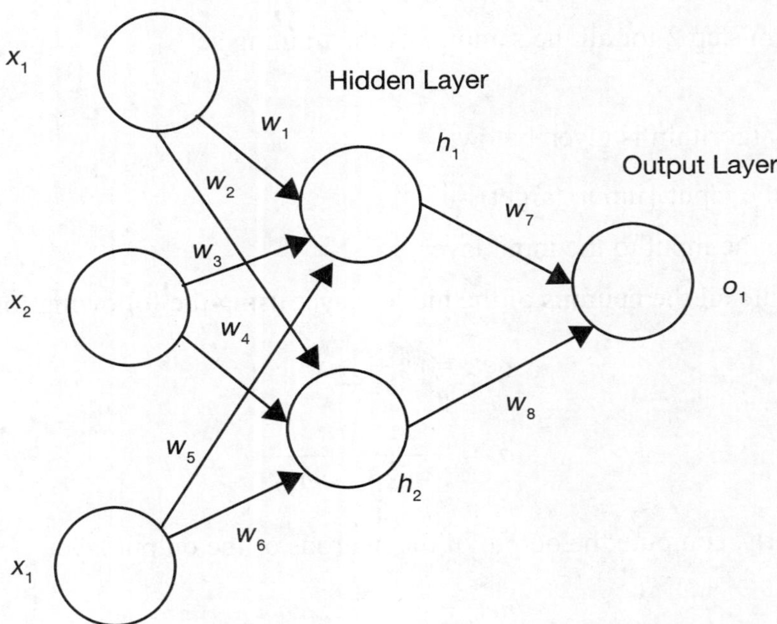

Figure 3.10 A Sample Multilayer Neural Network

There are two stages in multilayer neural networks:

(i) **Forward Stage:** In this stage, the data starts from the input and terminates with the output.

(ii) **Backward Stage:** In this stage, the weights and biases are modified based on the backpropagation model. Multilayer neural network also uses many non-linear activation models.

Backpropagation Algorithm

Multilayer neural networks use the generalized delta rule instead of the delta rule. Backpropagation is a variant of the generalized delta rule and is normally used to train the feedforward networks.

The algorithm can be informally given as below:

1. Input the vector {input, target}
2. For every input vector, do:
   2.1 Perform the forward sweep to the output
   2.2 Compare the target vector with the actual output
   2.3 If the error is not acceptable, then perform a backward sweep of the error vector
   2.4 Determine the weight change and update the vector
3. Perform step 2 for all the samples of the training set
4. Exit

The formal algorithm is given below:

1. Read the input {input, target)
2. Assign the input to the input layer
3. Compute all the neurons of the hidden layer using the following formula:

$$net_j = w_0 + \sum_{i=1}^{N} x_i w_i$$

$$o_j = \frac{1}{1+\exp(-net_j)}$$

   Similarly, compute the output of the neurons of the output layer.

$$net_j = w_0 + \sum_{i=1}^{N} x_i w_i$$

$$o_j = \frac{1}{1+\exp(-net_j)}$$

4. Compute the difference between the output and the target vector as an error. The error is given as

$$\delta_j = (t_j - o_j) o_j (1 - o_j)$$

   Similarly, calculate all the errors of all hidden layers using the formula.

$$\delta_k = o_j (1 - o_j) \sum_k \delta_k w_{kj}$$

5. The weights can be updated as

$$\Delta w_{ij} = \eta \times \delta_j \times o_i$$

The new weight is the old weight plus the increment $w_{ij} = w_{ij} + \Delta w_{ij}$

6. Go to step 2 and repeat all patterns till the convergence.

   The concept of backpropagation can be explained through the computational graph. While the backpropagation algorithm can compute gradients effectively, the weight updates can be effectively done with the optimizer functions. The optimizer functions are discussed in detail in the next chapter.

Summary

1. A traditional network that has one or two layers is called a shallow network.
2. A deep neural network has multiple hidden layers.
3. A multilayer neural network has three layers: an input, hidden, and output layer.
4. In feedforward networks, the data moves from the input layer to the output in one direction. The error moves in the opposite direction.
5. Activation functions mimic the firing of biological neurons.
6. Activation functions bring the non-linearity into the neural network.
7. The binary step function returns zero for the negative input and +1 for the positive input.
8. The output of the sigmoid function is between 0 and 1. The sigmoid function is a S-shaped curve.
9. Tanh is a non-linear activation function that returns a value between –1 and +1.
10. ReLU returns a value between 0 and infinity.
11. A dead neuron problem arises as ReLU suppresses all weaker signals, making it a zero.
12. The variants of ReLU are leaky ReLU, Parameterized ReLU, Randomized ReLU and Exponential ReLU.
13. The loss functions measure the error between actual and predicted values. It is an indication of the performance of the neural network.
14. Some regression loss functions are mean error, mean square error, and mean absolute error.
15. Binary cross-entropy is used for binary classification problems.
16. Multiclass cross-entropy is used for multiclass classification problems.
17. Computational graph is a visualization tool for observing the movement of data and gradients.

18. Backpropagation propagates the error back to update the weights and biases.
19. The backpropagation rule is a generalization of the delta rule.

Glossary

1. Shallow network – A neural network is called a shallow network because the number of hidden layers is just one or two.
2. Deep neural network – A deep neural network has many hidden layers.
3. Layer – A group of neurons is organized as a layer.
4. Feedforward network – A neural network whose acyclic graph does not form any cycles.
5. Dense network – A dense network is a fully connected network where a neuron in one layer is connected to all other neurons in the next layer.
6. Linearity – A condition where the input and output have a proportional linear relationship. If one changes, the other variable changes in a linear manner.
7. Non-linearity – A condition where the input and output do not have a proportional linear relationship.
8. Gradient – The first-order derivative of the function.
9. Activation functions – Activation functions take an aggregate value and produce an output.
10. Transfer Function – A synonym of activation functions.
11. ReLU – Rectified Linear Unit that returns the max of 0 and the input value
12. Leaky ReLU – The activation unit where the smoothing process is gradual and not abrupt.
13. Parametric ReLU – The parameter in this activation function is tunable.
14. Dead neuron – A problem of ReLU suppression of weak signals that creates more inactive neurons.
15. Softmax – An activation function that transforms a vector of integers to a vector of probability values.
16. Loss function – A loss function computes the error by taking the difference between the actual and predicted values.

17. Cost function – A cost function that computes the sum of all error values of all the losses of all the data points in the entire dataset.
18. Mean Absolute Error – The sum of all absolute errors of the data points.
19. Mean Squared Error – The sum of all the squared errors of all data points.
20. L_2 error – This is also known as the mean squared error.
21. Cross-entropy – Cross-entropy is a measure that computes the error of the categorical variables. This metric measures the difference between two random variables or events in the probability distributions.
22. Binary cross-entropy – This metric is also known as a log-loss. It measures the dissimilarity between two random variables or events in the probability distributions.
23. Categorical cross-entropy – It is a metric for measuring the dissimilarity between the predicted and the actual labels.
24. Computational graph – It is an acyclic graph that shows the graphical representation of a neural network.
25. Derivative – It is a measure of change in the output of the function with respect to the changes in x.
26. Gradient – A gradient is a vector of derivatives of a multivariate function.
27. Total derivative – Total derivative is a change in the function output with respect to all the variables.
28. Partial derivative – A partial derivative is a change in the function output with respect to a variable while keeping all other variables constant.
29. Chain rule – A rule that helps to find the derivative of a composite function.
30. Backpropagation – A mechanism of passing the error in a backward direction to update the errors.

Short Questions

1. What is the need for activation functions?
2. Why is ReLU popular in deep learning literature?
3. Why ReLU should be used only in hidden layers?
4. Distinguish between sigmoid and softmax activation functions.
5. Softmax is suitable for multiclass classifications – Justify.
6. What is the difference between regression loss and cross-entropy loss?

7. What is the difference between loss functions and cost functions?
8. What is a gradient?
9. State chain rule.

Long Questions

1. List out and explain activation functions.
2. List out and explain loss functions.
3. Explain the backpropagation algorithm with a neat example.

Numerical Problems

1. For $x = 7$, show the output of the following activation functions:
   (i) Linear function $y = 8x$.
   (ii) Sigmoid function
   (iii) tanh function
   (iv) ReLU function
2. Consider the following actual values {3, 4, 4, 5} and the predicted values {2, 2, 6, 8}, and show the mean square error, mean absolute error, and mean error.
3. Consider the following probability values {0.4.0.4, 0.2} for three colours given by the code {1, 0, 0}, {0, 1, 0} and {0, 0, 1}. Show the output of categorical loss.
4. Consider the following neural network shown in Figure 3.11.

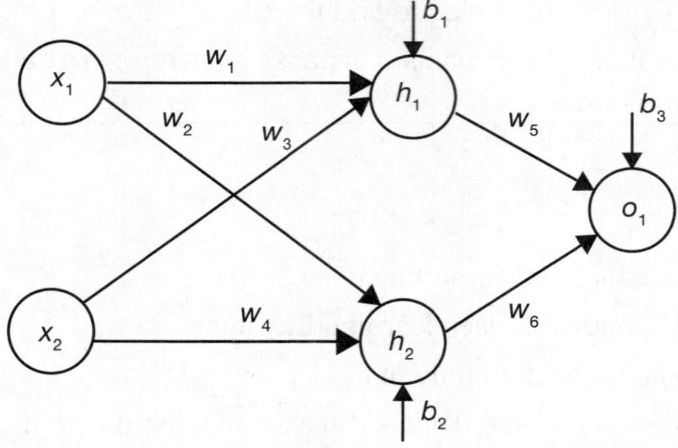

Figure 3.11 A Sample Neural Network

Assume all weights and biases as 1. What is the output at the hidden and output nodes when the following activation functions are used:

(i) Linear activation function

(ii) Sigmoid function

(iii) ReLU function

5. Consider the following neural network shown in Figure 3.12.

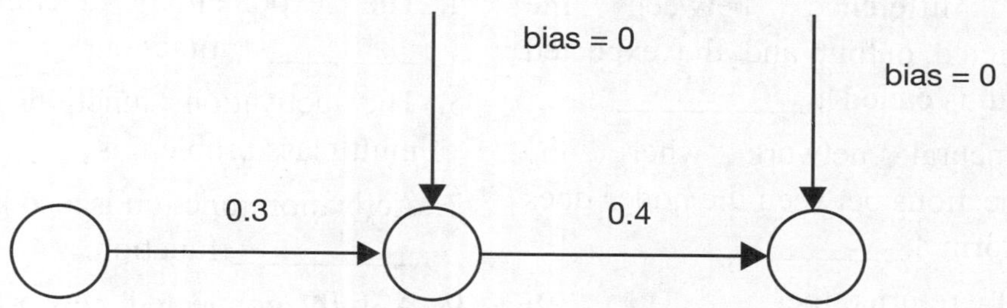

Figure 3.12 A Sample Neural Network

Let the activation function be a linear function and $x_1 = 2$. Apply the backpropagation algorithm assuming the output is 1.

Crossword

Across

2. Cross-entropy measures the difference between the predicted and actual output. (yes/no)
3. A fully connected network is also known as __________ network
6. The difference between the predicted output and the expected output is called a __________.
8. A neural network where the connections between the nodes does not form a __________.
10. ReLU returns the __________ of the 0 and the input value.
11. Multilayer neural network uses many activation functions. (yes/no)
13. Computational graph is __________.
15. A shallow neural network has one or two hidden layers. (yes/no)
16. Backpropagation is called __________ differentiation.
17. Are the loss function and cost function the same? (yes/no)
18. If the change in the input results in the change of output, they are said to be __________.

Down

1. The suppression of weaker signals by ReLU cause the problem of __________ neurons.
2. L2 error is the mean square error. (yes/no)
4. The exponential function is a __________ function.
5. The activation function used in multiclass problem is __________.
7. Activation function is also known as __________ function.
9. A fully connected network is one where neurons in one layer is connected to all neurons in the next layer. (yes/no)
11. The movement of the gradient is from the output layer to the input layer in the case of backpropagation. (yes/no)
12. A group of neurons are organized as a __________.
14. The chain rule is used for finding derivatives of __________ functions.

Jumbled Sentences

```
I F K U P M O C B Z H Q Q C H O Q X Z C J X W O J
H R H B M T A R G X H Y A P O Q I H S F L X Y W L
Q A N H J F O X Y Z S Q D L U M F G Z V A O B Y Y
K O M P I H E S I P Y V L L R T P Q I R P Z R K E
Q B D Q R R Q T O M W A X E A B V O A Y O E T M S
K J F E M O N W R F U T X M D Y T Z S T I Z G M Q
P S A K N C P U J A T M Q N C D E L X I N V J O Z
T Q S M A S M O O E N M X H J P J R M D T B C S Y
M E R S C J E J R H S S A G J L P U A D I E W Z E
Y N E R Y Q Z B N T U Z F X W R Q R I T D X G X S
L H V L C F A O J V I W I E B D E A D M T I C X Y
O V E J L B H S O E X O S L R A O A Y W W B Y F E
S D R Q I C S R M L L E N M Q H F I V S C T C W S
S H S T C F E J Q M Y Q S A B X Y Y Q P F Q L Q V
C Y E M K S B V H R W Y T E L F S S K X H C E U Q
C W W D F V V O A V F E W U Q N O N L I N E A R V
N W A P Z K E G O S E S O E I X Z N O D C N V Z D
```

yes
reverse
transfer
no

cycle
yes
maximum
yes

yes
layer
dead
yes

dense
proportional
softmax
acyclic

yes
nonlinear
loss
composite

Introduction to Optimization

CHAPTER 4

> Optimization techniques, whether linear or nonlinear, play a crucial role in virtually every aspect of science and engineering, helping us find the best possible solutions under given circumstances. — **Jorge Nocedal and Stephen Wright**

One of the major pillars of deep learning is the concept of optimization. Optimization algorithms are used to find the optimal model parameters for the neural networks. The model parameters include weights and biases. The learning algorithms involve hyperparameters that also need to be optimized. The careful selection of optimization algorithms is required to increase the accuracy and performance of the neural networks.

The learning objectives of this chapter are as follows:

- Understand the need for optimization algorithms.
- Know the types of optimization functions.
- Understand the first-order gradient descent algorithms.
- Know the types of gradient descent algorithms.
- Know about momentum.
- Know the types of momentum-based algorithms.
- Understand the second-order optimization algorithms.

4.1 Overview of Optimization

The training of neural networks is all about assigning optimal parameters to the model parameters based on the training dataset. The training process of the neural network involves these stages:

(i) Computation of the loss for every data element of the training data.

(ii) Compute the gradients of the loss function with respect to every model parameter.

(iii) The algorithms perform backpropagation to update the model parameters.

The parameters of the neural network are of two types.

(i) **Hyperparameters:** Hyperparameters are user-controlled parameters that can be tuned for the optimal performance of the neural networks. These hyperparameters are the parameters of the learning algorithm itself and, hence, are not learned from the data. These parameters are manually tuned or by algorithms like grid search for the better performance of the neural network.

(ii) **Parameters:** These are the model-controlled parameters that must be tuned by the learning algorithms for optimal performance by learning from data. For example, in a linear regression line fitting problem, y = mx + c, the parameters m and c are model-controlled and learned from the data automatically.

The manual exploration of optimal parameters is not feasible; hence, the study of optimization algorithms is important. What is an optimization problem?

4.1.1 Optimization Problems

Optimization, more precisely, functional optimization, is a subset of mathematical optimization theory. An optimization problem has an objective function and a set of constraints. An objective function is either minimization or maximization of a loss function of an optimization problem. The optimization problem is associated with a set of constraints. There are many feasible solutions called feasible solutions. An optimal solution satisfies the objective function without violating the constraints.

An optimization problem can be stated as finding the minimum of a function.

$$\min_{x \in \chi} f(x)$$

Here, f is the function that needs to be minimized and χ is the set of feasible solutions. x is the input of the function. The point x* is called the optimal value that minimizes the optimization function f. This point x* is called a local minimum if there exists $\delta > 0$ such that $f(x^*) \leq f(x)$ for all values of x where $\|x^* - x\| \leq \delta$.

In the case of deep learning, the optimization problem can be stated as

$$\min_{\theta \in \chi} f(\theta)$$

where θ is the model parameter, and $L(\theta)$ is the objective function, that is the difference between the predicted and the actual target values of the training dataset. The constraints can be related to data, regularization, or any condition imposed on the nature of data. Hence, the goal is to minimize this objective function over the entire dataset.

For a function of a single variable, the analytical methods are sufficient. The analytical method of a function of a single variable is discussed in Box 4.1.

Box 4.1 Analytical Solution of a Function with a Single Variable

Let us consider a univariate function f(x). To find the minima of the univariate function f(x), one needs to find the derivative. This derivative is the slope of the tangent line to the function at x. The derivative represents the rate of change of the function at x. The derivative of the function $f'(x)$ is given as follows:

$$f'(x) = \frac{df(x)}{dx}$$

The second derivative of the function is given as

$$f''(x) = \frac{d^2 f}{dx^2}$$

So, set the first derivative equal to zero and solve it. The solutions of this equation are called critical points. Substitute these critical values in the second derivative. If the result comes as

(i) positive, then the critical point x* is the local minimum.

(ii) negative, then the critical point x* is the local maximum.

(iii) zero, then the solution is inconclusive.

The following numerical problem illustrates the finding minimum analytically.

Example 4.1: Consider the following function $f(x) = x^2 + 2x + 1$ and find the local minimum analytically.

Solution

The given function is $f(x) = x^2 + 2x + 1$. The first derivative is obtained as

$$f'(x) = 2x + 2$$

Set the first derivative to zero ($f'(x) = 0$) and find the critical point x*.

$$2x + 2 = 0$$

$$x = \frac{-2}{2} = -1$$

One has to substitute this in the second derivative. The second derivative of f(x) is $f''(x) = 2$

This positive value of the second derivative confirms that the critical point x* is the local minimum and its substitution in the original expression.

$$f(-1) = (-1)^2 + 2(-1) + 1 = 1 - 2 + 0.$$

Therefore, the local minimum value is zero, and it occurs at x = –1. A plot of this function is shown below in Fig. 4.1. The aim is to find the point x_{min} where the function f is minimum.

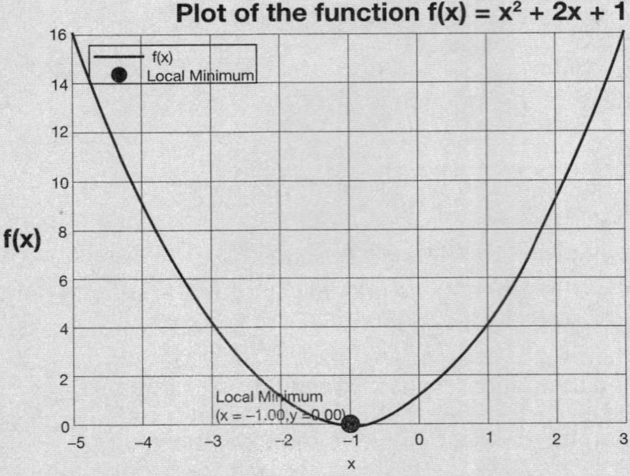

Fig. 4.1: Plot of the Objective Function f(x)

However deep learning involves neural networks of thousands of parameters. It is given as a multivariate function. A multivariate function is given as $f(x_1, x_2, \cdots, x_n)$. So, the problem involves finding the minimum of a multivariate function. The gradient of a multivariate function is given as $\nabla f(x_1, x_2, \cdots, x_n)$. It should be noted that the gradient is a vector where each component is the partial derivative of f concerning all the concerned variables. The gradient of the function is represented as $\nabla f(x_1, x_2, \cdots, x_n)$.

$$\nabla f(x) = \left(\frac{\partial f(x_1, \cdots, x_n)}{\partial x_1} \quad \cdots \quad \frac{\partial f(x_1, \cdots, x_n)}{\partial x_n} \right)$$

The second derivative of the multivariate function is the Hessian matrix, which is given as $\nabla^2 f(x)$ or in general as $\nabla^2 f(\theta)$ where θ refers to any parameter, say, weights, bias, or any other parameters.

The analytical or brute force methods will not work for multivariate functions. A brute force method is used to enumerate all the possible inputs and evaluate the target objective function for optima. This procedure is infeasible and takes so much time to check.

So, optimizers are required. An optimizer is an algorithm or method that is used to solve optimization problems.

4.1.2 Optimization Algorithms

The optimizer is an algorithm or method that is used to minimize the loss function to maximize the efficiency of neural networks. Some of the popular optimizers are stochastic gradient descent, ADAM, and AdaGrad. Optimizers do the parameter adjustment (weights, biases, and other hyperparameters) in an iterative process and help to get the optimal set of parameters by pushing the model towards it to get accurate predictions.

The role of optimizers is crucial for the following reasons:

(i) **Minimizing Loss Functions:** The role of optimizers is crucial for finding the optimal weights by minimizing the objective functions. The objective function of the neural network is to minimize the weights.

(ii) **Efficiency:** The manual exploration of solutions is not feasible; hence, the role of optimizers is crucial. Optimizers provide an automatic way of finding optimal solutions.

(iii) **Handling of Non-convex Functions:** Neural networks, especially with many multiple hidden layers, provide complex loss landscapes. So, the optimizers are necessary to navigate complex landscapes.

(iv) **Adaption to Data:** Optimizers are required to adapt to the data distribution of data by tuning the hyperparameters such as weights/biases and learning rates.

(v) **Convergence:** Convergence is an important property. A fast convergence of neural networks reduces time and improves efficiency.

4.2 Search Space

The optimization problems can be framed as search problems. The candidate solutions of an optimization problem form a search space. The search space is the universe of candidate solutions for the objective function. The optimization algorithms effectively search the search space and find the best solution. The maximum or minimum of the function is called the optima of the problem. In the minimization problem, the poor solutions are hills, and the good solutions are valleys. This reverse is true in the case of maximization problems.

The function that needs to be optimized may be a convex function or a non-convex function.

A convex optimization algorithm is defined for the convex functions over the convex set given as

$$\min_{\theta \in \chi} f(x)$$

such that

$$x \in C$$

A set C is convex if, for any two points, x_1 and x_2 of C, the line that connects them remains in C. It should satisfy the constraint,

$$f\left(tx_1 + (1-t)x_2\right) \leq t\, f\left(x_1\right) + (1-t)\, f\left(x_2\right)$$

where $[t \in [0...1]]$. Convex functions have only one global minimum (no local minima), and hence, the optimization of the convex function is a straightforward process. Also, it is easy to approximate the convex function as there are no saddle points or multiple local minima. Therefore, there is no risk of getting stuck in local minima as there is only one global minimum. One such convex function is shown in Figure 4.2.

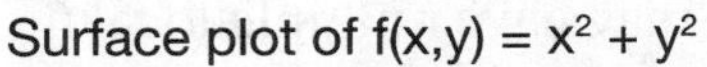

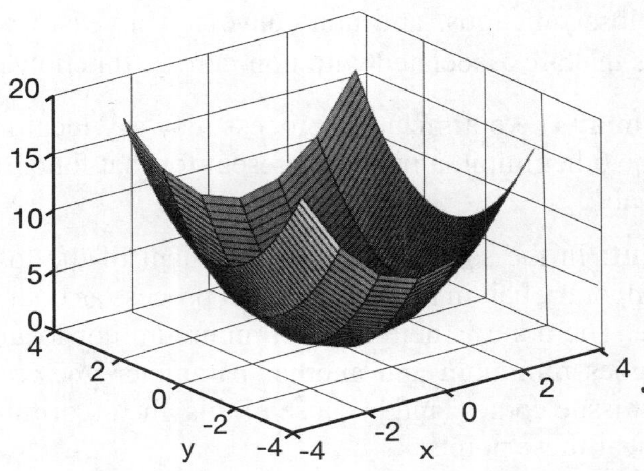

Figure 4.2 Surface Plot of a Convex Function

On the other hand, non-convex problems are very complex and involve many complicated scenarios. If the function has more than a single optimum and does not resemble a basin is called a non-convex function. In other words, the function has more than one hill or valley. A surface plot of a function is shown below in Figure. 4.3.

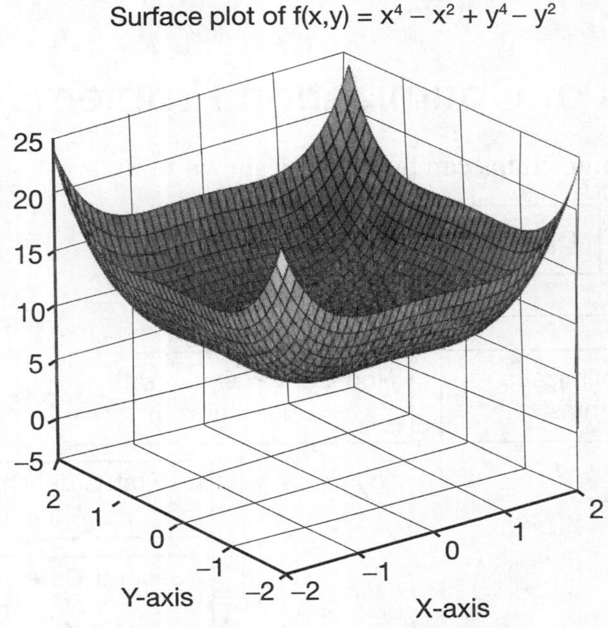

Figure 4.3 Non-convex Function

The non-convex function may have multiple local minima saddle points and complex irregularities, as shown in Fig. 4.3. Most deep neural networks with multiple layers have non-convex loss functions, and non-convexity increases with hidden layers. Some of the issues that are associated with non-convex function are listed below:

(i) **Local Minima:** The optimization process may say local minima when there may be some other minima/maxima present for that function. So, the solution is suboptimal.

(ii) **Saddle Point:** In the saddle point, the gradient of the loss function is 0. It causes a temporary halt in the optimization process as both ascent and descent are possible. The point is neither local minimum nor local maximum. If one parameter goes minimum and another parameter goes maximum, then the saddle point issue comes, and because of this, the algorithm becomes slow or gets stuck near these points.

(iii) **Plateau:** In the plateau, the gradient of the loss function is smaller or close to 0. The plateau landscape in the search space is a flat region. Here, the loss does not change significantly in the parameter space as gradients are very small. Plateau causes problems such as slow progress, and the algorithm may get stuck in local minima. Plateau poses a great challenge in optimization.

The role of optimizers is important in solving problems when non-convex functions are involved.

4.3 Types of Optimization Problems

The optimization algorithms can be given as shown in Figure 4.4.

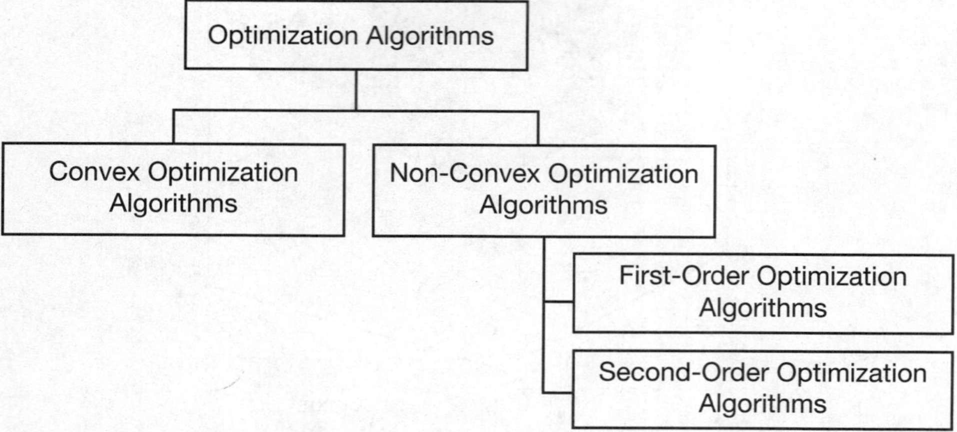

Figure 4.4 Types of Optimization Algorithms

One can categorize optimization problems also as convex and non-convex optimization problems. Convex optimization problems are easy to solve. In a region of search space, the algorithm finds the local minimum. In convex optimization problems, the local minimum is the global minimum. Non-convex algorithms are difficult to solve as the search space may have multiple local minimums and maximums. So, the local minimum is not a global minimum. Most of the deep learning optimization algorithms operate in this complex domain.

First-order methods include gradient descent methods. These methods are based on the gradient of the loss functions. The gradients are calculated using the partial derivatives of the weights and biases. Second-order methods use the first-order derivatives and their rate of change. The second-order methods include quasi-newton methods.

4.4 Hyperparameter Tuning

Hyperparameters are different from parameters. Hyperparameters are parameters of the learning algorithm itself and are not learned from the data. The users supply these parameters. In hyperparameter optimization, one needs to find a configuration so that the model works well for the training data as well as the testing data.

Some of the naïve algorithms for hyperparameter tuning are Random Search and Grid Search.

4.4.1 Random Search (Random Optimization or Random Sampling)

It is an algorithm where the hyperparameters are given a statistical distribution instead of a discrete value. The hyperparameter values are randomly sampled from the statistical distribution. The steps of the random search algorithm is given below:

1. Sample inputs randomly from the distribution.
2. Check for all combinations of input, evaluate the model, and check the results.
3. Pick the best combination of the inputs that generalizes the model well.

The advantage of this approach is that no assumption is made about the optimization function, and less memory is required for this procedure. The samples are independent of each other and hence the random search can be parallelized also. The disadvantage is that the computational complexity is very high as it involves checking all combinations of the input.

4.4.2 Grid Search

Grid search is another algorithm. It consists of the following steps:

1. Takes the hyperparameter with a discrete set of values.
2. Find all the combinations of the inputs.

   For example, if there are two inputs

   A = {0.1, 0.3} and B = { 0.1, 0.2}

   Then, four combinations are possible S = {(0.1, 0.1), (0.1, 0.2), (0.3, 0.1), (0.3, 0.2)}
3. Normally, a metric like accuracy is chosen for the evaluation of the model.
4. All the possible combinations are tested for accuracy (if that criterion is chosen for evaluation).
5. The best combinations are chosen for the hypermodel.

This algorithm works well. But the issues are if the discrete range of the hyperparameters is high and if the number of hyperparameters increases, the algorithm computation complexity increases.

Similarly, there are many such algorithms, such as the greedy approach (Select the first configuration), Exact search (Use algorithms like graph search algorithms to try out all possible combinations), Bayesian optimization (Sequential Model-Based Optimization (SMBO)) for hyperparameter optimization.

4.5 Gradient Descent Algorithms

The most popular algorithm of optimization is the gradient descent algorithm.

Gradient descent is a numerical optimization algorithm that aims to find the minimum value of model parameters. It minimizes the cost function during the training process. Various terms like loss or error function and cost function are used interchangeably. But the subtle difference is loss function should be used for a single sample and the cost function for the entire dataset.

The objective function is to minimize this loss function.

The way of looking for the minimum of a function is called gradient descent. The rate of change of a real-valued function at a given data point is called a derivative. The meaning of gradient is “slope” or “slant” of the surface. So, gradient descent is the descending in the slope to reach the minimum. In the case of a function of multiple variables, a vector of derivatives for every variable is formed. It is called gradient. The symbol ∇ is used to denote the gradient. The symbol ∇ is called del or nabla.

The objective of finding the minimum is achieved as follows:

(i) For example, consider a univariate function f(x). The derivative of the loss function is computed. The derivative of the parameter is given as $\frac{\partial f}{\partial \theta}$, where f is the loss function and θ is the parameter.

(ii) Gradient descent is an iterative algorithm that starts with an initial point, say w_0. Then, the slope (gradient in the case of a function of multiple variables) of the objective function is obtained with respect to each feature. If the function has more variables $x_0, x_{1,..}$, then the partial derivative of the loss function with respect to all these variables is computed and stored as a vector called the gradient.

(iii) The gradient of the multivariate function indicates two factors:

1. Magnitude that indicates how much change.
2. The direction of maximum change is called steepness.

The additional details about the gradient are given in Box 4.2.

Box 4.2 More Details about Gradient

A gradient is a derivative. It defines the effects of the variations of the input over the output of the function.

A gradient vector is composed of the partial derivatives of the network parameters. Partial derivatives compute each parameter's contribution to the change in the function value. So, the parameters can be individually updated. This fact is in contrast to the total derivatives, which take into account all the variables with respect to the function output and hence are not useful in deep learning.

A gradient indicates two things.

(i) Direction of the steepest ascent – The function f(x) at point x points to the steepest ascent (increase in the function value). If one looks for the minimum, then the model has to move in the opposite direction (in the direction of the steepest descent).

(ii) Magnitude or rate of change – The magnitude indicates the rate of change of the gradient. The larger magnitude indicates a steeper slope and, hence faster rate of increase in the function value. By moving in the opposite direction, a decrease in the function can be obtained.

For example, if there is a function f(x) that involves two variables, then the direction of the point (x_1, x_2) is given as $\left(\frac{\partial f}{\partial x_1}, \frac{\partial f}{\partial x_2}\right)$, and the Euclidean norm can give its magnitude as $\|\nabla f(x)\| = \sqrt{\left(\frac{\partial f}{\partial x_1}\right)^2 + \left(\frac{\partial f}{\partial x_2}\right)^2}$.

Suppose if the magnitude is m, then a small change in the input, say, Δr can cause a function change in value $m \times \Delta r$.

Example 4.2: Let the function be $f(x_1, x_2) = x + y$. Compute the magnitude and the direction of the gradient vectors.

Solution

$$f(x_1, x_2) = x + y$$

So, the gradient vector is $\nabla f(x_1, x_2) = \left(\frac{\partial f}{\partial x_1}, \frac{\partial f}{\partial x_2}\right) = (1, 1)$

The magnitude of the gradient vector is given as

$$\nabla f(x_1, x_2) = \sqrt{\left(\frac{\partial f}{\partial x_1}\right)^2 + \left(\frac{\partial f}{\partial x_2}\right)^2} = \sqrt{1+1} = \sqrt{2}$$

The direction of the gradient vector is the gradient vector itself, and it can be expressed in a normalized form as

$u = \frac{\nabla f(x_1, x_2)}{\|\nabla f(x_1, x_2)\|} = \frac{(1,1)}{\sqrt{2}} = \left(\frac{1}{\sqrt{2}}, \frac{1}{\sqrt{2}}\right)$ and the direction of the gradient vector is $\left(\frac{1}{\sqrt{2}}, \frac{1}{\sqrt{2}}\right)$.

The gradient descent algorithm starts with a point w_0. The derivative is obtained. The gradient descent algorithm forces the model to go in the opposite direction of the direction as the problem involved is of minimization of weights. The position is changed by subtracting the derivative of the starting point from the starting point as

$$\Delta w_0 = w_0 - \frac{\partial f}{\partial w_0}$$

Here, f is the cost function. It can be observed that the partial derivatives are computed for each parameter and subtracted from the parameter itself. This rule is called the parameter update rule.

One more parameter is introduced called η to control the update in the equation as follows:

$$\Delta w_0 = w_0 - \eta \frac{\partial f}{\partial w_0}$$

In general, the update is given as

$$\Delta w_{t+1} = w_t - \eta \frac{\partial f}{\partial w_t}$$

Here, the parameter η is called the learning rate. If η is small, then the movement of the model towards the minimum is in small steps. On the other hand, if η is large, then the model may overshoot the minimum value—large values η lead to more divergence and oscillations. This iterative process of gradient descent continues till the slope (or gradient in the case of multiple variables) is almost zero or leads to stability where the subsequent iteration produces a value that does not change.

Example 4.3: Let the function be $f(x) = x^2 + 2x + 1$. Show the first three steps of the gradient descent.

Solution

Let the function be $f(x) = x^2 + 2x + 1$, and hence, the derivative can be given as $f'(x) = 2x + 2$. So, start with the initial value as $x_0 = 0$. Let the learning rate (η) be 0.1

Iteration 1

The weight update is given based on that general formula for the variable x is

$x_{t+1} = x_t - \eta \frac{\partial f}{\partial x_t}$, Here, t is the iteration.

$$x_1 = x_0 - (0.1) f'(x_0) \quad : \text{with } f'(x_0) = 2(1) + 2 = 4$$
$$= 1 - (0.1 \times 4) = 1 - 0.4 = 0.6$$

Iteration 2

$$x_2 = x_1 - (0.1) f'(x_1) \quad : \text{with } f'(x_1) = 2(0.6) + 2 = 3.2$$
$$= 0.6 - (0.1 \times 3.2) = 0.28$$

Iteration 3

$$x_3 = x_2 - (0.1) f'(x_2) \quad : \text{with } f'(x_2) = 2(0.28) + 2 = 2.56$$
$$= 0.6 - (0.1 \times 2.56) = 0.024$$

It can be checked from problem 4.1 that the local minimum is −1. So, the above algorithm would proceed towards the goal. Slowly, the algorithm would converge. The result for 100 iterations is shown in the given plot as shown in Figure 4.5. It can be observed that the local minimum converges to −1, which is the correct answer.

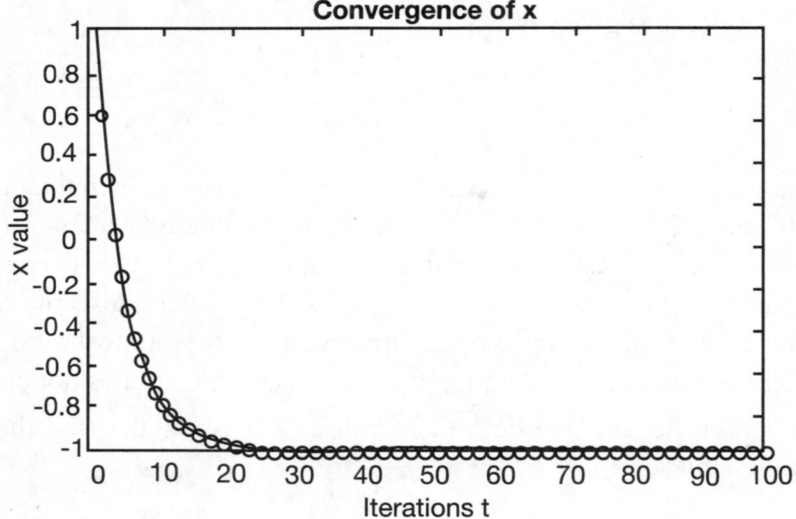

Figure 4.5 Plot of the Iterations

Box 4.3 Gradient Ascent Algorithm

Deep learning networks like GAN use gradient ascent algorithms. Gradient ascent algorithms look for the local maximum instead of the local minimum, and the algorithms implement the gradient that moves in the direction of the steepest ascent.

Hill climbing is one of the related algorithms, although hill climbing is a heuristic algorithm that does not require the derivatives. Instead, it uses the function values for finding the function maxima.

4.5.1 Batch Gradient Descent

Batch Gradient Descent is a gradient descent algorithm. The term gradient descent algorithm refers to batch gradient algorithm only. The neural network will have thousands or even millions of parameters in the case of deep neural networks. Hence, the objective function is the loss function of many variables. So, batch gradient descent computes the gradients of the cost function concerning the model parameters of the entire dataset.

The procedure for batch gradient descent is given as follows:

1. Initialize the model parameters θ with random values or with predefined values.
2. Initialize the learning rate η. The learning rate indicates the step size or learning rate. Initialize the number of iterations.
3. Repeat until iterations converge or the number of iterations is reached

   3.1 For the entire dataset, Compute the cost function as follows:

$$\nabla J(\theta) = \frac{1}{m}\sum_{i=1}^{m} \nabla J(\theta; x_i, y_i)$$

   Here, m is the number of samples in the training dataset. J is the cost function and θ is the parameter of the neural network. Here x_i, y_i is the current data point, and $\nabla J(\theta_t; x_i, y_i)$ is the gradient of the current point.

   3.2 Update the model parameters by taking the direction of negative gradient descent scaled by η as

$$\theta_{t+1} = \theta_t - \eta \times \nabla J(\theta_t)$$

   The symbol θ_t indicates the model parameters. t is the iteration.

4. Return optimal parameters and End.

   The advantages and disadvantages of the Batch gradient algorithm are given in Table 4.1.

Table 4.1 Advantages and Disadvantages of Batch Gradient Descent Algorithm

Advantages	Disadvantages
Convergence to global minima is smoother compared to stochastic gradient descent.	Computationally, it is intensive if the dataset is larger.
Stable convergence. Convergence is guaranteed for convex functions but not for all non-convex functions.	Memory requirement is higher if the dataset is large and complex.
Suitable for small datasets as there is only one update, and also, it is not a real-time update	This algorithm needs to adapt better and be suitable for online algorithms.

One of the major problems of the batch gradient is the amount of computations. Let us assume that there are 100 data points with 5 features. So, the number of computations is 100 X 5 = 500. If there are 100 iterations, then the number of computations is 100 x 500 = 50000. It can be observed that even if a computation taken is 1 second, the time involved in 50000 seconds. For larger networks, the computational complexity is heavy, and hence, stochastic gradient descent is preferable.

4.5.2 Stochastic Gradient Descent (SGD)

SGD is based on randomness. The word "Stochastic" means randomness. So, for this reason, the stochastic gradient descent, shuffles the dataset. It is used to minimize model parameters θ where θ is used to represent any parameter of the neural networks. It may be bias weight or any parameter related to the neural network.

The stochastic gradient descent algorithm takes only one random sample from the dataset for gradient computation and update. This random selection only introduces randomness in the optimization process.

The procedure for stochastic gradient descent is given as follows:

1. Initialize the model parameters with random values or with predefined values.
2. Initialize the learning rate η and the number of iterations

   The randomization is carried out by shuffling the dataset. Randomization is crucial for the success of the optimization process.
3. Repeat until iterations converge or the number of iterations is reached

   3.1 Shuffle the dataset.

   3.2 Take a training sample and compute the gradient of the cost for the current point with respect to the model parameters.

   3.3 Update the model parameters by taking the direction of negative gradient descent scaled by η as

   $$\theta_{t+1} = \theta_t - \eta \times \nabla J(\theta_t; x_i, y_i)$$

   Here x_i, y_i is the current data point and $\nabla J(\theta_t; x_i, y_i)$ the gradient of the current point.

   The symbol θ_t indicates the model parameters. t is the iteration.
4. Return optimal parameters and End.

   The advantages and disadvantages of the SGD algorithm are given in Table 4.2.

Table 4.2 Advantages and Disadvantages of Stochastic Gradient Descent Algorithm

Advantages	Disadvantages
Frequent update. Allows the use of large datasets as only one sample is updated. So, the usage of memory is less.	SGD, because of randomness, introduces noise. This randomness leads to noisy gradients as the resultant is oscillations. Because of the oscillations, the algorithm may fail to reach the local minima. Randomness also brings additional overhead.
Adaptive for online learning	The learning rate is constant.
Allows overcome of local minima with the help of randomness.	Computationally very expensive

4.5.3 Mini Batch

Mini-Batch Gradient Descent is another optimization algorithm. This algorithm is the trade-off between SGD and the Batch gradient algorithm. This algorithm achieves the compromise or balance by choosing a small set of training samples called mini-batch (k). Here, k is the user-defined hyperparameter that can be used to define the number of batches.

The procedure for mini-batch gradient descent is given as follows:

1. Initialize the model parameters with random values or with predefined values. The chosen parameter is the learning rate α, which indicates the step size or learning rate. k is the number of examples in each mini-batch.
2. Introduce the randomization by shuffling the data and creating a mini-batch with k data samples.
3. Repeat for a fixed number of steps or until convergence.

   3.1 Compute the gradient as follows:

$$\nabla J(\theta) = \frac{1}{k}\sum_{j=1}^{k} \nabla J(\theta; x_{ij}, y_{ij})$$

Here, k is the data sample of the mini-batch or mini-batch size and $\sum_{i=1}^{m} \nabla J(\theta; x_i, y_i)$ is the cost function of the mini-batch. A batch is a set of n-samples. Normally, the value of m is 50 to 256, and $\nabla J(\theta_i; x_i, y_i)$ the gradient of the current point.

3.2 Update the model parameters by taking the direction of negative gradient descent scaled by η as

$$\theta_{t+1} = \theta_t - \eta \times \nabla J(\theta_t)$$

4. Return optimal parameters and End.

The advantages and disadvantages of the Batch gradient algorithm are given in Table 4.3.

Table 4.3 Advantages and Disadvantages of Mini-Batch Gradient Descent Algorithm

Advantages	Disadvantages
The computational efficiency of the mini-batch is higher. The algorithm uses less memory compared to the batch gradient algorithm.	Noise due to randomness.
Adapt to the data changes and more steady and stable convergence.	There is no guarantee for convergence to the global minimum. Learning rate tuning is a challenging task.

Example 4.4: Suppose there is a dataset of 10,000 points. If the SGD, Batch Gradient, and mini-gradient algorithms are used, then how many weight updates would happen.

Solution

In Batch gradient, all the inputs are taken in a single batch, so there will be only one weight update. In stochastic gradient descent, there will be an update for every input. So, there will be 10,000 weight updates. In mini-batch, there is a compromise between stochastic and Batch gradient. If there are 1000 samples for a batch, then there will be 10 batches. So, 10000/1000 = 10 batches. A hyperparameter k dictates the selection. Say if k = 2, then 2 batches (2000 samples) are taken as input. So, there will be five updates.

4.5.4 Concept of Momentum

The major difficulties in traditional gradient descent algorithms are slow convergence, Oscillations due to step size, and the navigation of complex and poorly conditioned landscapes.

Momentum can be used to solve these problems.

The purpose of momentum is to accelerate the convergence process and to avoid local minima. This task is accomplished by collecting the gradients in a variable called velocity. Velocity is the smoothened version of the gradient. This momentum is added with the current update in the optimization algorithms.

The needs for the momentum are given below:

(i) Accelerated convergence – Momentum solves the problem of slow convergence by speeding up the algorithm in areas where the gradient consistently points.

(ii) Dampening oscillations – Momentum helps to remove oscillations or fluctuations. The oscillations occur in flat or shallow regions in the cost function.

(iii) Saddle Points – Momentum helps the algorithm to escape from saddle points.

(iv) Efficient navigation of the plateaus – The plateaus are the regions where the cost function has very small gradients. This effective navigation is done by accumulating velocity over flat regions.

(v) Improved generalization – Momentum helps in improved generalization performance and helps in overfitting.

4.5.5 Traditional and Nesterov Momentum

In momentum, all the previous updates are recorded and tracked using the variable called velocity (or momentum). One can say the current update and the fraction of the previous adjustments are done to the parameters for faster and smoother convergence.

There are two types of momentum, as shown in Figure 4.6.

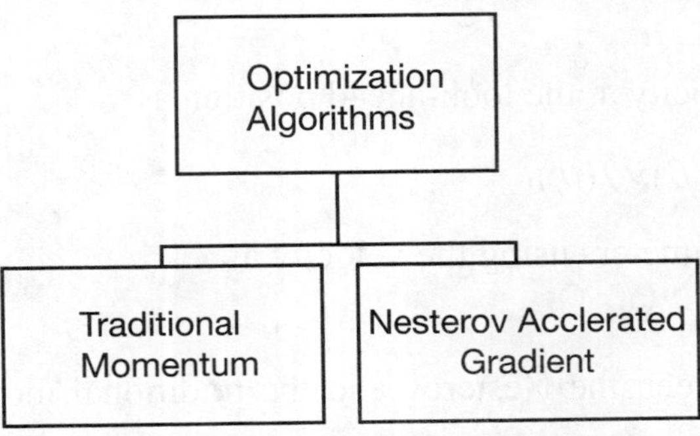

Figure 4.6 Types of Momentum

Traditional momentum

In the traditional momentum, the algorithm takes the current gradient and also the accumulated previous updates. The new velocity is the weighted combination of the current and previous velocity. The update is made as below:

$$v_t = \beta \times v_{t-1} + \eta \nabla J(\theta_{t-1})$$

Here, $\nabla J(\theta_{t-1})$ is the current update. The parameter $\nabla J(\theta_t)$ is the gradient of the cost function with respect to the model parameters.

β is the parameter called momentum coefficient. It determines how much the past updates should be taken into account. In other words, it controls the contributions of the current gradient and the accumulated past gradients, and its value ranges from 0-1.

Nesterov Momentum (Nesterov Accelerated Gradient)

Nesterov momentum is popularly used in neural network training in an algorithm called the Nesterov Accelerated Gradient Descent (NAG) algorithm.

Nesterov momentum is the modification of the traditional momentum to improve convergence. Nesterov momentum "looks ahead" at the future position of the parameters before computing the gradients. It estimates the direction of the next update. Hence, this method is based on both past as well as future updates, unlike the traditional momentum that depends only on past updates.

The Nesterov momentum procedure is given below:

1. Find the look ahead position.

   $\tilde{\theta}_t = \theta_{t-1} - \eta \beta v_{t-1}$

2. Compute the Gradient at the look-ahead position as

   $\nabla J(\tilde{\theta}_t)$

3. Update the velocity at the look-ahead position as

   $v_t = \beta v_{t-1} + (1-\beta) \nabla J(\tilde{\theta}_t)$

4. Update the parameters using the velocity as

   $\theta_t = \theta_{t-1} - \eta v_t$

The differences between the Nesterov and the traditional momentum are given in Table 4.4.

Table 4.4 Comparisons of Traditional and Nesterov Momentum

Nesterov Momentum	Traditional Momentum
First, the "look-ahead" parameters are computed before gradient computation.	
Adjustment of "future" parameters comes first before the gradients are computed.	First, the gradients are computed, followed by the adjustment of parameters based on the "past gradients."

4.5.6 Gradient Descent with Momentum

Gradient descent with momentum is another optimization algorithm that extends the traditional gradient descent algorithm with momentum. This algorithm includes the advantages of momentum, such as faster convergence and dampening of oscillations during the training neural network training process. The convergence is faster if all the gradients point in the same direction so that the algorithm rolls faster.

The procedure for the gradient with momentum is given below:

1. Initialize the model parameters θ with random or predefined values. Let η be the learning rate and β the momentum coefficient. Its value ranges from 0 to 1 and controls the accumulated gradients. Its typical value is 0.9.
2. Repeat until converge
   - **2.1** Initial steps are the same as SGD.
   - **2.2** Accumulate the gradients into velocity as

     $$v = \beta v - \eta g$$

   - **2.3** Apply the update rule as

     $$\theta = \theta - v$$

     v, which is the average of all past gradients.

4.5.7 AdaGrad (Adaptive Gradient Descent)

AdaGrad is another optimization algorithm designed by Duchi and Stinger in 2011.

One of the major problems of the gradient descent algorithms is that they use the same step size or learning rate for all the variables. If the features are sparse (most of them are zero, and very few are non-zeros) and also have fewer updates, then having a constant learning rate is not desirable. Hence, the first major aspect of AdaGrad is the adjustable learning rate.

Adaptive Gradients (AdaGrad) allow different step sizes in each dimension so that they adapt to different types of gradients seen by them. AdaGrad adapts suitable learning rates of the individual parameters during the training process. AdaGrad algorithm helps to find the step size dynamically that accounts for the local curvatures.

The idea of AdaGrad is to accumulate the square of the gradients in a normalization variable for every parameter. So, each parameter has a personalized learning rate. If the gradients are very large, then the learning rate would decrease over time. Similarly, if the gradients are small, then the learning rate would be larger. When the gradient is very large, then it is divided by the square of the gradients. Hence, the step size is controlled. This factor is amplified by η and ε (whose small number ensures that there is no division by zero).

The procedure for AdaGrad is given below:

1. Initialize

   The model parameters θ are initialized to zero or some random values. Let r be a vector that keeps track of the squared sum of the gradients that are initialized to 0.

2. Initialize the learning rate η and the parameter ε to 10^{-7} whose purpose is to avoid division by zero error.

3. Repeat until convergence

   3.1 The initial steps are similar to the Stochastic gradient algorithm.

   3.2 Accumulate the square of the gradients $(g \odot g)$ in r as

   $$r = r + g \odot g$$

   3.3 Update the parameters

   $$\Delta\theta = \eta \times \frac{1}{\sqrt{r} + \varepsilon} \odot g$$

   3.4 Apply the update

   $$\theta = \theta - \Delta\theta$$

The advantages and disadvantages are given in Table 4.5.

Table 4.5 Advantages and Disadvantages of AdaGrad Algorithm

Advantage	Disadvantage
Learning rate changes with iterations	Aggressive and monotonous
Adapt to data	The denominator keeps on increasing and hence may cause a vanishing gradient problem.

One of the major problems of squared gradients is that over a period, the learning rate becomes too small. This problem is called the learning rate decay problem. Also, the accumulation of squared gradients can lead to premature convergence.

Thus, the specialties of AdaGrad are:

(i) Personalized learning rate for every parameter.

(ii) Adaption is based on gradient history. So, the learning rate decreases over time.

(iii) Effective for sparse and higher dimensional data. Parameters with infrequent intervals will have larger updates and parameters with frequent updates will have smaller updates.

4.5.8 RMSProp

RMSProp (root mean square propagation) is an adaptive optimization algorithm introduced by the legendary Geoffrey Hinton in a lecture in 2012. It is designed to solve some of the issues of the traditional gradient descent algorithm by adjusting the learning rate adaptively. RMSProp provides an automatic adjustment of the learning rate and is, hence, often used when dealing with non-convex problems, thereby improving stability and convergence.

The key idea of RMSProp is to accumulate the squared gradients and also pick a fraction of the previous updates using an exponential weighted average decay factor (Refer to Box 4.4).

The disadvantage of AdaGrad is that it is very slow, as the step size computation takes a lot of time. It results in a slow learning rate and often ends in premature convergence. The main advantage of RMSProp over AdaGrad is that RMSProp uses an exponentially decaying average for the accumulated squared gradient so that the learning rate is not decreasing too rapidly as in the case of AdaGrad.

The differences between the AdaGrad and RMSProp are given below in Table 4.6.

Table 4.6 Differences between RMSProp and AdaGrad

RMSProp	AdaGrad
Decaying average or moving average of the partial derivatives.	The sum of the squared partial derivatives.
It uses the exponential weighted moving average that gives the larger weights for the latest updates.	The square of the partial derivatives grows monotonically and hence may lead to slow rates of convergence.

1. The key of the RMSProp is that the computation of the learning rate is adaptive based on the history of gradient magnitude using EWMA (Refer to Box 4.4). It uses a decay factor ρ that decays the history over time t. ρ is positive and less than 1. The decay factor and learning rate are hyperparameters, and choosing the hyperparameters is a difficult process.
2. Based on the exponential moving average (refer to Box 4.4) of the squared gradient for each parameter, this exponential moving average is the reason for its rapid convergence.

Box 4.4 Exponential Weighted Moving Average (EWMA)

The exponential moving average is a kind of weighted moving average. Suppose a cricketer scores 1,2,4,40,50,60, then it can be summarized as average. But the problem is it does the same weightage for all scores. But, if one wants to give more weightage for the latest scores, then weights can be assigned for each score, and this leads to the weighted average (WA). EWMA is one such method of weighted average where the weights are exponentially decreasing, and new values are given more weightage than old values.

This EWMA is required to smooth out data and to track the moving average.

What are the basics of EWMA? When the complete data is not available, then a rolling average or moving average can be useful. It accumulates some values and takes the average as the estimate of the current value. But the problem with this method is that it needs a memory buffer to store the past values and the average cannot be computed until all the points are accumulated.

Exponentially weighted moving average (EWMA) uses a recursive formula that need not store all the past values so that the average can be computed as soon new value is available. The recursive formula for the given sequence $x_1, x_2, \cdots, x_n$ is

$y_0 = x_0$ and

$y_n = \rho x_n + (1-\rho)y_{n-1}$

It can be observed that when ρ is zero, the value of $y_n = y_{n-1}$, it takes only the old data. And when ρ is 1 $y_n = x_n$, it takes only the current data. So, this ρ is the mixing factor of the old and new data. ρ is called the smoothing factor that determines the weights and is also called as exponential decay factor or decay rate. The advantage of EWMA is called exponential because the weights constantly decrease. The advantages of this method are that only the last value of the past is retained, the calculation begins as soon as the beginning of the sequence, and there is no need for the accumulation. This method is also known as ARIMA (Autoregressive Integrated Moving Average Model with no constant).

Example 4.5: Let us assume that $x = [x_0, x_1, x_2, x_3, x_4] = [5,10,12,14,16]$. Compute the EWMA assuming $\rho = 0.2$.

Solution

Apply the recursive solution,

$y_0 = x_0$ and

$y_n = \rho x_n + (1-\rho)y_{n-1}$

So, $y_0 = x_0 = 5$

$$y_1 = 0.2x_1 + (1-0.2)y_0 = 0.2 \times 10 + 0.8 \times 5 = 6$$
$$y_2 = 0.2x_2 + (1-0.2)y_1 = 0.2 \times 12 + 0.8 \times 6 = 7.2$$
$$y_3 = 0.2x_3 + (1-0.2)y_2 = 0.2 \times 14 + 0.8 \times 7.2 = 8.56$$
$$y_4 = 0.2x_4 + (1-0.2)y_3 = 0.2 \times 16 + 0.8 \times 8.56 = 10.048$$

So, the final values are 5, 6, 7.2, 8.56, and 10.048.

This makes the step size larger or smaller for the fast convergence of the algorithms. This algorithm provides more stability by preventing the learning rates from becoming too large. The problem with the large parameter is that it causes instability. The procedure for RMSProp is given below:

1. Initialization of vector of parameters θ, learning rate η, and ε. The parameter ε is used to control to prevent the division of zero. Its value is given as,

for example, 10^{-8}. The model parameters are initialized by picking the values randomly or by using a predefined method.

2. Init ρ, a parameter used to control the exponential moving average of the squared gradients.
3. Repeat the steps until convergence. The conditions for the convergence are either a maximum number of iterations or a desired level of loss.
   - **3.1** The steps are the same as SGD.
   - **3.2** Accumulate the exponential weighted moving average of the square of the gradient as
     $$r = \rho r + (1-\rho) g \odot g$$
   - **3.3** Update the parameters
     $$\Delta\theta = \eta \times \frac{1}{\sqrt{r+\varepsilon}} \odot g$$
   - **3.4** Apply the update
     $$\theta = \theta - \Delta\theta$$

The specialties of RMSProp are listed below:

(i) Adaptive learning rate for each parameter.

(ii) Handling non-stationary objectives by considering the recent history of the gradients.

(iii) Reduction in oscillations towards reaching the minimum. So, the convergence is stable and faster.

(iv) Computationally very effective.

4.5.9 ADAM

ADAM stands for ADAptive Moment estimation algorithm. ADAM is a combination of gradient descent algorithm with momentum and RMS prop. ADAM can be applied to non-convex problems as well. ADAM algorithm has many advantages, such as low memory requirements, appropriate for non-stationary objectives, large data, and large parameters.

The specialties of ADAM are listed below:

(i) Advantages of combining the advantages of AdaGrad and RMSProp gives more robustness and efficiency.

(ii) Adaptive learning rate for each parameter by combining EWMA of mean and variance. This yields faster convergence and the ability to solve the non-stationary targets.

(iii) Bias correction to remove the bias.

The focus of ADAM is to find the step size and it combines two moments that track the momentum.

(i) The first moment is mean. It refers to the mean of the gradients. It is also known as momentum in ADAM literature. EWMA is applied for mean. Here, v is the variable that keeps track of the exponentially decaying average of the past gradients.

(ii) The second moment in the variance. In ADAM literature, it refers to the squared gradients. EWMA is applied to variance also. The variable r tracks the historical squares of the gradients.

ADAM's specialty is bias correction. Bias correction is used to remove the bias by dividing the current update with $(1-\rho)^t$, where t is the iteration number. Since both the numerator and denominators are closer to 1, the division yields a small number and hence works well in practice.

The procedure for ADAM is given below:

1. Init the variables

The vector of the parameters $\Delta\theta$

Learning rate η

ε - a parameter used to control to prevent the division of zero. Its value is given as, for example, 10^{-8}.

ρ_1 and ρ_2 - These are mixing factors of the exponential moving weighted average. Initialize these values to a value between [0 – 1].

2. Repeat until convergence

2.1 Initial steps are the same as SGD.

2.2 Accumulate the exponential weighted moving average of the gradient as

$$v = \rho_1 v + (1-\rho_2)g$$

2.3 Accumulate the exponential weighted moving average of the square of the gradient as

$$r = \rho_2 r + (1-\rho_2) g \odot g$$

2.4 Since the variables v and r are initialized to zero, they are biased variables and hence need to be bias-corrected. Compute the corrected bias as

$$\hat{v} = \frac{v}{1-\rho_1^t}$$

$$\hat{r} = \frac{r}{1-\rho_2^t}$$

2.5 Compute the update as

$$\Delta\theta = \eta \times \frac{1}{\sqrt{r+\varepsilon}} \odot \hat{v}$$

2.6 Apply the update rule

$$\theta = \theta - \Delta\theta$$

ADAM performance depends on optimal values of and thus to be tuned based on the specific problems.

4.6 Second-Order Optimization Algorithms

Second-order optimization algorithms are algorithms that take the first-order information as well as the second-order information. It is denoted as $\nabla^2 f(x)$. Its origin lies in Newton's method. Newton was interested in finding optima using calculus where a function is taken and its derivative is computed. If it is difficult to find the analytical solution, then the approximation is carried out. If the initial weight is assumed to be w_0, then the new weight is computed as $w_1 = w_0 + \Delta w_1$. It should be noted that Δw_1 is the improved guess. This process is done iteratively to get stable solutions. If the second-order Taylor series approximates the function, then the solution is given as

$$f(w+\Delta w) \approx f(w) + f'(w)\Delta w + \frac{f''(w)\Delta w^2}{2!} + \ldots$$

Taking the first derivative and substituting that in the above equation and substituting its first derivative to zero gives the resultant,

$$\Delta w = -\frac{f'(w)}{f''(w)}$$

And

$$w_i^{t+1} = w_i^t - \frac{f'(w_i^t)}{f''(w_i^t)}$$

One can extend this logic to the matrices, and the second derivative of the loss function is given as a Hessian matrix, $H = \nabla f(x:w)$ and $\Delta w = H^{-1} g_i$ where $g = \nabla f(x:w)$ the vector of weight updates.

Hessian matrix is an important mathematical tool for optimization. It characterizes the second-order information and is useful for finding curvatures of the landscape. It is denoted as H. The components of the matrix H are the second-order partial derivatives of the cost function concerning the parameters. It is given as follows:

$$H_{ij} = \frac{\partial^2 J}{\partial \theta_i \, \partial \theta_j}$$

The positive elements of H represent the convex shape of the optimization landscape, and the negative value represents the concave shape. The value of zero in the Hessian matrix indicates the flat regions. Using H, one can find the saddle points, local minima, and maxima. For that, the Hessian matrix and its matrix are useful. Analyzing the Hessian matrix in terms of eigenvalues and eigenvectors provides more insides and guidance for neural network training.

The second-order optimization algorithms are of two types, as shown below in Figure 4.7.

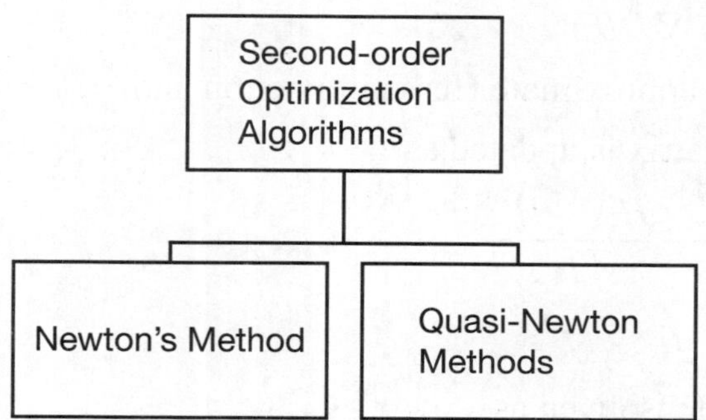

Figure 4.7 Types of Second-order Methods

4.6.1 Newton's Method

Newton's method is often not used because of the computational overhead involved in the calculation of the Hessian matrix and its inverse.

The updated formula for the Newtons method is given below:

$$\theta_{t+1} = \theta_t - (\nabla^2 J(\theta_t))^{-1} \nabla J(\theta_t)$$

Here, $\nabla^2 J(\theta_t)$ is the Hessian matrix and $\nabla J(\theta_t)$ is the gradient.
It can be observed that the computation involves the finding inverse of the Hessian matrix that involves excessive complexity.

4.6.2 Quasi-Newton Method

One of the quasi-newton methods is Broyden-Fletcher-Goldfarb-Shanno (BFGS) is an iterative optimization algorithm that finds minimum without any constraints. The procedure for BFGS is given as below:

1. Initialize model parameters θ with random values or using a predefined procedure.
2. Initialize the Hessian matrix
   $H_0 = 0$
3. Compute the gradient of the cost function at iteration t
   $\nabla J(\theta_t)$
4. [Update the parameters]
   $\theta_{t+1} = \theta_t - \alpha_t H_t^{-1} \nabla J(\theta_t)$
   Here, H_t is the approximate Hessian function and α_t is the step size.
   The Hessian matrix is updated as
   $$H_{t+1} = H_t \frac{y_t y_t^{-1}}{y_t s_t} - \frac{H_t s_t s_t^T H_t^{-1}}{s_t^T H_t s_t}$$
   Here, $s_t = \theta_{t+1} - \theta_t$
5. The final update is given as
   $y_t = \nabla J(\theta_{t+1}) - \nabla J(\theta_t)$
6. Repeat the steps till convergence is met. The convergence can be predefined iterations or a small change in the objective function.

The advantages and disadvantages of the BFGS algorithm are given in Table 4.7.

Table 4.7 Advantages and Disadvantages of BFGS Algorithm

Advantages	Disadvantages
Simplicity	It has memory limitations.
The algorithm provides stability and efficiency.	Computationally very intensive as the Hessian matrix and its inverse computation is very complex.

Summary

1. Optimization deals with finding optimal weights for the neural network.
2. The optimization algorithms or optimizers are used to minimize the loss function to maximize the accuracy of the neural network. The objective of the optimization algorithms is to minimize the error of the machine learning model.
3. The hyperparameters are user-controlled parameters and are set manually by the user. On the other hand, parameters are learned from the data by the algorithm.
4. A function is called convex if a line connecting two points of the convex set C also lies in the convex set. Otherwise, the set is termed as non-convex.
5. Some of the problems associated with non-convex optimization are the multiple local minima, saddle points, and plateaus.
6. Hyperparameter tuning includes random search and grid search methods.
7. Gradient descent is one of the popular optimization algorithms family to find a local minimum or maximum of a function.
8. The stochastic gradient descent algorithm uses randomness to select a random sample, and the weights are updated for every sample.
9. In batch gradient, the cost function is computed for the entire dataset, and weights are updated once.
10. Mini-batch is the trade-off between stochastic and Batch gradient algorithms where the weight updates happen in user-defined mini-batches.

11. The momentum is a process used to accelerate the convergence process by accumulating all the past gradients.
12. Nesterov accelerated gradient (NAG) is a look-ahead algorithm that finds the look-ahead position before computing the gradient.
13. A stochastic gradient descent with momentum is a process of changing the learning rate for faster convergence.
14. AdaGrad is an adaptive gradient descent that finds the optimal learning rate. This algorithm is useful when the features are sparse.
15. AdaDelta is a momentum-based algorithm used to update the weights using the moving average of all past squared gradients.
16. Adam combines the advantages of gradient descent and RMSProp to optimize the learning rate based on past gradients. It uses an exponential weighted moving average (EWMA) of mean and variance for weight updates.
17. RMSProp uses the past gradients to optimize the learning rate adaptively.
18. The second-order gradient methods use the Newton method and Quasi-Newton method.

Glossary

1. Optimization algorithms – This is also known as optimizers. These algorithms are used to find optimal weights for neural networks.
2. Optimization problem – A problem with an objective function that needs to be maximized or minimized with a set of constraints.
3. Optimization function – It is a function that needs to be fulfilled in an optimization problem without violating the constraints.
4. Candidate solutions – The set of feasible solutions are called candidate solutions.
5. Optimal solution – An optimal solution is the best solution that satisfies the object function without violating the constraints.
6. Optimal parameters – The learnable variables are the parameters that determine the behaviour and performance of a neural network. An optimal parameter is the best solution that achieves the objective function without violating any constraints.

7. Model parameters –Trainable weights and bias of neural network. These are structured parameters that are learned from the data and tuned by the learning algorithm without the intervention of the user.
8. Hyperparameters –These are user-controlled parameters that are the learning algorithm parameters. These should be tuned manually and are set automatically.
9. Derivate and gradient – The rate of change of a function is a derivative, and the gradient is a vector of all derivatives for a function of multiple variables.
10. Magnitude and direction – The maximum change in the function value that is measured is as magnitude, and direction guides the descent.
11. Learning rate – The parameter that guides how much weight/bias needs to be updated.
12. Cost function – The function that determines the differences between the predicted and actual value for the entire dataset.
13. Parameters: These are learnable parameters that are learned by the learning algorithm from the data.
14. Hyperparameters – These are parameters of the learning algorithm provided by the user.
15. Search space – A universe of all candidate solutions of the objective function.
16. Local minima – It is the smallest value of the function within a specified domain range. The global minimum is for the entire domain range.
17. Local maxima – It is a high point at which the function value is larger. The global maximum is for the entire range of domains.
18. Convex problem – A set of points where if anyone connects two points of the convex set C, then the line also lies within the convex set.
19. Non-convex problem – If the line connecting any two points on the surface lies outside the surface.
20. Saddle point – A point where the gradients of the loss function are zero.
21. Plateau: The gradient of the loss function is close to zero and represents the flat region of the function.
22. Epoch – The process of one cycle of training set.
23. Convergence – Converge is one condition where the model produces stable values for the optimal parameters with the termination of the algorithm.

24. Momentum – Accumulated past gradients are called momentum or velocity.
25. Momentum coefficient – It is a parameter that controls the mixing of old and new updates.
26. Random search – A technique of evaluating the objective function with the random input and checking whether it results in maximum or minimum using probability distribution.
27. Grid search – It is a process that searches exhaustively through manually specified data.
28. Gradient descent algorithm – It is an iterative first-order optimization algorithm to find a minimum or maximum value of a given function.
29. Batch gradient descent – Method to compute loss or cost function using the entire training data set.
30. Stochastic gradient descent – Method to compute loss or cost function using a single training data set.
31. Mini batch – Method to compute loss or cost function using a small subset of the training data set as specified by the user.
32. Traditional momentum – In the traditional momentum, the algorithm takes the current gradient and also the accumulated previous updates.
33. Nesterov momentum – Nesterov momentum "looks ahead" at the future position of the parameters before computing the gradients.
34. AdaGrad – It is an optimization algorithm that uses different step sizes and different types of gradients.
35. Adaptable learning rate – It is a personalized learning rate of every parameter that Is learned from the data during the training process.
36. RMSProp algorithm – It is an optimization algorithm that adapts to the sparse data and provides an automated adjustment of the learning rate.
37. Newton's method – It uses second-order derivatives to calculate the optimal parameter.
38. Quasi-Newton method – It is used to construct a quadratic model of the optimization function.
39. Hessian matrix – It is a matrix of second order derivatives to find the optimal values.

Review Questions

1. Define optimization algorithm.
2. Why are optimization algorithms required?
3. What is the need of optimization in deep learning?
4. Differentiate between hyperparameter and model parameters.
5. When does the critical point is called a local minimum?
6. List out some of the optimizers.
7. Distinguish between convex and non-convex functions.
8. List out the conditions for the convex function.
9. What is a saddle point? Is it a serious problem?
10. What is a plateau?
11. Define the magnitude and direction of the gradient vector $f(x, y) = x^3 + 2y^2$
12. Compare and contrast batch gradient descent, stochastic, and mini-batch gradient descent algorithms.
13. Define adaptable learning rate.
14. List the need momentum in the neural network perspective.
15. Explain the SGD algorithm.
16. What is the advantage of the mini-batch algorithm?
17. List out the advantages and disadvantages of ADAM.
18. How does ADAM update learning rates?
19. What are the specialties of the RMSProp algorithm?
20. Why is EWMA required for the update?

Long Questions

1. Explain in detail the SGD algorithm.
2. Explain the mini-batch SGD algorithm.
3. Compare and contrast gradient descent and stochastic gradient descent algorithms.
4. Explain AdaGrad in detail.
5. Explain in detail the ADAM optimization algorithm.
6. Explain the concepts of momentum.

Numerical problems

1. Find the local minimum of the $y = 2x^3 - 3x^2 - 6x$
2. Assume a function $f(x) = x^3 + 2y$ and compute the gradient vector. Find the magnitude and the direction of the gradient vector.
3. Apply the stochastic gradient descent algorithm for the function $y = 2x^3 - 3x^2 - 6x$ assuming the initial value as 1. Show the first three iterations.
4. Let us assume that $x = [x_0, x_1, x_2, x_3, x_4] = [1,3,5,8,12]$. Compute the EWMA assuming $\rho = 0.2$.

Crossword

Across

2. Convex optimization problems are easy to solve. (yes/no)
3. Gradient descent algorithms find local _______ (minimum/ maximum)
7. The components of an optimization problem are objective function, a set of constraints. (yes/no)
9. The weights and biases are _______ (parameters/Hyperparameters).
10. Optimization problems have many _______ solutions.
12. The steepness is the _______ of the maximum function changes.
14. Hyperparameters are user-supplied, and parameters are learned from data. (yes/no)

16. The factor that controls the mixing of past and current gradients in EWMA algorithm is called _______ rate.
17. Momentum is the gathered derivatives. (yes/no)
18. The learning rate can be both a hyperparameter ard a parameter. (yes/no)
19. The leaning rate is the _______ size.

Down

1. The matrix of the second order partial derivatives are called _______ matrix.
3. Optimal solutions are the best solutions that _______ or minimize the object function.
4. Plateau is not a major problem for optimization problems. (yes/no)
5. Adam accumulates the past gradients of two moments. They are _______ and variance.
6. Exponential weighted average can remove noise. (yes/no)
8. The word stochastic means _______.
11. The difference between a predicted and actual value of the single sample is called a _______ function.
13. The local minimum is not equal to the global minimum for convex optimization problems. (yes/no)
14. Non-convex function optimization problems have multiple minima or maxima. (yes/no)
15. The overshooting problem comes when the step size is _______.
17. Velocity smoothens gradients. (yes/no)
18. The magnitude of the gradient indicates how much the function changes. (yes/no)

Jumbled Sentences

```
H V Y S S C K Q F P J V T A H N L A R G E R X Y S
Y K E P I E Q H E R P S V F O R A N D O M N E S S
Q Y X R G R T S A H E J P C X H L F G C L F C F H
Y H D Z Q L I G S Y E Q U V Y J E T D M V S T E P
P E V I V D V J I Z O E V E P U G S N F U I J M S
Y E S K J Q Z C B D B M Y D X A C H S T H O M B Y
N W F G B D G U L E X A Y R Q J R D D I L G I K E
B M B D S J W A E T Z X Z P L V N A C O A F N D S
V E W T N O T U M R T I W Z Y O P H M E J N I E N
E A X J S N X K Y E S M A H I R T H X E N F M C W
Y N W H S Q H A E E N I M T T Q G U A S T Y U A R
O Y C E O N D H Y T I Z C B M T W Z K Q I E M Y Y
O G Y D U J Y V N O Y E O B L O S S X J R S R T E
M H F M G P D B K M R N X Y F L J J I F P I C S S
S G C U O B K I R I X W X U H S W V I R V A J O K
B B F Q G G Z R D J O D Z X R O F K K I E P Q Y P
O P S A J V B F H H K L A K R W V I X D P Z W F C
```

yes	feasible	maximize	loss	parameters	yes
yes	yes	no	no	randomness	minimum
yes	yes	decay	Hessian	yes	yes
direction	step	large	mean	yes	

Introduction to Regularization

CHAPTER 5

> The goal of regularization is to find a balance between fitting the training data well and keeping the model complexity in check, which helps in improving the model's ability to generalize to unseen data. — **Christopher M. Bishop**

Credits: © Christopher M. Bishop

One of the significant pillars of deep learning is the concept of regularization techniques. When a neural network is trained, the resulting model is expected to perform well for both training and testing data. However, if the model performs very well for the training data but fails poorly for unforeseen testing data, then this issue is called an overfitting problem. In extreme cases, the resulting model may not work for training and testing data due to a lack of data. This problem is called underfitting. Regularization techniques solve the problems of overfitting and underfitting. The learning objectives of this chapter are listed below:

- Understand the need for regularization.
- Know the types of regularization techniques.
- Understand the bias, variance, and its tradeoffs.
- Know about the weight initialization techniques.
- Know about explicit regularization techniques.
- Understand network configuration.
- Understand the heuristics of regularization.

5.1 Introduction to Generalization and Regularization

In data-driven systems, the model is constructed using a dataset. The data are in the form (input, output) called labelled data. The deep neural network takes the dataset as input and extracts the patterns. A pattern is a rule that captures the characteristics of the data. One of the patterns extracted is the relationship between the input and output variables represented in the form of a function. The extracted patterns are stored in a mathematical form called a model. The essential purpose of the good model is to learn the dataset's primary and general features by understanding the data underlying distributions. So, when the model encounters new data x, it should be able to predict correct y.

For example, in linear regression, the model will be in the form $y = ax + b$. Here, x is the input, the terms a and b are regression coefficients that are learned from the data, and y is the output. The purpose of the linear regression model is to predict the output, say y, correctly for unknown input x.

Generalization ensures that the model performs well for both training and unknown data. Generalization means that instead of memorization, the model understands the underlying patterns of the dataset and constructs a model out of these patterns. The opposite of generalization is called memorization. A poor model memorizes the data set instead of learning the patterns. It is something like a student memorizing answers for certain questions for examinations. The students perform well if the question is asked in the examination. Otherwise, his performance will be low. In memorization, the neural network memorizes the dataset, and hence, during testing, it fails to score on unknown data.

Generalization is used to evaluate the quality of the constructed model as generalization ensures that the model performs well for both training and unknown data. The error involved in the prediction is called a generalization error.

Finding the generalization error is easy if the actual value (ground truth) is known, as one can use the joint probability of predicted and actual values. However, in many circumstances, the actual values have yet to be discovered. So, one way to solve this problem is to divide the dataset into three types:

(i) **Training Dataset:** A set of samples for training purposes alone

(ii) **Validation Dataset:** A set of samples used to validate the experiment and the model and to perform the best model for model selection.

(iii) **Testing Dataset:** A set of samples for checking whether the model is good. One golden rule is that the testing data should never be training data. The split can be 60:20:20 or 80:10:10. More details of this data split are covered in the next chapter.

The error produced by the model for training data is called training error. The error produced by the model for the testing data is called a test error. If the training error is less than the testing error, then the constructed model is not good. On the other hand, if both training and testing errors are less, then the constructed model is good.

The difference between the test and training errors is called the generalization gap and indicates how good the quality of the model is. If the generation gap is low, it indicates that the model is not performing well or overfitting.

The reasons for this generalization gap are:

(i) The mapping between the input and output needs to be corrected due to a lack of data.

(ii) Noise and outliers of the input dataset dominate the model construction. This results in the discovery of unnecessary patterns, called noise and outliers.

(iii) The model gives sub-optimal solutions due to the need for more data.

The method of estimating the generalization is given in Box 5.1.

Box 5.1 Generalization Error

The generalization error is also known as the expected prediction error. The k-fold validation technique can be used to estimate the generalization error as often the ground truth is not available.

The process of k-fold cross-validation involves dividing the input dataset into k-folds. So, k-1 folds would be used as a training dataset for the learning algorithm, while the remaining fold serves as testing. This process is repeated for all the folds. The performance metric for each fold is computed. The average performance metric of all k-folds gives an estimate of the generalization error.

5.2 Overview of Overfitting and Underfitting

The two extremes of generalization are overfitting and underfitting. The generalization is also closely related to bias and variance. The details of bias and variance are given in Box 5.2.

Box 5.2 Components of Generalization

The components of generalization are bias and variance.

Bias

In the real world, problems are very complex. During the approximation process, the constructed model may not be able to capture the essence of real-world problems and can be too simplistic for prediction. The simplistic models cannot predict correctly. The error introduced by the approximation of the real-world problem leads to a systematic error where the predicted values consistently differ from the actual values.

There is a difference between error and bias. The difference between the predicted values and the actual values is called an error or residual. The bias, on the other hand, is a systematic error that shows how the average predictions of the model differ from the actual values.

Bias may be due to the following reasons:

1. Poor approximation of the real-world problems and not able to capture the important relationships of data.
2. Oversimplification of the problem by making too many assumptions.

Variance

Variance is the models' sensitivity to the small fluctuations in the input data. The reasons are noise and outliers that are present in the data. What is Noise? Any abnormal data that is different from normal data is called noise. These statistical fluctuations get amplified in deep neural networks and can cause variance in the model.

Variance in the model leads to erratic and inconsistent predictions when applied to the different training sets.

The generalization error can be crisply put as

Generalization error = $Bias^2$ + variance + Irreducibility error

Irreducible error is the noise in the dataset that the model can never reduce.

In Statistics, the term "fit" is used to explain how well the model's predicted values match with the ground truth values. The match indicates the quality of the model that explains how well the model is able to capture the underlying relationships between the variables. The best fit is one where there is a function available that approximates the data points correctly.

To explain the concepts better, let us take a linear regression example, where the data points are plotted as a scatter plot, as shown in Figure 5.1. The objective of linear regression is to fit a line to approximate the points. The linear regression works to adjust the weights to minimize the errors between the actual and predicted values. The "best fit" is one where the difference between the predicted and actual value is minimal to provide the closest match.

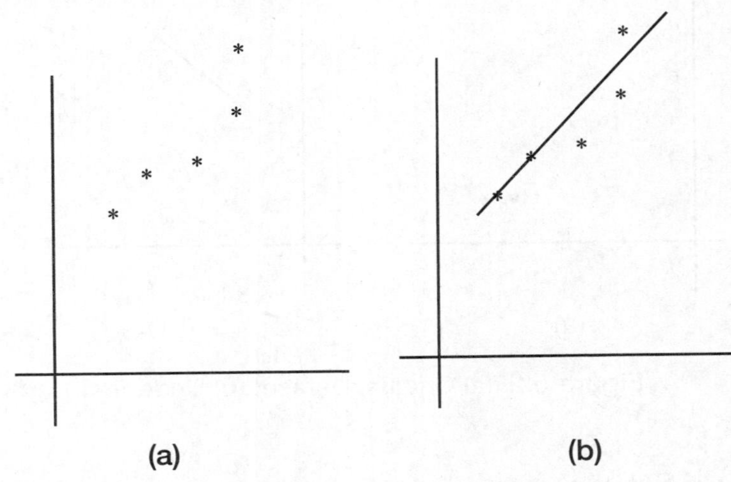

Figure 5.1 (a) Original Dataset (b) Best Fit

5.2.1 Underfitting

If the model is too simple, then the model may not capture the underlying structure of the data. It fails to recognize important patterns and relationships that are present in the data. As a result, the model may not be able to predict correctly for both training data as well as the new, unseen test data.

Overfitting is the case where the model memorizes the data and performs very well for training data but poorly for training data.

One can check Figure 5.2, where it can be observed that the fitted line is suboptimal as there is a lot of error between the points and the fitted line. Underfitting models are usually characterized by high bias and low variance (Refer to Box 5.2). The summary of underfitting models is listed below.

(i) An underfitting model is a too simplistic model. It cannot capture the underlying patterns in the data.

(ii) It does not reflect the real-world problems accurately. It makes many strong assumptions that result in the poor quality of the model.

(iii) The quality of the model is bad for both training data as well as testing data.

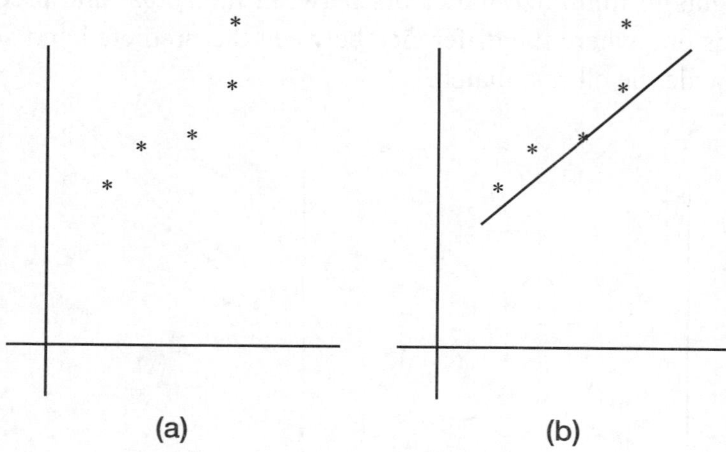

Figure 5.2 (a) Original Dataset (b) Underfit

5.2.2 Overfitting

The overfit model, unlike underfitting models, is too complex. Many times, the dataset may have noise and fluctuations. One can recollect that the undesired patterns are what one calls noise. Fluctuations are somewhere the model results vary for different datasets. So, the problem with the overfitting models is that they capture not only the underlying patterns among the data but also the noise and random fluctuations. So, the overfit model may work for training data, but the model will fail poorly for testing data. It does not generalize well.

Figure 5.3 is a case of overfitting. It can be observed that the model captures noise and random fluctuations instead of underlying patterns. It can be observed that the fit may look accurate, but the point is what we need is a fitting of data by a line and not the approximation by a polynomial of many degrees!

High variance and low bias characterize the overfitting models, and overfitting models are very sensitive to the training data. In short, for small datasets, the algorithm tends to memorize rather than learn from the data.

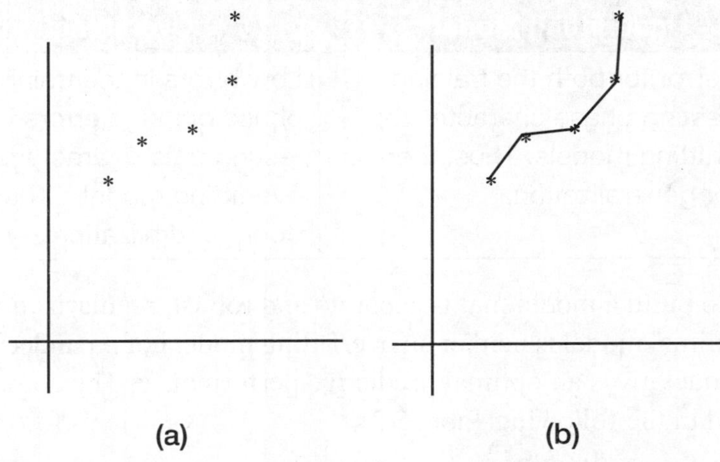

Figure 5.3 (a) Original Dataset (b) Overfit

The summary of overfitting models is given as

(i) An overfitting model is too complex model. It captures noise and fluctuations along with the underlying patterns in the data.

(ii) Overfitting models work well for the training data but poorly for unseen testing data.

The complete differences between underfitting and overfitting are given below in Table 5.1.

Table 5.1 Differences between Underfitting and Overfitting

S.no.	Underfitting Model	Overfitting Model
1.	The problem with the underfitting model is that it is too simplistic to capture real-world problems. The underfitting model fails to capture the underlying patterns in the data.	An overfitting model is a complex model that fits the data as well as the noise and fluctuations present in the dataset. Model complexity is very high and excessive.
2.	The model is characterized by high bias and low variance.	The model is characterized by low bias and high variance.
3.	The performance of the model during training as well as testing is poor	The performance of the model during training is good, but during testing, it is poor

S.no.	Underfitting Model	Overfitting Model
4.	High error for both the training and testing phase characterizes underfitting models. Thus, there is a poor generalization.	Low errors in the training data phase but high errors in the testing data characterize the overfitting models. Thus, there is a poor generalization.

As the goal is to build a model that is accurate and robust, regularization techniques are used. An optimal model is neither an overfitting model nor an underfitting model. The optimal model gives an optimal predictive performance. The above discussions are summarized in the following Table 5.2.

Table 5.2 Types of Bias-Variance Tradeoff

S.no.	Conditions	Model	Remarks
1.	High bias, low variance	Underfitting	Systematic error in predictions.
2.	Low bias and high variance	Overfitting	Sensitive to noise and outliers in the training data.
3.	High bias and High Variance	Useless model	There is no effective capturing of the patterns in the data.
4.	Low bias and Low variance	Desired model	Ideal model.

There are two ways the overfitting and underfitting can be compared. One is performance, and another is the model complexity.

(i) **Performance:** In underfitting, the model cannot learn data. In other words, the model is inefficient as the model tends to memorize. As a result, if an instance is encountered in the training phase, the model predicts it correctly, but when unknown data is encountered, the model stumbles.

(ii) **Model Complexity:** Underfitting is an oversimplification of the real-world problem. Underfitted models come with a solution that does not capture the complexity of the problem. On the other hand, overfitting means the problem is made overcomplicated. The model generated will be more complex than the simple model generated for the underfit condition. What is a simple and complex model? One way is to create a simpler model per Occam's razor principle (refer to Box 5.3).

Box 5.3 Model Complexity and Occam's razor Principle

Occam's razor principle, in the context of modeling, is that the balance between simplicity and complexity is essential. It suggests that simpler models should be preferred over complex models unless the complex models provide a better performance and are necessary.

For example, consider two models.

$M_1 = 2x^2 + 3$

$M_2 = 6x^4 + 7x + 2x^2 + 3$

Which one should be preferred? As per the Occam razor principle, the simple model is a model that has a lesser number of parameters without losing the capability of predicting better.

How to express it quantitatively? For this, the norms are used. Norms are the length of the vector. Some of the vector norms are

$$L_1 = |x_1\| = |x_1| + |x_2| + \cdots + |x_n|$$
$$= \sum_{i=1}^{n} |x_i|$$

The L_2 norm is given as

$$L_2 = \|x\|_2 = \sqrt{x_1^2 + x_2^2 + \cdots + x_n^2}$$
$$= \sqrt{\sum_{i=1}^{n} x_i^2}$$

The L_∞ norm is given as

$$L_\infty = \|x\|_\infty = \max_i (|x_1| + |x_2| + \cdots |x_n|)$$
$$= \max_i |x_i|$$

In general, the form is given as

$$L_p = \|x\|_p = \max_i (\sum_{i=1}^{n} \|x_i\|^p)^{\frac{1}{p}}$$

where $1 \le p \le \infty$

In the real world, one can illustrate concepts with complexity!

Walking to your friend's house next to your house is optimal!

Going to your friend's next house by car is luxury (Complex Model!) as it is overstated.

One can quantify complexity by numbers. For this, norms can be used. So, the quantification of the model $M_1 = 2x^2 + 3$ by L_1 is

$L_1 = \|2\| = 2$

The quantification of the model $M_2 = 6x^4 + 7x + 2x^2 + 3$ is

$L_1 = \|6\| + \|7\| + \|2\| = 15$

So, one can conclude that M_2 is more complex than the model M_1.

Example 5.1: Let polynomial equations characterize two models

$$M_1 = 4x + 9$$

$$M_2 = 8x^2 + 9x - 2$$

Determine which model is complex.

Solution:

One can apply the L_1 norm above to get

$M_1 = \|4\| = 4$

$M_2 = \|8\| + \|9\| = 17$

One can apply the L_2 norm above to get

$M_1 = \|4\|^2 = 16$

$M_2 = \|8\|^2 + \|9\|^2 = 145$

It can be observed that based on both norms, M_2 is a complex model compared to the model M_1.

5.3 Introduction to Regularization

The technique that is used to solve the problem of overfitting is called regularization. Regularization techniques penalize the excessive complexity and avoid the problems of overfitting and underfitting (Especially overfitting is more troublesome).

Some of the popular regularization techniques for solving the problem of overfitting and underfitting are shown in Figure 5.4.

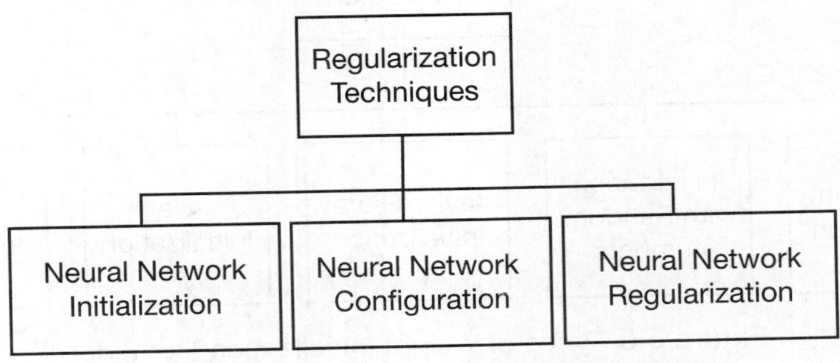

Figure 5.4 Regularization Techniques

Neural network initialization is an important aspect of convergence and vanishing gradient problems. If the value of the data becomes small in the forward process, its gradient will be too small for the backward propagation stage. As a result, the gradient values may become zero, and the network would never learn anything new or may not converge. Therefore, network initialization is an important topic.

Network configuration considers the heuristics that govern the number of layers, nodes, and architectures. Network configuration concerns how to make the models complex by adding the number of layers and neurons. The problem of underfitting and overfitting can be solved by controlling the number of neurons.

Neural network regularization is an important topic that avoids the problem of overfitting using regularization techniques.

Let us discuss them in the subsequent sections.

5.3.1 Weight Initialization

It is essential to initialize the neural network so that the neural network can give the best performance. If the weights are not initialized properly, it may lead to a vanishing gradient or exploding gradient problem. The weight initialization methods are shown in Figure. 5.5.

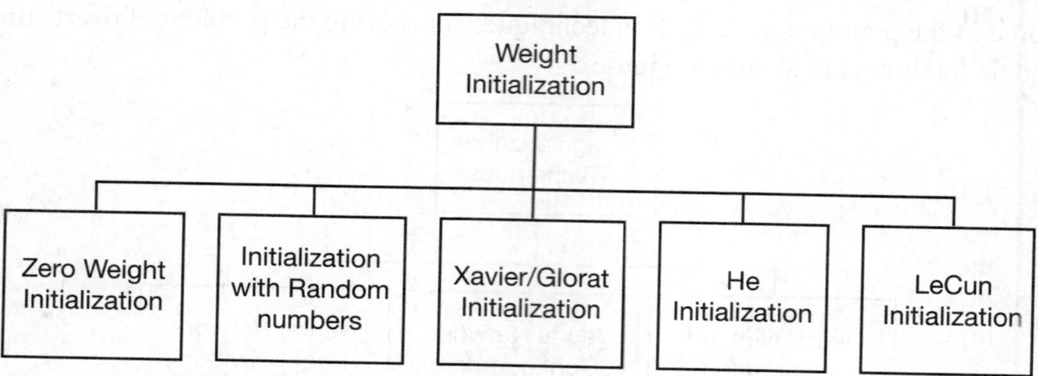

Figure 5.5 Types of Weight Initialization Methods

1. **Zero Weight Initialization:** In this method, the neural network weights are initialized to zero. Zero initialization makes neurons learn the same features in each iteration, which is not preferable.
2. **Random Initialization:** Random numbers are used to initialize the weights randomly, following the normal distribution.
3. **Xavier/Glorat Initialization:** Xavier uniform initialization is suitable for layers where sigmoidal activation functions are used.

$$\omega_i \sim U\left[-\frac{\sqrt{\sigma}}{\{fan_{in} + fan_{out}\}}, \frac{\sqrt{\sigma}}{\{fan_{in} + fan_{out}\}}\right]$$

Here, fan_{in} = the number of input paths toward a given neuron and fan_{out} = the output paths of the given neurons. The value of σ is 2 for sigmoid, but $\sigma = 6$ is recommended.

The Xavier normal initialization is given as

$$N(0, 1) \sim \frac{\sqrt{1}}{f_{in}}$$

The Glorat normal initialization is given by normal distribution with the standard deviation given as

$$\sigma = \sqrt{\frac{2}{fan_{in} + fan_{out}}}$$

4. **He uniform Initialization:** Weights are assigned from values of uniform distribution.

$$\omega_i \sim U\left[-\sqrt{\frac{6}{fan_{in}}}, \sqrt{\frac{6}{fan_{out}}}\right]$$

He Normal Initialization: The weights are assigned from values of normal distribution.

$\omega \sim \sim [0,\sigma]$ with a standard deviation given as $\sigma = \sqrt{\frac{2}{fan_{in}}}$

5. **LeCun Initialization:** LaCun initialization uses a Gaussian distribution with the mean and variance of $\frac{1}{fan_{in}}$ inputs. Here, the values are drawn from [-limit, limit], where the limit is given as $\sigma = \frac{\sqrt{3}}{fan_{in}}$.

5.3.2 Network Configuration

Network Configuration requires two parameters.

(i) Number of layers

(ii) Number of nodes

The solution to underfitting is to add more complexity to the neural network by adding more neurons and hidden layers and increasing the neural network's capacity (Refer to Box 5.4). If the constructed model exhibits underfitting, it is time to return to neural network design by making the models complex by increasing the neural network's width, size, and depth.

Box 5.4 Important Jargon

The following jargon is important

1. Width – The number of nodes in layers of a neural network.
2. Size – The number of nodes in the overall neural network model.
3. Depth – The number of layers in the Neural Network. If stacked, more layers indicate the depth, which is why one calls a neural network a deep neural network.
4. Capacity – The type of complex functions that the neural network can learn is called network capacity.
5. Architecture – The arrangement of layers and nodes is called the architecture of the neural network.

The number of hidden neurons (N_h) is given by

$$N_i \le N_h \le N_o$$

$$N_h < 2N_i$$

$$N_h = \frac{N_s}{Ni}(\alpha \times N_i + N_o)$$

where N_s is the number of samples and N_i is the size of the input layer and N_o is the size of the output layer and α is a hyperparameter in the range [2, 10].

5.4 Regularization Techniques

Regularization techniques bridge the gap between training and testing performance. If the dataset has abundant data, then regularization may not be necessary. But all the datasets are finite. In that context, regularization becomes crucial.

Regularization techniques prevent overfitting by penalizing the complexity of the network.

$$\text{Max / min } f(x)$$
$$\text{Subjected to } g(x) = c$$

Here, $g(x)$ is the constraint. This problem is called an unconstrained optimization problem. This kind of problem may be solved by the Lagrange multiplier method as follows:

$$f(x) + \lambda g(x)$$

Here, the term $\lambda g(x)$ is called the regularization term. It is also called the penalty term. The model with smaller weights is desirable compared to models with larger weights. So, the model with smaller weights needs to be encouraged. Here comes the role of regularization. The need to shrink the coefficients is solved by regularization. It can be observed that the penalty is a function in terms of the parameters of the model. It is a scalar that contributes to the loss function and regularization. It should be observed that the constraint is always the magnitude of the model parameters that are intended to produce simple models. Here λ is the penalty term. Thus, $g(x)$ is a scalar that returns a high value when the parameters are less preferred.

If λ is zero, then there is no difference between the model with or without regularization.

If λ is one, then all the weights are penalized.

In short, its value ranges between 0 and 1, and normally, its optimal value is chosen based on the cross-validation techniques.

The regularization types are shown in Figure 5.6.

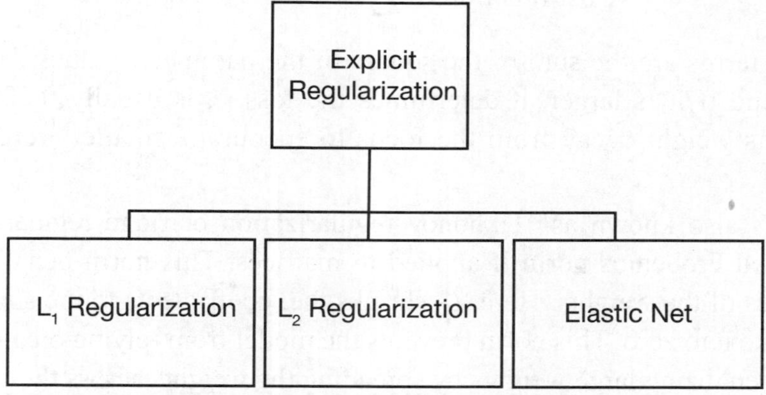

Figure 5.6 Types of Regularization Methods

5.4.1 L_1 Regularization

The L_1 norm is called LASSO (Least Absolute Shrinkage and Selection Operator). This norm is used to prevent overfitting and to select sparse features. Here, the cost function is given as

$$\sum_{i=1}^{n}(y-y')^2+\lambda\|w\|$$

The term $\lambda\|w\|$ is called L_1 norm. It is a penalty term. It can be observed that L_1 is the absolute value of the coefficients of the linear regression equation. L_1 norm penalizes the sum of the absolute weights to the extent of making the coefficients zero. So, it removes all less relevant features by making it to zero.

The advantages are:

(i) The model is simple and more straightforward to interpret.

(ii) The dataset has many irrelevant features that do not contribute significantly to predicting the output.

5.4.2 L_2 Regularization

L_2 norm is also called ridge regression. As per the above discussion, the cost function L_2 is given as

$$\text{Cost function} = \sum_{i=1}^{n}(y - y')^2 + \lambda \|w\|^2$$

The penalty terms are the sum of the square of the parameter values. Here, λ is the multiplier, and if it is larger, it determines the loss. λ is usually 0.0005. So, it is referred to as weight decay from the focus to encourage smaller weights (smaller weights).

This norm is also known as Tikhonov regularization or ridge regularization. This norm is called Frobenius norm if applied to matrices. This norm penalizes the sum of the squares of the weights. Here, L_2 shrinks the coefficients to the small value but does not make it to zero. This norm prevents the model from relying on a single or few features by penalizing large weights by spreading the weights across the features.

By adding the penalty, the partial derivative of that is added to the partial derivative of the loss function. This regularized loss function makes the stochastic gradient descent of the above equation is given in linear regression as

$$\omega_i = \omega_i - \eta \frac{\partial L}{\partial \omega_i} - \eta \lambda \omega_i .$$

Here, η is the learning rate and L is the loss function, and new term $\eta\lambda\omega$. The new term ensures that a small fraction of the weight is subtracted. This reduction makes the algorithm push the model weights towards zero as the training progress becomes η and λ are < 1.

The output of this regularization is non-sparse, unlike L_1 norm, which produces sparse output.

5.4.3 Elastic Net

An elastic net is a combination of both L_1 and L_2 norms. The cost function of the elastic net is given as

$$\text{cost function} = \sum_{i=1}^{n}(y - y')^2 + \lambda_{ridge} \|w\|_2^2 + \lambda_{lasso} \|w\|_1$$

The strength of the penalty is controlled by α. If it is zero, it is ridge regression or lasso.

The differences between L_1 and L_2 the norm are given in the Table 5.3.

Table 5.3 Differences between L_1 and L_2 norm

S.NO.	L_1 Norm	L_2 Norm
1	L_1 norm is the absolute value of the linear regression coefficients	L_2 is the squares of the magnitude of linear regression coefficients
2.	This norm is called LASSO.	This norm is called RIDGE.
3	This norm encourages sparsity by setting some model parameters to zero, producing a sparse output.	This norm produces a smoothness in the function by distributing the weight among all coefficients. But it does not make it zero. As a result, the output is non-sparse.
4.	Useful for feature selection or for building sparse models. This norm is applied when a subset of the features is relevant to the construction of the model.	This norm applies a quadratic penalty that makes the model less sensitive to extreme values of the coefficients and outliers. This model is chosen to avoid over-emphasis on certain features and to encourage a balance among many features.
5.	This norm applies an absolute or linear penalty.	This norm applies a quadratic penalty.
6.	Computing this norm is computationally inefficient.	Computationally efficient and analytic solutions are feasible.

The following example illustrates the concept of weight shrinking.

Example 5.2: let the weights be given as 4, 12, and 23. If $\lambda = 0.01$ is used as the penalty hyperparameter, explain how the weights are shrinked if the following policies are used:

1. Add $\lambda = 0.01$ to the negative coefficients and subtract $\lambda = 0.01$ from the positive coefficients. If the coefficient is zero, then ignore it.
2. Multiply by $(1-\lambda)$
   Show the effect of shrinking.

Solution

1. In the first method, the weights 4, 12, 23 would be shrinked as
   $= 4 - 0.01, 12 - 0.01, 23 - 0.01$
   $= 3.99, 11.99, 22.99$
   So, the shrinked weights are 3.99, 11.99, 22.99
2. In the second method, the weights 4, 12, 23 would be shrinked as
   $= 4 \times (1 - 0.01), 12 \times (1 - 0.01), 12 \times (1 - 0.01)$
   $= 4 \times 0.99, 12 \times 0.99, 23 \times 0.99$
   $= 3.96, 11.88, 22.77$
   If this continues for many iterations, the shrunk weights represent the model's different complexity.

5.5 Neural Network Regularization

The heuristics of regularization techniques are given in Figure 5.7.

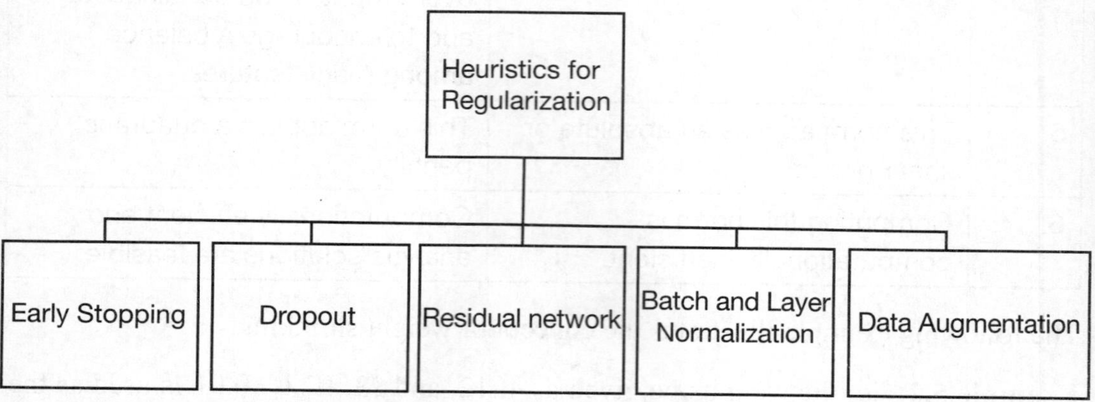

Figure 5.7 Types of Heuristics for Regularization

5.5.1 Early Stopping

Early stopping has an effect as L_2 regularization. The principle of early stopping is based on the monitoring of the model performance on the validation set. It is, hence useful for controlling the model complexity by halting the training process when the model starts learning the noise and outliers present in the dataset.

(i) The model's performance is evaluated based on the training data. The error of the model for training data is called training error. Normally, it is a curve that decreases continuously. One should also check the performance of the model on the validation dataset.

(ii) The model performance on the validation data is monitored. This error is called a testing error.

(iii) The moment the testing error stops improving and starts deteriorating, the "early stopping" is applied, and hence the training process is halted. The model at this point is stored ensuring that this model is the "best model" that is available.

Early stopping ensures that the coarse shape of the underlying function is captured but not the noise, and also the early stopping heuristics thus ensure that there is a balance between the model complexity and the generalization.

The model complexity graph plots the model's performance for training and validation errors. The x-axis of the graph is complexity, and the y-axis is error. There are only two curves – errors in both training and testing. The testing error is always a downside curve, and the validation error is a downside curve and may go up again. For example, two curves are given in the following Figure 5.8.

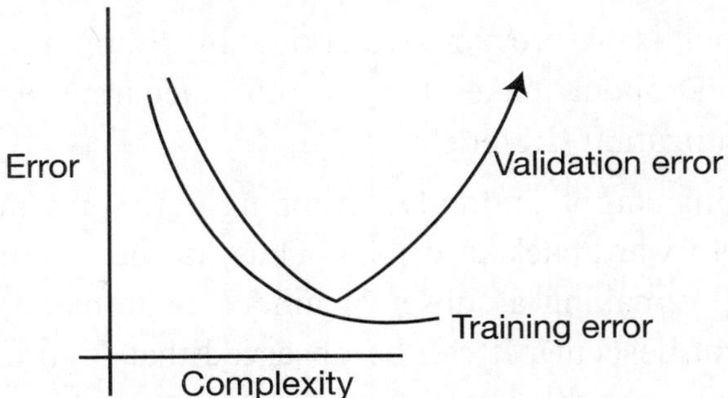

Figure 5.8 Model Complexity Graph

The meeting point illustrates the best degree where both the curves tend to be closer and indicates a solution for the overfitting problem.

This procedure has only one hyperparameter that can be chosen to stop the training procedure before it converges.

Example 5.3: Three models, M_1, M_2, and M_3 are given with training and testing errors as per Table 5.4.

Table 5.4 Model Selection

Model Name	Training Error	Testing Error
M_1	0.2	2.3
M_2	2.3	3.7
M_3	0.1	4.3

Can one predict the overfit, underfit, and best ft conditions from Table 5.4 above?

Solution

The model M_1 has the least training and testing errors. So, it may be the best fit. The model M_2 has both training and testing errors as high. Therefore, it must be underfitted, and M_3 exhibits low training error but high testing error. So, it is an overfit model.

5.5.2 Dropout

Dropout is a regularization technique. Dropout was introduced by Geoffrey Hinton in 2012.

The focus of dropout is to prevent overfitting by dropping random neurons in the neural network. Dropout makes the data less accurate but more robust, thus improving the generalization (Refer Box 5.5).

Dropout in the training stage, randomly "dropping out" some neurons in the neural network during the forward/backward pass. Thus, in the training stage, the neural network drops out (by making a subset of hidden neurons zero at every iteration of Stochastic gradient descent). It can be observed that Figure 5.9 shows a neural network and the resultant of the dropping of a neuron in Figure 5.10.

Box 5.5 Rationality for Dropout

Dropout is a technique that solves the problem of overfitting by solving the problem of co-adaptation. It is based on the fact that neurons rely too much on each other to learn specific patterns. This dependency leads to a co-adaptation situation where certain neurons are too specialized, and there develops some dependency on each other. As a result, the neurons work well when they are together but stumble individually upon the new data. This situation is called overfitting.

Dropout drops neurons "randomly" to break the co-adaptation. These dropping forces the neural network to learn the redundant representations robustly. Thus, the neural network encourages the neurons to learn independently the robust and global features. So, the steps of dropout are:

(i) Randomly select the neurons.

(ii) Drop a certain amount of neurons in the training phase.

(iii) After training is over, keep all the neurons for the testing phase and scale their activations by the dropout rate to account for the increase of neurons in the testing phase.

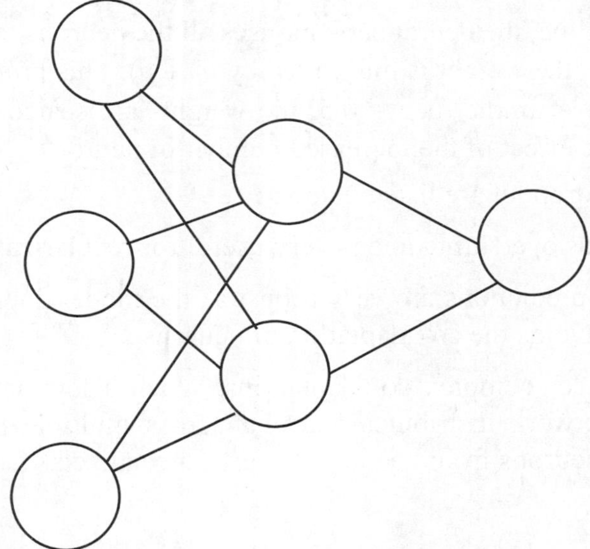

Figure 5.9 Original Network

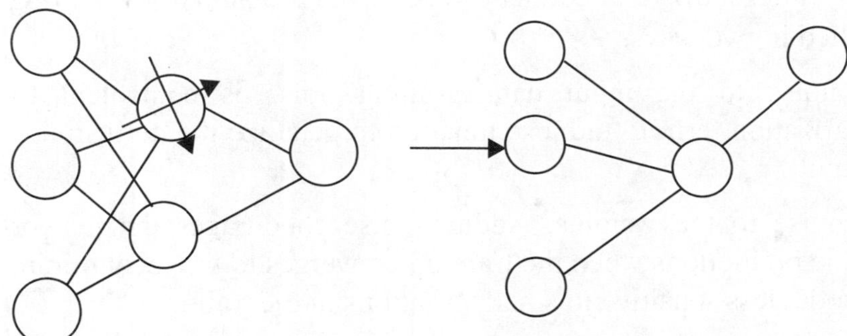

Figure 5.10 Dropping of a Neuron

How many neurons need to be dropped? The probability of randomly dropping the neurons is controlled by p. If $p = 0.5$, 50% of the neurons are dropped. By this, it is meant that the output of the neurons is set to zero. Usually, the value of p ranges from 0.2 – 0.5. For the layer ℓ, the dropping probability is p_ℓ. For each activation $a_j^\ell = a_j^\ell \times I_j^\ell$, for j = 1, 2, …, n it is given as

$$I_j^\ell = \begin{cases} 0 \text{ with probability } p_i \\ \dfrac{1}{1-p_i} \text{ with probability } 1-p_i \end{cases}$$

The advantage is that the dropping out introduces noise and prevents the network from relying on a few neurons. The deactivation of neurons differs for each training. Usually, dropout is applied to hidden layers more than to input and output layers.

During the testing time, the neural network uses all the neurons to make predictions. In the testing stage, the weight is multiplied by $(1 - p)$. This procedure is known as weight scaling. For example, if $p = 0.5$, the weights are scaled by ½. This weight scaling smooths the effect of the increased number of neurons.

The advantages of dropout are listed below:

(i) Dropout avoids overfitting and is very useful for regularization.

(ii) Dropout The predictions are very robust as the model does not rely on a few neurons and avoids the co-adaptation of neurons.

(iii) Dropout reduces complex co-adaptations. When a few neurons are inactive, the neural network distributes learning across multiple pathways. Dropout prevents the neurons from becoming overly specialized.

Adding Noise

Dropout is equivalent to applying multiple Bernoulli noises to the network activations, which shows that adding can solve the problem of overfitting. The noise can be applied in two ways.

(i) Add noise to the input data. Adding noise is equivalent to adding a regularization term to the loss function to penalize the derivatives concerning the input.

(ii) Add noise to the weights. Adding noise encourages the network to make sensible predictions when the training converges to the local minima. It makes the model less sensitive to small variations in the training data.

(iii) The noise can also be added to labels. The vacuum of the correct classes can be very large, and error classes would be associated with small values; this is called label smoothening and improves the generalization.

A hyperparameter should control the noise addition; only optimal noise should be added to the input.

5.5.3 Residual Network

Normalization ensures that the gradient is healthy and normal, and using the residual layer improves performance and eases the training of deep neural networks. Two problems are associated with the gradients shown in Figure 5.11.

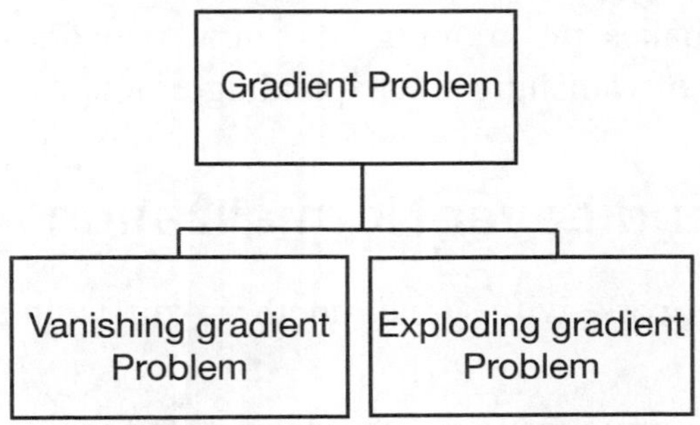

Figure 5.11 Types of Gradient Problems

It can be noted that, in the forward pass, the data is fed to the neural network. Then, the error is computed by taking the difference between the actual and output of the neural network. The partial derivative of the error is taken and backpropagated to update the weights.

(i) Sometimes, the gradients of the cost function in the backpropagation stage may be large and continue to increase may cause problems in parameter updating. The expanding gradients may cause the network to diverge instead of converge. This problem is called the exploding gradient problem.

(ii) The reverse problem is called the vanishing gradient problem, where the gradients become zero or very small in the backpropagation stage, making the network learn nothing or only one feature repeatedly.

Skipnets (Refer to Figure 5.12) do the regularization of these problems. It solves the vanishing gradient problem by using skip connections. Skip connection allows the network to bypass some of the paths directly using shortcuts.

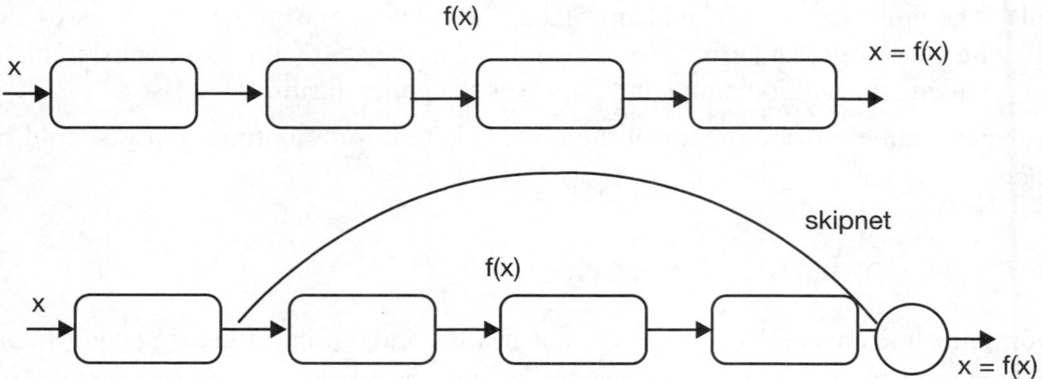

Figure 5.12 Example of Creating a Residual Network using Skip Connections

Skipping the layers makes the training of neural networks theoretically best by avoiding the problems of vanishing and expanding gradients.

5.5.4 Batch and Layer Normalization

Training a neural network with great depth is difficult. In that, using batch normalization helps.

The purpose of batch normalization is to ensure that the conditions of the training phase are maintained for the testing phase. This requirement is made possible by ensuring the data distributions remain the same.

Batch Normalization

Batch normalization addresses the problem of internal covariate shift. What is internal covariate shift? The distribution of test data often differs from the distribution of training data, even though the underlying rules that govern the data are the same. This concept of distribution change is called the covariate effect. This affects the performance of the learning models and generalization. When the magnitude of the input to a layer changes during the training process, the network has difficulty learning the weights in the next layer while accounting for the change in the magnitude of the input.

The problem of internal covariate shift is solved by batch normalization by normalizing the input, as the normalization keeps the gradients stable and prevents them from changing quickly.

The batch normalization algorithm normalizes the input by subtracting the mean and dividing it by the standard deviation of the batch. This is used to mitigate the internal covariate shift. The normalized values are adapted and scaled by the hyperparameters. This adaptability helps the model improve its expressibility by properly learning the suitable shifts and scales. This noise helps in the regularization process and avoids the dependency on the initial weights initialization. In short, these ensure an implicit regularization effect.

Batch normalization helps stabilize and set up the training process. It should be applied before the non-linear bias.

1. Determine μ and standard deviation based on activation vector z.
2. Compute mean $\mu = \frac{1}{n}\sum_i (z^i)$
3. Compute variance $\sigma = \frac{1}{n}\sum_i (z^i - \mu)$
4. Normalize the activation vector. $Z^i_{norm} = \frac{(z^i - \mu)}{\left\{\sqrt{\sigma^2 - \epsilon}\right\}}$

Then, compute the output.

$$z = \gamma \times z^i_{norm} + \beta$$

Here, γ, β are parameters used to adjust the standard deviation and bias.

The advantages of batch normalization are listed below:

1. Introduce noise to each layer's input, prevent overfitting, and improve generalization.
2. Batch normalization reduces the dependency on the weight initialization.
3. Reduces the need for dropouts

Example 5.4: Consider the following 2D data and apply the batch normalization process.

$$F = \begin{pmatrix} 1 & 2 \\ 4 & 1 \end{pmatrix}$$

Assume all other parameters α, β and ε are ignored for the sake of simplicity.

Solution

1. First, flatten the image as a one-dimensional vector (1 2 4 1).

2. Compute the mean of the image as

$$\mu = \frac{1+2+4+1}{4} = \frac{8}{4} = 2$$

3. Compute the variance as

$$\sigma^2 = \frac{(1-2)^2 + (2-2)^2 + (4-2)^2 + (1-2)^2}{4} = \frac{6}{4} = 1.5$$

4. Normalize the values as. Assuming ε as zero, one gets

$$\text{when } z = 1,\ z_{norm} = \frac{(1-2)}{\sqrt{1.5}} \cong -0.8165$$

$$\text{when } z = 2,\ z_{norm} = \frac{(2-2)}{\sqrt{1.5}} = 0$$

$$\text{when } z = 4,\ z_{norm} = \frac{(4-2)}{\sqrt{1.5}} = 0 \cong 1.63299$$

$$\text{when } z = 1,\ z_{norm} = \frac{(1-2)}{\sqrt{2}} \cong -0.8165$$

The reshaped normalized matrix would be $F = \begin{pmatrix} -0.8165 & 0 \\ 1.63299 & -0.8165 \end{pmatrix}$

If necessary, the transformations can be applied and ensure the input data in the testing stage is the same as the distribution in the training phase.

Layer Normalization

Layer normalization is the same as batch normalization. It normalizes the features within a layer, while batch normalization is across the layers. It contributes to normalization due to its normalization and introduction of noise in the neural network.

5.5.5 Data Augumentation

If the data is not large, then data augmentation should be used. In data augmentation, new data is generated by transforming the existing data. What is the need? The additional data prevents the model from overfitting and generalizing for the new data. This new data is thus used as a regularization technique for reducing model variance.

The advantages of data augmentation are

(i) To improve the generalization of the model

(ii) To artificially increase the size of the input dataset

(iii) To improve the robustness of the model

(iv) To prevent the overfitting of the model

(v) Solve the problem of internal covariate shift

Expanding the data set is called data augmentation. The aim is to increase the dataset by transforming the clip data while keeping the label the same. The augmentation operations such as rotation, blur, or color balance can be used to increase the dataset. For the text, the operations may be to substitute synonymous, translate to another language, and back. For audio, it may be amplification or attenuation of frequency.

The algorithm for data augmentation is given below:

1. Read input dataset data (x_i, y_i)
2. For each sample (x_i, y_i) do
   - 2.1 Select data augmentation operator
   - 2.2 Apply the data augmentation operator
   - 2.3 Add the resultant of step 2.2 to the dataset End for
3. Repeat steps 1–3 until the desired size is reached.
4. Exit

This chapter covered regularization techniques. The next chapter focuses on the data itself.

Summary

1. Regularization techniques solve the problem of overfitting.
2. The model predicts well for the training data, but testing data is called the overfitting model. The underfitting model works poorly for prediction for both training and testing data.
3. The bias is a measure of how well the model can be. It is the measurement based on the average error of the neural network output to the expected output. It is due to the problems in approximating the real-world problems.

4. Variance is a measure of how models are sensitive to the changes in the input. Variance leads to a greater difference when the model is applied to different datasets.
5. The bias-variance tradeoff is a way of ensuring the balance between bias and variance.
6. The model should be initialized properly for convergence of the neural network.
7. Network configuration provides guidelines for the number of neurons and layers used.
8. The regularization term can be assigned explicitly. L_1 and L_2 are some of the regularization schemes.
9. Early stopping is a heuristic rule ensuring the model captures only the coarse function, not the noises.
10. Dropout is a regularization technique that solves the problem of co-adaptation.
11. Batch normalization normalizes the activation vector just like data normalization.
12. Data augmentation increases the amount of data using the principle of self-generation.

Glossary

1. Regularization – Regularization techniques solve the problem of underfitting and overfitting in models.
2. Best Fit – When the predicted and actual values are closer.
3. Memorization – Model inability to generalize to unseen data.
4. Noise – A dataset that contains meaningless data or unnecessary patterns.
5. Outliers – A data point that is noticeably distinct from the rest of the data points.
6. Fluctuations – The conditions where the constructed models result vary for different datasets.
7. Occam's Razor Principle – Simple models should be preferred over complex models unless the performance of the complex model is very good.
8. Optimal Model – It is one where the model is sensitive to the patterns and generalizes to the new data.

9. Model – A model is a relationship among input and output variables that can be an equation.
10. Generalization – The ability of a model to predict correctly for an unknown instance is called generalization.
11. Generalization error – The error involved in generalization is called a generalization error.
12. Test error – The error produced by a model for testing data is called test error.
13. Training error – The error produced by the model for the training dataset.
14. Bias – The bias is the error introduced when approximating real-world problems by a simplistic model.
15. Variance – The model sensitivity towards the fluctuation in the input data is called variance.
16. Generalization gap – The difference between testing and training error is called the generalization gap.
17. Bias–variance tradeoff – The balance between bias and variance is called bias-variance tradeoff
18. Underfit -The model that performs poorly for both training and testing data is called the underfitting model.
19. Overfitting – The model that performs well for the training data and poorly for the testing data is called the overfitting model.
20. Penalty term – A term added to the loss function that penalizes the larger weights is called a penalty term.
21. Network width – The number of nodes in layers
22. Network size – The number of nodes in the model.
23. Network depth – The number of layers in the neural network
24. Network capacity – The type of functions that can be learned.
25. Early-stopping – Early stopping is a regularization technique where the model's training is stopped before convergence. The stopping is determined when the model's performance falls during cross-validation.
26. Loss function – The loss function is a function that computes the error by taking the difference between the actual and predicted values.
27. Cost function – The cost function is a function that computes the sum of all error values of the data.

28. Skip connections – A shortcut that helps to bypass the layers.
29. Vanishing Gradient Problems – In the backpropagation stage, the gradients become smaller and closer to zero, called the vanishing gradient problem. If weights become excessively large in the backpropagation, it is called the exploding gradient problem.
30. Normalization – It is a way of scaling the data to the same scale.
31. Skip Connection: A type of shortcut that connects the layers to avoid the problem of vanishing gradients.
32. Data augmentation – Data augmentation is a technique of adding new data by applying transformations to the existing data to get new but not identical data.
33. Transformations – Transformations are techniques of creating new but not identical data by operations like translation, scaling, rotation, and mirroring.

Review Questions

1. What is the need for regularization functions?
2. Define a model.
3. What is the need for generalization?
4. Differentiate between generalization and memorization.
5. Define the terms noise and fluctuation of the dataset.
6. What is a generalization error, and how is it quantified?
7. What is bias and variance?
8. What is the bias-variance tradeoff?
9. List out the heuristics for network configuration.
10. How does early stopping help in regularization?
11. What is batch normalization, and why is it needed?
12. What is the link between batch normalization and layer normalization?
13. Why does dropout help in batch normalization?
14. Why is data augmentation needed?

Long Questions

1. List out and explain regularization functions.
2. List out and explain L_1 and L_2 regularizations.
3. List out the weight initialization schemes. List out and explain the heuristic functions for regularization.

Numerical Problems

1. Let polynomial equations characterize two models
$$M_1 = 4x^3 + 9$$
$$M_2 = 8x^2 + 17x - 19$$
Determine which model is complex.
2. Let the weights be given as 16, 18, 34 and 72. If $\lambda = 0.01$ is used as the penalty hyperparameter, can you explain how the weights are shrinked using the vector norms?
3. Three models, M_1, M_2, and M_3, are given with training and testing errors as per Table 5.5.

Table 5.5 Model Selection

Model Name	Training Error	Testing Error
M_1	0.6	1.3
M_2	2.3	4.8
M_3	4.2	4.3

Can one predict the overfit, underfit, and best ft conditions from Table 5.5 above?
4. Consider the following 2D data and apply the batch normalization process.
$$\begin{pmatrix} 7 & 2 \\ 2 & 8 \end{pmatrix}$$
Assume all other parameters α, β and ε are ignored for the sake of simplicity.

Crossword

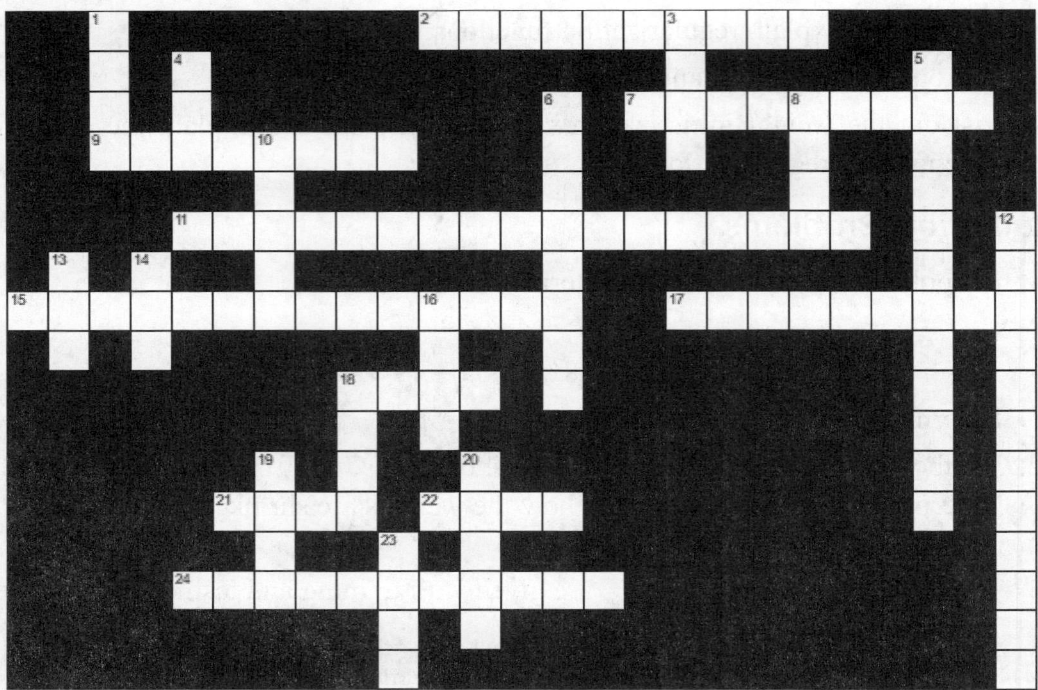

Across

2. The early stopping rule is applied when the __________ performance deteriorates.
7. Network capacity determines the __________ that can solve complex problems.
9. Dropout is an example of ________.
11. The model that is not working both for training and testing is a __________ model.
15. Model ability to predict the unknown instance is called __________.
17. Skip connections solve the problem _________ gradients.
18. Noise is not necessary for model construction. (true/false)
21. Generalization error can be evaluated by k-fold cross-validation. (true/false)
22. The number of the nodes in the neural network determines the _________ of the network.
24. The model that works fine for training data but not testing data is an example of __________ model.

Down

1. Normalization solves the problem of data scaling. (trure/false)

3. The depth of the neural network depends on the number of layers. (trure/false)
4. All neurons are retained in the testing phase of the neural network for dropout. (yes/no)
5. Data augmentation solves the problem of __________.
6. The model sensitivity is captured by __________.
8. The penalty term penalizes the weights of the model. (true/false)
10. The relationship between the input and output as a pattern stored in a _________.
12. The process of creating a new data similar to the old data is called data _________.
13. Regularization techniques are used to solve the problem of overfitting. (yes/no)
14. In best fit, the predicted and actual values are closer. (yes/no)
16. Generalization and memorization are the same. (true/false)
18. Good models should use minimal parameters as per Occam razor principle. (true/false)
19. The generalization gap is the difference between the training error and the testing error. (true/false)
20. The number of nodes in layer determine the _________ of the network.
23. How bad a model can be is indicated by _________.

Jumbled Sentences

```
M Q B N T N M O E E R C C K C U A A M T F J Y T Z
G A Y A O V E R F I T T I N G N N R N C R U S R C
J O S R U T R U E Q A B L W H D Z V P I P U M U E
R V D S I G R D P T R U E P B E K O L A T V E E U
G F Q B F S M O Z X U B W L K R S W F W R A E L N
A I U D E Z H E A K C F I M R F H A Z T U N T C D
S A E Y T C W G N I C J P A T I O G C V E I R A E
Y C N N R S R H T T U P D Q S T G G H M Q S U E R
E P S A U G E N E R A L I Z A T I O N I Q H E K F
S G E L E G S I Z E I T J E G I P K N R X I M K I
W A M L Y E S N Z K V X I G D N B B T N A N Z J T
O S B V S C C T L E Z A O O K G P D N C S G Z A T
Q B L D L F U N C T I O N S N M K L Y W E T B M I
L C E Q X Y R S H A I I K P E O Z K R I G R G O N
P K V A R I A N C E E Q L A C D V P S D O U I D G
A M O D K Q C X T D F I H K M E R X H T L E G E W
V A L I D A T I O N D N W V V L T L F H H W P L A
```

yes	yes	generalization	true	true
true	model	true	true	bias
variance	overfitting	underfitting model	true	width
size	functions	true	validation	ensemble
underfitting	true	vanishing	yes	augmentation

CHAPTER 6

Understanding Data

> Without data, you're just another person with an opinion. — **W. Edwards Deming**

Credits: © W. Edwards Demin

Deep learning algorithms involve large datasets to perform better. The quality and the quantity of the data is directly related to the performance of the deep learning algorithms. Therefore, it is necessary to understand data science concepts. The data preprocessing algorithms are required to clean the data to improve its quality. The concepts of preparing datasets are also essential to handle the deep learning projects.

The learning objectives of this chapter are:

- Understand the basics of data.
- Know about data management.
- Know about data preprocessing algorithms.
- Know about the performance measures of regression models.
- Know about the performance measures of classification models.

6.1 What is Data?

All facts are data. The singular for data is "datum". A datum is a piece of information that is an abstraction of a real-world entity. The entity can be a person, object, or event. For example, if one discusses a student, the student is an entity. An entity can be identified and is distinguishable from another entity.

Every entity has many attributes. The attributes are the characteristics of the entity. Attribute can be defined as the property or characteristics of an object. For example, the attributes of the students are name, age, address, and marks scored. The entity's characteristics can be measured, observed, stored, and transmitted for further processing.

Some entities and their attributes are shown in the following Table 6.1.

Table 6.1 Entity and its Attributes

Name of the Entity	Attributes
Patient	Patient ID, age, blood test, disease
Student	Roll number, register number, name, marks scored.
Iris	Leaf width, Leaf length, sepal width, sepal length.
Product	Product ID, Product name, Product number, Date of Expiry
Employee	Employee ID, name, age, Join date, Retirement Date

The decisions of the business organizations are based on the processing of data. The DIKW pyramid (Data-Information-Knowledge-Wisdom) is a framework that illustrates the processing of raw data and its conversion to knowledge and wisdom. The important jargon is given as below:

Data – Data is the raw facts and constitutes the basic building block. The raw facts are without any context or meaning.

Information – The data is processed to get information. Information is processed data with context and meaning. One can answer the questions like "Who," "What," and "Where" with the help of information.

Knowledge – Knowledge can be obtained from information by extracting the relationship and Insights. The deep learning algorithms can extract the patterns and models from the data to get rich insights into the data.

Wisdom – This is the last layer of the pyramid and refers to the application of knowledge to make decisions.

Though intelligence is not mentioned explicitly in the DIKW pyramid, it runs through the pyramid inherently.

6.2 Types of Data

Data stored by a single person or a small organization is called 'Small Data". These data are collected from several sources, integrated, and processed by a small-scale computer.

Examples of small data are the datasets of small business organizations, universities, and public datasets that are typically in GB's and MB's.

Deep learning and big data are directly related as the quality of the deep learning models is directly related to the quality and quantity of the data. Big data refers to the extremely large and complex datasets that are characterized by 3 V's and its details are given in Box 6.1. Examples of big data include social media data like Facebook, Twitter, and YouTube data.

Box 6.1 Small Data Vs. Big Data

Big data is characterized (by three V's)

(i) **Volume:** Volume refers to the 'size" of the data. The amount of data the algorithms generate, store, and process is referred to as volume. The Small data is often in Gigabytes and terabytes (TB). But Big data is measured in terms of Petabytes (PB) and Exabytes (EB). One Exabyte is 1 million terabytes.

(ii) **Velocity:** Velocity refers to the speed at which the data is generated and processed. Velocity is the term that is often refers to the processing speed of the real-time data.

(iii) **Variety:** Variety refers to the types of data processed by the algorithms. Deep learning algorithms use structured data, unstructured data, and semi-structured data. The variety may be related to various modalities like text, graphs, audio, video, maps, and other forms.

The comparisons of the small data and the big data are summarized in the following Table 6.1.

Table 6.1 Comparisons between Small Data and Big Data

Small Data	Big Data
Small datasets whose size is typically in MB and GB.	Big data is characterized by extremely large and complex datasets that are often in Petabytes and Exabytes.
Mostly structured data.	Big data includes structured data, unstructured data, and semi-structured data,
Data generation and processing is slow.	Big data is characterized by velocity, which refers to the high speed of data generation and processing.

Small Data	Big Data
Data quality is very high, and data cleaning is easy. Data cleaning requires simple tools.	Data quality varies. Data cleaning is not easy; and it is domain-dependent and requires NLP and Computer vision algorithms.
Creation and maintenance require less infrastructure.	Big data requires complex infrastructures in terms of hardware and software tools. Creation and maintenance require high costs.

One also classifies the data based on the nature of the data, as shown in Figure 6.1.

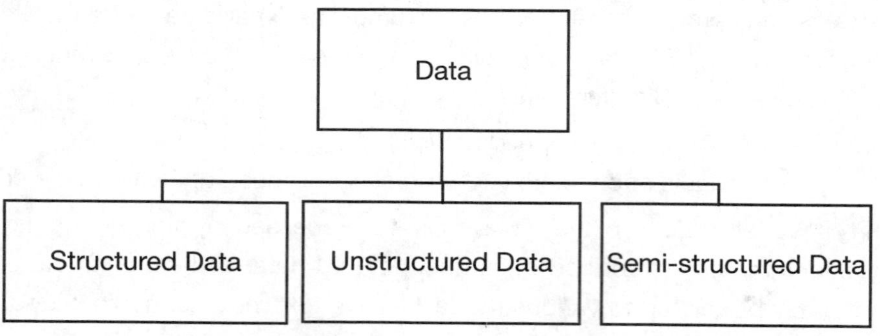

Figure 6.1 Types of Data

6.2.1 Structured Data

Structured data conforms with data model structures that can be stored in spreadsheets and databases and can be easily searched using SQL. The data present as tables in relational databases and Excel sheets, online forms, and log files are examples of structured data. The computer systems can readily process it. Only very little data is available in the form of structured data.

A table is the simplest representation of an entity and its attributes.

A sample table is shown in Table 6.2. Here, every row is called an instance. The other names often used are examples, cases, objects, entities, points, vectors, patterns, samples, observations, or records. The column is the property or characteristics of an entity. This kind of organization of the entities is the primary requirement of data science.

Table 6.2 Sample Student Table

Student Register Number	Name	Age	Physics marks	Chemistry mark	Biology Mark
#1	Daniel	17	70	80	90
#2	Jaya	17	65	50	40
#3	Raghav	17	72	76	79
#4	Radha	17	14	68	93

Tables can be stored in a flat file. Flat files are the simplest and most commonly available data source. A flat file is suitable only for storing small data sets and may not be possible for larger datasets. The dataset can be stored in a spreadsheet also. Some of the popular spreadsheet formats are listed below - CSV files – CSV stands for comma-separated value files and TSV files – TSV stands for tab-separated value files. Both CSV and TSV files are generic forms of storing data. Many tools, such as Google Sheets and Microsoft Excel, can process these files.

6.2.2 Unstructured Data

Unstructured data is not an organized data. There are no predefined structures or organizations in unstructured data. Unstructured data is not available in the form of tables or relational databases but is available in the form of text, images, and video. Text is a classic example of unstructured data. Images and video are also examples of unstructured data. Figure 6.2 shows an image as an example of unstructured data.

Figure 6.2 An image as an Example of Unstructured Data

Credits: Peter Senge

6.2.3 Semi-structured Data

Semi-structured data, too, like unstructured data, does not have any inherent structure. They lack any conformity with the structured data. However, semi-structured data has markers or tags to separate elements. Semi-structured data include emails, XML and HTML pages, binary executables, and zipped files.

The comparisons of structured, unstructured, and semi-structured data are given in Table 6.3.

Table 6.3 Comparisons Table of Types of Data

Structured Data	Unstructured Data	Semi-structured data
Structured data is highly organized data in the form of tables, spreadsheets, and relational databases.	Highly unorganized in the form of text, images, and video. There is no fixed schema present.	Some organizations are there, like tags and markers, but mostly unstructured data. There is no fixed schema present.
Searching is easy in the form of SQL.	NoSQL databases and complex tools do searching. Searching is difficult.	NoSQL databases and complex tools like XML and JSON Parsers are used for searching.
Processing is by ETL (Extract – Transform -Load) and minimal processing.	Processing is complex, and extensive processing is required.	Processing involves document DB, Parsers, and other complex tools that require extensive processing.
Feature engineering is often manual. The columns of the tables are manually identified.	Feature engineering is automatic. The deep learning algorithms extract the features automatically.	Feature engineering is automatic.

6.3 Data Variables and Scales

What is a variable? A variable holds information, such as attributes of an entity. Data variables are the building blocks of the data analysis. Data variables are required to perform statistical analysis and help to describe, summarize, and visualize data. The types of data variables are shown in Figure 6.3. The variables hold the actual data that can be processed.

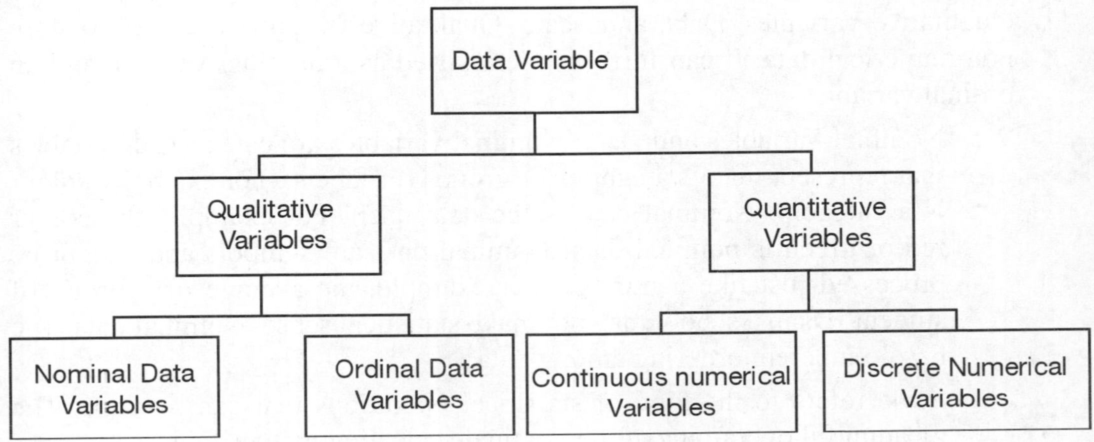

Figure 6.3 Types of Data Variables

Another related concept is called scale. Scale refers to the level of measurement. This measurement scale refers to the mathematical properties of the variables, like measurement, quantification, and comparisons. Scale also specifies the kind of statistical analysis that can be used for processing that kind of data.

Data scale – this indicates "how" one measures and the kind of processing that can be done.

The types of scales are given in the following Figure 6.4.

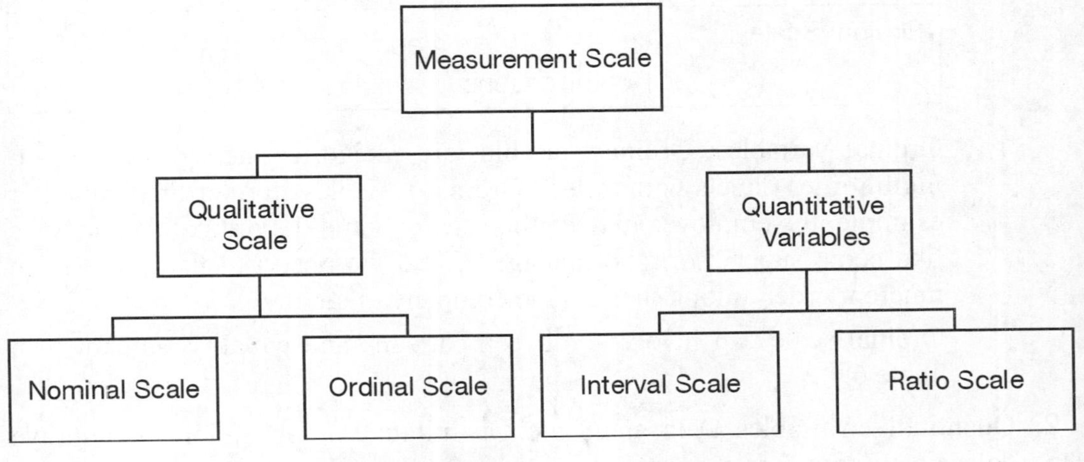

Figure 6.4 Measurement Scale

Broadly, the variables can be classified as qualitative and quantitative variables. Qualitative data are non-numerical data. The details are given below:

1. Qualitative Variables, Data, and Scale: Qualitative variables are used to store non-numerical data. It can further be classified as a nominal variable and an ordinal variable.

   1.1 Nominal Variables and Data: Nominal variables are categorical variables that represent many categories or groups (or labels). For example, colour is a category. Nominal data is the data itself. For example, the colour red or green is nominal data. Nominal data are symbols and cannot be processed just like a number. For example, the average of a group of student IDs in a school may not make statistical sense. Nominal data type has no inherent ordering among data.

   Scale refers to the kind of statistical operations that can be done. The meaningful operations of the nominal scale are given in Table 6.4.

Table 6.4 Categorical Data Operations

Name of the Data Type	Meaningful Operations	Remarks
Nominal Data	= and ≠	The rest of the operations are meaningless. For example, the average roll number of the student is meaningless.
Ordinal Scale	=, ≠, and comparisons	

   1.2 Ordinal Variables: Ordinal variables are categories that do have meaningful order (labels with order). Ordinal variables store ordinal data. For example, the employee may be the category, and the ordinal data may be like peon, supervisor, and manager. It can be observed that there is an inherent order among them in the company hierarchy.

   Ordinal scale can involve both comparisons and equality, as shown in Table 6.4.

2. Quantitative Variables, Data, and Scale: Quantitative variables store quantitative data. Quantitative data represent numerical values that are measurements of attributes.

2.1 Continuous variables store continuous data. The continuous numerical data are numbers that are taken from a range. For example, the height of the students is continuous data as the height has a lower and upper limit.

2.2 Discrete variables store discrete data. The discrete data are whole numbers and discrete. The countable data, like the number of rooms in a house, is an example of discrete data.

The scales of quantitative variables are interval scale and ratio scale.

(i) **Interval Scale:** Interval scale data has no true zero, and meaningful differences make statistical sense. For example, a temperature is an interval scale data, as zero temperature does not mean no temperature. Also, the differences are meaningful, as there is a difference between 30 and 40 degrees.

(ii) **Ratio Scale:** There is a true zero value for ratio data compared to the interval scale, and ratios are meaningful. For example, one can say 30 cm is thrice of 10 cm.

The ratio scale involves all comparisons, arithmetic operations, and ratio or proportion operations.

6.4 Data Encoding

Data encoding is one of the fundamental concepts of deep learning. Data encoding often refers to conversion, storage, transmission, and representation. Data processing often requires conversion from one form to another so that the statistical algorithms work. Data encoding is essential for algorithm compatibility, handling categorical data, efficiency, and reducing algorithm errors.

Some of the frequent encoding techniques encountered in deep learning are shown in Figure 6.5.

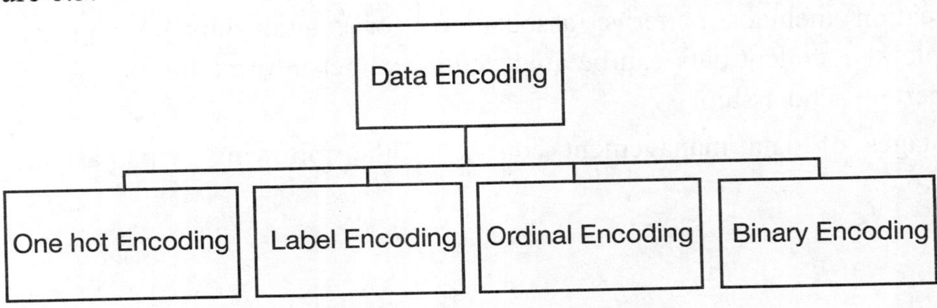

Figure 6.5 Types of Data Encoding

(i) **One-hot Encoding:** This encoding is also known as dummy encoding. One hot encoding allows the handling of categorical variables into binary vectors. Here, the binary matrix has each row as an observation, and each column has one category. Let us consider a simple example of colour.

Let colour = {R, G, B, O}

The colours are respectively red, green, blue, and Orange. One can assign a binary vector to these categories as follows:

R = {1 0 0 0}

G = {0 1 0 0}

B = {0 0 1 0} and

O = {0 0 0 1}

(ii) **Label Encoding:** Label encoding is used to handle categorical variables. Label encoding assigns a unique number (often integer) to each category of the categorical variables. For example, pet = {dog, cat}. The dog can be assigned a number 1 and a cat a number 2.

(iii) **Ordinal Encoding:** This encoding method assigns numerical values (integers) to the categories based on the ordinal position. Let employee = {peon, supervisor, manager}, then peon can be 0, the supervisor can be 1, and the manager can be 2. This number assignment is based on the ordinal position.

(iv) **Binary Encoding:** This encoding method assigns a binary code to an integer if required.

6.5 Data Management

Data by itself is meaningless. It has to be processed to generate information. Information includes patterns, associations, or relationships among data. For example, the student data can be analyzed to extract information on the eligibility for a certain scholarship.

The stages of data management consist of the following steps, as shown in Figure 6.6.

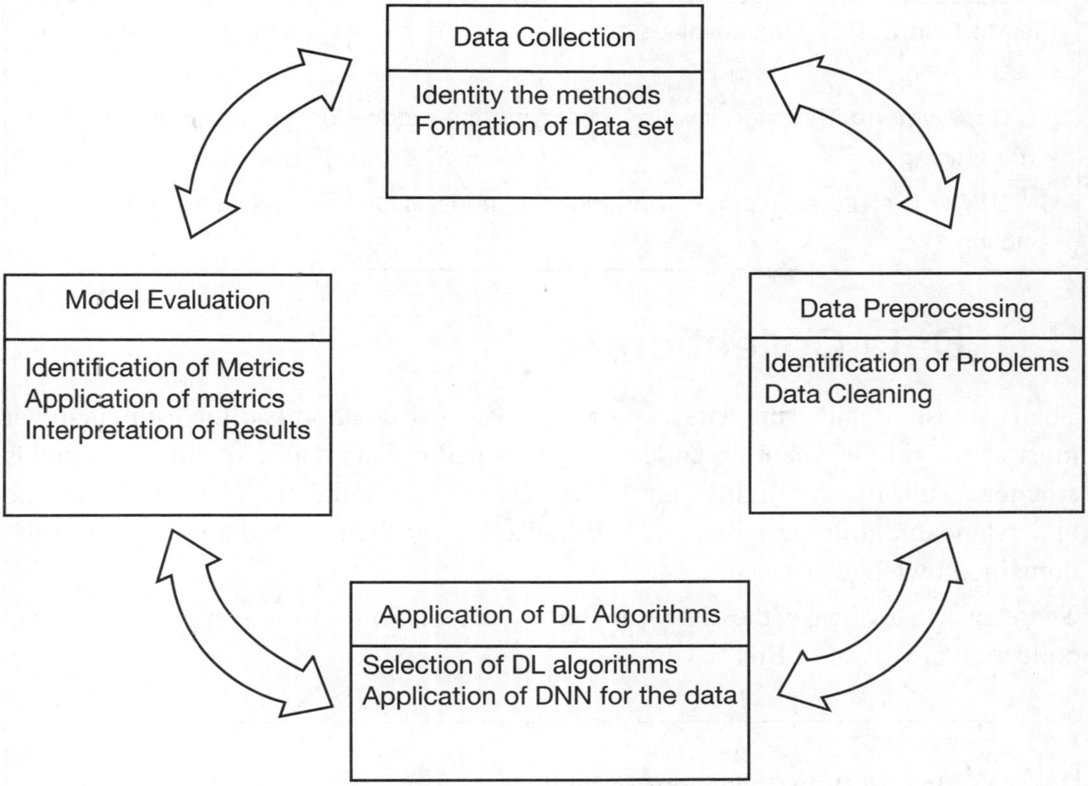

Data Collection
Identity the methods
Formation of Data set

Model Evaluation
Identification of Metrics
Application of metrics
Interpretation of Results

Data Preprocessing
Identification of Problems
Data Cleaning

Application of DL Algorithms
Selection of DL algorithms
Application of DNN for the data

Figure 6.6 Data Management

This iterative process is carried out permanently to ensure that data is suitable for data mining. Some of the Industrially accepted data management methodology is given in Box 6.2.

Box 6.2 CRISP-DM (Cross-Industry Standard Process for Data Mining)

CRISP-DM is one such standard for data analysis. This methodology has the following steps:

(i) Business Understanding: This step involves the understanding of the goal of the business organization,

(ii) Data Understanding: This step involves the problem statement and the requirements of data.

(iii) Data Preparation: This step involves data processing to clean the data, which is the preliminary requirement of deep learning algorithms.

(iv)Modeling: This step involves the creation of models such as regression or classification.

(v) Deployment: This step involves deploying the models on the customer site and further tuning.

CRISP-DM is an iterative process in which the model is tuned in real time to perfect the solution.

6.6 Data Collection

The first task of gathering datasets is the collection of data. It is often estimated that most of the time is spent on collecting good-quality data. Good quality data yields a better result. It is often difficult to characterize a 'Good data.' The data should be understandable, Interpretable, and self-sufficient for the required application as the domain knowledge engineer desires.

There are many ways the data can be collected. Some of the methods of data collection are given in Box 6.3.

Box 6.3 Data Collection Methods

Some of the methods that are available for data collection are given below:

(i) Questionnaires and Survey: Many times, the data can be collected using surveys.

(ii) Government and Statistical Sites: Governments normally provide many sites where valuable datasets related to census and voting preferences are available.

(iii) Open Data Sources: There are many types of sites where open datasets are available.

(iv) Social Media and the Internet: Social media sites like Twitter, Facebook, and YouTube provide lots of social media.

(v) Observational Data: Social science data is often collected based on observations and experiments.

(vi) Synthetic Data: Computer programs can be written to generate data artificially.

The need for the deep learning models should be understood first as the first step in deep learning model construction is the collection of data. Also, it should be noted that the quality of the data directly determines the quality of the models.

The steps of the data collection are given below:

(i) Identity the data requirements.

(ii) Identify the data sources. The source can be primary source where one can get data using sensors, surveys, experiments and questionnaires. The secondary sources may be the direct usage of existing databases, public repository, and API use to acquire data like twitter.

(iii) The data can be gathered manually or by using automatic collection tools like APIs, Web scrapping and sensors.

Then the data collected are use in the subsequent stages towards a successful creation of a dataset.

6.7 Preprocessing

The data cleaning process involves removing the bad data and preparing it for deep learning algorithms. This subject is very vast. Informally, there are two types of data – "Good" data and "Bad" data. Some of the "bad" data characteristics are given in Box. 6.4.

Box 6.4 "Bad data"

The "bad" data is incomplete, inaccurate and inconsistent data.

(i) Incomplete Data: This means that there are many missing data. There is much literature available for missing data analysis. Section 6.7.1 deals with missing data analysis.

(ii) Inaccurate Data: The data differs from the actual value. While this is due to various reasons, the primary reason is noise. Noise is abnormal data that differs from the normal values. For example, in a child database, an age of 76 is a noise and outlier. There are many noise removal algorithms available. Section 6.7.2 summarizes some of the noise and outlier removal algorithms.

(iii) Data Standardization: These are transforms that change data from one range to another so that the data is compatible with the deep learning algorithms.

Data preprocessing improves the quality of the data mining techniques. The primary idea of preprocessing is to clean the data so that the resultant data is suitable for deep learning algorithms. Some of the problems that are associated with the deep learning algorithms are given in Box. 6.5.

Box 6.5 Requirements of Deep Learning Algorithms

Some of the problems associated with deep learning algorithms are as follows:

(i) Insufficient Data: If there is not much data, the deep learning algorithms may not work correctly. Data augmentation can solve this problem by generating new data similar to the data present in the dataset.

(ii) Imbalanced Data: A dataset where samples of a particular class may dominate while there may not be any representatives for certain classes.

(iii) Noisy Data: Data has many discrepancies from the actual value for various reasons.

(iv) Data Transformations: The data may not be suitable for neural networks. Data transforms may involve normalization or standardization.

(v) Curse of Dimensions: Good data may require the removal of data that is irrelevant, which makes the dataset compact.

(vi) Private/ Confidential Data: Personal and confidential data may lead to some wrong decisions ethically.

Example 6.1: Consider, for example, the following student Table 6.5. Identify the problems that are associated with this dataset.

Table 6.5 Illustration of "Bad data"

ID	Student name	Age	DoB	Physics	Chemistry	Biology
#1	Geeta	21	10/01/1970	78	–1500	–10
#2	Raghav	36		90	70	30
#3	John	6	10/10/1980	90		80
#4	Peter	146		85	79	100

Solutions

Some of the mistakes identified with the above dataset are given below.

It can be observed that data like the absence of a chemistry mark for John needs to be completed. Students like Raghav and Peter have no DOB and need more data. John is six, but his DOB indicates it is 10/10/1980. This disparity is an example of inconsistent data. The chemistry mark for Geeta is -1500. A mark can't be less than 0. It is an instance of noisy data or a typographical mistake. Similarly, the age of Peter can't be 146. It might be a typographical error or data collection error. It is often desirable to distinguish between noise and outlier data.

6.7.1 Missing Data Analysis

Many times, in the dataset, the missing values can be replaced using the manual method. Here the domain expert can analyze the data tables, perform the analysis, and manually fill the values. But this is time consuming procedure and may not be feasible for the larger sets. So, some of the missing value removal algorithms are given in Figure 6.7.

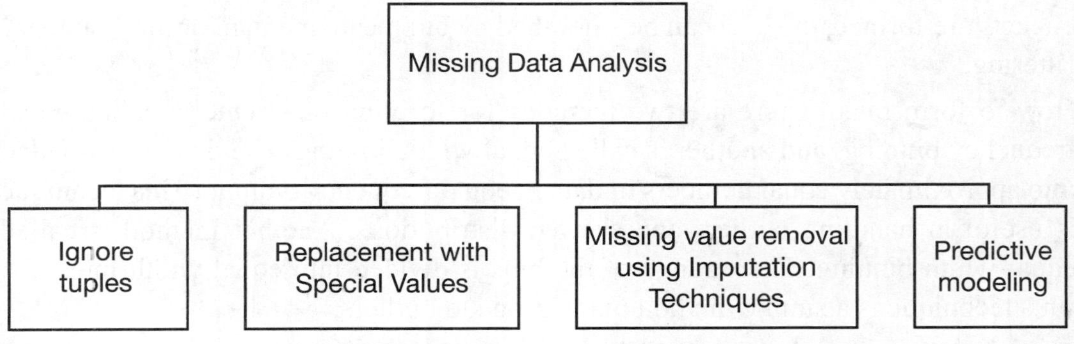

Figure 6.7 Missing Value Algorithms

(i) **Ignore the Tuple:** A tuple with missing data, especially the class label, is ignored. The entire row or column containing the missing data can be removed. This method is effective if the missing values are lesser but inefficient when the percentage of missing values increases because the deletion of more columns and rows leads to loss of information.

(ii) **Replacement with Special Values:** Special values can replace the missing values. The missing values may be substituted as "Unknown" or "Infinity." Special care should be taken in designing algorithms to handle these special values. Otherwise, the results may give spurious results by analyzing these labels.

(iii) **Imputation Techniques:** The missing value can be replaced by mean, median, or model. So, an example related to a missing age value can be the table's average age. In the case of time series data, the missing value can be replaced by forward fill (Just recent data in the forward direction) or backward fill (Just recent data in the backward direction). The missing value can also be replaced by using interpolation techniques.

(iv) **Predictive Modeling:** The missing value can be predicted using the available data using a classification algorithm.

However, it should be noted that the filled value may not be correct and is just an estimated value. Hence, the difference between the estimated and the original value is called error or bias.

6.7.2 Removal of Noisy or Outlier Data

Noise is a random error or variance in a measured value. The noise may be removed by using the binning method.

Binning is a method where the values are distributed into bins or buckets. Once the buckets are formed, the data can be smoothed by bin mean, median, or bin-boundary filtering.

How to form bins? There are two methods for forming bins. One is called equal frequency binning, and another is called equal width binning. The dataset is divided into approximately equal numbers of data in equal frequency binning. This technique is useful in handling outliers and skewed distributions. Another method is called equal-width binning. There range of the bins is divided into equal-width intervals. This technique is a simple method but is prone to outliers.

The following numerical example illustrates the formation of binning.

Example 6.2: Consider the following dataset

S = {2, 4, 6, 8, 10, 12, 14, 17, 20} and form bins using equal frequency and equal-width method.

Solution

In equal-width range, find the min and max of the set S. The min is two, and max is 20. So, the bin width can be calculated as the range/number of bins. Let us assume that the number of bins is 3. So, the bin width is 20 – 2/3 = 18/3 = 6.

So, the computed ranges are 2 – 8, 9 – 15, and 16 – 22. The bins are shown below:

Bin 1 = {2, 4, 6}

Bin 2 = {8, 10, 12, 14}

Bin 3 = {17, 20}

In the equal frequency method, the frequency is the total number of elements/ bins. So, frequency is 9/3 = 3. The bins are

Bin 1 = {2, 4, 6}

Bin 2 = {8, 10, 12 }

Bin 3 = {14, 17, 20}

So, it can be observed that all bins have the same (or approximate in general) data points in each bin.

Once the bins are formed, one can apply bin-mean, bin-median, and bin-boundaries methods. In bin-averaging, the average of a bin's data points replaces the bin's elements. Similarly, the bin-median algorithm replaces the data points by median and bin-boundary by the closest boundary value, which is nothing but the minimum and maximum of the bin.

The following numerical example illustrates the application of these algorithms,

Example 6.3: Consider the dataset

S = {2, 4, 6, 8, 10, 12, 14, 17, 20}

Solution

Use the equal frequency method and apply the bin-mean, bin-median, and bin-boundary methods.

1. First, sort the elements.
2. Form the bins as shown in Table 6.6.

Table 6.6 Illustration of Bins

Bin 1	Bin 2	Bin 3
2	8	14
4	10	17
6	12	20
Average = 4	Average = 10	Average = 17
Median = 4	Median = 10	Median = 17
Boundary = 2 and 6	Boundary = 8 and 10	Boundary = 14 and 20

If one applies the bin-mean algorithm, the bin values are replaced by bin-mean. So, the bins would become

Bin 1 = {4, 4, 4}

Bin 2 = {10, 10, 10}

Bin 3 = {17, 17, 17}

Similarly, replacement by median results in

Bin 1 = {4, 4, 4}

Bin 2 = {10, 10, 10}

Bin 3 = {17, 17, 17}

The bin-boundary method results in replacing the bin value with the closest boundary.

Bin 1 = {2, 6, 6}

Bin 2 = {8, 12, 12}

Bin 3 = {14, 20, 20}

6.7.3 Data Scaling

Data scaling is a preprocessing step for many deep-learning algorithms. The algorithms work better if the numerical values of the input are scaled to a standard range, say [0 – 1]. The need for data scaling arises because the scale and distribution of the input vary. Also, the inputs have many scales (different units). The larger number of inputs also creates instability in models, resulting in poor performance and generalization.

The other technique, called standardization, is a transform that modifies the distribution to have a mean zero and standard deviation of 1. Two types of data scaling are:

(i) Normalization

(ii) Standardization

The data scaling can be done for both input and output variables.

Normalization

The Min-Max procedure is a normalization technique where each variable X is rescaled to 0-1. The normalization is done as

$$y = \frac{x - x_{\min}}{range}$$

Example 6.4: If the minimum is 20 and the maximum is 40 means, the range is 40 – 20 = 20. Then, what is the output for x=38?

Solution:

The output would be

$$y = \frac{x - x_{\min}}{range} = \frac{x - 20}{20}$$

If x = 38, then, $y = \frac{38 - 20}{20} = \frac{18}{20} = 0.9$

Standardization

Standardization is called standard scaling. It aims to fit the observations to a Gaussian distribution with a mean of 0 and a standard deviation of 1 for the observed values. Standardization is used to solve the problem of scales. The standardization gives both positive and negative values around zero. Sometimes, one can normalize after the data is standardized. The standardized score is called the z-score. The formula for standardization is

$$y = \frac{x - \mu}{\sigma} = \frac{x - \left(\frac{1}{N}\sum_{i=1}^{n} x_i\right)}{\sqrt{\sum_{i=1}^{n} \frac{(x_i - \mu)^2}{N - 1}}}$$

If the mean is five and the standard deviation is 2, then the value x = 18 can be standardized as

$$y = \frac{x - \mu}{\sigma} = \frac{x - 5}{2} = \frac{18 - 5}{2} = 6.5$$

Example 6.5: Consider the mark list V = {10, 40, 70}, and convert the marks x = 70 into z-score.

Solution:

The list V's mean (μ) and standard deviation (σ) are 40 and 30, respectively. So, the z-scores of these marks are calculated as

z-score of 70 is = (70 – 40)/30 = 30/30 = 1

Hence, the z-score of 70 is 1.

6.8 Dataset Preparation

Many times, analyzing an entire population may be difficult or time-consuming. Hence, it is better to derive a small subset from the entire population for data analysis. It is called sampling. In other words, sampling is selecting representative data from the entire population.

Sampling is used so that the inferences can be made from the subset that explains the entire population. The process is explained in the following Figure 6.8.

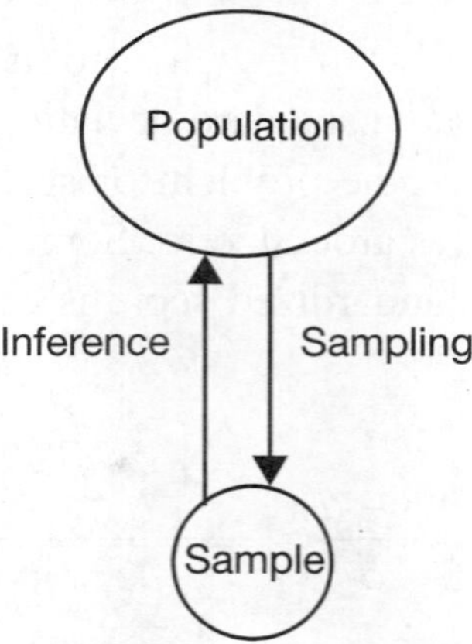

Figure 6.8 Sampling Process

6.8.1 Resampling

Resampling is a technique to select a model by reconstructing the training dataset and test dataset by randomly choosing instances by some method from the given dataset. Resampling is repeatedly drawing samples from the dataset with or without replacement to assess the variability, statistics, stability, and generalization. This method involves selecting different instances repeatedly from a training dataset to tune a model. It is done to improve a model's accuracy, assess the variability, and obtain robust estimates.

There are two types of resampling, as shown in the following Figure 6.9.

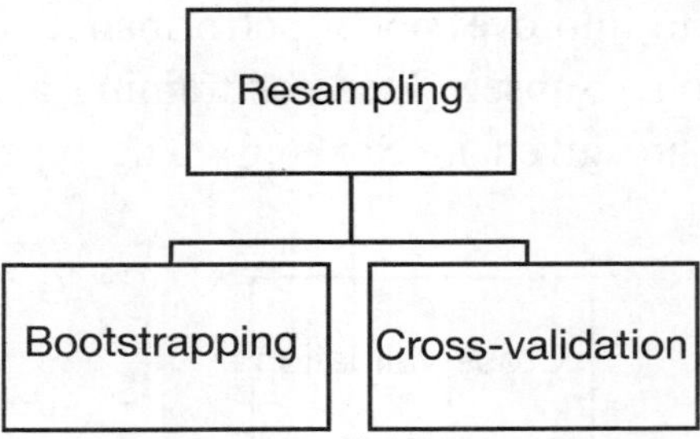

Figure 6.9 Types of Resampling

Sampling with replacement is called bootstrapping. Bootstrapping involves drawing random samples with replacements to the original set to assess the variability of the models. The bootstrapping process draws samples randomly with replacements to create multiple bootstrap samples. For example, consider the set {red, blue, Green}

Then, the replacement process is to randomly select with replacement and put it before the next selection as {red, blue, green, red}

The same data point can be chosen again and again as {red, blue, green, red, red}

Sampling without replacement is called cross-validation. Here, the samples are also selected but have yet to be considered further for subsequent selections. Cross-validation ensures the uniqueness of the sample within a single iteration. Cross-validation involves partitioning the dataset into subsets (folds). The process is repeated for multiple folds each time different folds are used for validation sets. Finally, the results are consolidated so that the results are more robust and the model exhibits more generalization. The idea is to test the model with "unknown" data instances to determine the performance. Cross-validation is used to assess variability, overfitting, and generalization.

Box 6.6 Data Splitting

Data splitting is about dividing the dataset for training/validation and testing.

Training dataset – This is used to train the machine learning algorithms.

Validation dataset – This dataset tunes the hyperparameters and avoids overfitting. It is also used to validate the model.

Test Dataset – This dataset evaluates the model to assess the algorithm's performance.

The dataset is split 70 – 30%, 80-20 %, or 90 – 10%. The major data is used for training and the rest for validation/testing.

Cross-validation is used to improve model performance. It divides the dataset into multiple subsets, with some subsets used for training and some for testing. (The details of the data split are given in Box 6.6). The types of cross-validation are shown in Figure 6.10.

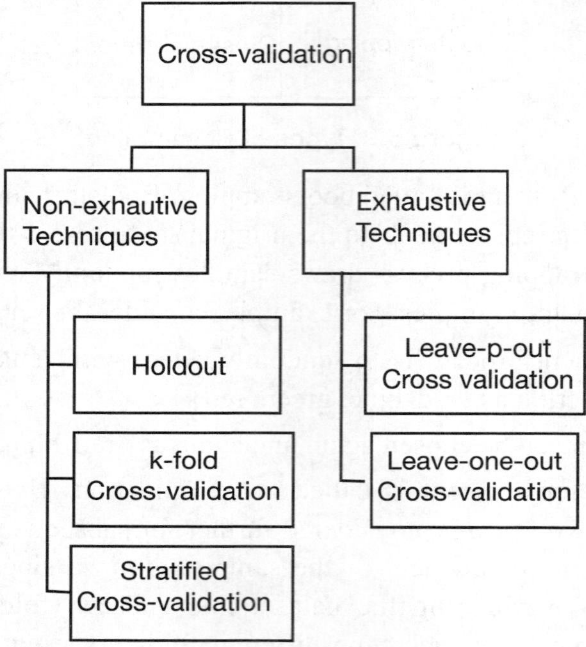

Figure 6.10 Types of Cross-validation

Non-exhaustive Methods

(i) Holdout: Holdout is about splitting the dataset into training and testing data. The split is about 70:30 or 80:20. This process involves shuffling the dataset randomly before splitting, training the model on different data combinations, and aggregating the results. This technique is useful for large datasets.

(ii) k-fold Cross-validation: Another way of cross-validating is using k-fold cross-validation, which will split the training dataset into k equal folds/parts. The process of cross-validation is given as follows:

1. Split the dataset into k number of folds
2. Use k-1 folds for training and kth fold for testing
3. Repeat until each k-fold has served as a training and testing dataset.
4. Average the k-recorded accuracy to get the cross-validation accuracy.

Cross-validation accuracy serves as the final estimate of the performance metric.

Example 6.6: Illustrate the k-fold validation idea with the data list S = {1, 2, 3, 4, 5, 6, 7, 8, 9}. Assume the value of *k* is 3.

Solution

Since k is 3, this is called 3-fold cross-validation. So, the dataset is divided into three folds {1, 2, 3}, {4, 5, 6} and {7, 8, 9}. One-fold is used as the test dataset, while the rest serves as the training dataset, as shown in Table 6.7.

Table 6.7 Illustration of 3-fold Validation

Iteration 1	Training data	Testing data
1	1, 2, 3, 4, 5, 6	7, 8, 9
2	1, 2, 3, 7, 8, 9	4, 5, 6
3	4, 5, 6, 7, 8, 9	1, 2, 3

It can be observed that a fold serves as both a training set and a testing test at different iterations.

(iii) **Stratified k-fold Cross-validation:** Sometimes, the split used by k-fold cross-validation may cause data imbalance. Stratification is a process of rearranging the data such that each fold is a good representative of the whole.

Exhaustive methods

(i) **Leave-p-Out Cross-Validation (LPOCV):** This method is called exhaustive because all p data point combinations are tested. If p is large, then there will be many combinations, and it will be exhaustive. The process involves the following steps:

1. Take p number of points from n. n is the number of total data points in the dataset.
2. Train the model (n – p) points and test the model on p points.
3. Repeat steps 1 – 2 for all possible combinations of p from the original dataset.
4. Average the accuracy for all the iterations.

(ii) **Leave-One-Out Cross-Validation (LOOCV):** This method repeatedly splits the n data instances of the dataset into a training dataset containing n-1 data instances and leaves one data instance for evaluating the model. This process is repeated n times, and the average test error is then estimated for the model.

Even though this model is expensive and time-consuming because it has to run for n times (i.e., n data instances in the dataset), it has less bias. For example, if the training dataset contains 100 data instances, 99 instances are used for training, and one instance is used to test or evaluate the model. This process is repeated 100 times, selecting a different instance as a holdout instance for testing in each iteration.

Example 6.7: Illustrate the leave-one-out cross-validation idea with the data list S = {1, 2, 3, 4, 5, 6, 7, 8, 9}. Assume the value of p is 1.

Solution

In the leave-out-one strategy, one sample is reserved for testing. The process is explained in Table 6.8.

Table 6.8 Illustration of Leave-one-out Cross-validation

Iteration 1	Training data	Testing data
1	1, 2, 3, 4, 5, 6, 7, 8	9
2	1, 2, 3, 4, 5, 6, 7, 9	8
3	1, 2, 3, 4, 5, 6, 8, 9	7
4	1, 2, 3, 4, 5, 7, 8, 9	6
5	1, 2, 3, 4, 6, 7, 8, 9	5
6	1, 2, 3, 5, 6, 7, 8, 9	4
7	1, 2, 4, 5, 6, 7, 8, 9	3
8	1, 3, 4, 5, 6, 7, 8, 9	2
9	2, 3, 4, 5, 6, 7, 8, 9	1

It can be observed that at every iteration, one datum is reserved for testing. The advantages of exhaustive methods are given in Table 6.9.

Table 6.9 Advantages and Disadvantages of Exhaustive Methods

Advantages	Disadvantages
All the data points are selected and used.	High variability
The exhaustive techniques lead to low bias of the model.	Exhaustive testing takes a lot of execution time.

Overall, the advantages and disadvantages of cross-validation are given in Table 6.10.

Table 6.10 Advantages and Disadvantages of Cross-validation

Advantages	Disadvantages
Overcome fitting	Computationally very expensive
Model selection	Time-consuming
Hyperparameter tuning	Bias-variance tradeoff
Data efficient	

6.9 Model Creation and Evaluation

One of the learning models is the regression model. The regression model models the relationships between the dependent and more independent variables. In its simplest form, it is about fitting a line.

$$y = b_0 + b_1 x + \varepsilon$$

Here, y is the dependent variable, and b_0, b_1 are independent variables and ε is the error. The focus is to estimate the model parameters such that the squared differences of the observed and estimated values of y are minimal. The output of the regression model is a number (i.e., a continuous variable). In other words, predictions like predicting the rent price of the car are all examples of regression models.

Another model is a classification model. Logistic regression is one of the simplest classification models where the output of the target variable is a binary outcome. The output of a logistical regression model is a probability $p(x)$ of the input value x. The equation does this is given below:

$$p(x) = \frac{1}{1 + e^{-(b_0 + b_1 x)}}$$

The input is classified as class 0 if $p(x) < 0.5$ and class 1 if $p \geq 0.5$.

The model evaluation phase is about analyzing the performance of the models using many metrics and selecting the best model.

These topics are covered in Chapter 7 of this book.

Summary

1. A datum is an abstract notation of a real-world entity. The entity can be any person, object, or event.
2. Attributes are characteristics of objects. It should be associated with a value.
3. A table is the simplest representation of an entity and its attributes. A row in a table is called an instance, and columns are characteristic of an entity.
4. A spreadsheet file can be used to store a table that can be stored in a format like a comma-separated value file (.csv) or Tab-separated value file (.tsv).
5. A variable stores or holds a piece of information.
6. The data variables are required to perform statistical analysis. It is categorized as qualitative and quantitative variables.
7. The qualitative variables can be subcategorized as nominal or ordinal variables. Nominal variables are categorical variables that do not inherent any order. Ordinal data has inherent order.
8. The quantitative variables can hold numbers that can be either continuous or discrete.
9. Data types refer to the classification of data variables based on the variables' content like integers, floats, characters, strings, or lists.
10. The data types are qualitative and quantitative. The qualitative data types include nominal and ordinal types. The quantitative data includes interval and ratio types.
11. Data Scale refers to the level of measurement. It is further classified into Nominal scale, ordinal scale, interval scale, and ratio scale.
12. In the interval scale, there is no true zero, and zero temperature does not mean any temperature, whereas in the ratio scale, there is true zero.
13. Data encoding refers to the conversion, storage, and representation of data.
14. The data encoding can be one-hot, label, ordinal, or binary.
15. Data management refers to data collection, data preprocessing, data analysis, and model selection/evaluation.
16. Data collection is gathering data.
17. Data collection methods are questions and surveys, government, and statistical sites, open data sources, social media and the internet, observational data, and synthetic data.

18. Data can be categorized as structured, unstructured, or semi-structured data.
19. Data preprocessing refers to cleaning the data to make it suitable for processing.
20. Missing data analysis can be done using missing value algorithms like ignoring the tuple, replacement with special values, imputation techniques and predictive modeling.
21. Noise is abnormal data. The binning techniques can be used to solve the problem of noise and outliers.
22. Data scaling algorithms convert data from one range of data to another.
23. The regression analysis finds the relationships between the dependent and one or more independent variables.
24. The regression model can be analyzed using metrics like error, mean square error, root mean square error, and r-squared error.
25. Min-max is a normalization technique, and standard scaling is a standardization technique.
26. Resampling is a technique of selecting a model by reconstructing a dataset by randomly choosing instances with or without replacement.
27. The sampling with replacement is called bootstrapping.
28. Cross-validation is another technique of partitioning the dataset into different subsets called folds to improve accuracy and generalization.
29. Different types of cross-validation are Holdout, k-fold Cross-validation, Stratified k-fold cross-validation, Leave-p-Out cross-validation, and Leave-One-Out cross-validation.

Glossary

1. Data – Raw facts.
2. Datum – A piece of information that is an abstraction of real-world entity.
3. Information – Processed data.
4. Entity – An entity is a real-world object, person, or event. An entity can be identified and distinguished from another entity.
5. Attribute – The properties or characteristics of an entity.
6. Table – The simplest representation of an entity and its attributes.

7. Instance – The row of a table is called an instance.
8. The measurement process – It associates every attribute with a value.
9. Variable – A variable holds attribute data.
10. Continuous variable – It holds a number with a fractional point.
11. Discrete variable – It holds whole numbers.
12. Nominal – A categorical variable with many groups or categories with no inherent order.
13. Ordinal – This is also a categorical variable like a nominal, except the categories have an inherent order.
14. Interval scale – Interval scale data has no true zero.
15. Ratio scale – True zero exists.
16. One-hot encoding – It converts a categorical variable with categories to a binary vector. It is also known as dummy encoding.
17. Label encoding – It assigns a unique number to each category of the categorical variables.
18. Ordinal encoding – It assigns a number to categories based on order.
19. Binary encoding – It assigns a binary code to an integer.
20. Insufficient Data – If there is not much data, the deep learning algorithm may not work correctly.
21. Imbalanced Data – A dataset where samples of a particular class may dominate while there may not be any representatives for a certain class.
22. Noisy data – Data has many discrepancies from the actual value for various reasons.
23. Data Scaling – It is a preprocessing step where input values are scaled to a standard range, say [0 – 1].
24. Missing data – It is the data omitted from the dataset intentionally or unintentionally.
25. Imputation – A name for removing missing data using mean, median, or mode.
26. Binning – A distribution technique of placing data into buckets called bins.
27. Three V's – In big data, it means volume, velocity, and variety.
28. Normalization – It is a data transform that scales a value to a range [0-1].

29. Standardization – It is a technique of transforming so that the distribution will have zero mean and standard distribution of one.
30. Resampling – A technique of reconstructing a dataset with or without replacement.
31. Cross-validation – A technique of splitting a dataset into many subsets (or folds) to improve accuracy and generalization.

Short Questions

1. Distinguish between entity and attributes.
2. Distinguish at least ten entities in the real-world.
3. Give some popular spreadsheet formats.
4. Define the terms – data variable, and data scale.
5. Is temperature an ordinal variable? Justify.
6. Compare and contrast interval and ratio scales.
7. What is the need for data encoding?
8. Differentiate between small and big data.
9. What are the sources of big data?
10. List out the techniques for missing data analysis.
11. In which situation forward or backward filling method is used?
12. Compare and contrast the normalization and standardization.
13. Mean and standard deviation cannot be the same. Justify.
14. What is meant by resampling?
15. How does cross-validation improve generalization?
16. Why is that k-fold cross-validation so popular?
17. In which situation is LOOCV preferred over the LPOCV method?

Long Questions

1. Explain the data management in detail.
2. Explain the various methods that are used to resolve incompatibility issues of data for statistical analysis.
3. Distinguish the factors that make bad data.
4. Explain the types of scale and explain it.

5. Explain missing data analysis.
6. Explain the bootstrapping techniques with an example.
7. Write down what type of missing value algorithm is used to fill the data for the following:
   a. When the numerical values are used
   b. When only certain data is entered
   c. When the entire row or column is faulty
   d. When data is sparse
8. Explain in detail about different cross-validation techniques.

Numerical Problems

1. Apply One-hot encoding for the following list of data, S = {Capital, State, District, State, Capital}
2. Apply one-hot encoding for the list of data, S = {Orange, Violet, Red}.
3. Consider the list of numbers, S = {1, 3, 5, 7, 6, 10, 12, 13, 14}. Apply equal-frequency and equal-width methods.
4. Apply the noise removal algorithms to the bins created in Q3 and remove the noise.
5. Find the result of replacing the bin values with a bin-average, bin-median, and bin-boundary method using the equal frequency method and also compare the resultant values when you use the equal-width method.
6. If min is 10 and max is 40, then what is the output of $x = 47$? Use the normalization technique.
7. Consider the list S = {10, 20, 40, 80, 120, 140}. Convert the mark 40 and 8 to z-score.
8. How many iterations are performed by LPOCV on the dataset, which has 10 elements and $p = 2$? And also find the difference in iteration if it is done by the LOOCV method.

Crossword

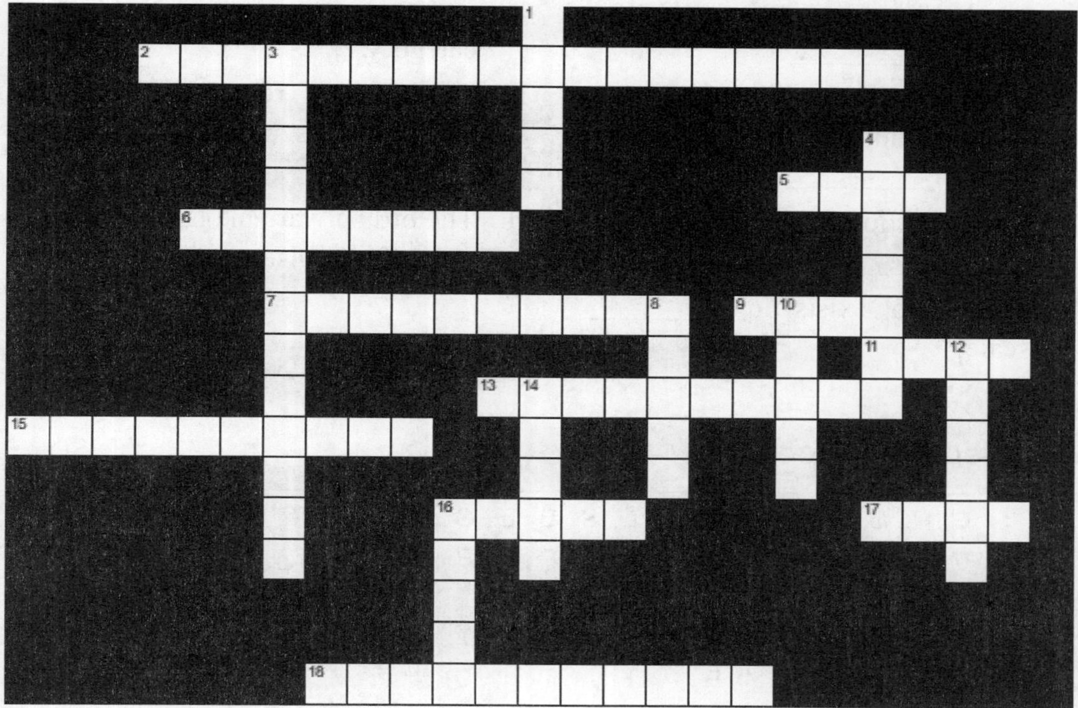

Across

2. The adjusting of distribution with specific parameters are called __________
5. Data are raw facts. (true/false)
6. Holdout split datasets into __________ and testing dataset.
7. The missing data filled with mean, median or mode is called __________ technique
9. The entity is a real-world object, person, or event. (true/false)
11. Nominal variable has no inherent order. (true/false)
13. The properties of the entities are called __________.
15. LPOCV is an __________ type.
16. The data variable and data scale are the same. (true/false)
17. Missing data is omitted data intentionally. (true/false)
18. One-hot encoding converts a __________ variable to a binary representation.

Down

1. A technique of reconstruction of a set without replacement is called __________ validation.

3. The technique of converting a number from one range to another is called ___________.
4. The k-fold cross-validatin involves the partitioning of datasets into folds or ___________.
8. The distortion of the value is called ___________.
10. True zero exists in ___________ scale.
12. Label encoding assigns an ___________ number to each category.
14. The simplest representation of an entity and its attributes are called ___________.
16. The ordinal variable has no inherent order. (true/false)

Jumbled Sentences

P	J	C	R	O	S	S	W	F	A	L	S	E	E	G	M	C	E	R	H	Q	T	P	S	R
I	I	U	E	L	K	Y	H	M	G	L	J	R	B	P	U	U	N	C	S	I	F	N	R	V
S	X	C	W	Q	F	H	P	G	H	S	H	P	U	X	R	I	O	U	D	E	D	O	T	A
S	I	W	O	J	P	K	P	M	H	W	I	I	N	T	Z	J	R	C	S	I	C	D	W	T
P	X	U	L	X	A	I	M	P	U	T	A	T	I	O	N	T	M	L	H	I	B	F	V	T
H	V	C	T	S	T	H	T	H	K	C	V	V	Q	K	S	R	A	E	J	D	R	M	N	R
C	W	E	C	K	Q	T	X	O	U	L	S	X	U	G	X	F	L	X	S	P	A	P	G	I
I	P	Z	A	P	J	O	B	G	Z	T	R	U	E	A	J	I	I	H	T	W	T	Y	B	B
X	B	D	D	B	B	Q	H	Q	X	S	F	M	I	N	X	R	Z	A	R	D	I	G	P	U
C	M	D	C	A	T	E	G	O	R	I	C	A	L	Y	I	X	A	U	U	J	O	R	E	T
G	A	A	M	W	W	F	N	O	I	S	E	L	K	Z	H	P	T	S	E	Y	R	S	A	E
S	R	G	B	P	T	A	B	L	E	Z	I	U	M	J	C	M	I	T	B	R	R	A	W	S
I	Z	V	Y	M	K	O	H	I	H	U	I	Q	S	Y	P	B	O	I	E	X	M	Q	F	K
A	D	Z	T	R	A	I	N	I	N	G	Q	X	Y	S	M	O	N	V	N	H	I	R	W	B
N	P	T	Y	A	C	L	S	U	B	S	E	T	S	J	V	N	Z	E	K	C	V	K	S	T
E	X	V	M	I	I	O	S	T	A	N	D	A	N	D	A	R	D	I	Z	A	T	I	O	N
T	R	U	E	T	O	T	B	T	V	R	Z	U	J	T	B	Z	R	H	W	I	O	E	O	C

true
false
categorical
imputation
subsets
true
true
unique
normalization
training
attributes
false
noise
standandardization
exhaustive
table
ratio
true
cross

Introduction to Regression and Classification

CHAPTER 7

> Science is prediction, not explanation. — **Fred Hoyle.**

Credits: © Fred Hoyle

Regression and classification problems are encountered in deep learning in topics such as object recognition, detection, and tracking. Regression is a statistical technique that helps predict by analyzing and understanding the relationships among the given variables. Prediction is estimating the value of the dependent variable based on the unknown values of the independent variables. Forecasting is often associated with time series data, where forecasting can identify and quantify future trends. Classification is about mapping the input data into labels of two or more categories. The focus of this chapter is on designing neural networks to solve regression and classification problems.

The learning objective of this chapter is as follows:

- Understand the basics of regression.
- Know the different types of regression.
- Designing neural networks for linear regression.
- Understanding logistic regression.
- Know about the classification.
- Understand the different types of classification.
- Designing neural networks for binary and multiclass classification.

7.1 Introduction to Regression

Often, there is a need to model the relationship between a dependent variable and one or more independent variables in statistics. The purpose is to study the variation in the independent variables that causes a change in dependent variables. The most common regression method is linear regression, where the relationship between the dependent and independent variables is linear. The relationship between the dependent variable (y) and one independent variable (x) is given as

$$y = a_0 + a_1 \times x + \varepsilon$$

Here, a_0 is the intercept of the line with the y-axis and a_1 is the slope of the line. The variables a_0 and a_1 are called regression coefficients. The term ε is the error term. The input x is called a feature, and the output y is called a label. In regression, it is a number. The linear equation is called a model.

Regression analysis is a statistical technique that can be useful for prediction and inference analysis. The purpose of the regression analysis is given below:

(i) To find the relationship between the dependent and independent variables. This ability of the regression analysis helps in modeling the complex relationships among variables.

(ii) It finds the strength of the relationships.

(iii) Understand the effect of the changes in independent variables over the dependent variable.

(iv) Regression analysis can be helpful as a decision-making tool as it can predict and forecast.

Everyone encounters regression analysis in our daily lives, as shown in Box 7.1.

Box 7.1 Regression Examples

Regression is helpful for prediction. One encounters many situations where prediction is required.

1. Predicting the time required to reach destination considering the distance, traffic, and vehicle type.
2. Predicting sales based on seasons and advertisements.
3. Prediction of college admission based on marks scored.
4. Prediction of Insurance claims based on age, location, and diseases.
5. Prediction of yield of crops based on fertilizer and water.
6. Determination of salary based on factors like education experience.

Some of the important jargon related to regression analysis is given in Box 7.2.

Box 7.2 Linearity and Nonlinearity

Linearity means that the relationship between independent and dependent variables is linear, and mathematically, this linear relationship can be represented as a linear equation as

$$y = a_0 + a_1 x$$

Here, x is the independent variable, and y is the dependent variable. a_0 is the y-intercept and a_1 is the slope. By linear, it means that the relationship between x and y is linear and can be represented close to a straight line. So, the change in the y is directly proportional to the change in x. The plotting of this would indicate that the data points are closer to a line.

By nonlinearity, it means that the variables x and y may be related by a nonlinear function that cannot be represented as a straight line. So, the change in y is not proportional to the change in X. Instead, the relationship among the variables is curvy or complex (such as logarithmic, exponential, polynomial). The nonlinear relationship among and y can be observed in the following equations:

$$y = 3x^2 + 4\cos(x)$$

$$y = 3x^2 + 4\log(x)$$

7.2 Linear Regression Techniques

Regression is classified into linear regression, multivariable linear regression, and logistic regression. Linear regression is applicable only if the relationship between the independent and dependent variables is linear.

7.2.1 Ordinary Least Square (OLS) Method

OLS is an analytical method for solving linear regression problems. The first method is based on the ordinary least square approach (OLS).

Assume that the problem is to predict the sales of an ice cream given daily data. If so, the first step is to collect all past N observations of the day, and sales are given. Linear regression can model the relationship between sales (x) and day(y), thus making the prediction possible for an unknown day.

The goal of linear regression is to "fit" a line to approximate the data points well such that it can fit the data points. The line is called a hyperplane. If the dimension of the input data is 2D, then a line can be used. For three dimensions, the hyperplane is called a place, and in general, for higher dimensions, it is called a hyperplane. Some additional details are given in Box 7.3.

The line equation is given as $y = a_0 + a_1 \times x + \varepsilon$

Box 7.3 Best Fit and Predicting Output

Predicting the output is done by the "Best fit" of the line. The first step is plotting the data points as a scatter plot. A scatter plot of Table 7.1 is shown in Figure 7.1.

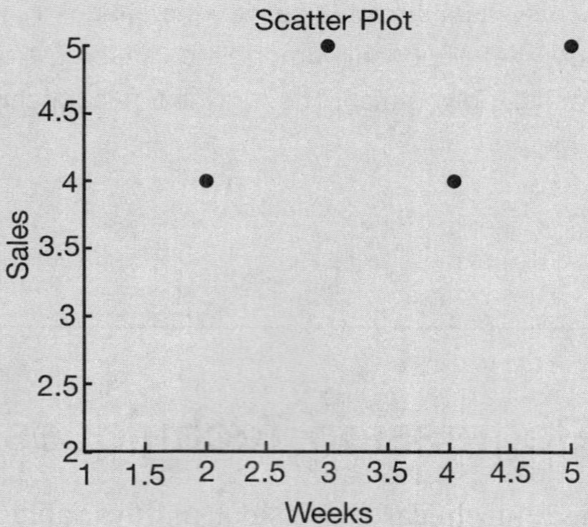

Figure 7.1 Scatter Plot of the Week and Sales Data

OLS finds a "best fit" line that fits these points. The best line is the line where the distances between the data points and the predictions are as small as possible. OLS minimizes the squares of these distances called residuals. The residual is the difference between the predicted value and the actual observed value. The residuals are shown in Figure 7.2.

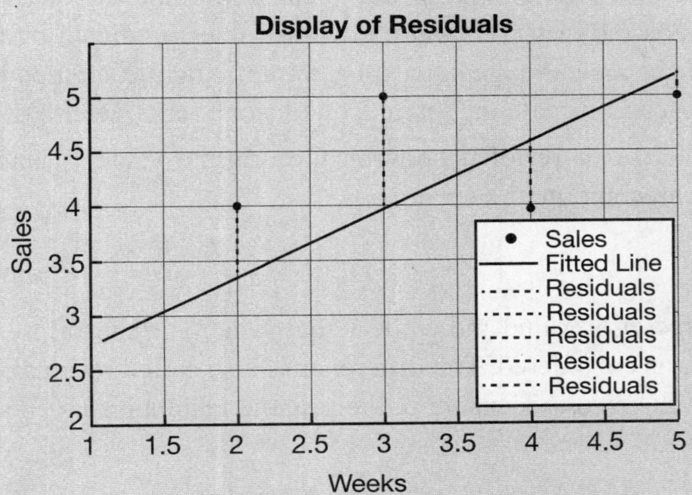

Figure 7.2 Illustration of Residuals

The smaller the residual then the fitted line is the best one. If the residual is positive, then the observed value is greater than the predicted value. If the residual is negative, then the observed value is lesser than the predicted value. It is zero when both are the same.

When would Linear regression work?

The assumptions of linear regression are:

(i) Linearity relationship between the independent values and the dependent value.

(ii) The observations are independent of each other.

(iii) The variance of all the errors is constant (called Homoscedasticity).

(iv) The errors are normally distributed.

(v) There is no high correlation among the variables (no multicollinearity or autocorrelation).

Here, a_0 is the intercept of the line with the y-axis and a_1 is the slope of the line. The variables a_0 and a_1 are called regression coefficients. The term ε is the error term. Here, y is the dependent variable, and x is the independent variable.

The fitting of a best-fitting line is that it can minimize the sum of the squared difference between the observed and predicted values predicted by the model. The squared differences are called residuals. By minimizing the squared differences, the linear regression can estimate the intercept and slope (parameters) of the model.

The amount of error or residual between the original value y_i and the predicted value $\widehat{y_i}$. One can compute the error as

$$\varepsilon_i = y_i - \widehat{y_i}$$

Here $\widehat{y_i}$ is the prediction value and y_1 the actual value. The subscript '*i*' indicates that the *i*th data point is considered. The difference is also called residual. The total error is the sum of all the errors. The sum of the squared residual is given as

$$SSR = \frac{1}{N}\sum_{i=1}^{N}\left(y_i - \widehat{y_i}\right)^2$$

Here, *N* is the number of observations. The object of the linear regression is to minimize the errors between the observed and predicted values, i.e., SSR. In order to minimize the function, one has to find the partial derivative of the objective function, and it is set to zero to find the optimal minimum of the parameters as

$$\min_{a_0, a_1} \frac{1}{N}\sum_{i=1}^{N}\left(y_i - \widehat{y_i}\right)^2$$

In this case, the minimization is done by differentiating the equation with respect to a_0 and a_1 and equating the equation to zero. This results in the equation

$$na_0 + a_1\sum_i x_i = \sum_i y_i$$

$$a_0\sum_i x_i + a_1\sum_i x_i^2 = \sum_i x_i y_i$$

This solution of the equation yields the coefficient values of a_0 and a_1.

$$a_1 = \frac{\overline{xy} - \overline{x} \times \overline{y}}{\overline{x_i^2} - \left(\overline{x}\right)^2} \text{ and } a_0 = \overline{y} - a_1 \times \overline{x}$$

Example 7.1: The following Table 7.1 shows the five week's sales data (in Lakhs). Apply linear regression technique to predict seventh- and twelfth-month sales.

Table 7.1 Sample Data for Regression

x (Week)	y (Sales in Lakhs)
1	2
2	4
3	5
4	4
5	5

Predict the 7th and 12th-week sales.

Solution:

The computation Table is shown in Table 7.2.

Table 7.2 Computation Table

n	X	Y	$x \times x$	$x \times y$
1	1	2	1	2
2	2	4	4	8
3	3	5	9	15
4	4	4	16	16
5	5	5	25	25
Sum	15	20	55	66
Average	$\overline{x}$ = 15/5 = 3	$\overline{y}$ = 20/5 = 4	$\overline{x_i^2}$ = 55/5 = 11	$\overline{xy}$ = 66/5=13.2

Let us compute the slope and intercept now using the following:

$$a_1 = \frac{\overline{xy} - \overline{x} \times \overline{y}}{\overline{x_i^2} - \left(\overline{x}\right)^2}$$

and

$$a_0 = \overline{y} - a_1 \times \overline{x}$$

Based on Table 7.2, the values can be computed as

$$a_1 = \frac{13.2 - 3(4)}{11 - 3^2} = 0.6$$

$$a_0 = 4 - 0.6 \times 3 = 2.2$$

Let us model the relationship as $y = a_0 + a_1 \times x$. therefore, the fitted line for the above data is $y = 2.2 + 0.6\,x$. The fitted line is shown in Figure 7.3.

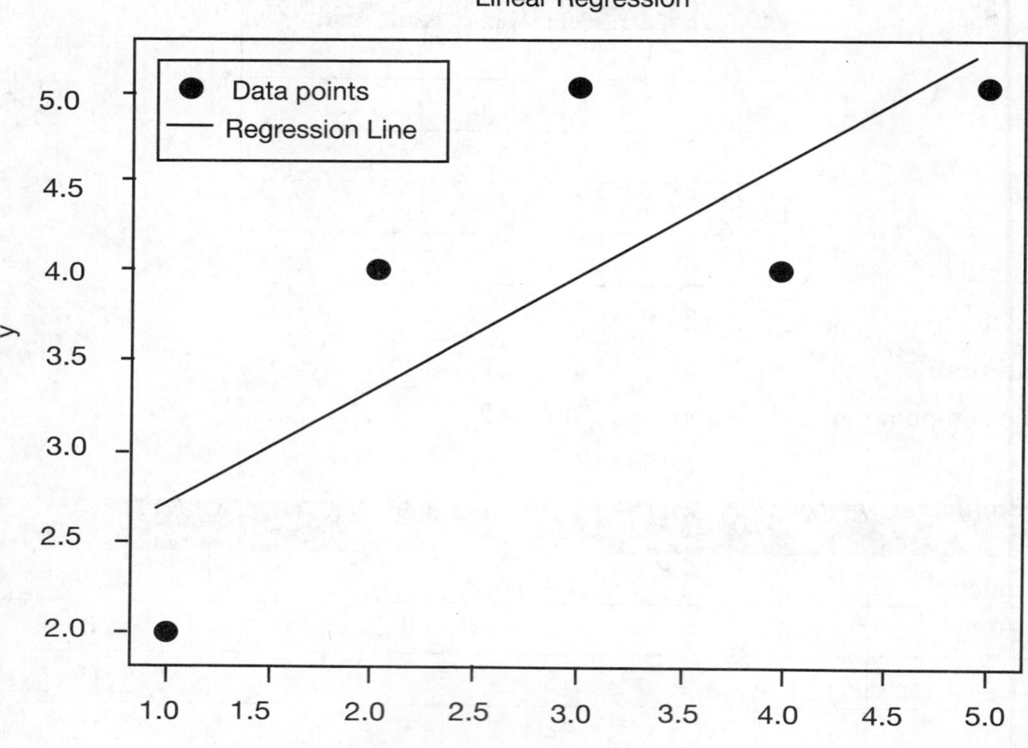

Figure 7.3 Fitted Line for the Above Data Points

The predicted seventh week sale would be (when $x = 7$) = $y = 2.2 + 0.6 \times 7 = 6.4$ lakhs and the twelfth month will be $y = 2.2 + 0.6 \times 12 = 9.4$ lakhs.

7.2.2 Matrix Methods for Linear Regression

Linear regression will be difficult to compute when there are many independent parameters—an alternate method to find the equation using a matrix so that the computations are compact and manageable. If there are 'n' observations and 'p' predictors, then matrices can be used for linear regression.

Let (x_i, y_i) be the set of data points. The regression equation is given by $y = a_0 + a_1x$. Group all the independent variables (y) as a n x 1 vector.

$$y = \begin{pmatrix} y_1 \\ y_2 \\ y_3 \\ . \\ . \\ . \\ y_n \end{pmatrix}$$

Similarly, group all the coefficients of regression coefficients as a single vector of size $(p + 1) \times 1$.

$$a = \begin{pmatrix} a_0 \\ a_1 \end{pmatrix}$$

Similarly, the data x_n can be augmented $x_n = \begin{pmatrix} 1 \\ x_n \end{pmatrix}$, a vector of $n \times (p + 1)$ matrix of independent variables. It should be noted that the first column is 1 for intercept. The grouping of the predictor variable x will be as follows:

$$X = \begin{pmatrix} x_1^T \\ x_2^T \\ x_3^T \\ \vdots \\ x_n^T \end{pmatrix} = \begin{pmatrix} 1 & x_1 \\ 1 & x_2 \\ 1 & x_3 \\ 1 & \vdots \\ 1 & x_n \end{pmatrix}$$

It can be observed that this is a $n \times 2$ matrix for our case. It can be observed that the first column is always 1, and the second column is the observation of x. ε is the vector of size $n \times 1$ of residuals. The matrix can be written as

$$y = Xa + \varepsilon$$

The objective is to minimize the sum of squared residuals (SSR). The SSR is given as

$$SSR = \varepsilon^T \varepsilon = (y - Xa)^T (y - Xa)$$

To find the optimal parameters, one has to take the derivative and substitute it to zero. The realignment of variables results in

$$X^T a = X^T y$$

So, the regression coefficients can be derived as below:

$$\hat{a} = \left(X^T X\right)^{-1} X^T y$$

The following numerical example illustrates the use of matrices for linear regression problems.

Example 7.2: Find linear regression of the following data of week and product sales (in Lakhs) as shown in Table 7.3 using linear regression in matrix form.

Table 7.3 Sample Data for Regression

n	*x* (Week)	*y* (Product Sales)
1	1	2
2	2	4
3	3	5
4	4	4
5	5	5

Solution:

Here, the independent variable *x* can be given as

$$x^T = [12345]$$

The dependent variable is given as follows:

$$y^T = ([24545])$$

Therefore, the optimal parameters are given as:

$$\hat{a} = \left(\left(X^T X\right)^{-1} X^T\right) y = \left(\begin{pmatrix} 11111 \\ 12345 \end{pmatrix} \begin{pmatrix} 1 & 1 \\ 1 & 2 \\ 1 & 3 \\ 1 & 4 \\ 1 & 5 \end{pmatrix}\right)^{-1} \begin{pmatrix} 11111 \\ 12345 \end{pmatrix} \begin{pmatrix} 2 \\ 4 \\ 5 \\ 4 \\ 5 \end{pmatrix}$$

$$= \begin{pmatrix} 5 & 15 \\ 15 & 55 \end{pmatrix}^{-1} \begin{pmatrix} 11111 \\ 12345 \end{pmatrix} \begin{pmatrix} 2 \\ 4 \\ 5 \\ 4 \\ 5 \end{pmatrix}$$

$$= \begin{pmatrix} 1.1 & -0.3 \\ -0.3 & 0.1 \end{pmatrix} \begin{pmatrix} 11111 \\ 12345 \end{pmatrix} \begin{pmatrix} 2 \\ 4 \\ 5 \\ 4 \\ 5 \end{pmatrix}$$

$$\begin{pmatrix} 0.8 & 0.5 & 0.2 & -0.1 & -0.4 \\ -0.2 & -0.1 & 0 & 0.1 & 0.2 \end{pmatrix} \begin{pmatrix} 2 \\ 4 \\ 5 \\ 4 \\ 5 \end{pmatrix}$$

$$= \begin{pmatrix} 2.2 \\ 0.6 \end{pmatrix}$$

Hence, the fitted line is given as $y = 0.6x + 2.2$. It can be observed that the results are the same as before.

The multiple regression model is an extension of the linear regression model that involves multiple predictors and models the relationship between two or more independent variables and one dependent variable.

Example 7.3: Apply multiple regression for the values in Table 7.4, where the amount and number of tomatoes and brinjals are given. Use a matrix approach for finding multiple regression lines.

Table 7.4 Sample Data

N	y (Amount)	x_1 (Tomato)	x_2 (Brinjal)
1	7	2	3
2	5	3	4
3	8	4	2
4	12	5	5

Solution:

Here, the matrix for y and x are given as follows:

$$y = \begin{pmatrix} 7 \\ 5 \\ 8 \\ 12 \end{pmatrix} \quad a = \begin{pmatrix} a_0 \\ a_1 \\ a_2 \end{pmatrix} \text{ and } x = \begin{pmatrix} 1 & 2 & 3 \\ 1 & 3 & 4 \\ 1 & 4 & 2 \\ 1 & 5 & 5 \end{pmatrix}$$

The regression coefficient can be calculated as follows:

$$\hat{a} = \left(\left(X^T X \right)^{-1} X^T \right) y$$

$$= \left(\left(\begin{pmatrix} 1 & 1 & 1 & 1 \\ 2 & 3 & 4 & 5 \\ 3 & 4 & 2 & 5 \end{pmatrix}^T \begin{pmatrix} 1 & 2 & 3 \\ 1 & 3 & 4 \\ 1 & 4 & 2 \\ 1 & 5 & 5 \end{pmatrix} \right)^{-1} \begin{pmatrix} 1111 \\ 2345 \\ 3425 \end{pmatrix} \begin{pmatrix} 7 \\ 5 \\ 8 \\ 12 \end{pmatrix} \right)$$

$$= \begin{pmatrix} 4 & 14 & 14 \\ 14 & 54 & 51 \\ 14 & 51 & 54 \end{pmatrix}^{-1} \begin{pmatrix} 1 & 1 & 11 \\ 2 & 3 & 45 \\ 3 & 4 & 25 \end{pmatrix} \begin{pmatrix} 7 \\ 5 \\ 8 \\ 12 \end{pmatrix}$$

$$\begin{pmatrix} 3.750 & -0.500 & -0.500 \\ -0.500 & 0.238 & -0.095 \\ -0.500 & -0.095 & -0.238 \end{pmatrix} \begin{pmatrix} 32 \\ 121 \\ 117 \end{pmatrix} = \begin{pmatrix} 1 \\ 1.683 \\ -55.341 \end{pmatrix}$$

So, the fitted regression equation is given as,

$$y = 1 + 1.683 x_1 - 55.341 x_2$$

7.2.3 Linear Regression Using Stochastic Gradient Method

Linear regression is a supervised learning. OLS method becomes computationally expensive for larger datasets. In that case, the stochastic gradient descent (SGD) can be used to estimate the parameters. It is an iterative method for minimizing the objective function to estimate the optimal parameters.

The problem of linear regression can be formulated as follows: Give N observations of pairs of (x, y). The problem of linear regression is to predict y for unknown x. The linear model is given as follows: $\hat{y} = a_0 + a_1 x$.

The focus is to estimate the parameters. The objective function has to be minimized. The objective function is given as the squared error between the expected and actual data and is given as:

$$J = (y - \hat{y})^2$$

So, the cost function,

$$L = MSE = \frac{1}{n}\sum_{i=1}^{n}(y - \hat{y})^2 = \frac{1}{n}\sum_{i=1}^{n}(y - (a_0 + a_1 x))^2$$

Compute the gradients of the loss function. The partial derivatives of the loss function L with respect to the parameters are given as:

$$\frac{\partial L}{\partial a_0} = -\frac{2}{n}\sum_{i=1}^{n} y_i - (a_0 + a_1 x_i))$$

$$\frac{\partial L}{\partial a_1} = -\frac{2}{n}\sum_{i=1}^{n} y_i - (a_0 + a_1 x_i) x_i)$$

Then, the update of the parameters is given as:

$$a_0 = a_0 - \eta \frac{\partial L}{\partial a_0}$$

$$a_1 = a_1 - \eta \frac{\partial L}{\partial a_1}$$

The procedure for regression using SGD is given as follows:

1. Initialize the parameters a_0 and a_1 to a small random number or zero.
2. The dataset is shuffled so that randomness is introduced in the dataset.
3. For each input (x_i, y_i) do
   - 3.1 Compute $\hat{y} = a_0 + a_1 x$
   - 3.2 Compute the gradients as

$$\nabla a_0 = -2(y_i - \hat{y})$$

$$\nabla a_1 = -2(y_i - \hat{y})x_i$$

   - 3.3 Update the parameters as

$$a_0 = a_0 - \eta \nabla a_0$$

$$a_1 = a_1 - \eta \nabla a_1$$

4. Repeat the above steps for a certain number of iterations or until convergence. At the end of the iteration, parameters should reach a stable value closer to the global minimum so that the error is minimal.

It is important to note that while this approach is computationally efficient, it requires fine-tuning hyperparameters, such as the learning rate, for optimal performance.

7.2.4 Neural Networks for Linear Regression

Neural networks are useful for solving regression problems. Neural networks help to find the complex relationships between independent and dependent variables. The neural network takes the input features as input, and the generated model captures the relationships among the dependent and independent variables.

The first step of the neural network is gathering data as a dataset. Since regression is a supervised technique, the dataset should have labeled data (input features and the target data). If necessary, the data should be preprocessed, such as normalization standardization.

Neural networks are ideal for regression tasks. (Refer to Box 7.4).

Box 7.4 Neural Network and Best Fit

Neural networks can recognize patterns that can assist in making decisions. Linear regression will not work on problems where there is a nonlinear relationship between the dependent and independent variables. In that case, a line cannot approximate the curvy or nonlinear relationships. So, the traditional regression technique uses polynomial fitting, cubic functions that fit the data. There can be a number of such functions, and picking the functions using manual means is an arduous task. Picking the wrong function may lead to the worst fit. The worst fit refers to a model that poorly approximates the given data points, which leads to high error.

So, the question reduces to finding the function that can "best fit" the data points and applying it so as to minimize the error thereby creating a model that can provide accurate predictions. Neural network reduces that burden by automatically finding the suitable function that can "best fit" the given data.

So, the regression is thought of as two layers – the representation layer and the task layer.

(i) **Representation Layer:** In representation, the hidden layers capture the patterns and relationships from the data and convert them into hidden representations. The hidden layers use the nonlinear activation functions to extract the complex representations from the input. This representation serves as the input for the last layer, called the task layer (which is the last layer before the output layer) that does regression or classification.

(ii) **Task or Regression Layer:** The task or regression layer uses the learned representations to predict the output continuous values.

Thus, the best fit of the data points leads to prediction, and the "beauty" of the neural network is that it "automatically" finds a function that does the best fit.

The neural network for the linear regression is shown in Figure 7.4.

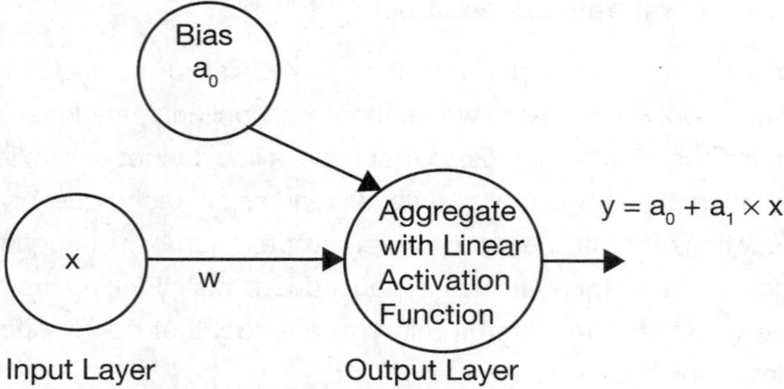

Figure 7.4 A Neural Network for Regression for a Single Input x

For a simple linear regression problem, there is a need for an input layer with neurons that equals the number of input features. There is no need for a hidden layer for regression problems if the data size is very small. However, the hidden layer can be added for complex problems involving a large dataset. There is no hidden layer since the data is small for the example problem (Refer to Figure 7.4). There is a need for only one neuron in the output layer. However, there is a linear activation for the output layer; hence, the neuron computes only the sum of the input and weights called aggregates.

In general, the neural network of Figure 7.4 can be extended for linear regression with 'n' inputs, as shown in Figure 7.5.

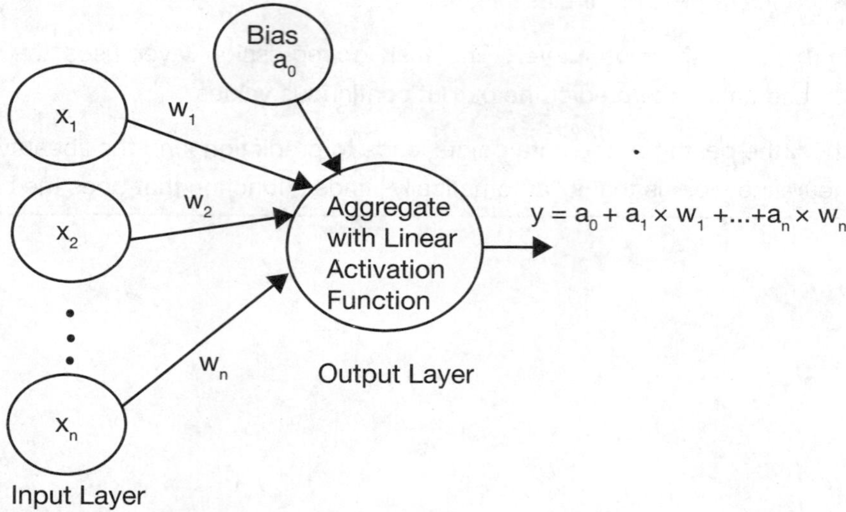

Figure 7.5 A Neural Network for Regression for *n* Inputs

The steps of the neural network training and testing are given below:

1. Initialize neural network weights randomly.
2. The input layer number is equal to the number of inputs. Input the data.
3. The output layer has one neuron equal to the input. The activation function is linear.
4. Compute the error. For a linear regression problem, the loss function can be mean square error, and the network can use stochastic gradient descent (or Adam) to propagate the partial derivatives backward and update the weights.
5. Repeat for all training set input by specifying data and the number of epochs until weights are converged.
6. Once the model is trained, the constructed neural network model can be evaluated using metrics such as mean absolute error or mean squared error.

7.2.5 Regression Model Evaluation

How to validate the regression results? The following metrics (Refer to Table 7.5) are used to validate the regression results.

Table 7.5 Regression Model Evaluation Metrics

Name of the Metric	Description	Remarks
Standard Error	The error is the difference between the actual (y) and predicted value ($\hat{y}$).	error = $y - \hat{y}$ For example, if the house construction estimation by the regression model is 75 lakhs, and the actual cost is 80 lakhs, which means the difference of 5 lakhs is an error.
Mean Absolute Error (MAE)	It is the average absolute difference between the actual and predicted values.	$\text{MAE} = \frac{1}{N}\sum_{i=0}^{N-1}(y_i - \hat{y})$ MAE is to ensure that the error is always positive.

Mean Squared Error (MSE)	It is the sum of the average squared difference between the actual and predicted values.	$\frac{1}{N}\sum_{i=0}^{N-1}(y_i - \hat{y})^2$ The purpose of squaring the difference is to ensure the amplification of the error.
Root MSE	The square root of MSE is called the Root mean square error.	$\sqrt{MSE}$
R-squared	This factor is called the coefficient of determination in the range [0-1]. A value of 1 indicates that the predictions are accurate.	$R^2 = 1 - \frac{\sum_{i=1}^{n}(y_i - \hat{y}_i)^2}{\sum_{i=1}^{n}(y_i - \bar{y}_i)^2}$ Here $\bar{y}_i$ is the mean of the observed values.

Example 7.4: The week and sales data are given as shown in Table 7.6

Table 7.6 Sales Data

Weeks (x)	Sales (y)
1	2
2	4
3	5
4	4
5	5

Find MSE, RMSE, MAE, and R-squared errors.

Solution:

The model parameters can be found as a_0 = 2.2 and (from Example 7.1), so the linear regression equation is given as

$$y = 2.2 + 0.6x$$

The model can be used for the prediction of the input data as:

$$x = 1, y = 2.2 + 0.6(1) = 2.8$$

$$x = 2, y = 2.2 + 0.6(2) = 3.4$$
$$x = 3y = 2.2 + 0.6(3) = 4.0$$
$$x = 4, y = 2.2 + 0.6(4) = 4.6$$
$$x = 5, y = 2.2 + 0.6(5) = 5.2$$

The predicted values are

$$\hat{y} = [2.8, 3.4, 4.0, 4.6, 5.2]$$

The quality of the regression can be assessed using the following metrics:

1. $MSE = \frac{1}{N}\sum_{i=1}^{N}\left(y - \hat{y}_i\right)^2$

$$= \frac{1}{5}\left[(2-2.8)^2 + (4-3.4)^2 + (5-4)^2 + (4-4.6)^2 + (5-5.2)^2\right]$$
$$= \frac{1}{5}[0.64 + 0.36 + 1 + 0.36 + 0.04]$$
$$= \frac{1}{5}[2.4] = 0.48$$

2. $MAE = \frac{1}{N}\sum_{i=1}^{N}\left|y - \hat{y}_i\right|$

$$= \frac{1}{5}\left[|2-2.8| + |4-3.4| + |5-4.0| + |4-4.6| + |5-5.2|\right]$$
$$= \frac{1}{5}[0.8 + 0.6 + 1 + 0.6 + 0.2]$$
$$= \frac{1}{5}[3.2] = 0.64$$

3. $RMSE = \sqrt{MSE} = \sqrt{0.48} \cong 0.6928$
4. R-squared error (Coefficient of Determination)

$$R - \text{squared error} = 1 - \frac{\sum(y_i - \hat{y})^2}{\sum(y_i - avg(y))^2}$$

The numerator can be computed from MSE calculation without diving by 5 as 2.4. The denominator can be found as

$$\sum(y_i - avg(y))^2 = (2-4)^2 + (4-4)^2 + (5-4)^2 + (4-4)^2 + (5-4)^2 = 6.$$

So, $R - \text{squared error} = 1 - \frac{2.4}{6} = 0.6$

It should be noted that the range is 0-1. Hence, the error indicates that accuracy is around 60%.

7.3 Logistic Regression

Logistic regression is suitable for binary classification problems. The goal of logistic regression is to take the input features of the data and produce binary outcomes or classes. For example, the logistic problem can be taking the number of hours practiced as input and producing an outcome whether the athlete won the cup or not. The outcome is a categorical variable whose value is zero or one. Like linear regression, logistic regression is used for modeling the relationship between the dependent and independent variables for classification.

The use cases of logistic regression are given in Box 7.5.

Box 7.5 Use Cases of Logistic regression

There are many applications of logistic regression. Some of the applications are listed below:

(i) Medical diagnosis

(ii) Granting of a bank loan.

(iii) Prediction of customer purchase.

1. The heart of logistic regression is the use of logistic functions. The logistic function is used to map the output values to a probability. A simple logistic function is called the sigmoidal function. The sigmoidal function is given as

$$\sigma(z) = \frac{1}{1+e^{-z}}$$

Here, z is given as the linear combination of the input features. For example, for a single feature input, the linear combination is given as

$$z = a_0 + a_1 x$$

Here, a_0, $a_1$are the parameters. The assumptions of linear regression are the same as linear regression, such as observations are independent of each other, the log odds are the combination of the input features and there is no multicollinearity. The mathematics of odds and its conversion to probability is given in Box 7.6.

Box 7.6 Odds and Logistic Function

In gambling and general, real-world problems involve odds. In betting, odds are used, say for a cricket team as 3:1. It actually means that for every bet of 1 Re, the better would get 3 Rs if the cricket team wins. Odds are another way of expressing the probability of winning. If the team has 60% of winning, the odds are $\frac{p}{1-p} = \frac{0.6}{0.4} = 1.5$. It means that there is 1.5 times more likelihood to happen for this event than not happen.

Let E be the event. One way to express the odds of E is to give the probability of even occurring to the probability of not occurring. So,

$$\text{odds} = \frac{\text{probability of } E}{\text{Probability of } E \text{ not occuring}} = \frac{p}{1-p}$$

Logit is the logarithm of odds and is expressed as the linear combination of independent variables. Logit transforms a probability into a value that ranges from $-\infty$ to $+\infty$. The logit is given as

$$\text{Log(odds)} = \text{logit(p)} = \ln\left(\frac{p}{1-p}\right) = a_0 + a_1 x$$

The logic of converting the odds back to the probability, instead of finding is directly as exponentials, is done by plugging the above into the logistic function as this is equivalent.

$$p = \frac{1}{1-e^{-\log odds}} = \frac{1}{1-e^{-(a_0+a_1x)}}$$

The above is the mapping of logit back to the probability). In the above equation, p is the probability that ranges from 0-1, and log odds are the linear combination of the independent variables.

If p is more than 0.5, then the input belongs to the positive class. Otherwise, it is a negative class.

2. Plugging this in the sigmoidal function gives

$$\sigma(z) = \sigma(a_0 + a_1 x) = \frac{1}{1 + e^{-(a_0 + a_1 x)}}$$

The above is the logistical regression model whose output is in the range 0 – 1. In a way, logistic regression is an extension of linear regression.

So, the procedure can be consolidated and is given below:

1. Find the model parameters a_0 and a_1, using model fitting.
2. Find the log odds as the linear combination of independent variables as

$$\text{logit}(p) = z = a_0 + a_1 x$$

3. Plug it into the logistic function to get the probability back by

$$p = \frac{1}{1 - e^{-\log odds}} = \frac{1}{1 - e^{-(a_0 + a_1 x)}}$$

4. Interpret the probability as

$$\text{class} = \begin{cases} 1 \text{ if } p \geq 0.5 \\ 0 \text{ if } p < 0.5 \end{cases}$$

The optimal parameters can be obtained as follows:

1. Find the likelihood of the given observations using the model. The likelihood means how well the model is able to predict such that the model prediction matches with the actual outcomes (Ground truth). If the predictions match, then the likelihood would increase. In the case of a mismatch, the likelihood would decrease.
2. To make computations simpler, log-likelihood is used. The log-likelihood function is given as

$$L(a_0, a_1) = \sum_{i=1}^{n} y_i (a_0 + a_1 x_i) - \ln(1 + e^{a_0 + a_1 x_i}))$$

3. The log-likelihood should be maximized to adjust the parameters as parameters need to be optimal so that the predictions of the model can match the actual outcomes. For this, the partial derivatives of the loss functions are obtained as

$$\frac{\partial L}{\partial a_0} = \sum_{i=1}^{n} y_i - \frac{e^{(a_0 + a_1 x_i)}}{1 + e^{a_0 + a_1 x_i}}$$

$$\frac{\partial L}{\partial a_1} = \sum_{i=1}^{n} x_i (y_i - \frac{e^{(a_0 + a_1 x_i)}}{1 + e^{a_0 + a_1 x_i}}))$$

4. The parameters are updated as

$$a_0 = a_0 - \eta \frac{\partial L}{\partial a_0}$$

$$a_1 = a_1 - \eta \frac{\partial L}{\partial a_1}$$

5. Repeat the above steps till the parameters converge to a stable value

   The above is the procedure to update the parameters. For the new values, the first step is to find the linear combination of the features and then plug it into the sigmoidal function. The outcome is probability. This probability can be compared with a threshold value of 0.5 to convert the outcome as a binary. Thus, logistic regression is used as a binary classifier.

Example 7.5: For the following sample data shown in Table 7.7, apply the logistic regression

Table 7.7 Cups Won Data

Weeks (x)	Cups Won (y)
1	0
2	0
5	1
8	1
10	1

Solution:

The intercept is given as $a_0 = -3.375$ and $a_1 = +0.914$. These values are using a linear regression method.

The logistic regression is given as

$$p(x) = \frac{1}{1 + e^{-(a_0 + a_1 x)}} = \frac{1}{1 + e^{-(-3.375 + 0.914x)}}$$

For $x = 1$,

$$p(1) = \frac{1}{1 + e^{-(-3.375 + 0.914 \times 1)}} = \frac{1}{1 + \exp(2.461)} \approx 0.0786$$

$$p(x=2) = \frac{1}{1+e^{-(a_0+a_1x)}} = \frac{1}{1+exp(1.547)} = 0.1755$$

$$p(x=5) = \frac{1}{1+e^{-(a_0+a_1x)}} = \frac{1}{1+exp(-1.195)} = 0.768$$

$$p(x=8) = \frac{1}{1+e^{-(a_0+a_1x)}} = \frac{1}{1+exp(-3.397)} = 0.981$$

$$p(x=10) = \frac{1}{1+e^{-(a_0+a_1x)}} = \frac{1}{1+exp(-5.765)} = 0.997$$

Multiplying by 100 gives the percentage of winning the cups.

7.3.1 Neural Networks for Logistic Regression

The linear regression model can be extended to predict labels instead of numbers. Hence, the logistic regression model is a classification model like binary classification. What is classification in neural networks? The details of classification as a function are given in Box 7.7.

Box 7.7 Classification as a Function Approximation!

Classification is about finding a function that maps the input data to a discrete variable. The process of finding the optimal weights of a function that maps the input data to the output label is called function approximation.

In short, $y = f(x)$

Here, $f(x)$ is the function that maps the input x, the features into output y, and the categorical variables that represent the class.

Thus, one can say that classification is about finding a function f that approximates the underlying functions that govern the data and maps the input data to classes. Thus, the "beauty" of the neural network is that it "automatically" finds a function that does the classification.

The concept of logistic regression can be extended for multiple categories as multinomial logical regression. Neural network solves both linear and nonlinear regression problems effectively (Refer to Box 7.8).

Box 7.8 Logistic Regression and Classification

One of the primary tasks of logistic regression is to find a line that separates the points into two classes. It is called linearly separable classes.

In reality, the linearly separable classes are not possible. So, finding a suitable hyperplane that separates the classes is a great ordeal. Neural networks come to our rescue again. It can automatically learn the function. It can learn a function as well as the parameters.

The neural network can be used for logistic regression, as shown in Figure 7.6.

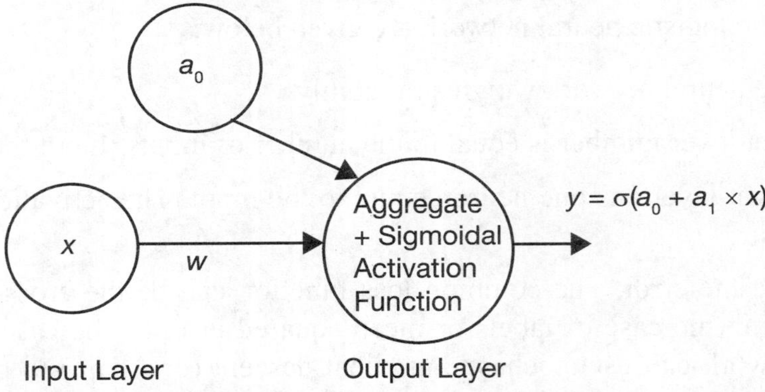

Figure 7.6 A Neural Network for Logistic Regression for One Input x

The differences between the construction of linear and logistic regression are given in Table 7.8.

Table 7.8 Differences between the Construction of Linear and Logistic Regression Networks

Linear Regression	Logistic Regression
There is no need for an activation function in the output layer. If used, it should be a linear activation function.	The sigmoid activation function is used in the output layer.
The output of linear regression is a number.	The output of logistic regression a label 0 or 1.

Linear Regression	Logistic Regression
Linear regression uses a loss function such as mean squared error.	Logistic regression uses loss functions such as binary cross entropy or categorical cross entropy (for multinomial problems).
The evaluation metrics are like mean absolute error and mean squared error.	The evaluation metrics are accuracy, precision, and recall.

The first step of the logistic neural network is gathering data as a dataset. Since logistic regression is a supervised technique, the dataset should have labeled data (input features and the target data labeled as 0 and 1). If necessary, the data should be preprocessed, such as normalization standardization.

The steps of the logistic neural network are given below:

1. Initialize neural network weights randomly.
2. The input layer number is equal to the number of inputs. Input the data.
3. The output layer has one neuron equal to the input. The activation function is sigmoidal.
4. Compute the error. The common loss function can be the cross-entropy loss function in the case of labels or mean squared error in the case of numbers. The network can use stochastic gradient descent (or Adam) to propagate the partial derivatives backward and update the weights.
5. Repeat for all training set input by specifying data and the number of epochs until weights are converged.
6. Once the model is trained, the constructed neural network model can be evaluated using metrics such as mean absolute error or mean squared error.

7.4 Introduction to Classification

In many areas, classification is important in daily life. In deep learning, classification refers to categorizing input data into distinct classes or categories based on certain features or characteristics.

The differences between classification and regression are given in the following Table 7.9.

Table 7.9 Differences between Classification and Regression

Classification	Regression
The output of a classification problem is a discrete and categorical variable. For example, predicting the brand of the car as Honda, Maruthi is a classification task.	The output of the regression problem is a number.
The output variable is categorical.	The output variable is continuous.
The classification evaluation is based on a confusion matrix and metrics like accuracy, precision, and recall.	The evaluation is based on errors such as mean absolute or squared errors.

The classification types are shown in Figure 7.7.

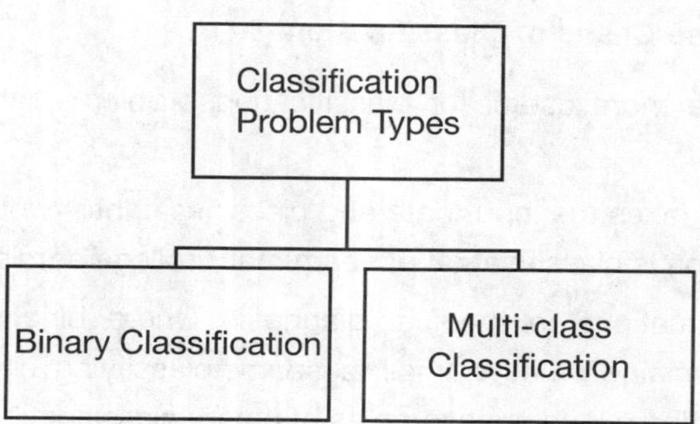

Figure 7.7 Types of Classification

The data can be classified into one of two class categories in binary classification. In binary classification, the output is denoted often as 0 or 1. In multiclass classification, the given data can be classified into three or more categories. Classification can be viewed as a function approximation, as given in Box 7.9.

Box 7.9 Function Approximation and Universal Approximation Theorem

It has been said earlier that classification is finding a function that maps the input data into labels or probability over the labels.

A neural network can find any function that classifies. This extraction of the function automatically is referred to as function approximation and informally as "function fit".

Do neural networks solve all problems? The answer is theoretically yes. The universal approximation theorem provides theoretical justification.

The universal approximation theorem states that any neural network that has a hidden layer with finite nodes can find approximates for any continuous function provided activation functions that are available with non-constant, bounded, and continuous functions.

Some of the use cases of classification are given in Box 7.10.

Box 7.10 Use Cases of Classification

Neural networks are more useful for classification problems rather than regression problems.

Binary classification takes the input data and classifies it into two groups. An example of binary classification is classification of spam mail, college admissions.

There are many situations in medical diagnosis where binary classifications are encountered. Determining whether mail is spam, classifying a tumor as benign or malignant, and granting a loan are examples of binary classification.

Multiclass classification is still more useful in various domains, including medical diagnosis, sentiment analysis, and fraud detection. Some of the multiclass classification problems are the recognition of handwritten digits, the classification of fruits into three categories – apple, orange, or banana, and the classification of vegetables.

7.4.1 Binary Classification

Binary classification is a fundamental task in deep learning, where the goal is to classify input data into one of two possible categories or classes. In binary classification, the input data is typically represented by a set of features or attributes, and each data point is associated with a binary label often denoted as positive (usually labeled as 1) and negative (usually labeled as 0).

The first step of the neural network is gathering data as a dataset. Since classification is a supervised technique, the dataset should have labeled data (input features and the target data). If necessary, the data should be preprocessed, such as normalization standardization. This dataset is split into training data, testing data, and validation data (refer to Chapter 6)

The neural network for binary classification can be designed as follows:

(i) The number of nodes equals the number of input parameters. Since the example problem has three inputs, the input layer has three nodes or neurons.

(ii) The output is binary, so one node is sufficient. Since this is a classification problem, the output node uses an activation function called sigmoidal function.

(iii) The hidden layer has neurons. However, there are no guidelines on how many neurons are required. The following network uses two hidden layers. The first hidden layer has four neurons, and the second has two. The neural network is shown in Figure 7.8.

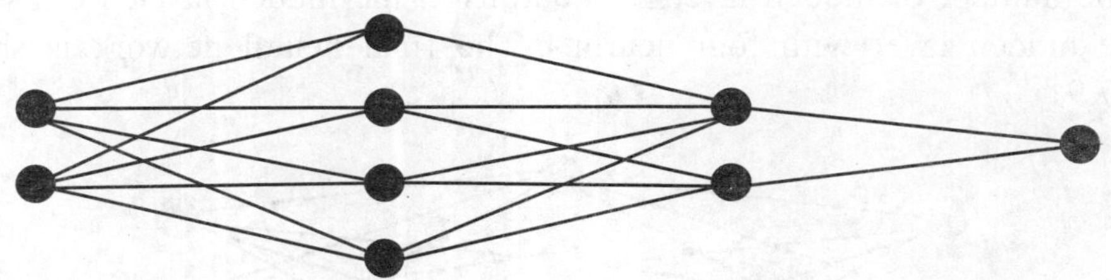

Figure 7.8 Neural Network for Binary Classification

The procedure of binary classification is given below:

1. Ensure that inputs are numbers. If the inputs are categorical, they must be converted to numbers.
2. Randomly initialize the weights of the neural network.
3. Give the input and evaluate the output. The difference between the output and expected output (d) is called an error (y). So, $\delta = d - y$, where d is the expected value and y is the actual value. If the involved quantities are categorical variables and are not numbers, then the loss functions, such as binary cross-entropy, are used to compute the error.

4. The partial derivatives of the error are propagated backward to the last hidden layer next to the input layer using an optimizer algorithm such as a stochastic gradient descent algorithm. A stochastic algorithm adjusts the weights.
5. Repeat the steps [3–4] for all the training set data.

Once the model is trained, the testing can be done. Finally, the model is tested with the unknown instance, and the model is evaluated. The concept of the classification model validation is given in chapter 6 of this book.

7.4.2 Multiclass Classification

Multiclass classification is a machine learning task where the objective is to categorize input data into one of three or more mutually exclusive classes or categories. Each data point can belong to only one class, and the model's output predicts the class label for each input.

Let us assume that for a hypothetical problem with the inputs and outputs as three. Then, the neural network can be designed as follows:

The input layer has neurons that equal the number of inputs. The output is three classes. Hence, the neurons of the output layer equal three. There is no guideline about the number of hidden layers or neurons in the hidden layer. Let us assume a single hidden layer with four neurons. The final neural network is shown in Figure 7.9.

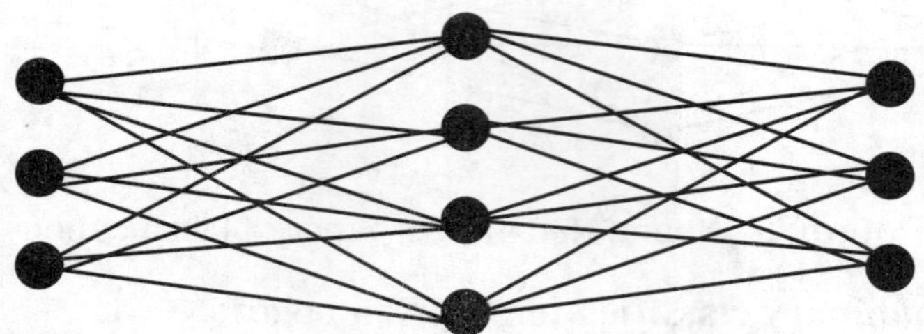

Figure 7.9 Neural Network for Multiclass Classification

The first step of the neural network is gathering data as a dataset. Since multiclass classification is a supervised technique, the dataset should have labeled data (input features and the target data). If necessary, the data should be preprocessed, such as normalization standardization. This dataset is split into training data, testing data, and validation data (refer to Chapter 6)

The procedure of a multiclass classification neural network construction is given below:

1. Randomly initialize the network weights.
2. Enter the input values to the networks. As the problem has three inputs, the given neural network has three neurons.
3. The number of neurons in the output layer should equal the number of outputs. Since the output of this problem is 3, the neural network has three neurons in the output layer. One-hot encoding is used to encode the output as follows:

$$\text{class}\,1 = [1 \quad 0 \quad 0]$$

$$\text{class}\,2 = [0 \quad 1 \quad 0]$$

$$\text{class}\,3 = [0 \quad 0 \quad 1]$$

   The activation function that should be used in the output layer is softmax. The softmax gives the probability of the classes.
4. Give the input and computer the error (δ). If the involved variables are categorical values, then the categorical cross-entropy is used to compute the error.
5. Propagate the error backward using the optimizer algorithm, such as the stochastic gradient descent method, to adjust the weights
6. Repeat steps [4-5] for all the data of the trained dataset.

   Once the model is trained properly, it can be tested with unknown input values, and the model evaluation can be done.

7.5 Classifier Model Evaluation

Classifier models are discussed in the subsequent chapters. This section focuses on evaluating classifier models. Classifiers are unstable, as a small change in the input can change the output. A solid framework is needed for proper evaluation. The framework for that is called the confusion matrix.

7.5.1 Confusion Matrix

Several metrics can be used to describe the accuracy of the classifier. It is done through a contingency table (Refer to Table 7.10). The contingency matrix is called a confusion matrix. A confusion matrix is a matrix that provides a summary of the predictions made by the model when the ground truth is available. For example, consider a test for detecting a disease, say Diabetes—a contingency table for this system prediction Vs. The expert prediction is given below in Table 7.10.

Table 7.10 A Contingency Table

Test Vs. Ground Truth (GT). GT is often the Expert Opinion	Has Diabetes?	Has no Diabetes?
Positive	Model prediction = Diabetes GT = Diabetes Both are in an agreement called True positive (TP).	Model prediction = Diabetes GT = No diabetes (Type I error called False Alarm or False Positive (FP)). Give a false alarm when the patient is normal.
Negative	Model prediction = No Diabetes GT = Diabetes (Type II error called False negative or FN). Fails to detect Diabetes. False Positive (FP)	Model prediction = No Diabetes GT = No Diabetes Both are in an agreement called True Negative (TP) and perfectly rules out a normal patient.

It can be observed that FP and FN are costly errors in this classification process. The metrics that can be derived from this contingency table are listed below in Table 7.11:

Table 7.11 Classification Model Metrics

Name of the Metric	Description	Formula Example
Sensitivity or recall or True Positive Rate (TPR)	The sensitivity of a test is the ability to find all positive cases (in our example, all diabetes patients) correctly. The sensitivity indicates how the model is sensitive to finding diabetes patients. TP value indicates how the model can catch all positive cases successfully! (No one can escape if they are positive!)	$\frac{TP}{TP+FN}$

Specificity or True Negative Rate (TNR) or recall	The specificity is the ability to accuse normal patients falsely. The model will identify no patient without Diabetes as a diabetes patient. (No false alarms)	$\frac{TN}{TN+FP}$
Positive Predictive rate (PPR) or Positive Predictive Value (PPV) or Precision	This metric indicates the ability of the model to measure the positive predictions. $\frac{\text{Correctly predicted postive patients as per ground truth}}{\text{Total number of positive predicted patients by the model}}$	$\frac{TP}{TP+FP}$
Negative Predictive rate or Negative Predicted Value	The negative predictive rate indicates how many are truly negative. $\frac{\text{Correctly predicted negative patients as per ground truth}}{\text{Total number of negative predicted patients by the model}}$	$\frac{TN}{TN+FN}$
Accuracy	Accuracy of the classifier	$\frac{TP+TN}{TP+TN+FP+FN}$
F1 score	F1 score of the classifier. A combination of harmonic mean of precision and recall is called F-measure or F1 score. The F1 score is useful in identifying the model skill for a specific threshold.	$2 \times \frac{(\text{precision} \times \text{recall})}{\text{precision} + \text{recall}}$

Example 7.6: Consider the following contingency Table 7.12 for test vs disease

Table 7.12 Contingency Table

4	1
1	3

Find the performance indicators of a classifier model.

Solution:

For the given table, TP is 4, TN = 3, FP = 1, FN =1

Accuracy is given as

$$\frac{TP+TN}{TP+TN+FP+FN}$$

Therefore, accuracy = 7/9 = 0.78.

$$\text{Precision} = \frac{TP}{TP+FP}$$

Therefore, precision = 4/5 = 0.8

$$\text{Recall (TPR or Sensitivity)} = \frac{TN}{TN+FP}$$

Therefore, recall is ¾ = 0.75

$$\text{F1 score is } 2\times\frac{(\text{precision}\times\text{recall})}{\text{precision}+\text{recall}}$$

Therefore, F1 score is 2 × (0.8 × 0.75)/1.55 = 2 × 0.6/1.55 = 0.77.

Example 7.7: Consider the output of a logistical regression model is {1, 0.3, 0.8, 1}. Let us assume that the model's actual output is {1, 0, 1, 1}. The details are given in Table 7.13. Find TPR and FPR.

Solution:

The details are listed in Table 7.13.

Table 7.13 Illustration of Threshold value 0.5

Model Output	Actual Output	Threshold value = 0.5
1	1	1
0.3	0	0
0.8	1	1
1	1	1

It can be observed that TP = 3, TN = 1, FP = 0, FN = 0. Therefore,

$$TPR = \frac{TP}{TP+FN} = \frac{3}{3+0} = 1$$

$$FPR = \frac{FP}{FP+TN} = \frac{0}{0+1} = 0$$

7.6 Multiple Classifier Comparisons

The classifier performance can also be computed as a distance measure. The classifier accuracy can be plotted as a point. A point in the northwest is a better classifier. The Euclid distance of two points of the two classifiers can give a performance measure. The value ranges from 0 to 1.

7.6.1 ROC Curve

A receiver-operated characteristic (ROC) curve is a graphical representation of a binary classifier's performance, plotting the true positive rate (TPR) on the x-axis and the false positive rate (FPR) or (1-specificity) on the y-axis.

The logistic regression model uses A cut-off value to classify p(x). All $p(x)$ values greater than the cut-off value are classified as positive, and all $p(x)$ values less than the cut-off are classified as negative. So, getting TPR and FPR for each cut-off value is possible. ROC depicts all possible scenarios for all cut-off values and plots it as a graph. The 45-degree line indicates the random guess.

The procedure for plotting the ROC curve is listed below:

1. Find different classification thresholds.
2. Compute TPR and FPR for every classification threshold.
3. Plot the curve as a graph by having TPR as the X-axis and FPR as the Y-axis.
4. Compute the area under the curve as the quantitative measure of classification.

Example 7.8: Let the test values be as given in Table 7.14.

Table 7.14 Illustration of ROC with Physics Marks

Physics Marks	34	47	49	66	39	68	29	29	38
Model Prediction	1	1	0	1	0	1	0	0	1
Threshold = 30	1	1	1	1	1	1	0	0	1

Show the ROC curve assuming a single threshold of 30.

Solution:

Generate one if the mark is greater than 30. Otherwise, it is zero. The ground truth is given for the physics marks. So, the TPR and FPR are calculated at the threshold and plotted as the curve (It can be seen if there is an agreement, the curve goes upwards and flat if there is a disagreement between ground truth and model prediction). The ROC curve is shown in Figure 7.10.

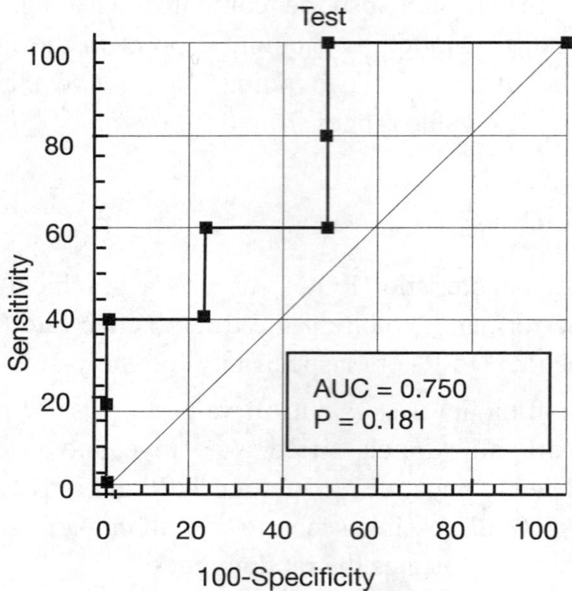

Figure 7.10 ROC Curve

In ROC, the plot's diagonal indicates the model with no skill or random classifier, and skillful models show the curve above the diagonal. TPR should be 1 for an ideal classifier, and FPR should be zero. By varying the threshold, one can evaluate the best performance of the classifier, and it helps to identify the optimal threshold value.

Another metric associated with the ROC curve is the quantity that measures the classifier's performance as an AUC (Area Under Curve) metric after constructing the TPR Vs. FPR, the area under the curve, is computed. This area calculation is done by forming the trapezoid by using the adjacent points of the ROC curve and finding the area. The value of ROC is between 0 – 1. A value of 1 indicates that the classifier is perfect, and 0.5 indicates that the model guesses the answer.

7.6.2 Precision-Recall Curve

The precision-recall curve is another method for evaluating the performance of the binary classifier. It is a graphical representation illustrating the tradeoff between precision-recalls at various thresholds. The x-axis of the precision-recall curve recall values at various thresholds, and the precision values indicate the y-axis.

Ideally, high precision and high recall are desired. But there will be a tradeoff across various classification thresholds. Precision-recall curves provide a good explanation for classifiers across thresholds. Similar to AUC, AUC-PR also can be computed. These curves are useful as a performance metric to indicate the imbalanced classes where the accuracy of the classifier may be misleading.

Summary

1. Regression is a statistical method used to model the relationship between a dependent variable and one or more independent variables. It is also used to predict the dependent variable's value based on the independent variables' values.
2. Linear regression can be done analytically by the ordinary least square method, the Machine Learning approach, and the Neural Network approach.
3. Linear regression is a fundamental statistical method used for modeling the relationship between a dependent variable and one or more independent variables.
4. Multilinear Regression, also known as multiple linear regression, is an extension of simple linear regression that involves more than one independent variable.
5. Ordinary least square is a method used to find the line (or hyperplane in higher dimensions) that best fits a set of data points by minimizing the sum of the squared differences between the observed values and the values predicted by the model.
6. Stochastic Gradient Descent is a popular optimization algorithm used in machine learning for finding a model's optimal parameters, mostly in high-dimensional parameter spaces.
7. Classification is a fundamental task in supervised machine learning where the goal is to predict the categorical class labels of new instances based on past observations.
8. Supervised learning is a type of machine learning where the algorithm learns from labeled data.
9. A confusion matrix is a matrix that summarizes a model's predictions when the ground truth is available.
10. The Ordinary Least square method uses a linear equation to generate the regression equation.

11. Matrix form is an easy way to handle regression problems.
12. When data is very large neural network can be used for regression
13. In a neural network, the initial weight, bias, learning rate, and threshold are randomly assumed, and through iteration, which is based on error value, is done
14. Logistic regression is another technique mostly used for classification problems and uses the sigmoid function.
15. There are two types of classification - binary classification and multiclass classification.
16. If the predicted class is of two categories, it is a binary classifier.
17. The universal approximation theorem suggests that the neural network with one hidden layer of fine nodes can find any function.
18. If the prediction is based on many classes, then it's multiclass.
19. ROC curve can be used to analyze the classifier performance. It is a graphical representation having TPR as the x-axis and FPR as the y-axis.
20. AUC (Area Under Curve) is another metric that can explain the performance of a classifier.
21. The precision-recall (PR) curve is a graph that visually illustrates tradeoffs of precision and recall at various threshold points.

Glossary

1. Independent Variable – It is also known as an explanatory variable. These are standalone variables not dependent on other variables.
2. Dependent Variable – It is also known as the response variable that is being studied or observed.
3. Supervised Method – It is a machine-learning approach where the model learns from a dataset of input-output pairs.
4. Aggregates – The sum of input and weights are called aggregates.
5. Best fit – A fit is called best fit if the approximation matches closely with the input data.
6. Logistic function – The logistical function converts odds to probability.

7. Classification – Classification is a mapping function that maps the input features to a categorical variable.
8. Function approximation – A neural network that can extract any underlying function from data to construct a model.
9. Sensitivity – The probability of producing a true positive result.
10. Specificity – The probability of producing a true negative result.
11. Accuracy – The ability of the model to correct classifications.
12. ROC Curve – The graphical plot of TPR and FPR that illustrates the performance of the classifiers.
13. AUC – The area under the curve is a metric that indicates the classifier's performance.
14. PR Curve – A graphical plot of precision and recall illustrates the tradeoff between precision and recall at various thresholds.
15. AUC-PR – Another metric that indicates the accuracy of the classifiers.

Short Questions

1. Difference between classification and regression
2. Differentiate between linear regression and logistic regression.
3. What are the common challenges or issues when training regression models in deep learning?
4. What are the assumptions of linear regression?
5. The best fit is related to prediction – Justify.
6. How does one assess the performance of a regression model in deep learning?
7. What is meant by function approximation?
8. Logistical regression works only on linearly separable data – Justify.
9. State universal approximation theorem
10. What is the fundamental difference between binary and multiclass classification problems in deep learning?

Long Questions

1. Explain the working principle of the SGD algorithm.
2. With a suitable example, explain logistic regression.

3. Consider a dataset consisting of 5 columns; you have to predict one response value based on the other four values. What type of regression method will you use for the prediction? Justify your answer.
4. Assume you are a stamp collector. You exchange stamps, sell stamps, and buy stamps. To predict the number of stamps in possession, perfectly, what type of regression will you use? Explain the process in detail.
5. Explain in detail about different types of classification.

Numerical Problems

1. The rent of a house depends on the area of the house. Here, rent is a variable that depends on the variable area. The following table gives the rent details based on the house's area. Find the best-fit line equation for the given data using the OLS method.

Area (in sq. ft.)	Rent (in rupees)
100	1000
120	1200
140	1400
160	1500

2. Using the matrices, find the linear regression for the following dataset of an athlete whose distance is covered in a given time.

Time Second (x)	Distance Meters (y)
5	40
7	120
12	180
16	210
20	240

3. Using a neural network, find the regression line equation for the following rain data.

	1	2	3	4	5	6	7	8
y	56	75	61	61	67	72	62	61
x	21	39	34	21	32	24	29	24

4. Find the linear regression equation for the following dataset using matrices. Here, x is the dependent variable, and y and z are the independent variables.

x	y	z
2	3	2
3	4	4
4	3	6
5	4	8

5. Apply regression for Table of Q1, and apply the regression performance metrics.
6. For the following sample data shown in below: apply the logistic regression

Weeks (x)	Sales Indicator
100	0
125	0
130	1
150	1
10	1

Apply classifier performance analysis and show the results.

Crossword

Across

1. Classification is a _______ of input variables to output category.
4. For binary classification, the activation function used is _______
6. In GLM, the residuals are not normally distributed (true/false).
8. The input data is called _______, and the prediction is a continuous variable in the regression.
10. In area under ROC ranges between 0-1. (True/false)
12. R-squared error is an estimation of accuracy, and its range is 0-1. (true/false)
13. Softmax is often used for _______ (multiclass/binary) classification.
15. A sigmoidal function is a _______ function.
16. The universal approximation theorem justifies the existence of a function for all problems. (true/false)
17. One predicts the independent variable in linear regression. (true/false)

18. Logistic regression can handle only linearly _______ problems.

19. ROC Curve is a graphical representation of TPR Vs _______

20. SGD can be used to estimate the parameters of linear regression. (true/false).

21. Neural networks can find any function. Is this true? (yes/false)

Down

2. The assumptions of linear regression are the linear relationship, the independence of variables, the variance is constant and the residuals have _______ distribution.

3. The sum of the product of weights and inputs are called _______

4. Regression is an example of _______ learning.

5. For linear regression, the activation function is _______ function.

7. The area under ROC gives the _______ of the classifier.

9. The independent variable is called _______ variable.

11. The dependent variable is called _______ variable.

12. Function approximation means finding a suitable function. (true/false)

14. Regression analysis finds the relationship between independent and dependent variables. (true/false)

16. Best fit is the core of prediction (true/false)

17. Odds is a probability value. (true/false)

```
B D O N F B T C J C A G A C O G Z U C N W E X Z Q
N K T R U E O T B I B Y L E W H T R U E S R X V A
K Y S L O G I S T I C M A P P I N G J L T C L R G
L Z Z S S U P E R V I S E D B S S R A G L H I A G
Z Y Z F Y I J F K J U N T A K V V F R R I E T C R
C S X K C M M T P S E P A R A B L E A O F X P Z E
J P W W E R B E N Q N T R U E C W E J S P P N H G
F Q E K S H F F G T Q X A Q C Q N X R V R L O S A
E T J R V A F R N R H B E R I I L N Y T T A R V T
A D U Q F F I V S U R F G R L Q R T R U E N M Q E
T E N T Q O A L F E I P Y C E M U G T B K A A H S
U I P R K L R L M U L T I C L A S S E V E T L G I
R D Z U S R A M S B F K R P H C V R E S P O N S E
E J E E S S W G A E B N H H K V W G B P A R J U I
S L A E C K G Q E N O P O U N Y L U L E T Y R J I
R F Y I O Q R V O T C D A J H D Z Q R G K T N F B
G A J A T R U E M P O E S I G M O I D A L F F Y V
```

true	explanatory	response	false	features	supervised	aggregates
logistic	false	separable	normal	true	true	true
yes	true	true	true	mapping	linear	sigmoidal
multiclass	FPR	true	performance			

Introduction to Computer Vision and Image Processing

> The ultimate goal of computer vision is to emulate the human visual system, achieving a level of understanding and interpretation of images that rivals human perception. — **Bernd Girod**

Credits: © Bernd Girod

Deep learning has become popular because of its higher performance in imaging applications. Deep learning is known for its best image classification and object detection performance. It is necessary to have some basics in image processing and machine vision to implement concepts related to Convolutional Neural Networks (CNN). The learning objectives of this chapter are

- Introduce the basics of Image processing.
- Explain the need for deep learning.
- Apply convolution for various image tasks.
- Illustrate feature extraction.
- Implement a deep neural network for image classification.

8.1 Introduction to Computer Vision

The AI system is supposed to perceive the environment and take action. Humans perceive the world through their eyes. The human brain interprets the images the eyes capture to understand the environment. Computer vision aims to provide the same capability to computers. Visual perception is the focus of computer vision. Visual perception is the act of perceiving patterns and objects through visual systems.

Computer vision and Image processing have played significant roles in developing image-based applications. Computer vision is a domain that enables the computer to interpret the external visual world. Computer vision includes the techniques for acquiring, processing, analyzing, and interpreting of visual world. Image processing is a domain whose main aim is twofold – to enhance the quality of the image and to interpret the image for pattern recognition tasks like classification and clustering. The image processing operations are image enhancement, image feature extraction, and image pattern recognition.

Computer vision perceives the world through images. First, through the camera, the physical models are constructed using machine learning, and then, the models are used by the machine learning algorithm. Finally, the computer vision pipeline interprets the images to interpret the images. The similarity of human vision and computer vision is given in the following Table 8.1.

Table 8.1 Comparisons between Human Visual Systems and Machine Vision Systems

Human Visual Systems	Computer Vision Systems
Eye to perceive the world.	Use sensors to acquire visual information.
Brain to interpret the visual information.	Use algorithms to Interpret visual information.
Humans have an innate ability to interpret patterns. Good in interpreting emotions and feelings.	Algorithms are used to understand the patterns. But, always limited by the training sets.
Humans can learn and adapt.	The training set limits them.
We use human visual systems for our daily activities for recognition.	It involves projects like image classification, segmentation, and object detection.

8.1.1 Image Processing Pipeline

Image processing is the preprocessing step of computer vision. Image processing aims to extract the image primitives like edges, corners, and shapes. Then, Machine vision uses these primitives and produces semantic descriptions based on the abstractions. The Image processing pipeline is shown here in Figure 8.1.

(i) **Image Acquisition:** This stage aims to obtain the digital image of the object.

(ii) **Image Enhancement:** This stage aims to improve the quality of the image so that the analysis of the images is reliable. Most of the real-time images are characterized by noise and blur. This stage focuses on improving brightness and contrast and removing the noise and blur in the image.

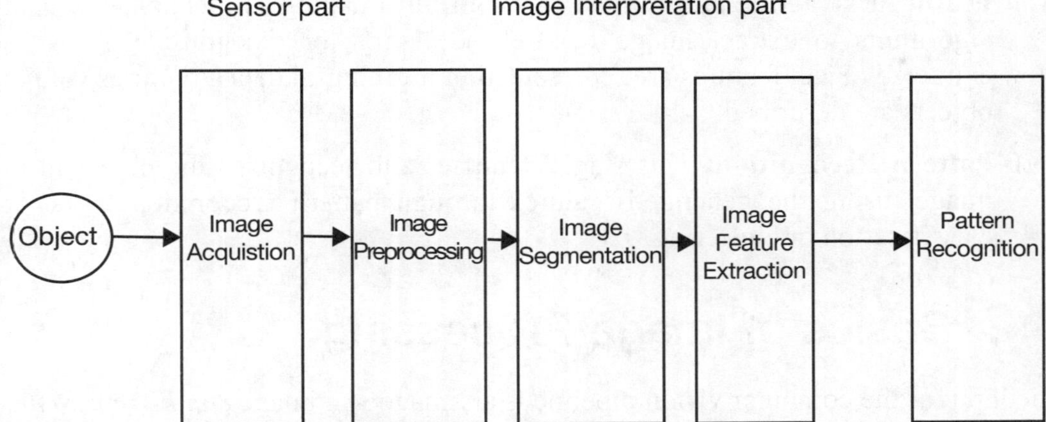

Figure 8.1 Image Processing Pipeline

(iii) **Image Segmentation:** This stage extracts the foreground object from the background. This operation is done by dividing the image into many sub-regions and extracting the necessary regions for further analysis. The unnecessary portions of the image, such as image backgrounds (dictated by the imaging requirement), are discarded, and only the ROI is extracted. Figure 8.2 shows a segmented image. Deep learning algorithms are effective in performing segmentation tasks like semantic and instance segmentation that can be used for counting objects. These concepts are discussed in Chapter 11 of this textbook.

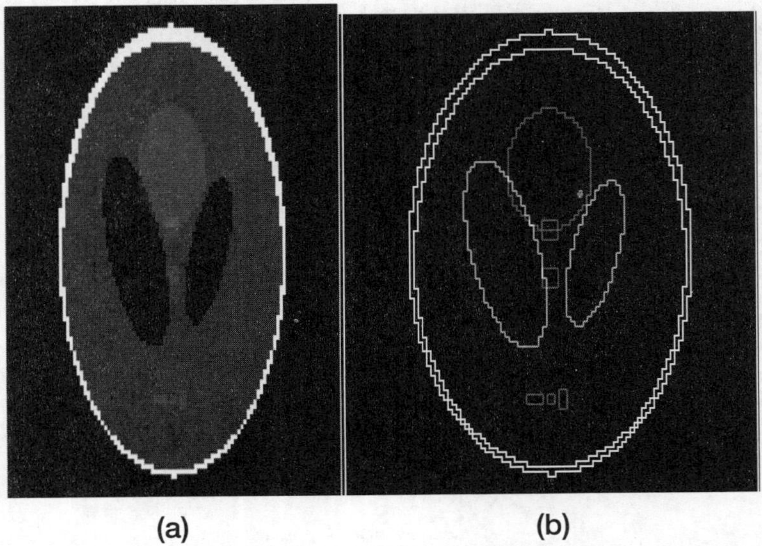

Figure 8.2 (a) Original Image and (b) Segmented Image

(iv) **Feature Extraction and Object Description:** Imaging applications use many algorithms to extract image features necessary for recognition. Then, the extracted object features are represented in meaningful data structures, and the objects are described.

(v) **Pattern Recognition:** This stage identifies and recognizes the object in the image, using the generated features through pattern recognition tasks like classification or clustering.

8.2 Basics of Image Processing

The input of the computer vision pipeline is an image. An image *can be represented* mathematically as $f(x, y)$. The intersection of rows and columns marks a pixel. A pixel is also known as pel or a picture element. A typical digital image consists of millions of pixels. Pixels are considered the building blocks of digital images. It is the basic unit that has colour or intensity value.

The number of rows and columns represents the physical dimensions of the image. It defines the size and resolution of the image. The rows represent the image width, and the columns represent the image height. The image size is often expressed in terms of the rectangular pixel dimensions of the array. Images can be of various sizes. Some examples of the typical image sizes (height × width) are 256 × 256, 512 × 512.

The number of pixels determines the spatial resolution of an image. The number of bits necessary to encode the pixel value is called *bit depth*. The bit depth is the number of bits used to represent the colour or greyscale of the image. Bit depth is always a power of two. Spatial Resolution = number of rows × Number of columns × bit depth

The value of the pixels indexed by row and column is called intensity of the image. The intensity is the amount of colour or light in each pixel. The higher the value of the pixel, the higher the intensity of the pixel.

The average pixel intensity of the image is called brightness. Brightness is the overall brightness and darkness of the image that is influenced by the intensity value of the pixel. Contrast refers to the finer details of the image. It is the difference in the luminance that distinguishes an object from other objects in the background of the image. The formula of contrast in terms of the intensity of the foreground and background object is given as

$$C = \frac{f_{object} - f_{background}}{f_{object} + f_{background}}$$

8.2.1 Types of Images

Images can be classified as grayscale (British spelling is greyscale), binary, true colour, and pseudo-colour images based on colour.

Greyscale and binary images are called monochrome images as there is no colour component in these images. True colour images support colours, and pseudo-colour images artificially add colours for processing convenience.

(i) **Greyscale Images:** The grayscale is the shades of gray that range from black to white. Most medical images, such as X-rays and ultrasound, are greyscale images with an intensity in the range of 0-255. Here, 0 corresponds to black, and 255 corresponds to white. Greyscale uses 8 bits to represent a pixel.

(ii) **Binary Images:** In binary images, the pixels assume a value of 0 or 1. So, one bit is sufficient to represent the pixel value. Thus, binary images are also called bi-level images. In image processing, binary images are encountered in many ways.

(iii) **Colour Images:** The pixel has a colour obtained in colour images by mixing red, green, and blue. Each colour component is represented by eight bits. Hence, colour images can be considered three-band images represented by 24 bits. The number of colours that are possible is 2553 (i.e., 255 × 255 × 255 = 1,67,77,216 colours).

Some image type conversions are given in Box 8.1.

Box 8.1 Colour Channels

Channels represent a specific colour or attribute. The image consists of many channels.

A true colour image is an RGB or 3- 3-channel image, and each channel has a colour. RGB is a 3-band image of red, green, and blue whose combination determines the colour of the pixel. A grayscale image is a 1-band image.

During the processing of the image, deep learning algorithms create more channels. Deep learning algorithms handle many higher-band images. But these additional bands do not represent the colours but features. So, often, these channels are called feature maps.

8.3 Image Operations

The following sections help to understand how these image operations are carried out. The role of image processing operations in deep learning is given in Box 8.2.

Box 8.2 Role of Image Operations in Deep Learning

The knowledge of image processing operations is required for a better understanding of deep learning algorithms. The roles of image processing operations are listed below:

(i) **Preprocessing:** Deep learning algorithms work very well if all the images are perfect. In reality, the acquired images have many flaws, such as noise, blur, and artifacts. Image processing operations are required for processing algorithms such as noise removal, brightness, and contrast enhancement.

(ii) **Feature Extraction:** Deep learning works on extracting the features from the images, such as points, lines, edges and corners, automatically. So, the knowledge of image processing algorithms is required to extract the features from the image.

(iii) **Data Augmentation:** The performance of deep learning algorithms would be less if the number of images are less. So, Data augmentation aims to increase the dataset by applying operations for contrast/brightness manipulation, operations like translation, rotation and mirroring to increase the number of images. The increase in number is carried out to increase the robustness or generalization of deep learning algorithms.

8.3.1 Image Arithmetic Operations

Remember, an image can be viewed as a matrix of values. So, the images can be subjected to arithmetic operations such as addition, subtraction, multiplication, and division. Some of the Operations are listed below in Table 8.2. These arithmetic operations can be used to manipulate the images that are necessary for deep learning algorithms. These operations are useful in creating new images for data augmentation also.

Table 8.2 Image Arithmetic Operations

Image Operations	Descriptions	Application of Operations
Image Addition	Two images can be added as given by $g(x,y)=f_1(x,y)+f_2(x,y)$	It can be used for adding noise to an image.
	$g(x,y)=f_1(x,y)+k$ Here, k is a scalar.	Brightness and contrast adjustment.
Image Subtraction	$g(x,y)=f_1(x,y)-f_2(x,y)$ or $g(x,y)=\|f_1(x,y)-f_2(x,y)\|$ or	It can be useful for finding the difference between two images and tasks like background elimination, brightness reduction, or change detection.
	$g(x,y)=\|f_1(x,y)-k\|$	Brightness and contrast adjustment
Image Multiplication	$g(x,y)=f_1(x,y)\times f_2(x,y)$	It can be useful for improving contrast, designing a filter mask, and highlighting important areas in an image.
Image Division	$g(x,y)=f_1(x,y)/f_2(x,y)$	It can be useful for change detection.

One of the image additions is shown in Figure 8.3.

(a) (b)

Figure 8.3 (a) Original Noisy Image (b) A Constant 100 is Added to all the Pixels to make it Bright

8.3.2 Logical Operations

The logical operations such as NOT, AND, OR can be applied to the image as shown in Table 8.3. These operations are used in creating binary masks that are useful in image segmentation.

Table 8.3 Image Logical Operations

Image Operations	Descriptions	Applications of Operations
NOT	$g(x,y) = 255 - f(x,y)$ for grayscale images, and NOT is used directly for binary images.	Digital Negative
OR Operations	$g(x,y) = f_1(x,y)$ OR $f_2(x,y)$	It is useful for finding the Union or merging of two images.
AND Operation	$g(x,y) = f_1(x,y)$ AND $f_2(x,y)$	It is useful for finding the images' intersection and designing filter masks.

8.3.3 Geometrical Operations

The geometrical operations are given in Table 8.4. The geometrical operations are translation (moving an object or image from a location to a new location), scaling (Enlarging or shrinking of an object), and rotation (Rotating the object in clockwise/counterclockwise directions). The image matrix can be multiplied with these matrices given in Table 8.4 to create the required effect. These operations are useful in deep learning applications and also for creating new images for data augmentation. These operations create new samples that make the deep learning algorithms more robust.

Table 8.4 Image Geometrical Operations

Image Operation	Mathematical Representation	Description
Translation	$[x',y',1] = \begin{pmatrix} 1 & 0 & \delta x \\ 0 & 1 & \delta y \\ 0 & 0 & 1 \end{pmatrix} [x,y,1]^T$	The translation is the movement of the image to a new location.

Image Operation	Mathematical Representation	Description
Scaling	$[x',y',1]=\begin{pmatrix} Sx & 0 & 0 \\ 0 & Sy & 0 \\ 0 & 0 & 1 \end{pmatrix}[x,y,1]^T$	Scaling means enlarging and shrinking the image. Here, a and y are the coordinates of the image and x' and y' are the new coordinate points.
Rotation	**x-axis** $[x',y',1]=\begin{pmatrix} \cos\theta & -\sin\theta & 0 \\ \sin\theta & \cos\theta & 0 \\ 0 & 0 & 1 \end{pmatrix}[x,y,1]^T$	An image can be rotated by degrees such as 90°, 180°, or 270°. By changing the sign of the degree, one can have the counterclockwise rotation of the image.
	Y-axis $[x',y',1]=\begin{pmatrix} \cos\theta & -\sin\theta & 0 \\ \sin\theta & \cos\theta & 0 \\ 0 & 0 & 1 \end{pmatrix}[x,y,1]^T$	Rotation along the y-axis.

An original and its rotated image by 90 degrees right is shown in Figure 8.4 as an illustration.

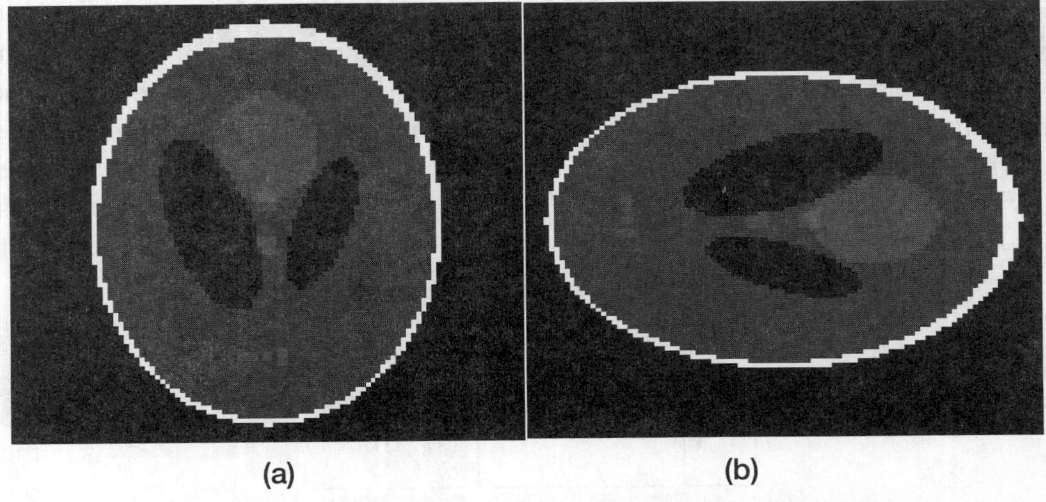

(a) (b)

Figure 8.4 (a) Original Image (b) Rotated Right by 90 Degrees

8.3.4 Additional Operations for Data Augmentation

Mirror or Reflection Operation

This function creates the reflection of the object in a plane mirror. The function returns an image in which the pixels are reversed. This operation is useful for creating an image in the desired order and for comparisons. The reflected object is the same size as the original object, but the object is in the opposite quadrant. In the homogeneous coordinate system, the matrices for reflection can be given, as shown in Table 8.5. The images can be multiplied by these matrices to get the desired result.

Table 8.5 Matrices for Mirror Operation

No	Reflection	Matrix
1	x-, y-, z-axis	$R_{y-axis} = \begin{pmatrix} -1 & 0 & 0 \\ 0 & 1 & 0 \\ 0 & 0 & 1 \end{pmatrix}; R_{x-axis} = \begin{pmatrix} 1 & 0 & 0 \\ 0 & -1 & 0 \\ 0 & 0 & 1 \end{pmatrix}; R_{origin} = \begin{pmatrix} -1 & 0 & 0 \\ 0 & -1 & 0 \\ 0 & 0 & 1 \end{pmatrix}$
2	Along a line	$R_{y=x} = \begin{pmatrix} 0 & 1 & 0 \\ 1 & 0 & 0 \\ 0 & 0 & 1 \end{pmatrix}; R_{y=-x} = \begin{pmatrix} 0 & -1 & 0 \\ -1 & 0 & 0 \\ 0 & 0 & 1 \end{pmatrix}$

Shearing

Shearing is a transformation that produces a distortion of shape. This operation can be applied either in the x-direction or the y-direction. Shearing can be done using the following matrices shown in Table 8.6. The images can be multiplied by these matrices to get the desired result.

Table 8.6 Matrices for Shear Operation

No	Reflection	Matrix
1	x-axis	$\begin{pmatrix} 1 & \lambda_x & 0 \\ 0 & 1 & 0 \\ 0 & 0 & 1 \end{pmatrix}$

No	Reflection	Matrix
2.	y-axis	$\begin{pmatrix} 1 & 0 & 0 \\ \lambda_y & 1 & 0 \\ 0 & 0 & 1 \end{pmatrix}$

Image Cropping

Cropping and resizing is one of the most important preprocessing tasks. This cropping is done by resizing the image dimensions. In Figure 8.5a, an original image is shown, and its cropped version is shown in Figure 8.5b.

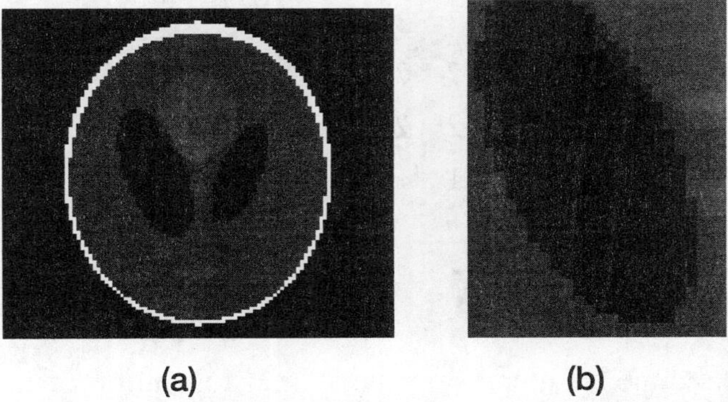

(a) (b)

Figure 8.5 (a) Original and (b) its cropped image

8.4 Downsampling and Upsampling

The quality of the image is determined by the resolution that depends on the spatial resolution. Resolution is the ability of the imaging system to produce minor discernible details.

8.4.1 Image Downsampling

Image downsampling is the reduction of resolution in the image by dropping the alternate pixels. The downsampling can be done by image filtering also. The simplest way is to drop the Nth pixel, where N is the downsampling factor. Downsampling is used to create a low-resolution image from the high-resolution image. Many deep learning algorithms like U-net and GAN use the concept of downsampling.

Example 8.1: Consider the image [1,2,3,8]. Create a downsampled image.

Solution:

One way of downsampling is to take the average of the neighboring pixels as

$$[1 \quad 2 \quad 3 \quad 8] = \left[\frac{1+2}{2} \quad \frac{3+8}{2}\right] = [1.5 \quad 5.5]$$

Or, the simple way is to drop the alternate pixels as

$$[1 \quad 2 \quad 3 \quad 8] = [1 \quad 3]$$

The same logic can be extended for 2D images also, as shown below:

$$\begin{pmatrix} 3 & 3 & 3 & 3 \\ 7 & 7 & 7 & 7 \\ 2 & 2 & 2 & 2 \\ 1 & 1 & 1 & 1 \end{pmatrix} \Rightarrow \begin{pmatrix} 3 & 3 \\ 2 & 2 \end{pmatrix}$$

8.4.2 Image Upsampling

Image upsampling is done by increasing the spatial resolution of the image using interpolation techniques like nearest-neighbor, bilinear, and bi-cubic interpolation. The zooming operation uses the image upsampling technique.

Example 8.2: Given the image, $F = [2\ 1\ 3\ 4]$. Upsample the image.

Solution

The image can be flattened as

$$F = [2\ 1\ 3\ 4]$$

Add zero as follows. It can be observed that the output would be (2*x* original number of samples)-1

$$F = [2\ 0\ 1\ 0\ 3\ 0\ 4] = \left[2 \quad \frac{2+1}{2} \quad 1 \quad \frac{1+3}{2} \quad 3 \quad \frac{3+4}{2} \quad 4\right] = [2\ 1.5\ 1\ 2\ 3\ 3.5\ 4]$$

Upsampling can be achieved by moving the average filter and applying a low-pass filter.

8.5 Convolution Operations

In deep learning, image convolution is one of the most important operations for deep learning. Convolutional neural networks are based on convolution operators only. Filters are also called spatial masks, kernels, templates, and windows. The spatial mask is convolved with the image to achieve the required smoothing or sharpening effect in the images or to extract useful features. A convolution is a mathematical operation that involves sliding the filter over the image and computing the dot product between the filter and the overlapped regions. The resulting image is called a feature map.

A sample 3 × 3 spatial mask is given below:

$$\begin{pmatrix} w_1 & w_2 & w_3 \\ w_4 & w_5 & w_6 \\ w_7 & w_8 & w_9 \end{pmatrix}$$

Here, w_1 to w_9 are mask weights. This mask is placed over the image, and the convolution operation is applied. Convolution is an operation that works on a group of input pixels of the given image and image mask and computes the resultant modified image by using the add and shift operation. The algorithm for convolution is given below:

(i) Superimpose a kernel or filter on the image.

(ii) Slide the image filter over the image.

(iii) Perform element-wise multiplication of the weights of filters and images and sum the element-wise products (or sum of dot products) to produce the output value in the resultant image called a feature map.

(iv) Repeat steps 1-3 for all the locations of the image by shifting the mask from left to right and top to bottom.

The convolution operation is useful for dimensionality reduction and for extracting the image features. The following numerical example illustrates the application of convolution operation.

Example 8.3: Consider a 1D data $I = [1,3,2,4,6]$ and kernel $F = [1,1]$ perform the convolution operation with stride = 1.

Solution: The 1D data = $[1,3,2,4,6]$ and Kernel $F = [1,1]$. The result is shown in Figure 8.6.

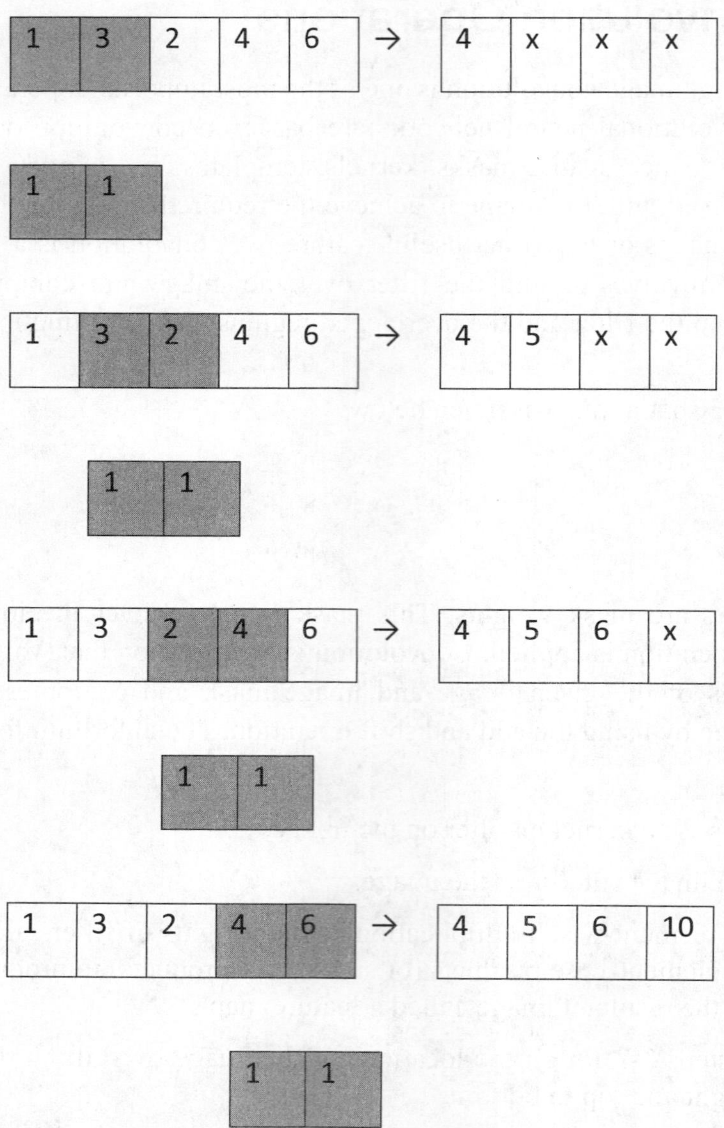

Figure 8.6 Application of Convolution

The result of the convolutional operation is [3,5.6,10].

Example 8.4: Consider the following image:

$$\begin{pmatrix} 2 & 4 & 3 & 4 \\ 6 & 8 & 10 & 12 \\ 14 & 11 & 8 & 9 \\ 6 & 6 & 3 & 2 \end{pmatrix} \text{ And mask } \begin{pmatrix} 1 & 0 \\ 0 & 1 \end{pmatrix}, \text{ Show the results of the convolution.}$$

Solution:

The convolution is obtained as shown in Table 4.6.

$$\begin{pmatrix} \boxed{2 \quad 4} & 3 & 4 \\ \boxed{6 \quad 8} & 10 & 12 \\ 14 \quad 11 & 8 & 9 \\ 6 \quad 6 & 3 & 2 \end{pmatrix} \Rightarrow \begin{pmatrix} 10 & ? & ? \\ ? & ? & ? \\ ? & ? & ? \end{pmatrix}$$

Shifting the mask right yields the following results:

$$\begin{pmatrix} 2 & \boxed{4 \quad 3} & 4 \\ 6 & \boxed{8 \quad 10} & 12 \\ 14 & 11 \quad 8 & 9 \\ 6 & 6 \quad 3 & 2 \end{pmatrix} \Rightarrow \begin{pmatrix} 10 & 14 & ? \\ ? & ? & ? \\ ? & ? & ? \end{pmatrix}$$

Shifting the mask right further yields the following results:

$$\begin{pmatrix} 2 & 4 & \boxed{3 \quad 4} \\ 6 & 8 & \boxed{10 \quad 12} \\ 14 & 11 & 8 \quad 9 \\ 6 & 6 & 3 \quad 2 \end{pmatrix} \Rightarrow \begin{pmatrix} 10 & 14 & 15 \\ ? & ? & ? \\ ? & ? & ? \end{pmatrix}$$

Lowering the mask down and applying the convolution operation gives the following results:

$$\begin{pmatrix} 2 \quad 4 & 3 & 4 \\ \boxed{6 \quad 8} & 10 & 12 \\ \boxed{14 \quad 11} & 8 & 9 \\ 6 \quad 6 & 3 & 2 \end{pmatrix} \Rightarrow \begin{pmatrix} 10 & 14 & 15 \\ 17 & ? & ? \\ ? & ? & ? \end{pmatrix}$$

Shifting the mask right yields the following result:

$$\begin{pmatrix} 2 & 4 \quad 3 & 4 \\ 6 & \boxed{8 \quad 10} & 12 \\ 14 & \boxed{11 \quad 8} & 9 \\ 6 & 6 \quad 3 & 2 \end{pmatrix} \Rightarrow \begin{pmatrix} 10 & 14 & 15 \\ 17 & 16 & ? \\ ? & ? & ? \end{pmatrix}$$

Shifting the mask right further yields the following results:

$$\begin{pmatrix} 2 & 4 & 3 & 4 \\ 6 & 8 & \boxed{10} & \boxed{12} \\ 14 & 11 & \boxed{8} & \boxed{9} \\ 6 & 6 & 3 & 2 \end{pmatrix} \Rightarrow \begin{pmatrix} 10 & 14 & 15 \\ 17 & 16 & 19 \\ ? & ? & ? \end{pmatrix}$$

Lowering the mask down and applying the convolution operation gives the following results:

$$\begin{pmatrix} 2 & 4 & 3 & 4 \\ 6 & 8 & 10 & 12 \\ \boxed{14} & \boxed{11} & 8 & 9 \\ \boxed{6} & \boxed{6} & 3 & 2 \end{pmatrix} \Rightarrow \begin{pmatrix} 10 & 14 & 15 \\ 17 & 16 & 19 \\ 20 & ? & ? \end{pmatrix}$$

Shifting the mask right further yields the following results:

$$\begin{pmatrix} 2 & 4 & 3 & 4 \\ 6 & 8 & 10 & 12 \\ 14 & \boxed{11} & \boxed{8} & 9 \\ 6 & \boxed{6} & \boxed{3} & 2 \end{pmatrix} \Rightarrow \begin{pmatrix} 10 & 14 & 15 \\ 17 & 16 & 19 \\ 20 & 14 & ? \end{pmatrix}$$

Shifting the mask right further yields the following results:

$$\begin{pmatrix} 2 & 4 & 3 & 4 \\ 6 & 8 & 10 & 12 \\ 14 & 11 & \boxed{8} & \boxed{9} \\ 6 & 6 & \boxed{3} & \boxed{2} \end{pmatrix} \Rightarrow \begin{pmatrix} 10 & 14 & 15 \\ 17 & 16 & 19 \\ 20 & 14 & 10 \end{pmatrix}$$

Since all locations of the image are processed, the convolution operation stops.

8.5.1 Variants of Convolution Operation

Dilated Convolution

Downsampling is done in deep learning algorithms like U-Net by atrous convolution (or Dilated convolution or Strided Convolution). The reason is that this convolution is less lossy while preserving the wider view of the image. Atrous convolution is a variant of covolution. Its word is derived from the French word "trou, " meaning a hole. So, unlike a normal convolution, the kernels of the atrous convolution have their elements placed at regular intervals, skipping some positions.

This convolution type allows the input data area to grow without increasing the parameters. This type of convolution is useful to capture objects at different scales. This spacing is controlled by a parameter called dilation rate. A dilation rate greater than 1 indicates the normal convolution process, and a dilation rate greater than 1 introduces the gaps in the kernel. If the dilation rate is higher, then the receptive field is larger.

Example 8.5: Consider a one-dimensional mask F = [1,2,3,5,7] and the kernel K be [1 1 1]. Show the output of atrous convolution.

Solution

Apply the convolution as it is we get

$$1\times 1+1\times 2+1\times 3=6$$
$$1\times 2+1\times 3+1\times 5=10$$
$$1\times 3+1\times 5+1\times 7=15$$

The computations are the same as convolution. The difference is in atrous convolution; the result is [6, ?, 10,? , 15]. Here are the positions,? , will be adjusted based on the padding operation.

Transposition Convolution

Deconvolution is also known as upsampling or transposition convolution. Transposed convolution is also called up-convolution or fractionally strided convolution. The transposition or transposed convolution takes a low-resolution feature map and gives an output in higher resolution. Here, zeros are introduced between the values, and a convolution operation is applied. The sliding filter is applied over the image and spreads values across the larger area.

The stride in the transposed convolution is equivalent to the dilation rate in atrous convolution.

8.5.2 Convolution and Preprocessing

Image enhancement is one of the most important classes of algorithms. The captured image may often not be of good quality because of noise, poor brightness, contrast, blur, or artifact.

(i) *Noise* is any unwanted signal. It is an unnecessary disturbance that causes fluctuations in the pixel values.

(ii) *Blur* is a disturbance that makes the image difficult to interpret. Blur is the systematic distortion of the image.

(iii) *Artifacts* are features of the object that are not true. These are observational errors, including dust and scratches on the image surface, complicating accurate interpretation.

Therefore, Image preprocessing algorithms focus on these problems in the acquired images. Some of the applications of convolution operations are listed below:

1. Image Filters for Denoising

Image filters are used to remove the unwanted information present in the image, such as noises, or to amplify the image features present in the image. Low-pass filters can be used to remove noise. The low pass filter removes each pixel with the average pixel values covered by the convolution mask and can be useful to remove the impulse and blur noise. All these filters are useful to remove the noise present in the image. All these filters can be applied using convolution operation. The matrices for the low-pass and high-pass filters are given in Table 8.7.

Table 8.7 Image Filters Masks

No.	Type of Filters	Spatial Masks Used
1.	High-pass Filter	$\begin{pmatrix} 0 & 1 & 0 \\ 1 & -4 & 1 \\ 0 & 1 & 0 \end{pmatrix}$
2.	Low-pass Filter	$\frac{1}{9}\begin{pmatrix} 1 & 1 & 1 \\ 1 & 1 & 1 \\ 1 & 1 & 1 \end{pmatrix}$

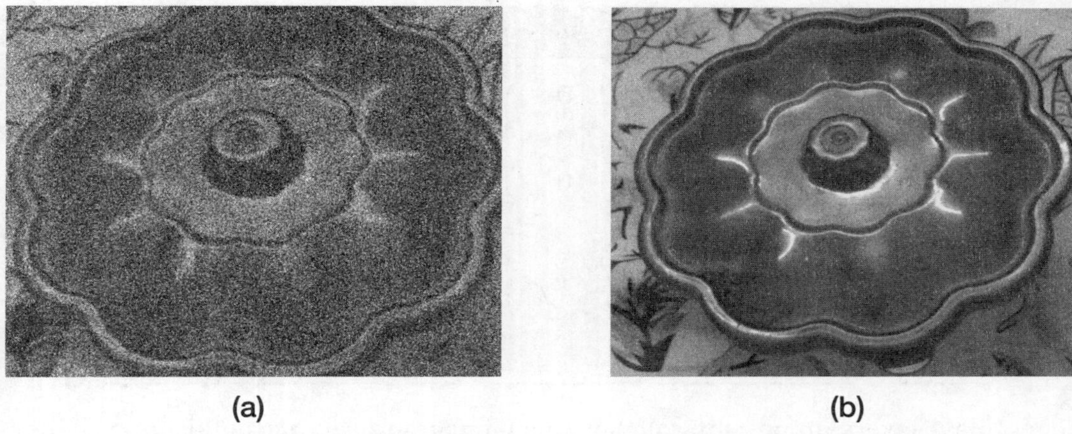

Figure 8.7 (a) Original Noise Image (b) Box Filter Used to Remove the Noise

It can be observed that the low pass filter removes the noise present in Figure 8.6 to get a clear image, as shown in Figure 8.7b. Denoising algorithms play an important role in deep learning applications like Generative adversarial networks for creating a new image.

8.5.3 Convolution and Feature Extraction

Image masks extract useful features like horizontal and vertical lines, points, and corners. These features are extracted by convolution operation by applying the mask to the image whose kernels and weights determine how important the pixel is in forming the important features. The following table 8.8. illustrates the masks used for extracting the points and lines of the image.

Table 8.8 Masks Extract the Points and Lines in the Images

No.	Type of Filters	Spatial Masks Used
1.	Point Extraction	$\begin{pmatrix} -1 & -1 & -1 \\ -1 & 8 & -1 \\ -1 & -1 & -1 \end{pmatrix}$

No.	Type of Filters	Spatial Masks Used
2.	Line Extraction	$\begin{pmatrix} -1 & 0 & 1 \\ -1 & 0 & 1 \\ -1 & 0 & 1 \end{pmatrix}$ for vertical lines and $\begin{pmatrix} -1 & -1 & -1 \\ 0 & 0 & 0 \\ 1 & 1 & 1 \end{pmatrix}$ for horizontal lines

Edges play a very important role in many image-processing applications. They provide an outline of the object. When the edge is detected, unnecessary details are removed, while only the important structural information is retained. In short, an edge is a local concept that represents only significant intensity transitions. Edge detection aims to find the difference between two neighbourhood pixels. If the pixels have the same value, the difference is 0. This value indicates that there is no transition between the pixels. The non-zero difference indicates the presence of an edge point. Edge detectors can be viewed as gradient calculators. The gradient of an image $f(x, y)$ at a location (x, y) is a vector that consists of the partial derivatives $f(x, y)$ as follows:

$$\nabla f(x,y) = \begin{bmatrix} \dfrac{\partial f(x,y)}{\partial x} \\ \\ \dfrac{\partial f(x,y)}{\partial y} \end{bmatrix}$$

or simply

$$\nabla f(x,y) = \begin{bmatrix} g_x \\ \\ g_y \end{bmatrix}$$

where $g_x = \left[\dfrac{\partial f(x,y)}{\partial x}\right]$ and $g_y = \left[\dfrac{\partial f(x,y)}{\partial y}\right]$. The magnitude of this vector, generally referred to as the gradient ∇f, is $\nabla f(x,y) = \text{mag}(\nabla f(x,y)) = \left[(g_x)^2 + (g_y)^2\right]^{1/2}$.

The edge magnitude indicates edge strength. The direction of the gradient vector is useful in detecting a sudden change in image intensity. The gradient direction can be given as

$$\theta = \tan^{-1}(\frac{g_x}{g_y})$$

Some of the important useful masks are given below in Table 8.9.

Table 8.9 First-Order Edge Detectors

S.No.	Name of the Edge Operator	Masks Used
1.	Roberts Operator	$g_x = \begin{pmatrix} -1 & 0 \\ 0 & 1 \end{pmatrix}$ and $g_y = \begin{pmatrix} 0 & -1 \\ 1 & 0 \end{pmatrix}$
2.	Prewitt Operator	$g_x = \begin{pmatrix} -1 & -1 & -1 \\ 0 & 0 & 0 \\ 1 & 1 & 1 \end{pmatrix}$ and $g_y = \begin{pmatrix} -1 & 0 & 1 \\ -1 & 0 & 0 \\ -1 & 0 & 1 \end{pmatrix}$
3	Sobel Operator	$g_x = \begin{pmatrix} -1 & 2 & -1 \\ 0 & 0 & 0 \\ 1 & 2 & 1 \end{pmatrix}$ and $g_y = \begin{pmatrix} -1 & 0 & 1 \\ -2 & 0 & 2 \\ -1 & 0 & 1 \end{pmatrix}$

Figure 8.8 illustrates the application of a Sobel edge operator of the original image.

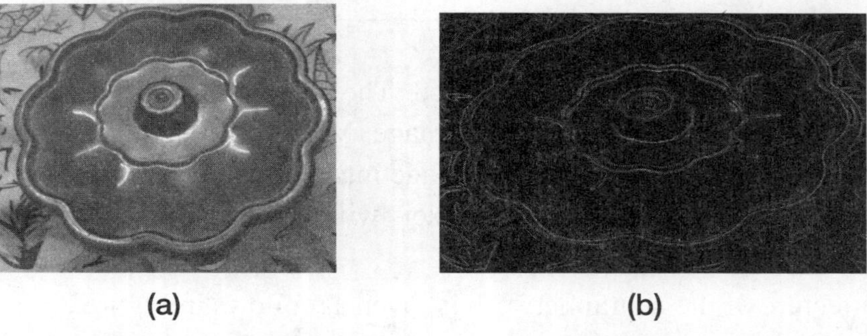

(a) (b)

Figure. 8.8 (a) Origianl Image (b) Edges of the original image

8.6 Image Classification using Multilayer Neural Network

Here, the simple way of image classification is illustrated. MLP consists of three layers. They are the Input layer, Hidden layer, and Output layer. Let us take, for example, a MNIST project. The project is about classifying digits 0-9 (10 Classes), and its details are given in Box 8.3. The neural network used to classify the MNIST image is a fully connected network (or called dense) because every neuron in the layer is connected to every other neuron in the subsequent layers. It is also a feedforward network as the graph of the neural network is acyclic and does not have any loops.

Box 8.3 MNIST Dataset

MNIST-Modified National Institute of Standard and Technology Database. MNIST was created by Yann LeCun, Corinna Cortes, and Christopher J.C. Burges. It is a benchmark machine learning and Computer Vision dataset for evaluating machine learning models for handwritten digit recognition tasks.

It consists of a handwritten set of handwritten characters 0-9 labelled 60,000 training and 10000 test grayscale images of size 28 x 28. Each pixel value is between 0 and 255, where 0 represents white and 255 represents black. The digits are in the center of the image. It is a simple and small dataset.

The image is acquired and pre-processed. The image in MNIST has a dimension of 28 X 28. Each image is a greyscale image. MLP can take data in one dimension only. So, the first step is to flatten the image into a single-dimensional vector of 784 elements, as there are 28 X 28 = 784 pixels will be there. This step is called image flattening.

The architecture of the neural network is given as follows in Figure 8.9.

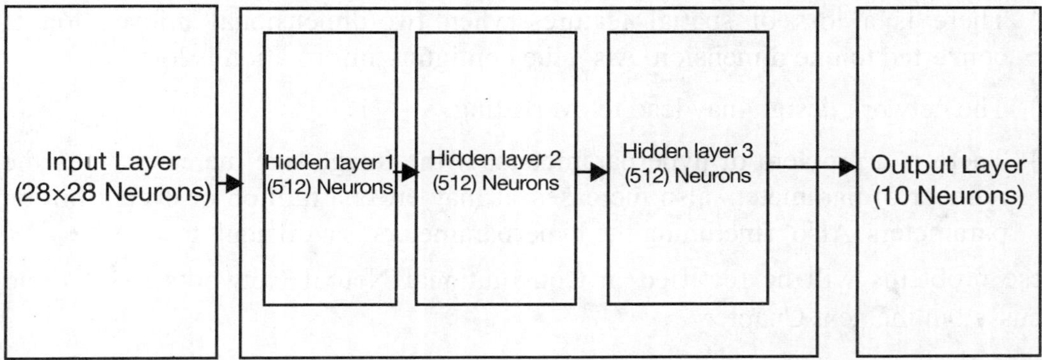

Figure 8.9 MLP for Image Classification

The neural network can use one or more hidden layers with the activation function reLU. The above neural network uses three hidden layers with 512 neurons. The number of layers and neurons would vary as per the design.

In the output layer, the number of nodes equals the number of classes. The output layer uses the softmax activation with 10 neurons that represent the digit 0-9. So, the summary of the network is

Input layer: 784 neurons

Hidden layer : 3 layers with 512 neurons

Output layer: 10 neurons

The activation function used in the hidden layer is ReLU, and the softmax is in the output layer.

The input data moves from the input layer to the output layer, and each layer output is the input for the next layer. The learning here is the adjustment of the weights and biases of the neurons. The loss function categorical cross-entropy is used as the measure of the difference between the true label and the output of the neural network. Optimizers like SGD or ADAM are used to update the parameters of the neural network using the backpropagation algorithm.

What are the drawbacks of Multilayer neural network-based classification? There are three disadvantages to this approach.

(i) There is a loss of spatial features when two-dimensional information is converted to one dimension. Also, the contiguity information is lost.

(ii) The network design may lead to overfitting.

(iii) There is a problem of hyperparameters. If the image size increases, then the number of parameters also increases. It may cross a million or even a billion parameters. Also, finetuning the hyperparameters is a difficult task.

These problems will be rectified in Convolutional Neural Networks (CNN) and discussed in the next Chapter.

Summary

1. Machine vision aims to provide vision capability to computers.
2. Visual perception is the art of perceiving patterns and objects.
3. The image processing pipeline includes image acquisition, preprocessing, image segmentation, extraction of image features, and finally, pattern recognition.
4. The images are of three types – greyscale, binary, and colour.
5. Data augmentation is a step of increasing the number of samples.
6. Image operations can be arithmetic operations, logical operations, and geometric operations.
7. Upsampling and downsampling algorithms are important to increase or decrease the number of pixels using image replication or interpolation. Deconvolution is also called upsampling.
8. Convolution takes a mask and an image and generates a new modified image using a shift-and-add operation. The convolution operator is useful for image preprocessing and feature extraction. Convolution operations help to extract the image features like points, lines, corners, and edges.
9. Image filters rename unnecessary information like noise and highlight some image features.
10. The edges can be extracted from the image using image gradients. Some of the edge detection operators are Roberts, Sobel, and Prewitt,
11. Multilayer Perceptron is useful for classifying an image. Multilayer perceptron takes a 2D image and converts it to a one-dimensional vector called image flattening. Multilayer perceptron uses a hidden layer and an output layer with neurons that equal the classes.

12. Some of the problems of multilayer perceptron-based classification are the loss of spatial information due to converting a 2D image to a one-dimensional vector and the increase in the number of hyperparameters.

Glossary

1. Computer vision – A computer domain that enables the computers computer to interpret visual information of the real world.
2. Image processing – A computer domain concerned with the preprocessing for enhancing the image quality and the extraction of features for pattern recognition tasks.
3. Pixel – A picture element present in the intersection of a row and column. A building block of the image.
4. Intensity – The pixel value is called intensity. The amount of colour or light information is quantified as a value.
5. Brightness – The overall brightness or darkness (or average pixel value) of the image.
6. Contrast – The finer details of the image that distinguish the image from the other objects present in the image.
7. Bit-depth – Bit-depth is the number of bits necessary to encode the image.
8. Spatial resolution – This is characterized as the number of pixels in an image.
9. Binary image – An image whose pixels have value – 0 or 1.
10. Greyscale image – An image whose pixel values range between 0-255. It uses 8 bits to encode a pixel.
11. Colour image – A 3-tier image, where 24 bits represent colours.
12. Channel – A representation of a specific colour and attribute.
13. Convolution – A mathematical operation that involves a sliding filter over the image and computing the dot product between the filter and overlapped regions. The resultant image is called a feature map.
14. Deconvolution – An upsampling operation that reverses the results of convolution.
15. Translation – Translation is the movement of an image from one location to a new location.
16. Scaling – The enlarging and shrinking of an image is called scaling.

17. **Rotation** – The rotation of an image is an operation where the image is rotated by a certain degree in clockwise or counterclockwise directions.
18. **Zooming** – The enlargement of an image is called zooming.
19. **Mirroring operation** – The mirroring operation that reflects the image in a plane mirror to produce a result.
20. **Convolution** – The convolution takes an image and mask and generates a new modified image using a shift-add operation.
21. **Noise** – Any unwanted signal is called noise. Blur is a systematic distortion of an image is called a blur. An artifact is an observational error in the image, such as scratches or dust in a medical image.
22. **Image filtering** – A filter that removes unnecessary noise and highlights some of the features.
23. **Edges** – The edge point is one with a transition point of intensity.
24. **Image flattening** – The process of converting a 2D image to a one-dimensional vector for multilayer perceptron is called image flattening.

Short Questions

1. Distinguish between computer vision and image processing.
2. List out the steps in image processing.
3. Why do preprocessing is necessary for image processing?
4. What is the difference between brightness and contrast?
5. List out some of the image processing operations.
6. What is the difference between scaling and zooming?
7. What is a convolution process?
8. List out the purposes of image filters.
9. Why is edge an important feature?
10. What is image flattening?

Long Questions

1. Explain the image processing pipeline.
2. Explain in detail the zooming process.
3. Explain the convolution process in detail.
4. Explain the concept of image gradients and their role in edge detection.

5. Explain multilayer perceptron for image classification.

Numerical problems

1. Assume a digital image whose dimensions are 256 X 256. What number of pixels would be if the image is greyscale or colour?
2. If the above image of Q1 is to be transmitted across a channel with 100 Bps, how much time it would take for image transmission.
3. Consider the image

   $F = \begin{pmatrix} 10 & 12 \\ 22 & 10 \end{pmatrix}$, perform translation by x-axis by ten units and y-axis by 15 units.

4. Consider the image

   $F = \begin{pmatrix} 10 & 2 \\ 22 & 13 \end{pmatrix}$, scale it three times in both x- and y-axis.

5. Consider the image

   $F = \begin{pmatrix} 10 & 2 \\ 22 & 13 \end{pmatrix}$, Rotate the image by 45 and 90 degrees clockwise and counterclockwise.

6. Consider the image

   $F = \begin{pmatrix} 1 & 2 & 4 \\ 1 & 3 & 5 \\ 1 & 6 & 7 \end{pmatrix}$ and mask $K = \begin{pmatrix} 1 & 0 \\ 0 & 1 \end{pmatrix}$. Perform convolution operation.

7. Consider the image

   $F = \begin{pmatrix} 1 & 2 & 4 \\ 1 & 3 & 5 \\ 1 & 6 & 7 \end{pmatrix}$ and with a new mask $K = \begin{pmatrix} 1 & 1 \\ 1 & 1 \end{pmatrix}$ and perform convolution.

8. Consider the image

   $F = \begin{pmatrix} 1 & 8 & 1 & 3 \\ 2 & 7 & 2 & 7 \\ 3 & 6 & 3 & 4 \\ 4 & 5 & 5 & 2 \end{pmatrix}$ and with mask $K = \begin{pmatrix} 1 & 1 \\ 1 & 1 \end{pmatrix}$ and perform convolution.

Crossword

Across

1. The number of bits that are required to encode the image is called __________.
4. The representation of colour or specific attribute is called a __________.
6. The overall brightness or darkness of the image characterized by the average pixel is called __________.
8. Sobel is useful for extracting __________.
9. The value is 0 or 1 in __________ image
12. The unwanted signal is called __________.
14. The building block of a digital image is called __________.
15. Deconvolution __________ the values to inverse convolution operation.
16. Feature engineering is __________ in image processing.
17. The other name for pixel is called picture element. (true/false)
18. The movement of an image from one location to another location is called __________.
19. The finer details that distinguish one object from the surrounding are called __________.
21. The rotation operations are useful in creating new samples called __________augmentation.
23. The spatial filter is also called as __________.

24. Convolution operation involves a sliding __________ over the image to perform dot product operation.
25. Image __________ are used to remove the noise.

Down

2. Image processing goals are image ______ and interpretation of image.
3. Colour image is ________ tier image.
5. The domain that deals with the interpretation of the visual world is called computer __________.
7. A point where there is a transition of intensity is called _________ point.
10. The greyscale ranges from 0 to 255 in __________ image.
11. The enlargement of an image is also called as __________.
13. Image __________ converts a 2D data into a single dimensional data.
20. The number of pixels characterizes spatial resolution. (true/false)
22. The fully connected layer is called as __________ layer.

Jumbled Sentences

D	A	T	A	T	Q	U	Q	G	C	N	L	U	R	K	O	G	F	V	Q	W	X	D	S	Y
I	H	Y	M	Z	P	C	S	E	U	I	C	O	N	T	R	A	S	T	J	J	N	X	U	L
K	G	E	D	B	R	I	G	H	T	N	E	S	S	D	N	W	Y	G	G	U	D	I	E	D
E	R	J	T	X	J	R	R	W	P	I	A	J	V	I	G	H	D	O	H	Q	C	X	X	E
R	A	A	R	H	W	E	K	N	W	G	R	W	Z	S	P	R	E	A	D	S	I	D	H	N
N	Y	Z	U	V	G	Q	J	C	H	A	N	N	E	L	N	C	X	S	W	P	W	K	Y	S
E	S	F	E	E	N	H	A	N	C	E	M	E	N	T	Q	U	E	B	K	L	H	A	G	E
L	C	Z	I	R	G	H	N	N	G	E	D	G	E	S	M	Z	J	P	T	Q	G	Z	H	N
I	A	O	N	L	V	A	K	J	Q	M	C	A	Z	Z	T	E	M	A	N	U	A	L	F	X
X	L	O	T	O	T	D	Y	Y	D	T	G	H	D	F	L	A	T	T	E	N	I	N	G	M
A	E	M	F	F	I	E	W	B	I	T	D	E	P	T	H	F	T	S	B	R	T	S	X	Q
B	T	I	L	S	N	S	R	L	L	S	B	N	F	I	L	T	E	R	S	Z	W	T	B	P
N	B	N	N	Y	U	T	E	K	O	Z	S	W	B	S	N	X	U	W	N	S	T	F	J	H
T	F	G	E	N	L	T	E	T	R	A	N	S	L	A	T	I	O	N	U	Z	H	B	B	Y
S	E	D	G	E	F	V	I	S	I	O	N	K	X	E	L	T	X	F	I	F	R	Z	T	C
Q	T	R	U	E	B	I	N	A	R	Y	I	M	A	G	E	J	F	R	J	S	E	A	R	H
L	E	M	J	D	T	W	C	C	Y	X	N	N	S	L	O	X	G	V	W	U	E	Y	A	L

vision	enhanement	pixel	true	brightness
contrast	bitdepth	true	binary image	greyscale
three	channel	filter	kernel	spreads
translation	data	zooming	noise	filters
edge	edges	manual	flatterning	dense

Convolutional Neural Networks

> Computer Vision is the automation of Human Visual System — **Jan Erik Solem**

Credits: © Jan Erik Solem

Image recognition is the fundamental component of computer vision, enabling machines to "see" and "identify" objects. In deep learning literature, the words Image classification and Image recognition are used interchangeably. Convolutional Neural Networks (CNN) play an important role in Image classification and help to solve many real-world problems. Hence, they impact many applications in the real world, and their impact on society in daily life is immense. This chapter focuses on the usage of convolutional neural networks for Image classification.

The learning objectives of this chapter are as follows:

- Understand the basics of convolutional neural networks.
- Understand the mathematics of convolution operation.
- Know the architecture of convolutional neural networks.
- Understand why parameters and hyperparameters are important.
- Know about LeNet-5 architecture.

9.1 Introduction to Convolutional Neural Networks (CNN)

Convolutional neural networks (CNN), called ConvNets, initiated the deep learning revolution. When it was initiated, CNN generated much interest in the society, which is the reason for deep learning revolution.

Computer vision tasks include image recognition. Image recognition is the ability of the system to identify objects, people, places, traffic signs, and actions within images. It involves detecting features or patterns in the image and classifying objects based on the extracted patterns. "Image recognition" and "Image Classification" are often used interchangeably in the deep learning approach. But there is a subtle difference between these two words. Image recognition is a much broader term that refers to image classification and object detection in the image. Image classification involves assigning a label to an image, and the labels are from categories, as shown in Figure 9.1.

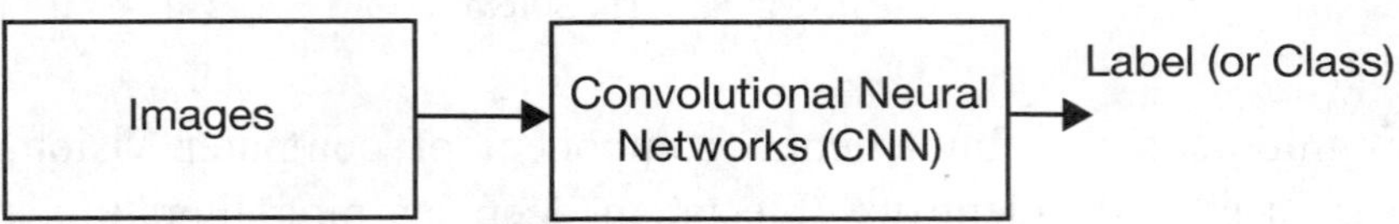

Figure 9.1 Image Classification

However, image recognition refers to identifying and labeling, often multiple objects, in the image (often termed object detection) associated with probability values. These probability values indicate the classifier's confidence about the detected object. One such example is shown in Figure 9.2.

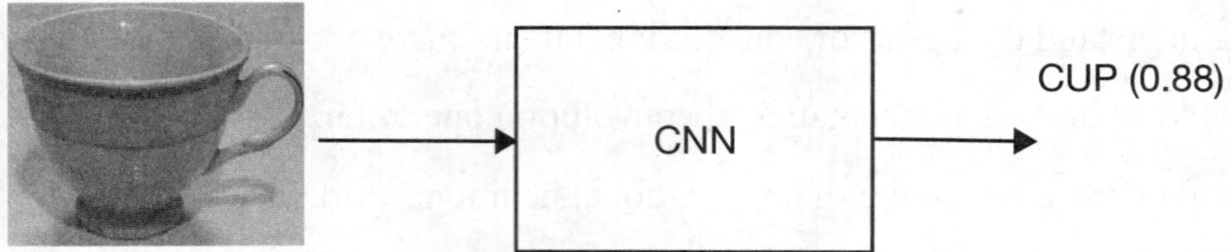

Figure 9.2 An Illustration of Image Classification

Figure 9.2 Illustrates the output of an image classifier where the input image is assigned a label "cup" with a value of 0.88. It indicates the confidence of the classifier in assigning the label.

The image classification using a multilayer network was discussed in Chapter 8. The training of deep nets is extremely slow, and the labeled datasets are few. Later, these limitations were overcome by the availability of big data. In 2010, many companies like Facebook, YouTube, and Twitter entered the scenario, and many datasets are available now. Also, the improvement in hardware in the form of GPU and TPU reduced the training time of the deep nets considerably. These advancements made CNN very effective in image classification. The history of CNN is given in Box 9.1.

Box 9.1 Evolution of CNN

The earliest inspiration for image recognition was Hubel and Wiesel's experiments. The roots of CNN are Neocognitron introduced by Kunihiko Fukushima in the early 1960s. The evolving Neocognitron resulted in LeNet, where Yann LeCun applied backpropagation algorithms to a neural network for digit recognition. This model was called LeNet-5. LeNet-5 is the first CNN that appeared in the Deep Learning revolution. LeNet-5 was introduced by Yann LeCun in 1998. The architecture was proposed by Yann LeCun, Leon Bottou, Yoshua Bengio, and Patrick Haffner in 1998.

LeNet marked a milestone in the history of deep learning by demonstrating the effectiveness of CNN in image recognition tasks.

LeNet-5 was designed to recognize digits specifically for handwritten numbers on the banks. Manual recognition is a time-consuming process CNN successfully demonstrated that it could automate it.

The revival of interest in deep learning was due to Quoc Lee, a Stanford University PhD student in 2011 who wanted to classify cat and dog images taken from YouTube thumbnails. He wanted to experiment the unsupervised learning without the labelling of the images. This project marked a renewed vigor in deep learning and Quoc Lee went on to become a researcher in the Google Brain project. His other contributions are CAPTCHA (Completely Automated Public Turing test to Tell Computers and Humans Apart) to verify whether the browser is a human or not and Duolingo, an app for learning languages that uses deep learning.

Some of the applications of Image classification are given in Box. 9.2.

Box 9.2 Applications of Image Classification

Image classification is useful for the following applications:

(i) Disease classification.
(ii) Object detection.
(iii) Semantic and Instance Segmentation (assigning labels to the pixels image).
(iv) Facial recognition in security applications.
(v) Handwriting Recognition like in LeNet-5.

(vi) Medical applications like object detection in X-ray, MRI, and CT images. Examples are tumor detection in CT images.

(vii) Object detection in autonomous vehicles like cars, trucks, roads, and pedestrians.

(viii) Visual image search.

9.2 Machine Learning Approach Vs. Deep Learning Approach

The basic difference between Machine Learning (ML) and Deep Learning (DL) classification is that feature extraction is done manually in machine learning. In contrast, in deep learning, it is done automatically. The image classification pipeline in machine learning is shown in Figure 9.3.

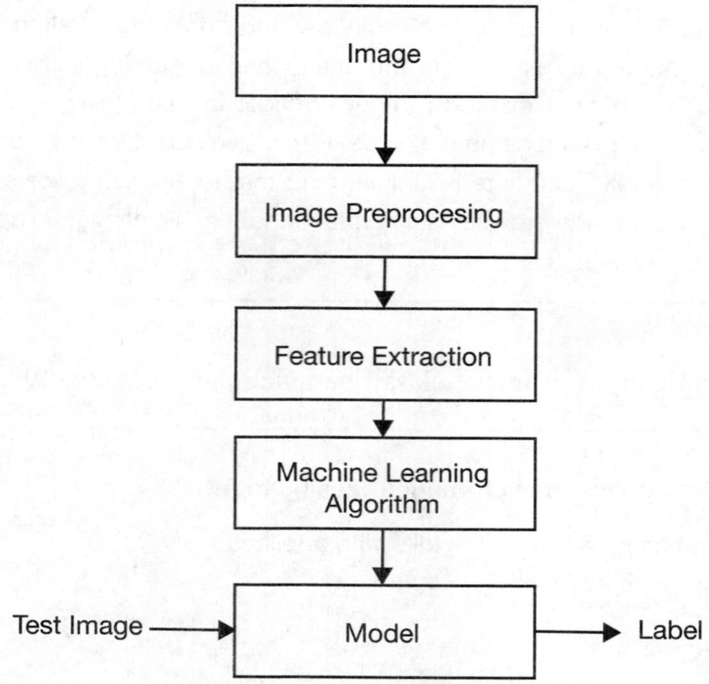

Figure 9.3 Image Classification Pipeline in Machine Learning

In machine learning, the given image is pre-processed first. As discussed in Chapter 8, the image's noise and artifacts are removed in the preprocessing stage to prepare a quality image for classification. If the given image has problems related to brightness and contrast, enhancements like contrast and brightness are done in the image preprocessing stage.

The important thing in machine learning-based image classification is that the features are extracted manually. This manual extraction of features is called feature engineering. Feature extraction quantifies features such as colour, spatial information, and texture. Feature Engineering in machine learning is a tougher task as it is

(i) Computationally very intensive.

(ii) Finding suitable features for certain problems is difficult.

Once the image features are extracted, the classifier, like SVM, is trained with these features to generate a model. The model then takes an unknown instance test image and generates a label.

The deep learning approach, on the other hand, automatically extracts the features. Feature extraction is done automatically in a deep learning approach thereby reducing the role of image feature engineering. As an option, manually extracted features can be added to enhance the performance. But mostly, it is optional. The feature maps are then fed to the fully connected neural network for generating a model. The model then takes an unknown test image and generates a label.

The deep learning approach to image classification is given below in Figure 9.4.

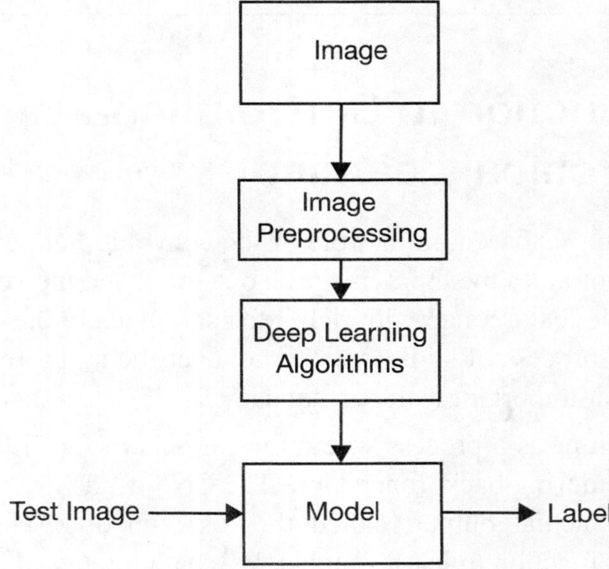

Figure 9.4 Deep Learning Approach for Image Classification

The differences between the machine learning approach and the deep learning approach-CNN are given in Box 9.3.

Box 9.3 Difference Between Deep Learning Approach and Machine Learning Approach

(i) Machine learning is a broader field, while deep learning is a narrower field.

(ii) In machine learning, the features are extracted manually and fed to the model for classification, whereas, in deep learning systems like CNN, the feature extraction is done automatically.

(iii) Deep learning models need more data than machine learning models to generate a good-quality model with better accuracy.

(iv) Deep learning models like CNN need more time for training and less time for testing for image classification compared to machine learning models.

(v) Deep learning models like CNN need higher-end machines to perform classification as the model performs feature extraction and classification.

(vi) In deep learning models like the CNN model, output interpretation is difficult as the hidden layers' role is yet to be discovered.

9.3 Introduction to Convolutional and Hierarchical Learning

Convolution learning is based on the role of the convolution operator. In CNN, the convolution operator takes the input image as one input and the kernel as the second input to produce the feature map with rich information about the features as output. Convolution is the process of sliding the kernel over the input image pixel by pixel to retrieve or extract important features that can classify the image.

Convolutional learning is a process where the weights of the filters in convolution layers are adjusted during backpropagation. The CNN finds the difference between the predicted and actual output, called the loss function. The neural network minimizes the loss function to learn weights. By changing the weights of the filters, the neural network learns to identify and extract the relevant features from the image for the given task.

CNN is inspired by the works of Hubel and Wiesel experiments (Refer Box. 9.4).

Box 9.4 Hubel and Wiesel Experiments

David Hubel and Torsten Wiesel conducted experiments in the 1950s and 1960s to "understand how we see.". This experiment involved the study of the brain's visual cortex. In 1981, Hubel and Wiesel received the Nobel Prize in Physiology and Medicine. This Nobel prize was shared with Roger Sperry for his research on the cerebral hemisphere's functional specialization.

This research proved to be a cornerstone in the brain's visual information research and the foundation of CNN. They focused on the cortex in cats and monkeys to understand how the visual parts of the brain work. Their main contribution is how the brain processes visual information in steps.

Their experiments proved certain facts listed below:

(i) Certain neurons respond to specific types of visual stimuli. For example, certain neurons are responsive to edges and lines. These are simple cells. For simple cells, Imagine a cell that gets excited only by vertical lines and not other visual stimuli say, diagonal lines.

(ii) These features serve as boundary blocks for more complex patterns. Their work demonstrated the hierarchical nature of the visual process. So, like a puzzle, the simple and complex cells cooperate to see the whole scene.

(iii) They also concluded that certain hindrance (such as covering the cat's eye) in critical periods impairs normal vision capabilities. If the young animal does not get visual experience during its primitive period, its visual experience will be damaged.

The transition from image to features in CNN is complex over many layers. This increased performance because CNN mimics the human brain's visual information processing. Human visual image processing is also hierarchical.

9.3.1 Hierarchical Learning

Hierarchical learning is the fundamental aspect of CNN's success in computer vision tasks.

Hierarchical learning is the process of learning representations or features hierarchically. These features range from simple to complex. Hierarchical learning facilitates CNN's automatic learning of multiple levels of abstraction, from simple to complex, as layers progress (Refer to Box 9.5).

(i) **Lower Layer:** The entry-level convolutional layers capture basic patterns like edges, colours, and simple texture, as each filter activates a visual feature. These captured features are generic.

(ii) **Middle Layer:** The middle-level convolutional layers combine basic features to get more complex features. The complex features are like shapes and specific features.

(iii) **Higher-level Features:** These higher-level convolutional layers synthesize the complex features to identify the whole object or scenes, and these features are highly specific to tasks like identifying particular plants or animals.

Box 9.5 Characteristics of Hierarchical Learning

The characteristics of Hierarchical Learning:

(i) The layered structures of CNN facilitate progressive learning. Progressive learning is an incremental learning that builds new features using the features gathered from the previous layers. This enables the composition of simple features to form complex features.

(ii) Automatic feature extraction, composition, and feature engineering.

(iii) Efficiency, generalization, and versatility.

9.4 Convolutional Neural Network Vs. Shallow Networks

Why does CNN perform better than shallow networks? This section focuses on the important points that differentiate CNN from shallow neural networks.

9.4.1 Differences in Architecture

There are differences between CNN and shallow networks in the architecture. A shallow network has few layers. The layers include input layers, and few hidden layers, and output layers. All the neurons are fully connected. In short, every neuron in a layer is connected to all neurons of the next layers. While this approach works for simple low-dimensional data, it will not work for higher dimensional data as the number of connections would grow exponentially, and many million parameters are required to model and train the network.

CNN approach differs from neural networks because it depends on the human visual cortex.

Connecting a pixel to a neuron is difficult as it requires more parameters. The working principle is that CNN breaks an image into several small pieces (or Chunks) and processes it individually. CNN is very effective compared to traditional shallow neural networks because it needs to process only the relevant parts of the image and not the whole image. This avoidance of fully connected images reduces the computational complexity of the image recognition process.

9.4.2 Translational Invariance

The neural network could not achieve translation invariance, such as size, distortion, or position in an image. Figure 9.5 illustrates an image along with its rotated versions.

Also, the shallow neural network does not possess the capability to recognize this kind of image. To make recognition possible, one can externally manipulate the images using scaling, translation, rotation, etc., before the image recognition stage. These operations ensure the input dataset is complete in all aspects (Data augmentation), and the neural network can recognize this. However, these approaches are computationally intensive tasks.

But CNN can detect these images without any problem. CNN once learned a feature, it can recognize the same feature in any different part of the image. The CNN can recognize these features irrespective of positions and orientations is called translational invariance. Translational invariance marks the major difference between the shallow networks and CNN.

Figure 9.5 Original Image and its Rotated Versions

9.4.3 Sparse Connectivity

CNN exploits the property called sparse connectivity. In this principle, pixels are not independent but linked by the spatial structure.

CNN divides the image into many sub-images or chunks. CNN tries to understand by analyzing individual chunks of images and how the image chunks are related to each other to understand the objects, shapes, and patterns. For example, the presence of the eye of a human indicates the presence of the other eye somewhere near is indicative of the spatial relationship. CNN captures these relationships very effectively. It also captures the neighborhood's patterns and tries to understand the whole picture.

In a shallow neural network, all the hidden layer's neurons are connected to the neurons of the previous layers. But, In CNN, a neuron (or units) is connected only to a small subset of the previous layers. In CNN, it is not fully connected. This kind of spatial connectivity is achieved because moving filters across the images focus only on small local regions at a time. The main advantage of this property is that it reduces the number of parameters and computations, making CNN more efficient compared to shallow networks.

9.4.4 Complex Tasks

CNN has many filters in the convolutional layers. Each filter is a specialized filter extracting features of the images in the form of a feature map. It stacks the feature maps as the layer progresses. This stacking of feature maps facilitates extracting more complex features in a hierarchy. This complex learning of the image's spatial and temporal hierarchical features makes CNN powerful.

Unfortunately, shallow networks cannot solve complex tasks as they do not have any mechanism of learning features in a layered or hierarchical form. So, using shallow networks to recognize complex patterns in the image or higher dimensional form is difficult.

9.4.5 Weight Sharing

CNN employs the principle of "weight sharing." If the features to be detected are of the same type, then the kernel weights are also the same. Hence, the weights are shared across spatial locations. This weight sharing allows the detection of features anywhere in the image. Also, the sharing of weights simplifies the process and promotes spatial invariance. It should be noted that even though the weights are shared, the biases can be either specific or shared.

The weights of the kernel are the same, irrespective of the location. The advantage of this approach are that

(i) The number of parameters is reduced.

(ii) This weight sharing facilitates backpropagation.

(iii) Facilitates the generalization.

(iv) Reduce the risk of overfitting

9.5 Generic CNN Architecture

A convolutional neural network consists of several layers, such as

(i) Input layers

(ii) One or more layers for extracting image features. These layers include:

a. Convolutional layers

b. Activation layers

c. Pooling layers

(iii) One or more fully connected layers for classification

(iv) Finally, the output layer gives the output.

Let us discuss each layer of CNN layers one by one in detail.

9.5.1 Input Layer

The input layer of CNN acts as an interface or initial stage where the input image is fed into CNN. The input image can be a single image or a series of images. A greyscale image is a single-channel image. For example, if the input is a single image of size 100 x 100 and of the single channel(greyscale) type, then the input layer would have a grid size of 100 x 100 x 1 neurons.

Colour images are three-channel images. To detect the colour images, a third dimension is added called "Channel." For example, a colour image has three channels—red, Green, and Blue—and each channel usually has different weights. If the input image is of size 100 x 100 and RGB format, then the grid consists of 100 x 100 x 3(3 channels- one channel for each Red, Green, and Blue) neurons.

The neurons in the input layer do not perform any computation; they act as an entry point for image data to the CNN model.

Many standard labelled datasets are available (Refer Box 9.6).

Box 9.6 Public Datasets for Image Classification

There are many public datasets available for image classification problems. These public datasets serve as benchmark data and a basis for comparing deep learning architectures.

MNIST Dataset

MNIST-Modified National Institute of Standard and Technology Database. MNIST was created by Yann LeCun, Corinna Cortes, and Christopher J.C. Burges. This dataset was discussed in Chapter 8 of this textbook.

CIFAR-10

Canadian Institute for Advanced Research (CIFAR) is a standard benchmark dataset. It has 60,000 color images of various subjects, such as automobiles, birds, and horses, i.e., 10 classes. There are many variations like CIFAR-100, with 100 classes available.

Kaggle

Kagle is another wonderful resource for finding public-domain datasets. Dogs vs. cats is one dataset often used for image classification problems. The dataset has 25,000 images of various resolutions.

Caltech-101

Caltech-101 is another dataset and is often used for object detection problems. The dataset has 8677 images of 101 categories. The images are varied, such as cycles, elephants, and balls.

9.5.2 Convolutional Layer

Convolution layers have a convolution operator that takes the input images and generates feature maps. This process helps to learn edges, textures, and other patterns in the data.

Convolution is a mathematical operation used to apply a small kernel or filter to the image. The application of convolution is called the filtering process. A convolution layer may have many filters. Each filter is like a magnifying glass that focuses on the small, localized region of the input image and extracts the features.

Convolution works by operating a kernel across all image channels simultaneously. The kernel is a small matrix that starts from the upper left of the image, moves from left to right and top to bottom, and ends in the bottom right corner of the image. This application of the convolution process is called the filtering process. Technically, this operation is cross-correlation in traditional signal processing. But by convention in deep learning is called convolution.

The following Figure 9.6 depicts the convolutional operation.

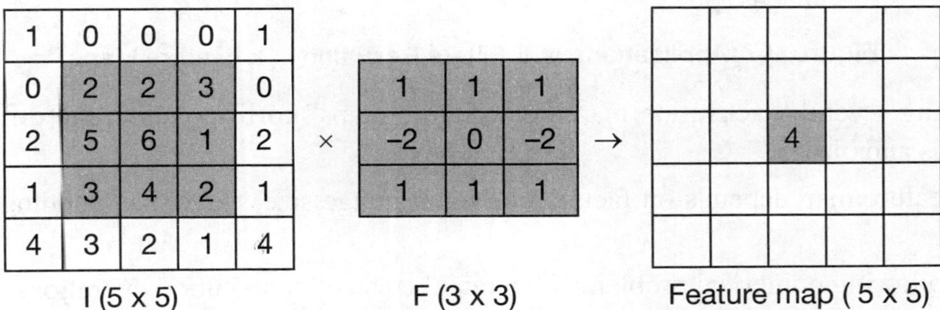

Figure 9.6 Convolutional Operation

Receptive Field and Feature Map

CNN takes an input image or feature map of the previous layers as input and generates the resultant feature map. In CNN, each neuron is connected to a small region called the receptive field and determined by the kernel size of the convolution operation. In sparse connectivity, the filter is connected to a small portion of the image and does not care about the other regions. In short, the convolution input is a receptive field, and the output is called a feature map.

Feature map has specific features or patterns of various locations in the input image. The unit's receptive field is the number of input image pixels connected to a unit. The receptive field influences the behavior of neurons. The receptive field grows, and the last layer will have wider receptive fields that cover the wider area of the image as they receive the aggregated information from the previous layers. Unlike traditional neural networks, these feature maps are stacked from simple to complex features.

For handling colour image channels, the filters should also be 3D, where the number of channels should match the number of channels. In short, the filter is also defined by height X width X number of channels. Each convolution layer has many filters. If one assumes that there are k filters, then the k filter application results in k feature maps that can be stacked, as shown in Figure 9.7.

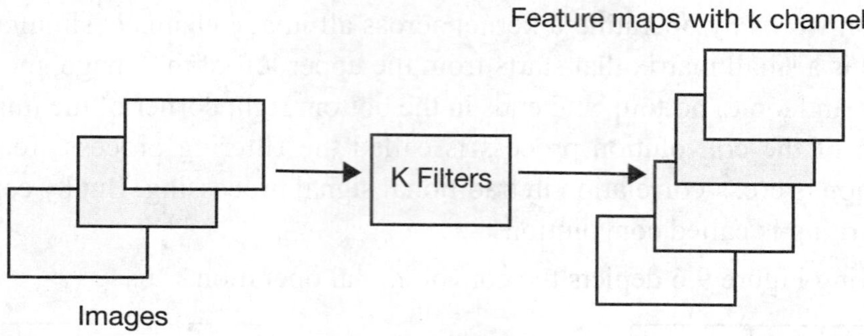

Figure 9.7 Applications of K Filters Resulting in k Feature Maps

Stacking several " activation maps" or "feature maps" corresponds to the different kernels and biases.

The feature map depends on factors like input image size, filter size, padding, and stride.

The following numerical problems illustrate the use of convolution operations.

Example 9.1: What will be the final feature map value after performing a convolution operation based on mask M on the given image (F)?

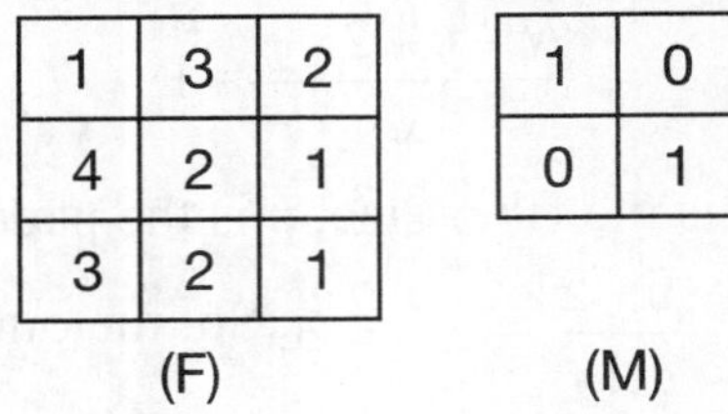

(F) (M)

Solution:

Step 1: $((1\times1)+(3\times0)+(4\times0)+(2\times1))=3$

1	3	2		3	x
4	2	1	→	x	x
3	2	1			

Step 2: $((3\times1)+(2\times0)+(2\times0)+(1\times1))=4$

1	3	2		3	4
4	2	1	→	x	x
3	2	1			

Step 3: $((4\times1)+(2\times0)+(3\times0)+(2\times1))=6$

1	3	2		3	4
4	2	1	→	6	x
3	2	1			

Step 4: $((2\times1)+(1\times0)+(2\times0)+(1\times1))=3$

1	3	2		3	4
4	2	1	→	6	3
3	2	1			

The final feature map values are [3, 4, 6, 3] after the convolution operation.

Example 9.2: Assume the input image size is 7 X 7 and the convolution kernel size is 5 X 5. If the stride (s) is 1 and the padding (p) is zero. Then, what would be the output size of the feature map?

Solution:

The output size is given as

$$\frac{N-n+2\times p}{s}+1$$

Here, N is the image size, n is the filter size, p is the padding, and s is the stride. So, substituting this one gets, $\frac{7-5+2\times 0}{1}+1=3$. So, the output size of the feature map is 3 X 3.

9.6 Parameters and Hyperparameters of CNN

In deep learning, a parameter is a local variable of the model that changes during the training process. Examples of parameters are weights and biases of the filters in the convolutional layers. These parameter values are initialized to random values and adjusted during backpropagation. Each kernel's weights are changed during the optimization process during the backpropagation. In short, the parameter values are learned directly from input data.

Hyperparameters are external values or configurations not learned from the input data but tuned manually or set based on grid search methods. These values do not change. Examples of hyperparameters are the number of layers, learning rate, and batch size. Hyperparameters guide the training process.

The hyperparameters of CNN are:

(i) Number of filters (or kernels)

(ii) Filter size

(iii) Strides

(iv) Padding

These weights are shared across the neurons. So, the results are the same.

9.6.1 Number of Filters and Kernel Size

Number of Filters (or Kernels)

Each layer of the convolutional layers has a different number of filters. The number of filters is dependent on the CNN architecture.

Kernel Size

Kernel size is a hyperparameter. The size should be specified and it varies as per the scenario. A typical size of a kernel is 7 X 7, 5 X 5, and 3 X 3. For example, if the image size is 28 X 28, then the usage of kernel 7 X 7 may be too large. Similarly, the kernel of size 3 X 3 is too small and too little and may have more overlaps.

9.6.2 Stride

Stride is the rate at which the filter slides over the input image to perform convolution operation or the number of pixels the filter matrix slides over the input image matrix. Usually there will be one stride or two strides operation. The region over which the filter slides is known as the receptive field. If it is one stride, the filter moves one pixel after each operation over the input image. If it is two strides, then the filter moves two pixels. Figure 9.8 shows how 1 and 2 strides are performed.

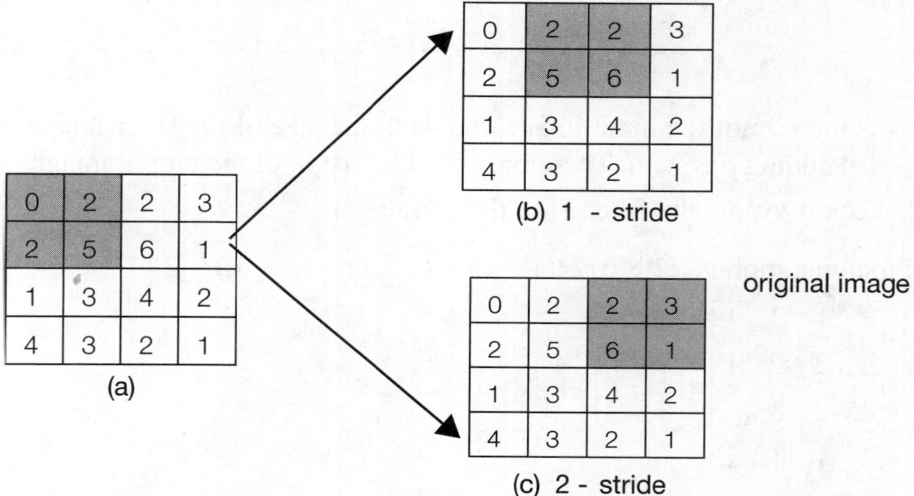

Figure 9.8 Stride Operation (a) The Original Image of Size (4 x 4), (b) Is the Image After One Stride of the Filter (c) Is The Two Stride of the Filter

If the stride value is large, it reduces the spatial dimensions of the output image. The output of one stride will generate an output image or feature map roughly the same size as the input image. When stride is 2, it makes the output image roughly half the input image size. This increase in stride reduces the computational complexity and memory requirements, fastens the computational process, and takes care of overfitting.

At the same time, larger stride values reduce spatial information. The reduction in size based on the strides is given as $\frac{\text{Input Size} - \text{Filter Size}}{\text{Stride}} + 1 = \frac{N-n}{s} + 1$. Here, N is the image size, n is the filter size, and s is the stride.

The following numerical problem illustrates this.

Example 9.3: Consider the following data: the image F and the filter M. Show the steps involved in the convolution operation where the stride is 1. Repeat the problem with stride = 2. Assume padding p is zero.

1	1	1	1
1	2	3	1
1	2	3	1
1	1	1	2

(a) Image F

0	1
1	0

(b) Filter F

Solution:

With stride 1, the size of the output image is given by the formula

$$\frac{N-n+2\times p}{s}+1=\frac{4-2+2\times 0}{1}+1=3$$

Here, N is the size of the input image, that is 4, the size of the filter image is 3, and stride = 1. Padding p is zero. Therefore, the dimension of the output image is 3 x 3. Let us check it. Apply the filter M to the image F.

1. First operation is $((1 \times 0) + (1 \times 1) + (1 \times 1) + (2 \times 0)) = 2$

$$\begin{bmatrix} 1 & 1 & 1 & 1 \\ 1 & 2 & 3 & 1 \\ 1 & 2 & 3 & 1 \\ 1 & 1 & 1 & 2 \end{bmatrix} \times \begin{bmatrix} 0 & 1 \\ 1 & 0 \end{bmatrix} \rightarrow \begin{bmatrix} 2 & x & x \\ x & x & x \\ x & x & x \end{bmatrix}$$

2. After this, the stride will move one-pixel position to the right. Then it perform the convolution operation $((1 \times 0) + (1 \times 1) + (2 \times 1) + (3 \times 0)) = 3$.

$$\begin{bmatrix} 1 & 1 & 1 & 1 \\ 1 & 2 & 3 & 1 \\ 1 & 2 & 3 & 1 \\ 1 & 1 & 1 & 2 \end{bmatrix} \times \begin{bmatrix} 0 & 1 \\ 1 & 0 \end{bmatrix} \rightarrow \begin{bmatrix} 2 & 3 & x \\ x & x & x \\ x & x & x \end{bmatrix}$$

3. The same process is continued again. After completing the first row, it starts from the second row.
$((1 \times 0) + (1 \times 1) + (3 \times 1) + (1 \times 0)) = 4$.

$$\begin{bmatrix} 1 & 1 & 1 & 1 \\ 1 & 2 & 3 & 1 \\ 1 & 2 & 3 & 1 \\ 1 & 1 & 1 & 2 \end{bmatrix} \times \begin{bmatrix} 0 & 1 \\ 1 & 0 \end{bmatrix} \rightarrow \begin{bmatrix} 2 & 3 & 4 \\ x & x & x \\ x & x & x \end{bmatrix}$$

4. $((1 \times 0) + (2 \times 1) + (1 \times 1) + (2 \times 0)) = 3.$

$$\begin{bmatrix} 1 & 1 & 1 & 1 \\ 1 & 2 & 3 & 1 \\ 1 & 2 & 3 & 1 \\ 1 & 1 & 1 & 2 \end{bmatrix} \times \begin{bmatrix} 0 & 1 \\ 1 & 0 \end{bmatrix} \rightarrow \begin{bmatrix} 2 & 3 & 4 \\ 3 & x & x \\ x & x & x \end{bmatrix}$$

5. $((2 \times 0) + (3 \times 1) + (2 \times 1) + (3 \times 0)) = 5.$

$$\begin{bmatrix} 1 & 1 & 1 & 1 \\ 1 & 2 & 3 & 1 \\ 1 & 2 & 3 & 1 \\ 1 & 1 & 1 & 2 \end{bmatrix} \times \begin{bmatrix} 0 & 1 \\ 1 & 0 \end{bmatrix} \rightarrow \begin{bmatrix} 2 & 3 & 4 \\ 3 & 5 & x \\ x & x & x \end{bmatrix}$$

6. $((3 \times 0) + (1 \times 1) + (3 \times 1) + (1 \times 0)) = 4.$

$$\begin{bmatrix} 1 & 1 & 1 & 1 \\ 1 & 2 & 3 & 1 \\ 1 & 2 & 3 & 1 \\ 1 & 1 & 1 & 2 \end{bmatrix} \times \begin{bmatrix} 0 & 1 \\ 1 & 0 \end{bmatrix} \rightarrow \begin{bmatrix} 2 & 3 & 4 \\ 3 & 5 & 4 \\ x & x & x \end{bmatrix}$$

7. $((1 \times 0) + (2 \times 1) + (1 \times 1) + (1 \times 0)) = 3.$

$$\begin{bmatrix} 1 & 1 & 1 & 1 \\ 1 & 2 & 3 & 1 \\ 1 & 2 & 3 & 1 \\ 1 & 1 & 1 & 2 \end{bmatrix} \times \begin{bmatrix} 0 & 1 \\ 1 & 0 \end{bmatrix} \rightarrow \begin{bmatrix} 2 & 3 & 4 \\ 3 & 5 & 4 \\ 3 & x & x \end{bmatrix}$$

8. $((2 \times 0) + (3 \times 1) + (1 \times 1) + (1 \times 0)) = 4.$

$$\begin{bmatrix} 1 & 1 & 1 & 1 \\ 1 & 2 & 3 & 1 \\ 1 & 2 & 3 & 1 \\ 1 & 1 & 1 & 2 \end{bmatrix} \times \begin{bmatrix} 0 & 1 \\ 1 & 0 \end{bmatrix} \rightarrow \begin{bmatrix} 2 & 3 & 4 \\ 3 & 5 & 4 \\ 3 & 4 & x \end{bmatrix}$$

9. $((3 \times 0) + (1 \times 1) + (1 \times 1) + (2 \times 0)) = 2.$

$$\begin{bmatrix} 1 & 1 & 1 & 1 \\ 1 & 2 & 3 & 1 \\ 1 & 2 & \boxed{3} & \boxed{1} \\ 1 & 1 & \boxed{1} & \boxed{2} \end{bmatrix} \times \begin{bmatrix} 0 & 1 \\ 1 & 0 \end{bmatrix} \rightarrow \begin{bmatrix} 2 & 3 & 4 \\ 3 & 5 & 4 \\ 3 & 4 & 2 \end{bmatrix}$$

The above is the final result of the convolution operation after applying one stride.

With stride = 2, let us apply the filter to the image. $\left(\frac{7-5+2\times 0}{2}+1=2\right)$, the output is a 2 X 2 image.

1. $((1 \times 0) + (1 \times 1) + (1 \times 1) + (2 \times 0)) = 2.$

$$\begin{bmatrix} 1 & 1 & 1 & 1 \\ 1 & 2 & 3 & 1 \\ 1 & 2 & 3 & 1 \\ 1 & 1 & 1 & 2 \end{bmatrix} \times \begin{bmatrix} 0 & 1 \\ 1 & 0 \end{bmatrix} \rightarrow \begin{bmatrix} 2 & x \\ x & x \end{bmatrix}$$

2. $((1 \times 0) + (1 \times 1) + (3 \times 1) + (1 \times 0)) = 4.$

$$\begin{bmatrix} 1 & 1 & 1 & 1 \\ 1 & 2 & 3 & 1 \\ 1 & 2 & 3 & 1 \\ 1 & 1 & 1 & 2 \end{bmatrix} \times \begin{bmatrix} 0 & 1 \\ 1 & 0 \end{bmatrix} \rightarrow \begin{bmatrix} 2 & 4 \\ x & x \end{bmatrix}$$

3. $((1 \times 0) + (2 \times 1) + (1 \times 1) + (1 \times 0)) = 3.$

$$\begin{bmatrix} 1 & 1 & 1 & 1 \\ 1 & 2 & 3 & 1 \\ 1 & 2 & 3 & 1 \\ 1 & 1 & 1 & 2 \end{bmatrix} \times \begin{bmatrix} 0 & 1 \\ 1 & 0 \end{bmatrix} \rightarrow \begin{bmatrix} 2 & 4 \\ 3 & x \end{bmatrix}$$

4. $((3 \times 0) + (1 \times 1) + (1 \times 1) + (2 \times 0)) = 2.$

$$\begin{bmatrix} 1 & 1 & 1 & 1 \\ 1 & 2 & 3 & 1 \\ 1 & 2 & 3 & 1 \\ 1 & 1 & 1 & 2 \end{bmatrix} \times \begin{bmatrix} 0 & 1 \\ 1 & 0 \end{bmatrix} \rightarrow \begin{bmatrix} 2 & 4 \\ 3 & 2 \end{bmatrix}$$

The above is the final result of the convolution operation after applying stride 2. It can be observed that the increased stride leads to a reduction in the output dimensions.

9.6.3 Padding

Padding is a hyperparameter. It is often denoted by p. Padding or Zero-padding the image, another important operation in CNN. Padding is nothing but adding a zero to the outer border of the image, as shown in Figure 9.9.

$$\begin{bmatrix} 1 & 1 \\ 1 & 1 \end{bmatrix} = \begin{bmatrix} 0 & 0 & 0 & 0 \\ 0 & 1 & 1 & 0 \\ 0 & 1 & 1 & 0 \\ 0 & 0 & 0 & 0 \end{bmatrix}$$

(a) (b)

Figure 9.9 (a) Image (b) Image After Padding

Padding is becoming essential for the following reasons:

(i) Padding addresses the problem of shrinking output. It is known that the convolution operation reduces the output size. If the shrinkage is allowed, the output image at the end would be very small. This shrinkage is not desirable. Hence, padding ensures that the shrinkage is avoided by adding extra layers of zeros.

(ii) Often, the edge information is essential. The convolution process reduces the dimension of the input image. So, most of the essential information is lost.

(iii) The padding ensures that a large kernel can be used to extract features.

If the image is padded with zero, the output size will not change. In CNN conventions, there are two types of padding – Valid or Same, as shown in Figure 9.10.

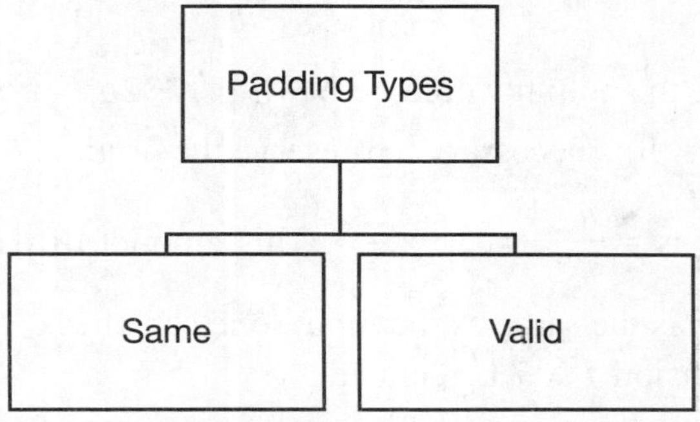

Figure 9.10 Padding Types

A convolution with no padding is called "narrow" or valid. Valid padding reduces the dimensions of the output. This name "valid" is used because only the valid data locations are used, and the edge information is ignored. To ensure the output size is the same as the input size, padding "same" is used. This padding is also known as "wide" padding. "same" padding ensures that the output has the same dimension as the input.

Valid Padding

The reduction of dimensions in "narrow" or "valid" padding is given as follows:

$$N - n + 1$$

N is the image size, and n is the filter size.

Same Padding

This same padding indicates that padding is done as much as possible so that the output size is the same as the input size. The reduction of dimensions in "same" or "wide" padding is given as follows:

$$N - n + 1 + 2p$$

Here, N is the image size, n is the filter size, and p is the padding. To ensure the dimensions of output are preserved, one should use a padding of

$$\frac{n-1}{2}$$

Here, n is the filter size. The following numerical example illustrates this fact.

Example 9.4: Let us assume that a filter 5 X 5 is used. Let the image size be 7 X 7. If the padding is the same, what are the dimensions of the output, and how much padding is required?

Solution:

If no padding is used, the output would be $N - n + 1 + 2p$, $7 - 5 + 1 + 2 \times 0 = 3$. The output would be 3 X 3. It is necessary to preserve the original dimension. Therefore, the required padding is $= \frac{n-1}{2} = \frac{5-1}{2} = 2$. This amount of padding is required to ensure the output size is the same as the input (one can check $7 - 5 + 1 + 2 \times 2 = 7$). So, the original dimension 7 X 7 is retained.

Example 9.5: Let us assume the size of the input image is 32 x 32, the filter size is 5 x 5, the stride (s) is 1, and the padding (p) is 2. What is the size of the feature map?

Solution:

The size of the feature map or activation map is given as $\frac{N-n+2p}{s}+1$ where:

N = size of the image, n = size of the filter, p = padding value and s = stride value

Feature map size = $\frac{32-5+2\times 2}{1}+1=32$. Therefore, the output would be 32 × 32.

9.6.4 Pooling

Each convolutional layer has many filters. As the process continues, the number of parameters grows exponentially. The pooling layer is used after the convolution layers. The purpose of pooling layers is that of subsampling (Refer to Chapter 8). Pooling is used to reduce the dimensions of the output of the convolutional layer. The pooling layer is required for the following purposes:

(i) Downsize or downsample the output of the filters.

(ii) Reduce the operations or parameters required for CNN.

(iii) Reduce the training time of CNN

(iv) To avoid the risk of overfitting

Also, the filters can be one-dimensional, two-dimensional, or 3D as the input data to process the image channels.

Pooling ensures that the feature detectors are more invariant of the input position. Pooling solves the important problem of "Translation invariance." and "rotational invariance." Translational variance means irrespective of the object orientation, the CNN would produce the same response.

Pooling also can be overlapped. Overlapped pooling helps to detect larger features that are relative to one another.

Two parameters characterize pooling:

(i) Pooling Type

(ii) Size of the polling window.

Four types of pooling are applied in CNN, as shown in Figure 9.11.

The size of the pooling windows is predefined and fixed before the training begins, and the size determines how the input feature maps are downsampled. Pooling has no parameters for backpropagation.

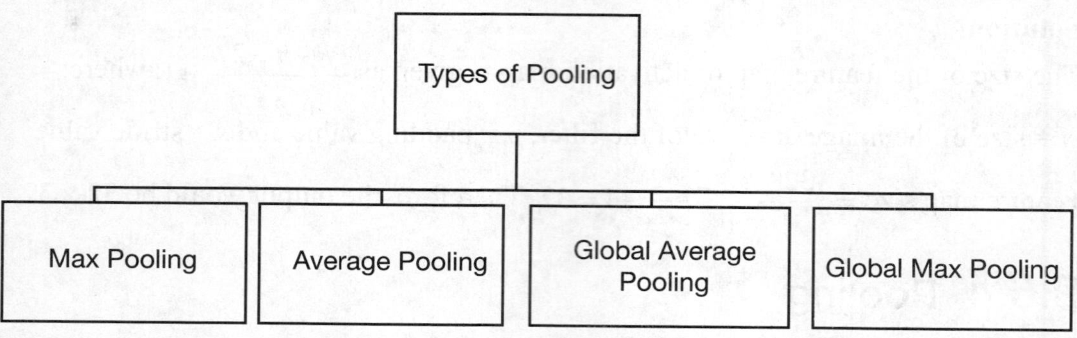

Figure 9.11 Types of Pooling

In pooling, the observation window is divided into subwindows or tiles based on the size of the pooling window and the subwindows element is reduced to a single element.

Max Pooling

In this type of pooling, the kernel slides over the feature map and identifies the maximum value in the window it covers. The advantage of max pooling is that it preserves the depth of the layer. Max pooling allows important global information, such as larger value, to be retained. Max pooling allows CNN to note the important information, and it should be noted that the exact positions do not matter. But instead only the relative positions are required. Also, max pooling does not go along with the padding.

Example 9.6: Consider the following image. Apply max pooling and show the output of max pooling.

$$\begin{bmatrix} 2 & 3 & 5 & 6 \\ 3 & 4 & 0 & 3 \\ 1 & 4 & 2 & 4 \\ 5 & 6 & 2 & 3 \end{bmatrix}$$

Solution:

In max pooling, the observation window is divided into subwindows or tiles based on the size of the pooling window and the subwindows element is reduced to a single element. Divide the 4 X 4 image into four 2 X 2 images and find the maximum value among them. That will be in the output image. Similarly, move the next four pixels and find the maximum in them. Continue the process till the end of the image.

$$\begin{bmatrix} 2 & 3 & 5 & \boxed{6} \\ 3 & \boxed{4} & 0 & 3 \\ 1 & 4 & 2 & \boxed{4} \\ 5 & \boxed{6} & 2 & 3 \end{bmatrix} = \begin{bmatrix} 4 & 6 \\ 6 & 4 \end{bmatrix}$$

On applying the max pooling kernel of size 2 x 2, the resultant feature map will be $\begin{bmatrix} 4 & 6 \\ 6 & 4 \end{bmatrix}$.

Average Pooling

In this type, the first 2 x 2 pixel value average is calculated, followed by the next, third, and fourth, and finally, all this is represented in a 2 x 2.

Example 9.7: Consider the following image. Apply average pooling and find the final feature map.

$$\begin{bmatrix} 2 & 3 & 5 & 6 \\ 3 & 4 & 0 & 3 \\ 1 & 4 & 2 & 4 \\ 5 & 6 & 2 & 3 \end{bmatrix}$$

Solution:

Apply the average pooling with mask 2 X 2.

Average of First 2 x 2 = (2 + 3 + 3 + 4)/4 = 3

Average of Second 2 x 2 = (5 + 6 + 0 + 3)/4 = 3.5

Average of third 2 x 2 = (1 + 4 +5 + 6)/4 = 4

Average of fourth 2 x 2 = (2 + 4 + 2 + 3)/4 = 2.75. the resultant feature map will be

$$\begin{bmatrix} 3 & 3.5 \\ 4 & 2.75 \end{bmatrix} = \begin{bmatrix} 3 & 4 \\ 4 & 3 \end{bmatrix}$$

Global Average Pooling

Instead of setting a window, Global average pooling calculates the average of the feature map pixel value.

Global Max Pooling

It also gives a single value as output, like global average pooling. Here, the maximum value of the pixel is considered and given as a resultant feature map.

Example 9.8: Consider the following image, apply the global max pooling method, and show the output.

Solution:

It finds the maximum value in the input image and gives it as an out image.

$$\begin{bmatrix} 2 & 3 & 5 & 6 \\ 3 & 4 & 0 & 3 \\ 1 & 4 & 2 & 4 \\ 5 & 6 & 2 & 3 \end{bmatrix}$$

The global max is 6. Therefore, the resultant of the image is given as [6]. The average of all values is $(2 + 3 + 5 + 6 + 3 + 4 + 0 + 3 + 1 + 4 + 2 + 4 + 5 + 6 + 2 + 3)/16 = 53/6 = 3.3125$, approximately equal to 3. It produces a single value for an image map irrespective of the size of the feature maps. But depth is maintained.

9.6.5 Additional Layers of CNN

These are the additional layers that increase the performance of CNN.

ReLU Activation Layer

The activation layer mimics the triggering of a perceptron. ReLU is proving to be a better activation function. One can recollect that ReLU takes a take negative number and converts it to zero. If the input is positive, the number is retained. ReLU maintains a wide range of input unlike sigmoidal or tanh activation functions that compress the input range to a smaller range like 0-1.

The output layer uses a sigmoidal function that provides multiple classes with a probability value.

Batch Normalization

The batch normalization layer is often present between the convolution layer (or fully connected layer) and activation layers. The purpose of the batch normalization layer is to normalize the data and solve the distribution drift.

Normalization ensures that the input of the activation layer does not bring the neurons to saturation or a dead state. Batch normalization layers fasten the neural network's convergence and solve the vanishing and exploding gradient problems. Batch normalization makes the training less dependent on the initialization of weights. Batch normalization facilitates a larger learning rate and faster training of convolutional neural networks.

Dropout

Often dropout layer is used to solve the problems of overfitting and the problem of "co-adaptation." Co-adaptation is the problem where a neuron response is adapted to the response of the other units according to a pattern in the dataset. Co-adaptation leads to a generalization problem as these weights are meaningless (Refer to Chapter 5 for more details on dropout).

Dropout solves the problem of overreliance on a particular neuron or feature by dropping the neurons at each epoch. For a probability of p>0, the neurons are dropped during the training phase. But in the testing phase, all units are activated and active.

9.6.6 Fully Connected Layers and Image Flattening

After extracting the features, they are given as input to the fully connected layer. The process of converting a 2D feature into a single-dimension vector is called image flattening. For example, if an image size is 3 pixels high and 3 pixels wide, it is represented by the following format, as shown in Figure 9.12.

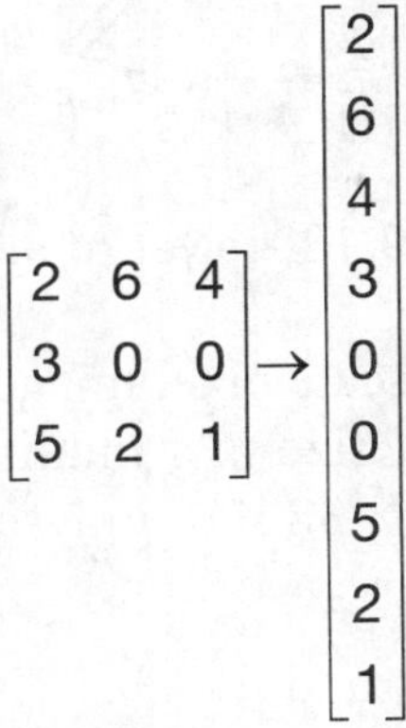

$$\begin{bmatrix} 2 & 6 & 4 \\ 3 & 0 & 0 \\ 5 & 2 & 1 \end{bmatrix} \rightarrow \begin{bmatrix} 2 \\ 6 \\ 4 \\ 3 \\ 0 \\ 0 \\ 5 \\ 2 \\ 1 \end{bmatrix}$$

Figure 9.12 Image Flattening (a) Original Image (b) Flattening Image

If the feature maps have 3 rows and 3 columns, then the flattened feature map is of size 1 x 9. The flattened vector is taken for a fully connected network (or dense). The fully connected network is one where every neuron of the layer is connected to every neuron of the subsequent layer. This dense network does the classification. This process is described in Chapter 8 of this textbook. The major disadvantages of image flattening are the loss of spatial information in converting matrices to vectors and additional parameters that are required and need to be tuned.

9.7 LeNet-5 Architecture

There are seven layers in LeNet (There are two convolution layers, two sub-sampling layers, two fully connected layer, and an output layer. Input Layer is not included). It has a set of convolution layers to extract the spatial features of the input image, which are subsampled by an average pooling layer. The tanh activation function is used in the feature extraction layer in the original implementation. Instead, sigmoidal or recent ReLU can be used. The extracted feature is then classified using dense layers.

The number of output layer neurons is based on the number of classification classes. For example, if we want to classify digits 0–9, then the output layer of LeNet will have 10 neurons in the output layer. The LeNet-5 architecture is shown in Figure 9.13.

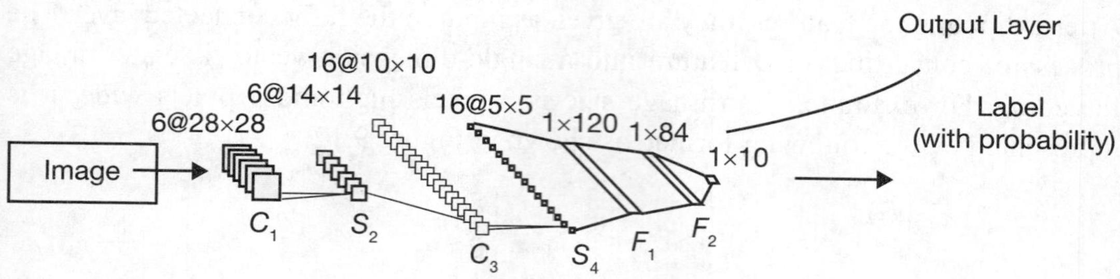

Figure 9.13 LeNet Architecture

1. The input to LeNet is a greyscale pixel image of size 32 × 32. The input image is a square. Often, the input size is a multiple of 16 and divisible by 2. The input image of leNet-5 is 32 × 32 if of grayscale type of image.
2. There are two convolution layers C_1, and C_3 two sub-sampling layers S_2 and S_4, two fully connected layers F_1 and F_2. There is one output layer.
3. The first layer is C_1. This layer has 6 filters of size 5 × 5. This convolution operation is carried out on the input image with padding = same and stride =

1. Based on the size calculation formula, the output image size is $(32 - 5 + 2 \times 0)/1 + 1 = 28$). The output of this layer is $28 \times 28 \times 6$ feature maps.

4. The second layer, S_2, is an average pooling or sub-sampling layer with size 2×2 kernels, stride 0, and padding = 0. A sigmoid activation function is applied to this layer. The output of this layer is 6 images of size $14 \times 14 \times 6$. The 2×2 receptive fields are non-overlapping, so feature maps S_2 have half the number of rows and columns as feature maps of the C_1 layer.

5. The second convolution layer (C_3) has 16 filters with kernel size 5×5. This results in the output of 10 X 10 X 16.

6. The fourth layer, S4, is the average max pooling layer with a stride of 2. The second pooling is also an average layer with size 2, resulting in the output $5 \times 5 \times 16$.

7. LeNet has two fully connected layers - F_1 and F_2.

   The first fully connected layer uses a tanh function in the original implementation. But ReLU or sigmoidal function can be used. The multiplication of $5 \times 5 \times 16$ gives 400. This fully connected layer has 120 neurons or nodes. So, 400 neurons have having full connection with 120 neurons.

   The second fully connected layer uses RBF in the original implementation. It can be a sigmoidal function. This fully connected layer has 84 nodes or neurons. The 120 neurons of the previous layer are fully connected with these 84 nodes.

8. The last layer is an output layer of 10 nodes, which uses the softmax activation function to classify the given image 0–9.

   Approximately 60,000 parameters are used for LeNet.

Summary

1. CNN is a deep learning-based image classifier.
2. Image recognition is the ability of the system to identify the objects, people, places, traffic signs, and actions in the images.
3. The basic difference between deep learning and machine learning approaches is that the features are extracted manually in machine learning. In the deep learning approach, the features are extracted automatically.

4. The CNN has two parts: Feature Extraction and classification.
5. Hierarchical learning is a process of learning representations or features from the image in a hierarchical manner – from low to high-level features.
6. The convolutional and pooling layers take care of the feature extraction part with the help of convolution operation.
7. The differences between the shallow networks and CNN are the differences in architectures, translational invariance, sparse connectivity and weight sharing.
8. Kernels or filters in the Convolutional layer extract the features.
9. Convolution is a mathematical operation to apply a small kernel to the image to get the sum of the dot product or overlapping regions of the image and the filter.
10. The output of the convolution operation is called the feature map, and the input of the image for the convolution process is called the response field.
11. The parameters are learned from the data, and the user sets the hyperparameters as part of the learning program. The hyperparameters are the number of filters, kernel size, stride, and padding.
12. The pooling layer is used to reduce the dimensions of the feature maps. Pooling reduces the size of the image, not its depth. The types of pooling are max, average, global max, and global average.
13. The stride is the step size of the kernel. Padding is about adding zero to the outer border of the image to solve the problem of shrinking output and to keep essential edge information.
14. The additional layers are ReLU, Batch normalization, and dropout.
15. The image-extracted features are flattened. The flattened image is given as input to the fully connected layer.
16. The activation functions used in convolutional layers of LeNet are either ReLU or sigmoid.
17. The final output layer has a softmax activation function.

Glossary

1. Image classification – The ability of the system to identify.
2. ConvNet – It is an alternate name for CNN.
3. Feature engineering – The art of designing input features for image classification.
4. Hypermeter – Parameters that are set before the learning or training process and are predefined.
5. Parameters – These are internal variables whose values change during the training process.
6. Convolutional learning – The learning of CNN using the convolution operator.
7. Hierarchical learning – The learning by CNN as a layered approach and building complex features out of simple features is called hierarchical learning.
8. Kernel or filter – A small matrix usually of size 3 x 3, 5x5, mostly square. The kernel convolves the image to generate the feature maps.
9. Convolution operation – This operation involves overlaying the kernel operation over the image and performing element-wise multiplication followed by summation.
10. Feature map – This is the output of the convolution operation performed over the image.
11. Receptive field – It is a region of interest of the input image where the kernel operates.
12. Translation invariance – The ability of the system to recognize, irrespective of the orientation of the object due to translation operation.
13. Stride – Stride is the step size of the kernel in convolution operation.
14. Sparse connectivity – The principle that the pixels are not independent but interlinked by the spatial structure.
15. Padding – Padding adds extra zero rows and columns to the input image to maintain size.
16. Activation function – It is used to bring the non-linearity in operations.
17. Dropout – It generalizes features by dropping certain neurons during training.

Short Questions

1. Why does CNN perform better than shallow neural networks?
2. What is meant by hierarchical learning?
3. List the differences between machine and deep learning approaches for image classification.
4. Define hyperparameters and list all the hyperparameters that are used in CNN.
5. Differentiate between hyperparameters and parameters?
6. Why small kernel size is used in CNN?
7. What is the purpose of the pooling layer in CNN?
8. Why is Image flattening done on CNN?
9. Define stride and padding.
10. What is the purpose of the pooling layer in CNN?
11. What is the purpose of the dropout layer in CNN?
12. Justify using ReLU, sigmoid, and softmax functions in CNN.
13. What are the salient features of LeNet-5 Architecture?

Long Questions

1. With a neat sketch, explain LeNet-5 architecture.
2. Explain hierarchical learning in CNN.
3. Explain how feature extraction is done in CNN.

Numerical Problems

1. Perform the convolution operation on the input image using the kernel with stride 1 and padding = 1.

1	0	2	3
2	2	3	4
5	6	3	2
1	3	4	2

1	0
0	1

2. What will be the size of the activation map if the image size is 50 x 50 and the kernel size is 4 x 4 with padding 0 stride = 2?
3. Calculate the feature map's dimension generated when a kernel of 5 x 5 is applied on the image of 7 x 7 with stride = 1, 2, and 3.

4. Apply different pooling operations on the image below and apply a pooling mask of dimension 2 x 2.

1	0	2	3
2	2	3	4
5	6	3	2
1	3	4	2

Crossword

Across

1. CNN is a dense network, like multilayer networks. (true/false)
3. LeNet in the final layer has ________ activation function.
9. The input image for the convolution is called the ________ field.
11. The building of complex features from the simple features is called ________ learning.
14. The pixels are related by spatial structure. This property is called ________ connectivity.
15. The principle of weight sharing helps to reduce the number of ________

17. Pooling helps in _______ reductionality.
18. The learning algorithm learns parameters. (true/false).
20. The advantage of deep learning over machine learning is learning of features in an _______ manner.
22. The Kernel or _______ is a small matrix used to slide the image.
23. LeNet - 5 is the _______ architecture for CNN.
25. The _______ function brings nonlinearity.

Down

2. Image classification assigns a _______ to the input image.
4. The advantage of ReLU over the sigmoidal function is that the range of ReLU is wider than 0-1. (true/false).
5. Stride is a _______ (parameter/ hyperparameter).
6. Dropout helps in _______
7. The padding adds extra _______ rows and columns to maintain the image size.
8. Convolutional learning is by the use of the convolution operator is also known as _______ learning.
10. The padding helps in preserving the _______ information.
12. The output of the convolution operation is called _______.
13. Hyperparameters are set by the users as part of the algorithm. (true/false)
16. Convolutional neural networks is also known as _______
19. The step size of the Kernel in convolution operation is called _______.
21. CNN provides translational invariance. (true/false)
24. The number of fully connected connected layers in LeNet is _______

Jumbled Sentences

```
O F T Y D C Q F H Y P E R P A R A M E T E R H F S
P H A B Y Q N G Y N L Y G I A F H R U G O K O S B
M C T R U E H L Q J W V F S H T Y Y A L A B E L F
P I E Z W Z D I M E N S I O N A S I U O U H A X X
A W G M T H T R U E E D G E J K S I A L W I U C K
R T X H R R U P R U K I Q Q K X A S Y C O E T O B
A B K H U M G E N E R A L I Z A T I O N A R O N R
M G V L E G F E A T U R E M A P L B J Z K A M V N
E S P A R S E U T U W B H F I L T E R S K R A N I
T F Z D Z Y C U W O D F A L S E S Y Q T P C T E N
E Q E V E Y F T O S X Q J B L F D B S H X H I T B
R A R K H I E R A R C H I C A L J R E L J I C N W
S B O A N L V U K A C T I V A T I O N B Z C C U P
R T O G H A W Z I F B U A O W F K Q K S F A G Z C
F R E C E P T I V E E G T J U K U Q A T K L Q Y L
O U D Q S O F T M A X V R J K C E L B Q W L O K M
B E K T S T R I D E F W M R U A O R M Z G X K M J
```

true
feature map
true
true
edge

true
receptive
generalization
false
dimension

hierarchical
stride
ConvNet
sparse
first

hierarchical
zero
label
parameters
softmax

filter
activation
automatic
hyperparameter
two

CHAPTER 10

Transfer Learning

> Knowledge transfer is the process by which one generation passes on skills, expertise, and wisdom to the next, ensuring that what has been learned and discovered is not lost but built upon. — **Peter Senge**

Credits: © Peter Senge

Image recognition is one of the most important computer vision tasks. Image recognition is a broader field that assigns labels to multiple objects in an image, while image classification assigns a label to the dominant object of the image. Building an image recognition model from scratch is costly as resources like labelled data and computing resources like GPU and TPU are costly. In this context, transfer learning becomes important. Transfer learning involves transferring knowledge in deep learning pretrained models to the models under development to reduce development time and improve performance.

The learning objectives of this chapter are:

- Overview of transfer learning.
- Understanding the relevance of ImageNet.
- Know the concept of Pretrained Models.
- Know Advanced CNN architectures.
- Know about AlexNet, VGGNet, InceptionNet and ResNet.
- Know the basics of transfer learning.
- Understand the techniques of transfer learning.

10.1 Overview of Transfer Learning

Human beings are known to transfer knowledge from one discipline to another.

Let us assume a hypothetical organization employs Tom. Let us assume Tom is assigned the task of photographing birds due to some reasons of change in company policy. Until now, Tom was an expert in wild animal photography of the organization, not birds. Will Tom survive in a new Job? Fine, Birds are different domain compared to the source domain of animals. But the knowledge of camera, lens, lights, and angles is mostly common despite some domain differences. Tom can reuse this knowledge to excel in a new job as shown in Figure 10.1.

The above scenario illustrates the transfer of knowledge in humans.

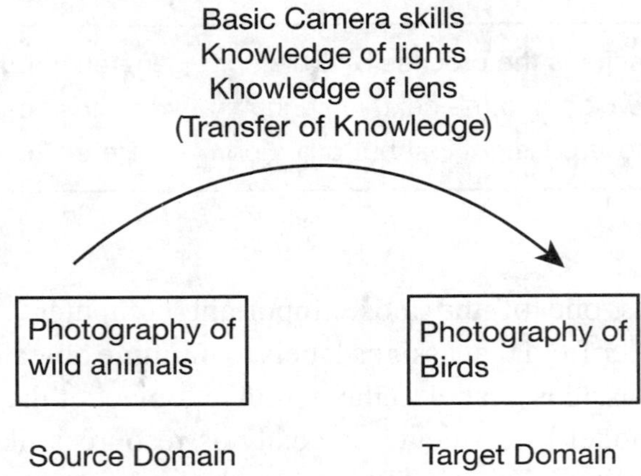

Figure 10.1 Transfer of Knowledge in Humans

For example, a specialized cook can branch from preparing one cuisine to another. Even though cuisine is different, certain basic cooking skills are the same. Similarly, the knowledge of riding a bicycle can be transferred to riding a motorcycle.

Similarly, one image classification model can be tuned to transfer knowledge to another model to improve classification performance. Let us assume that one user wants to classify flowers. Assume the user has insufficient data or resources like GPU to classify. Can the new project be done? Yes, the new project can be implemented if any pretrained model for a larger dataset like plants is available. Then, like a human knowledge transfer, one can reuse the pretrained model for the new problem of flower classification. This kind of re-usage of the pretrained model reduces the development time of the model for flower classification.

Thus, the motivations for transfer learning are given in Box 10.1.

Box 10.1 Motivation for Transfer Learning

The motivation for transfer learning is given below.

(i) **Data Problem:** Training a model from scratch requires lots of labelled data. It is very expensive to acquire the labelled data because manual annotation is a cumbersome task. Hence, whenever there is a shortage of data, transfer learning makes sense, where a pretrained model trained on a larger dataset can be used to transfer knowledge.

(ii) **Computation Problem:** It isn't easy to train deep learning networks as it requires many resources, such as TPUs and GPUs. Also, the training of models takes many hours, days, or even months. This requirement of heavy resources is unsuitable for many with fewer resources to work on model development.

Transfer learning makes sense whenever there is a data problem and a computation problem. Additionally, transfer learning solves the problem of poor generalization and overfitting.

Some of the advantages of transfer learning are given in Box 10.2.

Box 10.2 Advantages of Transfer Learning

The advantages of transfer learning are listed below:

(i) Transfer learning reduces development time as the models need not have to be developed from scratch. Transfer learning helps to save more time and resources.

(ii) Improve the target model's performance using the knowledge the pretrained model gained.

(iii) Transfer learning helps whenever there is data scarcity, domain shift, and higher task complexity.

(iv) Helps to deliver state-of-the-art technology models and make deep learning more accessible and efficient for common users.

10.1.1 Context of Transfer Learning

Transfer learning can be defined as follows: Transfer learning is a machine learning paradigm where knowledge gained from one/more tasks, domains, and datasets (referred to as source domain) is leveraged to solve a related task. This task may belong to a different domain, task, or dataset (called target domain).

Figure 10.2 illustrates the model construction in machine learning. It can be observed that the machine learning algorithms take the dataset as input and generate a model.

Once a model is constructed to solve a task, it is no longer useful for solving other related tasks. All the knowledge gained is thrown away as a new model is trained from scratch. There is no leverage of knowledge gained from the old models, and training new models from scratch takes more resources and time.

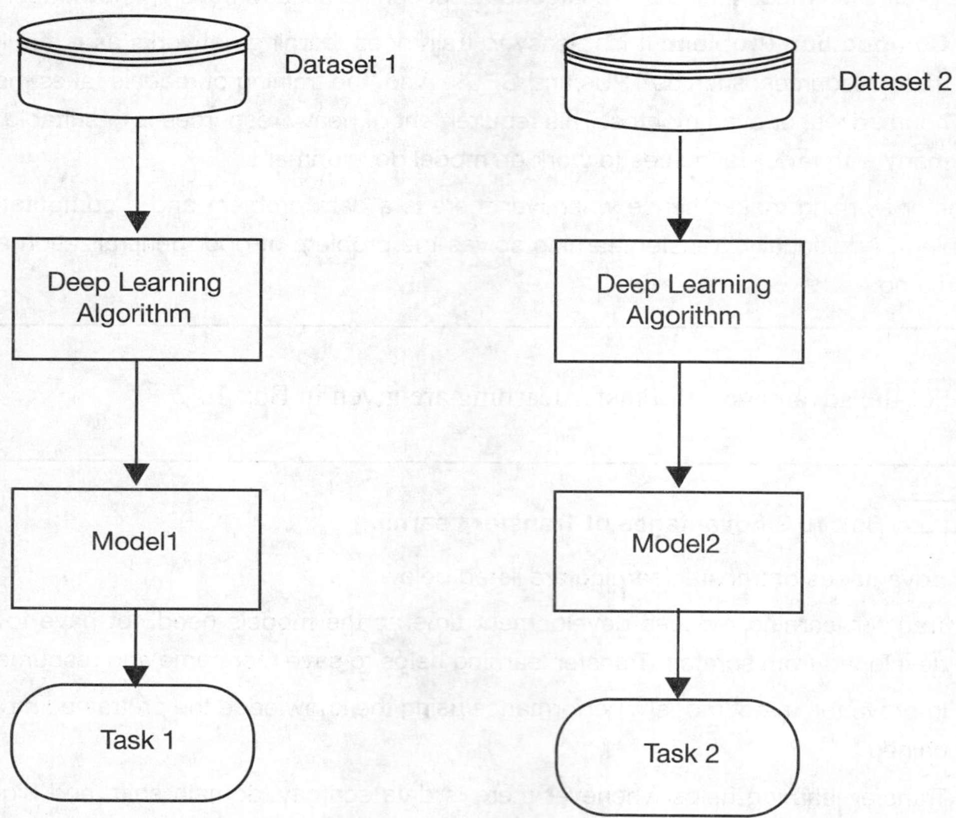

Figure 10.2 Scenario in Machine Learning

In deep learning, the scenario is different. In deep learning, algorithms train a model on a dataset for a task and use the model to solve another related task. The idea is to reuse the knowledge gained by solving a task, say task 1, and solve the task, say task 2. Figure 10.3 illustrates the mechanism of transfer learning in deep learning applications.

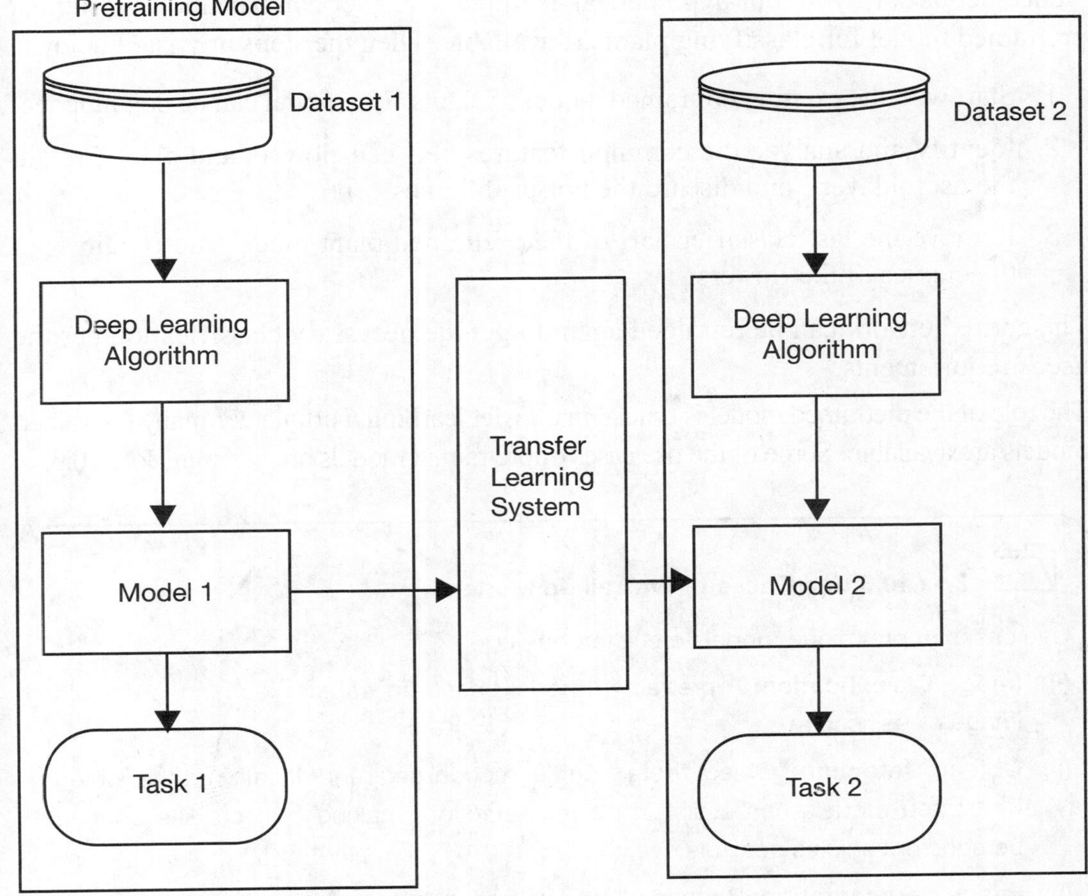

Figure 10.3 Transfer Learning Scenario

So, the stages in transfer learning are

1. Pretraining – Model 1 is created by deep learning using training on a larger dataset to solve task 1. This model is not thrown away and instead becomes a pretrained model to solve task 2.
2. Transfer of Knowledge – This meant reusing the learned features of model 1 to model 2.
3. Fine-tuning model 2 is a refining step for solving the new task, say task 2 more efficiently.

Here, the main core is the creation of a pretrained model. A pre-trained model is a model that has been trained on a larger dataset for certain objectives and can be saved for later use to solve other related tasks.

Hence, let us start with our hypothetical example of flower classification. Assume a pretrained model for classifying plants is available. Then the steps are listed below:

1. Start with the existing pretrained model of plants. The model can be downloaded.
2. Identify and analyze the common features between flowers and plants, retain the useful layers, and discard the not-useful ones.
3. Remove the last classifier part of the pretrained plant model and retrain with the classes of the flowers.

The entire network can be retrained again to get the necessary classification per the user's requirements.

The role of the pretrained model is crucial in transfer learning. Fortunately, many pretrained models are available. Some of the use cases of pretrained models are given in Box. 10.3.

Box 10.3 Use Cases of Pretrained Models

Use cases of pretrained models are listed below:

(i) **Image Classification:** A pretrained model based on transfer learning is useful in image classification.

(ii) **Object Detection:** Object detection is recognizing and localizing the object. Pretrained models can assist in object detection, making projects like counting persons or vehicles possible.

(iii) **Image Segmentation:** Pretrained models based on transfer learning are useful for image segmentation like sematic and segmentation.

(iv) **Generative Adversarial Networks:** Pretrained models are used to generate synthetic images.

(v) **Natural Language Processing:** Natural Language Processing also uses transfer learning-based pretrained models for applications like question-answering programs. Pretrained models help create customized models.

10.2 Framework of Transfer Learning

A domain D is a tuple of feature space and the marginal probability distribution of the input features $p(X)$. Here, X is the random data point. So, the domain can be represented as

$$D = \{X, p(X)\}$$

For example, the domain of natural scenes can be visualized as a collection of natural scenes with various objects. The feature space can be edges, textures, colours, patterns, and most abstract features like stems and leaves with pixel values and their derived features. The data distribution is the probability distribution function over all possible natural scene images in the datasets. Some of the examples of the domain and its feature space are given in the following Table 10.1.

Table 10.1 Example of Domain and its Feature Spaces

Example Domain	Feature Spaces
documents in the NLP domain	Some of the feature spaces are Word embeddings, Term frequency, and Inverted Document Frequency of the documents. The semantic features of the document constitute the feature space of a document.
Images (In the Computer vision domain)	Intensity, colour histograms, LBP features
Medical domain Images	Some of the feature spaces are Intensity, colour, shapes, Textures, and Landmark points.

A task is a tuple of label space γ and the objective f (The conditional probability of output (label) given the input features). The objective can be defined as P(γ/X). The task can be defined as a tuple as T = {γ, P(γ/X). Some examples of label spaces are given in Table 10.2.

Table 10.2 Example of Label Spaces

Example Domain	Feature Spaces
Documents in the NLP domain	Positive, negative, and Neutral sentiment (as in sentiment analysis) are labels. Topic categories (like cricket, Hockey) or entity types (Person, objects).
Images (In the Computer vision domain)	Sepal width, Sepal length (Like in Iris Classification), and Categories like wild animals and pet animals (Like in animal category) are examples of label spaces.
Medical domain Images.	Disease or condition categories like cancer types like melanoma, organ categories like brain or kidney, and disease types like fever, malaria, etc, are examples of labels.

So, the transfer function is the process of improving the target objective function and task using the knowledge transfer from the source domain or task.

10.2.1 Components of Transfer Learning and Types of Transfer Learning Models

The components of transfer learning involve:

1. Source domain – This involves a pretrained model trained on the dataset to learn task 1.
2. The knowledge, representation, or features are transferred to the target domain, which may have a different dataset, task, or objective.
3. Transfer mechanism – This is about fine-tuning the model for the target domain.
4. Objectives – Transfer learning aims to improve performance, efficiency, and generalization ability in the target domain using transferred knowledge.

What is transferred as knowledge? The optimal weights and biases are called knowledge. This scenario is shown in Figure 10.4.

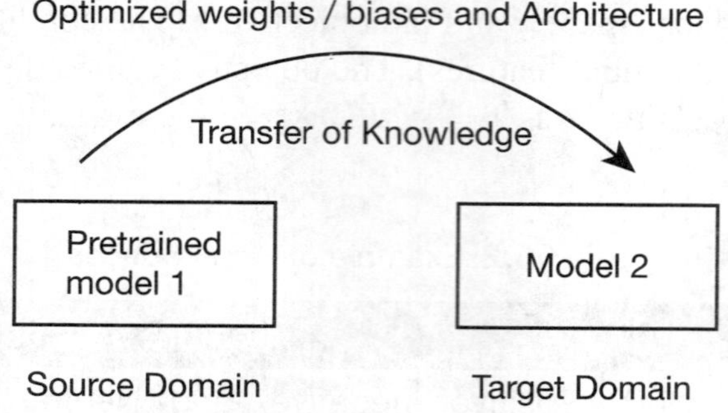

Figure 10.4 Knowledge Transfer

The additional details of knowledge are given in Box 10.4.

Box 10.4: Knowledge Transfer

The transferred knowledge is the data's latent and abstract/hierarchical features. The transferred knowledge can be summarized as follows:

(i) Learned Features: These are abstract and hierarchical features from the raw data, such as textures, shapes, or shapes.

(ii) Weights and Parameters: Weights represent the learned patterns and relationships.

(iii) Hidden Representation: These latent variables represent the different levels of abstraction that encode the rich information about the data.

(iv) Domain Knowledge: These are structures or characteristics of data, such as class distributions, semantics, or relationships.

(v) Task-specific Information: Task information, including attention mechanisms or task-specific weights, can be learned from the source domain to improve the performance of the target task.

Finally, two outcomes of the transfer learning are

(i) The architecture of the pretrained model.

(ii) The reusable knowledge. Note that the knowledge is a form of trained weights and biases.

So, the transfer learning can be categorized as shown in Figure 10.5.

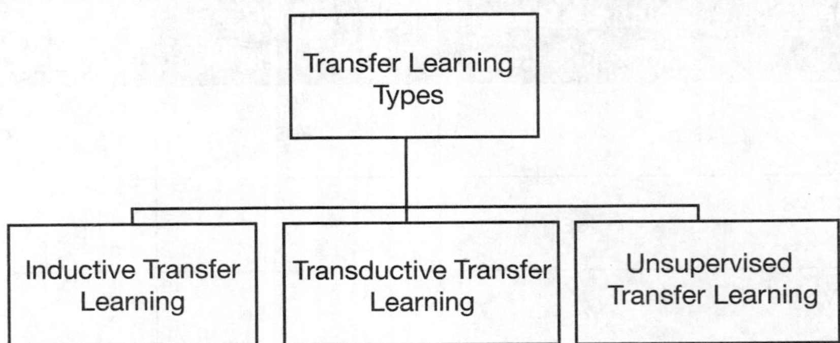

Figure 10.5 Types of Transfer Learning

(i) Inductive Transfer Learning: In inductive transfer learning, the source and target domains are related. But tasks are different

(ii) Transductive Transfer Learning: In transductive transfer learning, the source and target tasks are the same but in different domains. Here, the model needs to be adapted to work under different conditions or different kinds of data. This case is also called domain adaptation—for example, Product Sentiment analysis and YouTube comment sentiment analysis.

(iii) Unsupervised Transfer Learning: In unsupervised transfer learning, neither the source nor the target is labelled. In this case, the target model generates the content and is not involved in any prediction. So, the focus is learning in one domain and generating data in another.

Based on this, the transfer learning methods can also be categorized as

(i) **Feature-based Transfer Learning**, where the features are representations from the source to the target task by modifying layers/ architecture to adapt to the target domain.

(ii) **Parameter–based Transfer Learning**, where the parameters/weights between the source and target models are shared. This sharing is done with adjustments for fine-tuning.

(iii) **Instance-based Transfer Learning**, where some data is reused to train the model of the target domain. Many times, these instances are weighted differently as per the relevance.

The link between transfer learning methods and the types of transfer learning is given in Table 10.3.

Table 10.3 Link Among the Types of Methods and Types

Types	Features-Based Transfer Learning	Parameter-Based Transfer Learning	Instance-Based Transfer Learning
Inductive Transfer	Yes	Yes	Yes
Transductive Transfer	Yes	-	Yes
Unsupervised Transfer	Yes	-	-

10.3 ImageNet and Pretrained Models

ImageNet created many pretrained models in computer vision tasks like image recognition, object detection, and Image segmentation.

The pretrained model implies that the user can download the network architecture and the optimal weights. Pretrained models help developers develop efficient solutions with less data and computing power.

ImageNet has become a benchmark as the repository of images and the evaluation mechanism of state-of-the-art image-based applications. Most people need more data for their experiments, and finding millions of images is difficult. Professor Fei-Fei Li and her team at Stanford University created the ImageNet Project. It is a benchmark dataset created to remove the difficulties of shortage of data. ImageNet is a collection of a wide range of images. Professor Fei-Fei Li met Christiane Fellbaum, the creator of WordNet, the largest net of natural language processing. That is how ImageNet was born. Its popularity is due to a standard benchmark dataset and its ability to serve as an evaluation protocol. ImageNet and some of the public domain datasets are given in Box 10.5.

Box 10.5 ImageNet and Other Popular Datasets

ImageNet is a collection of 14 million Images. Based on Wordnet, where 1000 words are categorized as a set of synonyms. ImageNet, too, has 1000 images under each category (called synsets). ImageNet has 21841 subcategories. Most of the images are humanly annotated.

Fashion – MNIST

Fashion MINIST is a popular dataset with around 60000 training and 10000 testing images. These images are associated with ten classes that indicate the categories of images such as T-shirts, tops, and trousers.

CIFAR – 10

CIFAR is also a powerful dataset that has both colour and greyscale images. The colour images are 32 X 32 in ten classes. There are 6000 images in each class. Overall, there are 50000 training images and 10000 testing images.

Google Open Images

Google open Images is a project like ImageNet. It has 9 million images, most with bounding boxes that suit the object detection problem. Like ImageNet, Google also conducts an Open Images Challenge.

Kaggle

Kaggle is a powerful website that hosts many datasets for programming challenges.

MS COCO

MS COCO is one such dataset that is popular. MS COCO stands for Microsoft Common Objects in Context.

ImageNet conducts ImageNet Large-scale visual recognition challenges (ILSVRC), also called ImageNet challenges, and awards are given to the best models that excel in ImageNet challenges in computer vision. ILSVRC was introduced in 2010. The challenges primarily catered to Image classification and Object detection. Very soon, this competition became a cornerstone event in the domain of computer vision. Most of the challenge winners have become open-source models for public use as pretrained models, as the developers can use them to solve the related problem.

There are many pretrained models available in computer vision and natural language processing. Pretrained models have become the cornerstone of modern deep learning. It helps practitioners craft modern applications even though many have millions of quality data, GPUs, or TPUS to execute the work. The work of pretraining started as a separate field in the 2010s. In the 2010s, many pretrained models appeared in natural language processing. This area of pretraining models is improving faster with transformer models like OpenAI GPT series and Google BERT. Frameworks like TensorFlow, PyTorch, and Hugging Face have also been prolifically developed in computer vision.

AlexNet won the ImageNet challenge in 2012. Alex Krizhevsky, Ilya Sutskever, and Geoffrey Hinton created AlexNet, which won the competition with improved accuracy. AlexNet began a revolution in transfer learning, and every challenge produced many novel architectures.

In deep learning, many large-scale models can be used effectively to do specialized tasks easily. Such a model is called a pretrained model. These models ensure that the knowledge can be transferred to solving the related tasks. For example, to classify a new flower, a related plant pretrained model can be used by removing the plant classifier classification part with the classification part of the flowers. Then, this new neural network is trained on the "new" flower images. By constructing this, the new model would also classify the new images. This approach saves time, resources, and cost.

10.4 Advanced CNN Architectures

In computer vision, advanced CNN architectures like AlexNet, InceptionNet, VGG, and ResNet can be used as pretrained models (Refer Box 10.6). These are the subject of the discussion in the next sections.

Box 10.6 Motivation for Bigger CNN Architectures

The baseline CNN model is a set of convolutional layers/ pooling layers/activation layers for extracting the features from the images. These layers may include additional layers for regularization, like dropout or data augmentation. This part can be called as feature extraction part. The other CNN part is called a classifier, which has fully connected layers with a softmax layer.

The basic design template of CNN is given below in Figure 10.6.

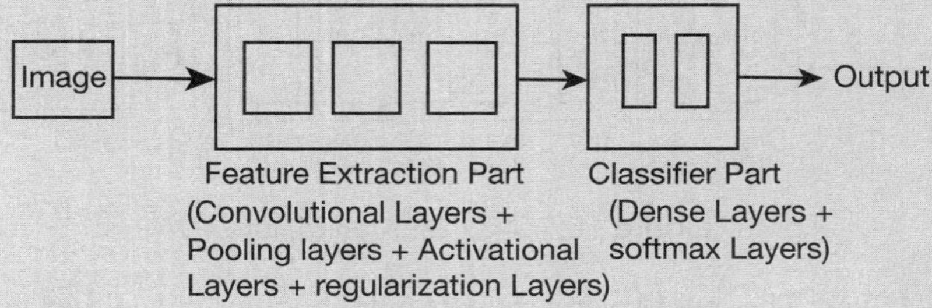

Figure 10.6 Design Template for CNN Network

The motivation for larger CNN architectures is to increase the depth of the network by increasing the number of layers and width of the network. Increasing the depth can cause vanishing gradient problems, making training the network difficult. So, the research focuses on removing these problems associated with increasing the depth and width of the network. The research results are amazing, and many architectures can be used as pretrained models now.

10.4.1 AlexNet Architecture

As discussed, AlexNet was the winner of the ILSVRC 2012 challenge. It is larger than the LeNet-5 architecture discussed in Chapter 9. AlexNet is very deep compared to LeNet, with around 8 layers. It has five convolutional layers and layers for max pooling, Local Region Normalization, ReLU activations, Dropout and fully connected layers.

The layers of AlexNet are listed below:

1. Input Layer
2. Convolutional Layer

3. Max pooling Layer
4. Local Region Normalization Layer
5. ReLU activation layer
6. Dropout layer
7. Fully connected Layers

The complete architecture of AlexNet is given in the following Figure 10.7.

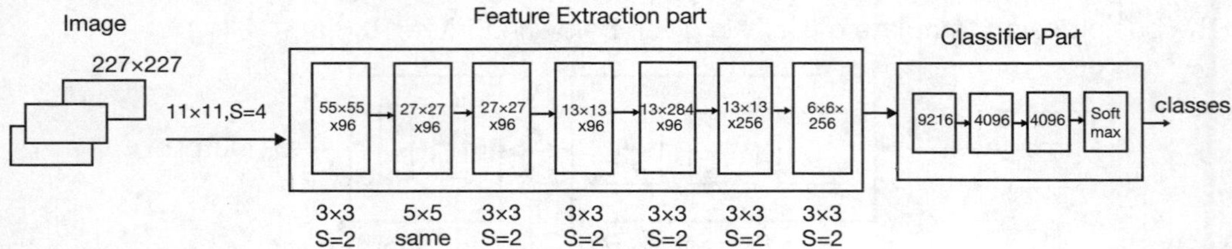

Figure 10.7 AlexNet Architecture

1. **Input Layer:** The input layer accepts an input colour image of size 227 × 227 with 3 colour channels, as RGB images are 3-band images. Feeding the input images to the input layer is the first task. The image size of AlexNet is 227 × 227 to ensure consistency among the images.

2. **Convolutional Layer:** There are five convolutional layers in AlexNet. Normalization and pooling later follow each convolutional layer. The first convolutional layer takes the image of size 227 × 227 × 3 and outputs the feature map of size 55 × 55

   The core of the convolution layer is filters. There are many filters in each convolutional layer. These filters capture the patterns and pass them to the next layers. The extracted features, like edges, textures, or colours, are basic at the initial level. Then, progressively, these features become very complex. Each convolutional layer builds upon the previous layers to get more complex features.

3. **Pooling Layers:** All the captured features are not necessary. So, keeping only the important features is necessary, and the rest of the unnecessary features can be discarded. In short, pooling layers perform dimensionality reduction. AlexNet uses overlap pooling to reduce overfitting.

4. **ReLU Activation Layer:** ReLU is a popular activation function used and popularized by AlexNet. The usage of ReLU increases the convergence of optimizers compared to other activation functions.

5. **Local Region Normalization (LRN):** This layer follows the first and second convolutional layers. Local response provides a lateral inhibition where an excited neuron suppresses the activity of the neighbouring neurons. This lateral inhibition creates competition among the neighbouring neurons for bigger activities. The local region normalization helps to remove the redundancy and co-adaptation. This local region normalization has the advantage of emphasizing the differences between features. Overall, the local region normalization improves the generalization of the model.
6. **Dropout Layer:** Dropout is a regularization technique where the neurons are randomly dropped. This layer follows all convolutional layers after the first two layers. The purpose of dropout is to make the network rely less on specific neurons or features, and introducing this layer increases network generalization.
7. **Fully Connected Layers:** AlexNet uses three fully connected layers. The purpose of the fully connected layer is to consolidate and integrate the features for classification.

The first fully connected layer of AlexNet has 4096 neurons, followed by ReLU and dropout. Fully connected layer 2 has 4096 neurons followed by ReLU and dropout layer. The final fully connected layer has 1000 neurons corresponding to the number of classes. The fully connected final layer uses the softmax activation function to generate the probability of the output classes.

The summary of AlexNet is given in the following Table 10.4.

Table 10.4 Summary of AlexNet

Layers	Num of Filters	Size of the Filter	Stride and Padding	Output Generated
Input Layer	RGB Images with size 227 × 227 × 3			
Convolution Layer 1	96	11 × 11	4	27 × 27 × 96
Max pool layer 1		3 × 3	2	27 × 27 × 96
Convolution Layer 2	256	5 × 5	Stride 1 and padding 2	27 × 27 × 256
Max pool layer 2		3 × 3	Stride = 2	13 × 13 × 256
Convolution Layer 3	384	3 × 3	Stride = 1, padding = 1	13 × 13 × 384

Layers	Num of Filters	Size of the Filter	Stride and Padding	Output Generated
Convolution Layer 4	384	3 × 3	Stride = 1, padding = 1	13 × 13 × 384
Convolution Layer 5	256	3 × 3	Stride = 1	13 × 13 × 256
Max pooling layer 3		3 × 3	Stride = 2	6 × 6 × 256
Fully connected Layer 2	Neurons 4096, ReLU with 50% dropout.			
Fully connected layer 2	Neurons = 4096, ReLU, Dropout = 50%			
Fully connected Layer 3	Neurons = 1000 for 1000 classes, Activation function Softmax.			

The highlights of AlexNet are given in Box 10.7.

Box 10.7 Highlights of AlexNet

AlexNet is very efficient and fast. Also, AlexNet can handle complex features and images. The highlights of AlexNet are listed below:

1. **ReLU Activation Function:** AlexNet introduced much popular ReLU activation function. ReLU activation function, unlike sigmodal functions, has a wide range of output and is instrumental in solving the vanishing gradient problem.
2. **Dropout Layer:** AlexNet used dropout layers to improve generalization.
3. **Data Augmentation:** AlexNet used data augmentation layers to improve generalization.
4. **Local Response Normalization:** Its purpose is to normalize the contrast of ReLU's output to enhance the generalization of the model.
5. **Weight Regularization:** Another specialty is weight regularization to improve generalization.
6. **Novel Reporting of Results:** AlexNet has a novel way of reporting the results, such as Top 5 error rates. It indicates the proportion of correct labels that fall apart from the Top 5 predicted labels. For example, if the correct label is kidney, the Top 5

predicted labels are brain, brain, leg, and hand. It can be observed that the correct label is not there in that Top 5 list. So, the error reported would be that the Top 5 error is 1, as the correct label is not in that list.

7. **Training on Multiple GPU:** The training of AlexNet is carried out using Stochastic Gradient Descent with a batch size of 128. The hyperparameter value of momentum is 0.9 with a weight decay of 0.0005.

10.4.2 VGGNet

Simonyan and Zisserman from the University of Oxford, with their team, created a convolutional Neural Network called VGGNet. VGG stands for Visual Geometry Group at Oxford University. They published a paper titled "Very Deep Convolutional Networks for Large-Scale Image Recognition: in 2014. VGG turned up as a runner in the ILSVRC competition in 2014. VGG is very influential as it is a backbone for many research projects, such as object detection and image segmentation.
The architecture of VGG 16 is shown in Figure 10.8.

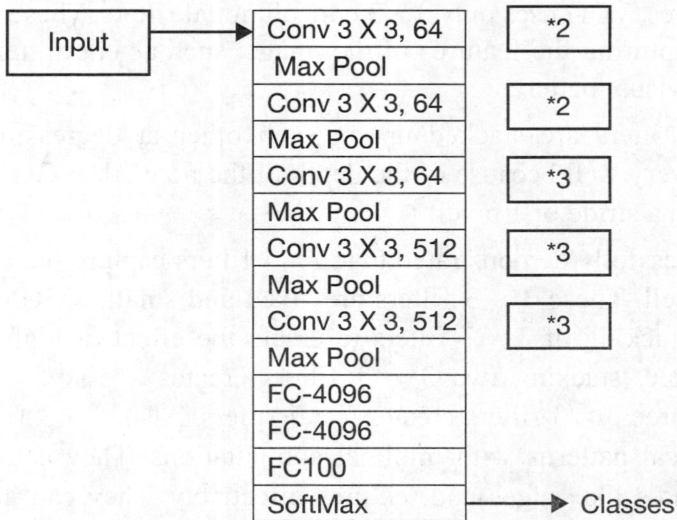

Figure 10.8 VGG16 Architecture

VGG 16 consists of 16 weight layers. As a convention, these 16 represent 13 convolutional layers and 3 fully connected layers. Usually, by convention, only convolutional and pooling layers are counted. VGG16 and VGG19 subsequently use 16 (13 convolutional and three fully connected layers with many pooling layers after the convolution layers) and 19 weight layers (16 convolutional layers and three fully connected layers with many pooling layers following convolutional layers). Both VGG 16 and VGG 19 are similar in all aspects. The only difference is that VGG 19 has three extra convolutional layers in decreasing depth of the network and captures more complex features at the expense of more parameters and resources.

The primary components of VGGNet are

1. Input Layer
2. Convolutional Layer
3. Pooling Layers
4. ReLU Layer
5. Fully Connected Layers

1. **Input Layer:** The input image is 224 × 224 RGB image in VGG. So, it is a 3 channel image.
2. **Convolutional Layers:** There are 13 convolutional layers in VGG16 and 16 convolutional layers in VGG19. Each layer, Unlike the other CNN architectures, VGG uses only 3 × 3 convolutional filters. These 3 × 3 filters are good at capturing the features of the image, such as edges, textures, colours, and other visual patterns.

   All these filters are stacked up on each other at decreasing depth. VGG performs very well because of the depth of the network. VGG uses only 3 × 3 filters with a stride of 1 pixel.

   VGG successfully demonstrated that 3 × 3 filters capture the directionality of patterns well. These 3 × 3 filters are fixed and small. VGGNet innovatively used the stacking of 3 × 3 filters to create the effect of higher-order filters. For example, stacking two 3 × 3 filters creates a 5 × 5 filter. Similarly, stacking three 3 × 3 filters creates 7 × 7 filters. Also, 3 × 3 filters effectively capture local patterns with minimal computations. They can capture lower-level features like edges and textures effectively. They can also capture the directionality of the patterns. Stacking 3 × 3 filters brings non-linearity into the model and captures many complex input and output mappings.

   The advantage of stacking is that it saves time by reducing the computations. For example, a stack of three 3 × 3 filters needs 3^3C^2, computations, where C is the number of channels. This results in many computations. But one 7 × 7 filter requires $7^2 \times C^2 = 49 \times C^2$ computations. As $27 \times C^2 < 49 \times C^2$, one can observe how much saving is done. One can now rationalize that stacking 3 × 3 filters yields fewer computations.

So, the advantages of stacking 3 × 3 filters are:

(i) More efficiency by stacking 3 × 3 filters with fewer computations.

(ii) Deeper architectures without excessive computations.

(iii) Improved training. This objective is achieved with incremental receptive field expansion.

(iv) As depth increases, it captures higher-level features while retaining local ones.

The first layer of VGG 16 has 64 filters; subsequently, the number of filters doubles after some layers. The final layer has 512 filters. These filters capture the image's hierarchical features.

3. **Pooling Layers:** A pooling layer follows a convolutional layer in VGG. The pooling layer uses a 2 × 2 filter with a stride of 2 pixels. The purpose of the pooling layer is to reduce the input size by half and to increase the number of channels.

The other layers that VGG use cases are listed below:

4. **ReLU Layer:** ReLU activations are used to be computationally very effective and solve the vanishing gradient problem.
5. **Global Average Pooling:** It is a layer that takes the average of the contents.
6. **Dropout Layer**: This layer is used with the first two fully connected layers to handle overfitting, and also, the weight initialization helps the network convergence. Dropout for first Fully connected with dropout ratio = 0.5
7. **Fully Connected Layers:** VGG uses three fully connected layers. The first fully connected layer uses 4096 neurons. The second fully connected network uses 4096 neurons. The final fully connected layer is the classification layer, with neurons equal to the number of classes. As ImageNet has 1000 classes, the final output layer has 1,000 classes.

Training of VGGNet

The training of VGG is done with a mini-batch optimization with a Gradient Descent optimizer with a momentum of 0.5. The learning rate is 0.01, which decreases by a factor of 10 when the validation frequency improves. The accuracy reported for VGG 16 is a top 5 error rate of 8.1%, and for VGG 19, The top 5 error rate is 7.4%

The highlights of VGGNet are given in Box. 10.8.

Box 10.8 Highlights of VGG 16 and VGG 19

VGGNet is very popular in the transfer learning community due to the following reasons:

(i) VGG is easy to use and implement as it is a homogeneous architecture of convolutional and pooling layers. VGGNet is known for its simplicity. VGG networks serve as a foundation model for many projects in computer vision. VGG16 and VGG19 are the most commonly used configuration.

(ii) VGG is the deepest architecture. For example, VGG19 has 19 layers.

(iii) VGG serves as a standardization of the convolution layer. It just uses a Stacking of 3 X 3 Filters with stride 1 and max pooling with a stride of 2.

(iv) It is highly effective in feature extraction.

(v) Transfer learning uses VGG more often for feature extraction is extremely popular.

(vi) VGG has become a benchmark for many applications related to computer vision.

The limitations of VGG are that the number of parameters and computational costs are high. Total number of parameters of VGGNet is approximately 135 million.

10.4.3 Inception

Inception is also called InceptionNet and GoogLeNet (It is not Googlenet!). Inception was introduced by Christian Szegedy and others from the Google team through a paper titled "Going Deeper with Convolutions" in 2014. InceptionNet introduced a modular approach to improving the efficiency of image classification. InceptionNet works almost at the human efficiency level and produced state-of-the-art results in the ILSVRC Challenge 2014.

InceptionNet focused on increasing the neural network's depth and width, and the Inception module fulfilled this objective. Inception is the fundamental building block of InceptionNet. It allows information to be collected through different-sized filters and combined so that objects of all scales are captured effectively.

The components of InceptionNet are given below:

(i) Layers

(ii) Inception module

(iii) Dimensionality reduction using 1×1 convolution filter

(iv) Auxiliary classifiers

(v) Global average pooling

InceptionNet is a deep network with 22 layers. It consists of traditional convolution, max-pooling, and regularization layers like AlexNet and VGGNet.

The architecture of InceptionNet is given as shown below in Figure 10.9.

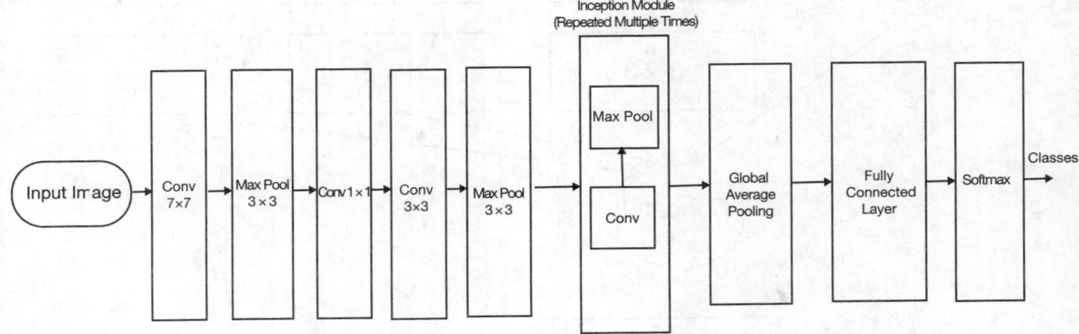

Figure 10.9 Types of Transfer Learning

The initial layers of InceptionNet resemble AlexNet. It has an input layer and a max pool layer. The latter layers of InceptionNet have a set of inception modules. The end layers of InceptionNet collect all the feature maps and use the Global average Pooling and Softmax layers to classify the image. Global average pooling reduces the number of parameters and replaces the fully connected network. The global average pooling can use feature maps directly to pass them to the softmax layer for classification.

The core idea of InceptionNet is the inception module. The idea is to capture objects in images of different scales. It is obvious that an object at a longer distance occupies a small space in the image; if it is closer, the space occupied by the image is more. So, a normal CNN can miss it. AlexNet uses a 7 × 7 filter, 5 × 5 filter, etc. The idea of the inception net is that "why not combine all the filters?" The collection of filters is called an inception block.

An inception block starts with an input and splits it into different paths. Each path has a different-sized filter or pooling. In short, the different receptive fields of the same image are obtained. The inception block finally concatenates all the output and passes it on to the next layers. The inception module's actual implementation is shown below in Figure 10.10.

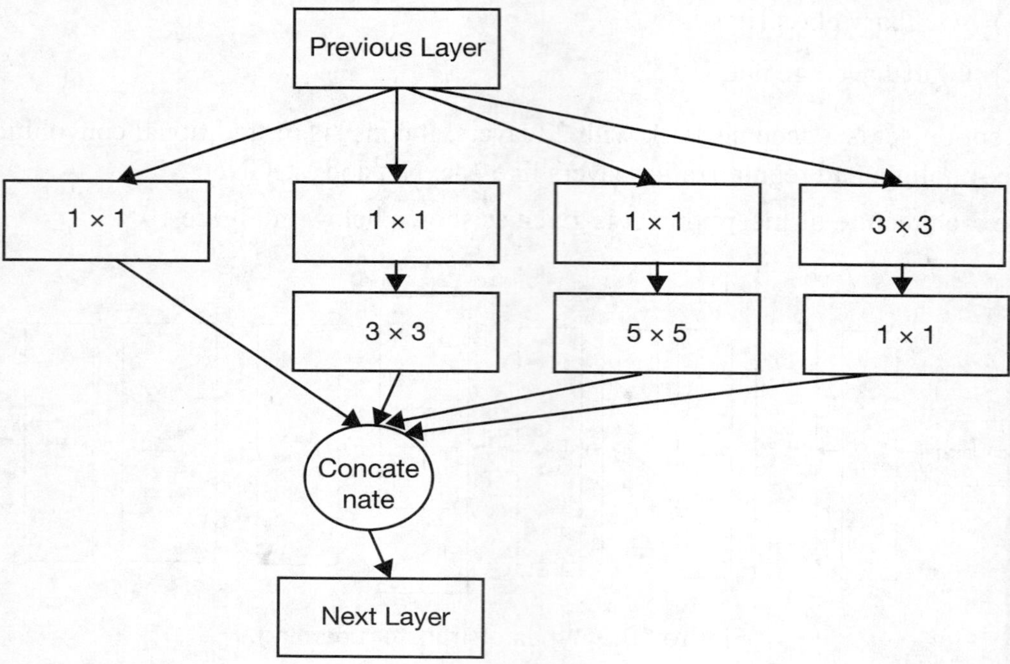

Figure 10.10 Inception Module

The inception module uses padding. Padding is used so that the input and output have the same shape. The different filters produce the results in different shapes, so all the results should be converted to the same shape. But the combination of filters results are quadrupled.

1 × 1 Convolutional Filter

A 1 × 1 convolution filter solves the exponential growth of the output. 1 × 1 convolutions are used to reduce the depth of each path. The following numerical problem explains the advantages of 1 × 1 layer. 1 × 1 layer is called a "reduce layer" or "bottleneck." Layer. Its purpose is to reduce the dimension, focusing on reducing computations. It does reduction by reducing the depth.

Example 10.1: Let's assume the input is 12 × 12 × 24. The convolution layer with 16 filters of kernel size, 5 × 5, is used. Find the number of computations involved. Also, apply a 1 × 1-dimensional reduction filter with 8 filters as intermediate and show that such an arrangement reduces the number of computations. Is the usage of 1 × 1 Justified?

Solution:

The suggested first arrangement is shown in Figure 10.11.

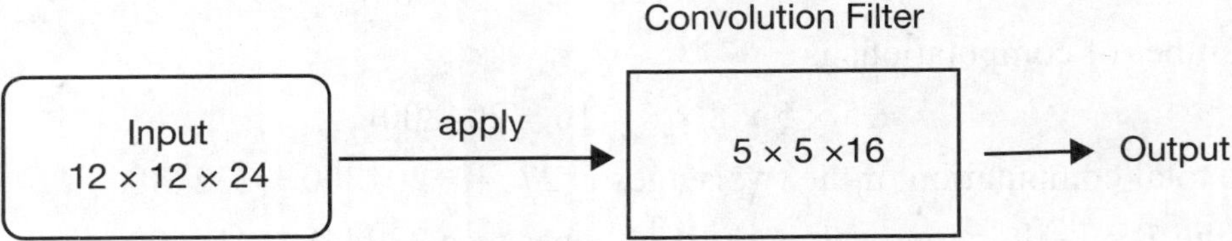

Figure 10.11 Initial Arrangement

The size of the output is computed as
$(W - F + 1) \times (H - F + 1)$. Here, H and W are the height and width of the input image, and F is the filter size. So, the Input height and width are 12 and 12, respectively. Substituting this, we get,

$$(12 - 5 + 1) \times (12 - 5 + 1) = 8 \times 8$$

The amount of computations is given as

$$\text{Filter width} \times \text{Filter height} \times \text{Input depth} \times \text{Input width} \times \text{Input height} \times \text{Number of filters}$$

$$= 5 \times 5 \times 24 \times 8 \times 8 \times 16 = 614400$$

Let us apply a 1 × 1 Filter between the above blocks, as shown in Figure 10.12.

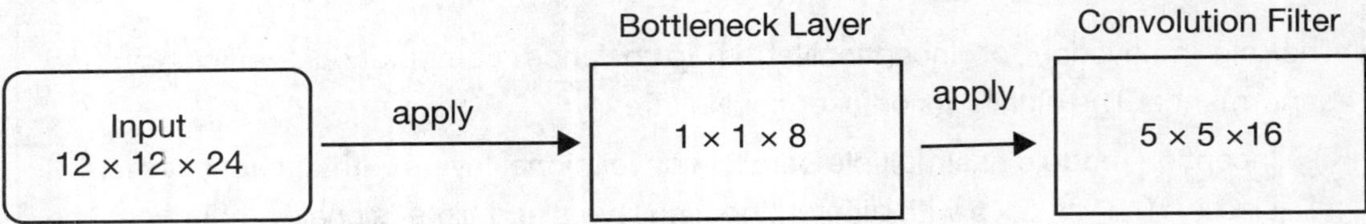

Figure 10.12 Types of Transfer Learning

1 × 1 layer preserves the spatial dimension. So, the input image width and height are preserved. 1 × 1 layer only changes the input depth and equals the number of filters used. So, the result of the first stage is 12 × 12 × 8.
The amount of the computation of the first stage is

$$\text{Filter width} \times \text{Filter height} \times \text{Input depth} \times \text{Input width} \times \text{Input height} \times \text{Number of filters}$$

$$= 1 \times 1 \times 24 \times 12 \times 12 \times 8 = 27648$$

Now, let us compute for the second stage, where the input is 12 × 12 × 8 (resultant of bottleneck layer) to the 5 × 5 × 16 layer. The size is

$$(12 - 5 + 1) \times (12 - 5 + 1) = 8 \times 8$$

The number of computations is

$$5 \times 5 \times 8 \times 8 \times 16 = 204800$$

So, the total computation of the two stages is 27648+204800 = 232448.

Using the 1 × 1 filter approach is justifiable because 232448 < 614400, as there is a saving of 381952 computations. Hence, 1 × 1 convolution is justified as dimension reduction.

Auxiliary Classifiers

InceptionNet also uses two auxiliary classifiers at intermediate levels. The final loss is the weighted sum of the auxiliary classifiers' loss and the real loss. The purpose of these auxiliary classifiers is that they are used to combat the problem of vanishing gradients. However, the final classifiers are not used for inference. Box 10.9 illustrates the highlights of InceptionNet architecture.

Box 10.9 Highlights of InceptionNet

The big motivation of InceptionNet is to balance computational efficiency and performance. The highlights of InceptionNet are:

(i) Inception module has multiple parallel convolutional layers with different kernels of size 1 × 1, 3 × 3, 5 × 5 with different pooling layers and dimensionality reduction. The usage of inception modules reduces the number of parameters.

(ii) The motivation is to design a deeper network.

(iii) Global average pooling to replace fully connected layers. The introduction of global average pooling is another innovation.

(iv) Using auxiliary classifiers at the intermediate stage to guide the final classification process, remove vanishing gradient problems, and improve regularization. The auxiliary classifiers at the intermediate stage are another innovation.

InceptionNet uses stochastic gradient descent with a momentum algorithm. The learning rate is 0.9. The learning rate decays at 4% for every epoch. InceptionNet displayed the result at a Top 5 error rate of 6.67%, almost closer to human-level performance.

10.4.4 ResNet

Microsoft introduced ResNet in 2015, and it won the ILSVRC competition in 2015. There are many versions of ResNet. Some versions are ResNet – 18, ResNet – 34, ResNet – 50, ResNet – 101 and ResNet – 152.

ResNet's idea is to solve the problem of training deeper architectures. The biggest problems here are the vanishing gradient and expanding gradient problems. These problems are discussed in Chapter 5 of this textbook. ResNet can solve the vanishing gradient problem by using shortcuts or skipping connections. Skip connections are the alternate paths for the gradient to flow through. The idea is to use a shortcut that directly skips one or more layers to the output, as shown in Figure 10.13.

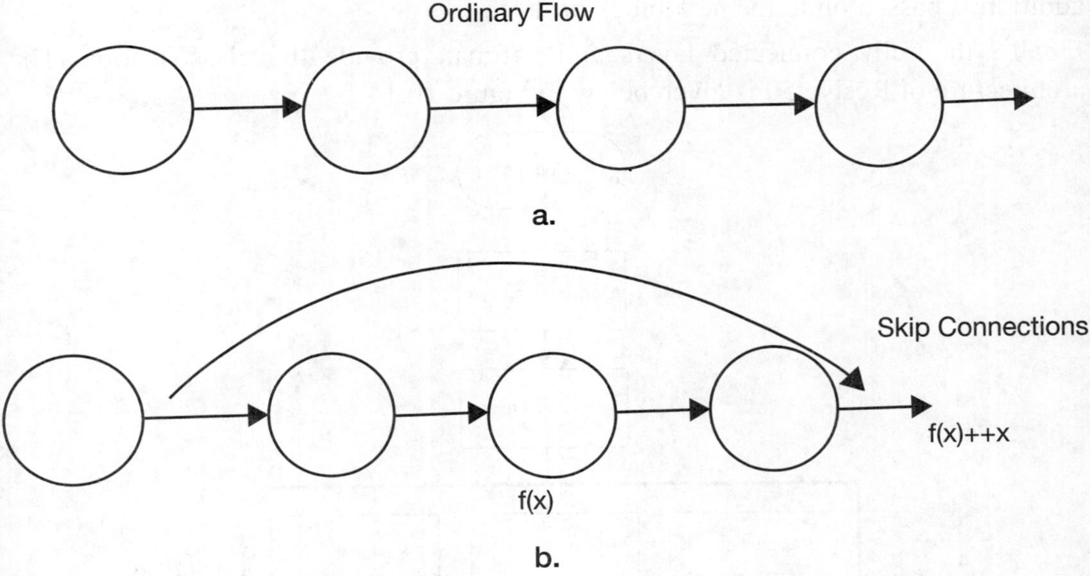

Figure 10.13 (a) Ordinary Flow (b) Flow of Gradients with Skip Connections

Skip connections allow learning of the identity function. If the input is x and the output is y. Then, the residual is the difference between y and x. $f(x) = y - x$. So, the network learns $f(x)$. For example, if $x = 60$ and $y = 70$, the residual is 10. So, the output is $x + f(x) = 60 + 10 = 70$, the same as the input. So, the idea is to learn the residual, and the network tries to learn the residual, that is, the difference between y and x, as $f(x)$. Skip connections allow for deeper networks, leading to better performance. In the above figure, $F(x)$ is the learned residual mapping, and x is the input. If the optimal function is closer to identity mapping, then the network pushes the weights approximately to zero so that the output is unity.

A branch consists of two paths – a main path and a shortcut.

The main path has convolutional layers and ReLU activation layers. This path allows ResNet to learn complex features. This path has as many residual blocks as many as possible. Batch normalization layers follow convolution layers and before ReLU layers. It helps to stabilize and accelerate the training process. Global average pooling is used instead of fully connected layers as these layers help to reduce the number of parameters and avoid overfitting.

The shortcut allows the input to bypass the main path to the addition operation. There is no change in the value in this path. The last part is the addition, where the input is added with the transformed data of the main path. This result is like the original data and the features learned along the main path. The resultant of the addition is passed on to the next block or layer.

Finally, the fully connected layers and softmax provide the classification. The architecture of ResNet50 is given below in Figure 10.14.

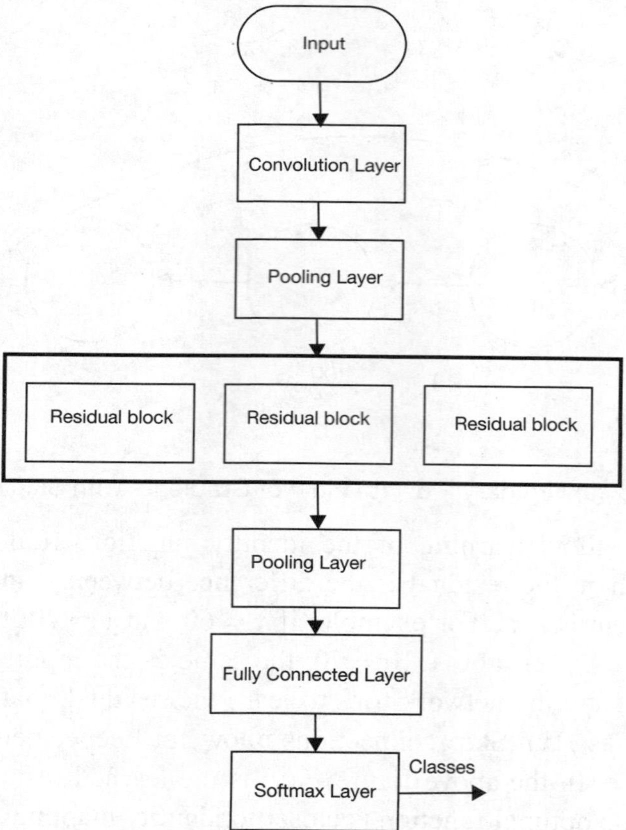

Figure 10.14 ResNet architecture

ResNet50 starts like AlexNet with the convolutional and pooling layers. However, it has multiple residual blocks and 50 layers in total (Stage 1: 7 × 7 convolutional layer = 1 layer, Stage 2: 3 residual block = 9 convolutional layer, Stage 3: 4 residual block = 12 convolutional layer, Stage 4: 6 residual block = 18 convolutional layer, Stage 5 = 3 residual block = 9 convolutional layer, Fully connected softmax layers = 1 layer = total 50 layers). The highlights of ResNet is given in Box 10.10.

Box 10.10 Highlights of ResNet

The motivation of ResNet is to remove the vanishing gradient problem. This task is achieved by adding shortcuts or skipping connections. The highlights of ResNet are:

(i) **Residual Learning** – Residual blocks with skip connections are an innovation. Skip connections enable learning residual mappings and optimizing them. By regulating the gradient flow, ResNet makes optimizing the network easier by reducing the number of parameters.

(ii) The motivation of ResNet is to develop deeper networks where the layers are in the 100s and 1000s and that can adapt to the tasks of different domains. The motivation is also to design a wider network.

ResNet was trained with mini-batch Gradient Descent with momentum 0.9, Learning rate 0.1, and L_2 regularization.

The search for better performing pretrained models is endless. Many such pretrained models are available for computer vision tasks (Refer Box 10.11). Some models are motivated to develop lightweight models, specifically for certain applications like edge devices and more pretrained models are given in Box 10.11.

Box 10.11 More Pretrained Models

Many pretrained models are available for computer vision tasks. Some of the models are motivated to develop lightweight models and for some specific applications like, such as edge devices.

Some of the pretrained models are listed below.

1. ZFNet – A model modified by AlexNet that won the ImageNet competition in 2013.
2. Xception – This model is a modification of ResNet that uses a 1 × 1 convolutional layer followed by depth-wise 2D convolution that replaces the Inception module. This model is referred to as 'eXtreme Inception".

3. DenseNet – A model that uses skip connections like ResNet that perform concatenation instead of addition as in ResNet.
4. SqueezeNet – This is a lightweight model.
5. ShuffleNet – A network that shuffles the parameters of a group of filters to improve the performance. The performance improvement is due to improved information flow due to shuffling.
6. MobileNet V2 – A lightweight model that uses skip connections and depth-wise separable layers.
7. DarkNet-53 – A popular pretrained model used in object detection tasks in YOLO.
8. EfficientNet – Another pretrained model to scale up images' depth, width, and input resolution.
9. AmoebaNet – A pretrained model that uses an evolutionary algorithm to identify the best neural architectures.

10.5 Transfer Learning Models

There are three major approaches to transfer learning. They are:

1. Using the pertained network as a classifier
2. Using pertained network features
3. Fine-tuning

10.5.1 Using a Classifier

Let us assume that one needs to classify an image, say a flower, for which there is little-labelled data. Assume a pertained model for classifying another type of flower is already available. As the domains are similar, one can use the pretrained model as a classifier for our flower images. The pretrained model is used as it is (Refer to Figure 10.15).

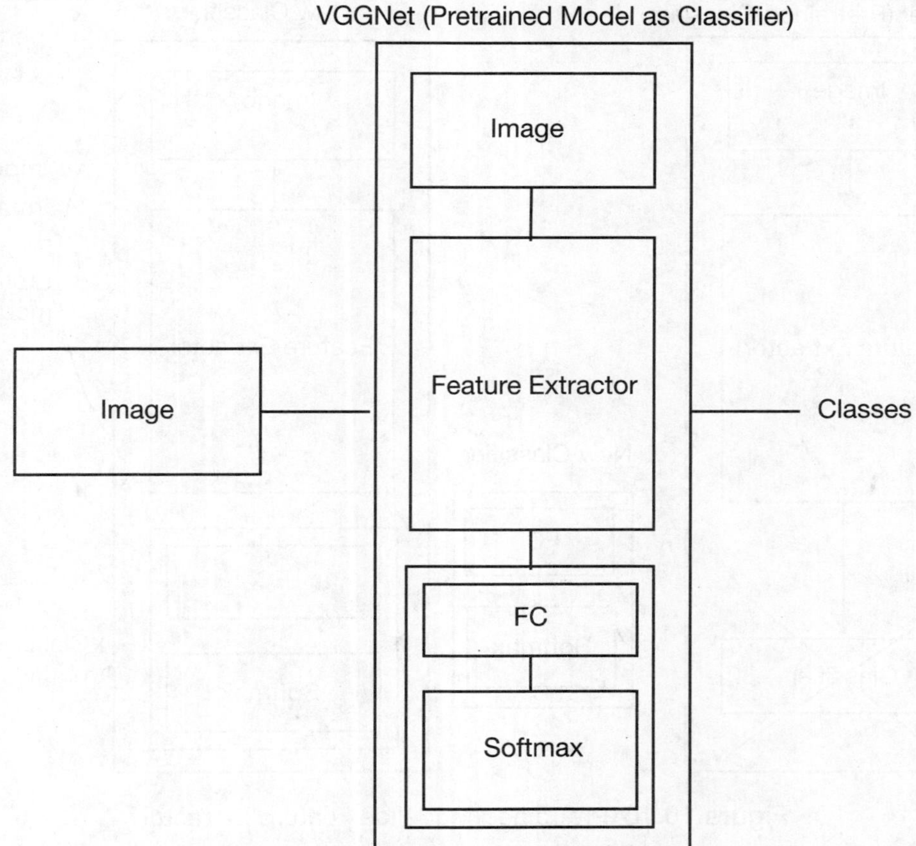

Figure 10.15 Pretrained Model as Classifier

10.5.2 Using as a Feature Extractor

A pretrained model can also be used as a feature extractor.

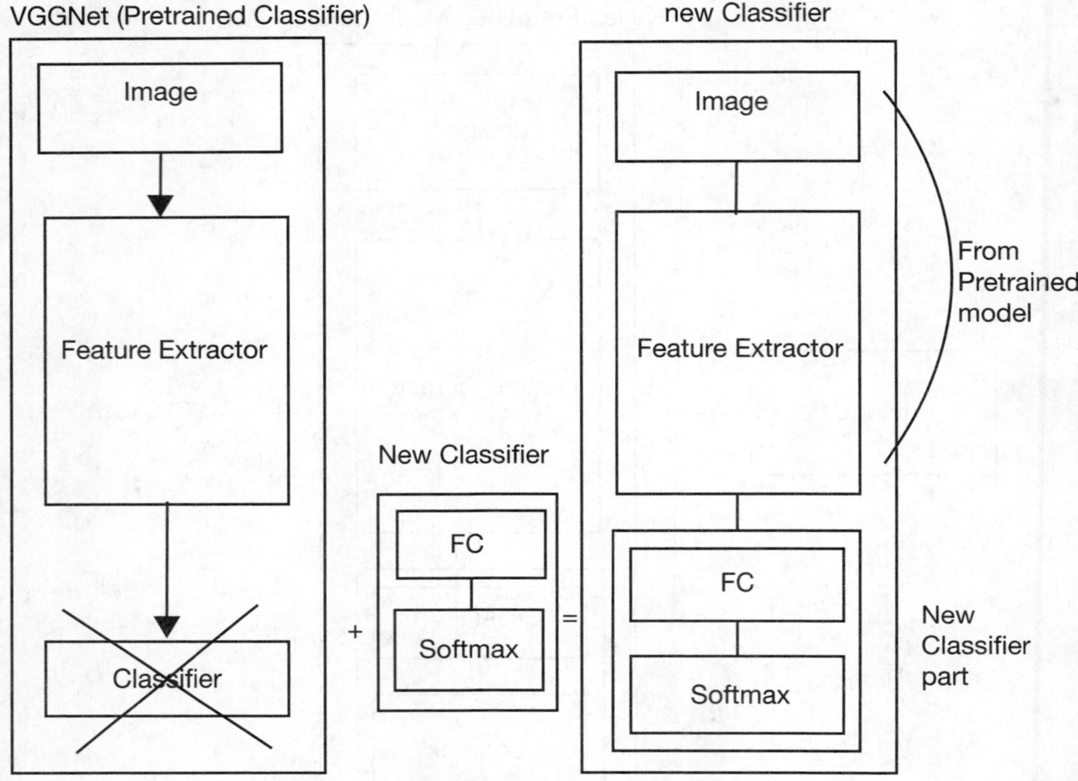

Figure 10.16 Pretrained Model as Feature Extractor

Figure 10.16 illustrates the arrangement of a pretrained model as a feature extractor. The steps of this arrangement are given below:

(i) Take a pretrained VGG model with its classifier part removed. Why? VGGNet is trained for ImageNet with 1000 classes.

(ii) A new classifier for classifying the new dataset is prepared by creating a classifier part with the requirements for three classes.

(iii) The pretrained classifier with the truncated classifier part is added to the new classifier to create a new classifier.

(iv) This created classifier is trained with labelled data of new data.

The advantage of the approach is that all previously learned feature maps are reused.

10.5.3 Fine-tuning

Fine-tuning is a category of transfer learning that helps a pretrained model solve a new task. Fine-tuning applies to a problem where the source domain differs from the target domain.

One may be tempted to start from scratch. However, starting from scratch is optional. Table 10.5 justifies fine-tuning rather than constructing the neural network from scratch.

Table 10.5 Justification of Fine-tuning over Development from Scratch

Fine-tuning Approach	New Neural Network Approach
Weights are already optimized. So, its usage reduces time and effort.	A new neural network starts with random values. So much time is required for its training.
The learning rate is optimized.	The learning rate in a new neural network starts with randomly initialized weights for the learning rate. So, the convergence of a new neural network takes much time.

These are the steps of fine-tuning.

(i) Use a pretrained model. Select a pretrained model that has already been trained on a large dataset.

(ii) Select the target task and dataset. The task needs to be solved, and it comes with a dataset called the target dataset.

(iii) Fine-tuning requires adjusting the model architecture. Here, the output layer of the pretrained model is replaced to suit the new target task. For example, the pretrained model must have been trained for the 1000 classes as in ImageNet, and the target requirement may be for only three classes. So, place the final layers of the pretrained model with the new layers tailored for the target task.

(iv) Fine-tune the model—Now, a decision about the level of freezing the layers has to be made. What is freezing? Freezing ensures that the weights of certain layers are not updated. The weights and biases are kept constant for the frozen layers and no weight update occurs in these layers during the backpropagation step of the training.

(v) The early layers of the model are generic, like edges, lines, and points. They are universal. These layers can be frozen. Similarly, the later model layers have higher-level features of the source dataset. The following Table 10.6 summarizes the learning of features by the convolution layers.

Table 10.6 Summary of Features Learning for Freezing Layers

Features	Examples of Such Features	Layers that Learn these Features
Low-Level features	Examples include lines, edges, and blobs. These features are not specific task related features but generic for all images. These apply to all tasks and datasets.	Entry-level convolutional layers capture the general features of the images.
Mid-Level features	Examples include Shapes, corners, and other geometrical shapes like squares and circles.	Middle convolutional layers capture these features based on the early convolutional layers' input. For example, a corner is an intersection of two edges.
High-level features	Examples include features like eyes, nose and face of human beings. These are not general features and are task-specific features.	The higher-level convolutional layers capture these complex features based on the feature composition of the earlier inputs.

(vi) A decision about the level of overfitting can be made. If the dataset is small, updating all the weights leads to overfitting as the training dataset learns the data with noise and outliers. Small dataset leads to poor generalization. Freezing the early layers may prevent this problem of overfitting.

(vii) Joint training is conducted after adding specific layers required for the problem.

(viii) Joint training is conducted for non-frozen layers and the newly added classifiers.

10.5.4 Level of Fine Tuning

The important task is the decision about the freezing of the layers. Two factors influencing this decisions are as listed below:

(i) Size of the target dataset.

(ii) Similarity of the domains.

1. The target dataset is small, and the source and target domains are similar

In this case, the original dataset is similar to the target dataset. In this case, both the general and higher-level features are relevant. So, the feature extraction part can be retained.

The classifier part should be retrained. There is no need for more fine-tuning, as it may lead to overfitting. Feature extraction on a smaller dataset is prone to overfitting. Since the dataset is very small, it may only cater to some of its features. If fine-tuning is too much, it could lead to more overfitting. Hence, more caution is required. Table 10.7 summarizes the actions that are required for this condition.

Table 10.7 Data is Small, and Domains are Similar

Scenario	Size of the Target Dataset	Similarity of the Target Domain and Source Domain.	What to Freeze?	Decision about Overfitting
1	Small	Similar	Use a pretrained model as feature extraction	More fine-tuning may lead to overfitting.

2. The target dataset is large target domain is similar to the source domain

In this case, the original dataset is similar to the target dataset. So, both general and higher-level features are relevant. So, keeping 60-80% of the pretraining model as relevant is better.

The target dataset is also large, so the model is not prone to overfitting. However, fine-tuning the entire network is optional. Table 10.8 summarizes the actions that are required for this condition.

Table 10.8 Data is Large, and Domains are Similar

Scenario	Size of the Target Dataset	Similarity of the Target Domain and Source Domain.	What to Freeze?	Decision about Overfitting
2	Large	Similar	Fine-tune with 60-80% frozen layer.	Overfitting is not an issue.

3. The target dataset is small, and the target domain differs from the source domain.

Here, the target dataset is very small, and the target domain differs from the source domain. In this case, it is better to freeze only the entry-level features, as the higher-level features may not be relevant to the task.

It is better to retrain from the very beginning or not to freeze any layers. Since the dataset is very small, the optimal decision would be to freeze the initial part of the network where generic features are available.

As the dataset is small, one should be careful about overfitting. Table 10.9 summarizes the actions that are required for this condition.

Table 10.9 Summary When Data is Small, and Domains are Dissimilar

Scenario	Size of the Target Dataset	Similarity of the Target Domain and Source Domain.	What to Freeze?	Decision about Overfitting
3	Small	Dissimilar	Fine-tune with the entry-level layers alone frozen.	More fine-tuning may lead to overfitting.

4. The target dataset is large, and the target domain is different from the source domain

Here, the target dataset is large and different from the source dataset. Fine-tuning applies to problems where the source domain differs from the target domain. Table 10.10 summarizes the actions that are required for this condition.

Table 10.10 Summary When Data is Large, and Domains are Dissimilar

Scenario	Size of the Target Dataset	Similarity of the Target Domain and Source Domain.	What to Freeze?	Decision about Overfitting
4	Large	Very different	Fine-tune through the entire network, as everything is different	Overfitting is not an issue.

Fine-tuning the entire network is necessary, as overfitting is not a major issue.

Summary

1. Human beings are known to transfer knowledge from one task to another.
2. Deep learning systems use pretrained models to transfer knowledge to solve another task.
3. A pretrained model is a model that has been trained on a larger dataset and can be stored and transferred for later use to predict another related task.
4. Transfer learning is a machine learning paradigm in which the knowledge gained from one or more tasks, domains, and datasets is leveraged to solve another task in the target domain.
5. Transfer learning's advantages include reducing development time and improving the baseline and final model performance.
6. Transfer learning is justified by data scarcity, domain shift, and higher complexity.
7. A domain is a tuple of feature space and the marginal probability of data point X.
8. A task is a tuple of label space and objectives.
9. Inductive transfer learning is the transfer of learning across similar domains but different tasks.
10. Transductive transfer learning involves transferring knowledge across different domains but the same tasks.
11. In unsupervised transfer learning, both domains have unlabelled data.
12. The knowledge in transfer learning may refer to the learned features, weights and parameters, hidden representations, and task-specific information.
13. ImageNet is a benchmark dataset with evaluation protocols.
14. The pretrained models are large-scale models that can be used for specialized tasks.
15. AlexNet is an advanced CNN architecture. AlexNet's specialties are convolutional layers with varied-size spatial filters, ReLU, a specialty introduced by AlexNet, and Local region normalization.
16. VGGNet is another deep convolutional layer. Its specialty is stacking 3×3 filters, which reduces parameters and saves time.
17. InceptionNet is also called InceptionNet. The inception module captures the features of the image using a set of varied-size filters.

18. ResNet uses skip connections to solve the problem of vanishing gradients. Learn identity mapping by using skip connections.
19. Skip connections help to build deeper deep-learning architectures.
20. Transfer learning can use pretraining models as a classifier if the source and target domains are similar.
21. Transfer learning using a pretrained model as a feature extractor.
22. Fine-tuning is adjusting the layers so that a pretrained model can be used to solve the target task.
23. The choice of fine-tuning is based on two parameters: the size of the dataset and the domain similarity of the source and target.

Glossary

1. Pretrained model – A large-scale model trained on a larger dataset and used for solving some related tasks.
2. Transfer – Reuse of the learned features of the source domain in the target domain.
3. Domain – It is a tuple of feature space and a marginal probability distribution of input features.
4. Task – A tuple of label (output) space and conditional probability distribution of label (output) given input features.
5. Inductive transfer learning – The transfer of knowledge among similar domains is called inductive transfer learning.
6. Transductive transfer learning – It refers to a Transfer of knowledge among dissimilar domains.
7. Unsupervised transfer learning – An example of unsupervised transfer learning is where source and destination domains have unlabelled data.
8. Local region normalization – It is the normalization of contrast enhancement of ReLU output for better classification.
9. Stacking of filters – Low dimensional filters stack to yield higher filter response.
10. Inception – The idea of using convolutional layers with filters of varied sizes.
11. Auxiliary Classifiers – A set of classifiers to predict labels and provide guidance for the final classification.

12. 1 × 1 layer – A layer called bottleneck layer for providing dimension reductionality.
13. Skip connections – This shortcut provides an alternate path for gradient flow.
14. Identity mapping – The idea of skip connections learning identity mapping.
15. Fine-tuning – A process of adjustment of layers to solve the target task.

Short Questions

1. What is transfer learning? What are the justifications for transfer learning?
2. What are the advantages of transfer learning?
3. List five domains with their feature spaces.
4. What is the framework of transfer learning?
5. How is ImageNet influential in modern transfer learning?
6. What is a pretrained model? List out five pretrained models for computer vision.
7. What are the specialties of AlexNet?
8. Why 1 × 1 convolution filter is important?
9. What is the global average pooling?
10. What is an inception?
11. How 1 × 1 filter does feature dimension reduction?
12. What is the role of auxiliary classifiers?
13. What is the need for skip connections?
14. What is fine-tuning?
15. What are the justifications for fine-tuning?

Long Questions

1. Explain in detail the framework of transfer learning.
2. Explain in detail AlexNet architecture.
3. Explain in detail InceptionNet architecture.
4. Explain in detail the specialties of VGGNet.
5. Explain in detail how ResNet is performing.
6. Explain in detail the fine-tuning process for different scenarios.

Numerical Problems

1. Show that stacking three 3 × 3 filters gives a 7 × 7 filter. How many parameters are saved?
2. Let the input be 28 × 28 × 8. Let the convolutional filter be 5 × 5, and the number of filters is 4. Justify the usage of a 1 × 1 filter in the arrangement and demonstrate that it reduces the dimensions.

Crossword

Across

1. In ___________ transfer learning, the domains are similar.
3. A tuple of label space and the conditional probability of label given input is called ___________.
5. Transductive learning involves domains that are ___________. (similar/dissimilar)
7. A large-scale model trained on a larger dataset and used for solving related tasks is called a ___________ model.
8. LRN promotes ___________ inhibition among neurons and helps to emphasize the input features.
10. The domain is a tuple of ___________ space and marginal

proability distribution of input features.

11. The process of adjustment of layers is called ____________ tuning.
13. AlexNet marked a revolution in the context of transfer learning. (true/false)
14. Professor Fei-Fei Lee is associated with ____________ project.
16. 1 × 1 layer is called a ____________ layer.
17. VGGNet is easy to use and implement. (true/false)
18. Skip connections provide an alternate path for ____________ flow.

Down

1. The idea of using convoluational filters of various size is called ____________.
2. Transfer learning solves the problem of data and ____________.
3. The reuse of features learned in one domain and used for another domain is called ____________ learning.
4. In unsupervised transfer learning the source and domain have ____________ data. (labelled/unlabelled)
6. ____________ of filters reduce parameters and yield higher filter response.
9. Auxillary classifiers guide correct classification. (true/false)
12. Skip connection learn ____________ mapping.
15. AlexNet won the competition of ILSVRC challenge in 2012. (true/false)

Jumbled Sentences

B	I	R	J	R	K	L	Y	I	D	E	N	T	I	T	Y	F	A	P	R	C	Q	Y	M	Y
O	Z	N	Y	L	G	K	C	C	E	Q	G	V	W	N	C	J	I	W	I	O	S	M	X	C
H	O	P	C	Z	A	V	A	I	X	X	T	H	D	D	I	V	S	J	L	M	Y	L	W	V
A	J	T	G	E	V	T	W	A	E	B	U	R	N	E	H	D	T	C	U	P	U	I	Y	K
U	U	D	R	D	P	F	E	A	T	U	R	E	U	D	D	D	A	Y	W	U	V	M	S	P
U	A	D	A	W	J	T	P	R	Y	G	X	R	J	E	G	I	C	H	Q	T	N	A	F	H
T	S	T	D	S	B	C	I	K	A	J	T	D	F	J	I	S	K	K	M	A	T	G	I	I
R	C	R	I	Q	C	V	R	O	G	L	E	T	I	R	N	S	I	Z	O	T	J	E	L	D
V	Q	U	E	J	A	H	J	H	N	N	H	F	N	N	D	I	N	C	Z	I	Z	N	N	T
C	Z	D	N	I	G	N	T	M	I	S	G	D	E	I	U	M	G	M	P	O	D	E	U	X
H	K	Z	T	S	O	T	G	A	E	F	P	F	K	S	C	I	L	I	J	N	J	T	B	Z
Z	S	O	L	C	V	Q	R	I	C	A	R	V	N	P	T	L	M	G	F	G	V	S	E	V
Q	W	H	W	H	T	T	W	T	H	H	X	W	V	X	I	A	Q	X	D	X	U	R	Q	D
L	I	V	B	C	E	B	A	P	W	H	Y	G	Z	E	V	R	H	S	N	Q	Q	D	J	D
T	R	U	E	R	V	X	T	R	U	E	M	X	C	A	E	Z	T	H	O	M	R	A	W	N
P	K	N	P	I	N	B	O	T	T	L	E	N	E	C	K	F	J	E	I	I	L	Q	Z	K
U	N	L	A	B	E	L	E	D	H	C	D	T	R	A	N	S	F	E	R	X	N	K	L	S

pretrained	transfer	computation	feature	task
inductive	dissimilar	unlabeled	true	lateral
stacking	inception	true	bottleneck	gradient
identity	fine	Imagenet	true	true

Introduction to Object Detection

> Computer vision gives machines the ability to recognize and analyze what they see in images and videos. — **Fei-Fei Li**

Credits: © Fei-Fei Li

Some important computer vision tasks are image recognition, object localization, object detection, and image segmentation. Image recognition takes an image as input and generates a label. CNN is very effective for image recognition. Object localization is about finding a single instance of the object with its type, along with the locations of its bounding box in the image. Object Detection is finding all the objects present in the image along with their type and location. Image segmentation is about the extraction of foreground objects from the background. Semantic and instance segmentation are some of the most important problems in computer vision. The learning objectives of this chapter are:

- Overview of object detection.
- Understand the types of object detection.
- Know about the R-CNN family of object detectors.
- Know about YOLO.
- Understand the need for Image segmentation.
- Know about semantic segmentation and instance segmentation.
- Know about masked R-CNN and U-net architectures.

11.1 Introduction to Object Detection

In computer vision, some important tasks are Image classification, localization, and detection.

Image recognition takes an image as input and generates a label for the dominant object of the image. If the image has multiple objects, then only the class label of the dominant object in the image is generated, and minor objects are ignored.

Object detection is also known as object localization. Normally, object localization is associated with detecting a single instance, and object detection is associated with detecting multiple instances. The output of localization is a bounding box around the object with the coordinates and the predicted class. The coordinates of a bounding box are given as (x_1, y_1, x_2, y_2). Here (x_1, y_1) is the coordinates of the top-left corner and (x_2, y_2) is the coordinates of the bottom-right corner. The bounding box also can be given as (cx, cy, w, h) where cx, cy represents the center of the bounding box, and w and h are the width and height of the bounding box.

One of the examples of object detection is shown in Figure 11.1.

Figure 11.1 Example of Object Detection Where Detected Objects with its Bounding Boxes

Object detection is one of the most important problems in computer vision. Object detection is the process of identifying or detecting objects in images and videos. This concept of object detection can be extended to video also. Object detection can detect an object as well as its location in images.

The list of information that is available after the object detection are:

(i) Class of the object. The object can be a person, a tree, or an animal.

(ii) The object detection algorithm returns a probability value that indicates the confidence of the object detector about the presence of the object. The value of the objectness score is in the range of 0-1. A closer value to 1.0 is desirable. In Figure 11.1, the objectness score is indicated along with the objects.

(iii) The algorithm returns the coordinates of the boundary box where the object is present. The boundary box is the smallest rectangle that fully contains the object.

The applications of object detection are given in Box 11.1.

Box 11.1 Use Cases of Object detection

There are plenty of applications for object detection. Some object detection applications are in video surveillance, face detection for applications like counting persons, robotic systems, driverless cars, and industrial applications like identification and tracking.

The difference between object detection and Image recognition is given in Table 11.1.

Table 11.1 Differences Between Object Detection and Image Recognition

Object Detection	Image Recognition
"Where" the object is located in the image is addressed by object detection.	"What" is the object in the image is addressed by Image Recognition.
The input image has many objects in it.	The input image has only one major object that must be labelled.
The output of the object recognition is a class label and a bounding box around the object.	The input is an image, and the output is the image's label.
The object detection should localize the object.	The classification takes all the images as a whole and generates a label.
The theory of object recognition is still not standardized.	The concepts of classification are well understood, and architecture is baselined.

11.2 Types of Object Detection

One of the naïve methods of finding objects in an image is a sliding window (also called a floating window) approach.

In sliding windows, the idea is to design a fixed window, slide it across the image, and classify the content of the sliding window, checking the presence of the object of interest. The steps of the naïve object detection method are given below:

1. Load the image where the object detection is required.
2. Define a fixed window of size width × height. Define the step size for the movement of the window. The step size determines the amount of window movement.
3. Slide the windows. Extract the contents of the window and classify it using the traditional CNN.
4. If the object is present, note the sliding window coordinates. Otherwise, reject it.
5. Use non-maximal suppression to eliminate the redundant and overlapping bounding boxes.
6. Output the resultant bounding boxes as output.

A modified approach can detect objects of all sizes. The idea is to detect the object regardless of the scale of the object – small or large. The procedure is as follows:

1. Take the images and generate the image in multiple resolutions.
2. Apply the naïve sliding window algorithm to detect the bounding boxes.

The advantages of the naïve sliding windows methods are given in the following Table 11.2.

Table 11.2 Advantages and Disadvantages of Naïve Object Detection

Advantages	Disadvantages
Guarantee the detection of the objects.	It is a slow process and takes a huge amount of time and hence practically not implementable.
Simple to visualize.	The algorithm is error prone.

Therefore, there is a need for better and more effective algorithms. The types of existing object detection algorithms are given in Figure 11.2.

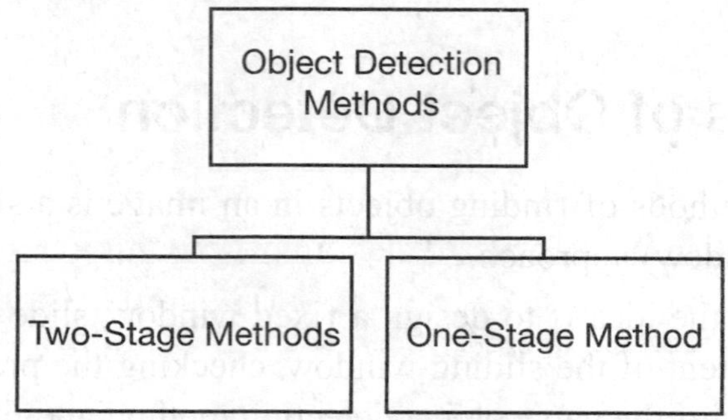

Figure 11.2 Types of Object Detection Methods

In two-stage object detection methods, there are two stages of detection. In the first stage, a special type of CNN proposes all possible regions where the object can be present. These proposed regions as potential objects are called region proposals. In this stage, there is no identification of the objects but only checking the object's presence. In the second stage, the object detector returns predictions for these region proposals. The R-CNN family of object detectors is a good example of a two-stage object detector.

In one one-stage object detection method, there is only one stage. In a single stage, the object detector makes predictions about the presence or absence of the image. This method is very fast but less accurate than two-stage object detector algorithms. YOLO is a good example of a one-stage object detector.

11.3 Object Detection Framework

Unlike image recognition, the framework of object detection is not standardized. However, there are four major components of an object detection network. The four major components of object detectors are:

(i) Region proposal mechanism

(ii) Feature extractor and detector

(iii) Non-maximal suppression

(iv) Object detection metrics

Let us discuss them now:

1. Region Proposals

An algorithm or a deep learning neural network generates proposed regions where the object is likely to be found. These proposed regions are also called the Region of Interest (RoI). These proposals can be generated using special selective search algorithms or neural networks.

The output of the region proposal component is the score called the objectness score. The classifier takes only regional proposals associated with a larger objectness score. If the objectness score exceeds a threshold value, the object is categorized as a foreground object. Otherwise, the object is categorized as a background object.

If the threshold value is too low, thousands of bounding boxes would be generated. This excessive generation of bounding boxes leads to more computational complexity. If the threshold is too high, many bounding boxes with objects might be missed. So, some tradeoff between accuracy and computational overhead must be associated with the bounding boxes.

2. Feature Extraction and Prediction

This module extracts the features from each bounding box. Feature extraction is by a predetermined CNN model to extract the features. Datasets like MS COCO or ImageNet are used to train these CNN networks (Refer to Box 11.2). The evaluation of whether the object is present or not is based on the extracted features. There are two predictors.

Box 11.2 Datasets Used for Object Detection

Object detection mostly uses datasets like MS COCO. MS COCO is an abbreviation of Microsoft Common Objects in Context (COCO). There are around two lakh images with 80 categories. All the images are annotated images with an average of 7.2 objects in the image.

Another useful dataset is PASCAL VOC. The dataset was created during the period 2005 – 2012. The dataset is a benchmark dataset with 11,530 images as part of training datasets and 27,450 images for validation dataset. There are images with twenty classes like person, animal, vehicles, etc, with 2.4 objects per image on average.

ImageNet has 4.7 lakhs of images with 1000 classes with an average of 1.1 objects per image. But ImageNet is mostly for image recognition rather than object detection.

1. Bounding box – The output is a vector with four components (x, y, w, h), where x, y are the center of the bounding boxes and w, h are the width and height of the bounding boxes.
2. Class prediction – The softmax function predicts the class probability of the bounding box. This class can be a person, tree, or any valid label.

3. Non-Maximal Suppression Algorithm

Sometimes, many bounding boxes would be generated around the object. The NMS module looks for a bounding box that predicts the object well. All the other overlapping bounding boxes are removed from consideration using some heuristic rules that are listed below:

1. The bounding boxes with predictions that exceed certain confidence threshold levels are removed.
2. Only the bounding boxes with the highest probability are considered.
3. The metrics, like the Intersection of Union (IoU), can be used to evaluate the bounding boxes by comparing them with the ground truth. The bounding boxes are rejected if IoU is less than some threshold value.

4. Object Detection Metrics

Some of the very important object detection metrics are listed below:

(i) Intersection of Union (IoU)

IoU indicates the localization performance of the object detector. IoU is also known as the Jaccard Coefficient. The intersection of Union (IoU) is evaluated as the area of overlap of the predicted bounding box with the ground truth bounding box to the union of the predicted bounding box and the ground truth bounding box. What is ground truth? The ground truth is the user-annotated coordinates of the object and object classes.

The IoU score is given as follows:

$$\text{IoU} = \frac{\text{Area of Overlap}}{\text{Area of Union}}$$

$$IoU = \frac{BB_{GT} \cap BB_{\text{Predicted}}}{BB_{GT} \cup BB_{\text{Predicted}}} = \frac{BB_{GT} \cap BB_{\text{Predicted}}}{|BB_{GT}| + |BB_{\text{Predicted}}| - |BB_{GT} \cap BB_{\text{Predicted}}|}$$

Here, *BB* is the bounding box. If IoU exceeds a threshold value, the prediction is considered true positive. Usually, a threshold value of 50% is considered. The prediction is considered false positive if the IoU score exceeds the threshold value.

Example 11.1

Let us assume that the ground truth box is given as (10, 10, 20, 40). Let us assume that (10, 10) is the bottom left coordinate point and (20, 40) is the top right point. Similarly, the predicted box is given as (10, 10, 40, 60). Find the IoU between the ground truth and the predicted box.

Solution:

The data that are given is given below:

$(x_1(pred), y_1(pred), x_2(pred), y_2(pred)) = (10, 10, 40, 60)$

$(x_1(GT), y_1(GT), x_2(GT), y_2(GT)) = (10, 10, 20, 40)$

The area of the predicted box is given as:

$(x_2(pred) - x_1(pred)) = 40 - 10 = 30$

$(y_2(pred) - y_1(pred)) = 60 - 10 = 50$

$\therefore$ Area of the predicted box = 30 × 50 = 1500

The area of the ground truth box is given as:

$(x_2(GT) - x_1(GT)) = 20 - 10 = 10$

$(y_2(GT) - y_1(GT)) = 40 - 10 = 30$

$\therefore$ *Area* of the ground truth box = 10×30=300

The area of the intersection box is given as

$$\text{left-top} = \max(x_1(\text{pred}), x_1(GT)), \max(y_1(\text{pred}), y_1(GT))$$
$$= \max(10, 10), \max(10, 10) = (10, 10)$$

$$\text{right-bottom} = \min(x_2(\text{pred}), x_2(GT)), \min(y_1(\text{pred}), y_1(GT))$$
$$= \min(40, 20), \min(60, 40) = (20, 40)$$

Therefore, the area of the intersection is (20 – 10) × (40 – 10) = 10 × 30 = 300.

So, the union area is computed as

$$\text{Area(union)} = \text{Area}(GT) + \text{Area(Predicted)} - \text{Area(Intersection)}$$
$$= 300 - 1500 - 300 = 1500.$$

Finally, IoU is computed as

$$\text{IoU} = \frac{\text{Area(Intersection)}}{\text{Area(Union)}} = \frac{300}{1500} = 0.2$$

It should be noted that the range of IoU is between 0 – 1. For this given problem, the overlap is approximately 20% and low.

(ii) Mean Average Precision (mAP)

IoU is fine. But the accurate measure of the overlapping windows is precision and recall.

Bounding box precision proves that the bounding box is the correct one. It should not be large as well be small. Class precision is about the correctness of the class. The class label should be correct and should not be wrong. Recall that the bounding box should not miss any objects. The focus should be that all objects should be detected.

The parameters like precision and recall can be found using the confusion matrix. The concept of a confusion matrix is well covered in Chapter 6 of this book. True positive (*TP*) is if IoU is greater than 50% and belongs to the same class. False negative (*FN*) is if IoU is greater than 50% with an incorrect class or no detection in the image. The false positive (*FP*) is if IoU is less than 50% or has a duplicate predicted box, and the true negative (TN) is if there is no detection by ground truth and the predicted class. True negative is not applicable for object detection.

The formula for computing precision and recall is given as follows:

$$\text{recall} = \frac{TP}{TP + FP}$$

And

$$\text{precision} = \frac{TP}{TP + FN}$$

Then, the precision and recall curve is drawn, and the area under the precision-recall curve is evaluated as average precision. The concept of *PR* curve is discussed in Chapter 7. *PR* curve of the model is evaluated at every threshold of coincidence. It is between 0-1. This value indicates the confidence of the detector. The area under the *PR* curve is the average precision, and it should be noted that it is for a single class.

This mAP is the average of all *AP* over all the classes. It is a metric that measures the average precision at different recall levels of all classes. The value of *AP* ranges between 0-100. The higher value indicates that the prediction is better.

Example 11.2: Let the object detector return outcomes as *TP, TP, TP, TP, FP* for five objects. Find the precision and recall value.

Solution:

In the above sequence, $TP = 4$ and $FP = 1$. Therefore, the precision and recall can be computed as

$$\text{precision} = \frac{TP}{TP+FN} = \frac{4}{4+0} = 1.$$

$$\text{recall} = \frac{TP}{TP+FP} = \frac{4}{4+1} = 0.8.$$

It should be observed that precision minimizes false positives, and recall minimizes false negatives.

Example 11.3: Suppose the precision and recall values for three classes are given in Table 11.3.

Table 11.3 Example Data

Class	Precision	Recall
Car	0.8	0.6
Lorry	0.7	0.6
Jeep	0.9	0.7

Find the average precision for each class and mean average precision (mAP).

Solution:

Average precision (AP) for the class car = precision × recall = 0.8 × 0.6 = 0.48

Average precision (AP) for the class lorry = precision × recall = 0.7 × 0.6 = 0.42

Average precision (AP) for the class Jeep = precision × recall = 0.9 × 0.7 = 0.63

$$\text{The mean average precision (mAP)} = \frac{0.48+0.42+0.63}{3} = \frac{1.53}{3} = 0.51$$

It should be noted that the higher the value and evaluates the overall performance of the object detector model.

(iii) Frames per second (FPS)

The number of frames or images provided by the camera or display system per second is called the frame rate. FPS is another useful metric for evaluating object detection algorithms. For example, Faster R-CNN can detect objects with an FPS of 5-7 frames. In contrast, YOLO predicts the objects with 59 frames per second.

11.4 Region-Based Convolutional Neural Networks (R-CNN) Family of Algorithms

Region-based Convolutional Neural Networks family has a set of models, R-CNN, Fast R-CNN, and Faster R-CNN for object detection. These frameworks are useful for object detection. Ross Girshick et al. introduced R-CNN. It is a framework based on two stages. Hence, it is called a two-stage framework.

(i) The first stage is called the region proposal stage. This stage generates a set of proposals where the object might be present.

(ii) The second stage is called the object classification stage, where the object is classified.

Fast – R-CNN and Faster-R-CNN are variations of the basic R-CNN framework. One more member of the family is Mask R-CNN, which is useful for image segmentation and is discussed later in this chapter. Let us discuss about R-CNN now.

11.4.1 Region-Based Convolutional Neural Networks (R-CNN)

R-CNN was proposed by Ross Girshick et al. in a paper titled "Rich Feature Hierarchies for Accurate Object Detection and Semantic Segmentation" in 2014. Region-Based Convolutional Neural Network (R-CNN) has three major components. The major components of R-CNN are listed below:

(i) Region Proposal Module

(ii) Feature Extraction

(iii) Object Classification and localization

1. The first module of R-CNN is the region proposal module. It takes an image as input and generates all possible regions where there are potential objects are present as region proposals. R-CNN removes the naïve sliding window approach and uses an external selective search algorithm to generate potential region proposals. Selective search is an algorithm that splits the image into many small regions. Then, the regions are hierarchically merged to generate region proposals. The details of the external search algorithm for region proposals are given in Box 11.3.

The regional proposal module generates approximately 2000 potential region proposals. The block diagram of R-CNN is given in Figure 11.3 below:

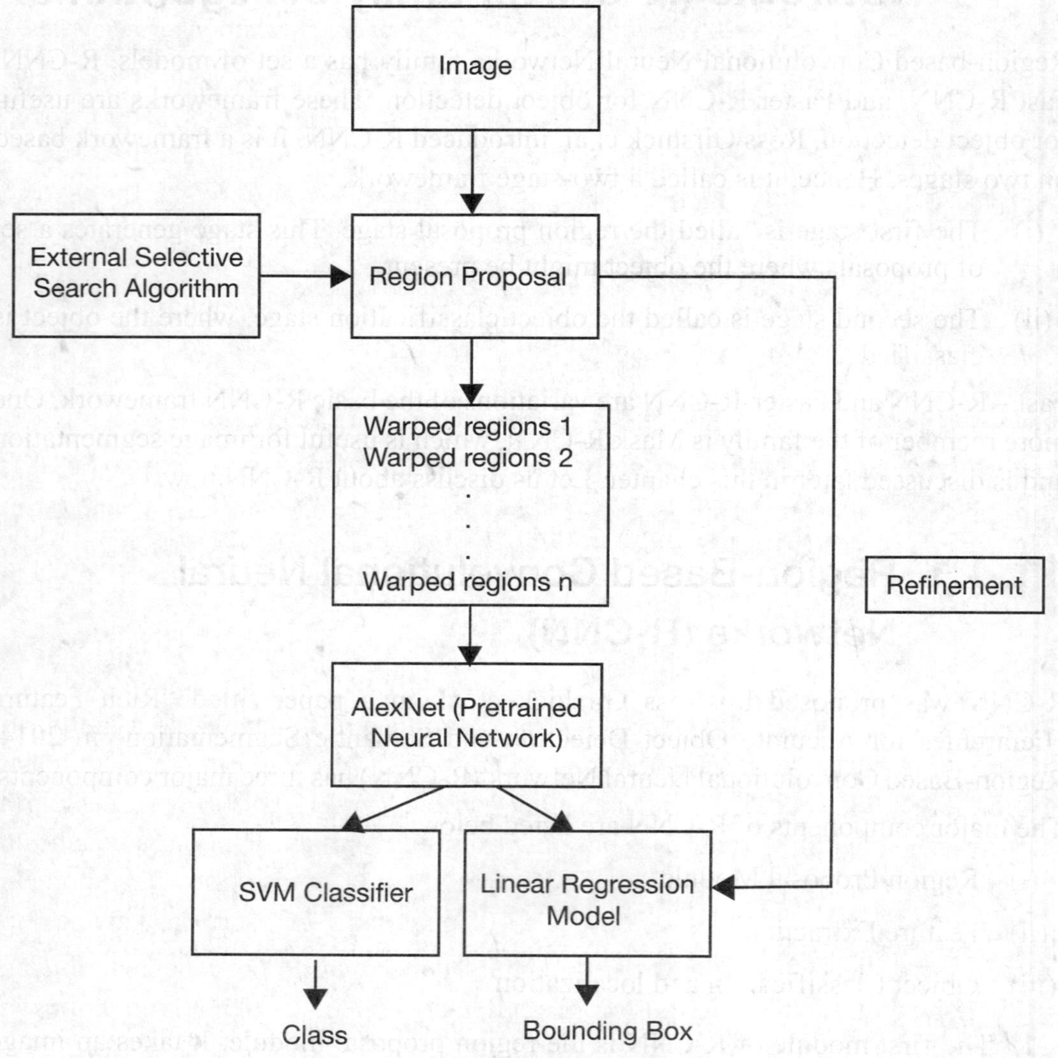

Figure 11.3 R-CNN

Box 11.3 External Search Algorithm for generating region proposals.

The selective search algorithm is a brute force method that searches the images and generates around 2000 region proposals. The idea is primarily from region region-growing algorithm of image processing.

(i) The selective search segments the input image into smaller regions. The criteria used for splitting the images are colour, texture, size, and shape. All the split smaller images are homogeneous in terms of colour, texture, or intensity.

(ii) The selective search algorithm then merges similar regions and groups them based on similarity. The similarity can be colour similarity, texture similarity, size similarity, or shape similarity.

(iii) similar regions are merged, and this chain of merging is done hierarchically. All the intermediate regions are stored as potential regions.

(iv) This merging is done at different scales of the image so that larger and smaller objects are identified as potential regions.

(v) All the sets of candidate regions are sent as region proposals.

2. The region proposals are the input for the warping regions. One has to note that the proposed region is of arbitrary size and shape (aspect ratio). The need is to warp the image regions to an expected input size after adding some padding to reduce the risk of the original cropping of the object. So, a warping (or resizing) is necessary so that the candidate regions are of the same fixed size as required by the CNN.
3. R-CNN uses a pretrained AlexNet. AlexNet uses a transfer learning concept for generating feature maps of the candidate regions.
4. R-CNN uses SVM classifiers to classify the objects. It must be noted that SVM is a binary classifier. It takes an output of AlexNet (A vector of 4096 features as input) and generates a binary class. SVM assigns a label for every object identified by the region proposals.
5. The next step is bounding box refinement. The focus is to generate a boundary box, aiming to increase the accuracy by taking care of scale and aspect ratio. R-CNN uses class-specific k logistic regression models to generate classes and k linear regression models. The bounding box refinement is done by taking the coordinates of the region proposal and 4096 features extracted by the CNN and accessing the complex information about the object, focusing on generating an accurate boundary box.
6. The last step is the output stage, where the final output of the bounding boxes, along with the class labels of the identified objects, are sent.

11.4.2 Fast R-CNN

R-CNN is slow in both training and testing. The first major improvement of Fast R-CNN comes because it takes an entire image as input and produces the feature map. Ross Girshick proposed this improvement in the "Fast R-CNN" paper. Fast R-CNN used VGG16 architecture and MS COCO Dataset.

The block diagram of Fast R-CNN is given in Figure 11.4.

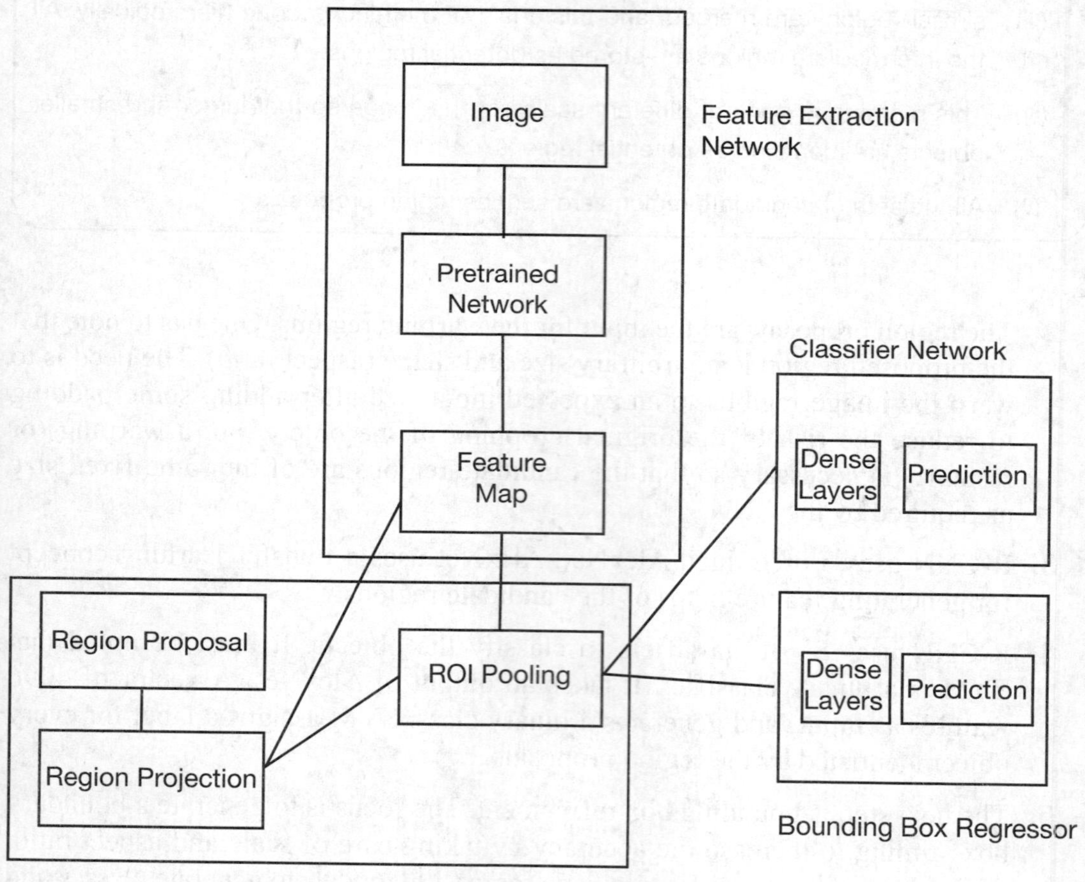

Figure 11.4 Fast R-CNN

1. The Region proposal is based on the feature map, not the original image. It takes the image as input and produces the feature map. Then, the region projection uses a size 4×4 window to take the image and the feature map for further processing to generate region proposals.

2. The second improvement of Fast R-CNN over R-CNN comes from the ROI Pooling layer.

   The Region of Interest (ROI) pooling removes the concept of warped regions in R-CNN. However, the generated region proposals are of different sizes, and fitting them into the full convolution layer is impossible. This need for fixed-size feature maps necessitates the RoI pooling layer, whose purpose is to downsample the feature maps with different sizes to generate feature maps of uniform size using max pooling.

   The ROI windows are divided into H × W cells. H and W are the height and width of the grid. It is a fixed one. The feature maps inside the H × W cell are converted to a fixed-size vector. The extracted fixed-size vector from the ROI pooling layer is sent to the convolutional layers.

3. The convolutional layers extract features and pass them to two heads:
   (i) Classification head – This is a set of additional convolutional layers with a softmax layer to predict N-Classes.
   (ii) Regression head – This is a set of convolutional layers with a linear regression layer that produces the four coordinates of the bounding box.

   The advantage of Fast R-CNN is its speed of training and testing. It is performance is also good as it yields a better mAP score.

The summary of Fast R-CNN is given in Box 11.4.

Box 11.4 Summary of Fast R-CNN

The working of Fast R-CNN is summarized as follows:

1. Fast R-CNN uses trained CNN to extract feature maps from the image.
2. The region proposal is done based on the feature map of the image.
3. The ROI pooling layer takes the different-sized candidate feature maps to a fixed-length vector and passes it into the next stage suitable for CNN.
4. The classifier takes the region proposals from ROI and generates a label for the proposed regions.
5. The regressor generates a boundary box for the region proposals.

11.4.3 Faster R-CNN

Shaoqing Ren et al. proposed this architecture in the paper titled "Faster R-CNN: Towards Real-Time Object Detection with Region Proposal Networks" in the year 2016. Faster R-CNN is much faster than Fast R-CNN as the main bottleneck of the previous framework characterized by selective search is removed. Instead, a separate special neural network called Region Proposal Network (RPN). RPN is a fully convolutional neural network that predicts the object bounds and objectness scores.

The architecture of Faster R-CNN is given in Figure 11.5.

So, there are two main components of Faster R-CNN. They are listed below:

(i) Region Proposal Network (RPN) for region proposals.

(ii) A detector network (Fast R-CNN) that operates on the region proposals.

Faster R-CNN is a single network of RPN and a detector network. The RPN and detector share a common set of convolution layers. This approach leads to more accuracy.

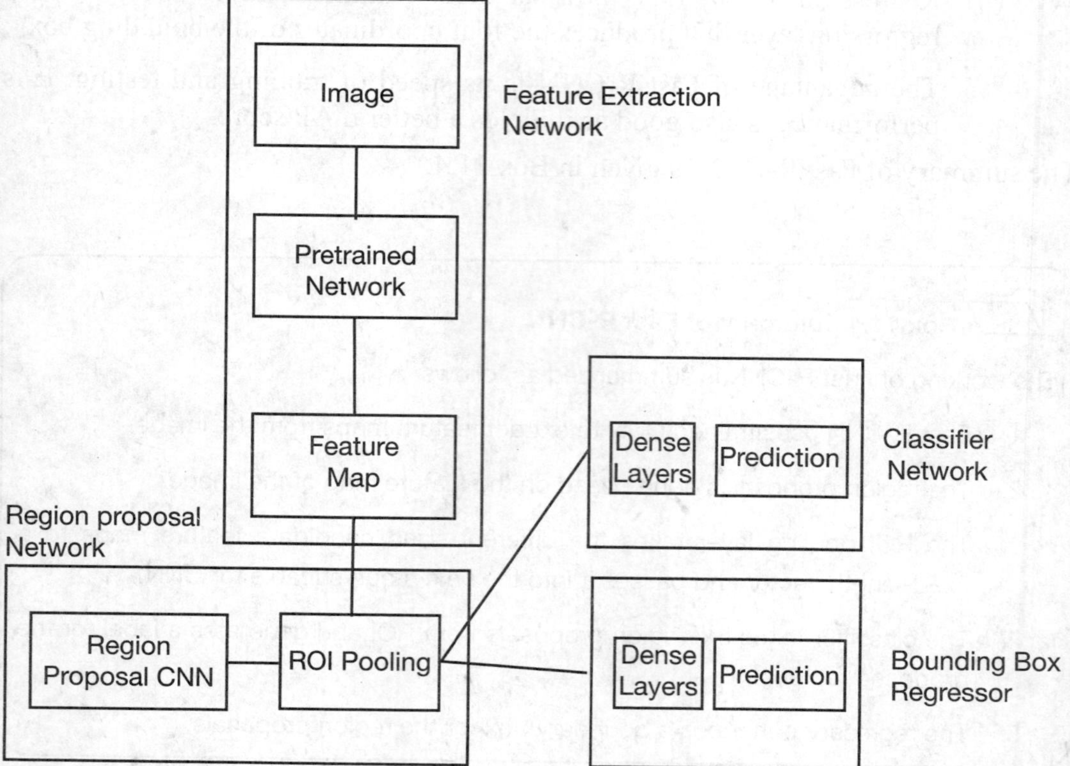

Figure 11.5 Faster R-CNN Network

RPN Network

A Region Proposal Network (RPN) is a small network that slides over the image and generates a region proposal. A region proposal has potential regions where the objects are present.

The steps of the RPN component are given below:

1. The pretrained classifier network takes the input image and generates a feature map.
2. RPN takes the feature maps as input and slides a small network over it. The network is a 3 × 3 convolution layer. The sliding window scans the feature map.
3. RPN generates multiple anchor boxes of different scales.

   What is an anchor box? The anchors are used to refine the proposals. Anchors are fixed-size bounding boxes for different scales and aspect ratios. Three different scales that are used are 1282, 2562, and 5122. The three different aspect ratios are 1:1, 1:2, and 2:1. Anchors filter the proposed proposals to remove all unnecessary bounding boxes. Approximately 6000 anchors are chosen for the given image.
4. RPN predicts the objectness score and bounding box coordinates.

   RPN predicts the objectness score of both objects as well as the background image. The objectness score is a binary that indicates the presence or absence of the object and background.

   The bounding box is calculated using another 1 × 1 convolution layer. The output is the center of the bounding box (x,y) and the width and height of the bounding box. These four values are adjusted or refined.

   RPN applies non-maximal suppression (NMS) to remove redundant and overlapping proposals. Only the best ones are preserved using the objectness score.
5. The last refined proposals are sent to ROI pooling and subsequent layers for further processing and classification.

Fast R-CNN (Detector Network)

The Faster R-CNN uses a Fast R-CNN as a detector network. It takes the proposals that are sent by RPN and classifies them using the classification head. The regression head takes these features and the feature map to generate the bounding boxes.

The components of Fast-CNN and their working principles are given below:

1. ROI Pooling

1. The RPN sends the proposed regions where the objects are present as input for the detector network.
2. The RPN proposals would have different sizes and aspect ratios.
3. These RPN proposals are the inputs for ROI pooling. The purpose of ROI pooling is to ensure that all regions are converted into fixed sizes. The reason is CNN can accept only the fixed-sized input.
4. ROI pooling divides the regions into a fixed number of images, say 7×7 or 14×14. These sizes are predetermined and fixed.
5. Max pooling is used for every grid summarizing the most important information.
6. The grid size, say $7 \times 7 \times C$, is the output of ROI pooling, indicating the size and colour.

The advantage of ROI pooling is that the output is of a uniform size suitable for CNN. It preserves the spatial information and its efficiency.

2. Classifier and Regressor Head

1. The classifier takes the output of ROI and generates the class of the object with the help of convolution layers.
2. The bounding box regressor does the refinement of the bounding boxes so that the bounding boxes are refined. The adjustments are done with the help of additional convolutional layers.
3. The final output is the class labels and refined bounding box locations.

11.5 One-Shot Detectors

Unlike two-stage detectors, single-shot detectors detect the object in a single stage. Examples of single-stage detectors are Single-shot Multibox Detector (SSD) and YOLO (You Only Look Once).

11.5.1 Single-Shot Multibox Detector (SSD)

Wei Liu et al. proposed a single Shot Detector (SSD) in a paper titled "SSD: Single Shot Multibox Detector" in 2016. SSD is a single-stage detector, as the classification layers directly detect objects in the image in a single shot. The block diagram of SSD is given in Figure 11.6.

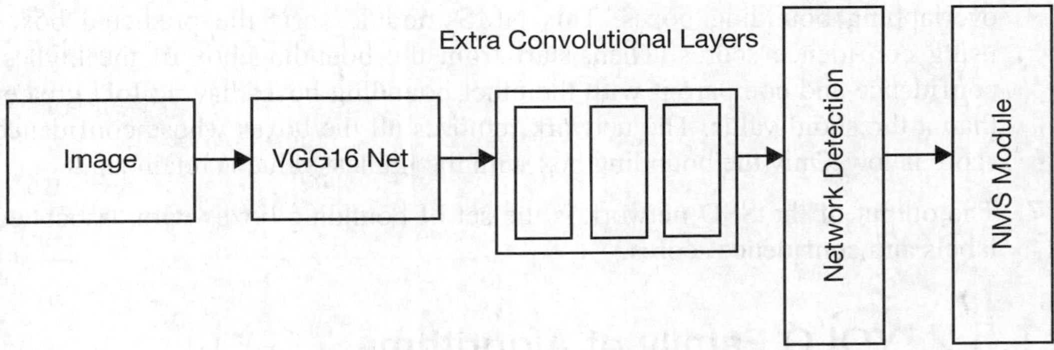

Figure 11.6 Single-Shot Detector

There are three major components of SSD. They are listed below:

(i) Base Network
(ii) Multiscale Features layer
(iii) NMS Module

The Single-shot detection algorithm works as follows:

1. The SSD deep neural network takes an image as input.
2. The base network is a standard predefined network. Normally, VGG16 is used as a predefined network for extracting feature maps.
3. SSD uses feature maps of multiple resolutions. A set of convolution layers is used to extract the features at multiple scales. This network enables the SSD network to detect the smaller objects as well as the larger objects.
4. SSD overlays a grid of anchors called priors around the image. An anchor box has a different aspect ratio and scale. A set of bounding boxes is used at every location of the feature map. The purpose of the anchor box is to guess the objects.
5. For every anchor box, the SSD network predicts
   (a) Objectness scores: The presence and absence of the object associated with the type of the object (indicated by the class).
   (b) Offsets: Offsets of the bounding box that may be required to refine the bounding box.
6. SSD network uses NMS (non-maximal suppression) to remove all overlapping, redundant boxes except the one that overlaps the most with the ground truth that has a high confidence score. NMS's purpose is to eliminate all unnecessary

overlapping bounding boxes. This NMS module sorts the predicted boxes using confidence scores. Then, start from the bounding box of the highest confidence and compare it with the other bounding boxes having IoU greater than a threshold value. The network removes all the boxes whose confidence score is low. Only the bounding box with the highest value is retained.

7. The output of the SSD network is the set of bounding boxes with associated labels and confidence scores.

11.5.2 YOLO Family of Algorithms

YOLO is an abbreviation of "You Only Look Once." YOLO is a one-stage object detector. Figure 11.7 shows the bird's view of the YOLO architecture. YOLO is an end-to-end deep neural network. It predicts bounding box and class probability in one stage. It is a state-of-art technology.

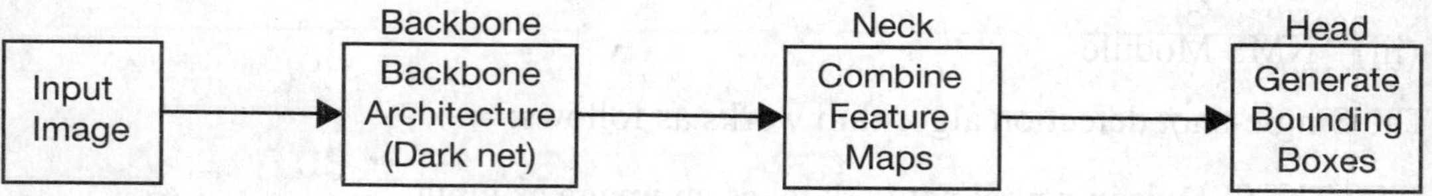

Figure 11.7 Bird View of YOLO Architecture

There are multiple versions of YOLO (Refer to Box 11. 5).

Box 11.5 YOLO Family

YOLO stands for "You Only look Once". There are many versions of YOLO. The original authors of YOLO were Joseph Redman, Santhosh Divvala, Ross Girshish, and Ali Farhadi. They published a paper titled "You Only Look Once: Unified, Real-Time Object Detection" in 2016. YOLO V1 was published as a Unified and Real-Time object detection method. Version 2 was called YOLO9000, and subsequently, Version 3 was released By Joseph Redman and Ali Farhadi. The recent version of YOLO is 9.0.

The following discussion is based on V3 of YOLO.

YOLO takes an image and uses a backbone architecture of Darknet to extract the feature maps. Then, the neck part of YOLO combines all the feature maps by downsampling and cropping, making it suitable for the head. The head takes those feature maps and generates the bounding boxes. Let us discuss them in detail now.

1. **Grid Division:** In YOLO, the image is split into a grid of S × S cells. The simplest grid is 3 × 3. An image with a grid of 5 × 5 is shown in Figure 11.8. If the object falls in the center of the grid, then it is the responsibility of the grid to detect the object.

Figure 11.8 An Image with a 5 × 5 Grid

2. **Bounding Box Prediction:** Each object is associated with a cell. Even if objects span multiple cells, it is the responsibility of the cell to identify the object if the object center falls within it. There will be B-bounding boxes and confidence scores for all these bounding boxes.

   There are three possibilities:

   (i) There is a chance that no object can be inside the cell.

   (ii) There is an association of 1:1 between the cell and the object.

   (iii) There is also a possibility of a 1 : n relationship where the cell is associated with two objects whose center lies within the cell.

   The grid cell generates a vector of elements as below:

$$\begin{pmatrix} b_x \\ b_y \\ b_h \\ b_w \\ p_c \\ c_1 \\ c_2 \\ \vdots \\ c_n \end{pmatrix}$$

Here $b_x b_y$ are the coordinates of the center of the bounding box. These values are normalized. The value b_n b_w is the bounding box height and width, respectively. An interpretation of [0.6, 0.4, 0.7, 0.8] means that the bounding box is of size 70 × 80 with the center located at (60, 40). This value is not an absolute value but a relative one.

The component p_c is the objectness score that ranges between 0-1. This value indicates the detector's confidence in the object within the cell. It is better if this value is 1.

The value $[c_1, c_2,\ldots, c_n]$ is the one-hot encoding of the object class. If there are two classes, the one-hot encoding is [1 0 and 0 1].

3. **Multiple Objects:** There can be multiple objects inside the grid cell. These objects are detected using the concept of anchor boxes. The anchor boxes are similar to R-CNN. The anchor boxes are predefined shapes and aspect ratios. These are called priors. The aim is to fit the anchor boxes to the object. The anchor box would have an objectness score of zero if there is no associated object. If there are multiple objects, then associate each anchor with the object. For example, with two anchors of size 5 × 5, one can detect a total of 5 × 5 × 2 = 20 objects. There is no computational overhead because only anchor boxes whose objectness score is near one are considered. All other bounding boxes are discarded.

4. **Combine the Predictions:** Here, the confidence score is multiplied by the class probability to get a final score. This score indicates the presence or absence of the object along with the labels.

5. **Thresholding and Non-maximal Suppression:** Non-maximal suppression removes the overlapping windows into a single bounding box using the

bounding box sort algorithm to remove the overlapping boxes. The procedure is as follows:

(i) Sort all the bounding boxes

(ii) Compute IoU with the other bounding boxes for all the bounding boxes.

(iii) Remove the boxes if $p_c < 0.6$ and also if IoU has a value greater than or equal to a threshold value. The threshold value is normally chosen as 0.5 – 0.9. If the IoU value is less than the threshold value, the boxes are discarded.

An example of a YOLO detector is given in Figure 11.9.

a.

b.

Figure 11.9 Example of YOLO Detection: a. Original Image and b. YOLO Output

11.6 Image Segmentation

Given an image F, Segmentation is assigning a label to each pixel. Depending on the image, the labels are like persons, trees, roads, or pedestrians. The details of the image segmentation are given in Box 11.6.

Box 11.6 Image Segmentation

Image segmentation is a subdomain of Image processing. It takes an image as input and groups all similar pixels or regions into respective labels. The image segmentation gives an outline of the foreground object that has both classes as well as localization. The segmentation process is shown in Figure 11.10.

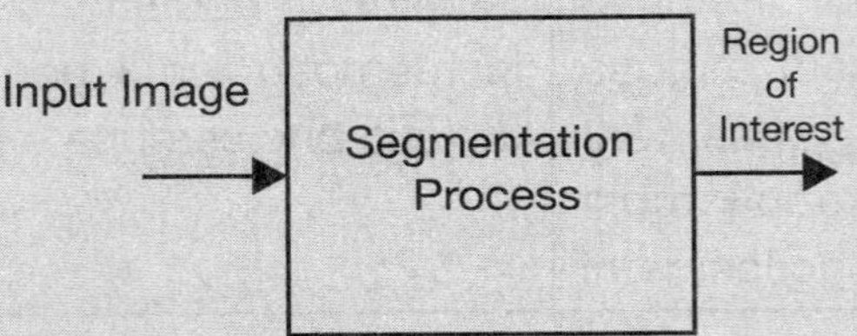

Figure 11.10 Input-Output of Image Segmentation

The segmentation has many useful applications like medical image segmentation for tumours and cancer tissues, segmentation of traffic signals, pedestrians, potholes in roads, and biometrics like faces in images.

Figure 11.11 shows an original image and its segmented image. It can be observed that only the foreground object is present and all the background parts are removed in the resultant image.

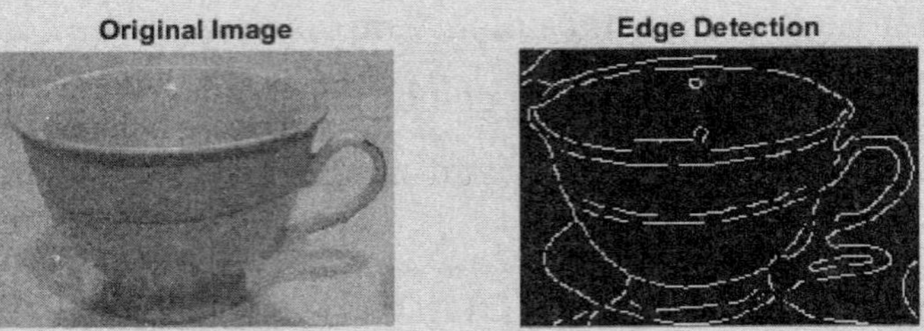

Figure 11.11 The Original and Segmented Image

There are two segmentation types available, as shown in Figure 11.12.

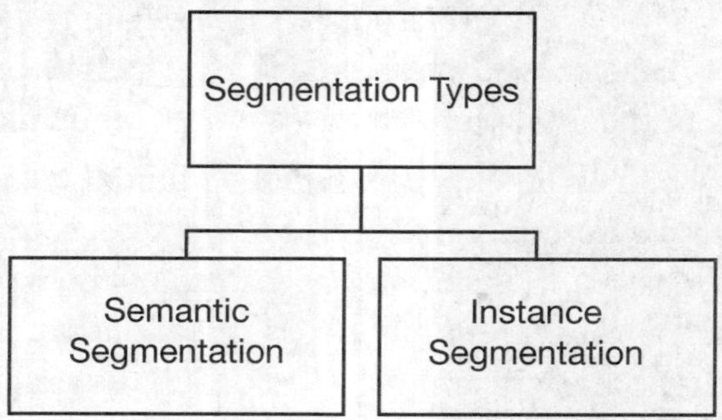

Figure 11.12 Types of Segmentation

The semantic segmentation assigns a label to each pixel but does not worry about the instances of objects. For example, if there are three tigers in the images, then all pixels of the tigers will have the same values. While this is useful to differentiate tigers from other objects, the counting of tigers in the image is impossible.

An output of semantic segmentation is shown in Figure 11.13. It can be noted that semantic segmentation uses the same shade or colour for both cups.

Figure 11.13 Example of Image Segmentation
a. Original Image and b. Semantic Segmentation

Instance segmentation assigns a label to each pixel of the image. Instance segmentation is like semantic segmentation. However, Instance segmentation can differentiate different instances of the objects. For example, a tiger is differentiated from another tiger by using different pixel values or colours. An example of instance segmentation is given in Figure 11.14, where multiple shades are used to differentiate the instances of the objects.

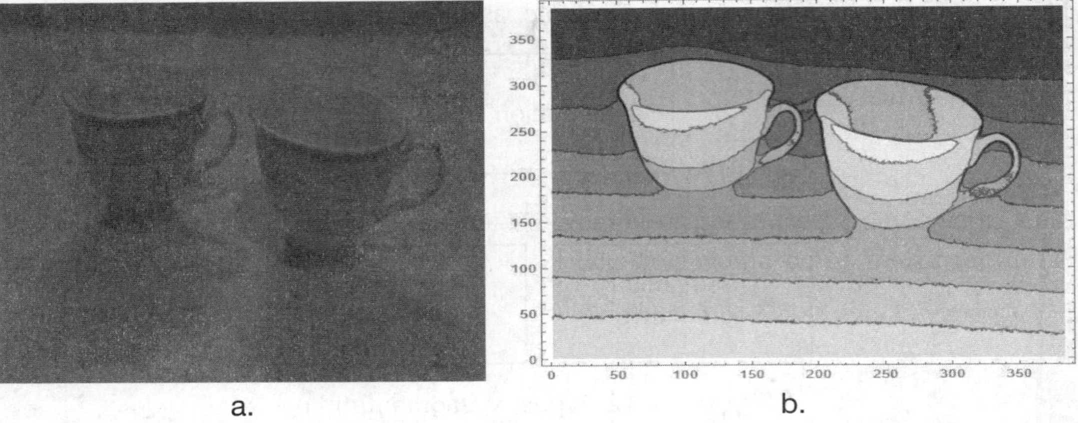

Figure 11.14 Example of Instance Segmentation:
a. Original Image and b. Instance Segmentation

The differences between semantic and Instance Segmentation are given in Table 11.4.

Table 11.4 Differences Between Semantic and Instance Segmentation

Semantic Segmentation	Instance Segmentation
Classify the pixel of the image into a specific category or class.	Classify the pixel to a specific category or class. In addition, it assigns a unique label to distinct objects.
All instances of the same classes are given the same labels.	All instances of the same class are given distinct labels.
There is no distinction between individual instances of the same class.	Instance segmentation distinguishes even if the pixels belong to the same category.
It helps in the overall understanding of the objects present in the image.	It helps provide a detailed view of the objects in the image and is a more challenging task.
IoU is primarily the evaluation metric.	IoU and mean Average Precision (mAP) are useful for finding segmentation accuracy.
Useful in applications like image understanding.	Useful in biomedical applications.

In the naïve approach, a sliding window can be used in either direction with slide one over the entire image, and a classifier is used. After the prediction, the classifier labels the label to the middle pixel of the input region. This approach is slow as the number of pixels is very large, so faster and more accurate algorithms are necessary.

11.6.1 Fully Convolutional Network (FCN) for Semantic Segmentation

A fully convolutional network (FCN) is an end-to-end convolution network used for image segmentation. It is called a fully convolutional network because, unlike CNN, all layers are convolutional layers and do not use the fully connected network at the end. The presence of only convolutional layers enables the processing of inputs of various sizes to produce segmented output.

(i) A fully convolutional layer network takes the input image for segmentation.

(ii) The encoder part of the network acts as the encoder. The convolutional layers with the pooling layers reduce the dimensions of the feature maps, allowing the network to learn hierarchical representations and capture increasingly abstract features. By varying the receptive fields, the network learns hierarchical representations very easily. The early convolutional layers capture the low-level features, while the deeper ones capture the high-level ones. As the network grows, the receptive fields grow, ensuring that the important contextual information is captured and the relations over larger spatial regions are understood.

(iii) The bottleneck layers, too, use convolutional layers to refine the features.

(iv) The decoders of FCN use upsampling to retain the spatial information. The upsampling is done by transposed convolutions (or deconvolutions). These details are given in Chapter 8.

(v) Skip connections are used to recover the fine details from the encoder layers after these details are lost in the decoder stage.

The training of FCN is done as follows:

(i) The image and the corresponding ground truth segmentation image are given as input for the FCN network.

(ii) The network processes the image and produces the predicted segmentation image.

(iii) The loss function is the difference between the ground truth and the predicted image.

(iv) The backpropagation algorithm is used to update the weights and bias.

(v) The above steps are carried out until the loss becomes minimal.

Once the network is trained, in the inference stage, one can give the test image as input to generate the semantic segmentation of that image.

11.6.2 U-Net

Olaf Ronneberger, Philipp Fischer, and Thomas Brox proposed U-net architecture in a paper titled "U-net: Convolutional Network for Biomedical Image Segmentation". The name of the architecture is U-net as the appearance of the architecture looks like the English letter U. It is a fully convolutional network.

The U-net was designed to do segmentation for biomedical images. U-net takes an image as input and generates a segmentation map as output in a single pass. The architecture of U-net is given in Figure 11.15.

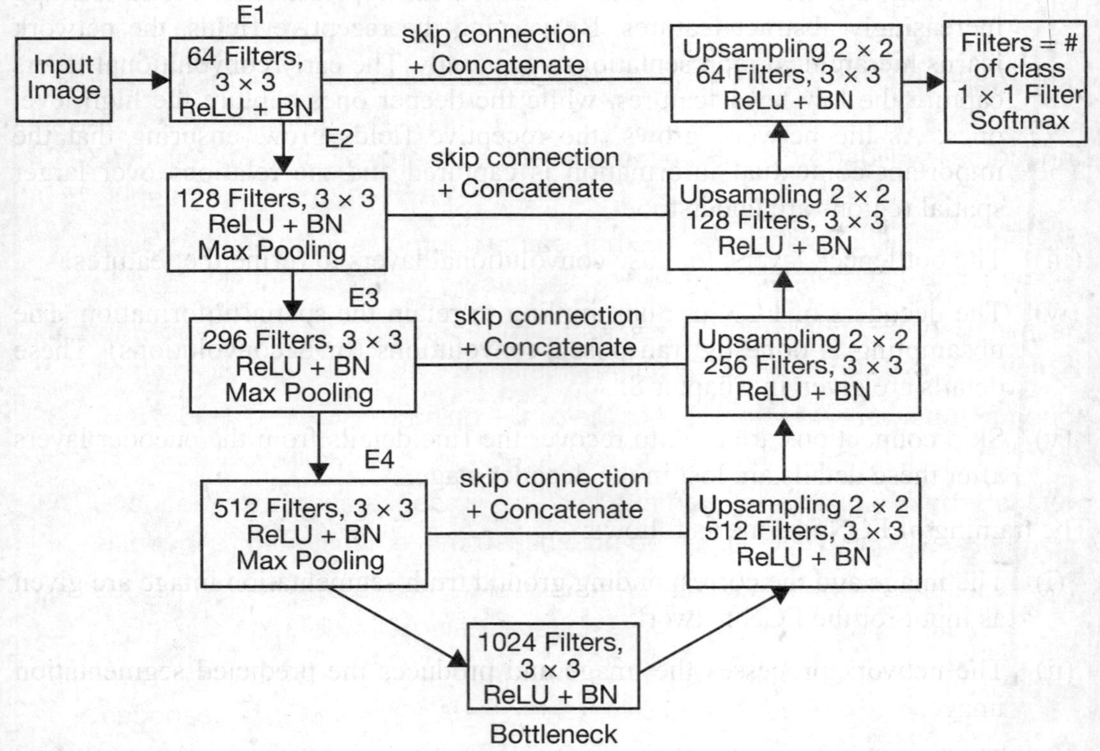

Figure 11.15 U-net Architecture

Three components characterize it:

(i) The left path of the architecture is called the contractive path. It is a fully convolutional network (FCN). It serves as the encoder.

(ii) A bottleneck layer. It also has only a convolution layer.

(iii) The right path is called expansive, and it serves as a decoder.

Contracting Path (Encoder)

The first part of the U-net is the encoder. An encoder is a repeated block of convolution layers followed by max pooling. The encoder's responsibility is to capture contextual information and learn highly abstract image representations. It takes the image as input and generates the latent space output.

Normally, the default input image size in U-net is 572 × 572. U-net's input can be of different sizes if the feature maps can facilitate max pooling with even dimensions. Otherwise, the output image would be distorted.

The encoder has four blocks.

Each encoder block has alternate convolutional layers with a small receptive field followed by max pooling. Encoders progressively downsample to capture the hierarchical structures.

The encoder components are listed below:

(a) Two convolution layers, with batch normalization, a cross channel 3x3 with stride one, and RELU activation

(b) Two max-pooling layers with a mask of size 2 × 2.

A downsampling operation reduces the spatial resolution but doubles the number of feature maps. It should be noted that the feature maps are increased with each downsampling. Downsampling is done by atrous convolution (Refer to Chapter 8). The final output of the encoder is a 1024, 28 × 28 feature map.

Bottleneck

A bottleneck is a stage where the given image reaches the lowest resolution. In this stage, the most abstract and high level features are captured and combine the information from different parts of the input image.

Decoder

The expansive path consists of decoders. A decoder is a set of transposed convolution layers with a ReLU activation function. The decoders take 28 × 28 feature maps and upsample them to 388 × 388 segmentation maps. The decoder is shown in the following Figure 11.16.

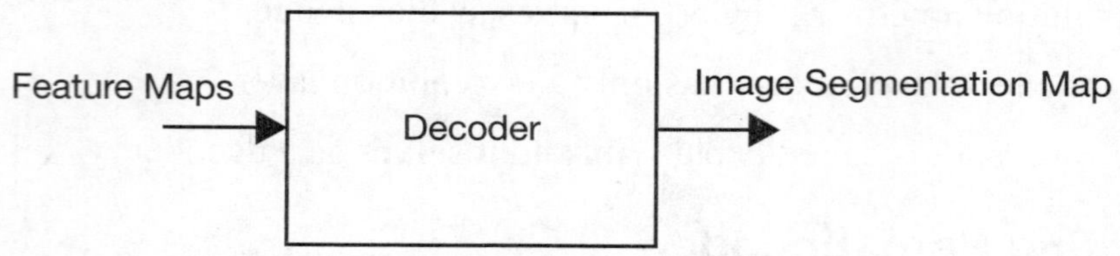

Figure 11.16 U-net Decoder

The decoders recover the spatial resolution using a special convolution operation called transposed convolution.

The decoder characteristics are:

(a) It has four blocks of decoders.

(b) The upsampling works with 2 × 2 transposed cross-channel convolutional with stride 2 (Refer to Box 11.6). Each upsampled step is concatenated with cropped high-resolution maps of encoders.

(c) Each transpose convolution (Refer to Chapter 8) is followed by two regular convolutions to smoothen the expanded representations.

(d) The upsampling halves the number of the feature map.

(e) The final layer is a 1x1 convolution layer that maps the 64-component feature map to the desired classes. The final output layer is a sigmoidal layer with the output 0 or 1. The output of 0 or 1 decides the classification class of the pixel.

Skip Connections

The role of skip connections is important. Skip connections address the issues of loss of spatial information by downsampling. These skip connections concatenate the feature maps with the layers of expansive paths. Skip connections ensure the network retains information at different scales to facilitate segmentation. Therefore, skip connections capture local and global contextual information, making U-net suitable for semantic segmentation.

Training of U-net

The loss function computes the difference between predicted segmentation and the actual ground truth. The errors can be backpropagated to adjust the weights and biases. This process is repeated till the loss becomes minimal. Once the network is trained, a test image can be given as input to get the semantic segmentation of the image as output.

In U-net, there will be a reduction in the size of the input. This size reduction is due to the unprecedented convolution; otherwise, many artifacts would be there. To avoid this, are can split the image into overlapping input tiles for better performance.

11.6.3 Mask R-CNN

Mask – R-CNN is an extension of faster R-CNN. Mask R-CNN was proposed by Ross Girshick in the paper titled "Mask R-CNN" in 2017. Mask R-CNN is used for instance segmentation.

The masked R-CNN is shown in Figure 11.17.

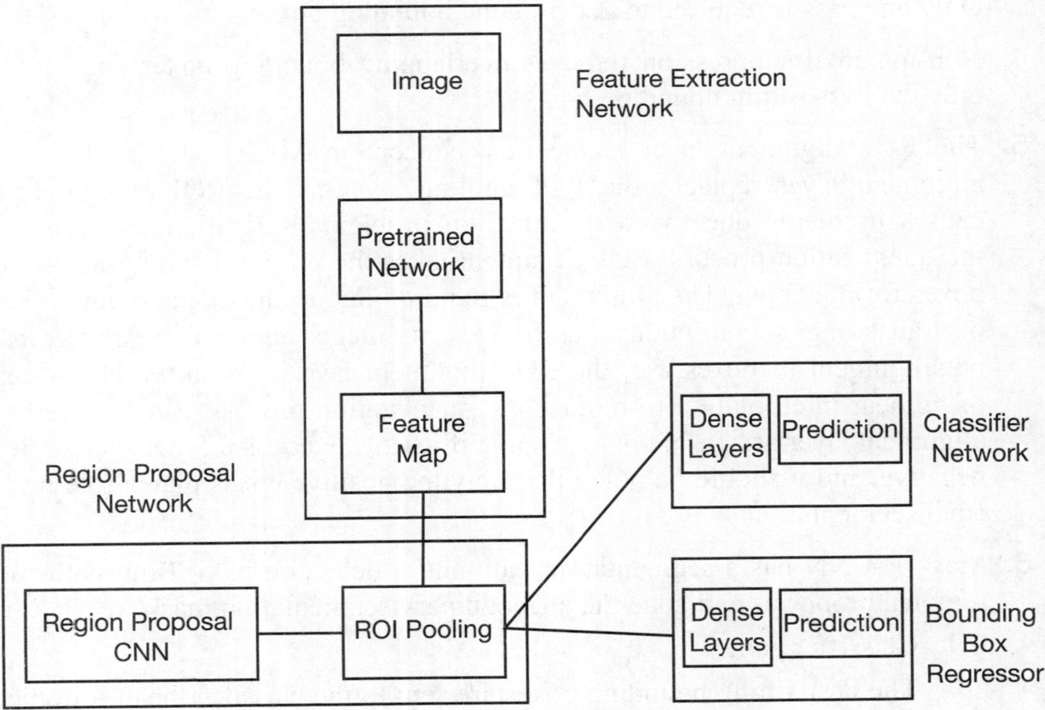

Figure 11.17 Mask R-CNN Architecture

1. The image is sent as input to the feature extractor.
2. The feature extractor is a pretrained network and is a dense classifier. It should be noted that the feature extractor is run only once. The output of the feature extractor is a feature map.
3. In mask R-CNN, RPN is a dedicated neural network that inputs the feature map and generates region proposals. Every region proposal indicates the locations of the likely objects in the image. It should be noted that only the region proposals containing the objects are sent for the final classification stage. In this way, the unnecessary computational overheads are reduced.

   How is it done? Mask R-CNN has a concept of anchors. Instead of splitting the image, the anchor boxes are used at every position or point. This avoidance of splitting the image ensures that the detector is fast but, at the same time, less accurate. A new component called a bounding box regressor is used to improve accuracy. The purpose of this regression regressor is to adjust the bounding box perfectly to fit the object by stretching or shrinking the bounding boxes.

   Only one pass is required to generate the bounding boxes.
4. Non-maximal suppression removes overlapping bounding boxes and returns only the best-fitting bounding box.
5. The ROI alignment layer is the new concept in Mask R-CNN. The ROI alignment layer replaces the ROI pooling layer as the ROI pooling layer causes problems due to its quantization problem. ROI alignment removes the quantization process. ROI alignment takes the proposals and uses anchor boxes for matching. The alignment is required due to the quantization effects of translating a continuous number to an integer number, resulting in a nonalignment of boxes. So, the ROI alignment layer introduces the concept of bilinear interpolation to remove the quantization process. Finally, the ROI alignment layer assigns a positive value if its IoU exceeds 0.5. Otherwise, it is negative, and it should be noted that only the positive boxes play a role in the final segmentation.
6. Mask R-CNN has a segmentation path and a detection path. Both paths use regional proposals and generate a final binary segmentation mask.

   6.1 Classifier path

   The best-fitting bounding boxes are sent to the classifier head for object prediction. The classifier is a dense layer followed by a softmax layer.

   6.2 Regressor path

   The best-fitted bounding box is given as output with its coordinates.

6.3 Segmentation path

One addition of mask R-CNN is the generation of masks for image segmentation. The extracted features are sent to a new CNN. This new CNN is also a set of convolutional layers. The new CNN generates a mask, which is stretched back over the bounding boxes that have been detected. Then, a mask is generated for each bounding box. This mask is used to assign a label for each pixel. Each pixel is assigned a label of a class. So, the pixels are labelled as true or false. It indicates that if the pixel is 1, the object is part of the image; otherwise, it is part of the background. The advantage of the mask is that it can be applied to images to filter the objects. This mask facilitates the counting applications, such as counting persons in an image.

Summary

1. Object recognition is the process of finding an object in an image.
2. The difference between object recognition and object detection is that object detection detects objects and their locations.
3. Object detection algorithms output the class of the object, the objectness score, and the coordinates of the bounding box.
4. The sliding window approach is a naïve method of moving windows and recognizing objects.
5. The proposed regions where the object is likely present are called region proposals.
6. The bounding box is a vector of the following components – the coordinates of the center of the box and the height and width of the bounding box. It can also be the lower left corner coordinates, height, and width.
7. Non-maximal suppression is a module that removes the overlapping windows and merges them to produce a single bounding box.
8. IoU is the metric that evaluates the overlapping ground truth and the predicted box.
9. mAP is the average of all average precision of classes.
10. R-CNN is a family of models for object detection. It includes variants like fast R-CNN, faster R-CNN for object detection, and fast R-CNN for semantic segmentation.

11. R-CNN has three major components. They are the region proposal module, feature extraction and network predictor module, and object detection module.
12. Selection search is an algorithm that sends RoI as proposals.
13. Fast R-CNN uses selective search on feature maps and, therefore, is faster than R-CNN.
14. Faster CNN uses a neural network for region proposals and Fast R-CNN for object detection.
15. Single-shot Detector (SSD) is a single stage object detector that takes the image as input and produces bounding boxes.
16. SSD uses a base network, multiscale detections, and an NMS module for object detections.
17. YOLO is of one-stage detector for object detection. It uses a backbone architecture for feature extraction, combining different-sized feature maps and generating bounding boxes.
18. The segmentation process takes an image and assigns labels to each pixel. The types of segmentation are semantic and instance segmentation.
19. The semantic segmentation assigns a label to each pixel. However, semantic segmentation does not distinguish similar objects.
20. Unlike semantic segmentation, instance segmentation assigns a label to each pixel and distinguishes between similar objects.
21. U-net is useful for the semantic segmentation of biomedical images. The encoder of U-net learns abstract representations of the image, and the decoder retrieves the original image using upsampling.
22. Mask R-CNN performs instance segmentation. It has two components – Faster R-CNN and FCN decoder to generate a binary segmentation mask.

Glossary

1. Object detection – The ability of the detector to detect object types and their locations of its bounding box in the image.
2. Bounding box – The rectangle box that surrounds the objects.
3. Objectness score – The confidence factor of the object detector about the presence of objects.

4. Sliding window – A moving window checks the presence of objects.
5. Region proposals – The proposed regions that contain the probable presence of objects are called region proposals.
6. Selective search algorithm –Selective search is an external algorithm that looks for potential objects in the image and proposes it for further processing.
7. Non-maximal Suppression (NMS) – NMS avoids overlapping windows by merging them into a single bounding box. NMS combines all overlapping bounding boxes into a single bounding box.
8. Intersection of union (IoU) – A metric for evaluating the quality of the bounding box by taking the ground truth and predicted bounding boxes. It is the ratio of the intersection of boxes to the union of the boxes.
9. mAP – A metric that measures the average precision at different recall levels of all classes.
10. Frames per Second (FPS) – It is a measure of the ability of the object detector to detect objects in real-time in a video.
11. Warped regions – The feature maps of different shapes are merged to get uniform-sized feature maps.
12. ROI layer – A layer that merges the different-sized feature maps by downsampling to get a uniform-sized feature map.
13. Region proposal network – It is a small neural network for generating region proposals.
14. Anchor – Anchors are windows with fixed size and aspect ratio used to generate region proposals.
15. Multiscale – The ability of the object detectors to find small and big objects in an image.
16. Grid – A fixed-size grid used by YOLO divides the image into cells.
17. Segmentation – The process of extracting the foreground object from the background.
18. Semantic segmentation – It is a pixel-level classifier that does not distinguish between similar objects.
19. Instance segmentation – A segmentation process that does pixel-level classification that differentiates similar objects by using different shades or colours.
20. Encoder – The encoder is a component that learns abstract representations.

21. Decoder – The decoder is a component that restores the image and generates the image maps.
22. ROI alignment – It is a component that aligns region proposals and anchor boxes that are not aligned due to quantization effects.

Short Questions

1. Distinguish between the terms – image recognition, object detection, and object localization.
2. List out the differences between object detection and image recognition.
3. List out the drawbacks of the sliding window approach.
4. State the selective search algorithm for region proposals.
5. What is non-maximal suppression? List out the rules for eliminating the overlapping boxes.
6. How is IoU computed? What is the relevance of IoU?
7. List out the differences between R-CNN, Fast R-CNN, and Faster R-CNN.
8. List out the differences between Fast R-CNN and R-CNN.
9. List out the differences between Faster R-CNN and Fast R-CNN.
10. What is an RPN network? What is the role of it?
11. What is darknet?
12. What is meant by semantic segmentation and instance segmentation?
13. What is the need for RoI alignment?
14. What is the need for transposed convolution?

Long Questions

1. Explain in detail the generic object detection framework.
2. Explain in detail R-CNN architecture.
3. Explain in detail Fast R-CNN architecture.
4. Explain in detail Faster R-CNN architecture.
5. Explain the implementation details of YOLO.
6. Explain U-net architecture in detail for semantic segmentation.
7. What is an instance segmentation? How is it done using Mask R-CNN?

Crossword

Across

3. Image segmentation is the extraction of foreground object from the _______
5. Mask R-CNN does _______ segmentation.
7. U-net does _______ segmentation.
10. A bounding box is a box around the _______ indicating its location.
12. The process of removing the overlapping bounding boxes is called non-maximal _______
14. The question of "where" in the image is achieved by _______ recognition.
15. The difference between R-CNN and Fast R-CNN is that the selective search works on a feature map instead of the image in Fast R-CNN. (true/false)
16. A bounding box is the _______ rectangle that fully contains the object.
17. One-shot detectors are SSD and _______
18. The point that the bounding box should not miss the objects is addressed as _______ (precision/ recall)
20. loU is also known as _______ coefficient.

21. YOLO is _______ (one/two) stage object detector.
22. Faster CNN region proposals are done by region proposal _______.
23. _______ segmentation facilitates counting of objects.
24. ROI pooling main purpose is to convert the variable-sized candidate regions into _______ size regions.

Down

1. _______ convolution layers does upsampling.
2. The algorithm that takes an entire image as input and generates a label is called _______. (recognition/detection)
4. The FCN in segmentation in semantic segmentation is Fully _______ network. (convolutional/ connected)
6. There are differences between Image recognition and object detection. (true/false)
8. The objectness score indicates the _______ of the object detector about the presence of the object.
9. One-shot detectors are _______ accurate than two-shot detectors.
11. The localization is about finding the location of a single object, and object detection is about multiple objects in the image. (true/false)
13. The region proposals of R-CNN is generated by _______ search algorithm.
16. Naive object detection uses a _______ window to detect the presence of the image.
19. The fixed size requirement of ROI pooling is because of CNN requirements. (true/false)

Jumbled Sentences

```
W C C C S V A B J T L V A O K J A C C A R D X Y X
S R L O Q R M A K G E K X A R E C O G N I T I O N
T Z O B E C G C X X S H I N S T A N C E M K C L X
V D W J Z D M K T N S U T I T R U E T N R R O O Z
R Z X E N K E G C S E M A N T I C S O D A T N D S
L R M C C E B R F H A G N K H Y E I E E I R F H X
F R E T T F E O O F H C N B L L S S J F Y U I L Q
L C O N V O L U T I O N A L L S O E V I E E D F M
Q G T Q J X T N S C I Q Z A E P P P Y N Y M E T S
D W S R Y Q W D E B W S M R S U U Y T S A Q N R L
O K L I U X O D L E Q S P N P F Q P N T F S C U I
I Y L P J E S N E T J P A Z N X W P E A I A E E D
Y R E C A L L I C J U R L C J I I B T N X Y E P I
B W M R F P D X T S T N R C G M A C W C E G H L N
G P O F T G K D I X K J Y O E H U S O E D N V D G
V K G K H Y A J V S O B J E C T T M R G Q Q B U R
O C R Q A R V O E L D R E S A S S L K K X X S X W
```

true recognition object confidence smallest true

object sliding suppression Jaccard recall selective

true fixed true network YOLO less

two background convolutional semantic instance Transposed

instance

CHAPTER 12

Recurrent Neural Networks

> Memory is the mother of all wisdom. – **Aeschylus**

Credits: © Aeschylus

A Recurrent Neural Network (RNN) is a neural network with a feedback loop that operates on sequence data. The feedback loop creates a form of memory that helps RNNs store and use the previous information to process new data. Therefore, RNNs are tailored to handle sequence data in applications like time series forecasting and Natural language processing. This chapter focuses on RNNs and the processing of sequence data.

The learning objectives of this chapter are as follows:

- Understand the basics of sequence data.
- Understand the working principle of RNN.
- Know the topology of RNN.
- Understand the mathematics of backpropagation through time.
- Understand the concepts of long- and short-term memory (LSTM).
- Know about LSTM architectures.
- Survey the applications of LSTM.
- Know about Gated Recurrent Units (GRU).

12.1 Overview of Sequence Data

Humans use memory. Humans use memory to make decisions. When one studies a storybook or watches a movie, the reader or viewer memory records the story plot inherently in memory. That is why one is able to understand the storybook or movie. Therefore, memory refers to the network's ability to retain information from past inputs to influence current decisions. This ability makes RNN powerful enough to handle sequences. Sequence data is a series of observed data collected over time and ordered specifically. Hence, the order of these data is important. This sequence data may represent a specific pattern, chronological order, or events happening one after another.

The order of the data arrangement is less important in non-sequential data. Table 12.1 gives the differences between sequence data and non-sequence data.

Table 12.1 Differences Between Sequence Data and Non-Sequence Data

Sequence Data	Non-Sequence Data
Order is important	Order is not very important.
Data that consists of elements that are temporal-based (Data exists at specific time intervals) or position-based (Spatial). For example, the data points occur at specific intervals in time-series data.	There is no temporal and spatial relevance in non-sequence data.
Examples of sequence data are time series data, video sequences, biomedical signals.	Examples of non-sequence data are static images, tabular data, spatial data, and demographic data.

Some of the examples of sequence data are given in Box 12.1.

Box 12.1 Examples of Sequence Data

Sequence data are used in various fields, like deep learning. Below are some of the most important sequence data usually encountered in the deep learning domain.

(i) DNA sequences

(ii) Music data

(iii) Text data

(iv) Time series data

(v) Video/audio signals

(vi) Event logs

The sequence data has certain unique characteristics, explained in Box 12.2.

Box 12.2 Important Characteristics of Sequence Data

1. Order matters in sequence data. Change of order causes problems. For better understanding, consider the sentence "I am reading." If the sequence of words is changed to "reading am I," it does not convey any meaning and is grammatically wrong.
2. Sequence data has either temporal or spatial relevance.
3. Sequential data requires sequential processing.
4. The length of the sequence data may vary.
5. The sequence may be homogeneous or heterogeneous.
6. The sequence data may have many multiple features at every time step t. These multiple features lead to the multidimensionality of data.

12.2 Need for RNN

Feedforward networks are represented by directed acyclic graphs. In other words, there are no cycles in feedforward networks.

Recurrent Neural Networks (RNN) allow information to persist. They are useful for performing sequential computation rather than parallel computation. RNN is a neural net with feedback, as shown in Figure 12.1. The feedback represents the recurrence in the computational graph and is shown as a cycle. This feedback creates a memory in the neural network that can store and leverage the stored information for suitable outputs. Hence, the feedback provides:

1. The notion of the time step is introduced.
2. RNN can adapt as the past stored data can influence the computation in the future.

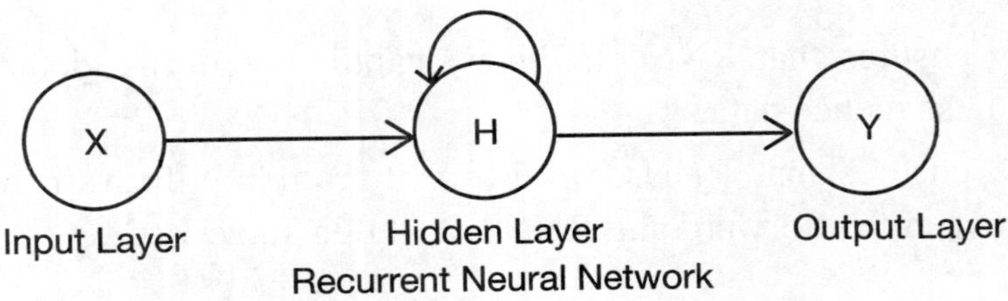

Figure 12.1 A Simple RNN

The recurrent loops introduce a notion of "memory," as shown in Figure 12.2. The left side representation is a folded version of RNN, and the right is an unfolded version, as shown in Figure 12.2.

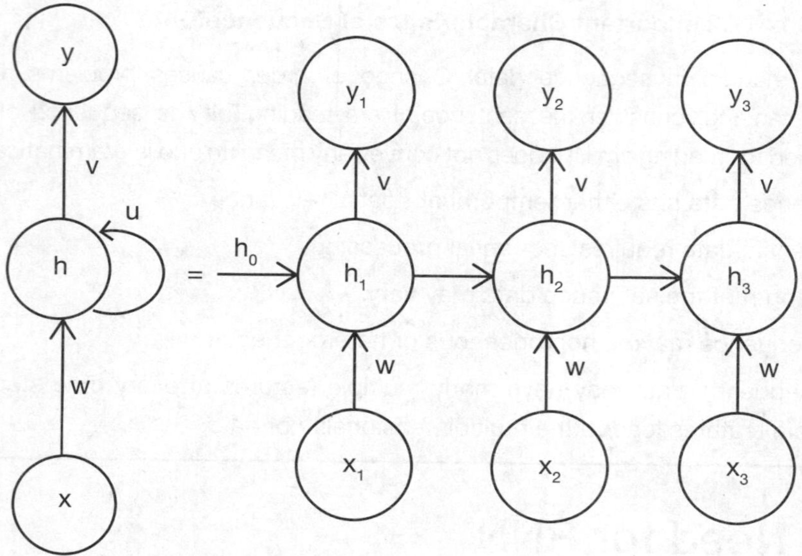

Figure 12.2 Unfolded Version of RNN

It can be observed that RNN is intimately related to sequential sequence data. Here x_1, x_2 and x_3 are the inputs, the terms y_1, y_2 and y_3 are outputs, and h_1, h_2 and h_3 are hidden values. At time t, the neuron takes the input and provides an output, creating hidden information. This information is used as input for the subsequent timestamps. At subsequent stages, the hidden information, along with the input, is used to create outputs. Thus, the information propagates from time t to time step t+1. Here, the time is not a clock time but an index to the data's sequence nature.

One can infer the following important points from Figure 12.2.

(i) The presence of recurrent connections is repeated.

(ii) There are shared weights across time steps.

This memory ensures that RNN effectively captures patterns, dependencies, and relationships in sequence data.

The feedback ensures that RNNs are different from Feedforward networks. The difference between feedforward and RNN is given in Table 12.2.

Table 12.2 Differences between Feedforward and RNN

Feedforward Network	Recurrent Neural Networks (RNN)
The feedforward neural network has a predetermined size of inputs and outputs.	RNN has no such constraints.
The feedforward neural network takes the current input and performs the task of classification, prediction, or regression.	The RNN considers current input and the previous observation as input to perform the task.
The feedforward neural network does not have a memory component.	The RNN has a memory component that helps them to forecast the future based on the past received input.
The inputs are independent of each other.	The RNN is designed to capture long-term dependencies in sequential data.

An RNN can be considered multiple copies of the same network, as shown below in Fig. 12.2. The hidden neurons are computed as follows:

$$h_t = f(h_{t-1}, x_t)$$

The output state is updated based on the input and the previous state.

$$x_{out}[t] = g[h_t]$$

12.2.1 Memory and Context

While discussing memory, it makes sense to note the difference between memory and context. Memory is the mechanism by which past information is stored. The context refers to the information used to make a decision. The context is the memory used to understand or predict the next element.

Historically, this feedback creates a memory. The memory is created in two ways historically in two networks called Elman and Jordon networks.

Elman networks are a special type of neural network where there is a feedback loop from the hidden state back to itself. This kind of feedback creates a context for the entire input sequence and hence creates a context that influences the processing of the new data. On the other hand, the Jordon network creates feedback from the network's output to the input. This network is good when the recently created output is needed for further outputs like music or a healthcare monitoring system. The differences between Elman and Jordon networks are given in Table 12.3.

Table 12.3 Differences between Elman and Jordon Network

Elman Network	Jordon Network
The feedback is from the hidden layer to the hidden layer itself.	The feedback is from the output to the input.
The hidden vector is the summary of all the input sequences.	This network contains the memory of the previous output. This storage helps make a quick decision on its last action.
This network can handle long-term dependencies and is suitable for applications like language translation.	This network can handle only short-term dependencies and is hence suitable for applications like time series forecasting and generating music.
The inputs are independent of each other.	The RNN is designed to capture long-term dependencies in sequential data.

RNN is very effective in prediction because it is based on the current input and previously stored hidden information. The previous hidden states capture the hidden information as memory. For example, consider the following problem: RNN needs to predict the next word, as shown in Figure 12.3.

The moon is visible at night _____.

Humans know the answer. The answer is the sky. Can RNN predict this? The following arrangement of RNN cells can predict this as humans do.

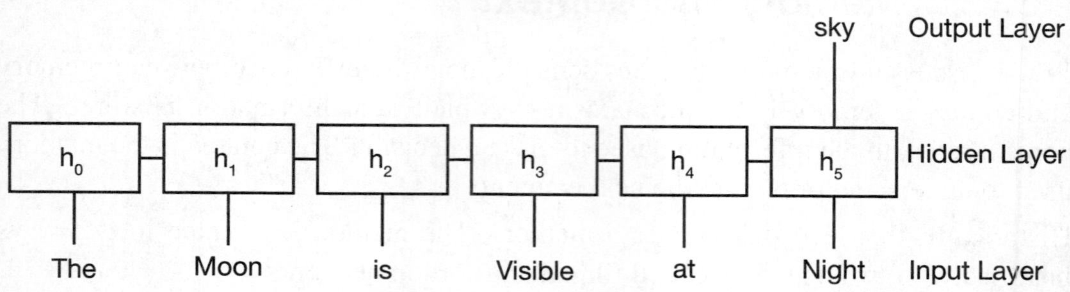

Figure 12.3 A Simple Example of RNN

It can be observed that words like moon and night influence the next word. So, context influences the decisions while memory refers to a mechanism of maintaining context. The use cases of RNN are given in Box 12.3.

Box 12.3 Use Cases of RNN

There are multiple applications of RNN. Some of the applications are listed below:

1. Finance – Applications that involve time series data like stocks.
2. Health care applications – Like biomedical signals like ECG, monitoring patients.
3. Natural language processing – Applications like language understanding, translation, sentiment analysis, text summarization, and question/answering.
4. Speech recognition

12.3 Topology of RNN

The above prediction problem shows how RNN cells can be combined to solve the problems. Similarly, the RNN cells can be arranged differently to solve problems effectively. This flexibility in RNN architectures, as shown in Figure 12.4, leads to many kinds of flexible architectures that can implement various tasks.

Some of the arrangements are given below:

a. **One-to-One:** This is the basic form of RNN, which takes one element as input and gives one element as output. For example, checking the word spelling falls under this category. The input is a single word, and the output will be whether the spelling is correct or wrong.

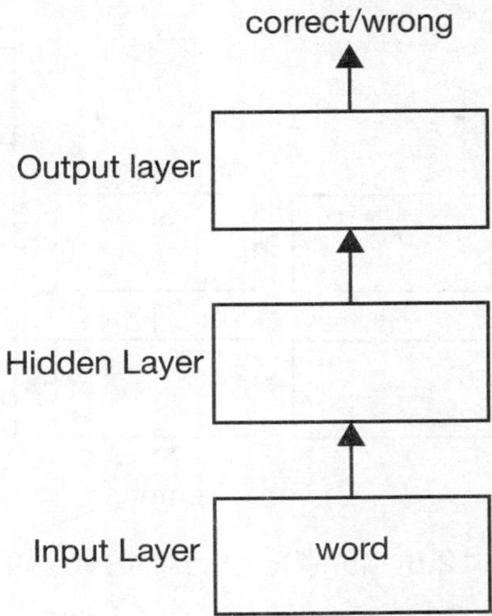

Figure 12.4 One-to-One RNN Architecture

b. **One-to-Many:** In this case, the input to RNN is one element, and the output is a sequence of elements. In the case of image captioning, the input is one image, and the output is a sequence of words that describe the image. This scenario is shown in Figure 12.5.

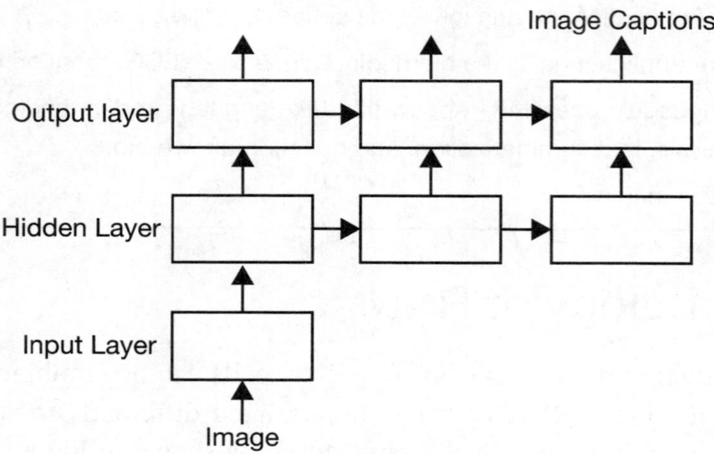

Figure 12.5 One-to-Many RNN Architecture

c. **Many-to-One:** In this type, the input to RNN is a sequence of elements, and the output is one element. The sentiment analysis is the best example of this type. In this case, the sentence or review command is given to the RNN, and the sentiment score is the output. This scenario is shown in Figure 12.6.

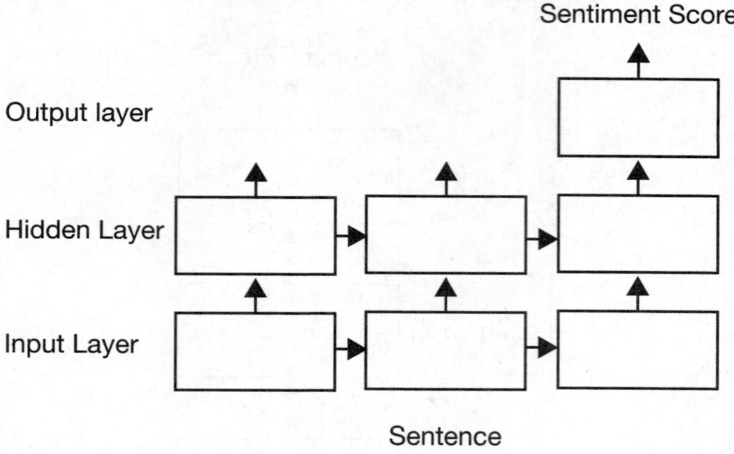

Figure 12.6 Many-to-One RNN Architecture

d. **Many-to-Many:** In this case, a sequence of elements is given as input, and the output is also a sequence of elements. Language Translation is an example of this type. This scenario is shown in Figure 12.7.

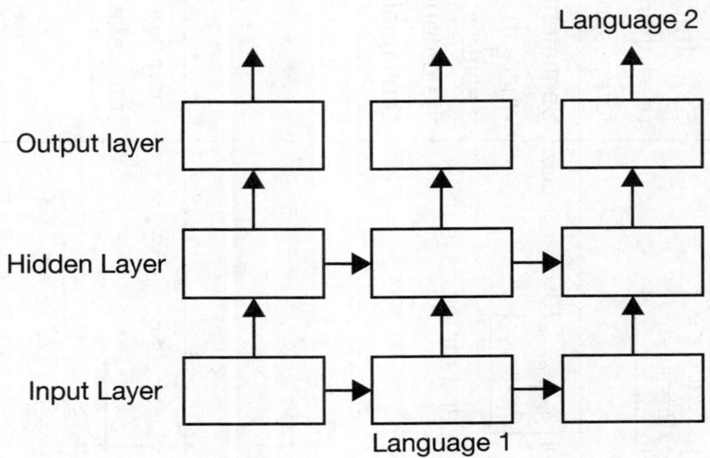

Figure 12.7 Many-to-Many RNN Architecture

All these RNN topologies are used to solve all kinds of sequence-related problems. Some of the sequence-related problems are given in the following Table 12.4.

Table 12.4 Example of Sequence Data Processing

Types of the Problem	Description	Diagram	Example Applications
Sequence prediction	This problem is to predict the next element in the sequence.	x[n-4], x[n-3], x[n-2], x[n-1] → Sequence Prediction → x[n]	Spell Checker, Stock market prediction, weather forecasting, etc.
Sequence classification	The main aim of sequence classification is to classify the input sequence to any one of the classes.	x[n-4], x[n-3], x[n-2], x[n-1], x[n] → Sequence Prediction → Sequence class The sequence is the input, and the class is the output.	Sentiment analysis, where the input is a sentence, and the output is the sentiment class.
Sequence Generation	Sequence generation is used to generate a sequence based on the input sequence.	Input Text → Sequence Prediction → Story	Story generation
Sequence to Sequence	This type is used in translating one language to another, also known as many-to-many. The input is a sentence sequence, and the output is a sentence sequence.	Sequence 1 → Sequence Prediction → Sequence 2	Language Translation

12.4 Backpropagation in Time Algorithm

The Backpropagation in Time algorithm works in two steps – Forward propagation and Backward propagation.

12.4.1 Forward Propagation

Let U be the weight matrix between the input and hidden layer. Let W is the weight matrix between the hidden to hidden layers. Let V be the weight matrix between the hidden to output layers.

Then, the hidden state h at any time step is computed as

$$h_t = \tanh(Ux_t + Wh_{t-1})$$

The output is computed as

$$\hat{y}_t = soft\max(Vh_t)$$

These activation functions are discussed in Chapter 3 of this textbook.

12.4.2 Backpropagation

This procedure implements all cells, and the final output is predicted. The error and loss function L is calculated at each time step *t*. The loss L at a time step is: $L_t = -y_t \log(\hat{y}_t)$. Here, y_t is the actual output and $\hat{y}_t$ Predicated output at a time step *t*. The final loss is the sum of all losses at each time step $L = \sum_{j=0}^{T-1} L_j$.

The weights are updated using the following equation.

$$V = V - \alpha \frac{\delta L}{\delta V}$$

$$W = W - \alpha \frac{\delta L}{\delta W}$$

$$U = U - \alpha \frac{\delta L}{\delta U}$$

12.5 Long Short-Term Memory (LSTM)

Sepp Hochreiter and Jurgen Schmidhuber proposed a sequence model LSTM to rectify the vanishing gradient problem (Refer Box 12.4) faced by RNN in 1997.

Box 12.4 What are the problems of RNN?

1. Vanishing Gradient Problem: In RNN, the vanishing gradient problem exists during the backpropagation stage. When the gradients are passed back, they become very small, often close to zero. These tiny gradients make the weight updates almost closer to zero. Recollect the fact from Chapter 5 that this closer zero weight update makes networks not learn anything at all. RNN have a severe problem of vanishing gradients.
2. The reverse problem of the vanishing gradient problem is called the exploding gradient problem. Here, the gradients make a very large update in weights. A large update diverges the learning process, and as a result, the networks may not converge.
3. RNN cannot handle long-term dependencies. As a result of the vanishing gradients problem, when the gradients diminish exponentially with the sequence length, RNN cannot learn connections with the distant events in a sequence. So, RNNs do have a problem retaining the earlier stage's information, and this causes problems in the later stage.

For example, consider the following sentence.

Ram lives in Tamil Nadu, and his mother tongue is Tamil. He is a skilled person. He knows poetry, too. He composes nice music, too. [...] He once wrote a nice ____ poem for his school students in his mother tongue.

In what language would that poem be? The answer is in the first sentence as Tamil. When the sentences, indicated as [...], become very large, RNN finds it difficult to remember the distant events.

The main benefits of LSTM are:

(i) It overcomes the vanishing and exploding gradient problem while training the model.

(ii) Memory is used to overcome the issues of long-term temporal dependency with input sequence.

(iii) It allows variable length input and outputs.

The use cases of LSTM are given in Box 12.5.

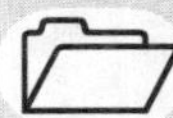

Box 12.5 Use Cases of LSTM

1. Many applications in NLP use LSTM.
   (i) Automatic image caption generation
   (ii) Automatic translation of text
   (iii) Automatic handwritten generation
2. There are many applications using time series data, like forecasting.
3. Speech recognition – Applications like speech to text.
4. Video analysis

12.5.1 LSTM Cell

The LSTM cell is a specialized unit of RNN that has a mechanism to regulate information and handle long-term dependencies or sequence data.

The comparisons between LSTM and RNN cells are given in Table 12.5.

Table 12.5 Differences between LSTM and RNN

	LSTM	RNN
1	It has both long and short-term memory.	It has primarily short-term memory.
2	It has three gates with a complex mechanism.	It has only one layer with no gate mechanisms.
3	The gates control the information flow with the cell state.	The process input with the previous state information.
4	It solves vanishing gradient problem.	It cannot solve the vanishing or exploding gradient problem.
5	Reliable and robust for longer sequence.	Computationally, less intensive and faster.

The details are given in Box 12.6. The specialty of LSTM is its long dependency that is achieved through long- and short-term memory.

Box 12.6 Human Long and Short-Term Memory

The memory can be divided into two types:

1. A short-term memory
2. Long-term memory

As the name indicates, short-term memory is short-duration and limited capacity. It can hold 7 ± 2 items for 20 – 30 seconds.

Long-term memory, as the name suggests, long-term memory holds information for the longest periods. It has a larger capacity and can include things that can be recalled or procedures like (car driving, shooting skills, etc.)

The core components of the LSTM are listed below:

1. **Cell State:** The cell state is a state vector that has the cell's internal memory. The gates update the information so the LSTM can retain or discard information. This cell state is a horizontal line that carries information through the LSTM cell.

   The cell state serves as a long-term memory. This cell state is a vector when the cell can read or write. The cell state records memories as the hidden layer of RNN and builds persistent memory. It accumulates the knowledge/patterns over the entire sequence. Hence, it helps LSTM to keep track of long-term redundancies/patterns of the sequence data and, therefore, helps to make accurate predication /context of input data.

2. **Gate Mechanisms:** Short-term memory is stored/managed through a combination of gates. The gates help LSTM capture short-term dependencies in the sequence data, which helps LSTM maintain and manipulate short-term memory. LSTM has three gates that regulate the information for the cell state.

3. **Hidden State:** LSTM maintains a hidden state vector that records the memory of the previous elements of the sequence. LSTM updates this value and passes it to the next cell, helping capture the sequence data's long dependencies.

4. **Input:** The input serves as the input for the LSTM cell. This input and the hidden states determine the output and the changes in the cell state.

5. Output: The output of LSTM includes

   5.1 **Hidden State:** The hidden state is the cell memory of the sequence up to that LSTM cell. This hidden state is passed on to the next cell, the final output layer, or LSTM. The focus of the hidden layer is to capture all the information about past elements of the sequences.

5.2 Cell State: Cell internal memory influences the hidden state of the LSTM.

12.5.2 LSTM Gates

The main feature of LSTM is to distinguish between the memory content, which data should be in retained long-term memory, and which data should be short-term memory. LSTM has three gates: a forget gate, an input gate, and an output gate that regulate information for long and short-term memory. LSTM also uses two activation functions: sigmoid and tanh functions and multiplication and addition operations.

Figure 12.8 depicts the basic architecture of LSTM. Each computational unit of the LSTM is called a memory cell or memory block. The top line in the memory cell is long-term memory, and the bottom is short-term memory. Due to this fact, it is called as long short-term memory. The data of both the memories are passed into the next LSTM cell based on the gates and activation function.

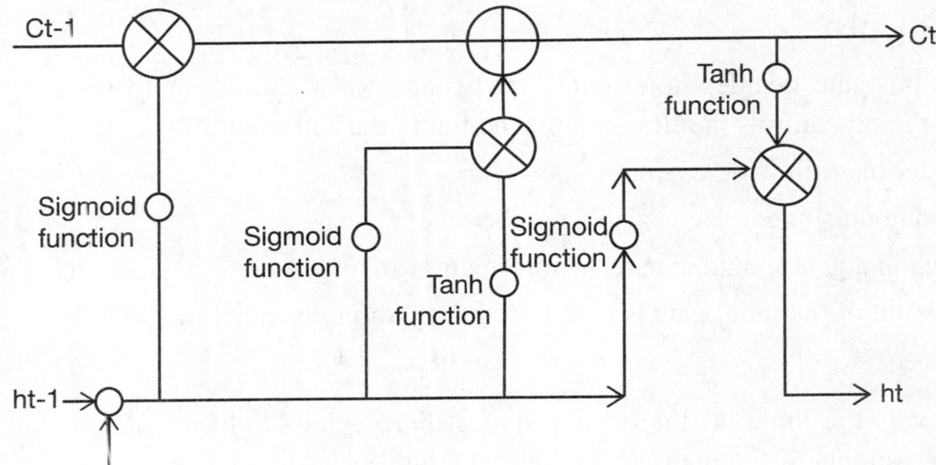

Figure 12.8 LSTM Architecture

Forget Gate

This gate is responsible for forgetting the information. Consider, for example, the following statement-

Raj is a good student. Peter is also a good student.

It can be observed that the focus now changes from Raj to Peter. The forget gate tries to remove Raj from the present context. The forget gate keeps the relevant parts and discards the irrelevant parts from the long-term memory.

$$f_t = \sigma(W_{xf}x_t + W_{hf}h_{t-1} + b_f)$$

Here, x_t is the input at time step t, h_{t-1} is the previous hidden state, W_{xf} and W_{hf} are the weights of the matrices to the input and hidden state, respectively. σ is the sigmoidal function and b_f is the bias.

The forget gate takes two inputs: previously hidden memory at time step t-1 and the newly input part of the current sequence x_t. Both inputs are mixed by taking a dot product between them and their corresponding weight. A sigmoid activation function is applied to the mixed data to filter out useless signals and enhance what seems important to keep and remember.

The resultant is a vector called the forget vector. It consists of values between 0-1. If the value is '1', the information should be retained fully; if '0', the information should be forgotten. The product of f_t and C_t determines how much of the past is forwarded to the current cell state.

Input Gate

The input gate decides how much newly input data should go to the long-term memory and controls the flow of information to the cell state.

Consider the following example-

Raj is a good student. He is also a good cricket player.

So, the input gate should update the information about Raj being a good cricket player.

The output of the input gate is based on the equation given below:

$$i_t = \sigma(W_{xi}x_t + W_{hi}h_{t-1} + b_i)$$

Here, x_t is the input at time step t, h_{t-1} is the previous hidden state, W_{xi} and W_{hi} are the weights of the matrices to the input and hidden state, respectively. σ is the sigmoidal function and b_i is the bias.

$\tilde{C}_t = \tanh(W_C[h_{t-1}, x_t] + b_C]$, creates new candidate values. Here, W_C and b_C are weights and biases, respectively.

Output Gate

The output gate determines what should be the short-term memory that passed to the next state $t + 1$. This gate regulates the part of the cell state that should go to the next hidden state.

The output gate decides which information should be output.

For example, consider the following statement,

John leaves for the U.S. Happy Journey ______!

The output should be John!

The input to the output gate is from long-term memory from the current state, short term from the previous state, and current inputted data. The long-term memory data is passed through the tanh activation function, and the mix of short-term memory and input data is passed through the sigmoid function. The results are multiplied by one another and then sent to the next state, t+1, as a short-term memory component.

$$o_t = \sigma(W_{xo}x_t + W_{ho}h_{t-1} + b_o)$$

Here, x_t is the input at time step t, h_{t-1} is the previous hidden state, W_{xo} and W_{ho} are the weights of the matrices to the input and hidden state, respectively. σ is the sigmoidal function and b_o is the bias.

The hidden state can be obtained as

$$h_t = o_t \times \tanh(C_t)$$

12.6 Various Models of LSTM

There are various models of LSTM.

12.6.1 Vanilla LSTM

It is the basic and default model of LSTM. It has an Input layer, a fully connected LSTM hidden layer, and a fully connected out layer. Figure 12.9 shows the Vanilla LSTM. This architecture is useful for sequence classification and sequence prediction problems.

Figure 12.9 Vanilla LSTM

12.6.2 Stacked LSTM

This model has multiple hidden layers, making the model deeper and giving an accurate output. As shown in Figure 12.10, LSTM cells are stacked over one after another. So, there are multiple layers of LSTMs. The additional layer of LSTM adds more level of abstraction of input over some time. The deeper network gives more accuracy on various challenging prediction problems. The last layer provides the important data to the fully connected layer, giving the task a final output.

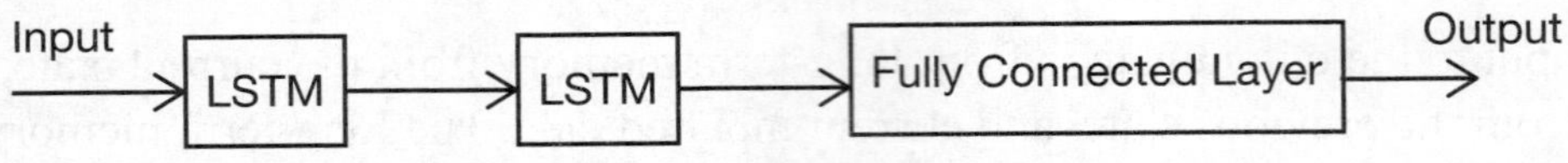

Figure 12.10 Stacked LSTM

One application of stacked LSTM is in speech recognition.

12.6.3 CNN LSTM

The CNN LSTM, as the name indicates, there is a CNN layer in this model.

This model is developed to handle visual time series prediction problems and for application image captioning (generating a textual description of an image). This model is applied to a variety of visual tasks involving many-to-may tasks.

As shown in Figure 12.11, The input image data is first fed into the CNN module to extract the feature map. The CNN part in this model is pre-trained on an image classification task that is reused as a feature extractor in this model. After this, the feature map is fed to the LSTM module. This model is both spatially and temporally deep.

This model is also used to handle problems like:

(i) Generating a textual description of an activity.

(ii) Generating a textual description from a sequence of images. For example, based on the video, they can tell whether it is about wildlife or historic places.

This CNN LSTM model is used on spatial and temporal input data to generate a sequence of output data, as shown in Figure 12.11.

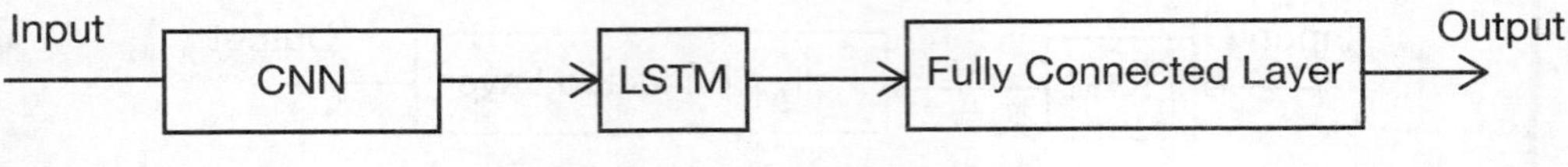

Figure 12.11 CNN LSTM

12.6.4 Encoder-Decoder LSTM

Figure 12.12 shows the architecture of encoder-decoder LSTM. This architecture consists of one encoder, a decoder, and a dense or fully connected layer. The encoder reads the input sequence and converts it into a fixed-length vector. Then, the decoder uses the fixed-length vector to output the predicted sequence. It is used in the statistical machine translation process.

This model is mainly used for the sequence-to-sequence prediction problem. This model may be one-to-many, many-to-one, or many-to-many type. The various applications of this model are machine translation(for example, Tamil to English), checking the output of programs, a question and answering system, and generating text from gestures.

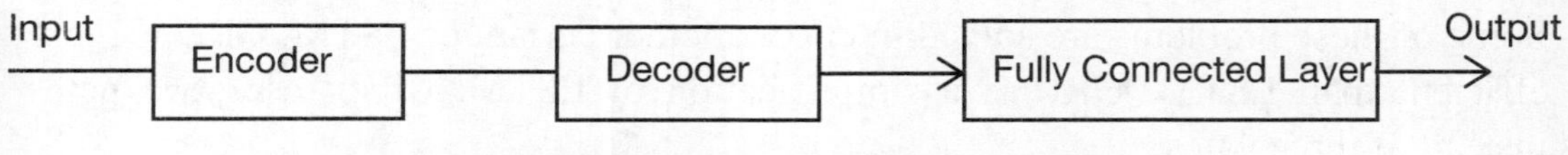

Figure 12.12 Encoder-Decoder LSTM

12.6.5 Bi-directional LSTM

For example, consider two sentences: Apple is good fruit, and The Laptop company name is Apple. The apple word is present in both sentences, but its context and meanings differ. Having the sentences and their reverse can provide this kind of enhanced context.

Bi-directional LSTM focuses on the problem of getting the most out of the input sequence in both forward and backward directions. In this model, the input sequence is duplicated into two. Both the forward and backward layers are side by side. The input to the forward layer is the same, but for the backward layer, the sequence is reversed and fed to it. Both the LSTMs return a probability vector as output. The fully connected layer considers both the output and gives the final output. The architecture of bi-directional LSTM is shown in Figure 12.13.

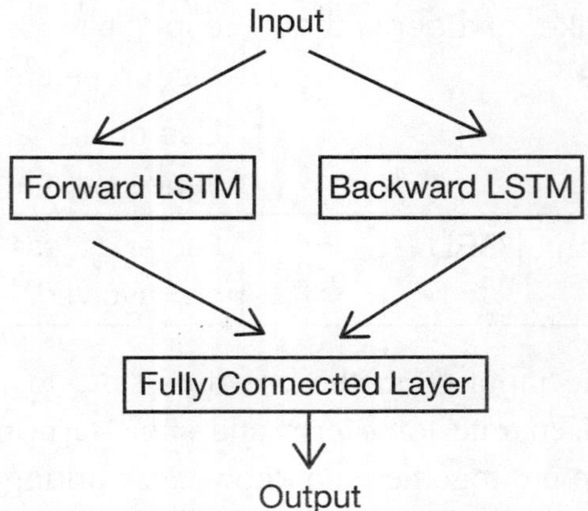

Figure 12.13 Bi-Directional LSTM

12.7 Gated Recurrent Units (GRU)

Some of the challenges of LSTM are:

(i) Computational complexity involved.

(ii) Huge data Requirements.

(iii) Hyperparameter selection mechanisms are complex as there are more parameters involved.

Some of these problems are solved in GRU, another variant of LSTM. GRU is more efficient than LSTM. GRU is a simplification of LSTM, which uses two gates instead of three gates

GRU has two additional gates that deal with "what to remember," "what to update," and "what to forget." The two gates of GRU are the reset gate and the update gate. It also uses sigmoid and tanh activation functions.

The differences between LSTM and GRU are shown in Table 12.6.

Table 12.6 Difference between LSTM and GRU

	LSTM	GRU
1	It is more complex, with three gates to regulate the information flow.	Only two gates (update and reset).
2	Cell state: for long-term memory. Separate cell and hidden state. So, LSTM has more control.	No cell state, only hidden state is provided.
3	Useful in handling long-term dependencies like next generation, time series data.	It is better with short sequences, especially when computational resources are limited. Useful in applications like time series data and NLP applications.
4	Slightly slower than GRU.	Faster as less number of parameters are involved.

There is only one single input from the previous state to the next state, contrary to LSTM, which has a separate long-term and short-term memory component. In GRU, both memories are put together and known as working memory.

The core components of GRU are listed below:

(i) Gate Mechanisms

(ii) Hidden state

(iii) New Hidden state that is the combination of input and updated hidden sate.

Some of the highlights of GRU are given in Box 12.7.

Box 12.7 Highlights of GRU

(i) They rely on single working memory. It is a combination of long-term and short-term memory of LSTM.

(ii) Cell states are processed repeatedly through a GRU cell itself. GRU is less complex than LSTM.

(iii) They are less capable when dealing with longer sequences than LSTM.

(iv) They are faster than LSTM.

(v) They outperform LSTM for less training data.

12.7.1 GRU Gates

1. Update Gate

This gate decides how much information from the previous time steps will be passed out to the future cells. It determines the influence of previous hidden states on the current hidden state.

$$z_t = \sigma(W_z \bullet [h_{t-1}, x_t] + b_z)$$

Here, z_t is the output of the update gate. W_z and b_z are the weight and bias of the update gate. $ht - 1$ is the previous hidden state, and x_t is the current input. The update gate decides how much of the previous memory will be maintained.

2. Reset Gate

This gate is useful to forget the irrelevant information of the past.

$$r_t = \sigma(W_r \bullet [h_{t-1}, x_t] + b_r)$$

W_r and b_r are the weights and biases of the reset gate.

The new candidate hidden state (output of reset gate + filtered through the gate current input) is the new content and is given as

$$\tilde{h}_t = \tanh(W[r_t \bullet h_{t-1}, x_t] + b)$$

Here, W is the weight matrix, x_t is the current input, h_{t-1} is the previous hidden state, and b is the bias.

The final hidden state, the (old hidden state + new candidate hidden state), is given as follows:

$$h_t = (1 - z_t)h_{t-1} + z_t \times \tilde{h}_t$$

where z_t is the old hidden state and $(1 - z_t)$ is how much the candidate state should be retained.

The reset gate takes two inputs one from the previous hidden state memory and the current input data. It applies a sigmoid function on the input, and the output of this function is multiplied by the working memory component. This mechanism enables the model to decide how much previous data can be forgotten. The reset gate decides how much new and previous information can be merged and remembered. The output of the reset gate is added to the working memory. The updated working memory is passed to the next state.

12.8 Case Studies for LSTM

Some of the LSTM applications are listed below for better understanding.

12.8.1 Case Study 1: Sentiment Analysis

Sentiment analysis is an application where the text is classified based on the word's sentiment. Sentiment analysis can be used for many applications like movie reviews, product reviews, and customer reviews of products.

The sentiments of a movie can be:

Positive: A review may have comments like "Movie is good." It is the same as the comment, "The movie is excellent." It is a positive sentiment. Therefore, the words can convey sentiment.

Negative: Similarly, words like bad or worse represent negative polarity.

Neutral: Certain words are neutral as it is neither positive nor negative. Based on the polarity values, the sentiment can be understood.

LSTM can be used for finding the sentiment value or emotional tone behind the sequence of texts. How? As LSTM remembers the full context of the input sentence, LSTMs are effective in sentiment analysis. The stages of sentiment analysis are given below in Figure 12.14.

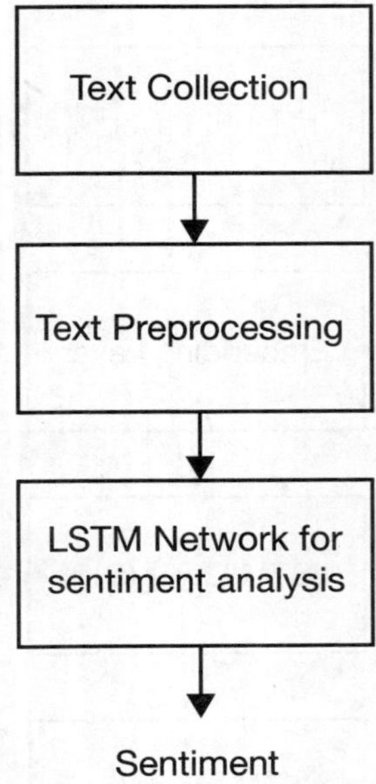

Figure 12.14 Sentiment Analysis

1. Data Preparation Stage: The first step is data collection. Movie or product reviews can be input, and review comments can be scraped from the web.
2. Text Preprocessing: The preprocessing steps include these tasks
   - All the unnecessary HTML tags, URLs, and non-numeric characters are removed.
   - Sentences are split into tokens. This step is called tokenization.
   - Stop words such as (a, an, and the) are removed as they do not convey useful information.
   - Stemming can be done to reduce the keywords to their base form. For example, writing and writing have a common stem of writing only.
   - The special characters, like punctuation marks, can be removed. Similarly, the numbers and white spaces can be removed.
3. Embedding: The important step is converting input data into a form that can be processed. One such conversion is called embedding, which captures the context of the input sentence.

4. Preparation of a Neural Network: LSTM can take the embeddings and update its internal states as it processes the input. It builds a context based on the previous words. Then, the final LSTM layer can be used to classify the sentiment of the text as positive, negative, or neutral. The neural network design is shown in Figure 12.15.

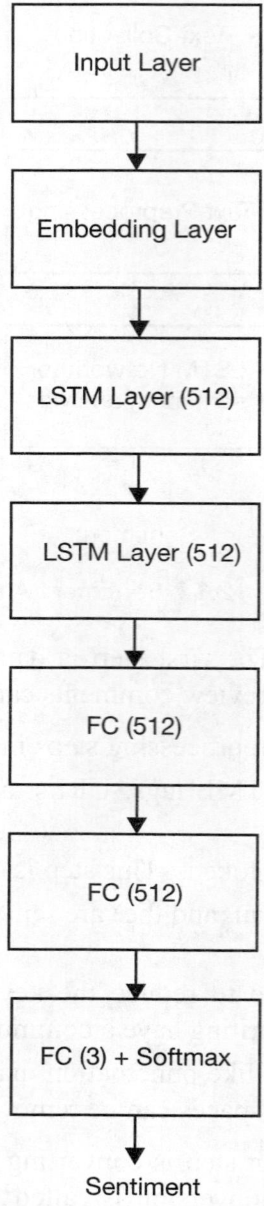

Figure 12.15 LSTM Architecture for Sentiment Analysis

1. The input layer takes less than 100 characters as input.
2. The embedding layer converts the input into embedding. Two parameters are
   - Vocabulary Size – This can be a pretrained parameter
   - Number of Embedding vectors – This can be the embedding size, say 100.
   - A Pretrained model like Word2Vec can be used for this.
3. LSTM layer
   - Two LSTM layers have 512 neurons.
4. Dense layers
   - There are three dense layers.
   - Two dense layers have 512 neurons, and the last dense layer has three neurons for three types of sentiments – positive, negative, and neutral. It uses softmax as it is a multi-class problem.

The LSTM is trained on a labelled dataset where ground truth is present. This training helps to learn patterns and word sequences corresponding to specific sentiments. The network can use ADAM as optimizers and categorical cross-entropy for finding the errors between the actual and output sentiment values.

12.8.2 Case Study 2: Language Translation using Encoder-Decoder LSTM

In applications like text generation, the input is small, and the generated output can be very big. The reverse is true for applications like text summary, where the input is very big, and the output is small compared to the input. So, there are two types of sequence data:

a. The sequence data whose length is fixed.

b. Sequence data whose length is varied.

Generally, this kind of processing can be called sequence-to-sequence or (Seq2seq models).

A seq2seq model is a neural network architecture using LSTM that can be useful for projects like language translation. The input can be a sentence in one language, say Tamil, and the output can be in another language, say Hindi.

A seq2seq model can be constructed using two LSTMs: encoder and decoder. The encoder encodes the input sentence to capture all its meaning or context. It facilitates the translation process. The decoder produces a coherent and grammatically correct translated statement.

The model for seq2seq is shown in Figure 12.16.

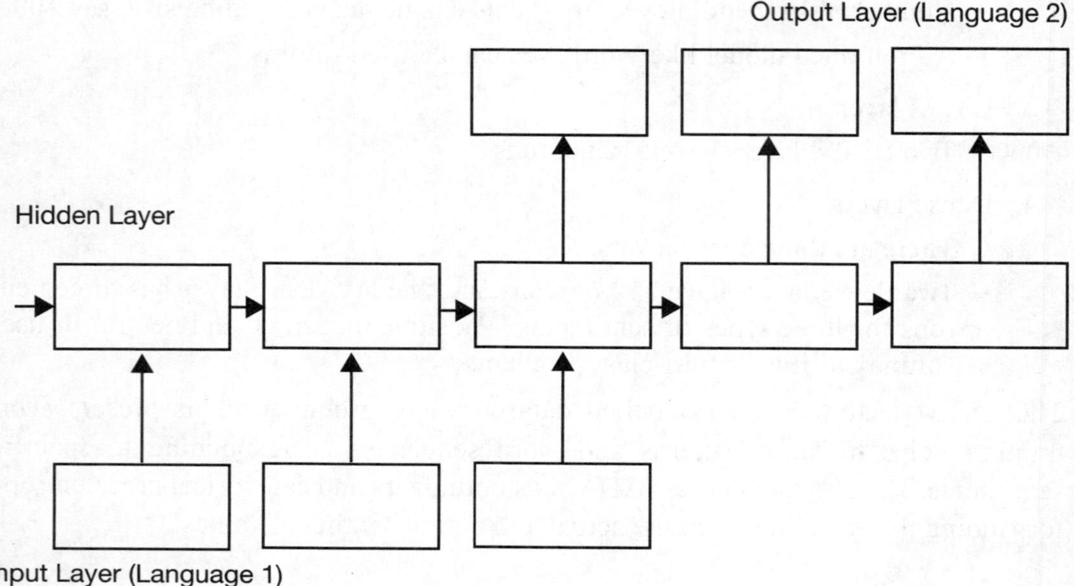

Figure 12.16 Many-Many models

Encoder: The encoder can be constructed using LSTM. LSTM aims to capture the input sentence's full meaning or context.

1. The input data is taken through an input layer.
2. The next layer is the embedding layer, where the embeddings are taken. The encoder takes these embeddings as input to produce the context vector. The encoder processes the variable input-sized data and converts that into a fixed-size context vector.

Context Vector: The size of the context vector is fixed. Essentially, the context vector is a summary of the input sequence. The encoder's hidden state represents the input sequence. Encoder LSTM takes two inputs: the input word and the hidden state of the previous unit. Then, it updates the hidden vector. This updated vector is passed to the next unit. The second unit repeats the same process. Thus, the encoder processes the input in time steps and updates the hidden state information.

The interaction of the encoder and decoder is shown in Figure 12.17.

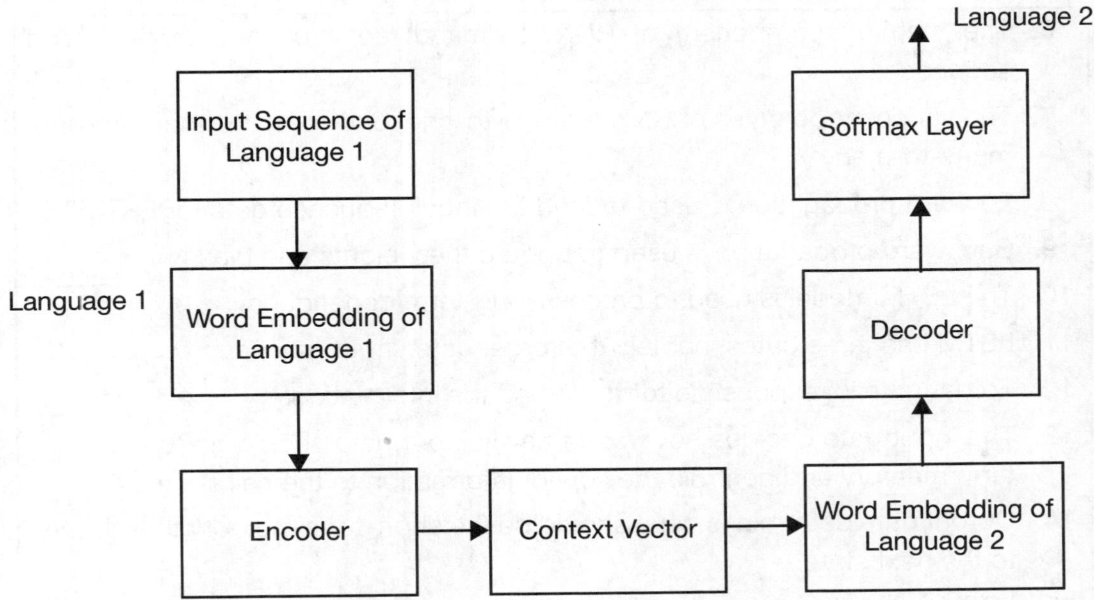

Figure 12.17 Encoder-Decoder Architecture

Decoder: The decoder is another LSTM.

The encoder processes the input sequence and gives the entire context vector to the first decoder layer. The decoder starts with <sos> tag, which indicates the start of the sequence. The whole purpose of the decoder is to predict the next word. For this, the decode takes the current and previous words generated already.

The output word's choice is based on all possible words. The context vector and all the previously generated words in the target sentence influence the appropriate word selection.

This process continues until the decoder outputs <eos>, a tag for the end of the sequence. The tag <eos> marks the end of the process.

Summary

1. Recurrent neural networks are modelled to process sequence data.
2. The order is important in sequence data.
3. The tasks that can be performed on sequence data are generation, classification, and prediction.
4. Text and video are sequence data.
5. RNN has a memory component that is used to process the sequence data.

6. The memory component of RNN is limited, so it cannot process long sequences.
7. The various topologies of RNN are one-to-one, one-to-many, many-to-one, many-to-many.
8. Forward propagation is used to feed the input sequence data for LSTM.
9. Backward propagation is used to update the weights and biases.
10. The LSTM model is used to process long-term dependency.
11. LSTM has three gates, namely the forget gate, input gate, and output gate.
12. Forget gate is responsible for forgetting the information.
13. The input gate decides how much newly input data should go to the long-term memory and controls the flow of information to the cell state.
14. Output gate determines what should be the short-term memory that passes to the next state.
15. LSTM gates use sigmoid and tanh activation functions to process the data.
16. LSTM is classified as vanilla, stacked, CNN, encoder-decoder, and bidirectional based on its architecture.
17. Vanilla LSTM is a basic model, a fully connected LSTM useful for sequence classification and prediction.
18. Stacked LSTM has multiple hidden layers, making the model deeper useful for speech recognition.
19. CNN-LSTM has a CNN module which is used to handle visual data prediction problem.
20. Encoder-Decoder LSTM consists of one encoder, one decoder, and a fully connected layer basically used for the statistical translation process.
21. Bi-directional LSTM handles information in both forward and backward directions.
22. GRU has two gates: update and reset gates.
23. Update gate decides how much information from the previous time steps will be passed out to the future cells.
24. Reset gate is useful for forgetting irrelevant past information.

Glossary

1. Sequence Data – A data set in which the elements, instances, or objects are ordered or arranged in a specific manner.
2. RNN – A recurrent neural network that has a feedback loop as memory.
3. Memory – It is a mechanism by which past information is stored.
4. Context – It is the memory used to understand or predict the next element.
5. Ellam Network – It is a special type of neural network where there is a feedback loop from the hidden state to itself.
6. Jordan network – It creates a feedback loop from network output to itself.
7. Vanishing gradient problem – A problem that exists during the back propagation stage. When the gradients are passed back, they become very small, often close to zero. These tiny gradients make the weight updates almost closer to zero making the networks ineffective in learning.
8. Long-term dependencies – Long-term dependencies are the ability to remember distant events in a long paragraph or a document. RNN cannot handle long-term dependencies.
9. Short- and long-term – These are the abilities to remember the short and long-term events in processing.
10. BPTT – An algorithm to compute the error and update the weights.
11. LSTM – A cell that provides a long-short term memory.
12. GRU –Gated Recurrent Unit that is a simplified version of LSTM.

Short Questions

1. Explain the different types of sequence tasks with suitable examples.
2. List out the applications of RNN.
3. List out the different topologies of RNN.
4. Differentiate between LSTM and GRU cells.
5. Is GRU better than LSTM? Justify.
6. List out applications of LSTM.
7. Explain the vanishing gradient problem.
8. List out the gates in LSTM.
9. List out the gates in GRU.

Long Questions

1. Explain in detail about the gates of LSTM.
2. Explain in detail about the working principle of LSTM
3. Explain in detail about BPTT.
4. Explain LSTM networks for sentiment analysis.
5. Explain language translation using LSTM networks.

Crossword

Across

2. The three gates of LSTM are __________, output and input.
6. RNN differs from CNN as it possess __________ to process sequence data.
7. The two gates of GRU are the update gate and __________ gate.
9. LSTM can process long-term dependencies. (true/false)
10. Stock market prediction is a __________ prediction problem.
11. Order is not important for sequence data. (true/false)
12. Memory and context are the same. (true/false)
13. Sequence data elements are temporal or __________ based.
14. LSTM uses __________ and tanh activation functions.

15. Cell state is a __________ term memory.
16. Sentiment analysis is a sequence __________ problem.

Down

1. GRU has __________ gates.
3. The number of gates LSTM possesses is __________.
4. Short-term memory can hold 7 plus or minus two items for 20–30 seconds. (true/false)
5. Some of the tasks that can be performed on sequence data are sequence __________.
8. GRU is a simplified version of LSTM. (true/false)
9. RNN cannot process long-term dependencies. (true/false)
12. Text is not sequential data. (true/false)
13. Event logs are __________ data.
15. Car driving skill is a __________ term memory.

Jumbled Sentences

X	I	O	D	X	M	F	B	L	Y	Z	Z	J	H	W	C	N	T	S	H	N	M	L	S	N
V	X	G	O	C	R	V	O	N	W	X	P	E	Z	X	V	C	O	M	E	O	D	O	K	N
A	N	D	E	Q	E	N	B	A	M	C	G	O	I	F	P	O	B	U	E	T	Y	N	O	Q
D	C	L	H	G	S	C	F	T	Y	Q	F	A	X	A	W	X	R	G	Z	M	Z	G	R	Z
S	C	S	Q	N	E	T	T	A	V	H	X	X	P	T	X	T	J	E	P	A	O	Y	F	E
S	Z	W	P	X	T	M	R	S	E	Q	U	E	N	C	E	R	E	N	L	P	A	R	G	R
W	Y	Q	M	A	F	Z	U	T	D	S	P	Z	R	I	L	N	E	E	P	H	Q	B	Y	P
K	P	U	S	T	T	E	E	M	Q	P	E	T	Q	D	X	Y	L	R	U	K	D	X	F	G
J	L	O	N	G	R	I	G	O	B	I	C	Q	T	U	X	V	V	A	H	Z	C	W	T	J
V	U	A	V	F	D	U	A	D	L	E	L	O	U	R	U	B	O	T	Y	C	Q	T	R	M
N	C	Y	E	D	A	C	E	L	J	H	U	Q	I	E	U	V	T	I	Y	I	E	D	U	B
X	N	T	V	Q	R	L	X	Z	B	G	B	O	R	Y	N	E	S	O	A	G	A	H	E	C
Y	P	M	U	V	R	O	S	B	V	D	D	Q	V	D	S	C	N	N	R	P	T	Q	G	H
L	F	H	U	X	U	G	Z	E	T	U	O	M	U	C	H	B	E	O	Y	V	S	K	B	L
A	U	Q	D	E	S	N	S	M	O	J	R	I	W	S	Z	W	F	Q	A	L	O	L	D	P
V	L	W	L	O	Z	C	C	L	A	S	S	I	F	I	C	A	T	I	O	N	B	R	L	T
C	A	T	S	Z	T	H	R	E	E	K	F	A	L	S	E	Y	S	I	G	M	O	I	D	P

spatial	false	memory	false	generation
true	true	three	forget	sigmoid
two	reset	true	true	sequence
sequence	classification	long	true	long

CHAPTER 13

Introduction To Autoencoders

> The ability of autoencoders to reduce dimensionality and find patterns in data is a cornerstone of many modern AI applications. — **Fei-Fei Li**

Credits: © Fei-Fei Li

An autoencoder is a type of neural network that can perform tasks like dimensionality reduction, denoising, and anomaly detection. It consists of core components – encoder, latent space, and decoder. The purpose of the encoder is to compress the input into a compact and smaller representation called latent space or code. The decoder's purpose is to reconstruct the original input using the latent representation. In that process, the autoencoder learns the important features of the input data. The learning objectives of this chapter are as follows:

- Explore the concepts of autoencoder.
- Know the components of autoencoders.
- Understand the types of autoencoders.
- Survey the application of autoencoders.
- Types of autoencoders.
- Provide an overview of autoencoder variants.
- Provide an overview of generative AI.

13.1 Overview of Autoencoders

Autoencoders consist of two words – auto and encoder. The word auto means self. Encoding refers to a way of representation. Autoencoder refers to a way of representing data using unsupervised learning. Geoffrey Hinton and his colleagues introduced the concept of autoencoders in 1986 and Yann LeCun contributed to its training methods like the backpropagation algorithm.

Autoencoders are a special type of artificial neural network for learning efficient representation of data. Autoencoders take higher dimensional data and compress it to a lower dimensional data called latent space, thereby capturing the most important details of input data. These representations are useful for applications like embedding, clustering, feature learning, and clustering.

The autoencoder learns using the concept of unsupervised learning. The details of unsupervised learning are given in Box 13.1.

Box 13.1 Unsupervised Learning

Unsupervised learning takes unlabeled data as input and groups similar items together. In that process, the learning program learns the hidden patterns and structures of the input data. Hence, unsupervised learning is useful in tasks like dimensionality reduction and clustering.

An autoencoder is a neural network that utilizes unsupervised learning specifically for learning efficient representations using unlabeled data. Autoencoder is a tool that utilizes unsupervised learning to compress the higher dimensional data into a lower dimensional latent space. Later, latent space is used to reconstruct the original data. In that process, autoencoders learn essential characteristics of data. These characteristics are utilized for various applications like denoising, dimension reductionality, and so on.

The autoencoders are data dependent and, hence, should be designed specifically for learning patterns from particular data.

The important thing about the autoencoder is representational learning. The details about the representational learning are given in Box 13.2.

Box 13.2 Representational Learning

In neural networks, we can broadly classify the architecture into the following two layers:

(i) **Representation Layers:** These are represented by the hidden layer, which is responsible for learning the data representations of the input data. The representations consist of rich information on features that can be exploited by the task layers for various tasks like classification, clustering, etc.

(ii) **Task Layer:** This corresponds to the output layer, which utilizes the representations for producing the final output, such as classification, regression, clustering, etc. Unsupervised learning takes unlabeled data as input and groups similar items together. In that process, the learning program learns the hidden patterns and structures of the input data. Hence, unsupervised learning is useful in tasks like dimensionality reduction and clustering.

The role of the autoencoder is directly with the quality of latent space. It is the component that takes the input data and compresses it to lower dimensional data, thereby capturing all the important latent representations. Therefore, the key role of autoencoders is to enhance the overall performance of the neural network by providing effective representations.

The details of the encoder and decoder are given below:

13.1.1 Encoder

The input data is fed to the encoder. The model constructed for the autoencoder is to decompose the data to learn the representations of the input data. The encoder part encodes the data into a lower-level representation called latent space (or latent representation or code). An encoder does this input data conversion into lower-level representation. The encoder compresses the input data using non-linear functions into a latent space representation h. The encoder function is given as

$$h = f(x)$$

Here, it can be observed that x is the input, and f is the mapping function that maps the input x to the latent space variable h. This encoding process can also be expressed as a conditional probability $p(h/x)$.

This autoencoder arrangement is shown in Figure 13.1.

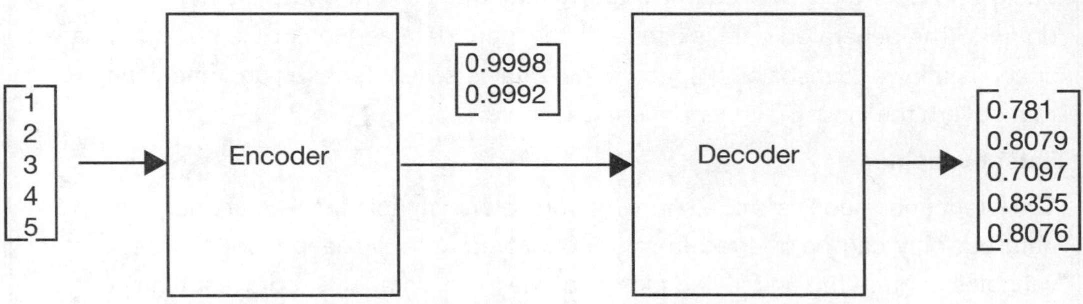

Figure 13.1 Arrangement of Encoder and Decoder

The size of the decoder layer should be the same as the encoder layer. For example, if the input data is (1, 2, 3, 4, 5), the encoder will have 5 neurons, and the decoder should have 5 neurons. The encoder takes the input and compresses it to a latent form, shown [0.9998, 0.9992] in Figure 13.1.

13.1.2 Latent Space (or Code)

The most important component of Figure 13.1 is the latent space. The latent space or code or bottleneck refers to a lower dimensional space with the essential features or information of the higher dimensional input data; in simpler terms, it is a compressed representation of the original data. The additional details of latent space are given in Box 13.3.

Box 13.3 Idea of the Latent Variables and Latent Space

Latest space contains important information representing the features of the input data. In latent space, all the similar items are grouped. This property is exploited in various autoencoder applications.

The relationships between latent space and latent variables are interdependent. Latent variables represent the hidden variables or facts that are present in the data. Latent variables are generated by the encoders that capture the essential features and patterns in compressed form. Latent space is a lower dimensional space where the latent variables that represent the input data exist.

What is a Latent Space?

A latent space is a set of points that reflects the input data. Each point is a compressed form of the original higher-dimensional input data. The chief characteristic of latent space is that all similar items are stored together. The encoder learns how to encode the input point in the latent space. One can manipulate the latent space. When mapped back, one gets the novel output data by taking the latent space points to the input domain. The generated data is similar to the input data and looks like real data. Latent space is a lower dimensional space that contains salient features and underlying rules that govern the input of higher dimensional data.

Latent Variables

The latent space consists of a set of random latent variables. These are not observable data but only can be inferred from the observed data. In deep learning, these latent variables capture the underlying factors of the input data. This representation contains the essence of important features and is useful for reconstruction.

Consider, for example, the student performance systems. The marks of the student are observable directly. So, they are observable features.

The unobservable patterns are like the motivation and interest of the student, as they are not directly measurable. These variables are used to reconstruct the original data.

The idea is to model the higher-dimensional space of observing the data using a lower-dimensional space called latent space. Then, the model takes the variables of the latent space and maps it back to the original domain, as shown in Figure 13.2.

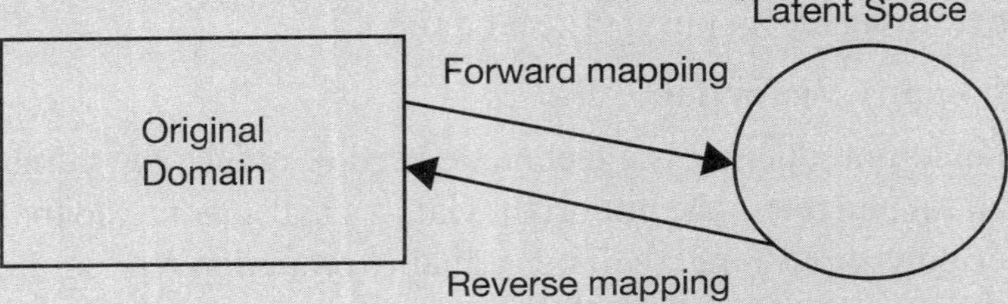

Figure 13.2 Mappings of Autoencoder

The latest space can be manipulated to generate new data or can be used for performing tasks like dimensionality reduction.

13.1.3 Decoder

The decoder, the other component, takes the latent form and reconstructs it into the original data. Hence, the purpose is to learn how to reconstruct the data without requiring the label. The input of the autoencoder is reproduced as an output. In other words, the input and output of the encoder are the same. A function whose output is the same as the input is called an identity function.

If so, what is the purpose of an autoencoder? The main purpose is to learn the hidden representations of the input data. In other words, this is similar to decompression. The decoder function is given as

$$x' = g(h)$$

Or as the conditional probability as $p(x/h)$.

The decoder reconstructs the input data from latent space variables. The decoder takes compressed representation and maps it back to the original data. It can be observed from Fig. 13.1 that the reconstructed input is given as [0.781, 0.8079, 0.7097, 0.8355, 0.8076].

13.2 Applications of Autoencoders

There are a variety of reasons for using autoencoders. Some of the important reasons are listed below:

1. **Find Patterns in Input Data:**

   Autoencoders use unsupervised learning and can be considered as a building block. Autoencoders can be used to capture the patterns in the input data. In a way, the patterns can be clustered together like a clustering algorithm. Hence, the primary usage is an unsupervised tool.

2. **Dimensionality Reduction:**

   Dimensionality reduction is a technique used to reduce the number of features in the dataset and retain the important features sufficient to do the classification or clustering task. In general, dimensionality reduction reduces high dimension to lower dimension, preserving the important or required features.

   For example, consider a dataset of basketball players' names, date of birth, age, and height to understand feature extraction. This dataset has four dimensions, of which three can be reduced by extracting the age from the date of birth data. The dimension is the number of features or columns of input data. By reducing the dimension, the time complexity and space complexity can be reduced. A new feature can be created by combining and transforming the original features in the feature extraction process.

   Dimensionality reduction can be performed in two ways: linear and non-linear. There are several methods for dimensionality reduction. Principal component analysis (PCA) and single Value Decomposition (SVD) are linear methods. The autoencoders come under the non-linear category, as shown in Figure 13.3.

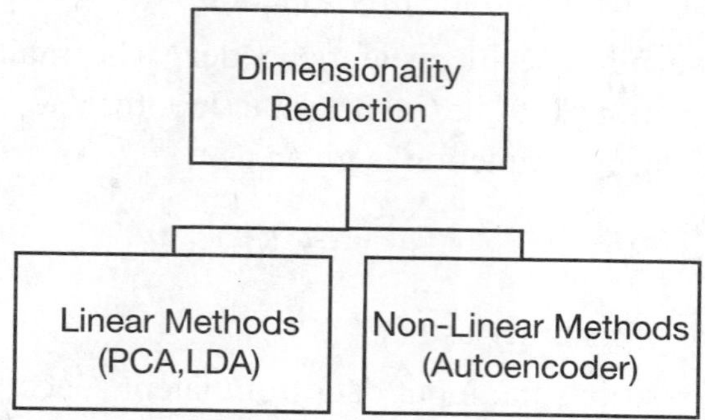

Figure 13.3 Types of Dimensionality Reduction Methods

The difference between the traditional dimensionality reduction technique and the autoencoder is autoencoder captures complex non-linear correlations in the data and does not require labelled datasets. They also reconstruct the input data from its lower dimensional representation.

3. **Compression:**

The encoder compresses the input data into an intermediate representation. What is a compression? Compression takes the data of larger size as input and compresses it to data that can take fewer bits. This compression is possible by removing the redundant data. For example, compression may take a file of size 1 MB and reduce it to 250 KB. The compression ratio is 4:1. If the reduced file can be restored to an original file without losing any information, it is called lossless compression. Otherwise, the compression is termed as lossy.

The autoencoder does the same. It takes the input data and compresses it. But the focus here is not to save memory space; instead, it focuses on reducing the dimensions of the intermediate representation, and by reducing it, it forces them to learn the internal representations of the input data that can be used to reconstruct the original data as closely as possible.

4. **Feature Learning:**

Autoencoders are useful for extracting the lower level as well as higher level features in the input data. The useful, meaningful, and robust features learned can be used for many applications. Autoencoders are used in some of the techniques like pretraining and transfer learning. These features can be used for information retrieval also.

5. **Embedding:**

In embedding, two sentences are grouped in latent space. This kind of grouping is useful in language translation. However, implementing this embedding is costly as innumerable pairs of pairs are possible across languages, say English and French. Autoencoders are useful tools for implementing this idea. Since the intermediate representation is of compact dimensions, autoencoders are forced to pair the items, making the intermediate representation more meaningful.

6. **Outlier Detection:**

Outlier data is abnormal data. For example, if the student's age is listed as {17, 18, 19, 17, 98}, then 98 is abnormal data. The loss is computed as the difference between the input and the reconstructed image or data. Hence, the loss is abnormal for data that is outlier. Autoencoders fail to reconstruct the outlier data and can be useful for detecting the outliers.

7. **Denoising:**

   Denoising is the process of removing noise in an image. Autoencoders are useful for removing noise in the image. Some of these details about noise are given in Chapter 8 of this book.

8. **Synthetic Data:**

   A variant of autoencoder called variational autoencoder can generate new data also that is similar to the input data in the training set. So, the generated data is a new one and is not obtained from the input using data manipulation.

   This data generation is useful for many creative applications and the generated synthetic data can be used for data augmentation.

9. **Data Clustering:**

   Autoencoders can be used to improve the quality of clustering algorithms by dimensionality reduction and noise.

   There are multiple such applications of autoencoders. Let us discuss implementing them in the subsequent sections.

13.3 Implementation of an Autoencoder Using Neural Networks

The neural network can be used to implement an autoencoder. The neural network has the following three layers:

(i) Input layer

(ii) Hidden layer

(iii) Output layer

The input layer receives the input data. The input data can be text, image, or any other data. The hidden layer can be fully connected (for any other data) or convolutional layers (in the case of image). Each hidden layer applies a transformation of the form

$$Y = wx + b.$$

Here, w is the weight matrix, and b is the bias.

Each layer is followed by the non-linear activation layers like ReLU that bring the non-linear into the computation.

The final hidden layer is the output layer that generates the latent representation.

A neural network-based autoencoder with four nodes is represented below in Figure 13.4.

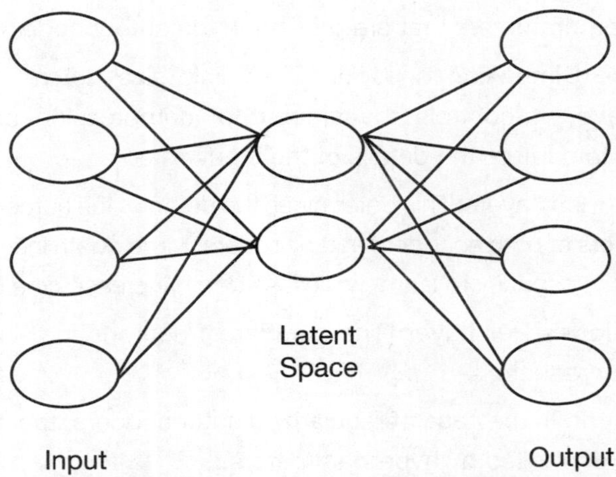

Figure 13.4 Neural Network Representation of Autoencoder

The decoder is responsible for the reconstruction of the output. It takes the output and transforms it back to the input. The decoder input is the latent space. The reconstructed data determines the activation function used. Normally, a sigmoidal function is used.

The training process of the vanilla autoencoder is given below:

1. Training involves presenting the network with unlabeled input data, passing it through the encoder to get the latent space (encoded representation), passing the encoded representation through the decoder to get the reconstructed input, and comparing the reconstructed input to the original input. The loss should be closer to 0.
2. Training aims to minimize the difference between input and reconstructed data. Training is carried out using backpropagation and gradient descent techniques. Autoencoders are trained to minimize reconstruction errors, often using a loss function such as Mean Squared Error (MSE) or Cross-entropy loss function between the input and its reconstruction.
3. During training, the weights or bias of the neural network are adjusted to minimize the loss function, and the process is typically performed using backpropagation. The hyperparameters of the autoencoder are given in Box 13.4.

Box 13.4 Hyperparameters

Some of the hyperparameters that are present in the autoencoder are:

a. **Latent Space Dimension or Code Size:** This size determines the size of the bottleneck layer. It controls the amount of compression and capacity of the autoencoder to capture the details of the input data.

b. **Number of Hidden Layers:** This determines the depth of the autoencoders. It is the total number of layers of both encoders and decoders. More depth increases the complexity of the encoder's capacity to learn, while less depth increases the processing speed.

c. **Number of Nodes Per Layer:** The number of neurons in a layer can control the dimensionality reduction.

d. **Penalty Amount:** In the case of regularized autoencoders, the amount of regulation or penalty is controlled by hyperparameters.

Example 13.1: Assume that there are 3 neurons in the input layer. Let the input be [1, 3, 4]. Let there be a single hidden layer with two neurons. Assume that all the weights are 1 and biases zero. Assume that the activation function used in $f(x) = x$. The constructed neural network is given below in Figure 13.5.

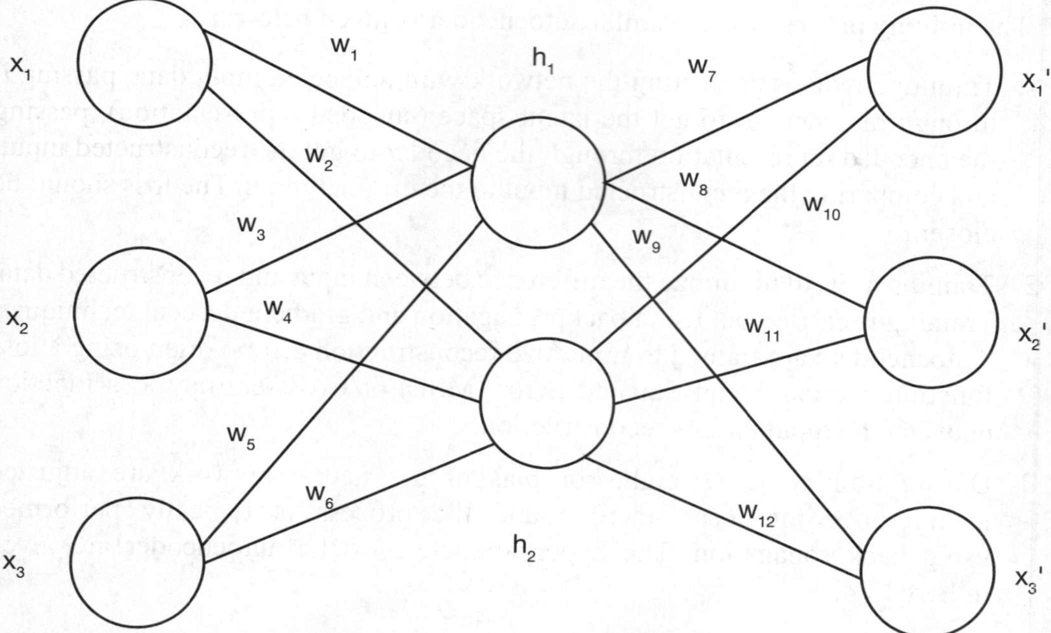

Figure 13.5 Example Problem with each link carrying a weight (x_1 to x_{12})

Solution:

The weights between the input layer and the hidden layer are 1. Similarly, all the weights between the hidden layer and the output layer are 1. All the biases are assumed to be zero. Let the activation be $f(x) = x$. The input is [1, 3, 4].

The linear activation function $f(x) = x$ is assumed for all encoders and decoders.

So, the computations for finding the hidden layer neurons are given below:

$$\begin{aligned} h_1 &= w_1x_1 + w_3x_2 + w_5x_3 \\ &= 1\times 1 + 1\times 3 + 1\times 4 = 8 \\ h_2 &= w_2x_1 + w_4x_2 + w_6x_3 \\ &= 1\times 1 + 1\times 3 + 1\times 4 = 8 \end{aligned}$$

Let the output neurons be x' for x. Then, the reconstructed neurons are given as

$$\begin{aligned} x_1' &= h_1w_7 + h_2w_{10} = 16 \\ x_2' &= h_1w_8 + h_2w_{11} = 16 \\ x_3' &= h_1w_4 + h_2w_{12} = 16 \end{aligned}$$

The reconstructed output is given as [16, 16, 16].

The reconstruction is not perfect, as the assumptions are too simplistic.

13.3.1 Undercomplete and Overcomplete Autoencoders

The autoencoder is classified as undercomplete and overcomplete, as shown in Figure 13.6.

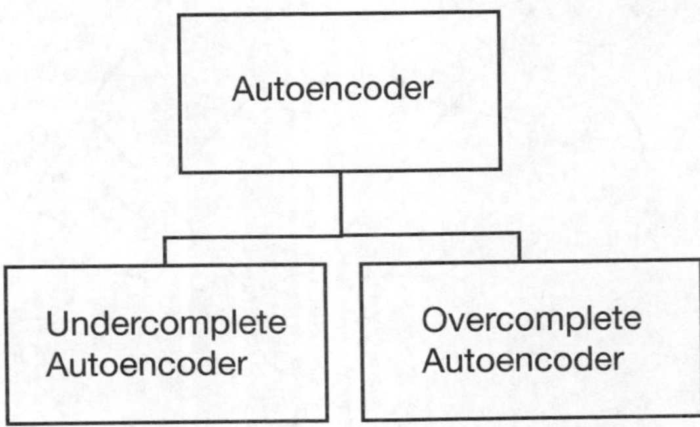

Figure 13.6 Types of Autoencoders

In an undercomplete autoencoder, the constraint is that the hidden layers have smaller dimensions than the input. An undercomplete autoencoder is shown below in Figure 13.7.

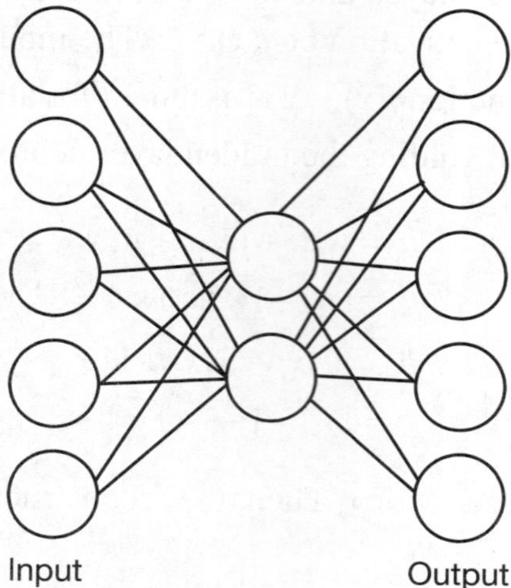

Figure 13.7 An Undercomplete Autoencoder

It can be observed from Figure 13.7 that the constraint here is that the hidden nodes have smaller dimensions than the input.

In contrast, in an overcomplete autoencoder the number of neurons in the latent space is more than the input neurons. An over-complete autoencoder is shown in Figure 13.8.

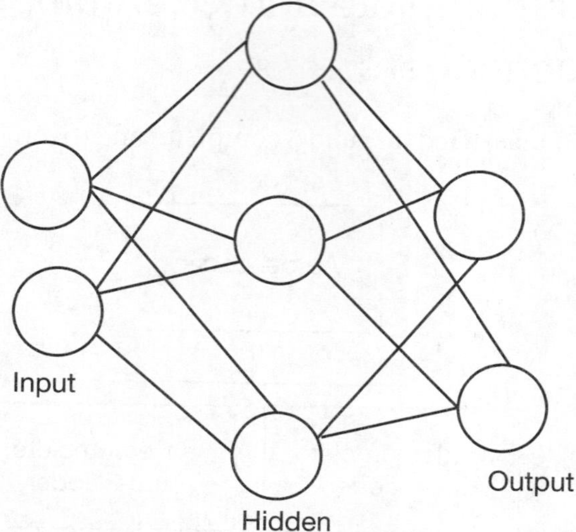

Figure 13.8 An Overcomplete Autoencoder

Here, the latent space has a larger dimension compared to the input. In other words, the code or latent dimension is more than the input dimension. The plain application of the above kind of autoencoder results in complete input learning and may result in identity function learning. But this is undesirable. Hence, regularization is normally applied so that only a few hidden layer neurons would be active. Regularization facilitates the learning of only important features of the input.

13.4 Autoencoder Variants

The autoencoder has various variants. Some of the most important variants are given below in Figure 13.9.

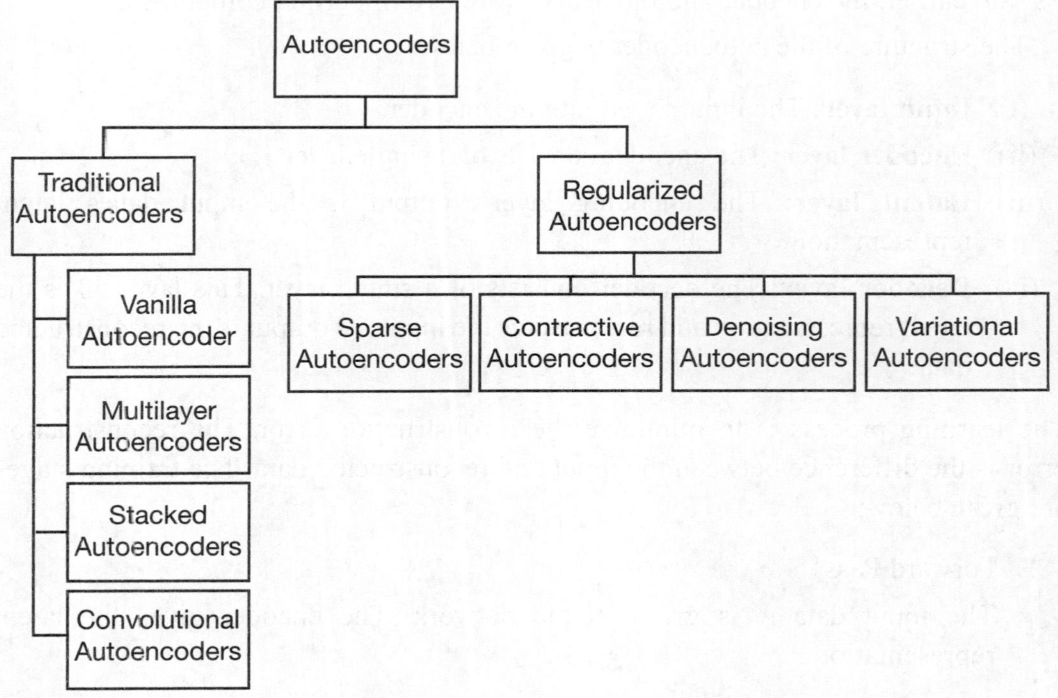

Figure 13.9 Types of Autoencoders

The subsequent sections discuss these important variants of the autoencoders.

13.4.1 Vanilla Autoencoder

A vanilla autoencoder is shown in the following Figure 13.10.

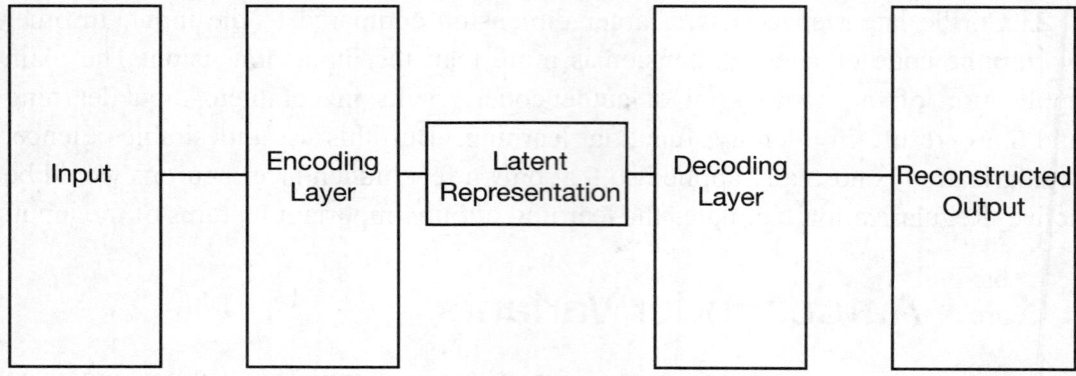

Figure 13.10 Plain Vanilla autoencoder

As said earlier, the encoder and the decoder are two important components.

The structure of the autoencoder is given below:

(i) **Input layer:** The input is fed into the encoder.

(ii) **Encoder layer:** The encoder consists of a single layer.

(iii) **Latent layer:** The encoding layer's output is the input data's latent representation.

(iv) **Decoder layer:** The decoder consists of a single layer. This layer takes the latent representation and reconstructs the input; its output is the reconstructed data.

The learning process is to minimize the reconstruction error. The reconstruction error is the difference between the input and reconstructed data. The training stages are given below:

1. Forward Pass

   The input data X is given to the network. The encoder gives the latent representation z.

$$z = \phi(w_e X + b_e)$$

   Here w_e and b_e are the weights and biases, respectively. Here, ϕ is the non-linear transformation created using the activation function.

   The decodes take z and generate the reconstructed input x'.

$$x' = \sigma(w_d z + b_d)$$

2. Compute the loss using the metric mean squared error in the case of numbers or cross-entropy in the case of labels.

$$loss = \frac{1}{n}\sum_{i=1}^{n}(x - x')^2$$

3. In the backward pass, the gradients of the loss are computed. The backpropagation algorithm is used to backpropagate the error, and the weights are updated using optimizers like ADAM.
4. Steps 1-3 are repeated for a fixed iteration (for a specific number of epochs) or until the loss becomes tolerable and acceptable.

13.4.2 Multilayer Autoencoder

It is a variant of the Vanilla autoencoder. When multiple hidden layers are added to the vanilla autoencoder, they are called multilayer autoencoder. Figure 13.11 shows the architecture of a multilayer autoencoder.

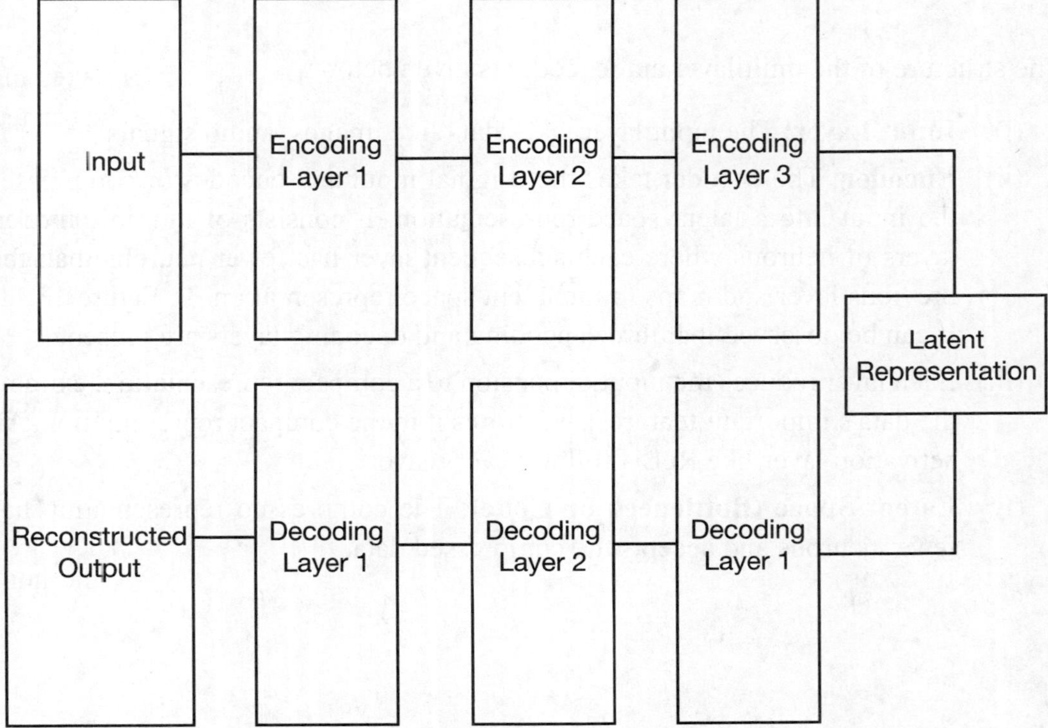

Figure 13.11 Multilayer Autoencoders

The differences between vanilla autoencoder and multilayer autoencoder are given in Table 13.1.

Table 13.1 Differences between Vanilla Autoencoder and Multilayer Autoencoder

Vanilla Autoencoder	Multilayer Autoencoder
There is a single hidden layer for encoder and decoder. It is just one-step encoding and decoding.	There will be multiple hidden layers for both encoder and decoder. It is a multiple step encoding and decoding.
Extracts only basic features from the input data.	Multilayer autoencoder can extract complex features from the input data.
It is suitable only for simple tasks as the created representation is very simple.	Suitable for very complex tasks and created latent representation is a very compact representation of very complex features of the input data.

The structure of the multilayer autoencoder is given below:

(i) **Input Layer:** The input layer takes data like images, audio signals, etc.

(ii) **Encoder:** The encoder takes the original input and encodes or compresses the input into a latent space representation. It consists of multiple hidden layers of neurons where each subsequent layer has fewer neurons than the previous layer and maps to the latent space representation. In Figure 13.11, It can be observed that three encoding and decoding layers are present.

(iii) Each layer reduces the input dimension to a compact representation, extracts the data's important features, and stores it in the compact representation. An activation layer like ReLU follows every layer.

(iv) **Latent Space (Bottleneck or Code):** The compressed representation has fewer neurons and accepts the compressed data.

(v) **Decoder:** The decoder receives the compressed representation from the latent space representation. It is the reverse process of the encoder. Like the encoder, the decoder has multiple layers, and each layer progressively increases the dimensions of the latent representation. The final decoding layer reconstructs the original input. The final dimension of the reconstructed image is the same as the encoder layer.

It is more useful in the complex task of extracting important features of the input data.

13.4.3 Stacked Autoencoder

A stacked autoencoder is composed of multiple autoencoders. In a stacked autoencoder, the autoencoders are stacked upon each other. In other words, one over the top of the other. The output of one autoencoder is used as the input for another autoencoder.

The differences between multilayer and stacked autoencoder are given in Table 13.2.

Table 13.2 Differences between Stacked Autoencoder and Multilayer Autoencoder

Stacked Autoencoder	Multilayer Autoencoder
It is a stack of trained autoencoders that are placed on one another like a stack.	There will be multiple hidden layers for both encoder and decoder.
Every layer is trained separately and is stacked.	The training is end-to-end with a backpropagation algorithm.
Every layer is trained locally and locally optimized.	They are globally trained and optimized.
Layerwise pretrained.	It is randomly initialized and trained.

The architecture of the stacked autoencoder is shown in Figure 13.12.

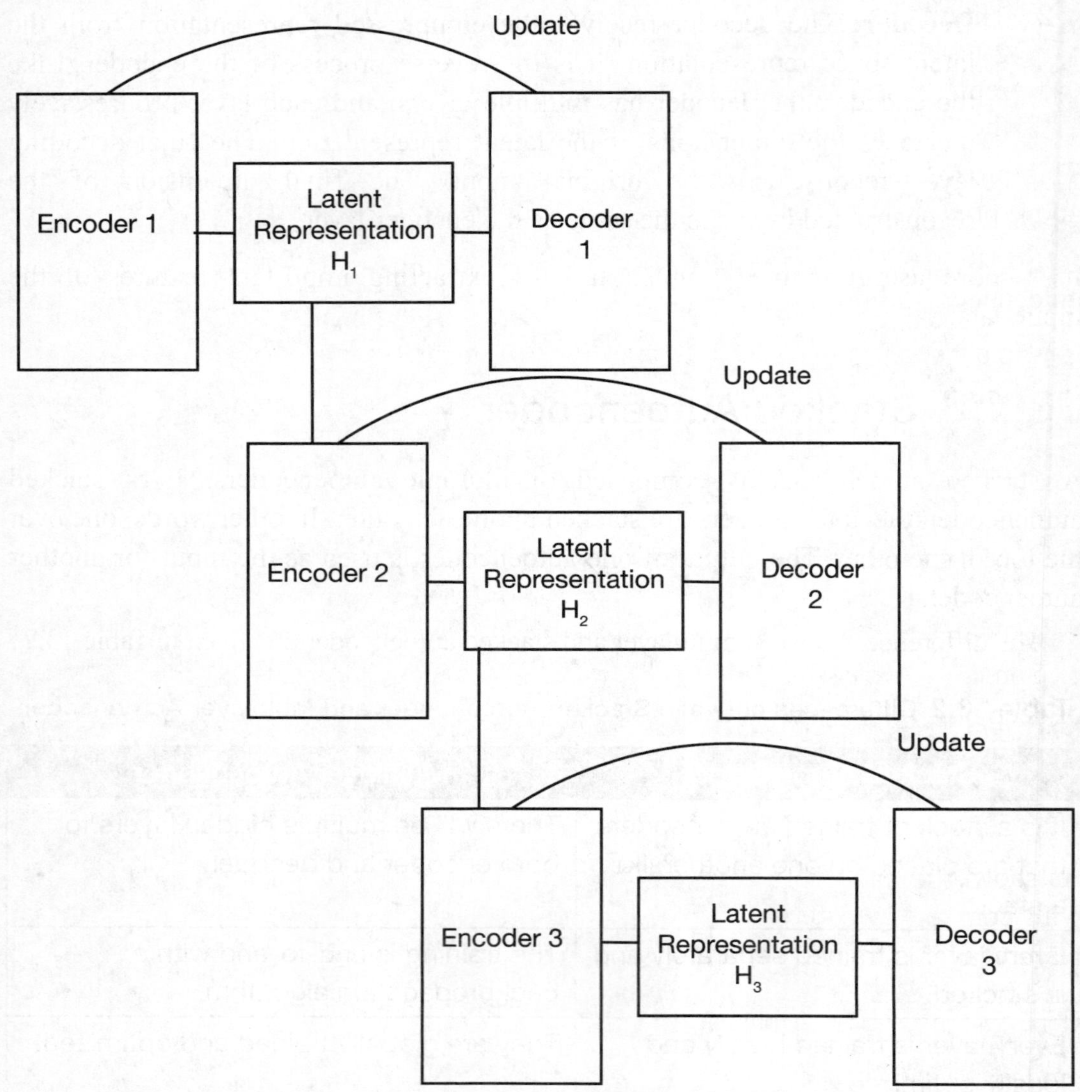

Figure 13.12 A Three-layer Stacked Encoder

Layer 1 of the stacked autoencoder is the first autoencoder.

1. The first autoencoder takes the input data X_1 and encodes it to a representation H1. The purpose of the decoder 1 is to reconstruct the data X_1. The training of this layer 1 is to minimize the loss between output and the predicted data.

2. The layer 2 of the stacked encoder is the second autoencoder. This encoder 2 takes the output H_1 of the first autoencoder as its input and encodes it into representation H_2. The decoder of this layer focuses on the reconstruction of the H_1.

This process continues for the further layers. There can be many layers, and the above process is repeated.

So, the training of the stacked encoder is different from the other types of autoencoders.

1. The first major difference is the layer-by-layer training. This training is unsupervised. This kind of training can capture all the important features of the input data, and this step can be used for initializing all the weights of the network.
2. Since all the encoders are stacked upon one another, the stacked autoencoder can be fine-tuned using supervised learning. The backpropagation algorithm is used for updating the weights. This weight updation is to ensure the overall reconstruction loss.

Some of the most important uses of the stacked autoencoder are the pretraining of deep neural networks, dimensionality reduction, and feature learning.

13.4.4 Convolutional Autoencoders

As shown in Figure 13.13, this autoencoder replaces the fully connected networks with convolution layers. The convolution layer is used to identify the important features of the image. Normally, the convolution layer is used to classify or it can be used to generate an image also.

Convolutional autoencoder combines vanilla autoencoder and convolutional models. This model combines supervised and unsupervised techniques as convolutional works based on supervised learning, and the vanilla autoencoder is based on unsupervised learning. This model is also known as a hybrid autoencoder.

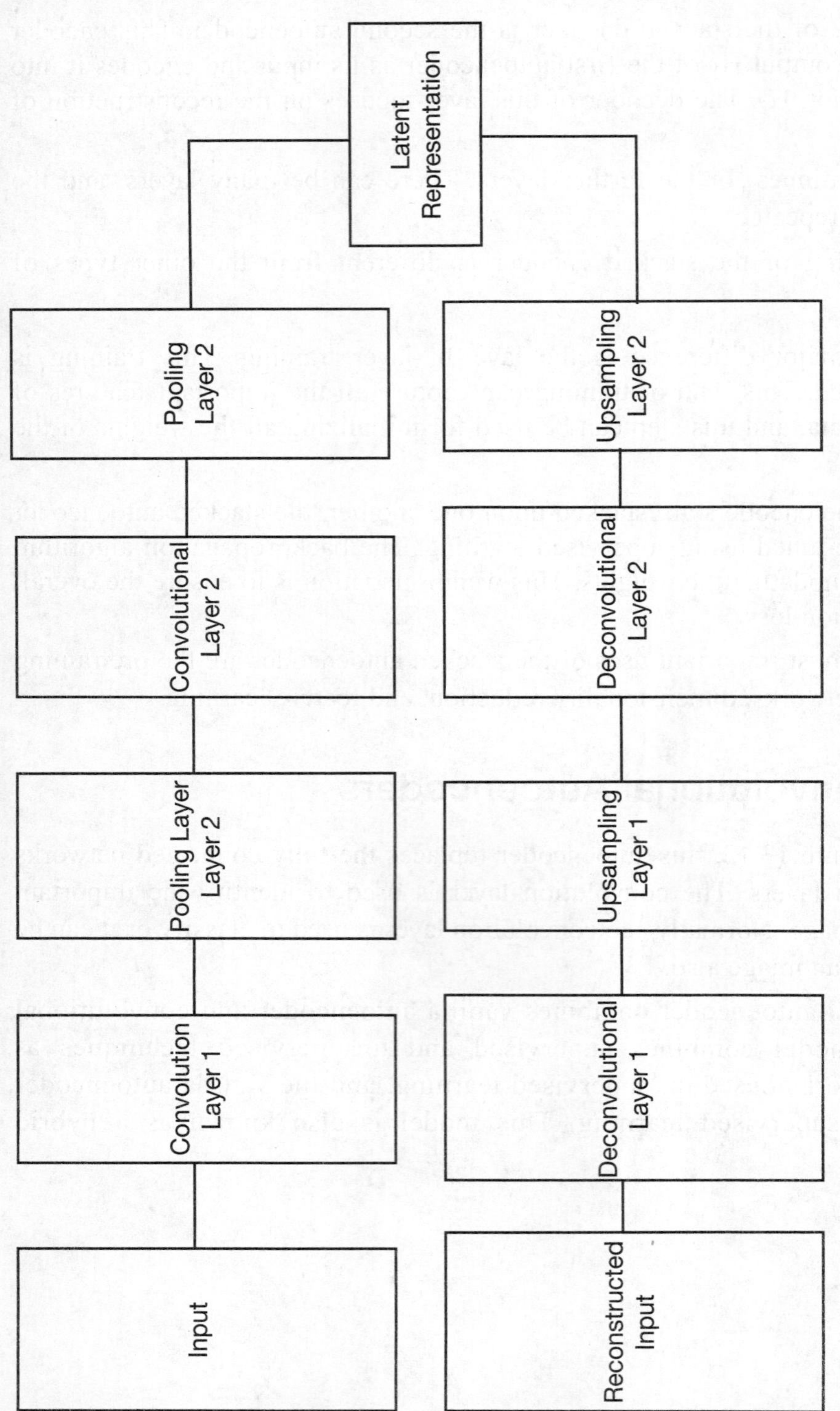

Figure 13.13 Convolutional Autoencoder

1. The encoder has convolution layers, as shown in Figure 13.13.
2. The convolutional layers extract the important features from the image. The max pooling ensures that only the important features are retained. Some of the useful hyperparameters are the number of filters, size of the filters, stride, and padding.
3. The convolutional and pooling layers create a latent representation with the important input image features.
4. The decoder has to reverse the latent representation closer to the original data. So, the decoder has components like upsampling to reverse the effect of pooling and convolution layers to reverse the effect of convolutional layers. The decoder uses upsampling to negate the effects of the encoders' convolution. It takes lower-dimensional data and upsamples to give higher-dimensional data. Similarly, the decoder uses transposed convolution as a deconvolution technique to negate the effects of the convolutional layers of the encoder. The decoder output is the reconstructed input data.

13.5 Regularized Autoencoders

One can recollect from the over-complete autoencoder discussion that the code or latent dimension is more than the input dimension. This flawless learning may result in identity function learning. But this is undesirable. Hence, regularization is normally applied so that only a few hidden layer neurons would be active. Regularization facilitates the learning of only important features of the input.

1. Regularized autoencoders are the extension of basic autoencoders. The extension is in the form of additional regularization constraints. These additional terms force the regularized autoencoders to
2. Learn useful, meaningful, and robust representations.
3. Regularization prevents overfitting and hence improves overall generalization. Some of the regularized autoencoders are shown in Figure 13.14.

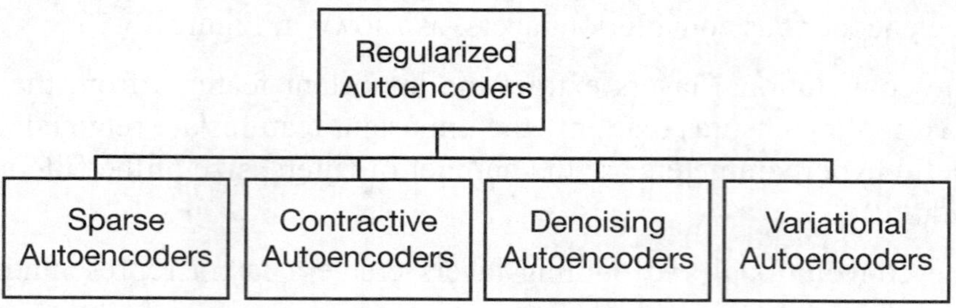

Figure 13.14 Types of Regularized Autoencoders

Let us discuss them now.

13.5.1 Sparse Autoencoder

In over-complete autoencoders, the number of nodes in the hidden layers is more than the number of nodes in the input. Rather than reducing the number of nodes in hidden layers, one can introduce a sparse constraint. A sparse autoencoder is an extension of normal autoencoders, and it imposes a sparse constraint.

The primary purpose of this autoencoder is to learn the sparse representation of the input data. By learning the sparse representation, the sparse autoencoder is designed to capture only important features of the input data. This task is accomplished by using a sparse constraint and sparse regularization.

Sparse Constraint

The sparsity constraint ensures that only a fraction of the hidden nodes (or encoded representation) are active at a time. How to inactivate the nodes? This deactivation of the hidden neurons is done by forcing their activations closer to zero. The sigmoidal function does this deactivation. The activated few neurons lead to sparse learning.

Sparse Regularization

Sparse regularization is an additional term in the loss function. The loss function between two distributions can be computed using the Kullback-Leibler divergence function. In this case, KL divergence is used to find the distance between the average activation level and the target sparsity level.

This implementation of a sparse autoencoder is done by adding the sparsity constraint as a penalty term to the loss function. This penalty is on the hidden layer neurons (Encoded representation) neurons. The loss function is shown as follows:

$$L = \|X - X'\|_2^2 + \beta \times sparse \text{ penalty}$$

The term β is the parameter that controls the importance of the penalty term.

It can be noted that the loss function has two components. The first component is the reconstruction loss. It finds the difference between the output and input data for weight updating. The second component is a penalty term for the neurons of the hidden layer, and its purpose is to encourage them to learn important features.

In sparse constraint, only a few nodes are activated, and it should be noted that only the activated neurons would learn important features. The deactivated neurons will not learn anything.

Sparse autoencoder logic is to keep the average activation of the hidden units ($\hat{\rho}$) closer to zero. The average activation of the node j is given as follows:

$$\rho_j = \frac{1}{n}\sum_{i=1}^{n}(a_j^{(h)}x^{(i)})$$

Similarly, the mean of all neurons is computed for the overall mean $\hat{\rho}$. The idea is to keep the average mean activation level $\hat{\rho}$ closer to the target level ρ. KL divergence can be used to measure the distance between two distributions characterized by ρ and $\hat{\rho}$.

The KL divergence is given as follows:

$$KL = \sum_{j=1}^{\ell(h)} \log\left(\frac{\rho}{\hat{\rho}}\right) + (1-\rho)\log\left(\frac{1-\rho}{1-\hat{\rho}}\right)$$

This KL defines the sparse constraint. So, the loss function of the sparse autoencoder is given as follows:

$$L = \|X - X'\|_2^2 + \beta \times \left(\sum_{j=1}^{\ell(h)} \log\left(\frac{\rho}{\hat{\rho}}\right) + (1-\rho)\log\left(\frac{1-\rho}{1-\hat{\rho}}\right)\right)$$

The sparse autoencoder ensures that the code will have a larger dimension but, at the same time, captures the important details.

13.5.2 Contractive Autoencoder

The focus of the contractive autoencoder is to learn the robust features of the input data. Robustness refers to the features that are less sensitive to the variations in the input data. For this, it is necessary to minimize the sensitivity of the hidden layer activations with respect to the data.

In the contractive encoder design, there is a contradiction between reconstruction error and variations error.

1. The reconstruction error minimizes the loss between the input and the reconstructed input. This loss should be minimal.
2. The contractive encoder should not be affected by the perturbations of the input. It means the input variations should not affect the output or the autoencoder should be insensitive to the input variations.

There must be a tradeoff between these two goals, and this serves as the core principle of the contractive autoencoder.

Jacobian matrix can solve this problem of variations in the input by ensuring the change in the hidden layer neurons with respect to the changes in the input data. The Frobenius norm of the Jacobian matrix can be computed and added to the loss function as a regularization penalty.

The loss function of the contractive autoencoder is now expressed as

$$L = \text{Reconstruction loss} + \lambda \times \text{Contractive penalty}$$

Here, the reconstruction loss is the difference between the reconstructed data and the input data. The term λ is the hyperparameter that controls the strength of the contractive penalty. The contractive penalty is given as

$$\text{Contractive penalty} = \sum_i \left\| \frac{\partial h_i}{\partial x} \right\|_F^2$$

Here h_i is the activation of the ith neuron. X is the input data.

The contractive penalty indicates the Frobenius norm of the Jacobian matrix of the hidden layers with respect to the input data.

The additional notes of the Jacobian matrix and Frobenius norm are given in Box 13.5.

Box 13.5 Jacobian Matrix and Frobenius Norm

Jacobian matrix is a matrix of the partial derivatives of output with respect to the input. In the context of the contractive autoencoder, the Jacobian matrix J can be given as

$$J = \frac{\partial h}{\partial x}$$

Here, x is the input vector, and h is the hidden layer activations. The hidden layer activations are nothing but the encoded representation. The purpose is to make the activations less sensitive to x. Frobenius norm is used to find the overall sensitivity of the latent representation. Frobenius norm is the measure of the size and magnitude of the matrix.

$$\|J\|_F^2 = \sum_{i,j} \left\| \frac{\partial h_i}{\partial x_j} \right\|_F^2$$

If there 3 inputs x_1, x_2, x_3 and two hidden neurons h_1, h_2, then the Jacobian matrix is given as

$$J = \begin{pmatrix} \frac{\partial h_1}{\partial x_1} & \frac{\partial h_1}{\partial x_2} & \frac{\partial h_1}{\partial x_3} \\ \frac{\partial h_2}{\partial x_1} & \frac{\partial h_2}{\partial x_2} & \frac{\partial h_2}{\partial x_3} \end{pmatrix}$$

The Frobenius norm gives a single number of a matrix that indicates the magnitude of the matrix, which is helpful in finding the overall sensitivity of the variables. For example, Frobenius norm of the matrix is given as $\begin{pmatrix} 1 & 2 \\ 2 & 1 \end{pmatrix} = \sqrt{1^2 + 2^2 + 2^2 + 1^2} = \sqrt{10} = 3.16$.

Thus, the Jacobian matrix and Frobenius norm are useful tools in measuring the sensitiveness of the features.

The contractive penalty is $\lambda \times \|J\|_F^2$. This term indicates that the autoencoder learns representations that are less sensitive to the changes in input x. The term here λ is the hyperparameter that controls the strength of the regularization.

13.5.3 Denoising Autoencoder

Denoising autoencoders are used to remove the noise in the image. Denoising autoencoders take a corrupted image as input and output a clear, denoised image. The process of denoising autoencoders is shown in Figure 13. 15.

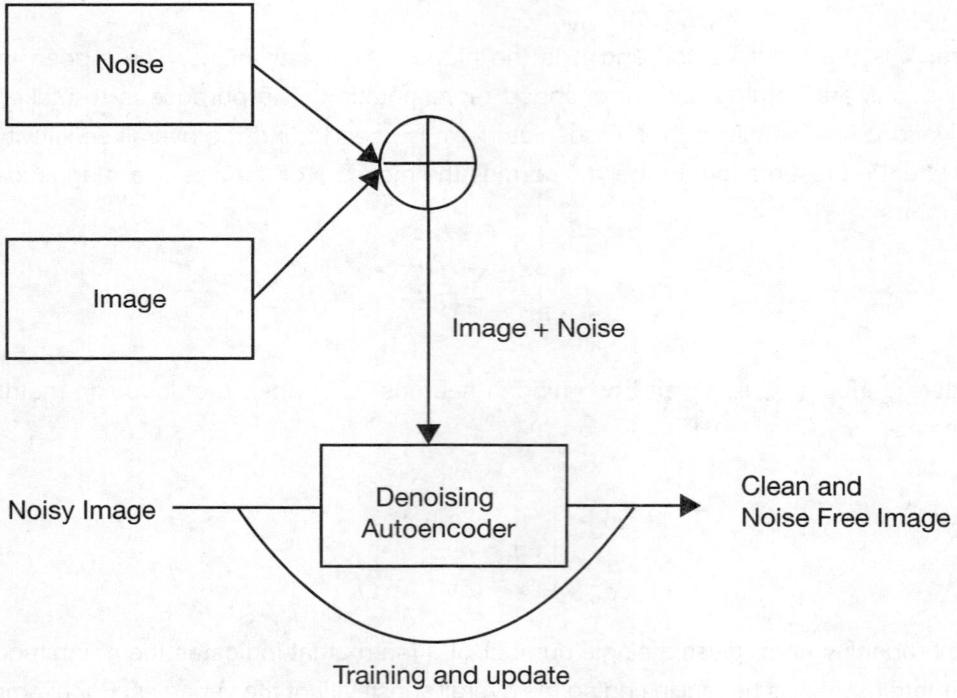

Figure 13.15 Denoising Autoencoder

Often, the ground truth images of the noisy image are not available. So, corrupting the image with a known noise is a practice and given as the autoencoder for training.

The encoder takes the noisy input and generates the output z as

$$z = f_\theta(\hat{x})$$

$$z = \sigma(\hat{x}\theta + b)$$

Here, $\hat{x}$ is the input x plus the added noise component.

It should be observed that the encoder considers the noisy information as irrelevant. Hence, the encoder can learn the compact representation that consists only of the necessary image information. So, the noise is unlearnt.

The decoder takes the information from the latent form as input and reconstructs the original image. The latent representation has no noise; hence, the decoder can reconstruct the uncorrupted image using the latent representation.

$$x' = g_{\varphi}(z)$$
$$x' = \sigma(\varphi z + b)$$

Here, x' is the reconstructed image.

13.5.4 Variational Autoencoder (VAE)

A generative model is an AI model that can generate new content with diversity (Refer Box 13.6). A variational autoencoder is like an autoencoder that learns the latent representation of the input data before decoding it back. In other words, VAE learns the distribution of the latent representation.

Box 13.6 Generative AI Model

Unlike the discriminative model, the generative model tries to learn the underlying distribution of the input data. It tries to learn the data and produces the probability density function. By sampling this distribution, one can generate a new (not obtained by manipulation or transformation of input data) with diversity. A generative model can generate text, images, video, audio, and even music.

An autoencoder is a base form of a generator. Variational autoencoder is a variant of an autoencoder and is a generative model. It can take a training set of data and can learn the probability density function. It can then generate new content.

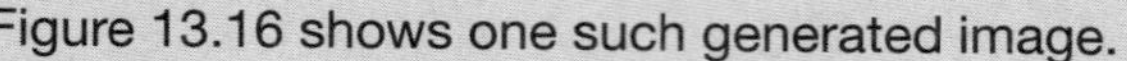

Figure 13.16 shows one such generated image.

Figure 13.16 Cinematic and Realistic Image of Cars on Road

Credits: AI Image © Pearson Education

Learning the data distribution and mapping it to known/unknown is the basis of generative modeling.

Encoder

The encoder part of VAE learns the input features in compressed form based on probability distributions. The variational autoencoder is shown in the following Figure 13.17.

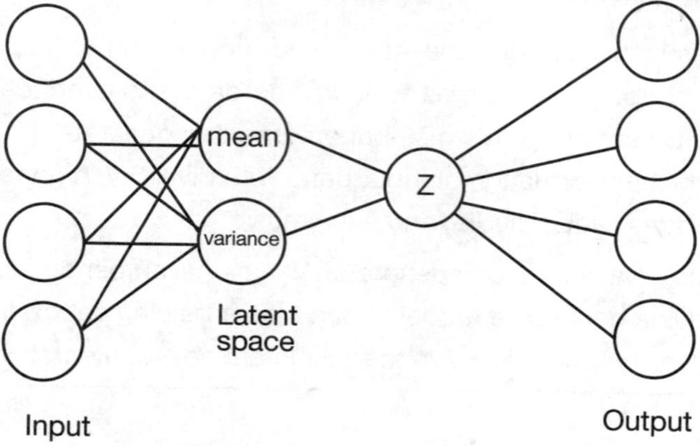

Figure 13.17 Variational Autoencoder

The generated output is assumed to be a normal distribution. Two parameters characterize the normal distribution – mean and variance. The variational autoencoder learns the mean and variance of the generated samples. The network learns the distribution with these two parameters. The advantages of learning parameters have certain advantages, like

1. Learning of the embedding space. The parameters reduce the amount of space or dimension of the data. The parameters allow the representation to be represented by simpler forms.
2. Ability to generate the latent spaces into new output.
3. This allows learning using only the input distribution and learning it back.

These help the generator to generate new samples. The decoder takes these samples and generates the new output.

The major difference between variational autoencoder and other types is that variational autoencoder learns in continuous latent space while others learn in discrete latent space. Variational autoencoders are discussed more extensively in chapter 16 of this book.

Summary

1. An autoencoder is a neural network that performs many tasks like dimension reduction and anomaly detection.
2. Autoencoder consists of key components – Encoder, coder, and Decoder.
3. Unsupervised learning takes unlabeled data as input and learns the underlying data representations.
4. The encoder decomposes the data into a lower-level representation called latent form (or code).
5. The decoder takes the latent form and aims to reconstruct the image closer to the original.
6. Latent space is low-dimensional data that has essential information about the data.
7. Some of the applications of autoencoders are dimension reduction, feature learning, compression, embedding, outlier detection, denoising, data generation, and clustering.
8. In an undercomplete autoencoder, the dimensions of the hidden layer are less than the input layer.

9. In an overcomplete autoencoder, the dimensions of the hidden layer are higher than the input layers.
10. Some of the autoencoder variants are Vanilla autoencoder, multilayer autoencoder, stacked autoencoder, and convolutional autoencoders.
11. The regularized autoencoders are sparse, contractive, denoising, and Variational.
12. The vanilla autoencoder has a single encoder and a single decoder.
13. The multilayer autoencoder has multiple layers of encoders and progressively reduces the dimensions of the input. Similarly, the decoder has multiple hidden layers.
14. The stacked autoencoder has one autoencoder placed on top of another.
15. The convolutional autoencoder replaces the fully connected networks with convolutional layers to capture the features.
16. Regularization autoencoder imposes a regularization constraint on the loss function. This regularization helps to learn important features.
17. The sparse autoencoder's purpose is to learn the sparse representation of the input data. The capturing is made possible by including the sparse constraint in the loss function.
18. The sparse regression has an additional term that is added to apply the penalty on the activations of the hidden layer neurons.
19. The purpose of the contractive autoencoder is to capture the features that are not sensitive to the small changes in the input.
20. Variational autoencoder is a special variant that can generate new content similar to the original data.

Glossary

1. Unsupervised learning – The concept of learning using unlabeled data.
2. Encoder – The encoder is a component of the autoencoder that takes an input and converts it into latent form.
3. Decoder – The decoder is a component of the autoencoder that reconstructs the original data using the latent form.
4. Latent space – The lower dimensional space is called latent space. It consists of latent variables. All similar items are stored together in latent space.

5. Latent variable – A latent variable is an unobserved data.
6. Dimensional reduction – Dimension reduction is a technique of reducing the dimensions of the data. The dimension refers to the number of features, say, a column of the input data.
7. Compression – Compression is a technique that takes data of a higher dimension and converts it into a lower dimension.
8. Undercomplete – The latent space has dimensions that are lesser than the input dimension and is referred to as undercomplete.
9. Overcomplete – The latent space has dimensions that are more than the input dimension and is referred to as undercomplete.
10. Sparse – A constraint that forces to have only a fraction of hidden neurons as active.
11. Sparse regularization – The presence of a penalty in the loss function to prevent overfitting.
12. Jacobian matrix – Jacobian matrix is a matrix of partial derivatives with respect to the input data.
13. Frobenius form – It is a measure that indicates the magnitude of the change.
14. Generative AI – A domain of deep learning models that can generate new content with diversity.

Short Questions

1. List the situations where autoencoders are preferred over PCA.
2. List out the applications of autoencoders.
3. What is the role of unsupervised learning in autoencoders?
4. What is the principal component analysis?
5. What is SVD compression?
6. Define latent space and latent variable.
7. Motivation is a latent variable in a student performance system – Justify.
8. Why is noise added to the image for denoising autoencoder?
9. What loss function is used for binary input autoencoder?
10. Which layer decides whether the autoencoder is overcomplete or undercomplete?
11. What is the purpose of regularization?
12. In what way does the stacked autoencoder vary from the multilayer autoencoder?

13. How are overfitting and underfitting scenarios avoided in autoencoders?
14. Differentiate between sparse and contractive autoencoder.
15. Define variational autoencoder.

Long Questions

1. Write the procedure for single-value decomposition.
2. With a neat diagram, explain the components of a vanilla autoencoder and how it varies from denoising autoencoder.
3. Discuss the convolutional autoencoder with a suitable example.
4. Tabulate the architectural differences of various types of autoencoder.
5. Explain in detail the sparse autoencoder.
6. Explain in detail the contractive autoencoder.

Numerical Problems

1. Assume that there are 3 neurons in the input layer of an autoencoder. Let the input be [1, 6, 8]. Let there be a single hidden layer with two neurons. Assume that all the weights are 1 and biases zero. Assume that the activation function used in $f(x) = x$. Show the output of the autoencoder.
2. Assume that there are 2 neurons in the input layer of an autoencoder. Let the input be [10, 12]. Let there be a single hidden layer with one neuron. Assume that all the weights are 2 and biases one. Assume that the activation function used is sigmoidal. Show the output of an autoencoder.

Crossword

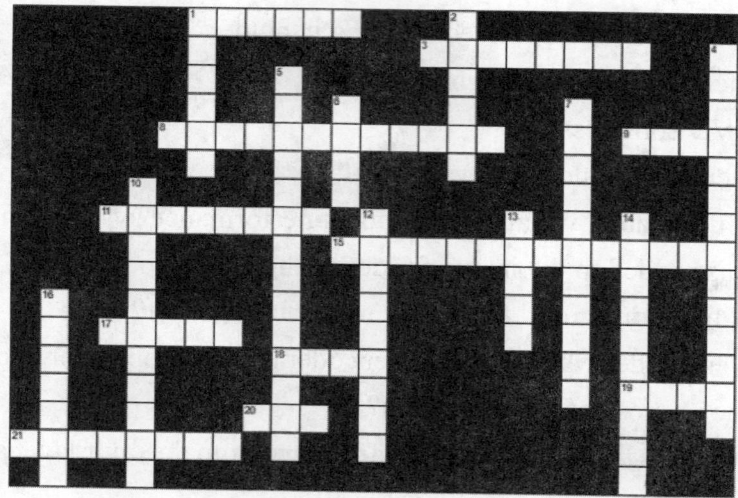

Across

1. Motivation is a __________ variable.
   (Latent/Observable)
3. The loss function between two probability distributions is measured by __________ Leibler divergence function.
8. Autoencoders use __________ learning.
9. Stacked autoencoders are composed of multiple trained autoencoders, (true/false)
11. The purpose of the encoder is to __________ the input data into latent space.
15. Code space is a __________. (parameter/hyperparameter)
17. Autoencoders cannot do embedding. (true/false)
18. An autoencoder is an ANN network that can perform dimensionality reduction, denoising, and anomaly detection, (true/false)
19. Convolutional autoencoders are used to capture the features of the input images, (true/false)
20. Latent space is a __________ level data representation.
21. Denoising means __________ the noise in the input image.

Down

1. The unobserved variable is called the __________ variable.
2. The dimensions refer to the column or __________ of features.
4. The amount of regularization is __________ (parameter/ hyperparameter).
5. Encoding is a data __________.
6. The latent space is a set of points that represents the input data, (true/ false)
7. The purpose of a sparse autoencoder is to capture the __________ features.
10. The robust features are captured by __________ autoencoder.
12. Autoencoders can generate __________ data.
13. The primary purpose of compression in the autoencoder is to compress the size. (true/false)
14. variational autoencoder is a __________ model.
16. The autoencoder removes the noise because noise is not __________ by it in training.

Jumbled Sentences

```
H Y P E R P A R A M E T E R L Q L Y F Z M B N U R
C J C B O S U Y J G N F L A T E N T D W J O F N D
A T R U E B R O G E W R C P P O U G Y V I S U S F
Z O B A Z A W F T N N A Z N Y H L F L T E H Q U W
L L D Y Y J M A O E I I N L V O D P A A B T C P X
T B E W T W L U T R L W N M J I Z T S L A P X E E
V H Y P E R P A R A M E T E R S N S Z T S I K R D
F A W X Y K U E L T R U E N B E E U S R Y E Q V N
G S S Y N T H E T I C X T O S R X O U G S K S I L
P S J M N C H R X V Y T J E P Y J T T H P F T S A
U S P Y N M H D W E Z T R M L T L L T X K G R E D
F H G N U M B E R Z B P O U H N S O W F B V V D F
O A H P O H D K F J E C F I E Q N W P S F A L A A
Q R E M O V I N G R Q H G X E K U L L B A C K S L
L E A R N E D N C J T R X B Q K O J X J J C U I S
C U J S C O N T R A C T I V E G D J T R U E H X E
B T S W A S P E C I A L I Z E D D W B P Q P C P H
```

true	representation	unsupervised	low	compress
latent	true	latent	number	false
false	synthetic	hyperparameter	hyperparameter	true
true	specialized	contractive	kullback	removing
learned	generative			

Natural Language Processing for Deep Learning

> The limits of my language mean the limits of my world. – **Ludwig Wittgenstein**

Credits: © Ludwig Wittgenstein

Natural Language Processing (NLP) is a promising field. Natural language processing, as a domain of Artificial Intelligence, provides the necessary theory, algorithms, models, and methodologies that make the interaction between humans and computer systems possible. Most of the NLP tasks involve the processing of text. Text is unstructured data that lacks a predefined structure or organization. Deep learning provides many algorithms that help to process text.

The learning objectives of this chapter are:

- Understand the basics of natural language processing.
- Need for text encoding algorithms.
- Know about word embeddings.
- Know about the vectors in processing embeddings.
- Know about the pretrained models for creating embeddings.
- Know the outline of the sentiment analysis.
- Know about the seq2seq models.

14.1 Motivation for Natural Language Processing

Humans communicate in natural languages like English, Hindi, or Tamil. A language is necessary to communicate with the machines as well. The primary question in natural language processing is - Is it possible to communicate with computers in a natural language?

NLP is a domain of Artificial Intelligence (AI) that provides the necessary theory, algorithms, models, and methodologies that make the communication between machines and humans feasible. In practice, most of the NLP projects focus on processing textual information to develop applications that are useful for humans.

What is text? Text is unstructured data that is used to convey information. Unstructured means it lacks a predefined format or organization. It is a sequence of characters used for communication. Text is everywhere! (Refer to Box 14.1). Text is the integral component of NLP, and most NLP applications use text for input and output to assist other applications.

Box 14.1 Textual Data

The current book that is read by you now is an example of how texts can be helpful in communication. Examples of text include emails, blogs, microblogs, Twitter tweets, Facebook Posts, LinkedIn Profiles, YouTube comments, and advertisements are all examples of text data. There is also much textual information offline, such as books, documents, and technical reports.

Technically, the text is unstructured data as it does not have any predefined format or organization, unlike tables or Excel sheets. Nevertheless, the text is essential to communication as humans reads around 200 million words in his life!

The role of deep learning comes into the picture as many deep learning algorithms are used to process text.

Some of the NLP applications are given in Box 14.2.

Box 14.2 NLP Applications

Some of the deep learning applications listed here show the impact of NLP in our day-to-day lives.

- Text Classification – The classification of news as genuine or fake news.
- Topic Modelling (or Topic Identification) – Assigning a topic to documents. Topic modelling also implies grouping documents under a heading and is an example of unsupervised learning.
- Machine Translation – Translation of documents from one language to another language.

- Sentiment Analysis – This is about the classification of text based on positive and negative sentiments.
- Text to Speech – The focus is on converting text to speech.
- Speech-to-text – The focus is on the speech-to-text conversation.
- Question/Answering – Interpret the questions and answer the query.
- Entity Recognition – Identification of entities like pin code in postal address. Country and its capital name in travel catalogues.
- Text Summarization – The summary of large documents into documents of smaller documents with a lesser number of words.
- Natural Language Generation – Generation of text documents or text documents with multimedia components like images or any other data type.
- Chatbots – The user can interact with the machine using dialogues for a restricted domain.

Textual understanding by humans is a complicated process. To be done by computers is still more complex, and NLP provides many methods to perform complex tasks on linguistic objects. Some of them are speech, words, phrases, and meaning—some of the levels of NLP where the processing is required for text understanding are given in Box 14.3.

Box 14.3 NLP Levels

Some essential NLP levels where the processing is required are given below:

1. Phonetics – Phonetics is the identification of sounds and phonemes to form a word. One interprets the speaker's acoustic signal and the basic units called phonemes and converts them to word sequences. This level deals with language models to recognize the phonemes and words to form a word.
2. Morphology – Morphology is about forming a word from the smallest units called morphemes. For example, students mean – student + s, where a student is a stem and "s" indicates that the word is plural.
3. Lexicon – The validation of a word, correct or otherwise, is called lexicon. The lexicon is about the functioning of the word.

4. Syntax – Syntax explains how the words are joined to form a sentence. Syntax deals with rules of the formation of a sentence, which are referred to as the language's grammar. The syntax varies as per the language. Normally, a parser is used to extract the underlying grammar structures of a sentence.
5. Semantics – Semantics refers to the literal meaning of the word. Semantics can be at the word level or the sentence level. A sentence constructed using a valid grammar rule may be meaningless. The two sentences, X bites Y and Y bites X, give different meanings. Similarly, different ordering or words can give a different meaning. Semantics deals with context also.

   John goes to the Bank to deposit money.

   Daniel's Blood Bank is nearby.

   Here, the word "Bank" has different meanings as the context differs.
6. Linguistics – Linguistics is used to understand the structure and meaning.
7. Reasoning – Reasoning refers to the requirement of understanding the reader's communication based on words and intent, which is called reasoning. The association of a language with actions is called pragmatics. This reasoning approach is called pragmatic analysis.

Let us discuss the ways of processing textual information now.

14.1.1 Basics of Text Analytics

Text mining or text analytics are interchangeable words. Text analytics is a domain of AI that incorporates the concepts of NLP, Information retrieval (IR), Machine learning, and deep learning concepts to process huge amounts of textual information to create models of NLP applications (refer to Box 14.2).

The steps of text analytics are shown in Figure 14.1.

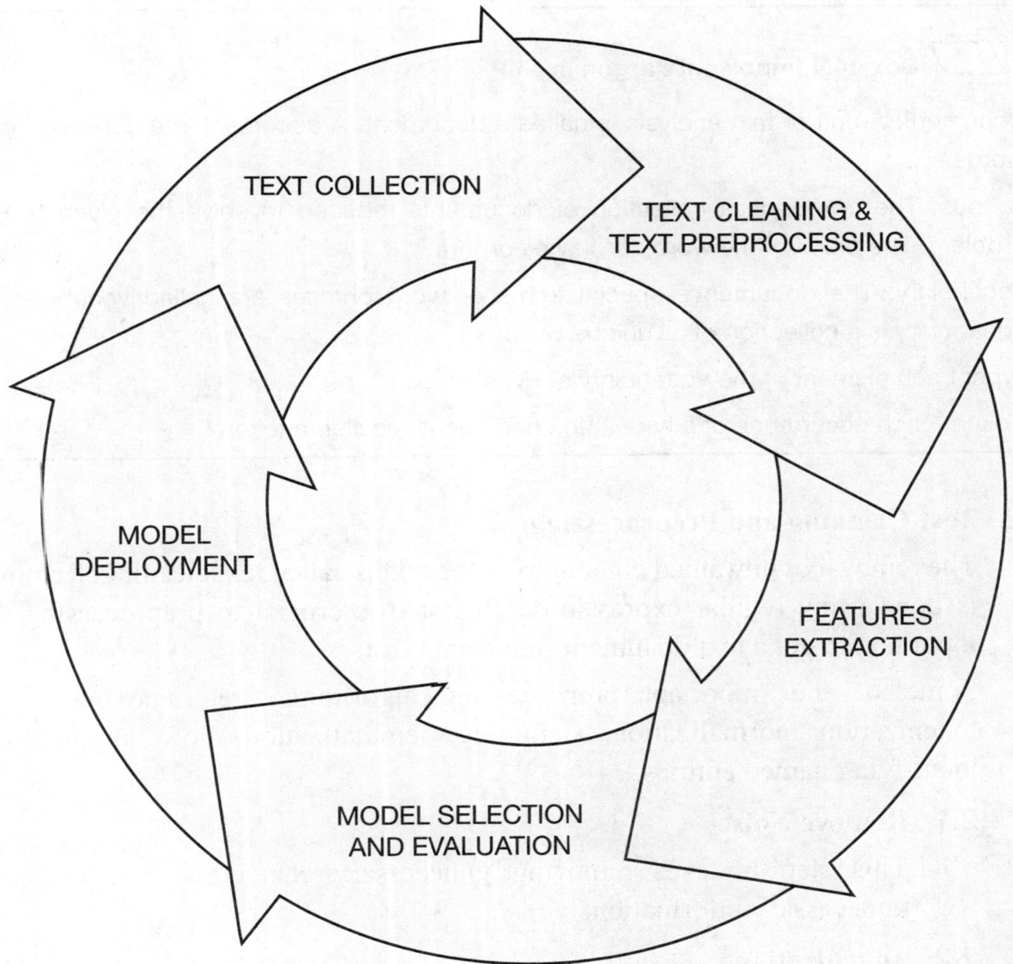

Figure 14.1 The Steps of Text Analytics

1. **Text Collection**

   Text analytics requires a huge collection of data. The textual data may be related to websites, documents, emails, and blogs. The text collection step involves importing data as flat files or databases. Some of the important jargon related to text collection, like documents, vocabulary, and corpus, are given in Box 14.4.

Box 14.4 Important Jargon in NLP

Document: A unit of text analysis is called a document. A document is a collection of words.

Corpus: The corpus is a collection of documents required to solve the given NLP problem. The plural of the word corpus is corpora.

Vocabulary: The document's special terms or word phrases are called vocabulary. Vocabulary is a collection of all unique words.

Type: Each element of the Vocabulary set V is called a type.

Token: Each occurrence of a type in the document is called a token.

2. Text Cleaning and Preprocessing

The removal of unwanted content from the text is called text cleaning. Removal is done using regular expressions. This step is crucial to preprocessing the input text to get a text document free from errors.

Some of the important preprocessing algorithms are removing noise, tokenization, normalization, stemming, lemmatization, PoS tagging, and identifying named entities.

2.1 Remove Noise

This step involves removing unnecessary characters, symbols, and unnecessary information.

2.2 Tokenization

This step splits the text strings into a list of individual words called tokens. In writing, often, the words are delimited by white spaces. Sometimes, this may not be so, as a comment can end with an exclamation mark such as - Happy!! So, caution needs to be exercised to extract the tokens. Some of the important jargon related to tokenization, like vocabulary, types, and tokens, is given in Box 14.4.

The process of extraction of a word is called tokenization. The equivalent task is splitting a document into a set of sentences.

Example 14.1: Consider a document that has one sentence:

"This sentence is a good sentence"

Identify the types and tokens of this document.

Solution:

The type in the sentence is {This, sentence, is, a, good}. Types include punctuation marks also. There is no redundancy as the word "sentence" is ignored as it is already encountered.

The token in the sentence is {This, sentence, is, a, good, sentence}. There can be a duplicate in a token list.

2.3 Normalization

Normalization is a domain-specific preprocessing step that refers to transforming a text to a uniform or standard consistent format suitable for processing. Some of the normalization techniques are listed below:

(i) Converting all the text to upper case/lower case

(ii) Removing the punctuation marks

(iii) Removing the numbers

2.4 Stemming and Lemmatization

Stemming and lemmatization are morphological analysis tools (refer to Box 14.3). By this, a word can be split into stem and prefixes/suffixes.

Stemming means reducing the word to its original roots. For example, "compute" is the base form for the word "computer." The word running can be split as run + ing, where the word "run" is the stem. Stemming may cause interpretation problems as it tries to remove everything except the base form. Sometimes, the base form word may be meaningless. In that, the Lemmatization technique is applicable.

Lemmatisation is a morphological process of NLP that returns a word to its canonical form. A canonical form is a standard or normalized form. The document may have many words, such as want, wants, wanting, and wanted. The base form of all these words is "want." In that case, lemmatization is helpful as this step reduces the word to its stem word, which is a standard dictionary word.

2.5 Stop Word Removal

Some words like a, is, am, he, she, or they are not required in NLP applications. For example, there is no difference between "a park" and "the park" from a computing perspective. So, the idea is to identify a set of words and remove a group of words that are not useful is called stop word removal.

Any ignorable word is called a stop word. Generally, the determiners like "a," "the," and "an" are stop words, and hence the stop words can be removed. Alternatively, one can substitute a special symbol for these stop words in NLP applications.

2.6 Parts of Speech (PoS) Tagging

Many persons, actions, and qualifiers characterize the English language. PoS identifies verbs, nouns, and pronouns in sentences and assigns a tag using tagging. PoS is the process of identifying parts of speech called PoS tagging or parsing. PoS is a lexicon (Refer Box 14.3) analysis that aims to capture the relationships of words and the role of the word as it can be a noun or verb, depending on the context.

Some of the PoS tags are N (Noun), V (verb), DET (Determiners), ART (Articles), and P (Preposition). For example, in the sentence "A dog bites a person," dog and person are nouns, bites are the verb, and "a" is a determiner.

Certain nouns and verbs that contribute more are called content words or open words. Words that contribute less, like propositions, are called closed words or function words.

2.7 Named Entities

Named Entities Recognition (NER) is the task of seeking the information and arranging it in a predefined domain-specific format. For example, the sentence

"Selvam (200011375) is writing a physics test" can be converted to a predefined format as

Name: Selvam

Register no: 200011375

Test: Physics

It can be observed that the format is domain-specific. NER is useful for locating postal addresses.

3. Features Extraction

The text encoding algorithms are applied to the text, and all relevant features are extracted.

4. **Models Selection and Evaluation**

   NLP tasks like regression or classification can be done using trained data. In evaluation, the output of the model is interpreted using statistical tests. Also, this step is crucial to converting the result to text if necessary.

5. **Deployment**

   In this stage, the application is deployed and tuned.

   The above is an iterative process and is repeated until the model output is as expected.

14.2 Text Encoding

There is a need to convert text into numbers before it can be processed (How can one do apple + orange?)

As said earlier, text encoding algorithms convert the text into numbers or in a form suitable for performing operations. In this context, vectors become more relevant. (Refer to Box 14.5)

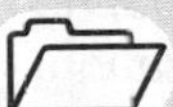

Box 14.5 Vectors and Vector Space Models (VSM)

Text should be converted to a numerical representation to manage and process it. This conversion uses Vector Space Models (VSM) by text encoding algorithms. Vector space models permit the representation of document features in higher-dimensional form as a vector. The advantage of using vectors is that vectors can be processed using traditional vector algebra.

A vector is a list of numbers. An example of a vector is given as follows:

$$v = (a_1, a_2, a_3, a_4)$$

Here are the scalars. This vector can also be represented as a column vector.

$$v = \begin{pmatrix} a_1 \\ a_2 \\ a_3 \\ a_4 \end{pmatrix}$$

Any data can be represented as a point in n-dimensional space, where 'n' is the number of dimensions. Finally, the text encoding algorithms convert a text string into a vector. A collection of N-vectors is called a matrix. This matrix will be in the form given below:

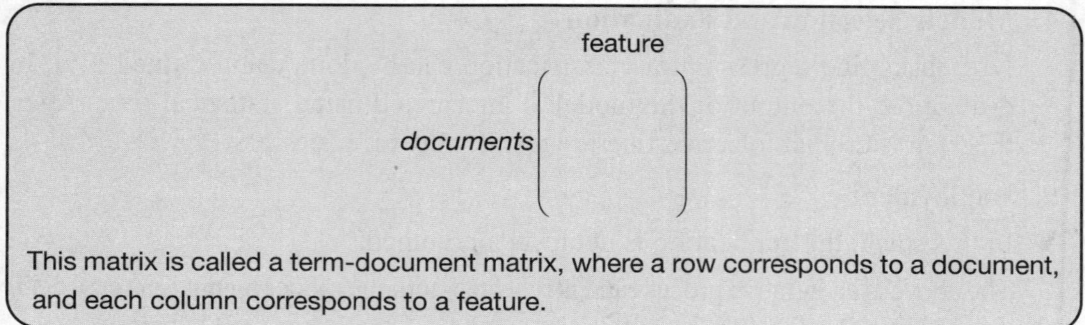

This matrix is called a term-document matrix, where a row corresponds to a document, and each column corresponds to a feature.

The types of text representation models are given in Figure 14.2.

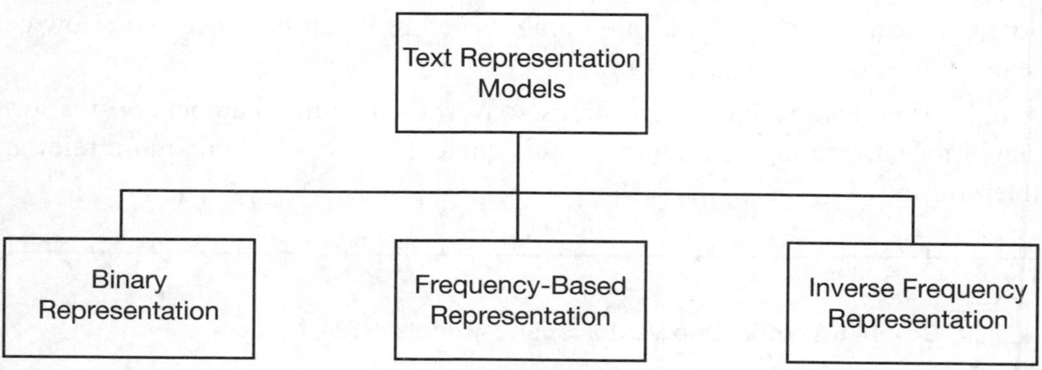

Figure 14.2 Types of Text Representation Models

In the binary-based representation, the document is encoded as a vector of Boolean elements that indicates the presence and absence of the vocabulary word in the document. One-hot encoding is a classical approach to producing this textual model. In frequency-based representation, the vector element is based on the frequency of the word in the text. Algorithms like Bag of Words are useful to produce frequency-based textual models. The inverse frequency-based approach considers the ratio of unique words in a single document and the individual words in the entire corpus. TF-IDF is a classic algorithm that is used to create this model.

14.2.1 One Hot Encoding

One-hot encoding is one of the simplest algorithms for producing the binary representation of text. This one-hot encoding method is implemented through these steps:

1. Initially, vocabulary or a dictionary is constructed with all unique words of the corpus. The document collection is called corpus.
2. Assign a unique index number to each unique word. Any unique index number can be assigned without any restrictions. The index number may start with 0.
3. Construct a vector of size $|V|$ with zero elements. Here, V is the size of the vocabulary. The length of the binary vector is equal to the vocabulary size. Then, the document's words are encoded as a binary vector as 1(hot) and 0(Cold) based on the presence or absence of the word of vocabulary in the specific documents.

   It must be noted that the assignment of 0 or 1 is unique for every word. In that sense, one-shot encoding distinguishes the phrases "the" and "The" as the assignment is case-sensitive. The following numerical illustrate this concept.

Example 14.2: Consider the sentence "Deep learning is a subject". Apply one-hot encoding and show the result.

Solution:

Document 1: Deep learning is a subject

Document 2: Every subject is important

A vocabulary of the above documents is constructed as part of the first step. The vocabulary is given as {Deep, learning, is, a, subject, every, important}. It can be observed that the words "is" and "subject" are removed in the second document as it is already present in the vocabulary. The assignment for the document's words is given below in Table 14.1.

Table 14.1 Assignment for One-hot Encoding

	Deep	Learning	is	a	subject	Every	important
Index	0	1	2	3	4	5	6
Document 1: Deep learning is a subject	1	1	1	1	1	0	0
Document 2: Every subject is important	0	0	1	0	1	1	1

It can be observed that the resultant is a term-document matrix given as

$$\begin{pmatrix} 1 & 1 & 1 & 1 & 1 & 0 & 0 \\ 0 & 0 & 1 & 0 & 1 & 1 & 1 \end{pmatrix}$$

In this matrix, a row represents a document, and every column represents the unique words (index numbers).

Example 14.3: Consider the following three hypothetical documents –

Document 1 – Ram likes oranges.

Document 2 – Geeta likes apples.

Document 3 – Peter likes both.

Perform one-hot document encoding.

Solution:

First, the dictionary is constructed with unique words. The dictionary is the corpus. The constructed dictionary would be like

{both, apples, oranges, likes, Geeta, Ram, Peter}

It can be observed that there are seven unique words in the dictionary. Therefore, the size of the vector would be 7. The vectors of the sentences can be constructed by comparing the sentence with the corpus. The word in the document would be encoded as 1 or 0 based on the presence or absence of words. For example, one-hot encoding of the above documents is shown in Table 14.2.

Table 14.2 Assignment for One-hot Encoding

	Both	Apples	Oranges	Likes	Geeta	Ram	Peter
Index Number	0	1	2	3	4	5	6
Ram likes Oranges	0	0	1	1	0	1	0
Geeta likes Apples	0	1	0	1	1	0	0
Peter likes Both	1	0	0	1	0	0	1

It can be seen wherever the words are present in the document; its value is 1. Otherwise, the value is zero. This assignment results in a term-document matrix as given below:

$$\begin{pmatrix} 0 & 0 & 1 & 1 & 0 & 1 & 0 \\ 0 & 1 & 0 & 1 & 1 & 0 & 0 \\ 1 & 0 & 0 & 1 & 0 & 0 & 1 \end{pmatrix}$$

14.2.2 Bag of Words (BoW)

The binary representation approach would work well if the number of unique words is less in the dictionary. However, the vector becomes sparse when the number of unique words becomes more extensive. A related approach is called frequency-based vectorization, where the frequency of the word can be noted instead of just presence and absence. Bag of Words (BoW) is a frequency-based text encoding technique.

BoW is one of the familiar and oldest approaches. The frequency or counting-based approach focuses on giving importance to each word. The importance is given by counting the number of words in the document. In BoW, the order is irrelevant, and only the occurrence matters. The output of the text encoding is the representation of a document as a vector. One element of the vector is the unordered elements, and another is its frequency.

The procedure is as follows:

(i) Construct a vocabulary. A vocabulary is the collection of all unique words in a document. It is also known as corpus.

(ii) The vector is constructed where each element of the document is the element that is present in the vocabulary, and another element of the vector is the frequency of the elements.

(iii) Finally, collect all the vectors for all the documents in the corpus as a document-term matrix. In this matrix, each row is called a document, and each column represents a word in the vocabulary.

BoW gives the output in sparse form as all the words in the document will not be present in the vocabulary. While BoW has many advantages such as simplicity and oldest technique for representing the documents, there are some disadvantages that are listed below:

(i) It does not pay any attention to word order.

(ii) It ignores all grammatical rules.

(iii) It ignores all structural information.

Example 14.4: Show the representation for the following sentence

"This sentence is a better sentence."

Solution:

The count vector is

Sentence: 2, This: 1, is: 1, a: 1, better: 1

The result is shown in Table 14.3.

Table 14.3 Document-Term Matrix

	This	sentence	Is	a	Better
This sentence is a better sentence	1	2	1	1	1

This assignment results in a term-document matrix as

$$(1 \;\; 2 \;\; 1 \;\; 1 \;\; 1)$$

Here, a row is a document, and a column is a unique word in the vocabulary (index numbers).

14.2.3 N-gram Approach

N-gram is a popular approach. It is helpful for word embeddings and is used in many "state of the art" word embedding algorithms such as sentiment analysis and language modelling. Mainly, this approach is useful for capturing semantic and contextual relationships.

The main difference in this approach is how the dictionary or vocabulary is constructed. It is constructed as unique N-grams, where N can be any number. If the value of N is 1, then it is called unigram (or 1-gram). If N = 2, it is a bigram; if N = 3, it is called a trigram, and so on.

- Unigram – Individual words are called unigrams.
- Bigram – A bigram is a sequence of exactly two words with the condition that they are adjacent to each other in the dataset. (In other words, they must be contiguous). What is the advantage? The advantage is that the bigram captures the relationships between two adjacent words.
- Trigram – A trigram is a sequence of exactly three words with the condition that they are adjacent to each other in the dataset.
- N-gram – A N-gram represents N-contiguous items.

The following numerical example illustrates this concept of N-grams.

Example 14.5: Consider the sentence

I like to eat Orange.

Construct 2-gram, 3-gram.

Solution:

The 2-gram would be like 2-contiguous words.

1. I like
2. like to
3. to eat
4. eat Orange.

And the 3-gram would be like 3-contiguous words.

1. I like to
2. like to eat
3. to eat Orange.

What is the advantage of N-grams? The advantage is that it helps determine the context word from a sequence of words. For example, consider the following sentence:

Ram sits on the floor.

If the word sits is missing, like Ram ________ on the floor. Then, the missing word can be predicted based on the learning from the corpus. The prediction is based on the context words on the left and right. Thus, instead of creating a dictionary of unique words, a glossary of N-grams is made in this approach. This N can be any integer.

Example 14.6: Consider the corpus of three sentences

He came

He saw

He won

Then, for the sentence, He ________, what would be the second word of this incomplete sentence?

Solution:

Take the probability of the bigram as follows. The probability of the missing word can be calculated by finding the occurrence of the word "He" in the corpus as 3. "He came" has a frequency of 1. Therefore, the probability is 1/3. This probability implies that the missing word would come with a probability of 1/3. Based on this, the probability of the missing word being "came" is 1/3.

14.2.4 TF-IDF Approach

Frequency-based algorithms give importance based on frequency. Is it possible to give more priority to certain words than some other words? This concept leads to the concept of weights. TF-IDF is an approach that aims to find "interesting" words by giving a larger weight. So, the weights are not based on just counting but use a strategy to indicate the importance of the words.

Term frequency (TF) – Term frequency is the frequency of the term in a document. It can be formally defined as the number of times the word appears in the document.

$$w(i,j) = TF(i,j)$$

$TF(i, j)$ is the frequency or the number of times the term i appears in document j. If *TF* is high, the high-frequency word may be a document topic. If *TF* is low, then the word may be rare.

But, TF does not reflect the word's relevance in the corpus. The idea is to impose a penalty whose value is greater if the word is present more in the corpus. In this approach, the natural frequency (Term frequency) weights are adjusted by IDF. The implications are that the moderately frequent words in a document but only a few in other corpus documents will get the highest score. The word is frequent in the document, and the corpus will have a low score. All the stop words have a low score if this algorithm is used.

Inverse Document Frequency – IDF computes the importance of the term across the corpus. IDF computes the weights given below:

$$IDF(i) = \log\left(\frac{N}{DF(i)+1}\right)$$

Here, N is the number of documents in the corpus, and $DF(i)$ is the document frequency that indicates the number of documents where the term i is present. Logarithm reduces IDF value as millions of documents are usually present in the corpus. Sometimes, there is a possibility of division by zero as the term of a document may not be present in the other corpus documents. So, one is added to avoid division by zero. This approach is called the Laplacian smoothing approach.

TF-IDF – Finally, the weights of the terms using *IF-IDF* are computed as the product of *IF* and *IDF*.

$$w(i,j) = TF(i,j) \times IDF(i,j)$$

However, it must be noted that there are many variations in the calculations of TF-IDF. One more way of computing is by using this formula for normalized values.

$$\text{smooth TF} = \log(\text{TF(word)} + 1)$$

$$\text{Smooth IDF} = \log\left(\frac{N}{DF(\text{word}) + 1} + 1\right)$$

Here, DF is the document frequency. The following numerical example illustrates these concepts.

Example 14.7: Consider the following hypothetical documents.

Doc1 – Deep Learning is a core subject.

Doc2 – English is a preferred subject.

Apply the TF-IDF approach and find TF and IDF.

Solution:

One can calculate the frequency of the word "is" in

$$TF(is, document\ 1) = \frac{\text{Number of times the word "is" is present in document 1}}{\text{Number of terms in the document}} = \frac{1}{6}$$

It can be observed that there are six terms, and the word "is" is present once. Similarly, one can find TF in the second document as

$$TF(is, document\ 2) = \frac{\text{Number of times the word "is" is present in document 2}}{\text{Number of terms in the document}} = \frac{1}{5}$$

IDF is an abbreviation for Inverse Document Frequency. Let there be *N* documents (Here, in this problem, $N = 2$), and k is the number of documents that contain the given word called document frequency (DF (word)). The inverse document frequency can be computed as the log of the Total number of documents (*N*) divided by the document frequency of the word.

$$IDF(is) = \log\left(\frac{\text{Total number of documents}}{\text{Document frequency("is")+1}}\right) = \log\left(\frac{2}{3}\right) = -0.17$$

It can be observed that the word "is" is present twice in the corpus of two documents, and its frequency is 2. Hence, it is log 2/3 that implies IDF is less than zero. What is the inference? If the IDF value is high, then the word is irrelevant. If the IDF value is small, the word's relevance is high.

TF-IDF is the product of TF and IDF. It is a measure of the relevance of the word. TF-IDF is the product of TF and IDF. It is given as

$$TF - IDF(is) = TF(is, document\ 1) \times IDF(is) = \frac{1}{6} \times -0.17 = -0.028$$

for document 1.

$$TF - IDF(is) = TF(is, document\ 2) \times IDF(is) = \frac{1}{5} \times -0.17 = -0.034$$

for document 2.

14.3 Word Embedding (or Text Vectorization)

Word embedding is the distribution of words in a continuous vector space. Word embeddings imply the mapping of words and phrases to a vector of real numbers in a continuous vector space. These dense vectors are called context vectors. Unlike the vectors of text encoding that have no relevance to the real world, the word embedding vectors capture semantic relationships between words. These vectors represent the word as well as their properties as of the real world.

The details of the differences between text encoding and word embedding are given in Box 14.6.

Box 14.6 Difference between Text Encoding and Word Embeddings

There are a lot of differences between text encoding and word embeddings (Or Text Vectorization). Text encoding represents a set of discrete text features that can be computed. On the other hand, word embeddings (text vectorization) use a neural network to convert text with context to a vector or real numbers that capture the context and semantic relationships. The differences between text encoding and text vectorization are given below in Table 14.4.

Table 14.4 Differences between Text Encoding and Word Embeddings

No.	Text Encoding	Word Embeddings
1.	Text encoding converts a sequence of characters to a number or a suitable representation for processing.	Word embeddings capture the semantic relationships among the words.

No.	Text Encoding	Word Embeddings
2.	There is no role for context in text encoding.	Context plays a vital role in word embeddings. Embeddings capture the context and semantic relationships.
3.	Text encoding does not track any grammatical aspects of the text.	Grammatical and sentence structures are taken care of by the word embeddings.
4.	One can interpret the text encoding algorithms.	It is not possible to interpret the word embeddings.
5.	The output of the text encoding algorithms is a vector that can be sparse or dense.	Word embeddings are dense vector representations.
6.	Text encoding results are vectors that represent higher dimensions.	Word embeddings are dense vectors and represent lower dimensions.
7.	Text encodings are directly applied to the raw text. Hence, text preprocessing is unnecessary.	Word embeddings require pretrained models.
8.	Examples include BoW, n-grams, and TF-IDF.	Examples include Word2vec, GloVe, and fasttext.

Distributed representation is based on the distributional hypothesis. A distributional hypothesis states that if the words are similar to each other, they should be from a similar context. In other words, if the words are semantically related, then their vectors are closer to each other in the vector space.

The advantages of word embeddings are given in Box 14.7.

Box 14.7 Advantages of Word Embeddings

What is the advantage of word embeddings? First, it can be recollected that word embeddings are also known as vector-space embeddings. It also captures location and meanings. Here, each word is assigned to a space called vector space. A space can have multiple dimensions called N-dimensions. Therefore, a word is represented as a point in vector space as a vector of floating numbers.

There are many advantages of word embeddings. Some of them are listed below:

(i) Embedding provides contextual information.

(ii) Embeddings can be useful as a semantic representation.

(iii) Embeddings can provide contextual information.

(iv) Word embeddings can be task specific.

(v) Many tasks, like the similarity of words and analogy, can be done using word embeddings.

What is a Context?

Consider the following example,

Daniel goes to River Bank to deposit money.

The apartment is located on the river Bank.

John's Blood Bank is famous in the city.

It can be observed that the meaning of the word "Bank" varies in each sentence based on the context. John Rupert Firth, a famous linguist, succinctly captured this principle: "You will know a word by the company it keeps."

Word embeddings are used to capture context. There may be many circumstances for the need to find the similarity of words. For example, flat, apartment, studio apartment, building, villa, home, and house are synonymous words. Technically, these words should occur together in the vector space.

The following Figure 14.3 shows two vectors of words A and B in the vector space. What is the closeness of the words?

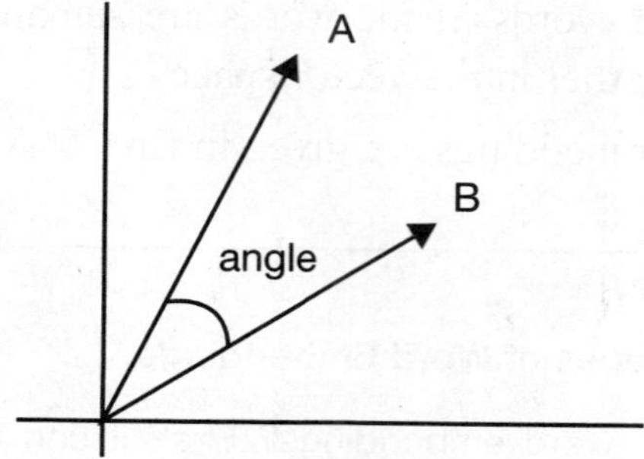

Figure 14.3 The Similarity of the Words A and B

The similarity of the vectors can be found using vector arithmetic. The lengths of the vectors are immaterial. Vector arithmetic finds the similarity among the documents using the vector difference. The vector difference can be used to find the difference. If $a = (a_1, a_2)$ and $b = (b_1, b_2)$, then the vector c can be given as

$$c = (a_1 - b_1, a_2 - b_2)$$

A better solution would be using cosine similarity. The cosine angle between the vectors is a better measure of the similarity. It must be noted that cosine $(0^\circ) = 1$ and cosine $(90^\circ) = 0$. If the angle between the vectors increases, the cosine value decreases. Thus, cosine similarity is a metric used to find the similarity between two vectors in inner product space. It aims to find the similarity by finding the cosine angle between the vectors. It ranges from –1 to +1.

1. If the cosine similarity is +1, the vectors are the same. It indicates the maximum similarity.
2. If the cosine similarity is –1, then it indicates the vectors are in the opposite direction, and it indicates the maximum dissimilarity.
3. The cosine similarity value 0 indicates that the vectors are orthogonal and is an indication of dissimilarity.

In reality, it isn't easy to visualize the cosine angle as embeddings usually have more dimensions, such as 256 or 512. So, the angle can be calculated with the help of linear algebra as:

$$sim(X,Y) = \frac{X \bullet Y}{\|X\| \times \|Y\|} = \frac{\sum_{i=1}^{n} X_i \times Y_i}{\sqrt{\sum_{i=1}^{n} X_i^2} \times \sqrt{\sum_{i=1}^{n} Y_i^2}}$$

The numerator is the dot product of the vectors A and B. The denominator is the product of the norm of vectors A and B. The following numerical example illustrates the finding of cosine similarity for three-dimensional vectors.

Example 14.8: If the given vectors are $X = \{1, 1, 0\}$ and $Y = \{0, 1, 1\}$, then what is the cosine similarity?

Solution:

The cosine similarity is given as $sim(X,Y) = \frac{X \bullet Y}{\|X\|\|Y\|}$

The dot product of the vector $X \bullet Y$ is given as $1 \times 0 + 1 \times 1 + 0 \times 1 = 1$.

The norm of the vectors $X = \sqrt{1^2 + 1^2 + 0^2} = \sqrt{2}$ and $Y = \sqrt{0^2 + 1^2 + 1^2} = \sqrt{2}$.

So, the cosine similarity is given as $\frac{1}{\sqrt{2}\sqrt{2}} = \frac{1}{2} = 0.5$

What are the uses of embedding vectors? The embedding vectors are useful in context creation and vector arithmetic.

1. **Context Creation**

   A context can help in prediction. For example,

   The Sun ________ in the East always.

   The appropriate prediction is "rises" based on the context in which the sentence is mentioned as "East." So, the above prediction can be written as

   The Sun (Actions) _______ in the East always.

   Here, it can be seen the potential candidates of the fill-in-the-blanks are the "rises" and "sets." The context of 'East" forces the model to pick rises.

   This above process can be viewed as moving a vector closer to "rises." This context creation process is given in Box 14.8.

Box 14.8 Context Creation using Word Embeddings

In the prediction, word embeddings are useful.

Consider the following sequence of statements.

1. Apple is a reputed company selling desktops.
2. I like to eat apples.

So, it can be observed that the context of "Apple" is different. In the first sentence, it refers to a company, and in the second sentence, it refers to fruit.

So, if the prediction for the sentence, "-------- is a good fruit" and needs to be done, then we have to push the vector of the new sentence to the second context of fruits, as shown in Figure 14.4.

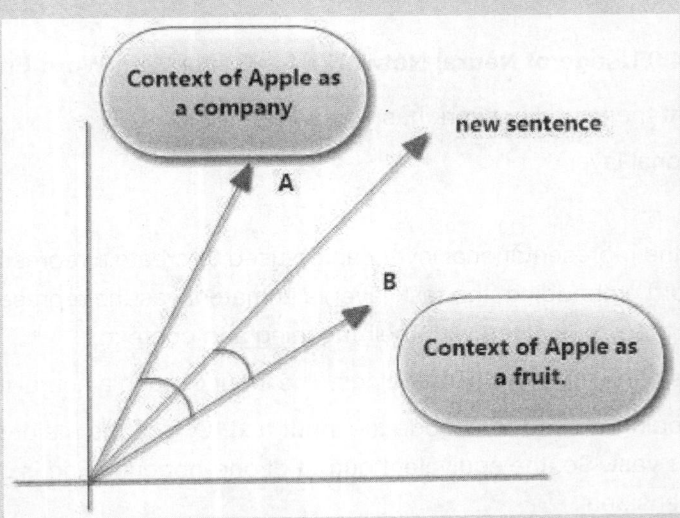

Figure 14.4 Mapping of the Correct Context

Mathematically, this can be done by the linear combination vector operation. Some percent of vector A and some percent of vector B can be taken to express the linear combination of the new sentence. It also must be noted that the length of the vectors is not important. Only the angles are important. The linear combination of vectors is the best way of creating contexts.

2. **Vector Arithmetic (King – Man + Women = Queen)**

   Another advantage of vector notation is that one can manipulate the vectors. For example, Vectors allow us to reason like this.

   $$V_{king} - V_{man} + V_{women} \approx V_{queen}$$

   Surprisingly, the values are almost close. Vector operations enable the performance of word arithmetic that uses embedding spaces and reason.

14.4 Pretrained Models for Word Embedding

The aim is to generate vector representations of words such that words with similar contexts will be closely represented in the vector space. In graphical terms, if the word is represented as a vector with the origin as one point, the angle between the vectors should be close for similar words. Neural networks are required to generate word embeddings (refer to Box 14.9).

Box 14.9 Usage of Neural Networks for Generating Word Embeddings

It was noted that the neural network has two parts:

1. Representational layer
2. Task layer

The outputs of the representational layer can be used to create a representation for the task layer. In word embedding, the task layer is immaterial as the representational layer output embeds the words along with their meaning and context.

Neural networks generate word embeddings. The input of such a neural network is text.

1. One-hot encoding is used to encode the input text. One of the major disadvantages is that the text is vast. So, the equivalent output of one-hot encoding is quite large as it is of higher dimensional.
2. Word embedding techniques, instead, keep the dimensional low as it is a hyperparameter controlled by the user. Typically, dimensions of 256 or 512 are used for embedding.
3. Finding labelled data for embedding is difficult. So, one mask the known word (For example, Ram goes to school is marked as Ram goes to _______), and the network is expected to predict the missing words.
4. The loss is computed between the predicted word and the actual word. This loss is propagated back to adjust the weights. This process is continued till the parameter values do not change much.
5. Once a trained network is available, then the words can be sent as input, and the outputs of the representational layer can be taken as embeddings.

Training a neural network for word embeddings is a difficult task as it requires a huge corpus and computational time. The most common approach is to use the concept of pretrained models.

14.4.1 Word2Vec

Word2Vec is a pretrained method of finding word embeddings. Word2vec is a method proposed by Mikolov et al. and presented in the paper "Efficient Estimation of Word Representation in Vector Space." Word2Vec focuses on capturing the meaning and semantic relationships between words in a sentence.

Word2Vec is a neural network model to produce a low dimensional vector called word embeddings. The model takes a corpus of words as input. The text is divided into sentences and then words. The word analysis is made to extract the context. Hence the focus is to predict the correct target words and context words.

The components of Word2Vec as a 3-tier neural network are:

(i) **Input Layer:** In this layer, the target word or context words are given as continuous vectors in a higher dimensional space.

(ii) **Projection Layer:** This is a hidden layer with no activation functions. This layer gives the weights that project the input to the output word, which can be a target word or context words that surround the target word.

(iii) **Output Layer:** This layer is also called the softmax layer, and the output layer will have the exact dimension of the input layer. This layer will be used to predict target words or context words. This prediction is done by computing the probability distribution of the entire vector space.

The types of Word2Vec are shown in Figure 14.5.

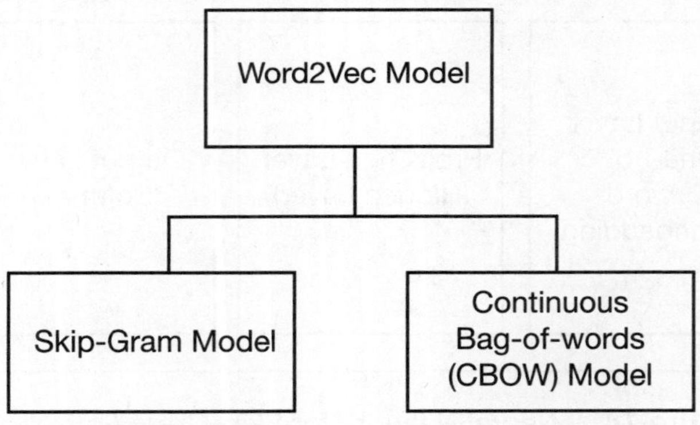

Figure 14.5 Types of Word2Vec Models

Skip-Gram Model

The skip-gram model predicts the context words given the target word. The context words are the words that surround the given target word.

The skip-gram model's input and output are shown below in Figure 14.6.

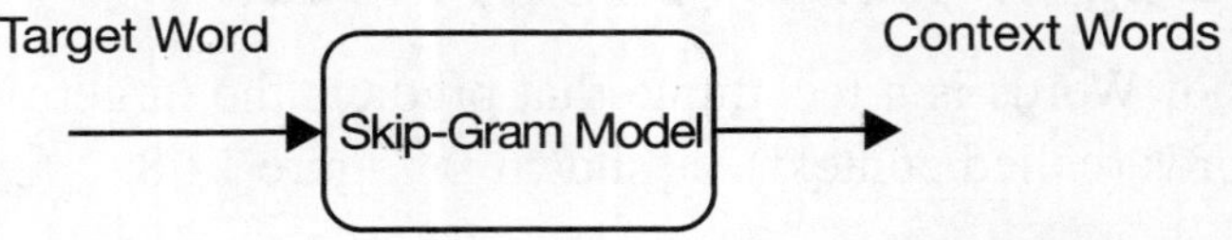

Figure 14.6 Input-Output of Skip-Gram Model

Skip-gram model focuses on predicting the context of words using the missing word. The Skip-gram model is given as follows:

1. Input Layer – As discussed earlier, the neural network input layer neurons correspond to one-hot encoding or embeddings of the target word. The input layer will have no bias term. There will be no activation function between the input and hidden layer.
2. Projection layer – This is the hidden layer. The neurons in this layer contain weights that connect the input target word to the output context words. The weights would be adjusted in the neural network training. In short, the hidden layer works like a look-up table that takes the weighted sum of the input and projects that to the output layer.
3. Output layer – A softmax layer that computes the probability of the context words that appear adjacent to the given target word.

The neural network is given as shown in Figure 14.7.

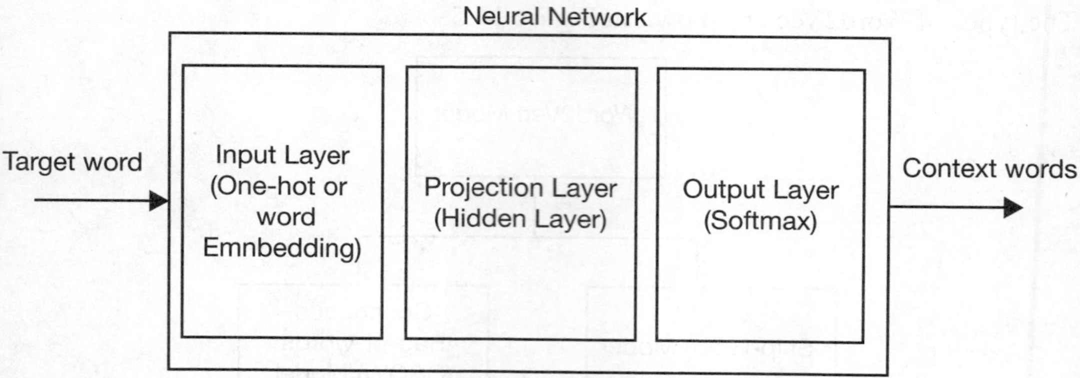

Figure 14.7 Neural Network for Skip-Gram Architecture

This neural network aims to maximize the probability of the predicted context words given the input target word. This model requires a lot of training to adjust the weights to maximize the probability (or to minimize the negative likelihood of the loss functions). Skip-gram model effectively captures the semantic relationships and similarity among words in a small dataset.

Continuous Bag-of-Words (CBoW) Model

Continuous Bag of Words is a technique that predicts the target word based on the neighbouring words (called context), as shown in Figure 14.8.

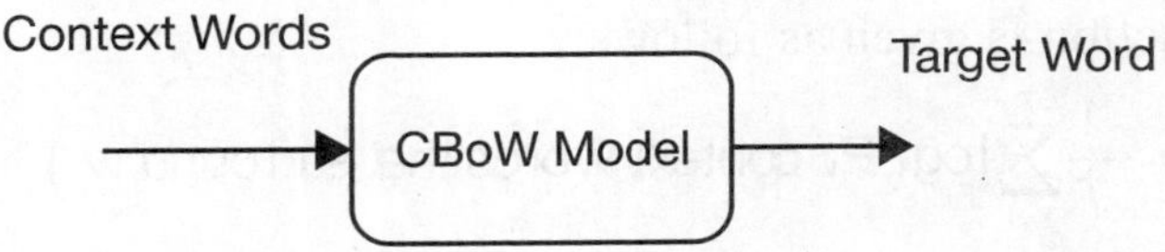

Figure 14.8 CBoW Architecture

The context words are the surrounding words of the target. For example, consider the sentence.

The Sun always rises in the ________

If the prediction of the East is required in the fill-in-the-blank and hence the target word and all the surrounding words are context words. In general, if the target word is w_t, where t is the time stamp. Then all the words "$w_{t-1}, w_{t-2}, \ldots$," and "$w_{t+1}, w_{t+2}, \ldots$," are called context words. The context words are extracted using a sliding window of a certain size. The size should be optimal as the larger window size makes it difficult to predict if the search space grows.

The CBOW neural network architecture is given as follows:

1. Input Layer – As discussed earlier, the neural network input layer neurons correspond to one-hot encoding or embeddings of the context words.
2. Average/Merge Layer – This layer performs the average or merging of all input context words.
3. Projection layer – This is the hidden layer. The neurons in this layer contain weights that connect the input context words to the output target word. The weights would be adjusted in the neural network training.
4. Output layer – A softmax layer that computes the probability of the target word given context words.

The architecture is shown in Figure. 14.9 below:

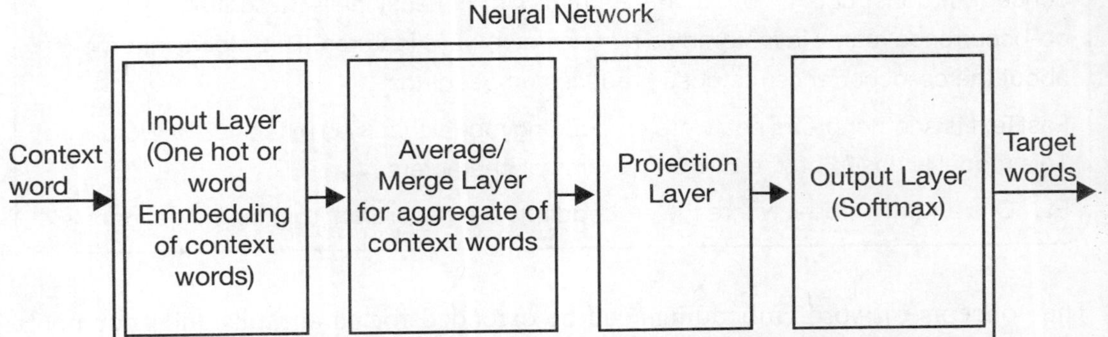

Figure 14.9 Neural Network for CBoW Architecture

The objective function is given as follows:

$$\frac{1}{T}\sum_{t=1}^{T}\log(P/\text{context words that surround } w_t)$$

Here w_t is the target word, and T is the total number of words in the corpus for training the model.

The training of neural networks achieves the objective of finding the target word using context words. The training is carried out with the largest corpus of words. The focus is to maximize the log probability of predicting that target word given the context words.

For example, the output for the prediction task for the sentence, The Sun always rises in the _________ The output may be as shown in Figure 14.10.

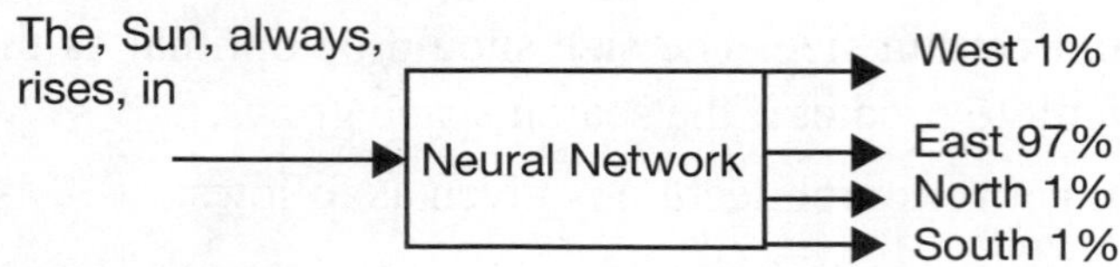

Figure 14.10 A Hypothetical Softmax Output for Prediction

The other types of pretrained word embedding models are given in Box 14.10.

Box 14.10 Other Pretrained Word Embedding Models

The GloVe (Global Vectors for Word representation) is an alternative pretrained model that can be downloaded and used using the transfer learning concept. GloVe is based on a vast corpus. The documents may span various languages also. The difference between GloVe and Word2vec is that GloVe uses a global context instead of a local concept. It constructs a co-occurrence matrix of dimensionality x-contexts. Then, the co-occurrence matrix is factored as a matrix of x-word features. This global information about the co-occurrence matrices produces embeddings.

FastText is another pretrained word embedding model that is an extension of Word2vec. This model is based on the bag of N-grams of characters.

ELMO is another model where the embeddings are generated from language models.

The concepts of word embeddings can be extended for paragraphs and documents also.

14.5 Case Studies for NLP

Word embeddings can be used for many practical applications. Some of the NLP applications are discussed below.

14.5.1 Sentiment Analysis

Sentiment analysis is an application where the text is classified based on the word's sentiment. There are many circumstances where user feedback can be collected, and sentiment analysis can be applied. Sentiment analysis provides the mood and sentiment of the users. This analysis can be applied to IMDB movies or, in general, to any product.

The sentiments can be:

Positive: A review may have comments like "Book is good." It is the same as the comment, "Book is excellent." It is a positive sentiment. Therefore, the words can convey sentiment.

Negative: Similarly, words like bad or worse represent negative polarity.

Neutral: Certain words are neutral as it is neither positive nor negative. Based on the polarity values, the sentiment can be understood.

The process is shown below in Figure 14.11.

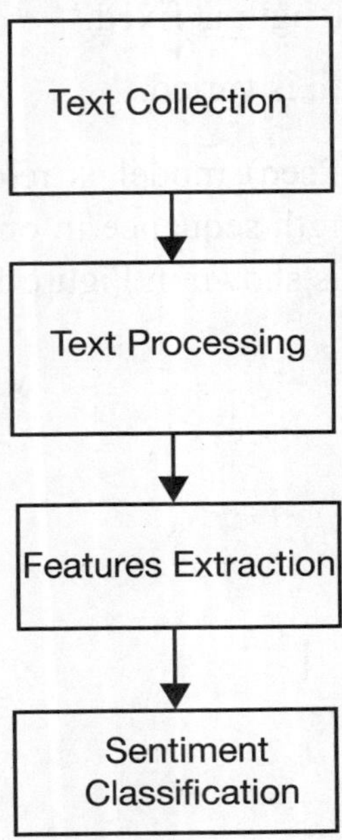

Figure 14.11 Steps of Sentiment Analysis

1. **Text Collection:** The input is the movie or product reviews. The review comments can be scraped from the web also.
2. **Text Preprocessing:** The preprocessing steps include these tasks
   - Sentences are split into tokens. This step is called tokenization.
   - Stop words can be eliminated as they do not convey useful information.
   - Stemming can be done to reduce the keywords to their base form.
   - The special characters, like punctuation marks, can be removed. Similarly, the numbers and white spaces can be removed.
3. **Features Extraction:** Techniques like Bag of Words, TF-IDF, and Word embeddings can be used to extract features.
4. **Sentiment (text) Classifier:** A classifier can be trained using the term-document matrix, resulting in the words' polarity.

14.5.2 Seq2seq Models

A seq2seq model is a neural network architecture to handle variable-sized sequence data. It is useful for machine translation, text summarization, and dialogue generation. Text data is sequence data where every part is time-stamped. There are two types of sequence data.

(i) The sequence data whose length is fixed.

(ii) Sequence data whose length is varied.

The sequence-to-sequence (seq2seq) model is relevant if the data is varied. The input for seq2seq is a varied-length sequence in one language, and the output is in another. The model for seq2seq is shown in Figure 14.12.

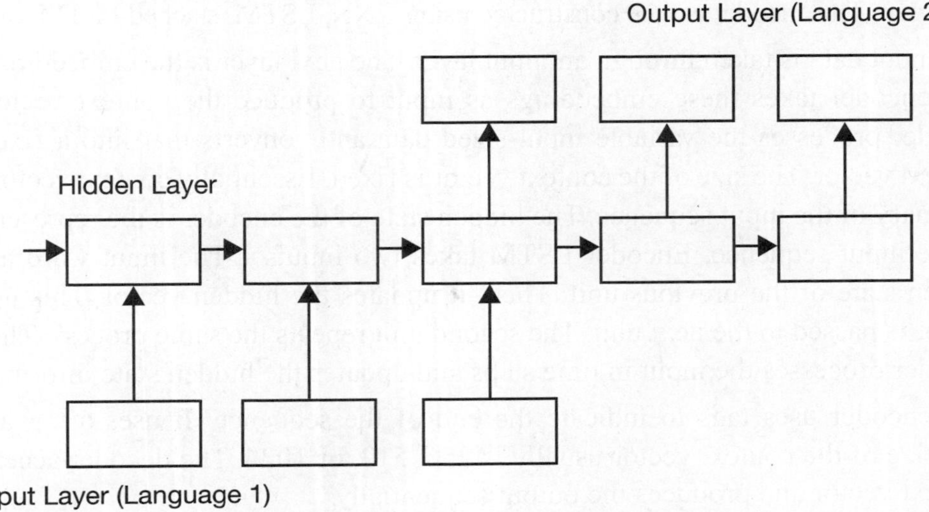

Figure 14.12 Many-to-Many Model

The input for the model is the next sentence of varying length, and the output is the LSTM output of the text in another language. The model has two major components, namely Encoder and Decoder. The interaction of the encoder and decoder is shown in Figure 14.13.

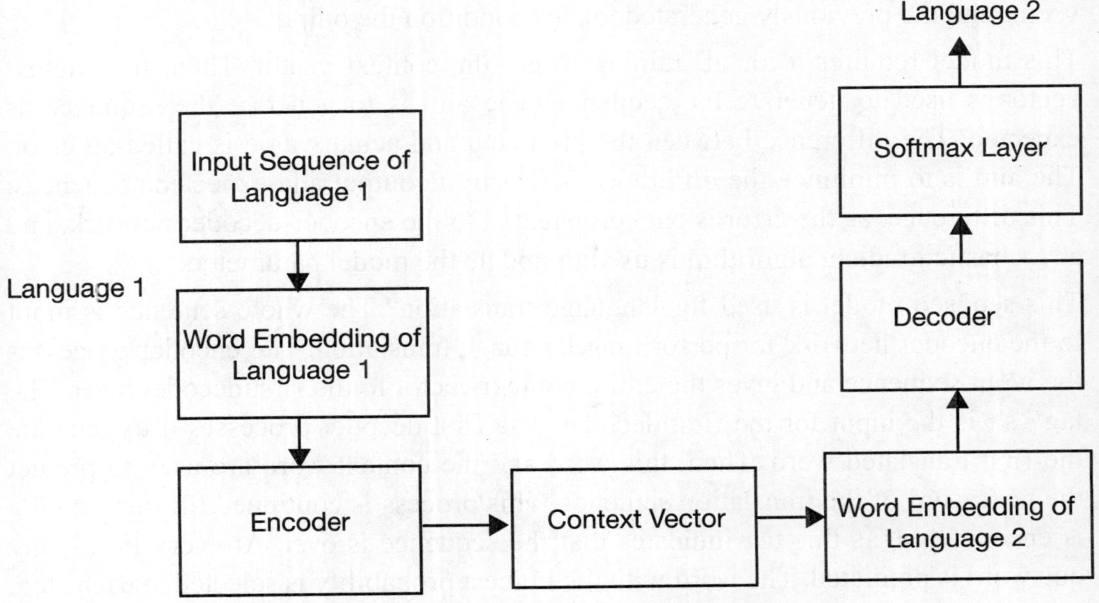

Figure 14.13 Encoder-Decoder Architecture

Encoder: The encoder can be constructed using RNN, LSTM, stacked LSTM, or GRU. The input data is taken through an input layer. The next layer is the embedding layer. The encoder takes these embeddings as input to produce the context vector. The encoder processes the variable input-sized data and converts that into a fixed-size context vector. The size of the context vector is fixed. Essentially context vector is the summary of the input sequence. The hidden state of the encoder is the representation of the input sequence. Encoder LSTM takes two inputs – The input word and the hidden state of the previous unit. Then, it updates the hidden vector. This updated vector is passed to the next unit. The second unit repeats the same process. Thus, the encoder processes the input in time steps and updates the hidden state information.

The encoder uses tags to indicate the end of the sequence. It uses a tag as <s>. The size of the context vector usually is 256, 512, or 1024. The decoder accepts the context vector and produces the output sequentially.

Decoder: The decoder can also be RNN, LSTM, stacked LSTM, or GRU. Here, an LSTM takes the hidden cell states in a context vector. The context vector is given to the embedding layer where the embeddings of the target language would be present. The closest words are identified, and the decoder takes this information. The next layer is the softmax layer, which generates the probability of the words. Based on the probability, one can get the best output based on the context vector. The context vector and the previously generated tokens condition the output.

This model requires a lot of training to get the context vector. Then, the context vector is used to generate the sequence. The aim is to generate the sequence as expected. The difference between the predicted and actual value is called an error. The aim is to minimize the difference between the output and expected sequences. This difference, as the error is backpropagated to the encoder-decoder network, and a stochastic gradient algorithm is used to update the model parameters.

This seq2seq model is used for language translation? The whole sentence is input to the encoder network for performing language translation. The encoder processes the input sequence and gives the entire context vector to the first decoder layer. The tag <s> is the input for the first decoder. The first decoder processes it to generate the first translated word. Then, this word and the context word are used to predict the next word of the translation sentence. This process is continued till the tag </s> is encountered, as this tag indicates that the sequence is over. At every time, only one word is predicted. The word with the highest probability is selected at each step. This method is called greedy decoding.

The attention mechanisms can be used to improve the model's performance and are dealt with in the next chapter.

Summary

1. NLP investigates the methodologies that can formalize the interaction between computers and humans.
2. Text is unstructured data.
3. The essential granularity of text analysis is a document. A document is a collection of words. The corpus is the collection of documents.
4. The process of extraction of a word is called tokenization.
5. "Stemming" means reducing the word to its stem or base form.
6. PoS is the process of identifying parts of speech called PoS tagging or parsing.
7. N-gram is a technique of creating a vocabulary from N-adjacent words. For example, if the value of N is 1, then it is called 1-gram. If $N = 2$, it is a bigram; if $N = 3$, it is called trigram.
8. The TF-IDF approach considers the number of occurrences of the given word and the number of documents containing the given word.
9. Distributed representation is based on the distributional hypothesis. It means that if the words are like each other, they should be from a similar context.
10. Word embedding is creating a dense vector of floating-point numbers for every word. These dense vectors are called context vectors.
11. Continuous Bag of Words is a technique that predicts the center word based on the neighbouring words (called context).
12. The Skip-gram model predicts the context words using the missing words. The Skip-gram model is relatively slow but more accurate for finding low-frequency words.
13. Word2vec is a distributed representation of a word. It focuses on capturing the meaning and semantic relationships between words in a sentence.
14. GloVe is an alternative pretrained model that uses a vast corpus. The difference between GloVe and Word2vec is that GloVe uses a global context instead of a local context.

Glossary

1. Structured data – Data organized in a predefined form or format like tables and Excel sheets are called structured data.
2. Unstructured data – Data that does not have any predefined structure or form.
3. Text – Text is a form of unstructured data.
4. Syntax – Syntax explains how words combine to get a sentence or paragraph.
5. Semantics – Semantics refers to the meaning.
6. Normalization – Normalization is an application-specific task like converting text to a uniform form so that it can be analyzed.
7. Tokenization – This process of extraction of a word is called tokenization.
8. Stemming – Reduce a word to its stem or base form.
9. Lemmatisation – Like stemming but instead gives meaningful words.
10. Stop word removal – Identify and remove words that do not contribute. This process is called stop word removal.
11. Tagging – Identifying and assigning nouns, verbs, and grammatical aspects to the words are tagging.
12. Named entity recognizers – Semantic entities can be identified by Named entity Recognizers (NER).
13. Text encoding – It represents a set of discrete features that can be computed from text.
14. Word embedding – Captures context and semantics as a vector.
15. One-hot encoding – It is a technique of converting categorical data to the binary vector indicating the presence or absence of the word.
16. Bag of Words (BoW) – A frequency-based approach where the count of the occurrence of a word is computed as an unorganized list.
17. N-gram – A N-contiguous word that is useful to analyze the structure of a text.
18. TF – TF is the term frequency that quantifies the frequency of the term or word in a document.
19. IDF – It is used to weigh the importance of the word in a collection of documents.

20. TF-IDF – It is a statistical metric that measures the importance of the word in a document relative to the collection of documents.
21. Distributional semantics – The semantic relatedness of context is called distributional semantics, which implies that the words that occur in a similar context tend to have similar meanings.
22. Continuous Bag of Words – This technique predicts the target word based on the neighbouring words (called context). It is a technique for learning word embeddings.
23. Skip-gram model – This model predicts the context words given the target word.
24. Cosine Similarity – It is a metric for finding the similarity among the documents.
25. Document embeddings – The idea of extending the word embedding where documents are embedded in the vector space model like words.
26. Sentiment analysis – It is a text classification based on the word's sentiment.

Short Questions

1. Distinguish between structured and unstructured data.
2. List out at least five major NLP applications.
3. List out the differences between text encoding and text vectorization.
4. What is a BoW approach?
5. List the differences between the count-based and weighted approaches like TD-IDF.
6. What is a distributional hypothesis?

Long Questions

1. Explain the models for word embedding.
2. Outline the details of the implementation of sentiment analysis for a movie review.

Numerical Problems

1. Use a one-hot encoding technique for the following sentences.

   Doc 1: New Delhi is the capital of India

Doc 2: New Delhi is located in North India

Doc 3: Madurai is located in South India

2. Identify the tokens and types in the following sentence.

   Chennai experienced a mild tremor today.

3. Use the BoW approach for the following sentences.

   Doc 1: The Sun rises in the East.

   Doc 2: Kanyakumari is a favourite spot for sunset.

   Doc 3: Sun restaurant is my favourite in east Chennai.

4. Use the TF-IDF approach for the following sentences.

   Doc 1: Sun rises in the East.

   Doc 2: Kanyakumari is a favourite spot for sunsetting.

   Doc 3: Sun restaurant is my favourite in east Chennai.

5. Compute cosine similarity for the two sentences that are represented by the vectors.

   Vector 1: 1 0 0 1 1 1

   Vector 2: 0 1 0 0 1 1

Crossword

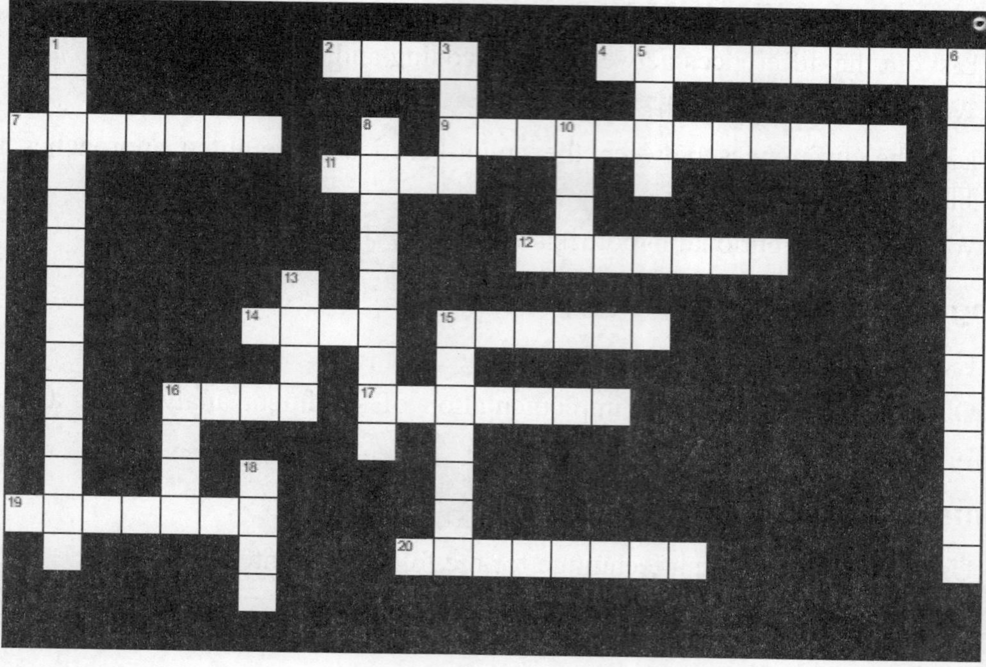

Across

2. __________ encoding refers to the set of discrete features that can be computed.
4. A table is an example of__________ data.
7. Identifying and assigning tags to the grammatical aspects to words is called __________.
9. Text is an example of __________ data.
11. One-hot encoding is a process that assigns a value to the presence or absence of a word. (true/false)
12. Semantics refer to __________.
14. The technique of creating a vocabulary form N-adjacent words is called N-gram. (true/false)
15. __________ similarity is a technique for finding the similarity among the documents.
16. IDF can be used to weigh the importance of the word in a collection of documents. (true/false)
17. This technique predicts the center words based on the neighboring words is called __________.
19. Word embedding captures the __________.
20. Reducing a word to its stem or base form is called __________.

Down

1. Sentiment analysis is text __________.
3. The semantic entity is called a named entity. (true/false)
5. Unstructued data does not have any predefined form or format. (true/false)
6. The semantic relatedness of context is called __________ semantics.
8. BoW is a __________ based approch.
10. Syntax explains how the words are combined to get a sentence or paragraph. (true/false)
13. TF is term frequency that quantifies the frequency of the term or word. (true/false)
15. Skip-gram model predicts the __________ words using the missing word.
16. TF-IDF is a statistical metric that measures the importance of the word in a document to the collection of documents. (true/false)
18. Removing the unnecessary words that do not contribute is called __________ word removal.

Jumbled Sentences

V	A	W	Q	Q	T	H	J	R	D	Y	X	A	I	Q	P	F	C	H	T	R	U	E	Z	U
Q	K	I	W	P	Z	K	O	G	I	J	J	W	L	I	J	U	K	G	D	T	E	X	T	Z
C	F	K	Z	S	I	W	Z	R	S	H	Z	H	K	R	V	N	L	D	Y	C	L	S	K	R
L	A	C	R	T	I	T	A	I	T	R	S	F	D	K	Y	S	V	P	O	O	J	T	Y	O
A	F	I	Y	O	Z	R	J	Z	R	C	J	Q	Y	W	N	T	Q	Y	J	S	K	E	X	H
S	L	O	E	O	G	U	M	T	I	H	D	Q	J	E	Y	R	S	Z	C	I	I	M	G	Q
S	R	L	Q	D	Y	E	O	C	B	V	L	H	I	I	E	U	T	V	O	N	L	M	J	H
I	A	M	E	A	N	I	N	G	U	J	W	O	F	T	M	C	R	C	N	E	R	I	K	N
F	Y	A	S	P	Q	Z	H	T	T	T	Y	X	G	R	J	T	U	Z	T	F	W	N	W	Y
I	Q	T	C	J	L	F	X	B	I	C	R	L	U	U	J	U	C	G	E	L	P	G	C	D
C	S	R	K	O	M	E	O	E	O	M	C	U	S	E	H	R	T	E	X	Y	Y	N	D	V
A	G	U	T	G	T	T	B	F	N	I	T	E	E	K	M	E	U	J	T	V	E	R	H	L
T	H	E	I	N	Z	K	R	D	A	E	H	J	Q	M	V	D	R	J	P	U	S	V	I	H
I	H	J	O	T	R	U	E	U	L	H	K	K	S	R	U	B	E	O	Q	S	S	E	E	Q
O	S	C	D	T	T	V	E	P	E	I	S	U	M	N	S	B	D	E	N	U	G	B	X	D
N	C	O	N	T	E	X	T	V	G	E	G	E	D	E	A	O	R	T	A	G	G	I	N	G
V	A	S	T	O	P	T	H	A	S	W	K	R	U	L	R	F	H	J	B	T	T	R	U	E

structured	true	unstructured	true	meaning
stemming	stop	tagging	true	text
context	true	frequency	true	true
true	true	distributional	context	context
cosine	classification			

Transformer Architecture and Large Language Models

Attention is all you need. — **Vaswani et al., 2017**

Credits: © Vaswani et al

Traditional deep neural networks like LSTM cannot be expected to solve many natural language processing (NLP) problems efficiently. Transformers are an alternative way to solve those complex NLP problems. Many natural language processing tasks can be implemented effectively using transformer architecture. Large Language Models (LLMs) are based on transformers. BERT and ChatGPT are neural models that are the focus of this chapter. The learning objectives of this chapter are:

- Study the need for attention networks.
- Know about Transformers.
- Understand large language models.
- Understand BERT concepts.
- Know the training mechanism of BERT.
- Know about GPT architectures.
- Understand prompt engineering.

15.1 Overview of Transformers

The transformer is a new class of language models. Transformers are alternate architectures designed to process sequential data like RNN or LSTM. It is a replacement for seq2seq models, which use RNNs and LSTMs. LSTM or RNNs have limitations such as sequential processing and memory. But transformers are designed to work in parallel using self-attention mechanisms and for handling huge amounts of data called scalability and can handle long-range dependencies.

Transformers are primarily used for natural language processing tasks. However, the transformer's scope is extended to many other domains, such as vision, audio, and speech processing. The use cases of transformers are given in Box. 15.1.

Box 15.1 Use cases of Transformers

Transformers are effective in applications such as:

1. **Natural Language Processing:**

   Some applications where transformers are used are machine translation (such as google translate), text summarization, language modeling, and sentiment analysis.

2. **Speech and Audio Processing:**

   Conversion of speech to text, speech synthesis.

3. **Computer Image and Video Processing:**

   Image classification, image captioning, video generation, video understanding, medical image analysis and video surveillance.

4. **Recommender systems:**

   Netflix and Amazon book recommendations.

The story of transformers started from the classical paper "Attention is All You Need" by Vaswani et al. in 2017 (NIPS'17: Proceedings of the 31st International Conference on Neural Information Processing Systems December 2017). Before the arrival of transformers, the sequential data processing was done using RNN / LSTM networks. The limitations of LSTM are listed below:

(i) It is applicable for only small sequences. LSTM cannot remember very long sequences.

(ii) Context vector cannot encode all the information of all input timestamps. Therefore, storing all the information in the context vector is not practical. This limitation of the context vector is known as the bottleneck problem.

(iii) LSTM suffers from the vanishing gradient problem.

Transformers have become foundational models for many natural language processing tasks. Some of the important characteristics of transformers are:

(i) Transformers can handle sequence data effectively and efficiently using a self-attention mechanism.

(ii) Transformers handle sequential data in parallel and are faster.

(iii) Transformers also handle longer dependencies, capturing complex and contextual relationships within the data.

(iv) Transformers are scalable as it has more layers and parameters.

The summary of the differences between transformers and LSTM networks is given in Table 15.1.

Table 15.1 Differences between LSTM Networks and Transformers

Transformers	LSTM Networks
Transformers use attention mechanisms to process sequential data.	Use recurrent loops to process sequential data.
Faster because of parallel processing.	Slower because of sequential processing.
Suitable for large amounts of data.	Suitable for less amount of data.
Handle long sequences and their long dependencies.	LSTM networks face the problem of vanishing gradients and hence, suitable only for short sequences.
More memory is required, and computationally, transformers are very complex.	LSTM networks require less memory and possess simpler architectures.
Transformers require less training time as it does parallel processing over texts.	Longer training time due to the sequential nature.

15.2 Attention Mechanisms

The basis of attention is visual attention. If one watches an image, the immediate eye movement to certain parts of the image can reveal the subject's attention. The aspects of the image that grab the attention are called visual cues. This visual cue can be colour, shape, corners, intensity, edges, or motion. These are also called visual attributes that characterize the salient aspects of the image.

There is a connection between memory and attention. The human brain has limited memory, so only important details must be stored. What is to be stored is determined by the attention mechanism. The attention mechanism selects the important information that needs to be stored in the memory. Box 15.2 gives more details of visual attention.

Box 15.2 Attention Mechanism in Humans

William James proposed an attention model for attention based on visual cues. What is a cue? A cue is something that brings the subject's attention to a part of the image. For example, coloring a part of an image to highlight it create a cue. Similarly, a shape is a cue.

There are two types of cues.

1. Subjects do voluntary (volitional or intentional) cues by focusing on the target.
2. Involuntary (non-volitional) cues are the mechanisms that grab the attention of the subject. For example, a building painted in a unique color, say red, distinct from other buildings is an involuntary cue.

Volitional cues correspond to the queries, and non-volitional cues correspond to keys. The sensory inputs correspond to values.

The three components of human attention are given in Fig. 15.1.

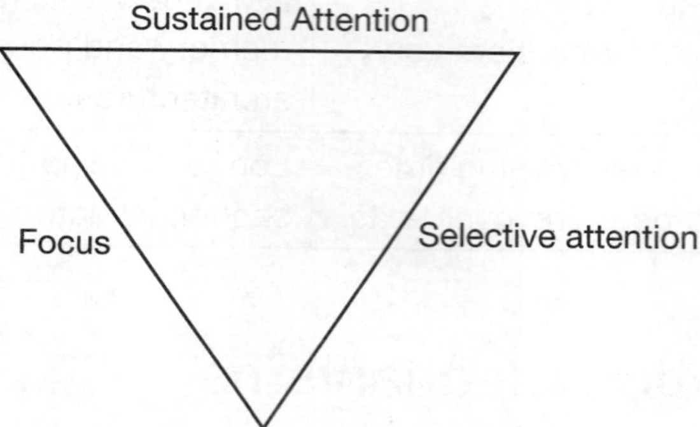

Figure 15.1 Three Components of Attention Mechanism

a. The first component is called focus. It means focusing on a specific stimulus by avoiding all the distractions. The equivalent deep learning component of focus is called a query.
b. The second component is sustained attention. It indicates the ability to focus over a longer period. It is deep learning, it is implemented for all the inputs for the given sequence.

c. The third component is called selection attention. Selective attention is the ability to concentrate on a specific aspect, ignoring all others. In deep learning, this is provided by the query and key vectors.

In deep learning, attention is achieved by focusing on certain words while ignoring other insignificant words. Like humans solving a puzzle, the model focuses on solving the problem by concentrating on certain sentence details and avoiding all irrelevant details. The advantage of the attention mechanism is that.

- Savings in memory
- Computation time
- Parallel Processing

Attention can be applied to natural language processing tasks.

Let us consider another sentence - "George Eats Yellow Banana." The following Table 15.2 illustrates the spotlights of each word.

Table 15.2 Illustration of Spotlights of Attention

Words	Spotlight
George	"eats" as the query may be what George eats "Banana" as "What is eaten" "Yellow" is a description of the banana.
Eats	"George" and "Banana" as eats is a connecting word of these two.
Yellow	"Yellow" is drawing attention as colour information. It is a description of a banana.
Banana	"eats" as it is the effect on banana "George" as George is acting. "yellow" possibly as a description.

15.2.1 Context Creation

The exploitation of attention is called context creation. One way is to visualize the attention mechanism as context creation. It should be noted that all the words should be included in the context creation, which is done in parallel. The context creation in transformers depends on all the words of the text.

Consider the following sentence:

George eats yellow ________.

The word "eat" is very important to predict the word in the blank. So, the missing word should be related to eating. Hence, it should be an eatable item. So, one should take a linear combination of "yellow" with all other words. The context creation can be viewed as turning the vector (Narrowing down to eatables and whose colour is yellow) towards the vectors of the influencing words. So, the logic is to take the linear combination of "yellow" with all other vectors of all the words but ensure that the proportion of "eats" is larger. In other words, it is paying more attention to the important words.

15.2.2 Self-Attention

Self-attention takes a sequence and computes the representation of each element of the sequence in relation to all other elements in the sequence. The focus here is to capture the context that finds the dependencies of all the elements. It uses a database approach called the Q(Query), K(Key), and V(Value) to compute the attention scores. The focus of Figure 15.1 corresponds to the query. The sustained attention corresponds to the key and value. The attention scores determine the contribution of each element to the representation.

1. **Query:** First, a request to the system is called a query. Query is the vector representation corresponding to the input's specific part. It is used to evaluate the relevance of other input parts to this word. A query of a word is how important other words that can influence the query word.

   For example, consider the sentence – Chennai is a city.

   The query for "Chennai" focuses on how much information the words of the sentence (is, a, city) contribute to the contextual relevance of Chennai.

2. **Key:** Next, the description is called a key. The key is a vector used to assess each part's influence on the other parts of the sentence. The key is the reply of other words in the input sequence, indicating their relevance to the keyword.

   Key vectors determine how much attention should be paid to each word. It also quantifies the relevance or importance of the word. Also, the key vector determines the contextual influence, taking the dot product of the query and the key vector that gives the attention needed to update of query word.

3. **Value:** Finally, the content is called a value. Value is a vector representation of each word. It is the value the other words bring to the word in query.

A query is issued, and the similarity between the query and the key vector is called a scoring function or attention function. The scoring function gives a numerical value. Let there be N key/value pairs. $(k_1, v_1), (k_2, v_2), \cdots, (k_n, v_n)$, and let α be the scoring function. The scoring function measures the query and the key's similarity and returns the scores $a_1, a_2, \cdots, a_n$ corresponding to the keys $k_1, k_2, \cdots, k_n$. Then, the scoring function can be computed as

$$a_i = \alpha(q, k_i)$$

Softmax ensures that the sum of the weights equals 1. The final score is the weighted sum of the values. The value of the scoring function is significant if the similarity is greater. One can apply the softmax function to attention scores as

$$B = \text{softmax}(a)$$

The output is the weighted sum of the attention weights and values

$$o = \sum_{i=1}^{n} b_i v_i$$

The steps of finding the weights are as follows:

(i) The sentences are broken into tokens or words in the input stage.

(ii) The scores are obtained for each word, indicating the attention the word should give to the other words.

(iii) The weighted combination of the words given the weighted importance.

(iv) The output of the self-attention mechanism is the mix of the word and context. The subsequent layers process this information. The final layer gives more complex embeddings of the input sentence.

The scoring function for computing attention scores is given below:

1. **Dot Product Method:**

   One of the most specific functions with no learnable parameter is computed as follows:

   $$\alpha(q.k) = q \bullet k$$

   Here, q and k are query vectors and key vectors, respectively.

2. **Luong Method:**

   The scoring function is computed as

$$\alpha(q.k) = v^T \tanh(W_k \times k + W_q q)$$

3. Scaled Dot Product or Multiplication Method:

Another way of computing the score function is by using the dot product of the query and key vectors. This method was proposed by Vaswani et al. The scoring for the attention can be calculated as follows:

$$\alpha(q.k) = \frac{q \bullet k}{\sqrt{d_k}}$$

The above formula also has no learnable parameters. The *qkv* approach is shown in Figure 15.2.

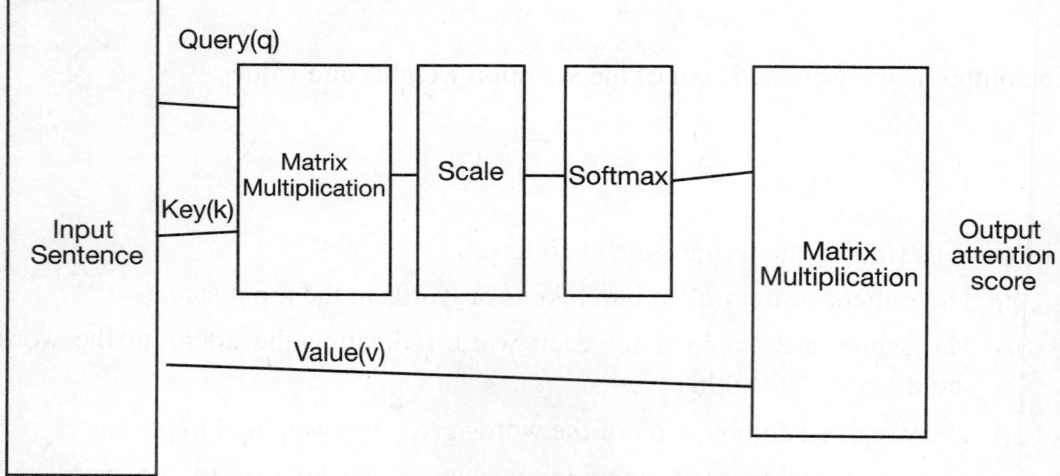

Figure 15.2 Scaled Dot Product Method

The procedure for scaled dot product is given below:

- Three neural networks are used to compute *qkv* tensors.
- First, the query, key, and value vectors are calculated by multiplying the input query vector with three weight matrics: $W(q)$, $W(k)$, and $W(v)$. The resultant are vectors.
- Multiply the vectors q and k using an inner product.
- Divide the score by the square root of the word embedding dimensions ($\sqrt{d_k}$) of the query and key vector. Here d_k is the dimension of the word embeddings. This division is to ensure that the scores are small.

- Apply the softmax function on scores. This softmax step ensures that the value is not too large or small. Softmax aims to provide the influence of close matches.
- Multiply the modified softmax function score with the value vector v.
- Sum up the weighted value vectors to give the self-attention output for each word.

In summary, the attention score is given as follows:

$$Attention(q,k,v) = soft\max\left(\frac{qk^T}{\sqrt{d_k}}\right)\times v$$

The advantage of the *qkv* attention mechanism is that it can be applied in parallel.

Example 15.1: Consider the sentence "Chennai is a city". Assume the dimension of the word embedding as 1 and implement the above formula.

$$Attention(q,k,v) = soft\max\left(\frac{qk^T}{\sqrt{1}}\right)\times v = \text{softmax}(qk^T) \times v$$

Find the attention scores of the word Chennai.

Solution:

Let the index be as shown in the following Table 15.3.

Table 15.3 Embeddings as One-Hot Vector

Word	Index
Chennai	[1 1 0 0]
is	[0 1 1 0]
a	[0 0 1 1]
City	[1 0 1 0]

Solution:

Let the query be Chennai. Then,

$$\text{Scores ("Chennai", "Chennai")} = 1 \times 1 + 1 \times 1 + 0 \times 0 + 0 \times 0 = 2$$

$$\text{Scores ("Chennai", "is")} = 1 \times 0 + 1 \times 1 + 0 \times 1 + 0 \times 0 = 1$$

$$\text{Scores ("Chennai", "a")} = 1 \times 0 + 1 \times 0 + 0 \times 1 + 0 \times 1 = 0$$
$$\text{Scores ("Chennai", "city")} = 1 \times 1 + 1 \times 0 + 0 \times 1 + 0 \times 0 = 1$$

Assume the dimension is 1. So, 1/sqrt(1) = 1.

Apply softmax for Chennai = [2, 1, 0, 1].

The results of the Softmax are:

$$\text{Sum} = \exp(2) + \exp(1) + \exp(0) + \exp(1) = 7.389 + 2.718 + 1 + 2.718 = 13.825$$

So, the softmax score of

$$\text{Chennai vs. Chennai} = 7.389/13.825 = 0.534$$
$$\text{Chennai vs. is} = 2.718/13.825 = 0.197$$
$$\text{Chennai vs. a} = 1/13.825 = 0.072$$
$$\text{Chennai vs. city} = 2.718/13.825 = 0.197$$

It can be observed that the highest score of Chennai is on itself. This way is called self-reference or self-focus. The above example can be extended for matrices also. The following numerical example illustrates this concept.

Example 15.2: Consider the sentence "orange apple grapes." Assume the dimension as 3 and implement the embeddings of orange.

Solution:

The first step is the one-hot encoding of the above as

Orange [1 0 0]

Apple [0 1 0]

Grapes [0 0 1]

The next step is the embedding step. Let us assume hypothetically, the embedded matrix is given as W randomly as

$$W = \begin{pmatrix} 0.2 & 0.1 & 0.1 \\ 0.4 & 0.3 & 0.2 \\ 0.2 & 0.1 & 0.1 \end{pmatrix}$$

Then, the embedding of orange is given as

$$
\begin{aligned}
[1\ 0\ 0] * W = [\ & 1 * 0.2 + 0 * 0.1 + 0 * 0.1 \\
& 0 * 0.4 + 0 * 0.3 + 0 * 0.2 \\
& 0 * 0.2 + 0 * 0.1 + 0 * 0.1\ ] \\
= [0.2\ & 0\ 0]
\end{aligned}
$$

Suppose the position encoding is [0 0 0]; then, the vector can be added immediately with word embedding to give the input X.

$$X = [0.2\ 0\ 0] + [0\ 0\ 0] = [0.2\ 0\ 0]$$

15.2.3 Multihead Attention

Similarity can be determined by different factors such as sound, syllables, or patterns. Hence, multiple scoring functions can be used on a word. Multiple scoring functions are computed using various networks. Each network is called a head. The multihead attention mechanism is shown in Figure. 15.3.

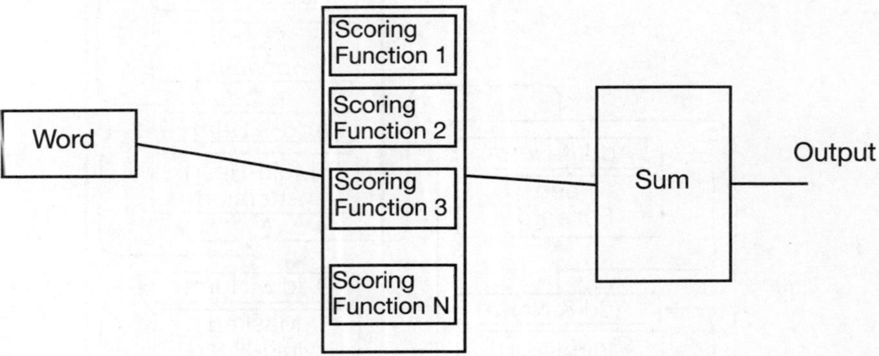

Figure 15.3 Multihead Attention

The implementation of the multihead attention mechanism is as follows:

(i) The input sequence is linearly projected to create multiple sets of keys, values, and queries. This projection is called h.

(ii) The attention scores are computed for each head, and the weights are obtained using the softmax activation function.

(iii) All the head outputs are combined into a single vector.

(iv) The single vector is projected again to get the final output of the multihead attention mechanism.

Initially, a network is initialized differently. Then, each head operates individually and computes its scoring function. Scoring functions are added to increase the quality by considering various criteria if necessary.

15.3 Architecture of Transformers

Transformers can understand and generate text based on context. Transformer architecture has two components – Encoder and Decoder.

The encoder-decoder arrangement is given in Figure. 15.4.

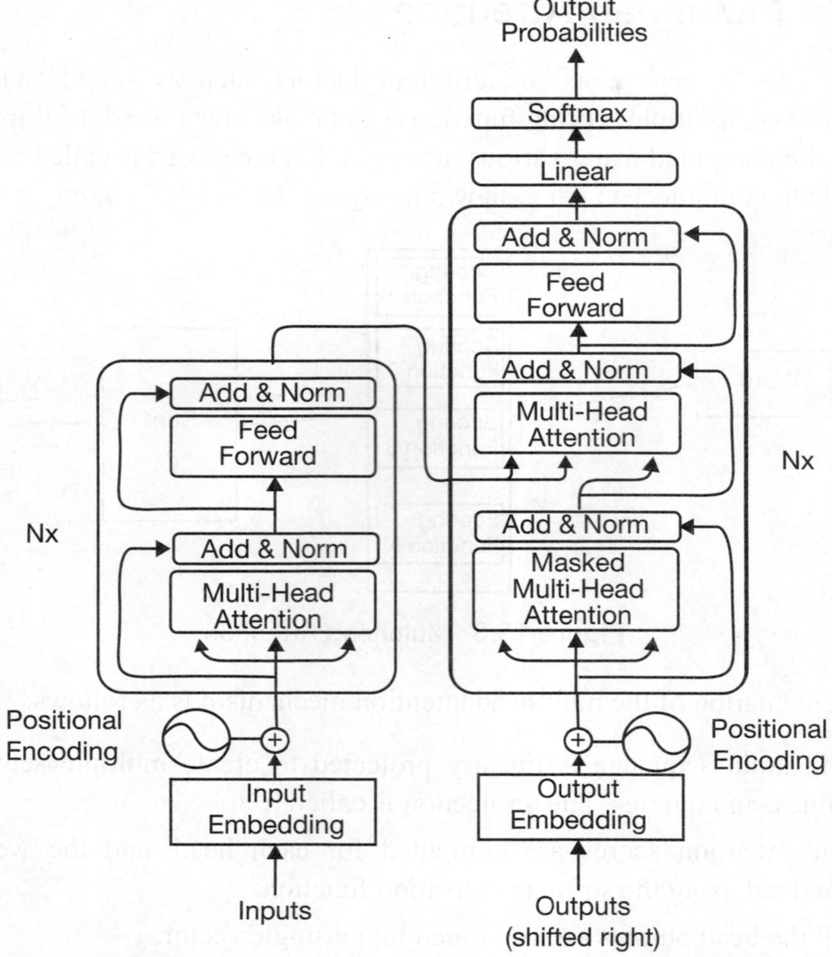

Figure 15.4 Transformer Architecture (https://arxiv.org/pdf/1706.03762)

The above architecture is called Encoder-Decoder architecture. The encoder-decoder architecture aims to transform the input sequence of varying lengths and structures into an output sequence per the requirement. For example, in a machine translation task, the transformer can accept a sentence in one language, say Hindi, to the output sequence, say English.

The transformer achieves this using the components – encoder and decoder.

15.3.1 Encoders

What is the purpose of an encoder? The purpose of the encoder is:

1. Conversion of raw data into data into a suitable representation. This process is often called data preprocessing.
2. The encoder can capture the contextual relationships of the input sequence using attention mechanisms.
3. The focus of the encoder is to prepare a suitable context-aware representation suitable for the output. The components of an encoder are shown in Figure 15.5.

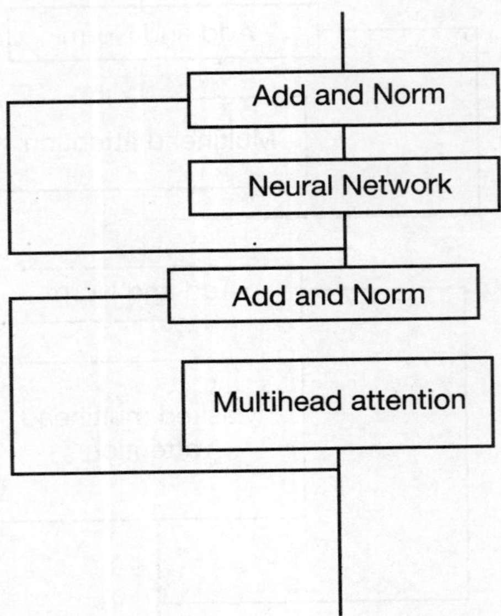

Figure 15.5 Encoder Architecture

It can be observed that the encoder has a layer of Multihead attention followed by another layer of feedforward neural networks, as shown below in Figure 15.5. In transformer architecture, often there will be many encoders, often six layers of encoders.

15.3.2 Decoders

The decoder's purpose is to:

(i) Process the input from the encoder in the encoded representation.

(ii) The decoder decodes the input representations using cross-attention and self-attention mechanisms to generate the output sequence.

(iii) A typical output of a decoder is to predict the next word based on the previously generated words and the input representations from the encoder in the case of language translation or the probability as in the case of text classification.

The decoder is shown in Figure. 15.6. There will be multiple decoders in transformers. Typically, six identical decoders would be present in a transformer.

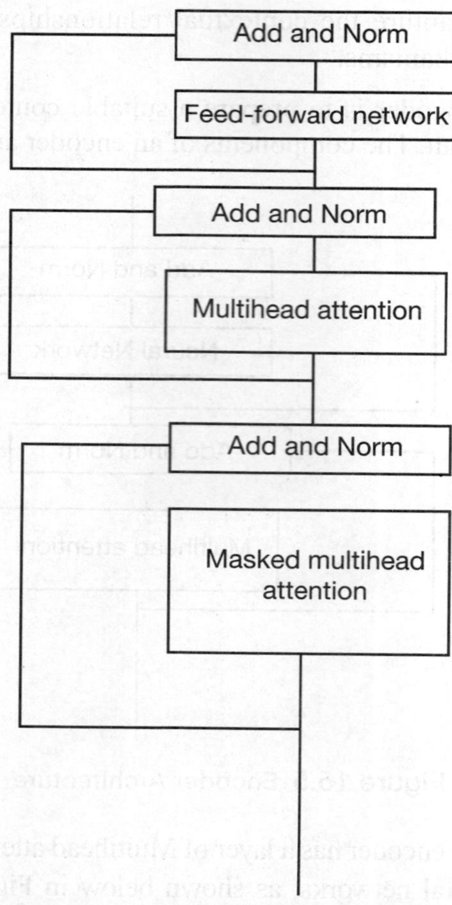

Figure 15.6 Decoder

The combined encoder-decoder structure thus handles the complex sequential transformations, can handle various lengths and structures, and provides versatility across domains such as image captioning, where the input is an image, and the output is text.

It can be observed that some of the components are the same in both the encoder and decoder. Let us discuss the interaction of encoder-decoder now.

15.3.3 Source and Target Representations

The first step is tokenization of the sentences. The source and target sentences are tokenized, and their representations are created using word and position embeddings.

Let us discuss them now.

Word Embeddings

Word embedding is the first step. The main focus is to understand the meaning of the words.

The words are converted into a form the computers can understand and operate on. This conversion is made possible by embeddings. In embeddings, all items that are similar and have similar codes are stored together.

For example, the words happy and overjoyed are similar in sentiment as both words share positive intent. Similarly, sad and depressed are similar.

This embedding step covers the sentences of length L to a matrix W of dimensions (L, d). Word embeddings take a word (or token) and generate a vector that captures the context. The embeddings are discussed in detail in the previous Chapter 14. Let us discuss the positional encoding now.

Positional Encoding

Positional encoding refers to the relative and absolute positions of the tokens in a sequence. Positional encoding is required because of the parallel processing of texts by the transformers.

Positional encoding represents the order of the words in the sequence.

Positional encoding is required because transformers process all data in parallel. So, transformers need to track the order of the words. A better system uses a mathematical function to create a unique vector for each position in a sequence. The mathematical function converts an index into an amazing set of elements. The aim is then to associate these lists to the input index.

(i) Sine/cosine functions are generally used with different frequencies along dimensions.

(ii) The dimension is chosen as the dimensionality of the word embedding.

Instead of appending, the vectors are added to get an output. The output is the same as the input and does not use additional bits. This approach is called positional encoding. However, this addition may cause some loss of information. This disadvantage is removed by adding this loss in the architecture as a form of addition. This addition ensures that the embedded information is added back after each processing.

The positional encoding for each position is given in terms of dimensions as follows:

$$\text{For odd dimension } 2i = \sin\left(\frac{p}{10000^{2i/d}}\right)$$

$$\text{For even dimension } 2i+1 = \cos\left(\frac{p}{10000^{2i/d}}\right)$$

Here, p is the position. 'i' is the index, and d is the dimension. It can be noted that for odd dimensions, sine function and for even dimensions, cosine functions are used. It can be noted that the odd positions are given as $2 * i$, and the even positions are given by $2 * i + 1$.

$$PE\,(p, 2i) = \sin\left(\frac{p}{10000^{2i/d}}\right)$$

$$PE\,(p, 2i+1) = \cos\left(\frac{p}{10000^{2i/d}}\right)$$

For 2-dimensions, $i = 0$ (as only two dimensions are used). The formula is reduced to

$$\text{For even dimension } d = 0,\ PE\,(p, 2i) = \sin\left(\frac{p}{10000^{0/2}}\right) = \sin(p)$$

$$\text{For odd dimension, } d = 1,\ PE\,(p, 2i+1) = \cos\left(\frac{p}{10000^{0/2}}\right) = \cos(p)$$

Example 15.3: Consider a simple sentence – "I like Chennai". Assume the dimensions as two for simplicity.

Solution:

So, the sentence to be encoded is – "I like Chennai."

1. The position of "*I*" is $p = 0$. $i = 0$ and $d = 2$. The dimension is 2, so the formula is reduced to sin(*p*) and cos(*p*), respectively.

$$PE\ (p, 0) = \sin\left(\frac{0}{10000^{\frac{0}{2}}}\right) = \sin(0) = 0$$

$$PE\ (p, 1) = \cos\left(\frac{0}{10000^{0/2}}\right) = \cos(0) = 1$$

2. The position of "Like" is $p = 1$. $i = 0$ and $d = 2$.

$$PE\ (p, 0) = \sin\left(\frac{1}{10000^{\frac{0}{2}}}\right) = \sin(1) \simeq 0.841$$

$$PE\ (p, 1) = \cos\left(\frac{1}{10000^{0/2}}\right) = \cos(1) \simeq 0.540$$

3. Position 2 ("Chennai") is $p = 2$, $i = 0$ and $d = 2$.

$$PE\ (p, 0) = \sin\left(\frac{2}{10000^{\frac{0}{2}}}\right) = \sin(2) \simeq 0.909$$

$$PE\ (0, 1) = \cos\left(\frac{2}{10000^{0/2}}\right) = \cos(2) \simeq -0.416$$

So, the positional encoding tags for '*I*' are (0, 1), "Like" is (0.841, 0.540), and "Chennai" is (0.909, –0.416).

In reality, the dimensions used for larger and many values of I are used using cosine and sine functions. This higher dimension helps to generate positional encodings at the higher dimensions.

Finally, the final input X concatenates W and *P*., i.e., $X = W + P$.

15.3.4 Attention Layers

As discussed in the last section, attention mechanisms derive query, key, and value from the input embeddings using linear transformations. Then, the attention score is obtained by the dot product of the query and key vectors. Softmax is applied to normalize the values. The normalized values are called weights. The weights are used to find the weighted sum of values. The weights are the output of the attention mechanism.

Self Attention

The next step is to project input x_i into three matrices W_q W_k, and W_v. The weight matrices are randomly initialized, and weights are learned during training. The computation can be done using the formula:

$$attention(Q, K, V) = soft\max\left(\frac{QK^T}{\sqrt{d_k}}\right)V$$

Multihead Attention

Multihead-attention means the input sentence is split into multiple parts. The attention mechanism is applied to each part separately. Here, the transformer used h parallel self-attention heads. Normally, the value of *h* is 8. Each head operates on different aspects of the information. Each head learns separately.

This learning is given as a formula as below:

$$head_i = attention(W_q^i Q, W_k^i K, W_v^i V)$$

The final result is the combination of all heads. Multihead attention helps to capture the different types of relationships across the various parts of the sentence.

All head outputs are concatenated and multiplied with the weight W_o to get the final matrix z_i. The value z_i is the output of input x_i.

Masked Multihead Attention

The decoder's masked multihead attention mechanism (Refer to Figure 15.4) aims to predict the next word or character. Masked multi-attention helps pay attention selectively to certain positions placed before the "Mask" while ignoring the rest of the future ones. Thus, this masking is done so that attention is paid only to the words encountered so far and not the future words.

This concept is implemented by assigning infinity to all the weights in the weight matrix. The masked attention is given as follows:

$$maskedattention(Q,K,V) = soft\max\left(\frac{QK^T + M}{\sqrt{d_k}}\right)V$$

The scaled values are used for the past values and zero is the future tokens.

Cross Attention

Cross-attention is a distinct mechanism. It handles two sequences. Normally, it is useful for translation. Let us consider the translation of English to German.

1. The input sequence is an English sentence.
2. The output sequence is a German sentence.
3. The query is from the output of the decoder.
4. The key and values come from the output of the encoder.

Here, the query vectors from the target sentence and key/values are used for the entire input sequences. The dot product of the queries is done with the keys, and scaled output is sent to softmax. The output of the softmax gives the attention weights. Then, the weighted sum is computed.

The purpose is to learn the attention relationship between the entire input sequence and target output at a time. Cross-attention allows one sequence to attend the other sequences.

So, the influence of English words is computed in the translation. Based on this, the relevant parts of the German are considered. Based on this, the next word is predicted in the output German sentence. This process is continued until the sentence is complete.

15.3.5 Add and Normalize

The purpose of normalization is to make the data uniform across the networks. This normalization process involves:

1. Computation of mean and variance.
2. Subtracting the mean from input and dividing that by variance. It is given mathematically as

$$\frac{x-\mu}{\sigma+\varepsilon}$$

Here, x is the input data, μ is the mean, σ is the standard deviation, and ε is a small constant intended to avoid the division by zero error.

The output of the transformations is combined with the original input through a residual connection. This step is called "Add".

The skip connections are also known as residual connections. The motivation is to reduce the required amount of work. The residual networks lead to a smaller network, ensuring faster computations. This idea ensures that one can skip the nodes by ignoring specific nodes.

In add-norm, the output is the transformed output and the original input. The input x is short-circuited with z and passed as input for the add and norm layer. This layer aims to ensure the smooth flow of gradients in backpropagation, help capture the complex relationship in input data, and generalization. Hence, this layer provides an overall stability of the learning process.

15.3.6 Feedforward Networks

The Feedforward stage comes after the attention layers. This feedforward network complements the attention mechanisms. The main purpose of the feedforward networks is to bring the non-linearity into the system. The focus of feedforward networks is to

i. The feedforward networks act upon the output of attention mechanisms independently. Hence, the local/complex transformations can be done independently.
ii. Attention mechanisms are linear. Neural networks bring the non-linearity into the system. Hence, the transformers can capture more complex patterns

and dependencies that are missed by the attention mechanism. Also, neural networks add more depth and complexity to the transformers.

iii. Ensure that specific adjustments can be done locally. This attention mechanism and feedforward network combination balances global processing and local feature transformations.

15.3.7 Output

The output of the final encoder layers is the input sequence's complex, high-level embeddings.

There are some limitations of transformers. Some of them are listed below.

1. Attention can deal with only fixed-length text strings. So, splitting the variable-length text into fragments of fixed length is necessary. After fixed-length vectors are formed, it is fed into the system.
2. The splitting can cause "context fragmentation," as splitting may result in the loss of context.

15.4 Overview of Large Language Models

Large Language Models (LLM) are AI models designed to understand the natural languages. LLMs are advanced deep-learning models to mimic human capabilities in text generation. The "large" in LLM refers to the fact that neural models are trained over vast text data. A language model is designed to understand and generate human language. Some of the popular LLMs are shown in Box. 15.3.

Box 15.3 Popular LLMs

LLMS are used in day-to-day life. Some of the popular LLMs are listed below:

1. Virtual Assistants – Apple Siri, Google Assistant, Amazon Alexa
2. Chatbots – Google BARD, Claude, Jasper AI.
3. Language Translation – Google Translate is a popular LLM that converts a language to another language.
4. Email Composing – Gmail smart email composing is another example of LLMs.
5. Search Engines – Google uses BERT, an LLM, to refine search queries and deliver accurate content.

6. Education – DuoLingo is another popular LLM.
7. Recommendation Systems – LLM can offer recommendations like Netflix, Amazon, and Personalized News Channels.

Also, some of the listed LLMs are famous.

1. ChatGPT – An LLM for text generation.
2. BART Series – A Google LLM
3. T5 – A text-to-text transformer.
4. XLNet – Developed by Google.
5. OpenAI Codex – GPT-based code generation.

LLMs are generative models that generate text, images, and even video. Some of the capabilities of LLM are given below:

1. Text prediction:
   LLM can estimate the probability distributions of different possibilities of the words and can predict the next word or sentence. This ability helps in text generation.
2. Text generation:
   LLM can generate texts.
3. Understanding of a context:
   LLM can capture the context meaning or relationships among the words.
4. Generalization:
   LLM can generalize the training data to perform various NLP tasks like:
   i. Text Generation
   ii. Text Summarization
   iii. Text Classification
   iv. Text Translation
   v. Sentiment analysis
   vi. Chatbots / Assistants
   vii. Question / Answering

The advantages and disadvantages of LLMs are given in the following Table 15.4.

Table 15.4 Advantages and Disadvantages of LLMs

Advantages	Disadvantages
LLMs can generate, summarize, and translate text.	Ethical considerations are there as the generated texts may be unreliable or biased due to the poor quality of the training data.
LLMs can be used as conversational agents.	The accuracy of the output may be a problem.
LLMs can be used for human-computer Interfaces.	The hallucination of facts where the LLMs are not trained for this kind of data,
	Huge amounts of resources are required like energy requirements.

15.4.1 Architecture of LLM

LLMs can be constructed in many ways. Some of the LLMs constructed are shown in Figure 15.7.

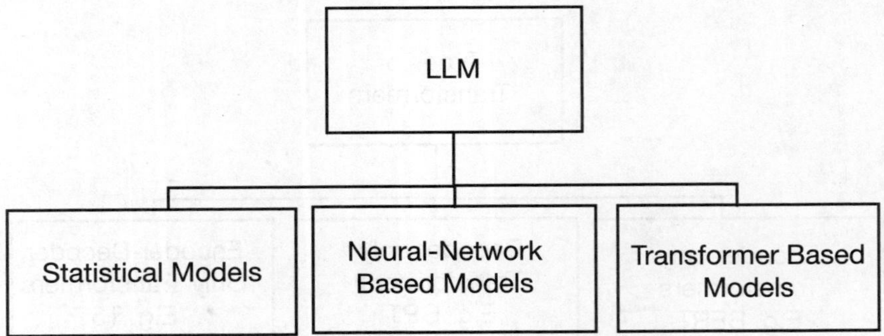

Figure 15.7 Types of LLM Models

But transformers-based LLMs are the state-of-the-art models. Primarily, all modern LLMs are transformer-based architectures.

A typical LLM architecture is shown in the following Figure. 15.8.

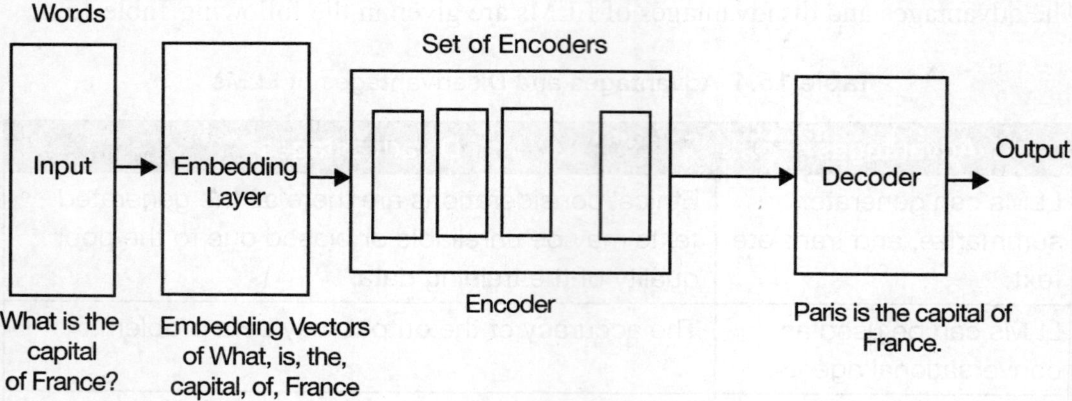

Figure 15.8 Architecture of LLM

It can be seen that two major components of LLM are encoders and decoders.

The encoder creates a context and introduces non-linearity in the prediction process.

The role of the decoder is to generate a context based on the context produced by the encoder context and the output of the words generated so far. The decoder generates one word at a time based on the probabilities.

LLMs can be constructed using encoders or decoders only, or both. Some of the LLMs that are constructed based on transformer architecture are shown in Figure 15.9.

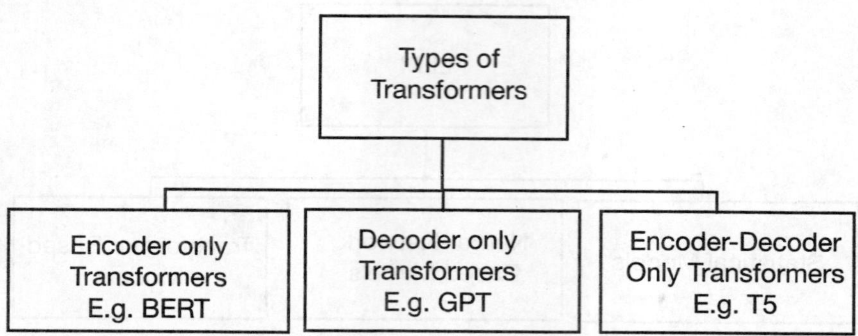

Figure 15.9 Types of LLMs based on Transformers

BERT is constructed only encoders, and there are no decoders in BERT. GPT uses only decoders, and T5 uses both encoders and decoders.

15.4.2 Process of LLMs

The LLM process is given in Figure. 15.10.

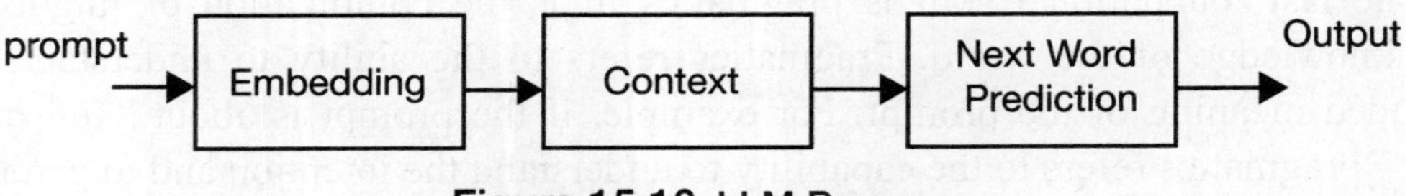

Figure 15.10 LLM Process

The input for LLM is a prompt. The next important is the embeddings. As discussed, the need is to transform the inputs into embeddings. Context generation is the most important stage. The attention scores are used to weigh the value vectors of each word. Then, the context vectors are used to predict the probability of the next word. Finally, the word is generated. The output of LLM is the probability distribution that can be sampled to generate the text.

15.4.3 Pretraining and Fine Tuning of LLMs

The main focus of the LLM training is to capture the syntactical aspects, linguistic aspects, knowledge of the world, and language pragmatics. These four aspects of the language are called the foundational capabilities of LLM.

The four foundational capabilities are listed below:

i. Syntactical aspects of the language.
ii. Lexical aspects of the language.
iii. Knowledge of the world.
iv. Pragmatic aspects of the language.

Consider an application like sentiment analysis. The focus of LLM is to understand the prompt and to generate coherent replies. Here, The LLM focuses on generating a well-formed and grammatically correct sentence. This generation requires the knowledge of syntax and grammar and is called the syntactic aspects of the language. The generated sentence's nouns, subjects, verbs and adverbs should be well placed as a human-generated language. Proficiency in using the words is called lexical aspect.

Some queries like comparisons require knowledge of the world. For example, to compare the flowers, one must know all the flowers. Hence, LLM should know the world and its usage of the existing knowledge to make sense.

The last foundational skill is pragmatics. It is the combination of linguistics and knowledge of the world. Pragmatics refers to the ability to understand the intended meaning of the prompt. For example, if the prompt is about "Tell me a Joke," pragmatics refers to the capability to understand the intention and to generate sentences based on the context.

Training

LLMs require the foundational capability. Hence, LLMs should be trained in many books, articles, social media sites, and news. The data should be very large, and its learning requires many parameters.

It is not easy to get the labelled data. So, LLM uses a self-supervised method. For example, consider the sentence, The Sun sets in the west. This sentence is posed as -

- The Sun sets in the _______.

The masked word is west. It is known to us. This knowledge serves as the ground truth for checking the validity of LLM. This kind of learning is called the self-supervision method.

The stages of LLM training are similar to the normal neural network training. The steps are given below:

1. In the forward pass, the input is given.
2. The error is computed between the actual output word and the expected word.
3. The gradient of the loss function is computed.
4. Based on the gradient, the parameters are adjusted.
5. The network is checked for convergence.

Once the neural network is converged, the training process is over. Two variations in LLM training are there as shown in Figure 15.11.

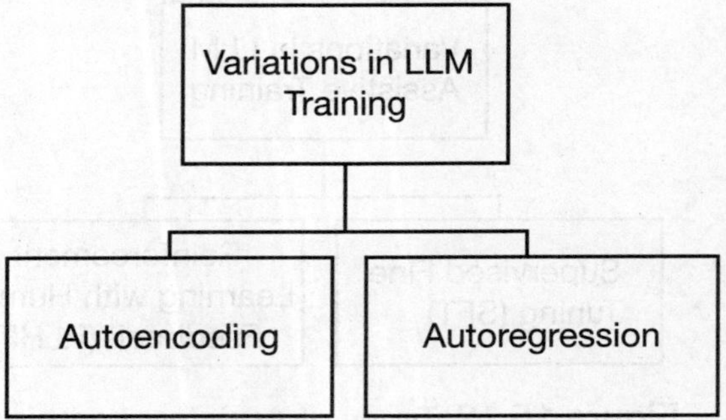

Figure 15.11 Variations in LLM Training

In autoencoding, the model can see both the words before and after the blank to predict the missed words.

For Example, The Sun _______ in the west in all countries.

Here, the model can check the context of the words before and after the word that needs to be predicted.

LLMs use autoregressive language modelling and are trained to predict the next word. For this, consider the example.

The Sun sets in _______.

Only the words before the blank must be checked to generate the next word in the autoregression method.

Fine Tuning

LLMs, after training, can be adapted for task specific tasks. This kind of adaptation is called assistive capabilities. The generation of the next word should capture the following aspects:

1. The purpose of the prompt.
2. The tone of the language.
3. The level of the language.
4. The ethical considerations like no bias towards gender, race etc.

The compliance of the above is called assistive capability. While the foundational training is self-supervised, the assistive training is supervised learning. Assistive training takes little effort as the data amount is relatively less than the foundational training as it caters to only some aspect of the task.

Two popular methods of assistive capability are shown in Figure 15.12.

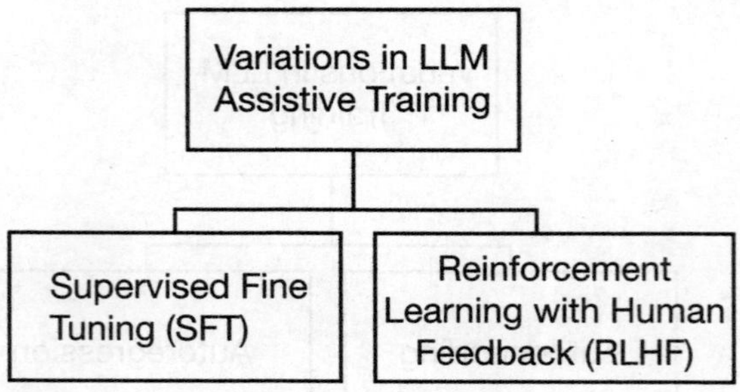

Figure 15.12 Types of Assistive Learning

Supervised Fine Tuning

The scenario of supervised fine-tuning is given in Figure 15.13.

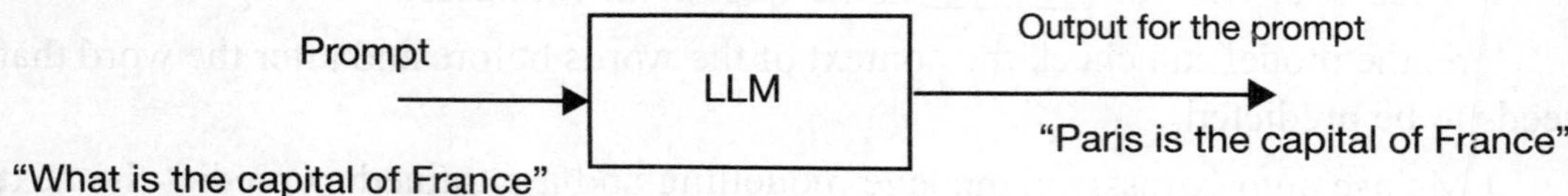

Figure 15.13 Supervised Fine Tuning

Unlike the training phase, fine-tuning is supervised learning. Fine-tuning is an example of LLM's efficiency and adaptability. In SFT, the input is given, and the actual and expected outputs are used to compute the loss. Then, the loss gradient is computed and used to update the parameters. This process is repeated till the loss nears zero. This process does not guide the next word generation but corrects the output.

Reinforcement Learning with Human Feedback (RLHF)

Reinforcement learning works by rewards and punishments. The core idea is to reward useful actions and to penalize the operations that are not desirable. This model can be implemented by modifying the SFT model by incorporating the feedback mechanism shown below in Figure 15.14. Here, the responses are used to train the model.

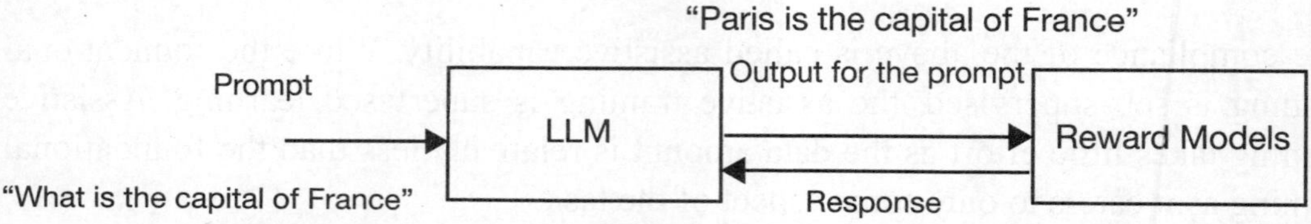

Figure 15.14 Reinforcement Learning with Human Feedback

The model reinforces the correct behaviour as the correct responses carry high rewards.

15.5 Google BERT

BERT (Bidirectional Encoder Representations from Transformers) is a transformer-based architecture aiming to generate word representations that include context.

What is the need for BERT? The problem with the sequential data is that it must be processed sequentially. Bidirectional LSTM solves this problem to some extent. Google designed BERT, using which many machine learning tasks are possible. The advantage of BERT is that it can be fine-tuned as a single layer to do state-of-the-art machine-learning tasks.

BERT was developed and published by Jacob Devlin, Min-Wei Chang, Kenton Lee, and Kristina Toutanova in a paper titled "BERT: Pretraining of Deep Bidirectional Transformers for Language Understanding" in 2018. BERT is a type of AI model and is good for understanding language by fully understanding the context of all words in a sense.

BERT's specialty is that it processes the text in a bi-directional (Left to right and right to left), thereby capturing the context of a word by looking at the words that come before and after that. Thus, BERT captures context in both directions.

The variants of BERT are given in Box 15.4.

The result is improved performance in search engines, natural language translation, Text summarization, and question/answering.

Box 15.4 variants of BERT Architectures

There are two variants of BERT models.

One model is Base 12, with 12 attentional heads and 110 million parameters.

The Base 24 configuration has 24 encoders, 16 attention heads, and 340 million parameters.

BERT is a task-agnostic model and can be installed as a service and a family of Bert models as Bert Base, uncased, Bert large-cased, Base-Cased, Large-uncased, Base-multilingual, Base-Multilingual- old, Bert-Chinese. Based on BERT, many models like ALBERT, ROBERTA, SCIBERT, and ERNIE are available in the literature.

15.5.1 BERT Architecture

BERT is a transformer-based architecture that uses only encoders. Each encoder has two mechanisms.

1. Multihead self-attention
2. Position wise feedforward networks

BERT uses a bidirectional transformer coder where attention is done in both directions – left and right. The capacity of BERT architecture is characterized by:

1. Number of layers L.
2. The size of the hidden layer representation H.
3. The number of bidirectional self-attention heads.

BERT is trained on huge amounts of data. This process involves a collection of many datasets.

The first step is the tokenization of the input data. The tokenization used by BERT is a complex process shown in Figure 15.15.

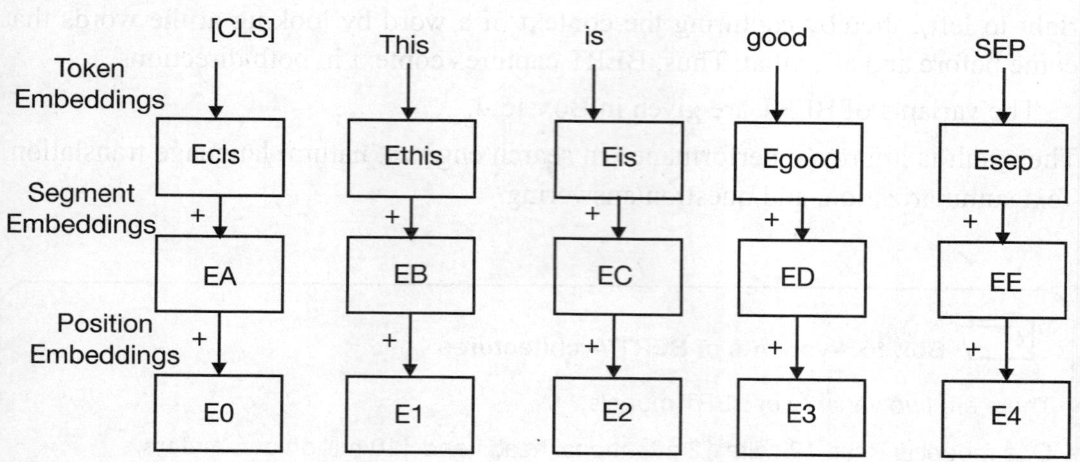

Figure 15.15 Illustrations of BERT

It can be observed that three mechanisms are used.

1. **Token Embeddings:** These are embeddings of the specific word. There are some special tokens like [CLS], a special token that is used for classification.

Similarly, a special token [SEP] separates two sentences. Later, attention mechanisms are used to differentiate these special tokens from the actual tokens.

2. **Segment Embeddings:** Specific words are taken as segments, and embeddings are created.

3. **Positional Embeddings:** BERT learns and uses positional embeddings to express the position of words.

The sentence is tokenized, embeddings are carried out, and words are combined to get segments. Then, segment embedding is done. Then, finally, positional embeddings are carried out.

The tokens are converted to BERT vocabulary using a BERT tokenizer. The input of BERT is restricted to 512 tokens. If a sentence exceeds 512 tokens, the input sequence is split to fit 512 tokens. In reality, the 128 tokens limit is used for computational performance. The above-said process is the process of padding or truncating the length to be of a fixed length.

The final input representation is obtained by adding all these three types of embeddings. This final representation is used for pretraining.

These input tokens are sent to the masked attention mechanism of BERT of the pretraining stage.

15.5.2 Pretraining of BERT

BERT is a pretrained model where the training is carried out on Wikipedia (2500 million words) and Book Corpus (800 million words). BERT takes a sentence or a pair of sentences as input. BERT uses unsupervised learning on the huge corpus of text.

Two techniques are used to improve the performance of BERT. One mechanism is the masked language model, and another is the next sentence prediction.

Let us discuss them now:

Masked Language Model (MLM)

In MLM, the model randomly masks some percentage of words and predicts the masked words based on the context.

In the masked language model, certain words are masked. For example, for the sentence

I like orange fruit.

The word "Orange" is masked and posed as

I like ---------- fruit.

Then the aim is to predict it by the missing token using right and left context. This process is repeated repeatedly. The method of the masked-language model is implemented as follows –

1. Randomly masks the token; the objective is to determine the vocabulary identification number from both contexts.
2. Use the left and right context and use them for pretraining

   However, the process of masking all the words and predicting is a time-consuming task. So, only 15% of the words are masked. A softmax layer can be used to predict the masked words. The performance is better if the predicted words are closer to the actual data. All the predicted words will have the exact word embeddings.

How are the masked words selected? One approach is to use 80% of words masked with [MASK] tokens. For Example, My rose is [MASK].

In this example, 10% of tokens are masked with random words like My rose is milk. Masked sentences add noise to the dataset. Otherwise, the model would not learn and instead may plagiarise as it is. The 10% of the training is with the actual words, like – my rose is beautiful.

Next Sentence Prediction

In this step, the focus is on understanding the relationship of sentences. Generally, it is used as a pair of sentences. The model receives a pair of sentences. The focus is to check whether the second sentence is the pair of the first sentence in the original document.

So, for example, if the BERT generates two sentences, A and B, the aim is to learn whether sentence B is the following sentence in the corpus or whether B is a random sentence.

This stage's input is sentences tagged with [CLS] and [SEP].

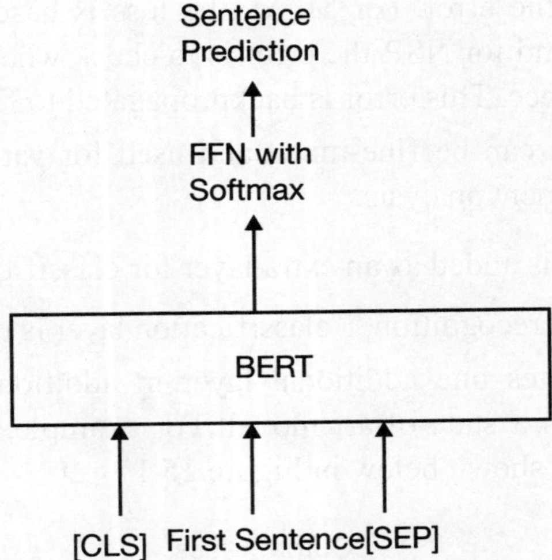

Figure 15.16 Next Sentence Prediction

The next sentence prediction is shown in Figure 15.16. The Feedforward network and softmax function classify and tag sentences as "IsNext" and "NotNext."

It is necessary to choose 50% of the pairs as following actual sentences, and for the remaining 50%, the second sentence should be random. For example,

[CLS] Peter went to [MASK] mall [SEP]
He bought a nice dress [SEP]

It would be a tag 'ISNEXT' as buying a dress is more appropriate for sentence A if the predicted word for the [MASK] is shopping. On the other hand,

[CLS] Peter went to [MASK] mall [SEP]
He bought a nice dress [SEP]

One can conclude that the second sentence is random, and its tag should be "NotNext."

Fine-Tuning

The created models enable understanding the patterns and structures that can be fine-tuned. In this stage, a limited task-specific dataset is used. The loss functions are used to compute the error. For MLM, the loss is based on how well the next tokens are predicted and for NSP, the error is to check whether the second sentence follows the first sentence. This error is backpropagated to find optimal parameters.

The created model can be fine-tuned and used for various tasks ranging from classification to sentiment analysis.

1. A softmax layer is added as an extra layer for classification.
2. For named entity recognition, a classification layer is used to identify the NER.

   Fine-tuning creates one additional layer in addition to the existing layers. This step creates a state-of-art model. For example, fine-tuning is done for classification, as shown below in Figure 15.17.

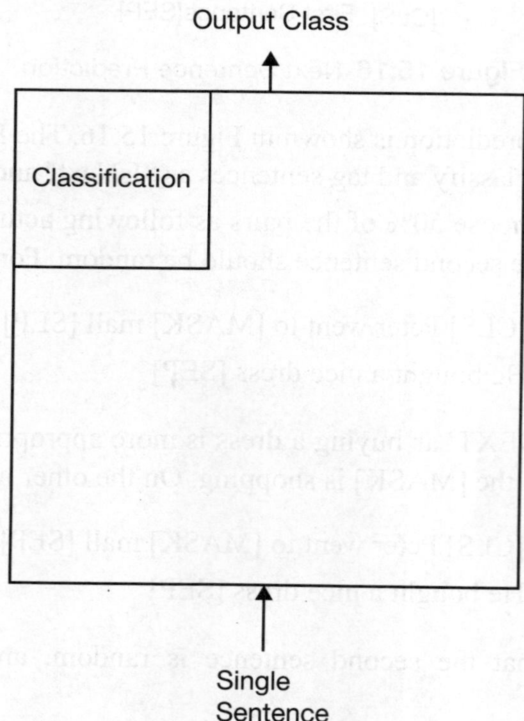

Figure 15.17 BERT Classification Model

BERT can be used to classify texts as Not spam and spam. The outline of the project would be as follows:

- Data scrubbing for data

- The preprocessing step is where the data is conditioned in 3D form.
- Use the hugging face transformer that creates a classification model.
- Fit the data.
- Evaluate the results.

15.6 ChatGPT

GPT-3 is a decoder model. The model consists of a series of transformers that operate on word embeddings. GPT is a decoder-based transformer-based model as it uses only the decoders of a transformer. It uses a series of layers comprising self-attention mechanisms and neural networks (Refer Box 15.5)

Box 15.5 History of GPT

GPT stands for Generative Pretrained Transformer. It is a transformer-based architecture. It aims to generate a text that is coherent and contextually appropriate,

OpenAI released GPT-1 This and pretrained on a dataset of 40 GB. It used 1.5 billion parameters.

GPT-2 was released in 2019. It was trained on 570 GB of text data and used 1.5 trillion parameters.

GPT-3 was released in 2020. The sequence length is 2048 tokens long. The batch size of tokens is 3.2 million. GPT-3 uses 96 transformers. It uses 96 attention heads. This model was trained on 570 GB of data and has 175 billion parameters.

GPT-4 was released in 2021. It was trained on many TB of data with 500 billion parameters.

The only purpose of this model is to generate a word at a time based on the words that come before and not after that. Hence, they are called autoregressive models.

GPT style is an autoregressive model. For example, consider a sentence.

"India is a beautiful Country"

The probability of the full sentence is given as

Pr("India is a beautiful Country") = Pr(India) * Pr(Is/India) * Pr(a/India is) * Pr(beautiful/India is a) * Pr(Country/India is a beautiful).

It can be observed that the joint probability of N tokens $\Pr(t_1, t_2, \cdots, t_n)$ is given as

$$\Pr(t_1, t_2, \cdots, t_n) = \Pr(t_1) \prod_{n=2}^{N} \Pr(t_n / t_1, t_2, \cdots, t_{n-1})$$

The focus is maximizing the tokens' log probability to generate the next word.

15.6.1 Pretraining and Finetuning of GPT

GPT is trained on a large corpus of data. GPT uses unsupervised learning using a vast amount of books, websites, and other sources of websites. Then, this knowledge is used to generate the next word.

The training process of GPT is given as follows:

1. The input text is tokenized.
2. The tokens are converted into embeddings.
3. The embeddings are the input to the masked attention. So, only the current and previous tokens are attended. All the future words have no relevance. The goal is to predict the next word.
4. The linear layer maps each word embedding to the vocabulary size.
5. The loss is computed
6. The loss is propagated back to minimize the error.
7. Finally, Softmax converts this into a set of probabilities.

Fine-tuning

GPT is fine-tuned for specific tasks to adapt a particular application style. This fine-tuning is limited to a small task-specific dataset.

15.6.2 Prompt Engineering

Prompts are used to elicit useful and accurate responses from the model.

P Tell me about Indian mathematician Ramanujan in five lines

R Here's a brief overview of Srinivasa Ramanujan:
Ramanujan was an Indian mathematician who made significant contributions to number theory.He self-studied mathematics and traveled to Cambridge University, where he worked with G.H. Hardy.
Ramanujan discovered the'taxicab numbers' and made important findings on elliptic curves and infinite series. Despite poor health, he published over 300 papers during his lifetime. Sadly, Ramanujan passed away in 1920 at just 32 years old due to illness.

Figure 15.18 Prompt and its Response

In the Gpt4all, an open-source GPT (https://gpt4all.io/index.html) is shown in Figure 15.18 illustrates a prompt and its response. The prompt is "Tell me about Indian Mathematician Ramanujan in five lines, " and its output is shown in Figure 15.18.

To generate the response for any text generation system like GPT is a prompt. A starting point is a token. This token is called a prompt. Some essential requirements of the prompts are accuracy, relevancy, and consistency.

This prompt is fed into the network, and then the output is the probability over all possible subsequent tokens. The most likely token or any token from the probability distribution can be picked. This sequence is again fed to the network to generate the next token. This process is continued till the large body of the text is generated.

Prompt Engineering is the art and science of designing prompts that require knowledge and strategy. For example, the output generated is huge if one removes the words in five lines in the above prompt, as shown in Figure 15.18.

1. In autoencoding, the model can see both the words before and after the blank for predicting the missed words.

   For Example, The Sun -------------- in the East in all countries.

   Here, the model can check the context of the words before and after the word that needs to be predicted.

2. In Autoregressive language modelling, Only the words before the blank must be checked to generate the next word. Consider the Example.

   The Cat is --------.

Beam Search

How to generate the next word? One strategy the model uses is beam search with top-k words.

Beam search is a heuristic method algorithm used to predict the next word. This algorithm constructs and explores a graph by explaining the promising nodes. This explanation is limited to only a fixed number of nodes. This fixing of exploring a range of nodes is called beam search. Then, the methods keep only Top-k words at each step and prune all other nodes.

For example, consider the following Mathematica script, where the prompt is given as

"Ramanujan was a great Mathematician". The Top 5 probabilities of the next word and its histogram are given in Figure 15.19.

```
In[6]:= topProbs = lm["Ramanujan was a great Indian Mathematician",
        {"TopProbabilities", 5}]

Out[6]= { but → 0.0219882,  who → 0.129204,
         . → 0.187816,  and → 0.205444, , → 0.219619}
```

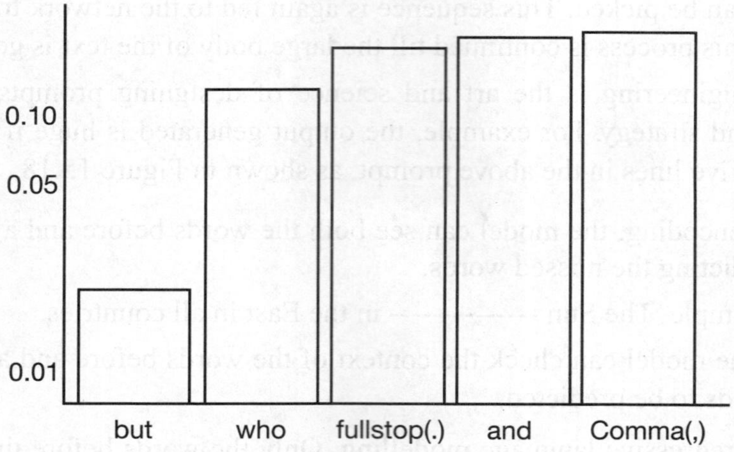

Figure 15.19 Histogram of the Predicted Words

It can be seen the top 5 tokens are given in Figure 15.19. It can be observed that the most likely word is "comma (,)" in the output.

The beam search strategy ensures a balance between width and consistency.

15.6.3 Zero-Shot and Few-Shot Learning

The focus is to generalize the model from a relatively smaller amount of data, usually a few minimal examples. This ability of the model to learn from a few examples per class makes GPT training very attractive. The learning strategies of GPT are listed as

1. **Zero-Shot:**
   In this case, GPT requires no examples. The model is expected to predict a new example that has never been seen before in the training dataset. What will it do? The model uses existing information (Semantics and class information) to infer the class of the new data. Zero-shot allows the model to generalize without the need for any examples.
2. **One-Shot Learning:**
   One-shot learning is a deep learning technique where the model is trained to learn from a single example to predict the class of the new example along with the existing knowledge.
3. **Few-Shot:**
   A few examples and existing knowledge are used here to make sense of the new query and produce results.

Summary

1. Transformers are replacements for LSTMs for handling sequence data.
2. Transformers can handle longer dependencies and capture complex contextual patterns.
3. Attention mechanisms focus on certain words while ignoring the rest of the words.
4. Attention mechanisms use self-attention mechanisms.
5. Scoring functions measure the similarity between the query and key vectors.
6. Some self-attention algorithms are dot product, scaled dot product, Long, and multiplicative algorithms.
7. The multihead mechanism measures multiple scores and increases the quality.
8. Transformer architectures have two components – encoder and decoder.
9. Positional encoding encodes the positions of the words in a sentence.
10. Masked multihead mechanism aims to predict the next character or word.
11. Cross-attention measures the attention relationship among input and output sequences.

12. Layer norm is a regularization step.
13. LLMs are designed to understand and generate texts.
14. LLMs are transformer-based architectures.
15. LLM process involves input, embedding, context generation, and the next word generation.
16. The foundational capabilities of LLM are syntactical, lexical, knowledge of the world, and pragmatic aspects of the language.
17. LLM uses the self-supervised method for training.
18. The variations in LLM training are autoencoding and autoregression.
19. In autoencoding, the models use the words before and after the masked word to capture the contextual information.
20. In autoregression, LLM uses only words before masked words for prediction.
21. Fine-tuning is a kind of adaptation of the model for certain tasks. Two variations in fine-tuning are supervised fine-tuning (SFT) and reinforcement learning with human feedback (RLHF).
22. In SFT, the loss is computed between the predicted and actual words, and this process is repeated till the error becomes zero. RLHF is a feedback mechanism to tune the model.
23. Bidirectional Encoder Representations from Transformers (BERT) is a transformer-based model. BERT is an example of an encoder-only transformer. The inputs for BERT are token embeddings, segment embeddings, and positional embeddings.
24. The techniques used for BERT are Masked Language Models (MLM) and Next Sentence Prediction (NSP).
25. BERT can be fine-tuned for tasks like text classification, summarization, Sentiment analysis, and Question/Answering.
26. GPT is a decoder-based transformer model. GPT is trained on a large corpus of data.
27. Prompt Engineering is the art and science of designing prompts for LLMs.
28. Prompts elicit useful and accurate responses from the model.
29. The strategies are beam-search and Top-K.
30. Zero-shot learning is based on existing knowledge and description.
31. In few-shot learning, a few examples and existing knowledge are used to make sense of new queries and produce results.

Glossary

1. Transformer – Transformer is a new class of language models.
2. Attention and Attention Mechanism - The ability to focus on certain words and ignore others is called attention.
3. Query – A query focuses on the contribution of other words for the context.
4. Key – Determine the attention that must be paid to the query.
5. Value – The content is called the value.
6. Scoring function – The scoring function measures the similarity between the key and query vector.
7. Self-reference – The attention of the word upon itself is called self-reference.
8. Encoder – Encoders encode the input in a suitable for data representation.
9. Decoder – Decoders decode the encoded information for producing output.
10. Positional encoding - Positional encoding is a technique to encode the words' positions in a sentence.
11. LLM – An AI model designed to understand and generate natural languages.
12. Foundational capabilities – The syntactical, lexical, knowledge of the world and pragmatics are called foundational capabilities.
13. Autoencoding – The model's ability to use the missing words for prediction.
14. Autoregressive models – The model can use words before and after the blank to find the missing word.
15. Supervised fine tuning (SFT) – SFT is a supervised technique for fine-tuning LLM.
16. Reinforcement learning-based human feedback (RLHF) – A reinforcement learning-based technique for fine-tuning LLM.
17. Bidirectional encoder representations from transformers (BERT) – An encoder-only-based transformer-based architecture.
18. Masked language model (MLM) – The MLM model is a self-supervised technique for training BERT.
19. Next sentence prediction (NSP) – The NSP model is a self-supervised technique for training BERT.
20. Generative pretrained transformer (GPT) – A decoder-based model to generate the next word.

21. Prompt – Input to elicit useful and accurate responses.
22. Prompt engineering – The art and science of designing and using prompts.
23. Beam search – A technique for choosing the most likely word.
24. Top-k – A technique for choosing a word randomly from top-k possibilities.
25. Zero-shot – Zero-shot is a technique of using the existing knowledge to give the response.
26. Few-shot – Few-shot is a technique of using only a few examples along with the existing knowledge to do NLP tasks.

Short Questions

1. List out the limitations of LSTM.
2. Compare and contrast transformers with LSTM.
3. What is an attention mechanism?
4. List out the ways of finding self-attention mechanisms.
5. What is a scoring function? What does it do?
6. What is a multihead attention?
7. What is an embedding?
8. Why is positional embedding required?
9. What are the components of encoders and decoders?
10. What is masked attention?
11. List out the relevance of cross-attention.
12. What is LLM?
13. Explain the LLM process.
14. What are the variations in LLM training?
15. What is SFT? Why is it required?
16. What is RLHF? Why is it required?
17. What are the specialties of BERT?
18. Explain MLM and NSP.
19. What are the specialties of GPT?
20. What is a prompt engineering?
21. Explain zero-shot and few-shot learning.
22. Explain beam-search and top-k mechanisms.

Long Questions

1. Explain in detail the transformer architecture.
2. Explain the architecture of LLM.
3. Explain the LLM process.
4. Explain the fine-tuning process of LLM. Why is it required?
5. Explain the BERT model and how text classification can be applied.
6. Explain the pretraining of the BERT model.
7. Explain the architecture of GPT.

Numerical Problems

1. Assume a dimension of one and compute the attention score of Delhi in the following sentence = "New Delhi is the capital of India."
2. Use a 3 × 3 order matrix and implement the attention score of the above sentence.
3. Use two dimensions and implement positional encoding for the above sentence.

Crossword

Across

2. A __________ function measures the similarity between the query and key.
8. Transformer is a new class of language model, (true/false)
9. The __________ of the transformer does the data representation of the input.
10. __________ is used to elicit useful and accurate responses.
11. NSP predicts the continuity among the random lines, (true/false)
12. The LLM is used to understand and generate natural languages, (true/false)
13. The most likely word is obtained using __________ search.
14. Transformer cannot implement seq2seq models. (true/false)
16. BERT uses only __________ in its architecture.
19. The value and __________ correspond to the selective attention of human beings.
20. The syntactical, lexical, pragmatic, and knowledge of the web is called the __________ capabilities of LLM.
22. The query corresponds to __________ in human attention.
23. BERT is an abbreviation of Bidirectional Encoder __________ from Transformers.

Down

1. The contribution of a word can be captured by in a context.
2. SFT uses __________ learning technique for LLM.
3. The attention of a word upon itself is called self __________.
4. Top-k picks top-k likely words randomly for the next word prediction, (true/false)
5. The art and science of designing and using prompts is called __________ engineering.
6. The techniques for predicting the missing word in a sentence are autocoding and __________.
7. Encoding keeps tracks of the position of the word in a sentence.
11. GPT is an LLM. (true/false)
15. The ability to focus on certain words while ignoring all other words are called __________.
17. Zero-shot uses the __________ knowledge to give a response.
18. The MLM uses a __________ supervised technique fortraining BERT
21. __________ determine the attention that must be paid to the query.

Jumbled Sentences

H	P	Q	F	O	C	U	S	S	E	E	T	R	U	E	Z	F	N	S	R	E	F	P	C	J
U	W	T	Y	H	J	I	F	Q	L	F	M	S	U	P	U	O	C	V	Z	R	U	C	F	S
A	N	R	Z	O	P	T	D	C	D	B	C	A	K	J	M	U	T	R	U	E	K	G	M	U
P	O	U	Y	N	O	X	A	B	N	U	O	U	H	T	K	N	O	L	E	P	V	O	P	D
U	A	E	R	Q	S	Q	A	U	X	U	P	T	R	R	D	D	C	U	N	R	F	F	R	S
O	I	S	B	Y	I	K	K	E	Y	V	D	O	D	N	Y	A	R	V	C	E	Q	O	O	U
G	M	E	O	A	T	G	E	E	H	D	M	R	T	H	H	T	Y	D	O	S	Q	H	M	P
D	M	L	E	X	I	M	Y	Y	B	S	F	E	U	V	Z	I	L	P	D	E	W	P	P	E
E	L	F	L	Y	O	A	T	S	R	I	Y	G	V	W	C	O	Y	R	E	N	S	Z	T	R
D	M	E	Z	A	N	T	R	F	E	M	L	R	T	E	P	N	P	O	R	T	E	O	K	V
K	J	N	R	L	A	T	U	A	F	I	L	E	C	K	N	A	D	M	J	A	X	E	R	I
J	B	C	D	X	L	E	E	L	E	L	H	S	A	U	B	L	Y	P	Y	T	I	E	H	S
A	E	O	L	L	D	N	K	S	R	A	S	S	O	U	D	V	V	T	A	I	S	W	Y	E
K	A	D	B	W	G	T	D	E	E	R	B	I	T	Q	U	E	R	Y	L	O	T	G	T	D
K	M	E	O	D	N	I	B	L	N	I	V	O	E	T	N	T	T	C	G	N	I	C	P	W
E	M	R	W	H	A	O	S	L	C	T	X	N	C	E	B	W	T	R	Y	S	N	K	A	U
Q	W	B	E	H	O	N	H	K	E	Y	D	E	S	T	R	V	W	J	S	H	G	X	J	Z

true	false	attention	query	focus
key	key	similarity	reference	encoder
positional	true	foundational	autoregression	supervised
encoder	self	true	true	prompt
prompt	beam	true	existing	Representations

Generative AI and Generative Adversarial Networks

> Generative Adversarial Networks open up the exciting possibility of machines that can imagine and create. — **Andrew Ng**

Credits: © Andrew Ng

Generative AI is an advanced area of computer vision where deep learning models are used to generate new images, audio, and video. GAN is a new type of neural architecture that can generate new images. The learning objectives of this chapter are:

- Introduce the concept of Generative AI.
- Introduce the architecture of GAN.
- Introduce generator and discriminator components of GAN.
- Explain the training of GAN.
- Understand the evaluation of GAN.
- Study the GAN variants.
- Introduce the variational autoencoders.
- Introduce diffusion models.
- Overview of transformer-based image generation.

16.1 Overview of Generative AI

Often, it is thought that creativity and imagination are the domain of humans. Humans can imagine and create new poems and drawings to display their higher form of intelligence. Humans can paint and create new music that can entertain others and display intelligence. To mimic this in computers is a challenging task. Many thought these tasks were impossible for machines to imitate human beings. No more! Now, computers can generate new images, paintings, videos, audio, and music. The domain that deals with generating new content is called generative AI or Gen AI.

Generative AI (Gen AI) is a domain of artificial intelligence for creating new content. The primary characteristics of generated new content are that the generated content should resemble the training images in style, composition, or content. The second important characteristic is that the generated content should be diverse.

Gen AI can generate many synthetic data such as virtual environments. For many applications, the data is not available. So, generative modelling is a necessity. The developments in Generative AI are a driving factor for many domains.

Generative AI is a challenging task because of the following facts:

1. Handling the higher-dimensional data is huge and challenging.
2. Also, data generation is a higher form of intelligence, usually considered an exclusive domain of humans.

One must review the types of deep learning models to understand generative AI. The two types of deep learning models exist, as shown in Figure 16.1.

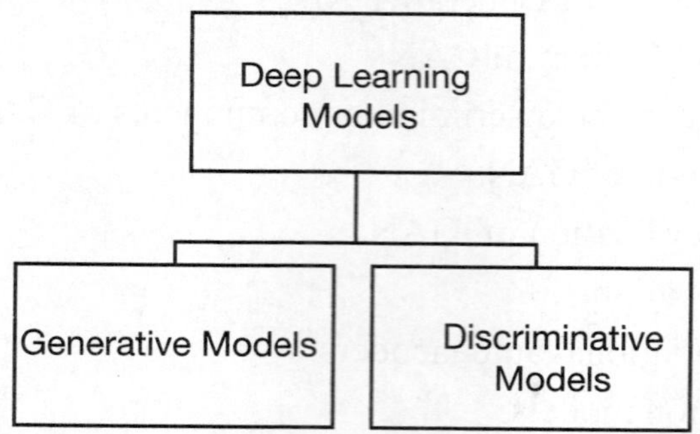

Figure 16.1 Types of Deep Learning Models

A discriminative model is a statistical model that is used to identify the distinct classes or categories in the dataset. The classification models, like classification and prediction, are discrimination models. The steps of the discriminative models are given below:

1. Each observation in the training data has a label. E.g., to classify an email as normal or spam, one has to label the data as normal or spam
2. The learning used by the discriminative model is supervised learning

3. The model learns to estimate $p(y/x)$, where y is the output label, and x is the input data. The classification or prediction models are called discriminative models. They typically take the input x and generate labels y.

The new generative modelling workflow is shown in Figure 16.2.

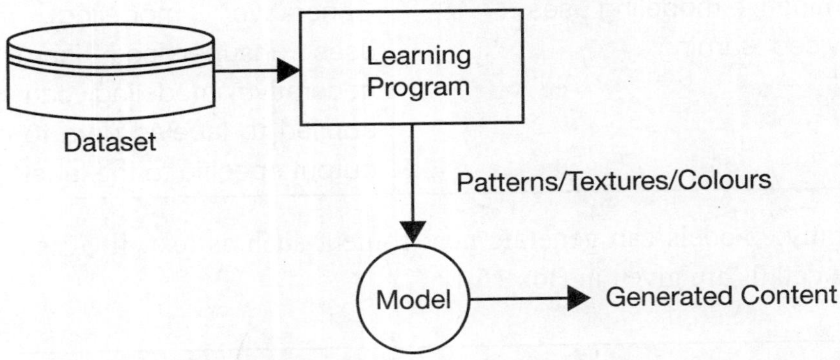

Figure 16.2 Generative Model

For the generative model, the following steps are required.

1. First, a dataset is required. The dataset has many samples of training data. Each data is called an observation data
2. The learning program generates a probabilistic model from the training set. The model is probabilistic rather than deterministic, as the model involves a random element that influences the generation process
3. The generated model learns the probabilistic distribution of the training data. The focus is to mimic the actual distribution as closely as possible. The generative model estimates $p(x)$, the probability of observing x. If labeled data is used, it ignores y in $p(x/y)$.
4. Sampling of the generated model gives new observations that look alive to the training data

The differences between discriminative and generative modelling are given in Table 16.1.

Table 16.1 Differences between Discriminative and Generative Modelling

Discriminative Modelling	Generative Modelling
1. The mathematics of discriminative modeling is finding the conditional probability $p(y/x)$, where the probability of x belongs to y. Here, x is the input, and y is the label.	The mathematics behind generative modeling is to estimate $p(x)$, the underlying distribution of input data x.

Discriminative Modelling	Generative Modelling
2. Discriminative modeling uses labeled data	Generative modeling uses unlabeled data
3. Discriminative modeling uses supervised learning.	Generative modeling primarily uses unsupervised learning. But generative modeling can also be applied to labeled data to generate output specific to the label.

The generative models can generate new content such as text, images, video, and audio. The details are given in Box 16.1.

Box 16.1 Generative Data Types

Generative models can generate a variety of outputs. Some of the data generated by Gen AI models are given below:

1. Text – Generative models can generate coherent and context-sensitive data. A good example is ChatGPT.
2. Images – Generative models can generate new and enhanced images.
3. Audio – The generative AI can generate speech, music, and sounds.
4. Video – Generative AI can generate video or enhance video.
5. 3D model – Generative AI models can generate game and virtual reality environments.
6. Synthetic data – Generative AI models can generate synthetic data for machine learning models.

Some of the popular AI generative models are given in Figure 16.3.

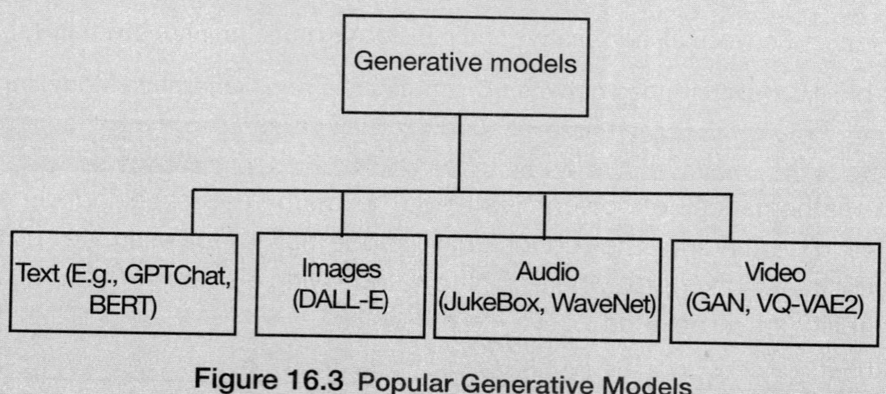

Figure 16.3 Popular Generative Models

Some models that can generate text are popular GPTChat and BERT. The details of text generation are covered in Chapter 15 of this book. Dall-E is a popular deep-learning model that can generate images. Similarly, audio and video can be generated by deep learning models.

The mathematics behind generative modelling is given in Box 16.2.

Box 16.2 Mathematics of Generative Modelling

The mathematics behind GAN is given below:

1. The GAN model takes a dataset of observations X.
2. The input data x is assumed to have an underlying distribution p_{data}.
3. The focus is to estimate a new distribution p_{model} to mimic the underlying distribution p_{data}.
4. If p_{model} is available, then this probabilistic model can be sampled to generate the new data with the following characteristics.
   a. The generated data should be similar to the images of the training data.
   b. The model should generate new data that has more diversity.

Some of the important jargons related to probability are given below:

1. Sample Space – A set of all possible observation data *x*.
2. Probability density function – *p*(*x*) is a probability density function that maps the data of *x* to a number between 0 – 1. If one sums all the numbers, it equals 1 if the distribution is well-defined.

For an observational data *x*, many distributions are possible. So, one has to find the parametric model $p_\theta(x)$, a family of distributions that can be explained using parameters θ.

The Likelihood function and the maximum likelihood function can be used to estimate the parameters θ in $p_\theta(x)$.

Some of the use cases of generative AI are given in Box 16.3.

Box 16.3 Use Cases of Gen AI

Generative models have many advantages. Some of the domains where Gen AI can be used are listed below:

1. Art and Design
2. Fashion – Clothing and Articles design
3. Entertainment
4. Medical Imaging
5. Image completion by filling in some of the missing parts of the image.
6. Picture-to-Picture Translation can convert black and white images to colour images and vice versa, Creating high-resolution images.

Some of the challenges of Gen AI are the misuse of the generated content (like DeepFakes), Ethical considerations, quality and realism of the generated content, required computational resources, and the control of the generated content.

16.2 Overview of GAN

The types of generative models are as shown in Figure 16.4.

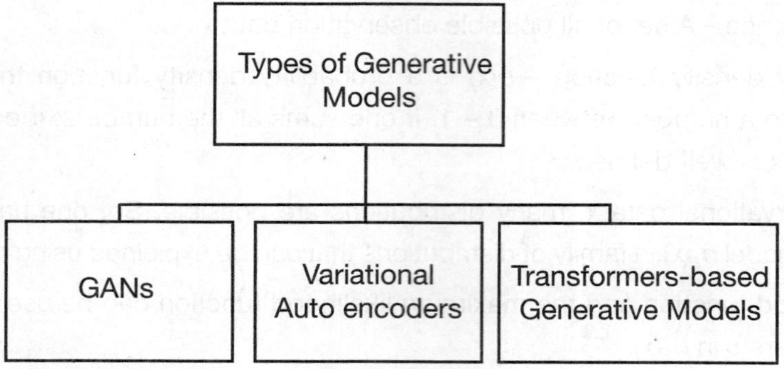

Figure 16.4 Types of Generative Models

In 2014, the Generative Adversarial model (GAN) was introduced by Ian Goodfellow and his colleagues, including Yoshua Bengio, at the University of Montreal. Ian Goodfellow published a paper titled "Generative Adversarial Nets" at the Neural Information Processing Systems (NeurIPS) conference in 2014, marking the emergence of one of the exciting technological innovations of this century.

GAN can generate new images, videos, and text. GAN has two components generator and discriminators to generate images. GANs are discussed in the next section. Variational Encoders use two components, an encoder and a decoder, to generate new images using the concept of latent spaces. Transformers–based generative models use transformers to generate the output like text. Some of the popular examples are GPTChat and BERT.

GANs are very popular, and the advantages and use cases of GANs are given in Box. 16.4.

Box 16.4 Use Cases of GAN

GANs have many advantages, such as they generalize well with small data. They can generate new content, such as high-quality images and synthetic data.

Some of the domains where GANs are used are listed below:

1. Image generation – This is also called Image synthesis. GAN can generate images and virtual environments in many domains like art and design.
2. Data Augmentation – GAN can create more images whenever the data is limited.
3. Super-resolution – GAN can create high-resolution images from low-resolution images.
4. Style Transfer – GAN can modify the content/video to reflect a style for the original content.
5. Text to Image synthesis – The textual descriptions can be converted to an image by GAN.
6. Cyber security: creating fake images
7. Entertainment – GAN can be used to create realistic characters.
8. Marketing – GAN can be used to generate advertisement content, product designs
9. Education – GANs are adept at generating educational content.

16.2.1 Principle of GAN

GAN is based on the principle of adversarial training. The purpose of adversarial training is to create robust models by giving deceptive, corrupt, or challenging examples to train a robust model. Robust models can handle tricky inputs of the real world. GAN is two neural networks that compete with each other. One neural network is called a generator, and another component is called a discriminator.

The purpose of a generator is to generate a fake image by converting a random noise into an image similar to the original image. The purpose of the discriminator is to check whether the generated image is genuine or fake. The competition among the generator and discriminator helps GAN to mimic the data distribution effectively for image generation. The relationship between the generator and discriminator is one that of counterfeiter and cop as shown in Figure 16.5.

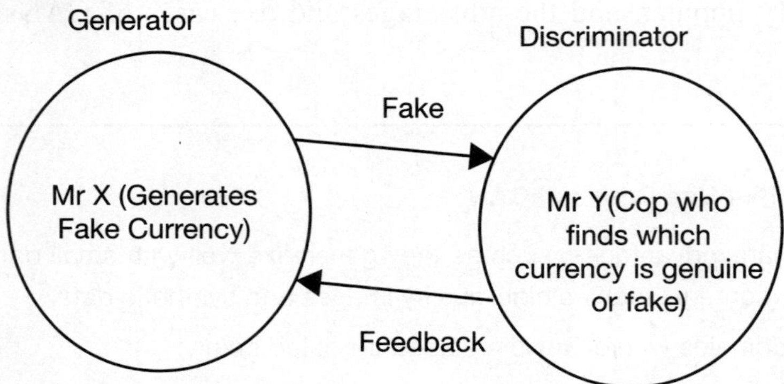

Figure 16.5 Relationship Between Generator and Discriminator

Let Mr. X be a counterfeiter (Generator) whose aim is to print the fake currency. But, Mr. Y, a cop, has to detect which one of the currencies Mr X produced is fake and which is genuine. The purpose of Mr. X is to fool Mr. Y, and Mr Y aims to avoid mistakes. The competition among these persons is that Mr. X can generate very good fake currency over time, so that Mr Y may need help distinguishing. This kind of training is called adversarial training, a repetitive process that will continue until the generator becomes adaptive in generating the content (in this case, currency!) similar to the original.

16.2.2 Implementation of a Discriminator and Generator

Consider, for a moment, the typical classification process. Let us assume that one wants to design a classifier that takes a real horse image and a fake horse image to generate a real or fake image. For this to happen, a classifier must be trained on the real and fake horse-labelled datasets (with real horses labelled as 1 and fake horses as 0), as shown in Figure 16.6.

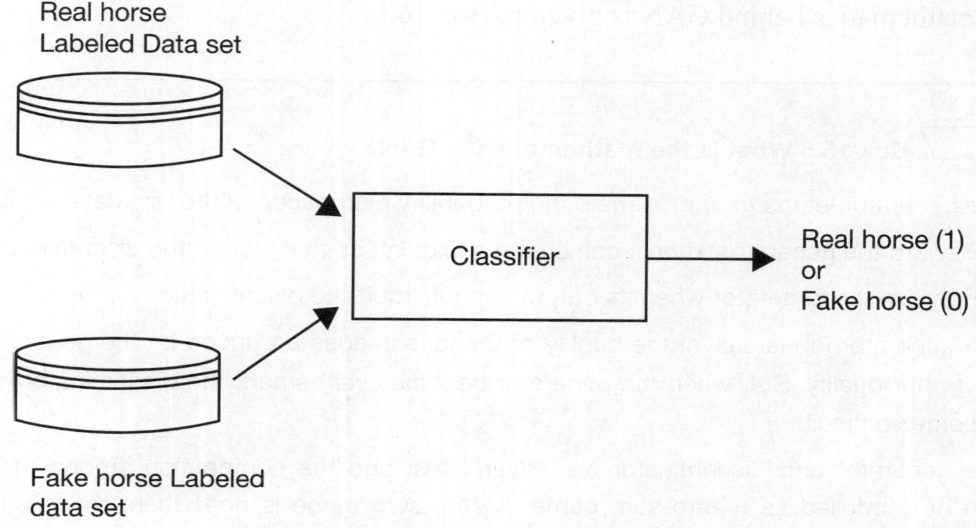

Figure 16.6 A Typical Classification Problem

Now, let us remove the fake dataset by a generator component. The generator aims to take a random noise as an input and generate fake images similar to the training set, as shown in Figure 16.7. A discriminator replaces the component classifier. The role of a discriminator is the same as that of a classifier. The purpose of the discriminator is to differentiate the real image that comes from the training set and the fake image that comes from the generator. The discriminator can be considered a cop, and the generator as a counterfeiter.

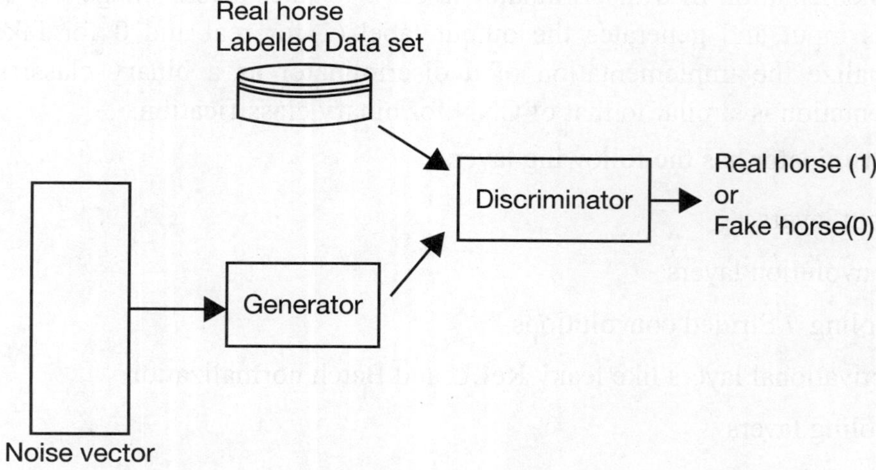

Figure 16.7 General Diagram of a GAN

The mathematics behind GAN is given in Box 16.5.

Box 16.5 What is the Mathematics of GAN?

The generator learns to approximate the probability distribution of the real data.

1. Reward the generator when it can create a fake image that "fools" the discriminator.
2. Penalize the generator when its output cannot "fool" the discriminator.

The generator job is easy if the quality of the fake images produced by the generator is of poor quality. But, when the generator becomes very smart, the discriminator job becomes difficult.

The generator and discriminator are adversaries, and the competition among them can be modelled as a zero-sum game. A zero-sum game is one where there is no competition among the players. This mathematics is modelled after game theory.

How to implement the generator and the discriminator? The neural networks can be designed to implement the generator and discriminator. The implementation details are discussed in the subsequent section.

16.2.3 Architectures of Discriminator and Generator

The implementation of a discriminator is easy. It takes a real image and the fake image as input and generates the output label (1 for real and 0 for fake). One can visualize the implementation of a discriminator as a binary classifier. The implementation is similar to that of CNN for binary classification.

The discriminator has the following layers.

1. Input layers
2. Convolution layers
3. Pooling / Strided convolutions
4. Activational layers like leaky ReLU and Batch normalization
5. Pooling layers
6. Output layers

A stack of convolutional layers can do this verification with a sigmoidal function. In a sense, the discriminator works as a binary classification problem. If the generated output is 1, the image is real. Otherwise, it is fake. The flow diagram of the typical discriminator is shown in Figure 16.8.

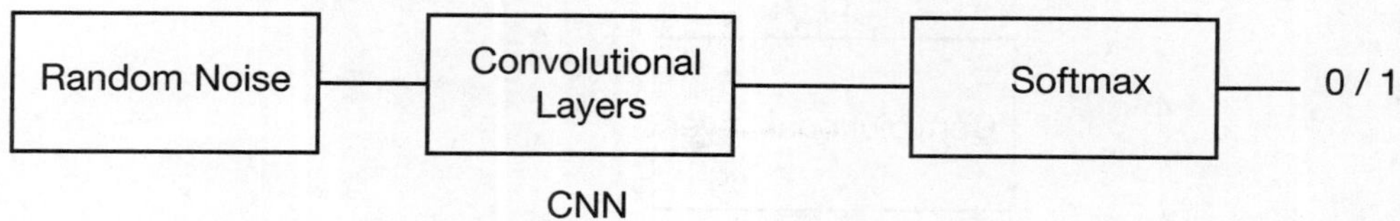

Figure 16.8 Discriminator

While the implementation of a discriminator is easy, the implementation of a generator is a little tricky. One can view a generator as an inverted CNN. The purpose of the generator is to learn the input data distribution. Then, it uses the distribution to generate new data similar to the given data.

The characteristics of the generator are to

1. Generate a new sample similar to the input data.
2. To create a diverse data.

The architecture of the generator should include the following layers as shown in Figure 16.9.

1. Input layer
2. Hidden layers
3. Reshaping layers
4. Convolutional Layers
5. Additional layers like Batch normalization and activation layers.
6. Output layer.

The details of these convolutional layers are given in a detailed manner in Chapter 9 of this book.

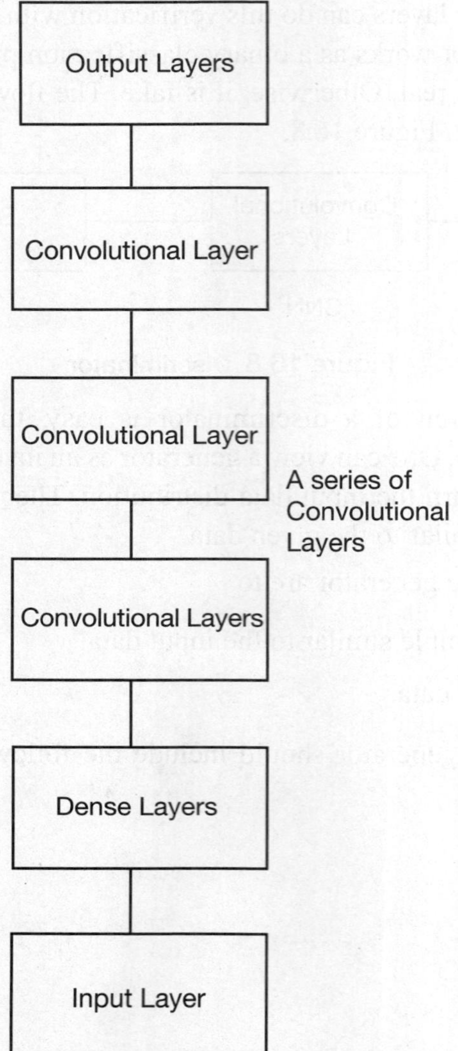

Figure 16.9 Architecture of an Image Generator

The input layer starts with a random noise generated by the Gaussian distribution. The noise vector's size is smaller than the image's size. In other words, the generator takes a random noise as input and reshapes it into a cube. Normally, the input is a 100-dimensional vector.

The dense layer takes the noise vector as input. The dense layer is a fully connected network that aims to increase the input dimensionality suitable for restructuring.

The reshaping layer takes the output of the dense layers and converts that into a 3D array or cube with height, width, and depth.

The generator's core is the convolutional layers with a series of deconvolutional layers (Transposition convolution) to upsample the input data. The lower dimensional space is converted to a higher dimensional space by increasing the spatial dimensions. The additional layers include batch normalization and activation layers. The activation function used in the generator is ReLU. The purpose of ReLU is to bring non-linearity.

The output layer uses Tanh or a sigmoidal function that produces the output. The output at this stage will equal the dimensions of the input upon which it is trained.

The generator workflow is given in Figure 16.10.

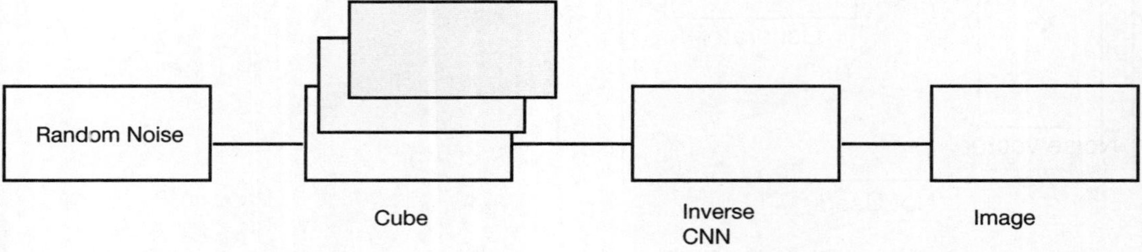

Figure 16.10 Image Generator

The training details of GAN are given in the subsequent sections.

16.2.4 Adversarial Training of GAN

The purpose of the discriminator is to differentiate the real and fake data. The network is given a labelled image. The training of the discriminator is easy. It is done using the supervised method.

Step 1: Show the real images of the database to the discriminator to generate label 1, indicating that these images are real. The loss is computed and used to update the discriminator. The training process of the discriminator flow is shown in Figure 16.11.

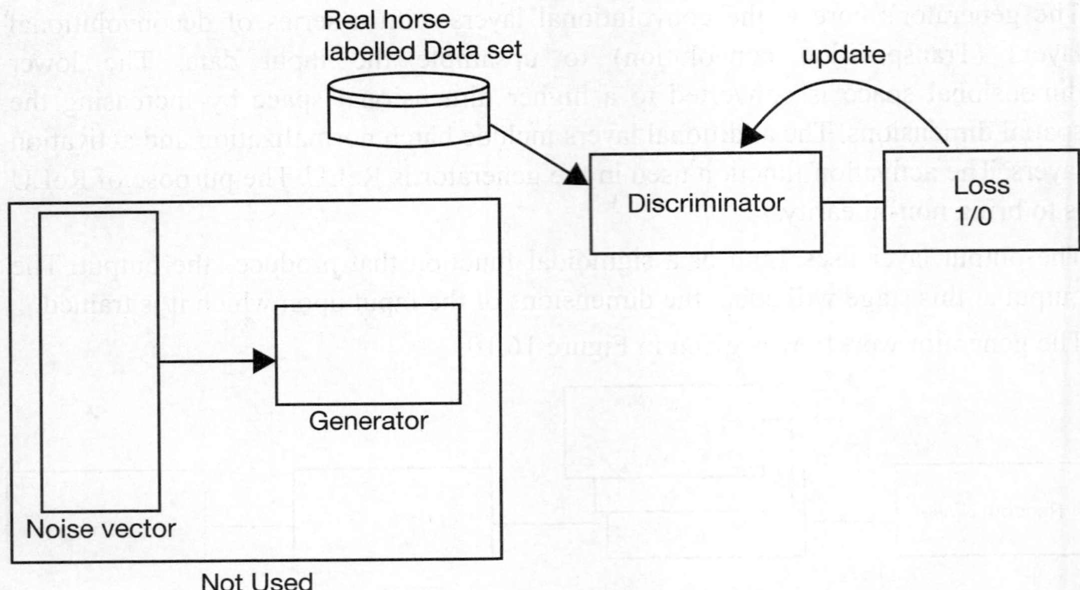

Figure 16.11 Training of a Discriminator

1. The first step of the discriminator training process is the collection of the training data. The data is the labelled one. The label is 1 if the data is from the training set and 0 if the data is from the generator.
2. The batch training is used for input data, which mixes real and fake data. The discriminator result is the label of the image - fake or original.
3. The GAN network finds the error between the correct and generated images. The focus is to minimize the probability of assigning a correct label. The loss is computed using the binary cross entropy.
4. The loss is computed separately for real and fake data. The total loss is the sum of both real and fake data loss.
5. The gradient of the loss function is backpropagated. The weights are adjusted to minimize the loss.
6. The GAN network uses a sigmoidal function to generate the output.
7. The process is iterated with new batches of training data until the discriminator distinguishes between real and fake data loss.

It can be observed that the above procedure is similar to the procedure of the binary classification.

Step 2: Training a generator is a tricky process.

The fake images of the generator are given to the discriminator, forcing it to output as 0. This output 0 indicates that the output image is fake. The error between the actual input and the 0 is computed and used to update the discriminator only. The generator is not updated as one does not want to reward the generator as it is not producing convincing fake images. The scenario is shown in Figure 16.12.

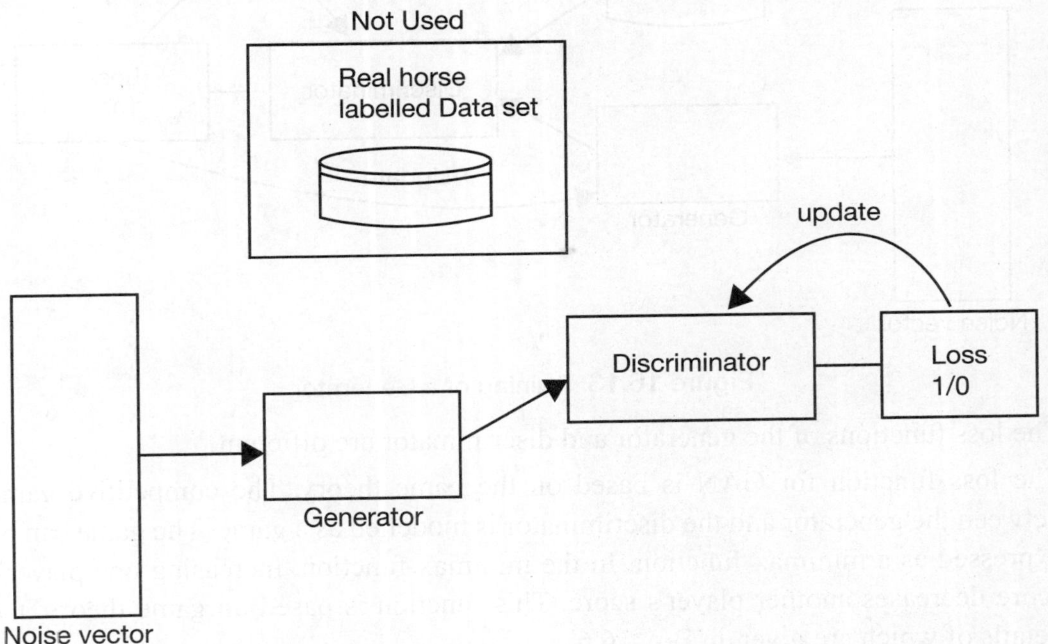

Figure 16.12 Training of a Generator

Step 3: In this stage, the generator generates the image. The discriminator outputs 1. The aim is to strengthen the generator to generate fake images convincingly. In this case, the discriminator is not updated because one does not want to encourage the discriminator to get the classification wrong. The generator training is shown in Figure 16.13.

Ideally, the training should continue to the stage where the generator and the discriminator reach equilibrium or until computing resources like GPU time or memory are available. This endpoint of the adversarial game is that neither the generator nor the discriminator can improve their strategy further. This saturated point, called Nash equilibrium, marks the termination of the adversarial training process.

The convergence can be monitored manually or by using performance metrics such as the inception score and Frechet Inception distance or the subjective evaluation of the image quality generated by the generator.

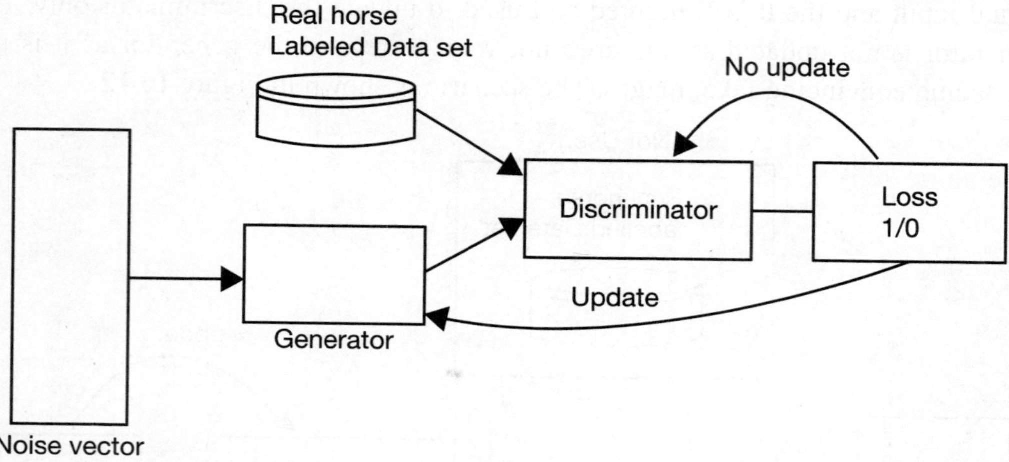

Figure 16.13 Training of a Generator

The loss functions of the generator and discriminator are different.

The loss function for GAN is based on the game theory. The competitive game between the generator and the discriminator is modelled as a game/ The game can be expressed as a minimax function. In the minimax function, increasing one player's score decreases another player's score. This function is based on game theory, the details of which are given in Box 16.6.

Box 16.6 Game Theory

Game theory is a branch of mathematics that deals with games. John Nash formulated this exciting field. The game theory is relevant to GAN because GAN components, generator, and discriminator are modelled as a two-player game.

The game is structured as a zero-sum game. A game is a zero-sum game where there is no cooperation among competitors. In GAN, the generator and discriminator are modelled as adversaries; hence, their interactions are modelled as a minimax game. The loss function is called minimax loss and is derived from game theory. The purpose of the generator is to minimize the loss, and the discriminator is to maximize the loss.

The endpoint of the adversarial game is that neither the generator nor the discriminator can improve their strategy any further. At that time, the generator can produce realistic data, and the discriminator can only guess randomly. This saturated point is called Nash equilibrium.

The loss function has two components: the generator loss and discriminator loss.

The discriminator tries to maximize the ability to detect real and fake images. The generator minimizes the discriminator wins as the generator wants the discriminator to fail.

The minimax function is given as follows:

$$\underset{G}{Min}\,\underset{D}{Max}\,V(D,G) = \mathrm{E}_{x\sim p_{data}}\left[\log D(x)\right] + \mathrm{E}_{z\sim p_z(z)}\left[\log(1 - D(G(z))\right]$$

Here, G is the generator. D is the discriminator.

1. In the first part $\mathrm{E}_{x\sim p_{data}}\left[\log D(x)\right]$, the real data is x. The P_{data} is the actual data distribution. $D(x)$ is the ability to determine real x as real. It is the expectation of the real data.
2. In the second part $\mathrm{E}_{z\sim p_z(z)}\left[\log(1 - D(G(z))\right]$, z is the random noise with noise distribution P_z. $G(z)$ is the fake data. $D(G(z))$ is the discriminator probability estimate of the fake data. G wants to maximize $D(G(z))$ so that it reduces the effectiveness of $1–D(G(z))$.

In short, the discriminator wants to maximize the function max (log($D(x)$)) and minimize log(1–$D(G(z)$)). Log($D(x)$) is the probability output of the discriminator for the real data.

The generator wants to maximize log(1–$D(G(z)$)) or minimize –log(1–$D(G(z)$)).

16.2.5 Evaluation of GAN

There are two commonly used evaluation metrics for GAN. They are:

1. Inception score
2. Frechet Inception score

These metrics involve finding the differences between two probability distributions, P and Q, using Kullback-Leibler divergence (KL divergence). KL divergence measures how one probability distribution, say P, diverges from the other Q. KL divergence quantifies the difference between P and Q.

The formula for the *KL* divergence is given as

$$KL(P \| Q) = \Sigma_i P(i) \times \log_e \left(\frac{P(i)}{Q(i)} \right)$$

The *KL* divergence is always a positive value; its value is zero if and only if *P* equals *Q*. The following numerical example illustrates the way of computing *DL* divergence.

Example 16.1: Let there be two distributions, *P* and *Q*, whose values are given below:

$P : P = \{0.2, 0.8\}$

$Q : Q = \{0.5, 0.5\}$

Compute the *KL* divergence.

Solution

As per the problem,

$P(1) = 0.2, P(2) = 0.8, Q(1) = 0.5$ and $Q(2) = 0.5$.

The *KL* divergence formula is given as

$$KL(P \| Q) = \Sigma_i P(i) \times \log_e \left(\frac{P(i)}{Q(i)} \right)$$

All logarithms are base 2 as KL divergence is measured in bits. But, one can use natural logarithms also. When $i = 1$,

$$P(1) \times \log_e \left(\frac{P(1)}{Q(1)} \right) = 0.2 \log_e \left(\frac{0.2}{0.5} \right) = 0.2 \times \log(0.4) \cong -0.1832$$

When $i = 2$,

$$P(2) \times \log_e \left(\frac{P(2)}{Q(2)} \right) = 0.8 \log_e \left(\frac{0.8}{0.5} \right) = 0.2 \times \log(1.6) \cong 0.376$$

So, KL divergence is given as

$$KL(P \| Q) = -0.1832 + 0.376 \ = \ 0.19274$$

Inception Score

The inception score is based on two facts. One is the high predictability of the generated image. If the generated image is good, then the inception score is high. Second, the distribution of the generated images should be diverse. In simple words, no single class of images should dominate.

Example 16.2: Let the training dataset consist of only three images with the output probability given as

Image 1: [0.2 0.3 0.5]

Image 2: [0.1 0.6 0.3]

Image 3: [0.2 0.5 0.3]

Compute the Inception score. The logarithm base is e.

Solution

Compute the marginal distribution $p(y)$ as follows:

$$p(y) = \frac{1}{3}([0.2\ 0.3\ 0.5) + [0.1\ 0.6\ 0.3] + [0.2\ 0.5\ 0.3])$$
$$= \frac{1}{3}([0.2 + 0.1 + 0.2], [0.3 + 0.6 + 0.5], [0.5 + 0.3 + 0.3]))$$
$$= [0.167\ 0.467\ 0.367]$$

The KL divergence can be computed for the image 1 as follows:

$$KL(p(y/x_1) \| p(y)) = \left(0.2 \times \log_e\left(\frac{0.2}{0.167}\right) + 0.3 \times \log_e\left(\frac{0.3}{0.467}\right) + 0.5 \times \log\left(\frac{0.5}{0.367}\right)\right) = 0.0667$$

$$KL(p(y/x_2) \| p(y)) = \left(0.1 \times \log_e\left(\frac{0.1}{0.167}\right) + 0.6 \times \log_e\left(\frac{0.6}{0.467}\right) + 0.3 \times \log\left(\frac{0.3}{0.367}\right)\right) = 0.0627$$

$$KL(p(y/x_2) \| p(y)) = \left(0.2 \times \log_e\left(\frac{0.2}{0.167}\right) + 0.5 \times \log_e\left(\frac{0.5}{0.467}\right) + 0.3 \times \log\left(\frac{0.3}{0.367}\right)\right) = 0.0391$$

The inception score can be computed as

$$\exp\left(\frac{1}{3}(0.0667 + 0.0627 + 0.0391) = 0.0562\right) = \exp(0.0562) \cong 1.058$$

If the score is higher, then the generated image is better. It has to be done on larger datasets to compute accurately.

Frechet Inception Score

The activations for a real/generated image are computed as multivariate Gaussian. They are measured as the distance between two distributions, called Frechet or Wasserstein distance.

The FID formula is given as

$$FID = \left\|\left(\mu_r - \mu_g\right)\right\| + Tr\left(\Sigma_r^2 + \Sigma_g^2 - 2 \times \sqrt{\sigma_r^2 + \sigma_g^2}\right)$$

A low score indicates that the generated image is of good quality. The challenges of

GAN are given in Box 16.7.

Box 16.7 Challenges of GAN

Some of the GAN challenges are listed below:

1. Oscillating Loss: The oscillation between the generator and the discriminator should be less. The loss of the discriminator and generator starts oscillating wildly, then there would not be any stability, and the convergence becomes an issue.

2. Mode Collapse: Statistically, a mode is data that comes frequently. If the generator generates the same data repeatedly, then the output is dominated by a single observation (called mode). Simply put, a particular class of images dominates the outputs, affecting output diversity.

3. Uninformative Loss: The lack of correlations between the generator loss and the image quality results in uninformative loss. This factor complicates GAN training.

4. Hyperparameters: GAN has a larger number of hyperparameters. A small hyperparameter change can affect the GAN as GANs are very sensitive. Handling the hyperparameters is a huge challenge.

16.3 Popular GAN Architectures

Some of the popular GAN architectures are given below:

16.3.1 Stacked GAN

One primary application of Gen AI is generating text based on images. The input is a set of textual descriptions, and the output is an image.

In stacked GAN, there will be multiple GAN levels on each other. This type of GAN is also useful for creating photorealistic images in art and improving the image's resolutions.

A stacked GAN is shown in the following Figure 16.14.

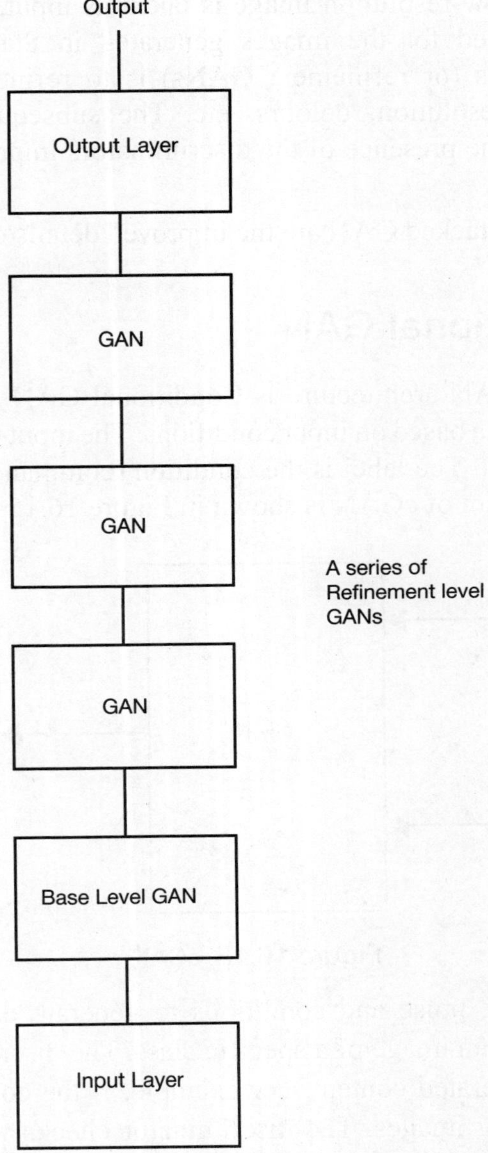

Figure 16.14 Stacked GAN

The stacked GAN works in two stages:

1. Based on the textual generations, generate a primitive shape and colours of the object. This generation is the job of the base GAN. Based on the random noise, the base level GAN can generate an image that is usually of low resolution and has only primitive properties.

2. In Stage 2, the low-resolution image is taken as input, and a high-resolution image is generated for the images generated in Stage 1. The job of the subsequent GANs (or refinement GANs) is to refine the content at every level, such as resolution, colours, etc. The subsequent GANs also have discriminators. The presence of the discriminators improves the quality of the generators.

The advantages of the stacked GAN are the improved details/quality and modularity.

16.3.2 Conditional GAN

The second popular GAN architecture is Conditional GAN. Conditional GAN (or cGAN) can generate data based on input conditions. The input to cGAN is the random noise along with a label. The label is the condition (commands like only flowers or trees). The block diagram of cGAN is shown in Figure 16.15.

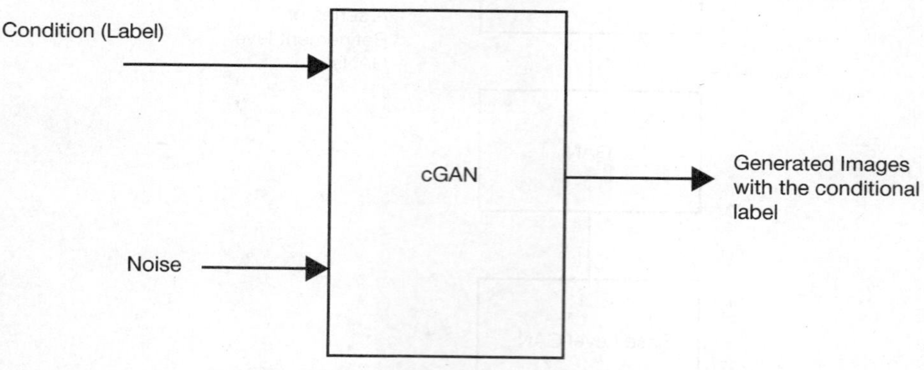

Figure 16.15 cGAN

The generator takes the noise and conditions to generate data. For example, the condition may generate an image of a specific class. The discriminator also receives the labels with the generated content. For example, if the condition is a dog, then cGAN can generate dog images. The discriminator checks whether the generated content is that of the labels in addition to whether the image is real or fake. The training of the generator/discriminator goes on till the generator can generate realistic images that satisfy the given condition.

Pix2pix is a cGAN. This GAN uses a generator/discriminator that transforms one type of image into another type. For example, it can transform one type of image into another type. Some use cases of pix2pix GAN are image enhancement, colorization of black and white images, and style transfer.

For example, to convert a black-and-white image to a colour picture, pix2pix can be used as follows:

1. The images (black and white or colour) are taken.
2. The generator tries to create an image that matches the target type.
3. The discriminator, as usual, classifies the image as fake and real.
4. This process goes on till the ability of the generator to generate a target image is achieved.

16.3.3 Neural Style Transfer

An alternative for pix2pix is the neural style transfer. Unlike GAN, this uses primarily a CNN. The style transfer is done by taking the content and style images as input and blending them by embedding the style image over the content image. The resultant image will have the content as well as the style image. Gatys et al. proposed this idea in a paper titled "A Neural Algorithm for Artist Style." This idea was proposed as an alternative to pix2pix GAN.

The neural style transfer is shown in Figure 16.16.

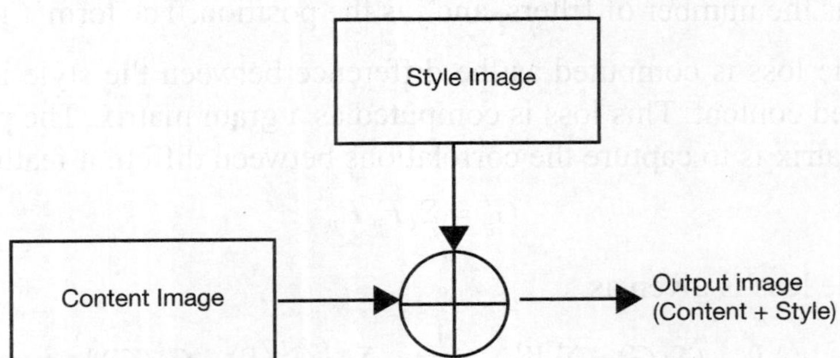

Figure 16.16 Neural Style Transfer

This idea uses a CNN to get three components:

(i) **Content image (C):** In the content image, the details are preserved.

(ii) **Style Images (S):** This Image has the style that needs to be applied to the content image.

(iii) **Generated Image (G):** The output image combines content and style images.

Neural style transfer uses a pretrained VGG19 architecture. As one knows, the architecture of this predefined CNN architecture are:

(i) Input layers

(ii) A set of convolutional layers

(iii) Pooling layers

(iv) Fully connected layers

The complete details of CNN are available in Chapter 9 of this book.

The higher-level convolutional layers provide the content, as the higher-level layers are adept at capturing high-level structures and objects. The style is defined as the textures and the correlations across the feature maps. The lower and middle-level convolutional layers capture this style.

The loss is computed as three types of losses.

1. The content loss is the difference in content between the generated image and the content image. Mathematically, this loss is given as

$$L_{content}(C,G) = \frac{1}{2}\Sigma_{i,j}\left(F_{ij}^{\ell}(C) - F_{ij}^{\ell}(G)\right)^2$$

   Here, i is the number of filters, and j is the position. The term ℓ is the layer.

2. The style loss is computed as the difference between the style image and the generated content. This loss is computed as a gram matrix. The purpose of the gram matrix is to capture the correlations between different feature maps.

$$G_{ij}^{\ell} = \Sigma_k F_{ik}^{\ell} F_{jk}^{\ell}$$

   The style loss is given as

$$L_{style}(S,G) = \Sigma_{\ell} W_{\ell} \frac{1}{4N_{\ell}^2 M_{\ell}^2} \Sigma_{ij}\left(G_{ij}^{\ell}(S) - G_{ij}^{\ell}(G)\right)^2$$

   Here N_{ℓ} is the number of feature maps, M_{ℓ} is the style of the feature maps, and W_{ℓ} the weight of the layer.

3. The total variation loss is a loss that is added to encourage the smoothness in the generated images. The purpose of this loss is to penalize the large differences between the adjacent pixels.

$$L_{total-variation}(G) = \Sigma_{ij}\left(\left(G_{i,j+1}(S) - G_{ij}\right)^2 + \left(G_{i+1,j} - G_{ij}\right)^2\right)$$

The total loss is computed as

$$L_{Total} = \alpha L_{content} + \beta L_{style} + \gamma L_{total\,variation}.$$

Here α, β, γ are the weights.

The procedure is defined as follows:

1. Load the pretrained VGG19 CNN architecture.
2. Extract the feature maps of the images.
3. Compute the content and style.
4. Initialize the generated that needs to be generated.
5. Iteratively update to minimize the loss.
6. The generated has minimal loss.

The use cases of neural style transfer are given in Box 16.8.

Box 16.8 Use Cases of Neural Transfer

Some of the uses of style transfer are in the domains of

1. Art and creative design
2. Augmented reality
3. Neural transfer helps to produce surrealistic and psychedelic images.

16.3.4 SuperResolution (SRGAN)

Christian Ledig introduced this type of GAN, which converts low-resolution to higher-resolution images. SRGAN focuses on improving the low-resolution image to quality high-resolution images. SRGAN can improve unavailable high-resolution images' quality, details, and cases.

1. The generator takes a low-resolution image and creates a high-resolution image.
2. The above is achieved by upsampling, convolutional layers, and upscale learning. Upscale learning refers to the ways of improving the details and texture.
3. The discriminator distinguishes between high and low-resolution images.

4. The loss functions are:

    4.1 **Content Loss:** The loss between the generated image and the contents of the original image.

    4.2 **Adversarial Loss:** This is the loss between the generated and the input image regarding realism.

Some use cases of SRGAN are image enhancement and medical imaging, which aim to increase the images' resolution and improve video resolutions.

16.4 Diffusion Model

A diffusion model is a generative model. It can generate an image by transforming a noise progressively. Diffusion models are a powerful group of generative models that can generate a good-quality image from the noise.

There are two components of the diffusion models. They are:

1. Forward (Diffusion) process
2. Reverse (Denoising) process

The diffusion model is shown in Figure 16.17.

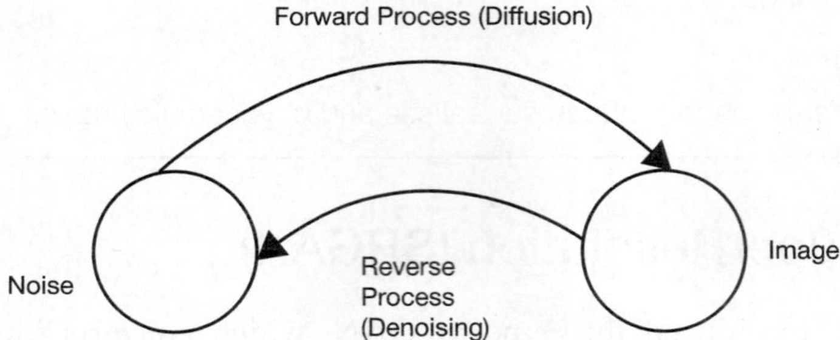

Figure 16.17 Diffusion Models

16.4.1 Forward (Diffusion) Process

The forward (diffusion) process is a fixed process where the noise is added to the original image in small steps. The data is corrupted by adding the noise over different time stamps until the noise fully corrupts the image.

The Markov process can be used to model the diffusion process. The details of the Markov process are given in Box 16.9.

Box 16.9 Markov Chain

Markov chain is used to model the forward diffusion process. A Markov chain is a stochastic process that models the forward diffusion process. Mathematically, the Markov chain can be stated as

$$P(X_{t+1} / X_t, X_{t-1}, \cdots, X_0) = P(X_{t+1} / X_t)$$

Markov Chains are based on the Markovian assumption. Markovian assumption means that the future state is based on the current state, not the past states that lead to the present state.

Markov chains are suitable for modelling the diffusion process where the noise is added incrementally. Later, the main focus is to formulate a reverse process where every step concerns only the removal of noise introduced in the previous step.

The advantages of the Markov chain are:

1. The predictability and control of the process.
2. Efficiency in computations.
3. A solid mathematical foundation for the diffusion process.

The forward diffusion process is given as follows:

$$q(x_1 / x_0), q(x_2 / x_1), \cdots, q(x_\tau / x_{\tau-1})$$

Here, at each step, a noise is added to the previous step. The forward diffusion process is modelled as follows:

$$q(x_t \mid x_{t-1}) = N(x_t; \sqrt{\alpha_t} x_{t-1}, (1-\alpha_t) / I)$$

Here x_0 is the original data, x_1, a noisy version of the data at time stamp t, α_t is the amount of noise, N is the normal distribution and I is the identity matrix. Here, α is the coefficient controlling the noise addition process, and $N(.)$ is the normal distribution. The term I indicates the identity matrix that ensures that the noise is isotropic. The resultant of the application noise to the original image is shown in Figure 16.18.

Figure 16.18 A Gaussian Noise is Added to the Image to Get a Diffused Image at Stage 1. In Reality, This Process Would Continue till the Image is Entirely Corrupted.

16.4.2 Reverse Process

This stage is a denoising stage. This step is the opposite of the forward (diffusion) process. It aims to generate data by reversing the diffusion process. This stage predicts the noise and removes it to reconstruct the original data.

The main focus of the forward process is to learn the noise distribution. It is important to learn the noise distribution to do the denoising. Also, the addition of noise ensures that effective denoising process.

The learning happens when a noise is added and removed. This learning process helps to generate a new image. It starts with pure noise and refines it progressively to coherent data.

Thus, learning and reversing the noise leads to a loss of function. This simple loss function computes the mean square error of the noise added in the forward process and the predicted noise in the reverse process.

The aim is now to generate an image using the repeated application of the reverse process to the noise image to a coherent image.

16.4.3 DDPG Algorithm

The Denoising Diffusion Probabilistic Model (DDPG) is a generative model to generate high-quality images. It consists of two phases:

Forward Phase

The forward phase starts with the initial state x_0. At every time step (1 to T), a random Gaussian noise is added to the image. This forward phase can be represented as shown in Figure 16.19.

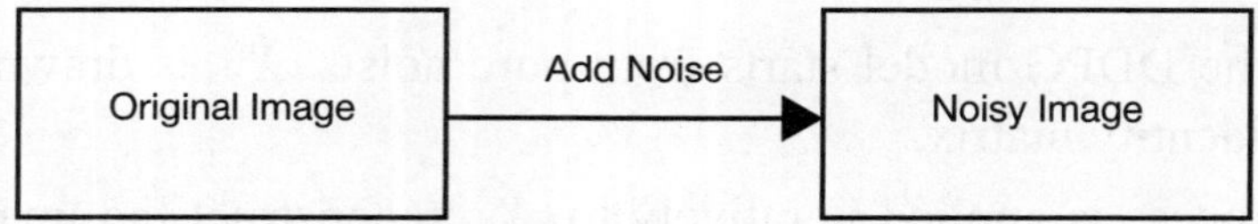

Figure 16.19 Diffusion Process

Here, x_t (the data at step t) is the noise variance. The is derived from $N[0-1]$, a normal distribution.

$$x_t = \sqrt{1-\beta_t} \times x_{t-1} + \sqrt{\beta_t} - \varepsilon$$

Reverse Process

This reverse process is a denoising step. It uses the neural model to predict the noise. This phase reconstructs the original data from pure noise. It is given in Figure 16.20.

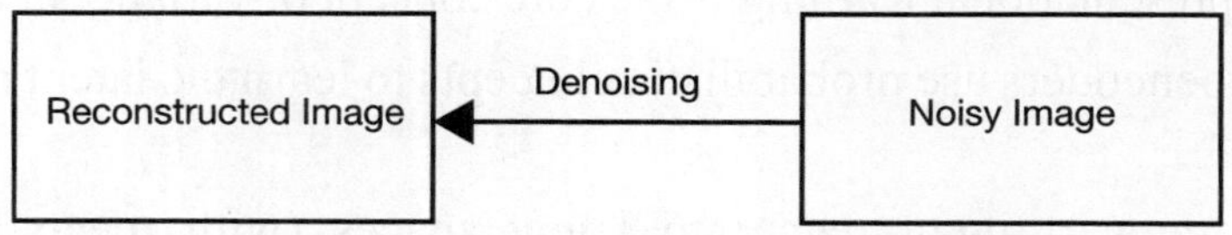

Figure 16.20 Reverse (Denoising) Process

The reverse process estimates the error. The focus is estimating the noise epsilon added in the forward process and using that to reconstruct the data.

Given the noisy data x_t, the model estimate using the parameterized function is given as

$$\hat{\varepsilon}_t = \varepsilon_\theta(x_t, t)$$

Mathematically, this reverse update is given as

$$x_{t-1} = \frac{x_t - \sqrt{\beta_t} \times \hat{\varepsilon}_t}{\sqrt{1-\beta_t}}$$

The objective function is to minimize the difference between ε_t and $\hat{\varepsilon}_t$.

The objective function is given as

$$L(\Theta) = E_{t,x_0,\varepsilon_t}\left[\left\|\varepsilon_t - \varepsilon_\theta(x,t\right\|^2\right]$$

Loss functions: The loss is the mean squared error between the actual noise added in the forward pass and the predicted noise in the reverse process.

This process is repeated till the loss becomes minimal.

Generation Process

In this stage, the DDPG model starts from pure noise. X_T is drawn from *N*[0–I], where *I* is the identity matrix.

The reverse process is applied iteratively to X_T reconstruct the image X_{T-1}. This step involves estimating the noise.

Use the estimated noise to compute X_{T-1} from X_T. By repeating the process until T reaches 1, generates the new image.

16.5 Variational Autoencoders

The concept of autoencoders is discussed in a detailed manner in Chapter 13. Variational autoencoders are mentioned here because variational autoencoders are generative models. VAE is based on the concept of encoder-decoder architecture to generate images. The representational learning is the core concept of variational encoders.

Variational autoencoders use probabilistic concepts to learn the latent representations of the data.

The encoders convert input data into latent spaces (with mean and variance), which describe the latent space probability distribution. The encoder outputs the distribution for the input data. By sampling this, one can provide different encodings for the same input. This distribution is the reason for the variability and robustness of the variational autoencoders.

The decoder takes the latent space data and reconstructs it to the original data as close as possible.

Let x be the input data (Observed data). The encoder maps the input x and outputs the latent space. Hence, the concept is to map the higher-dimensional space to a lower-dimensional space called latent space. The representational learning learns the feature that describes the observational data. The learning algorithms learn the complex mapping functions of the latent space back to the original domain to generate the data.

The autoencoder maps the image to a single point (Refer to Chapter 13). But, in the variational autoencoder, the input is mapped to a multivariate normal distribution around a point in the latent space.

The normal distribution is given as

$$f(x \mid \mu, \sigma^2) = \frac{1}{\sqrt{2\pi\sigma^2}} \exp(-(x-\mu)/2\sigma^2)$$

Two parameters that characterize the normal distribution are mean and variance.

VAE assumes that there is no correlation among dimensions. Hence, VAE encodes the image to mean and variance vectors only assuming no covariance among the dimensions. Two parameters characterize the distribution of the latent space: mean and variance.

This latent distribution is given as $q_\theta(z/x)$. This distribution approximates the true posterior distribution $p(z/x)$.

$$q_\theta(z/x) \sim N(\mu_\theta(x), \sigma_\theta^2(x))$$

Instead of sampling directly from $N(\mu, \sigma^2)$, the variation autoencoder uses a reparametrization trick to sample from

$$z = \mu + \sigma \times \varepsilon$$

"ε" is the parameter derived from the standard normal distribution $N(0, 1)$. Some of the interesting operations that can be performed in the latent spaces are given in Box. 16.10.

Box 16.10 Latent Space Arithmetic

The data in the latent space can be manipulated for various applications. Some of the applications are listed below:

1. Image Morphing: An image can be morphed into another image using VAE. This kind of morphing is done by manipulating the latent variables. For example, assume that the requirement is to morph image A to image B. The transformation does this

$$z_{new} = z_A \times (1-\alpha) + z_B \times \alpha$$

Here α is the blending factor.

2. Change of Features: Is it possible to change the features of the image? Say, for example, to change a laughing image to a non-laughing image. For that, the average of the laughing image and the average of the non-laughing image can be taken. The difference between the average laughing and the non-laughing image gives the non-laughing image.

The transformation is given as

$$z_{new} = z + \alpha \times \textit{feature} \text{ vector}$$

The decoder takes the latent variable z and reconstructs the input x. The decoder defines $p_\theta(x/z)$ a probability distribution of the reconstructed data. The objective of the VAE is to maximize the ELBO (Evidence Lower Bound) is the log-likelihood of data. The difference between the approximate posterior distribution $q_\theta(z/x)$ and the prior $p(x)$ is computed by the KL divergence.

It can be observed that the multiple inputs are summarized as the distribution of the single point. The term ε brings randomness, and hence, multiple reconstructions are possible.

The loss function consists of two terms:

1. **Reconstruction Loss:** The reconstruction loss is the difference between the decoded and the original input. This loss can be estimated using mean square error or binary cross-entropy.

2. **KL Divergence:** Kullback-Leibler (KL) divergence aims to find the difference between the $p(z)$ and $q(z/x)$ distributions. Here, $p(z)$ is the original distribution, and $p(q/x)$ is the learned distribution. KL divergence measures how one distribution differs from the other and serves as the loss function.

Sampling and Generation

After the training, sample the distribution p(z) and pass the samples to the decoder. The decoder generates the new samples for these inputs.

The complete procedure of VAE is given as follows:

1. The input image has three channels – Red, Green, and Blue as the output of VAE is an image.
2. The latent space is assumed with more dimensions (For example, 200 instead of 2)
3. There is a convolution layer for upsampling. There is a batch normalization layer after the convolution layers.
4. In this case, the reconstruction loss is computed between the generated and input data as image difference.
5. The training process goes on till all the hyperparameters are updated.
6. Using the learned mappings, The generator feeds the output based on the latent spaces.

The advantages and the use cases are given in Box 16.11.

Box 16.11 Advantages of VAE and Use Cases

The advantages of VAE are:

1. Image generation / reconstruction
2. Data denoising
3. Anamoly detection

16.6 Transformer-Based Image Generation

The transformers can be used for image generation. They are encoder-decoder-based architectures. The encoder encodes the input, and the decoder generates the image based on the input encodings—the additional notes in Box 16.12.

Box 16.12 Popular Transformer-based Image Generators

Some of the popular transformer-based image generators are listed below:

1. iGPT: This takes pixels as input and uses transformer-based architecture to generate realistic images.

2. DALL-E: DALL-E is a variant of GPT for generating creative and innovative images from textual descriptions. Dall-E is named after the famous surrealist artist Salvador Dali and the Pixar animated robot Wall-E. DALL-E is based on GPT-3 architecture developed by OpenAI.

3. VQ-VAE-2: This neural model is an integrated variational autoencoder and a transformer. It is a model to enhance the image generation quality for generating high-fidelity images.

4. ViT: Dosovitsky et al. proposed Visual Transformer (ViT) in their paper titled 'An Image is Worth 16 X 16 Words: Transformers for Image Recognition at Scale" in late 2018. It is a state-of-the-art technology for image-related tasks. Visual transformers divide the images into patches. ViT uses a transformer-based approach to generate images.

5. The state-of-the-art technology is now stable diffusion and latent diffusion models that effectively employ transformers.

Some of the steps of this process are given below:

1. **Data Preparation:** The input images are divided into many patches or a sequence of pixels. This pixel is equivalent to the token of a sentence in NLP.
2. **Embeddings:** The input data is converted to embeddings.
3. **Encoding:** The input for the encoding process is the embeddings. The output is encoding these in a suitable representation for the decoder.
4. **Decoder:** The decoder generates an image pixel-by-pixel or patch-by-patch using autoregressive modelling.
5. **Output:** The final output of the reconstruction is from the generated pixels or patches.

The advantages of the transformer-based image generation process come with the advantages of transformers handling long-term dependencies, scalability, and versatility.

Summary

1. Generative AI is a domain of AI for creating new content like images, video, audio, or sound.
2. Generative models can generate text, images, audio, video, 3D models, and synthetic data.
3. Generative AI is useful in art, design, fashion, entertainment, medical imaging, and image processing.
4. The types of generative models include GANs, variational encoders, diffusion models, and transformer-based models.
5. In GAN, two neural networks, a generator, and a discriminator, compete in adversarial training.
6. The generator takes a random noise vector and uses reshaping and multiple convolutional layers to generate output.
7. The discriminator model aims to take the input and generate the real or fake label.
8. The core success of the GAN is based on adversarial training where the generator and discriminator compete with each other.
9. The loss function used in GAN is called the minimax function. The discriminator wants to maximize the ability to detect real and fake images. The generator wants to minimize the loss.
10. GANs use the inception score and Frechet Inception score for evaluation.
11. Some popular variants of GAN have stacked GAN, Conditional GAN, and super-resolution GAN.
12. A diffusion model is generative for generating high-quality images from noise.
13. The diffusion model has a forward process (called the diffusion process) and a backward process (called the denoising process).
14. A diffusion model is a generative model for generating high-quality images.
15. One of the popular algorithms for diffusion models is DDPM (Denoising Diffusion Probabilistic Model).
16. The purpose of a variational autoencoder is to generate images using an encoder-decoder structure.
17. Transformer-based image generation models are encoder-decoder-based algorithms to generate images.

Glossary

1. Discriminator models – A model discriminates data to generate a label.
2. Generative model – A generative model is a model that can generate data.
3. Gen AI – A domain of AI that can create new content.
4. GAN – A generative model that generates images using two competing neural networks: generator and discriminator.
5. Adversarial training – A kind of training of a model with deceptive, corrupt, or challenging examples to make a robust model.
6. Generator – A component that takes the random number input and generates an image.
7. Discriminator – A component that classifies the input as real or fake.
8. Game Theory – A branch of mathematics used to design games or competing entities in GAN.
9. Zero-sum game – A game where there is no cooperation among players.
10. Minimax function – A function used in game theory to minimize the error.
11. Inception score – The inception score is an evaluation score that indicates the quality and diversity of the images.
12. Frechet Inception score – FIP is a scoring method whose score indicates image quality.
13. Conditional GAN – A conditional GAN takes a condition as input and generates the content that satisfies the conditions.
14. Diffusion models – Diffusion models are a group of algorithms that can generate a good-quality image from noise.
15. Diffusion model – Introducing noise to corrupt the image is called diffusion.
16. Encoder – The encoder of VAE takes an input and transforms it into a latent space.
17. Decoder – The Decoder of VAE takes a point of the latent space and generates output.
18. KL divergence – KL measures the distance between two probability distributions.

Short Questions

1. What is Gen AI?
2. What are the outputs of a generative model?
3. List out some of the domains where Gen AI is used.
4. Explain the adversarial training process.
5. What is a generator?
6. How will one evaluate GAN?
7. What is cGAN?
8. What are the uses of SRGAN?
9. What is stacked GAN?
10. What is a diffusion model?
11. List out the steps of transformer-based Image generation.

Long Questions

1. Explain the deep learning architecture of a generator.
2. Explain the deep learning architecture of a discriminator.
3. Explain in detail the adversarial training process of GAN.
4. Explain the DDPM algorithm in detail.
5. Explain the working of a variational autoencoder.
6. Explain the concepts of transformer-based image generation.

Numerical Problems

1. Consider the training set of the images

   [0.1 0.2 0.3] [0.1 0.3 0.6] [0.2 0.3 0.5] [0.2 0.4 0.4] [0.3 0.5 0.2] [0.3 0.4 0.3]

   Compute the inception score for this limited set of images.
2. Let there be two distributions, P and Q, whose values are given below:

   $P : P = \{0.3, 0.7\}$

   $Q : Q = \{0.4, 0.6\}$, Compute the KL divergence.

Crossword

Across

4. __________ score indicates the quality of the image generation.
6. The encoder component of VAE takes an input and transforms it into __________ space.
7. A game is called a __________ sum game if there is no cooperation among players.
11. GAN consists of two competing networks called generator and discriminator. (true/false)
13. Conditional GAN takes a __________ as an additional input that generates content according to the condition.
14. __________ function is used to minimize the error.
15. A classifier is a __________ (discriminative/generative) model.
16. The decoder takes the latent space as input and generates __________.
17. Gen AI can generate images and videos. (true/false)
18. KL measures the distance between two __________ distributions.
19. The training used for GAN is called __________ training.

Down

1. Ian __________ designed the concept of GAN.
2. The __________ component of GAN classifies the input as real or fake.

3. ___________ inception score indicates the image quality.
5. DALL-E is named after artist ___________ Dali and the Pixar animated robot WALL-E.
8. The input for a generator is a ___________ number.
9. A model that generates new content is called the ___________ model.
10. ___________ model introduce noise to corrupt the images.
12. ___________ theory is the branch of mathematics that provides basis for training a GAN.

Jumbled Sentences

R O B A N H L K R P C D I S C R I M I N A T O R H

W L H H E T G O O D F E L L O W O L A T E N T S E

E C C P I I I M I N I M A X E U E A A G Y O H V W

O I F R J S E Y J C O N D I T I O N T U R Y I J F

W L O T T A B J G H B I J Y B N O G J E O T Q T X

N E M Z C D U M D H B E K E S A B X Z G A R E J Q

O H Y D B V X T O R C U Q M Z P C P R N E H Z Q P

J M I N C E P T I O N H Z W A K B A I K C T M E R

L S J K C R T N S N N T R U E N W M B E C W V E O

V Y A S A S A L V A D O R Y O G I N R M Y I A C B

A T M T Y A U C H C W D I I T R F F E X T N F C A

W N W H W R K V U I M V S T C W H R M A W Q T V B

G A M E F I G A G O M U E S X K H L R O U U Q E I

Z F X A F A F V D X F C I O N A G E W D P M G J L

D I E P I L T N D F E D N E Z O N B Q T W S L U I

B Q J D U E A R I M T R U E N E T L U O A F I I T

D Q U A S R F D J N X R W Y G O K O M B F G G R Y

discriminative	generative	true	true	adversarial
random	discriminator	Game	zero	minimax
Inception	Frechet	condition	diffusion	latent
output	probability	Goodfellow	Salvador	

Boltzmann Machines and Deep Belief Networks

> The life contest is primarily a competition for available energy.
>
> — **Ludwig Boltzmann**

Credits: © Ludwig Boltzmann

Restricted Boltzmann Machine (RBM) is important from a historical point of view. The purpose of RBM is to take input data to generate/predict/approximate the probability distribution curve of the input data. RBM is a building block of many deep learning networks, such as deep belief networks.

This chapter focuses on RBM and the construction of Deep Belief Networks (DBN). The learning objectives of this chapter are:

- Understand Boltzmann machines.
- Understand the differences between Boltzmann machines (BM) and RBM.
- Know the training of RBM.
- Survey the applications of RBM.
- Know the basics of Deep Belief Networks (DBN).
- Understand the training of DBN.
- Survey the applications of DBN.

17.1 Introduction to Boltzmann Machines

Boltzmann machines are named after Austrian physicist Ludwig Boltzmann. Boltzmann distribution implies that the specific configurations of a system are related to an energy function.

The Boltzmann machine is an unsupervised, stochastic, recurrent neural network. Geoffrey Hinton, a university professor at the University of Toronto, and Jerry Sejnowski, a professor at Johns Hopkins University, invented Boltzmann machines in the 1980s. The history of Boltzmann machines is significant. Boltzmann machines belong to the class of Markov random fields. The principles of deep learning and physics, especially statistical mechanics, inspired the Boltzmann machines.

Boltzmann machines are, unlike other neural networks, are stochastic. The term "Stochastic" implies that the operations of Boltzmann machines incorporate certain randomness or probabilities, so the machine's behaviour is not deterministic, as the computations involve certain random variables and probabilistic decision rules. The popularity of RBM, a variant of BM, is attributed to Netflix for its recommendation systems.

Autoencoders now replace RBMs. The difference between RBM and autoencoders is shown in Table 17.1.

Table 17.1 Differences Between RBM and Autoencoders

RBM	Autoencoders
A fully connected network of neurons forms RBM. The connection between neurons is bidirectional and asymmetric.	Encoder-decoder network.
Focus on the generative model to learn the joint probability distribution. The output of RBM is a probability density function.	Focus on minimizing the reconstruction error. The aim is to learn the compact representation of input data by capturing the salient features of input data. The output of an autoencoder is a number.

The salient feature of the Boltzmann machine is that it looks like a graph unlike the neural networks seen so far, like feed-forward or recurrent neural networks. A sample Boltzmann machine is shown in Figure 17.1. Here, the shaded nodes are hidden units whose values cannot be observed directly but only can be inferred. The remaining units are called visible units, whose value can be observed directly. The words neurons, units, and nodes are the same and used interchangeably.

1. The neurons of Boltzmann machines are binary units. They can take only two states on (1) or off (0). Every node is on or off. The state depends on the weights/biases. Each node is aware of all other nodes that trigger it. The trigger depends on the previous input and its weights.
2. The neurons in Boltzmann machines are categorized as visible nodes (or units or neurons) and hidden nodes. They are arranged as two layers - visible layers

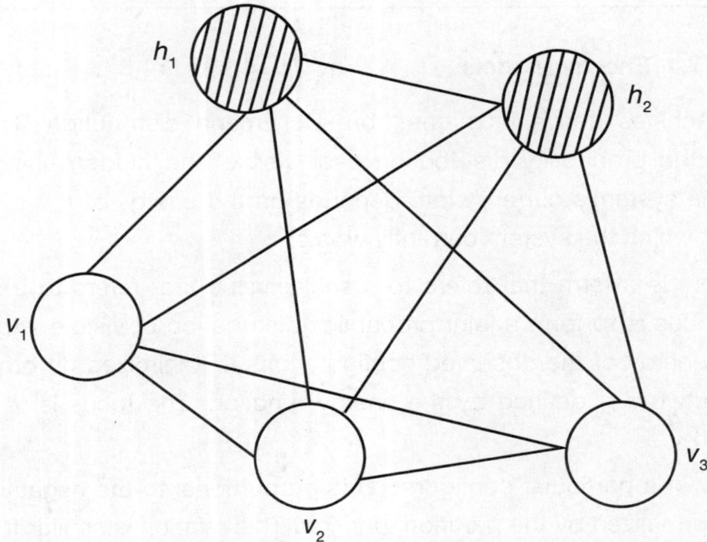

Figure 17.1 A Sample BM with No Weights Shown. Here, h_1 and h_2 are Hidden Units, and v_1, v_2, and v_3 are Visible Units

and hidden layers. There is no output layer. The user can see the values of the visible layers, and the values of the hidden neurons cannot be seen and can only be inferred. The hidden variables are also known as latent variables.

3. The connections among the neurons have symmetric weights. For example, the weight between neuron *i* and neuron *j* is the same as the weight between neuron *j* and neuron *i*.
4. All the links or edges between neurons are bidirectional, and the edges are unidirectional.
5. The neurons update weights 0 or 1 stochastically based on activation functions and external parameters like the weighted sum of the inputs.
6. The Boltzmann machines are based on energy-based models (Refer to Box 17.1). The logic is to define an energy function over the network states. Then, the probability is used to minimize the energy function. The energy determines which states are on or off. The goal of the Boltzmann machine is to minimize the energy connection between units (weights) to reduce the energy of the desired state.

   By exploring the various probabilities, the machine learns patterns as the patterns are low-energy states.

Box 17.1 Energy Models

Boltzmann machines derive its name from Boltzmann distribution. The Boltzmann distribution is the probability distribution over visible and hidden units. As per that distribution, the system's current state depends on the energy of the system and the temperature at which the system currently works.

The energy here is a term that refers to a scalar value that refers to the state of the system. The focus is to form a joint probability distribution of visible and hidden units such that the energy of the observed configurations is minimized. In other words, the state of the network is defined by the energy function. The focus is to minimize the energy function.

The probability of a particular configuration is proportional to the negative exponential of its energy normalized by the partition function. This relation is similar to the system's energy and probability of a particular system state.

7. The machine can learn the weights in such a way as to match the model distribution and the empirical data distribution of the training data using the stochastic gradient descent algorithms.

   The purpose of Boltzmann machines is to input data to generate/predict/approximate the probability distribution curve of the input data. The probability distribution curve is the mathematical function that provides the probability of the different outcomes. Therefore, Boltzmann machines are generative and unsupervised models. Boltzmann machines can generate images and text data. One of the major applications of Boltzmann machines is their ability to do tasks like associative memory. It takes the incomplete input and retrieves the closest one of the similar training samples. This mechanism is called an associative memory. The details of associative memory are given in Box 17.2.

Box 17.2 Associative Memory

The information retrieval using key or partial information of the data itself instead of the memory location is called associative memory. BM implements associative memory that takes an incomplete input and restores it to the complete one.

Traditionally, the information is stored in memory and accessed by using the memory location where it is stored. In short, the way of retrieving is by using memory location.

Imagine you know your friend's telephone number starts with 729. Then, the brain tries to work the fill-in-the-rest like a fill-in-the-blank problem. The rest of the telephone number is filled with some learned patterns—the ability of the brain to compute tasks like puzzles by patching various associations. In short, associate memory is to recollect information using its parts.

Based on the data and cost function, the neurons make stochastic decisions about turning it on or off. The Boltzmann machine minimizes the loss between the input and reconstructed data. By learning this, the machine discovers interesting features when input data is given by capturing the hidden relationships.

The use cases of Boltzmann machines are given in Box 17.3.

Box 17.3 Use Cases of Boltzmann Machines

Boltzmann machines are suitable for solving two types of problems, as shown in Figure 17.2.

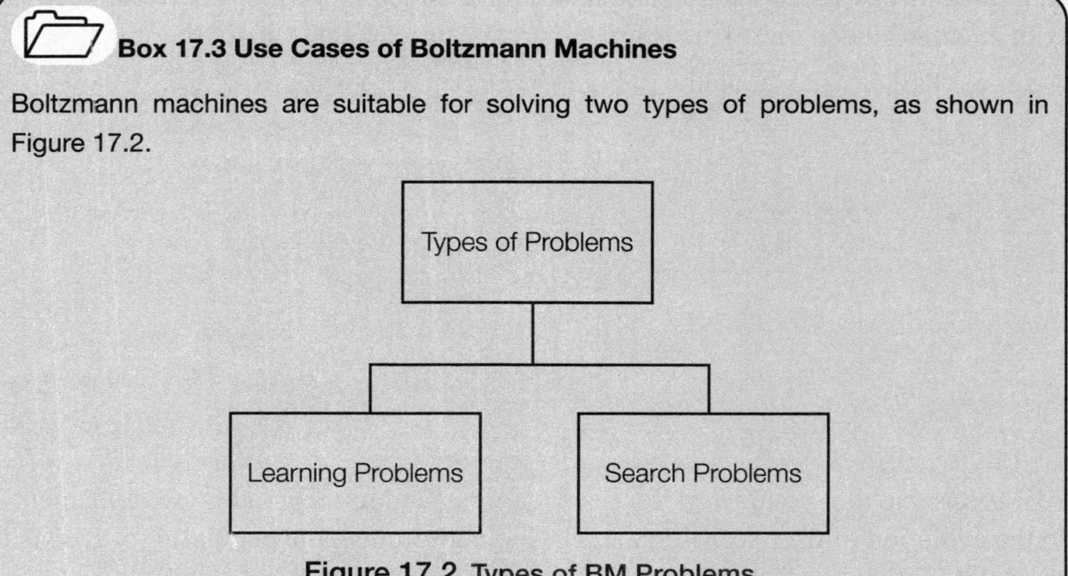

Figure 17.2 Types of BM Problems

Boltzmann machines can learn by finding some of the important features of the input data. Boltzmann machine can also help in finding missing data. Boltzmann machines can also solve search problems, such as optimization problems. Boltzmann machines can solve constraint optimization problems where the goal (or objective function) is associated with many constraints. The focus is to find a solution satisfying all the constraints.

(i) BM implements associative memory that takes an incomplete input and restores it to the complete one.

(ii) Boltzmann machines are good at solving optimization problems.

(iii) Boltzmann machines are useful in dimensionality reduction problems.

17.1.1 Restricted Boltzmann Machines

Restricted Boltzmann Machine (RBM) is called Generative deep neural networks or Harmonium. It takes the sample data and approximates it to a probability density function.

RBMs are simplified "restricted" versions of BMs by restricting their architecture. The restriction is that there cannot be any Intra-layer connections. In a sense, a visible unit can connect with only hidden units and vice-versa. In other words, a visible unit cannot connect with another visible unit, and a hidden unit cannot have connections with another hidden unit. This restricted architecture enables faster training.

A simple RBM is shown below in Figure 17.3.

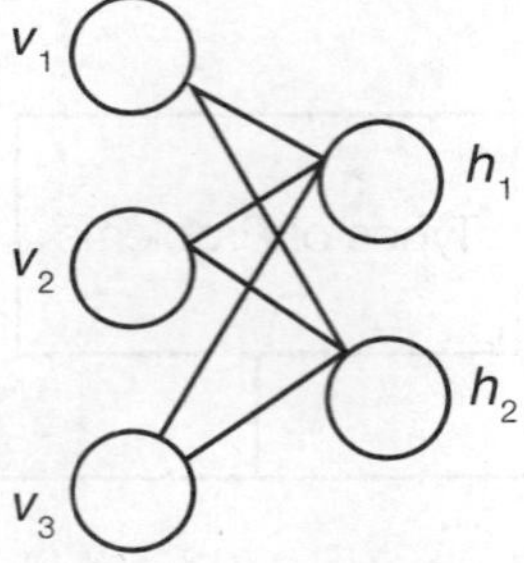

Figure 17.3 Architecture of a Simple RBM

RBMs has laid the groundwork for deep learning, and its techniques are fundamental in the evolution of deep learning models and algorithms. The popularity of RBMs is due to the following reasons:

(i) Efficient training due to its restricted architecture and due to stochastic gradient descent-based algorithms

(ii) RBMs perform unsupervised learning by capturing the useful representations from the input data.

(iii) RBMs are generative models. It can generate new samples from the learned distribution. It can generate new samples that resemble input data. It can generate images or text.

(iv) RBMs are popular as RBMs are building blocks for Deep belief networks and Deep Boltzmann machines.

(v) RBMs are popular as they are versatile in handling multimodel data such as text, images, and structured data.

The use cases of RBM are given in Box 17.4.

Box 17.4 Use Cases of RBM

RBM can be used in several applications. Some of the well-known applications of RBM are

(i) Disease Classification
(ii) Feature Learning and representation.
(iii) Collaborative filter
(iv) Dimensionality Reduction.
(v) Noise reduction
(vi) It can reduce the time for large-scale and real-time classification of other networks by learning the optimal weights using unsupervised learning.

1. In RBM, the units or neurons are organized as visible and hidden layers as a bipartite graph. Bipartite means the nodes of RBM are divided into two subsets of visible and hidden layers. Hence, the connection is only across them. It can be observed that the nodes are divided into two sets where there is no connection among nodes of the same layer.
2. The connections between neurons of visible and hidden layers are symmetric and bidirectional. This fact implies that the flow of information is bidirectional.

   The types of RBM are shown in Figure 17.4.

   Binary RBMs are popular as Gaussian RBMs are very complex. In practice, Binary RBMs are mostly used.

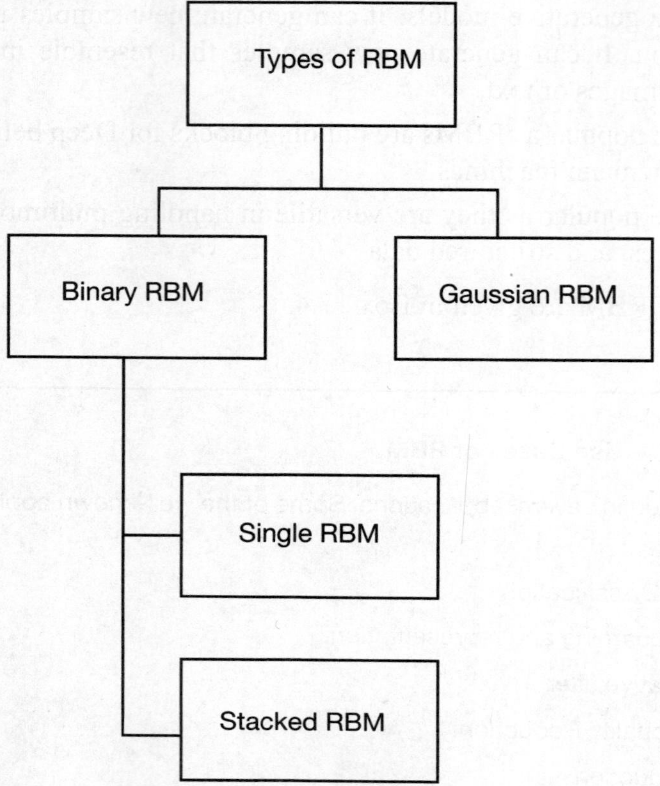

Figure 17.4 Types of RBM

In Binary RBM –

(i) The visible layers take binary inputs.
(ii) The nodes make decisions about whether to allow input or not
(iii) The hidden units serve to increase the expressiveness of the model.

One can view this as a parameterized model that learns by maximizing the likelihood function of the input data since the goal is to learn the probability distribution function.

RBMs are as effective in implementing associative memory as Boltzmann machines. RBM can handle noisy, incomplete data (Details are given in Box 17.5).

The restoration details of associative memory are given in the Box. 17.5.

Box 17.5 RBM and Restoration of Input Data

Like BM, RBM also implements associative memory. The input of RBM is not complete data. RBM computes the probability of the specific value given to the input data by trying to minimize the biases of the input data. When the input data has many missing values, RBM can be applied, and RBM finds the probability distribution function of the input data.

One form of restoration is as follows:

1. Let x_1, x_2, x_3, ..., x_n be the training example. Let x be the unknown example, then the restoration can be $x \rightarrow x_i$

   Where x_i is the closest vector that approximates the unknown vector x. This mechanism can be viewed as retrieving the closest training sample.

2. The second restoration method is finding the closest cluster prototype. The procedure is as follows:

   a. Cluster the N training samples into m clusters. Let the clusters be c_1, c_2, c_3, ..., c_m. Then, the associative memory is a process of restoring the unknown vector x to the closest prototype as

   $$x_1 \rightarrow c_i$$

   One can visualize this as a classification by the 1-nearest neighbour method.

17.2 Training of RBM

There are two steps in training of RBM as shown in Figure 17.5.

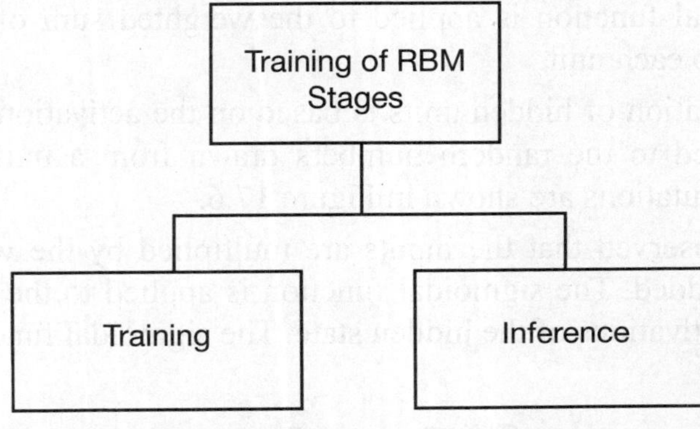

Figure 17.5 Stages of RBM Training

1. Training

The visible values are vector, $v = [v_1, v_2, v_3 \ldots.v_d]$. Here, d is the dimensionality. The hidden values are $h = [h_1, h_2, h_3\ldots.., h_k]$. It should be noted that the connections between the input layer and the hidden layer are complete. If w_{ij} is the connection between i^{th} visible node and j^{th} hidden node, then the weight matrix is given as

$$W = \begin{pmatrix} w_{11} & \cdots & w_{1d} \\ \vdots & \vdots & \vdots \\ w_{k1} & \cdots & w_{kd} \end{pmatrix}$$

The difference between RBM and BM is that the connection can exist between only visible and a hidden variable.

The procedure for training an RBM is given below:

1. **Data Preprocessing:**

   The input data must be pre-processed. The preprocessing steps include normalization, scaling or any techniques necessary.

2. **RBM Initialization:**

   The input is given only to the input variable. The edges associated with the visible and hidden values are assigned random or zeros. Normally, the weights from the Gaussian or other suitable distributions are used to initialize the weights and biases.

3. **Computer Hidden Unit Activations:**

   RBM uses the output to predict the probability P(a|v: w) of finding "a" given weighted x. The hidden node unit values are computed by the product of input values and weights (or the product of previous hidden values/weights). Then, the sigmoidal function is applied to the weighted sum of the visible units connected to each unit.

   The computation of hidden units is based on the activations. The activations are compared to the random numbers drawn from a uniform distribution. These computations are shown in Figure 17.6.

   It can be observed that the inputs are multiplied by the weights. Then, the biases are added. The sigmoidal function is applied to the outputs to decide about the activations of the hidden state. The sigmoidal function is given as

$$\sigma(x) = \frac{1}{1+e^{-x}} = \frac{e^x}{1+e^x}$$

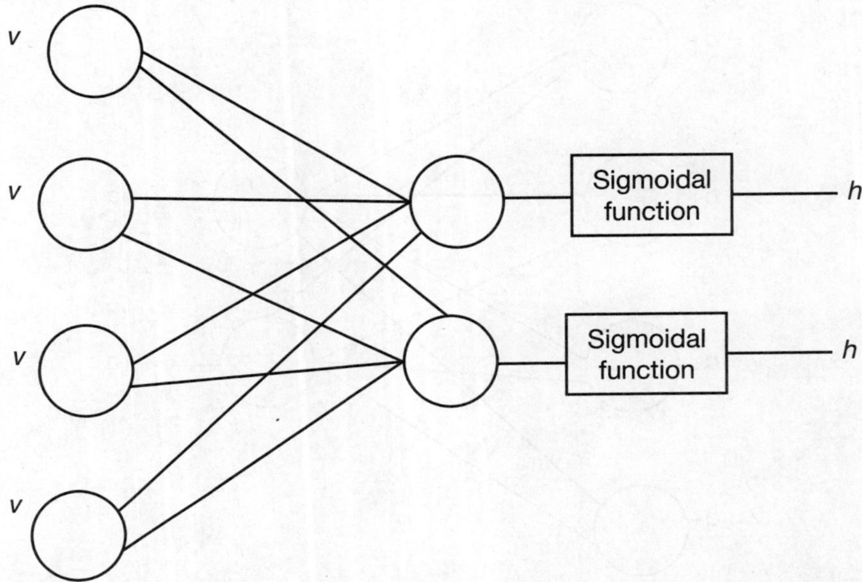

Figure 17.6 Hidden Layer Computation with Vector *h* of Activations "*a*"

Given the input visible vector v and the weight matrix w_{ij}, the hidden values are computed as

$$h_i = \sum_{j=1}^{d} w_{ji} \times v_j + a$$

The above equation can be viewed as the product of the weight matrix and the visible vector

$$h = \sigma(w.v + a)$$

Here, v is the input vector, a is the hidden layer labels, and h is the corresponding hidden layer vector.

4. **Reconstructed Visible Computation:**

   The input is activations and is trying to guess the probability of x given activations a. This probability is given as $p(x|a;w)$ probability of estimate x given activations a, which are weighted by the weights using the first pass These estimates are the joint probability of inputs x and activations a $p(x, a)$. The restored value is again computed for the visible nodes as the product of hidden values and weights (product of previous visible values and weights). This computation is done in the opposite direction. Here, the activations of the hidden units and the corresponding weights are used, as shown in Figure 17.7.

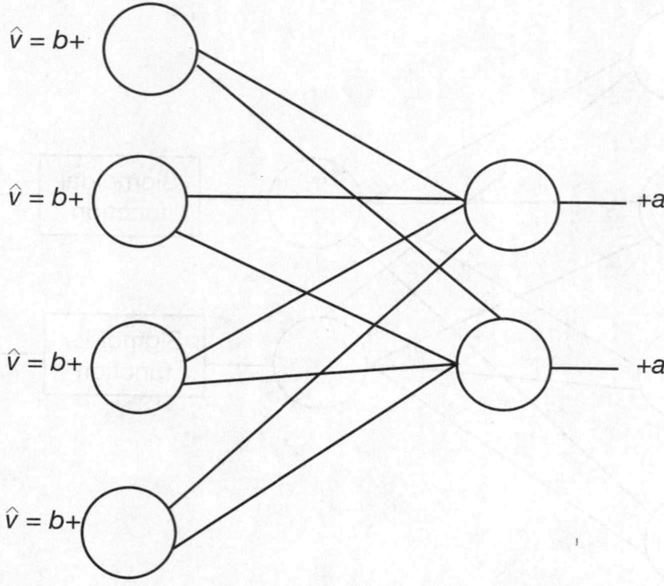

Figure 17.7 Illustration of Reconstruction of Visible Vectors

The two types of visible vectors are:

(i) Target visible vector

(ii) Computed visible vector

The process of computing the visible input from the hidden vector is given as follows:

$$\hat{v}_i = \sum_{j=1}^{k} w_{ji} \times h_j + b$$

Here, $\hat{v}$ is the set of reconstructed x's shown in Fig. 17.7. The above can be denoted as a dot product as

$$\hat{v} = \sigma(h.w + b)$$

Here, $\hat{v}$ and h are the vectors of the visible and hidden layers. 'b' is the bias of the visible unit.

5. Error Computation:

The error is computed between the initial visible values and the restored (or computed) visible values. The error is the difference between the input vector v and the restored input vector $\hat{v}$. The loss function is given as follows:

$$E = \frac{1}{2}(v - \hat{v})^2$$

The error minimization is carried out, and updates of weights are carried out. The weight is adjusted in each iteration to minimize the error as

$$w_{ji} = w_{ji} - \eta \frac{\delta E}{\delta w_{ji}}$$

The learning rate controls the magnitude of the weight and bias. The equation for updating the weight is given as

$$w_{ji} = w_{ji} + \eta h_i \left(v_j - \hat{v}_j \right)$$

6. The above steps are repeated for multiple iterations, or a convergence is obtained. The alternative updating of weights is shown in Figure 17.8.

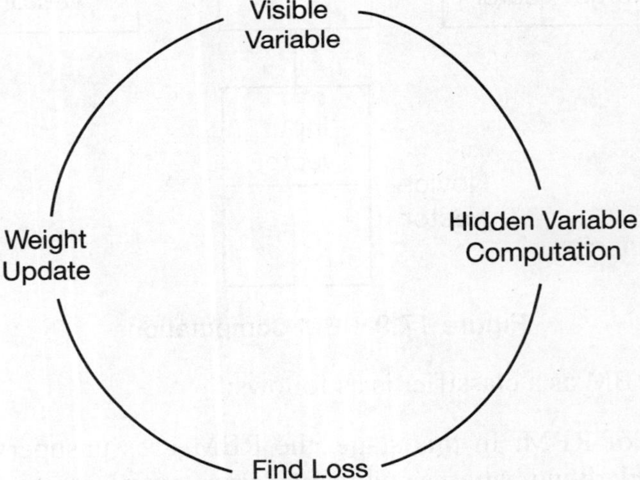

Figure 17.8 Illustration of the Update Process

Inference: Once training is over, then the inference can be made about the unknowns.

17.2.1 RBM as a Classifier

The RBM can be used as a classifier. The RBM typically consists of two layers:

(i) Visible layers

(ii) Hidden layers

The input vector is augmented with its target visible vector. Initially, it is assigned with zero. Let the input vector's dimensions be d and the augmented vector is m. So, the visible vector is d + m. The RBM training process is applied.

The hidden vector is computed from the visible vector. Similarly, the visible vector is computed from the hidden vector. The difference between the target and the computed vector is called an error. The weights are updated to minimize the error.

The unknown input has only an input vector augmented with a zero vector. The computation of the hidden vector is computed from this input vector plus the augmented vector. The augmented part answers the classification problem, as shown in Figure 17.9.

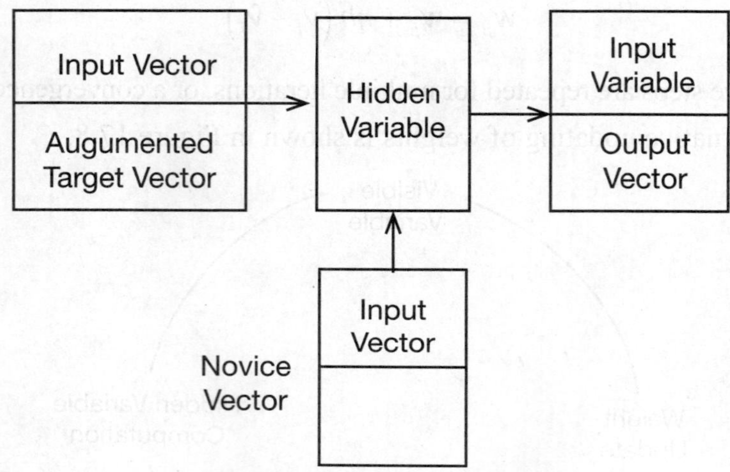

Figure 17.9 RBM Computations

So, the steps of RBM as a classifier is as follows:

1. Pretraining of RBM. In this stage, the RBM uses unsupervised learning to learn the underlying patterns and feature representations.
2. Adding a classification layer and the network is finetuned using labelled data.
3. For new input, the softmax layer computes the probability of each class and assigns the highest probability to the input class.

17.2.2 Stacked RBM

A stacked RBM is multiple layers of RBM stacked on each other. The stack of RBM is sequenced so that the output of one RBM is input for the next RBM.

A stacked RBM can be given, as shown in Figure 17.10.

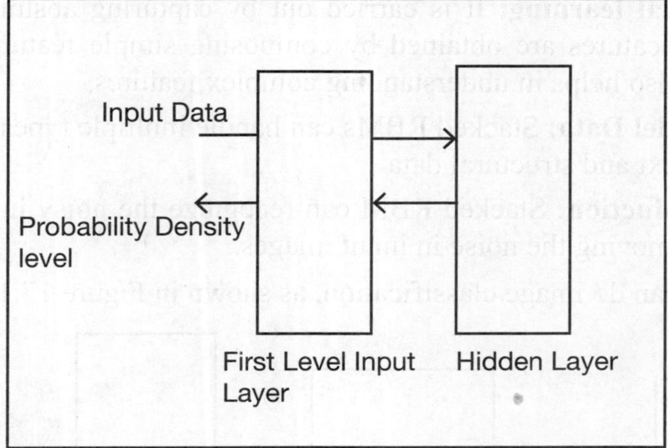

Figure 17.10 A Stacked RBM

The single RBM can be expanded to include multiple RBM. The single RBM consists of two layers – visible and hidden layer.

The multiple RBM has one visible and multiple hidden layers. The output hidden layer is in the input (visible layer) to the next RBM. The final hidden layer is computed using the multiple hidden layers, and the visible layer is computed backwardly.

Let the hidden layers be J and $J + 1$, then the value of the hidden layers is computed as

$$h_i^{j+1} = \sum_{r=1}^{|J|} w_{ir} h_r^j$$

It should be noted that the weights are updated in the forward direction. Initially, the weights are random. Firstly, the hidden values are computed forward between the visible layer and the last hidden layer. Then, the visible layer is computed backward from the last hidden layer to the visible layer.

The advantages of stacked RBMs are

(i) **Layer-wise Pretraining:** Stacked RBMS solves the problem of vanishing gradients. Layer-wise pretraining ensures faster convergence. Layer-wise training also ensures efficiency and manageability as one layer deals only with the previous layer. One can add/remove layers. This facility adds more flexibility in the construction of stacked RBM.

(ii) Hierarchial learning: It is carried out by capturing abstract features, and complex features are obtained by composing simple features. Hierarchical learning also helps in understanding complex features.

(iii) Multimodel Data: Stacked RBMs can handle multiple types of data, such as Images, text and structural data

(iv) Noise Reduction: Stacked RBM can recognize the noisy inputs also. It can help in removing the noise in input images.

Stacked RBMs can do image classification, as shown in Figure 17.11.

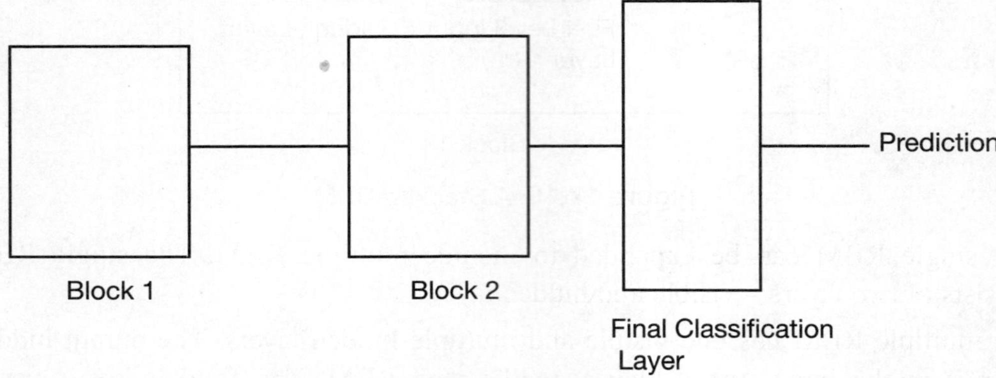

Figure 17.11 Stacked RBM as a Classifier with Every Block is RBM

The training of the stacked RBMs for classification is as follows:

(i) Each RBM is trained independently for unsupervised learning. The input data is fed to the first RBM. Based on the input data, the hidden layer activations are computed. These activations serve as input for the next RBM. The weights and biases are adjusted so that likelihood is maximized. This pretrained stage is unsupervised.

(ii) The second step is called fine-tuning. Once all RBMs are stacked, it is fine-tuned for supervised learning. One extra layer called the softmax layer can be added. The softmax layer computes the probability of each class for the given input. The class with the highest probability is the class of input.

(iii) The networks can be fine-tuned now with the labeled data and the backpropagation algorithm. Here, the goal is to minimize the loss by adjusting the weights/biases.

(iv) Then, the test data can be given and classified.

17.3 Mathematical Interpretation of Training of RBM

Contrastive divergence is an optimization algorithm used for training RBM. Geoffrey Hinton developed this algorithm. Contrastive divergence is a modification of Gibbs sampling is called contrastive divergence. The Gibbs sampling method is used to reduce the divergence between the model and data distribution.

The joint configuration of visible and hidden units is an energy function. RBM is called an energy model, as any configuration of the machine depends on the energy function's negative exponentiation.

Let v and h be a visible and hidden neuron, then the probability of the pair is given as

$$p(v,h) = \frac{1}{z}\exp\left(-\hat{E}(h,v)\right)$$

where z is the normalization constant and is the sum of all possible constants and is the sum of all possible combinations of neurons of visible and hidden neurons.

$$z = \sum_{v}\sum_{h}\exp\left(-\hat{E}(h,v)\right)$$

$$\hat{E}(h,v) = -\sum_{i=1}^{m}\sum_{j=1}^{n} w_{ij} v_i h_j - \sum_{i-1}^{m} v_i b_i - \sum_{j-1}^{n} h_j d_j$$

Here, m is the number of visible nodes, and n is the number of hidden nodes. b_i And d_j are biases of visible and hidden nodes, respectively. RBM assigns a scalar energy to each configuration of the hidden and visible variables. The probability distributive function is used to describe the energy of the system. The lower energy configurations are more probable. The sum of all probability distribution functions of all possible states is infeasible for larger systems. This sum is difficult because the computation involves an exponential number of terms.

Contrastive divergence does not aim to find the partitioning function. Instead, it focuses on adjusting model parameters so that the probability of the observed data increases if the probability generated data becomes less. Contrastive Divergence uses the Gibbs sample procedure to generate samples. Then, the samples are used to estimate the log-likelihood gradient concerning the model parameters. Then, these are used to update the parameters in the direction that improves data representation.

So, the minimization of error is carried out concerning the log probability. This formula leads to a learning rule as follows:

$$\Delta w_{ij} = \alpha\left(\left\langle v_j, h_j\right\rangle_{data} - \left\langle v_j, h_j\right\rangle_{model}\right)$$

Here α is the learning rule.

The procedure of contrastive divergence is given below:

1. Start with a training sample, compute the probability of hidden data
2. Sample the hidden configuration to reconstruct the data
3. Find the differences between the outer products of original and reconstructed data
4. Update the model parameters to minimize the difference

The advantages and disadvantages of the contrastive divergence algorithm are given in Table 17.2.

Table 17.2 Advantages and Disadvantages of Contrastive Divergence

Advantage	Disadvantage
1. Efficiency	1. The approximation method depends on the Gibbs sampler, so it may not be perfect.
2. Simplicity	2. suboptimal models
3. Effective in practice	3. mode collapse that leads to divergence
4. Scalability	4. Performance deterioration when used for Deep belief networks.

17.4 Deep Belief Network

Deep Belief Networks (DBN) is a generative stochastic model. It is like a complex brain structure that can learn given the huge input data. Here, "Belief." refers to probabilistic learning and inference. Belief indicates the confidence of the machine about its states and its outcomes. DBNs have become popular as DBN can handle large amounts of data, have Faster training, and can find the global minima.

The applications of Deep Belief networks are given in Box. 17.6.

Box 17.6 Applications of Deep Belief Networks

Deep Belief networks can be helpful in projects like

(i) Image generation
(ii) Image classification
(iii) Object detection
(iv) Natural Language Processing
(v) Pose detection
(vi) Dimensionality reduction
(vii) Collaborative filtering

Deep Belief Networks is a probabilistic generative neural network. The architecture of DBN is a stack of RBMs where each layer has a link with the previous and subsequent layers. It can be visualized as a set of multiple hidden layers. In a sense, the output of an RBM is an input for the next RBM. Each model produces an output that is a non-linear input transformation and, in turn, serves as input for the next RBM. So, the representation of every RBM is different.

The components of DBN are given below:

(i) The building blocks of DBN are RBMs.
(ii) A RBM has two layers – visible and hidden. Each visible unit is connected to only a hidden unit and vice versa,
(iii) The stacking of RBM is such that the hidden layer of one RBM is the visible unit for the next RBM. This stacking enables DBN to capture the complex representations of the input data.
(iv) The connections between the units are undirected.

The additional notes on DBN are given in Box 17.7.

Box 17.7 DBN is not Stacked RBM

Is DBN a stacked RBM? No, stacked RBM and Deep Belief Networks have many differences. The differences between stacked RBM and Deep Belief networks are given in Table 17.3.

Table 17.3 Differences Between Stacked RBM and Deep Belief Networks (DBN)

Stacked RBM	Deep Belief Networks
In stacked RBM, every layer is treated independently.	The First two layers form RBM; subsequent layers are considered probabilistic neural networks. The first two layers are Fully connected. The rest have Feedforward neural networks.
Each layer forms an undirected graph model.	Only the first two layers are undirected. The rest of the layers are directed.
No fine-tuning across unless at an extra step.	Fine-tuning is done for backpropagation through all layers.
Simple training as there is no intercommunication between successive layers.	More complex, especially for backpropagation.
Stacked RBM is used mainly for feature extraction and dimensionality reduction. It can be used for classification with added layers or finetuning.	Deep belief networks are mainly used for feature extraction, classification, and generative modeling.

DBNs are not Bayesian neural networks. The differences between Bayesian and DBN are given in Table 17.4.

Table 17.4 Differences Between Bayesian Network and DBN

Bayesian Networks	Deep Belief Networks
Bayesian networks are Directed acyclic graphs. Here, the edges denote the conditional dependencies, and the nodes are random variables.	Deep belief networks are hybrid hierarchical graph models with a stack of RBMs that are undirected graph models.

Bayesian networks compute posterior probabilities given prior probabilities.	Deep belief networks use layer-wise pretraining and finetuning.
The probabilities are computed explicitly in Bayesian networks.	The focus is on learning hidden representations, not probabilistic modeling among random variables.

DBN can learn step by step. It starts learning simple features and starts by combining the simple features, DBN can learn complex features. DBN can do layer-wise learning. Then, in the fine-tuning stage, all layers cooperate to learn together by fine-tuning all they know. This kind of learning helps DBN to recognize the objects in an image.

17.4.1 DBN as a Classifier

A deep belief network can be constructed by stacking RBM for Classification, as shown below in Figure 17.12.

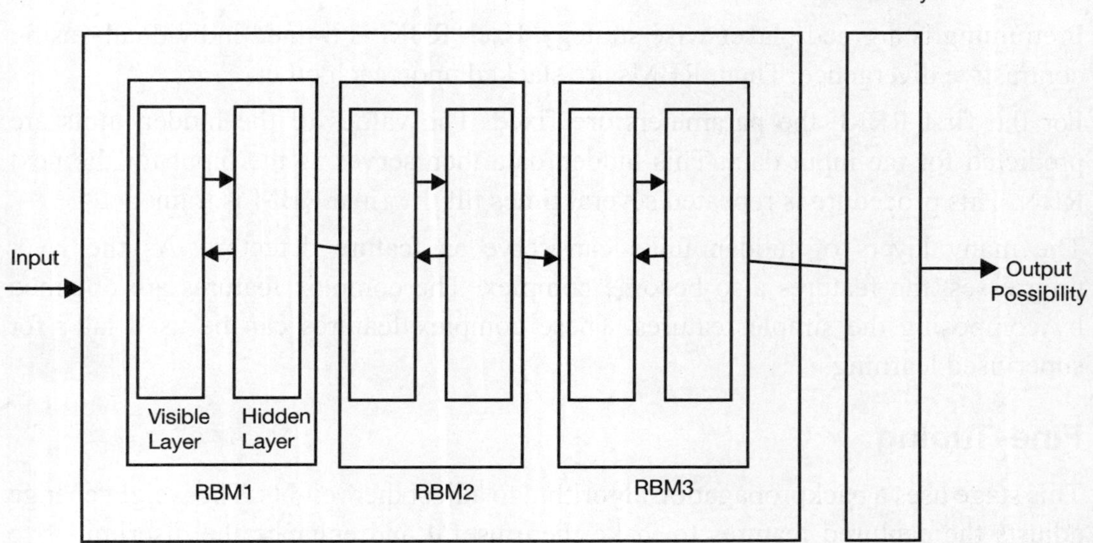

Figure 17.12 Deep Belief Networks

One can visualize Figure 17.13 as a neural network as below. It can be observed that the links are bidirectional.

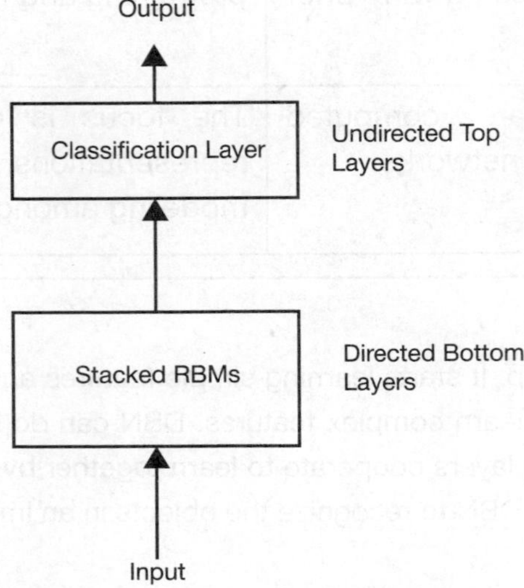

Figure 17.13 Equivalent Neural Network Representation

The DBN training has two steps – Pretraining and Fine-tuning.

Pretraining

Pretraining is a greedy layer-wise strategy. Each RBM is trained individually using contrastive divergence. Then, RBMs are stacked upon each other.

For the first RBM, the parameters are fixed. The values of the hidden units are predicted for the input data. This hidden data then serves as the input for the next RBN. This procedure is repeated several times till the final RBM is trained.

The many layers of hidden units can serve as feature detectors. As the layer progresses, the features also become complex. The complex features are obtained by composing the simple features. These complex features can be used later for supervised learning.

Fine-Tuning

This stage uses a backpropagation algorithm to adjust the weights. The weight change adjusts the captured features to make them useful and enhance the discriminative ability. This change in weights is done by minimizing the error. The error is the computed differences between the predicted and actual class.

The classifier may use a softmax layer for creating multiclass labels. Softmax layers learn the joint probability of the features and labels. Fine-tuning is a supervised model that requires labelled data.

After this, test samples can be given to the network and forwarded through the softmax layers.

Deep belief networks can be used as solutions to solve the problems of traditional networks like slow learning. It can find a joint Probability density function and serve as a generative model. The advantages and disadvantages of Deep belief networks are given in Table 17.5.

Table 17.5 Advantages and Disadvantages of Deep Belief Networks

Advantages	Disadvantages
Efficient use of hidden layers.	Deep Belief Networks require a lot of hardware and huge data.
Deep belief networks can be useful for classification and other applications.	Expensive to train.
DBN can handle huge amounts of data.	Complexity is huge.

Summary

1. RBM takes an input and approximates the input data as a probability distribution.
2. Boltzmann machines are unsupervised, probabilistic, and energy-based models.
3. Boltzmann machines implement associate memory.
4. Boltzmann machines have only two layers – Visible and hidden layers.
5. In Boltzmann machines, all nodes are connected to all other nodes.
6. Boltzmann machines can solve both learning and search problems.
7. In RBM, there is a restriction between connections. There are no inter-layer connections.
8. RBM takes input data and approximates the probability distribution curve of input data.
9. One form of restoration is to approximate the incomplete data to the nearest training vector or the nearest cluster prototype.

10. RBM aims to compute hidden layers from visible layers and vice versa. It aims to find the joint probability distribution of both visible and hidden layers.
11. The probability distribution curve can be mathematically obtained using Gibbs sampling, Kullback-Leibler, and contrastive divergence.
12. RBM can be used as a classifier by augmenting the input vector with its target vector.
13. A DBN is a stack of RBMs and is a probabilistic generative neural network.
14. The training of RBM has two stages – Pretraining and Fine-tuning.
15. DBN can be used as a classifier.

Glossary

1. Boltzmann machines – Boltzmann machines are unsupervised, stochastic machines that take input data and generate the probability distribution curve.
2. Stochastic – It implies that the operations involve random variables and are probabilistic. The operations of a stochastic machine are random.
3. Associative memory – It is where information can be accessed using its parts or keys.
4. Visible layer – A visible layer is a layer of observable nodes.
5. Hidden layer – A hidden layer is a layer of nodes that are not observable.
6. Symmetric weights – The concept of a weight between unit I and unit J is the same as unit J and unit I is called symmetric weight.
7. Learning problem – A technique for learning the important features.
8. Search problem – An optimization problem.
9. RBM – A machine where there is no intra-layer communication.
10. Bipartite graph – The nodes are divided into two subsets, and connections are across the sets.
11. Joint probability distribution – The joint probability of both visible and hidden layers.
12. Deep belief networks – DBN is a network of stacked RBMs.
13. Pretraining – The stacking of pretrained RBMs constitutes the pretraining.
14. Fine-tuning – Fine-tuning is configuring to do a specific task, say by adding an extra softmax layer for classification.

Short Questions

1. What is a Boltzmann distribution?
2. What is an associate memory?
3. How is RBM different from autoencoders?
4. How are RBMs trained?
5. What is DBN?

Long Questions

1. Explain in detail the training procedures for RBM.
2. Explain in detail the DBN-Based classifier.

Crossword

Across

1. The RBM are ________ (Stochastic / Deterministic) machines.
8. RBM is a special type of autoencoder. (true/false)
9. Boltzmann machines are named after ________ Boltzmann. He was an Austrian physicist.
11. Boltzmann machines are ________ models.
14. The term energy is related to ________ of the system.
15. RBM cannot learn the hierarchical features. (true/false)
18. RBM is also called as ________.
19. The nodes in the BM are divided into ________ and hidden units.
20. The purpose of RBM is to learn the probability ________ function.
22. DBN is a ________ model.

23. The advantage of stacked RBM is layer-wise training. (true/false)
24. Stacked RBM and DBN are the same. (true/false)

Down

2. The focus is to form joint probability density function of visible and _______ units.
3. DBN can be used for collaborative filters. (true/false)
4. RBM can be used for _______, feature learning, collaborative filter, and dimensionality reduction.
5. RBM is effective in learning data representations. (true/false)
6. The Restricted Boltzmann machines look like a _______ structure.
7. RBM uses _______ learning.
10. RBM can handle _______ data.
12. The idea of retrieving data using key or partial information is called _______ memory.
13. RBM can handle _______ data.
16. BM can solve learning and _______ problems.
17. Contrastive _______ is a modification of Gibbs sampling.
21. The word "belief" refers to probabilistic learning and inference. (true/false)

Jumbled Sentences

```
P X Y K G R T O U O D E N S I T Y D C C T L Z K B
J I P U V K Q S G I C Z N O D A Q L U D W I G P M
D B X C E T Q H D I B I P A R T I T E U Y C H E P
O W Q S T V R D B Q N X I O Z N T K I T R U E C S
X J L A I S E A R C H Z Z G E N E R A T I V E B R
G A H A R M O N I U M K T T R U E S T A T E E J D
F L H S B O D P C V Q P Z M C A N P X I J M F L Y
H O C X N Y I N C O M P L E T E F E Q E M U F A J
W S K Q A S S O C I A T I V E H I D D E N M C S M
O I H K T Y Q G V C L A S S I F I C A T I O N W C
I F I H S V I S I B L E Y P C F A L S E J Z K F Y
O P Y Z F L E A A J G E N E R A T I V E S C G R E
P J X U A U T R U E W U N S U P E R V I S E D U O
X X L S R Z O G M U L T I M O D A L R J D T R V D
R H G T F A T U M L J H P U Z F C J A U S T J T U
K C T S X Z E C H Z J N O D W D I V E R G E N C E
O U G D D S T O C H A S T I C F M D U A Z L R Y J
```

Ludwig	unsupervised	stochastic	bipartite	visible	state
hidden	density	generative	associative	harmonium	search
true	classification	incomplete	true	true	false
multimodal	divergence	generative	true	false	true

CHAPTER 18

Deep Reinforcement Learning

Reinforcement learning is the closest thing we have to a plausible model of how humans and animals learn. — **David Silver**

Credits: © David Silver

Reinforcement learning is a branch of machine learning. Reinforcement learning is a type of machine learning where an agent interacts with the environment to learn. Learning is the interaction of the agent with the environment, and the agent learns by performing actions to maximize the rewards. The agent interacts with the environment, receives feedback, and adjusts the actions based on the rewards. In deep reinforcement learning, the deep neural networks are combined with reinforcement learning. There are many applications of reinforcement learning, such as games, robotics, and resource management. This chapter aims to provide the basics of reinforcement learning.

Learning Objectives

- Overview of reinforcement learning.
- Learn the basics of Markov decision process.
- Know about model-free methods.
- Introduce Q-Learning algorithm.
- Understand deep Q-Network (DQN) algorithm.
- Understand the need for policy gradient methods.
- Know about the REINFORCE algorithm.

18.1 Overview of Reinforcement Learning

Reinforcement Learning (RL) mimics human beings. Humans interact with the environment to get information through our sensory organs. The senses of humans are vision, hearing, taste, smell, and touch. For example, through our eyes, humans get visual information. The brain processes this input visual information for processing. This processing leads to actions and decision-making.

Reinforcement learning is one branch of AI closest to what humans do. Reinforcement learning is a branch of machine learning that deals with agents learning by performing actions to maximize the rewards. An agent can be a human or a program. The agent interacts with the environment, receives feedback, and adjusts the actions based on the rewards. A positive reward would reinforce the agent's behaviour (Such as awards encourage one student to study harder) and a negative reward (such as punishments) deter the agent from avoiding the behaviour.

The similarities of reinforcement learning and the human beings are listed below:

(i) Both human beings and machines learn by trial and error. Human beings perform an action and by observing the consequences of actions, learn. Similarly, the machines learn by observing the rewards and penalties.

(ii) Both human beings and machines adjust strategies based on feedback.

(iii) Both human beings and machines are goal oriented. Humans maximize rewards or minimize pain to select actions. In the same manner, the machines maximize the rewards over a longer period to learn.

The history of Reinforcement learning is given in Box 18.1.

Box 18.1 History of Reinforcement Learning

Reinforcement learning is one of the major subareas of machine learning. It is a domain that draws inspiration from many areas like computer science, psychology, neuroscience, and control theory.

The origin of reinforcement learning started with the trial-and-learning algorithm in the 1950s. The major motivation is dynamic programming proposed by Richard Bellman. The earliest RL machine designed was MENACE by Donald Mitchie.

Richard Sutton and Andrew Barto formulated the TD learning method. In 2010, a Deep Q learning algorithm was proposed.

A major revival in reinforcement learning started in 2015. Mnih et al. of DeepMind used Deep-Q Networks (DQN) for Atari games. A major boost came in 2016 when AI agent AlphaGo made history by beating the GO champion Lee Sedol in a complex game of GO with a score of 4-1. This event marked a revival of interest in reinforcement learning. In 2016, DeepMind used the AlphaGo Zero agent without any human training to beat AlphaGo with a score of 100-0.

The gaming domain remains a popular domain in reinforcement learning because games have some standard fixed rules. It is also easy to simulate games.

Deep Reinforcement Learning (DRL) combines deep learning and reinforcement learning principles, enabling an agent to learn using trial-and-error algorithms. Deep neural networks are used to approximate the functions to decide actions that can maximize the rewards.

The application of reinforcement learning is given in Box. 18.2.

Box 18.2 Applications of Reinforcement Learning

There are many applications of RL. Some of the application domains where reinforcement learning is used are listed below:

- Industrial automation
- Personalized news recommendation systems
- A/B testing of websites
- Customized applications
- Driverless cars
- Games like chess and Go
- Planning of travel itinerary
- Scheduling of jobs

18.2 Components of Reinforcement Learning

The components of Reinforcement Learning (RL) include:

(i) Agents

(ii) Environment

(iii) Actions
(iv) State
(v) Feedback

The components of reinforcement learning are given in Figure 18.1.

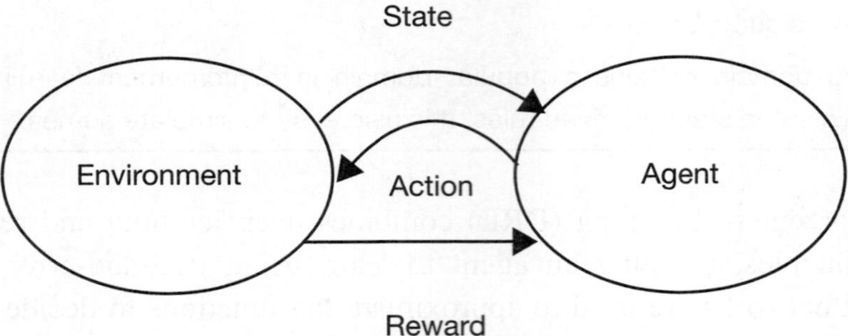

Figure 18.1 Basic Components of RL

1. Agent: An agent is an autonomous body that interacts with the environment and takes action. The agent can be a human, system, or program. One can say the agent is an entity that interacts with the environment. The learning happens with the interaction of the agent with the environment using the trial-and-error method. The agent chooses actions to influence the environment.
2. Environment: The environment is the context where the agent interacts with the environment. It has
   (i) States: A state represents the configuration that the agent can observe. It is statistical information based on that, the agents take a decision. A set of all possible states that the agents can observe is called a state space.
   (ii) Action: An action is a decision or a move by the agent to influence the environment. An action is a decision or choice that an agent can take. The set of all possible actions that the agent can perform is called action space.
   (iii) Dynamics: The rules and mechanisms that govern how the system can change in response to the agent's action. Transitions capture the state change in response to the action. The transition probability is the probability of moving from one state 's' to another state called (s') while performing an action.
3. Feedback or Rewards

   The reward indicates the performance of the system. Reinforcement learning is reward-based learning, where the rewards reinforce a behaviour. The reward is a function given as r(s, a, s') and is the agent's reward for state transition. The rewards can be positive or negative. The agent is forced to execute similar actions to get the maximum benefits, and negative rewards are a deterrent.

Example 18.1: Consider the simple maze shown in Figure 18.2. The problem is navigating the robot from home to school. Identify the state, actions, and rewards.

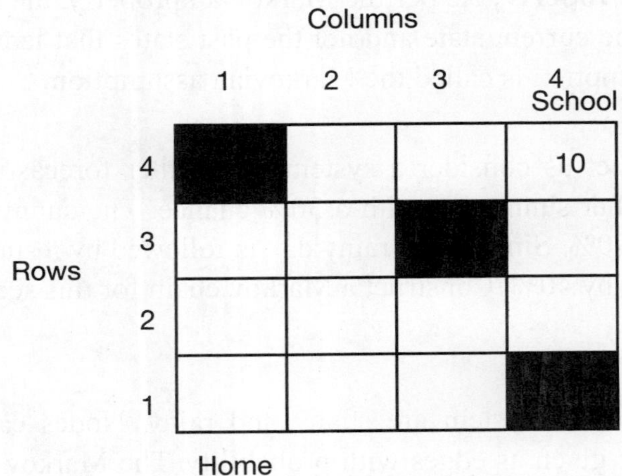

Figure 18.2 **A Simple Maze: Red is the danger zone with a reward of -10, and the Goal state is a reward of +10, with top and right moves carrying a reward of 2 and down and left with a reward of +1.**

Solution:

The robot is the agent. The states of this maze game are the grid or cells. The cells {(1, 1), (1, 2), (1, 3), (1, 4), …, (4, 4)} are states.

The starting state is home (1, 1), and the goal state is school (4, 4).

The actions can be – up, down, right and left. The reward of red is –10, and the goal is +10. The actions top and right are 2, and the down/left is 1.

18.3 Markov Decision Model

Markov Decision Process (MDP) is a mathematical framework to model the environment for the decision-making process to make decisions under uncertainty. The main purpose of the model is to formulate a reinforcement problem in terms of states, actions, transitions, and rewards. Then, by using the model, an optimal policy can be obtained by maximizing the returns. MDP is an extension of the Markov chain or Markov process. Markov models are named after Andrey Markov. The key features of the Markov chain are:

(i) **States:** The environment is modelled as finite and infinite states.

(ii) **Transition Probability:** Transition probability is the probability of moving from one state to another. The transition probability matrix for a system represents the dynamics of the environment.

(iii) **Markov Property:** As per the Markovian property, the future state depends only on the current state and not the past states that led to the current state. This assumption is called the Markovian assumption.

Example 18.2: Let us consider a system of weather forecasting. A sunny day is followed by another sunny day with a 30% chance. The sunny day is followed by the rainy day by 70%. Similarly, a rainy day is followed by a sunny day by 60% and another rainy day by 40%. Construct a Markov chain for this scenario.

Solution

The two states of the system are sunny and rainy. Nodes can represent it. The transitions can be given as edges with probability. The Markov chain for the above scenario can be given in Figure 18.3.

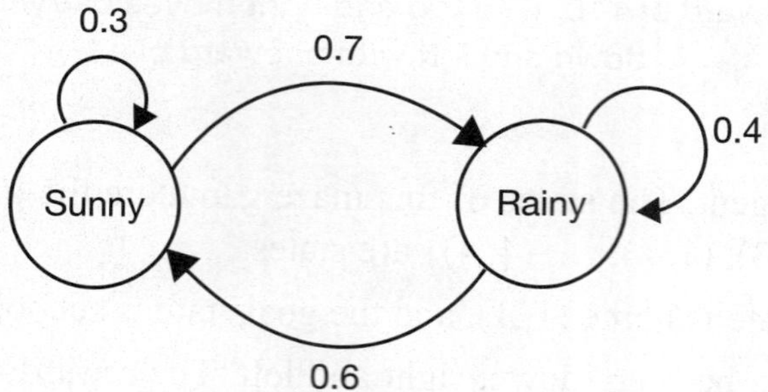

Figure 18.3 Markov Chain

The transition probability matrix can be given as a matrix also as shown in Table 18.1.

Table 18.1 Transition Probability Matrix

	Sunny	Rainy
Sunny	0.3	0.7
Rainy	0.6	0.4

Markov reward model is an extension of the Markov chain where, in addition to the state transitions, rewards can be assigned. The key components of the Markov reward model are states, transition probabilities, and rewards.

Markov decision process is another extension of Markov reward process. It is used for modelling decision-making where the outcome is partly random and partly under the control of the agent. The key components of the Markov decision process are the states, actions, transition probabilities, rewards, and policy.

So, a model is the mathematical representation of the system dynamics that help to determine the future states and rewards.

A simple learning algorithm in reinforcement learning is given, as shown in Figure 18.4.

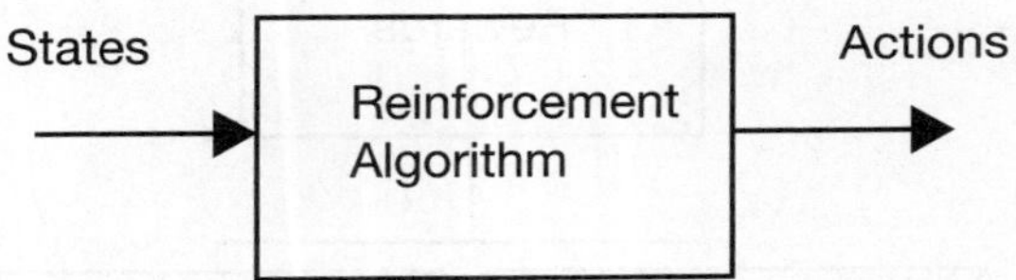

Figure 18.4 Input and Output of a Reinforcement Learning Algorithm

The inputs of the RL algorithm are state or state variables. The output of the RL is the program's actions. The algorithm that maps the input states to actions, the program/algorithm, is called a policy. The learning algorithm is a method used to improve the policy or value over time based on the rewards. One can consider the equivalent of an algorithm as policy.

A policy is a strategy that determines the behaviour or decision-making of an agent. A policy can be a rule or strategy that maps the states to actions. Its purpose is to govern the behaviour of the agent in the environment. The agent takes action based on the strategy and the current state of the environment. The policies are of two types. They are shown in Figure 18.5.

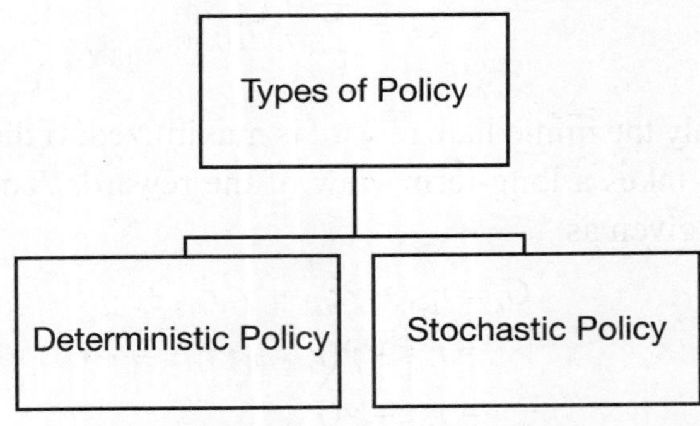

Figure 18.5 Types of Policies

In deterministic policy, the strategy specifies a single action that needs to be taken. Mathematically, a deterministic policy is given as $\pi(s) = a$. Here, s is the state, and a is the action.

In stochastic policy, the policy has a choice of many actions and the probability of selecting an action. It can be represented as $\pi\left(\frac{a}{s}\right) = P\left(A = a/_{S = s}\right)$ where $\pi\left(\frac{a}{s}\right)$ is the probability of taking an action 'a' in state 's.'

Rewards are associated with state-action pairs. The reward is the benefit or cost associated with each transition. The rewards are of two types, as shown in Figure 18.6.

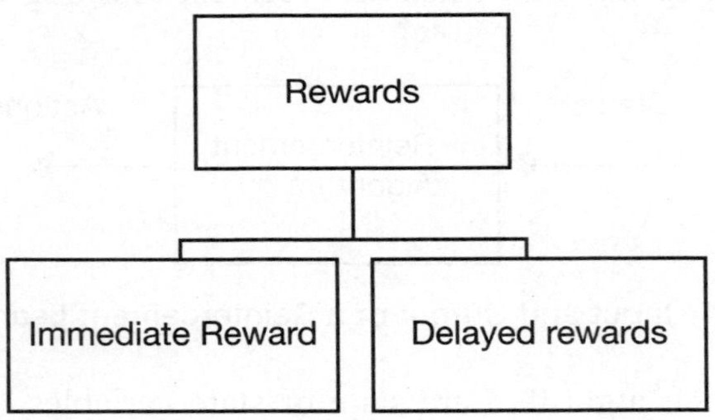

Figure 18.6 Types of Rewards

Immediate rewards are rewards that come after the execution of an action. Delayed rewards occur in the future only, for which the agent should balance short-term and long-term strategies. The return is the sum of all rewards. It is given as

$$G_t = r_{t+1} + r_{t+2} + \cdots + r_\tau$$

A discount factor can discount the rewards (γ). The return is given now as

$$G_t = \sum_{k=0}^{\tau-t-1} \gamma^k r_{t+k+1} .$$

If γ is zero, then only the immediate reward is maximized. If the factor γ approaches zero, the algorithm takes a long-term view of the rewards. The rewards in terms of discount factor are given as

$$\begin{aligned} G_t &= r_{t+1} + \gamma r_{t+2} + \gamma^2 r_{t+3} + \cdots \\ &= r_{t+1} + \gamma(r_{t+2} + \gamma r_{t+3} + \cdots) \\ &= r_{t+1} + \gamma G_{t+1} \end{aligned}$$

The above relation is the recurrence relationship between G_t and G_{t+1}.

Example 18.3: let γ be the discount factor be equal to 0.3. Let us assume that the reward sequence is given as $r_0 = 3$, $r_1 = 4$, $r_2 = 2$ and $r_3 = 1$. Compute the total reward where a factor of discounts the future rewards γ.

Solution:

The total reward is given as

$$\begin{aligned}\text{Reward} &= r_0 + \gamma r_1 + \gamma^2 r_2 + \gamma^3 r_3 \\ &= 3 + (0.3) \times 4 + (0.3)^2 \times 2 + (0.3)^3 \times 1 \\ &= 3 + 1.2 + 0.18 + 0.027 = 4.407\end{aligned}$$

The following example illustrates the reinforcement learning problem formulation.

1. Learning and Update

   The agent learns from experience, collects data, and updates the transitions and rewards—the interaction of an agent with the environment by performing an action and getting a reward. The interaction from the start to the final state (goal or terminal state) is called an episode. The episode is also known as Trajectory and is denoted by τ.

   A return is the sum of the rewards obtained by the agents in an episode.

   The interactions of an agent with the environment are modelled as MDP, which performs the following actions:

   - Observe the current state s_t
   - Performs the action a_t
   - Gets the reward $r(s_t, a_t)$
   - Enters a new state s_{t+1}

   The state transition probability is given as follows:

$$P_{ss'}^{a} = \{s_{t+1} = s' \mid s_t = s, a_t = a\}$$

   It indicates the moving from states to s' after taking an action 'a'. In other words, given a state 's', it is the probability of the occurrence of the next state s'. One can also represent it as a state transition matrix where each row indicates the transition probability from one state to another. The expected value of the reward is given as:

$$R^a_{ss'} = E\{r_{t+1} \mid s_t = s, a_t = a, s_{t+1} = s'\}$$

The agent focuses on maximizing the total rewards accumulated over time called returns.

The following problem illustrates the formulation of a reinforcement problem.

Example 18.4: Consider the following path problem shown in Figure 18.7. The path problem states that an autonomous system should start from city A and reach city D. The goal is reaching city D. List some episodes.

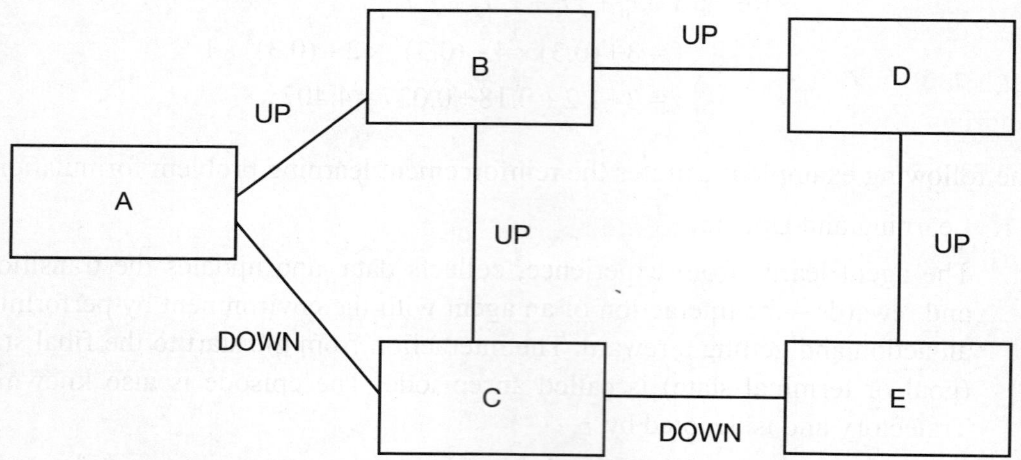

Figure 18.7 A Sample Game with Actions UP and DOWN

Solution:

The states are A, B, C, D, and E. Here, A is the special city where the journey starts. The node A is called "Start" state. The goal node is the final destination or target node given as D.

1. The goal node D is called the terminal node. All other nodes are called non-terminal nodes.
2. Start is the initial state. All other cities are called just states.
3. The action of the game is – up and down.

   An episode starts randomly in a state and explores. Some of the episodes are A-C-B-D, A-B-D, A-C-E-D.

These episodes are known as trajectories also. An episodic task is one where the episodes have a terminal state. A-B-C-D and A-B-D, A-C-E-D are episodic tasks. The continuous task is one where there are no episodes or terminal nodes.

18.4 Dynamic Programming

Dynamic programming is a design strategy proposed by Richard Bellman. Dynamic programming is used to solve the optimization problems. It takes the problem and divides it into subproblems. It uses the principle of optimality. Using the principle of optimality ensures that the computations are done in the best possible way.

Dynamic programming helps to solve model-based reinforcement learning. As discussed earlier, a model is the mathematical representation of the system dynamics that help to determine the future states or rewards. Dynamic programming plays an important role in the value and policy iteration method.

The main advantage of dynamic programming is that.

(i) It uses the solutions of the subproblems so that recomputation is avoided.

(ii) Dynamic programming guarantees to find the optimal solution if the model is known.

18.4.1 Value Iteration

Value iteration estimates *V*(*s*) for every state. *V*(*s*) is the quality or usefulness of how good that state is!

Step 1: This is the first step. Here, *V*(*s*) is determined for every state.

Step 2: This step finds the optimal value.

$$V_{k+1}(s) = \max_{a \in A} \left(\sum_{s'} P\left({s'}/{s,a} \right) \left[R(s,a,s') + \gamma V_k(s') \right] \right)$$

The relationship between *Q* and *V* is defined as the optimal value $V^*(s) = \arg\max_a$ $Q^*(s,a)$.

In the above equation, $V_k(s)$ is the value of the state '*s*,' '*a*' is the action, *s*' is the successor state, $P\left({s'}/{s,a} \right)$ and is the probability of executing an action a and moving from state *s* to *s*'. The discount factor is γ and $R(s,a,s')$ is the reward obtained after changing from state s to *s*'.

Step 3: The difference between $V(s)$ and $V^*(s)$ is obtained and checked for the convergence. The convergence is done till $V(s)$ settle into the optimal value.

Step 4: return $V(s)$

The other algorithm is called policy iteration.

In the policy iteration algorithm, there are two stages. One is called policy evaluation, and another is called policy improvement.

Policy Evaluation

Step 1: An initial policy π is determined.

Step 2: Using this policy, determine the value function,

$$v^{\pi}(s) = \sum_{a} \pi\left(\frac{a}{s}\right) \sum_{s'} P\left(s'/_{s,a}\right)\left[R(s,a,s') + \gamma v^{\pi}(s')\right]$$

Here $\pi\left(\frac{a}{s}\right)$ is the probability of taking action 'a' at state s and moving to s' using the policy π.

Policy Improvement

Step 1: In this stage, the existing policy is improved from π to π'.

$$\pi'(s) = \arg\max_{a} \sum_{s'} P\left(s'/_{s,a}\right)\left[R(s,a,s') + \gamma v^{\pi}(s')\right]$$

Step 2: Check whether there is any difference between policies π and π'. If there is more difference, repeat policy evaluation till a stable policy is obtained.

18.5 Model Free Methods

In model-free methods, there is no complete knowledge of the environment. So, there is no model. Learning in a model-free environment is based on the experience through direct interactions with the environment.

The Monte Carlo method is one method that allows to agent to interact with the environment using Monte Carlo simulation methods. The details of the Monte Carlo method are given in Box 18.3.

Box 18.3 Monte Carlo (MC) Method

The interaction of an agent with the environment gains experience. The experience is divided into many episodes. The sequence that starts from the start node to the goal node is called an episode. The Monte Carlo algorithm collects the reward at the end of the episode. The return is calculated as the empirical mean. The return of many episodes divided by the total number of episodes gives the average.

The procedure of the MC algorithm is given below:

Repeat for all episodes

Generate an episode for policy π

Compute the average returns for a state *s* in the episode

Update the returns.

Monte Carlo methods are not that much relevant for the Q-learning algorithm. TD is one of the foundations of the Q-learning method. In TD, one need not wait for the full episode to end. Instead, the knowledge about the environment is updated after each action. TD is an alternative to the MC method and is directly in the Q-learning algorithm (Box 18.4)

Box 18.4 Temporal Differencing (TD) Method

Temporal differencing is a learning method where an agent learns from every step of its actions instead of waiting for the complete action sequence. For example, In the game of chess, the winning or defeat is known only at the end of the game. So, one cannot wait till the end. Instead, one needs to compute the reward at every move. TD learns from the experience at the end of every single step rather than waiting until the end of the episode.

After executing an action, the learning happens by immediately updating the belief about its future. The update is based on its current action experience and its future reward expectations. TD learning of an agent is the difference between "What is expected to happen" and 'What actually happened?" This difference helps to adjust the expectations and decision-making.

This difference is called temporal because the difference involves two different points of time. The difference is the new estimate and the state-action is updated for every step. This difference is called TD error and indicates how the current Q-value deviated from the estimated value.

If TD is high, it is a 'surprise factor' and denotes the highest reward. If TD is less, it represents the 'frustration' factor and denotes the lesser reward. In other words, TD is a sort of 'reward.' It is initially high and slowly gets minimized as it reaches the end of the training when it reaches the final goal.

The temporal difference at time '*t*' is done using the update:

$$TD(s,a) = r(s,a) + \gamma \max_{a'}(Q(s',a') - Q(s,a))$$

Here, *r*(*s*, *a*) is the immediate reward obtained by performing action *a* and $Q(s_{t+1}, a)$ is the estimate of the best action at state s_{t+1} i.e., *s*', and Q(*s*', *a*') is the Q-value of the action a at state *s*. Here, the best action performed at future states discounted by a discount factor (γ) is $\gamma \max_{a'}(Q(s',a') - Q(s,a)$.

TD learning allows us to update values after every step. The advantages of TD learning are as follow:

(i) It lets the algorithm learn optimal policies in complex environments without a model.

(ii) There is no need to wait for a long sequence of actions called episodes.

(iii) TD allows the continuous learning of the agent and adjusts its strategy after each action.

18.6 Q-Learning

Q-learning is an off-policy method. Here, "*Q*" refers to the quality or quality of action. Each action at a particular state is indicated by a quality of value called Q-value. Q-learning algorithm is a model-free algorithm that aims to learn the value of an action in a state' *s*' and returns the actions that must be performed to maximize the cumulative reward. Q-learning algorithm is useful when a model is unavailable, if the model dynamics are unknown, or if the environment is too complex. Q-learning does not need any model; it indirectly learns the optimal policy by learning the best actions.

In reinforcement learning, the estimation of every action is carried out. This estimation of Q enables the agent to pick the best actions to be carried out as the agent learns the best strategy to maximize the cumulative rewards.

The steps of the Q-learning algorithm are as follows:

The first step is the constriction of a Q-Table. Q-Table is the fundamental concept designed to store and update the Q-values. The focus of Q-Table is to store the knowledge of the agent about the environment. Q-value is the total reward an agent is expected to get by acting on an optimal policy. The rows of the Q-Table are the states and the columns are actions that an agent can choose. The intersection of row and column is called a cell. Each cell stores a Q-value of a state and action, which indicates the expected future rewards for taking an action 'a' by following the optimal policy. Q-Table is shown in Figure 18.8.

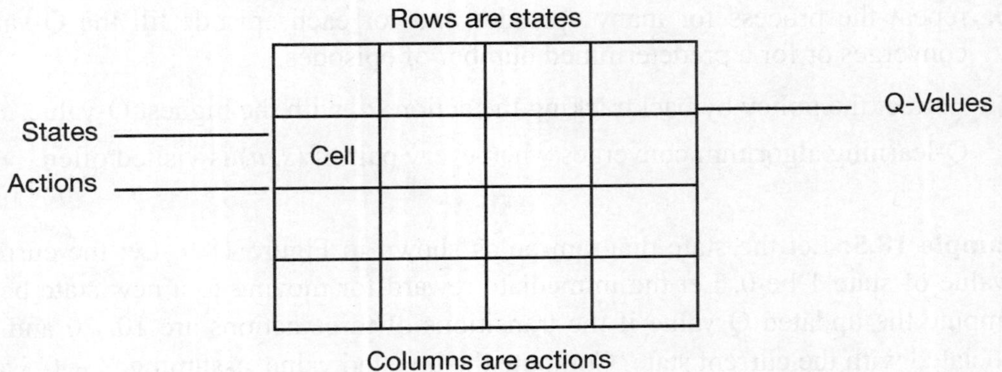

Figure 18.8 Q-Table

The Q-Table is consulted whenever an agent needs to do an action. The agent picks an action associated with the maximum Q-value (Exploitation) or a random action (Exploration) to discover new information.

The Q-learning algorithm is given as follows:

18.6.1 Algorithm Q-Learning

1. Initialize the Q-values $Q(s_t$, a) for all state-action pairs (s, a) to zero or a small random number.
2. Use an epsilon-greedy algorithm to choose an action "a" from state "S" using the current value. The performance of the action "a" leads to a new state s' and fetches the reward r.
3. Update the Q value as shown below:

$$Q(s,a) = Q(s,a) + \alpha[r + \gamma \max_{a'}(Q(s',a') - Q(s,a))]$$

This equation is equal to

$$Q(s,a) = Q(s,a) + \alpha \times TD(s,a)$$

Here α is the learning rate, r is the reward of choosing an action at state s, γ is the discount factor, and $\max_a(Q(s',a'))$ is the maximum Q-value. It is between 0 and 1. If α is zero, nothing is updated, and there is no learning. The learning happens fast when setting it to a higher value, such as 0.9. γ is the discount factor. It is in the range 0–1. It should be less so that the algorithm can converge.

4. update the state: set the current state $s = s'$
5. repeat the process for many episodes and for each episode till the Q-value converges or for a predetermined number of episodes.
6. Extract the policy by backtracking the action '*a*' with the highest Q-value.

Q-learning algorithm converges when every pair of (*s*, *a*) is visited often.

Example 18.5: Let the state diagram be as shown in Figure 18.9. Let the current Q value of state 1 be 0. Let the immediate reward for moving to a new state be 5. Compute the updated Q value if the transitions of three actions are 10, 20 and 25 associated with the current state. Compute the updated value, assuming $\gamma = 0.5$ and the learning rate ($\alpha = 1$.)

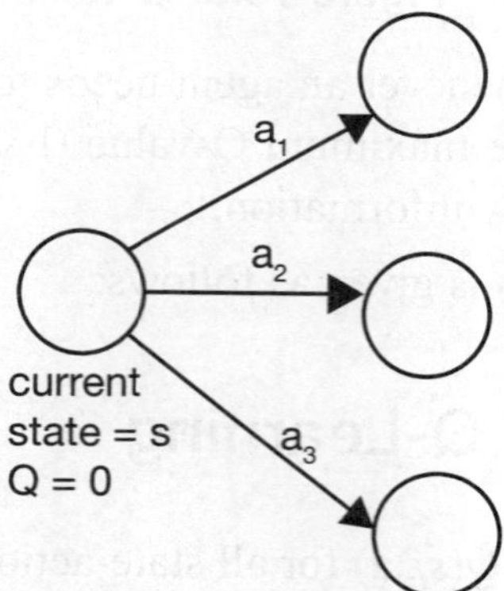

Figure 18.9 State Diagram

Solution:

The current value of Q is 0. So, $Q_{old}(s,a) = 0$. The updated value would be

$$Q_{new}(s,a) = Q_{old}(s,a) + \alpha((R + \gamma \times \max_{a'}(s',a')) - Q_{old}(s,a))$$

The maximum reward is max (10, 20, 25) = 25. So, the updated Q value is

$$Q_{new}(s,a) = 0 + 1 \times ((5 + 0.5 \times 25) - 0) = 17.25$$

18.7 Deep Q-Network (DQN)

Deep Q-Network learning combines the concept of Q-learning with deep neural networks. Q-learning is ineffective if the number of states and actions is large, as it would be difficult to construct a Q-table. The larger table creates two problems.

(i) The amount of memory for saving and updating is increasing exponentially.

(ii) The amount of time is quite large and unrealistic.

So, the idea is to replace the Q-learning algorithm with neural networks.

The essential components of Deep Q-Network are listed below:

1. There are two neural networks. One is called a predictor network, and another is called a target network.
   a. Predictor network: This network aims to approximate the Q-function. So, the idea is to replace the table using a network—the input and output of the Deep Q-Network illustrated in Figure 18.10.

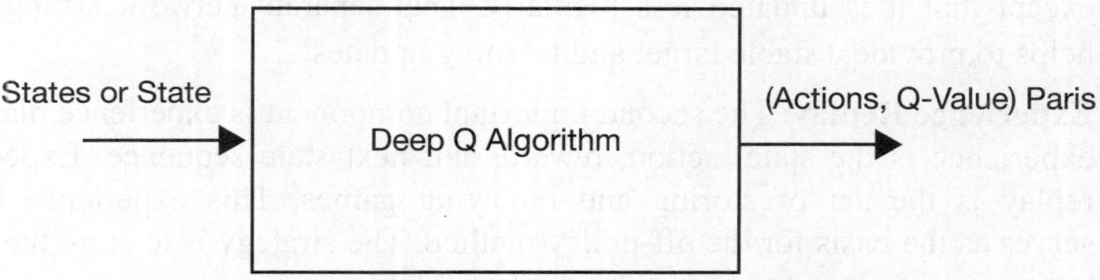

Figure 18.10 Input-Outputs of Deep Q Algorithm

   The input is the state(s) or observations from the environment, and the output is the set of all possible actions. This network is doing exactly the basic Q-algorithm in reinforcement learning.

   b. Target Network: The problem associated with the above equation is the non-stable (or moving target). This moving target is mainly because the same network is computing the predicted and target values. One can use two networks to solve the problem. The first network, a target network, predicts the target value, and a prediction network predicts the value.

   This arrangement is shown in Figure 18.11. The main and target networks can be constructed using dense layers with ReLU activation functions.

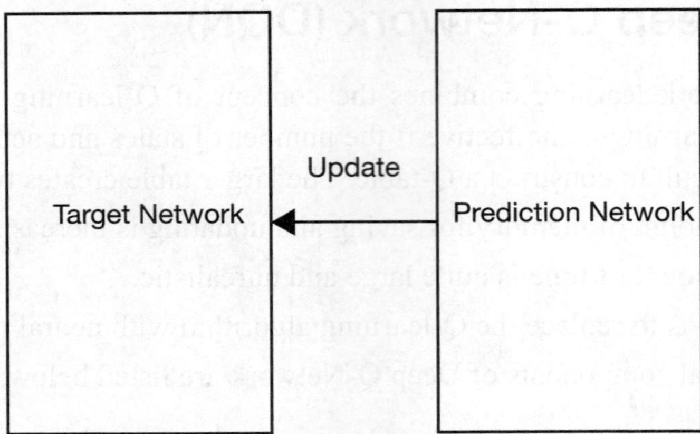

Figure 18.11 Relation Between Target and Prediction Network

The parameters from the prediction network are copied to the main network periodically for every *C* iteration.

The architecture of the target network is the same as the predictor network, except that it is updated less regularly. This separate network arrangement helps to provide a stable target and learning updates.

2. **Experience Replay:** The second important component is experience play. The experience is the state, action, reward, and next state sequence. Experience replay is the act of storing and replaying games. This experience replay serves as the basis for the off-policy method. The strategy is to store the agent experiences as $e_t = (s_t, a_t, r_t, s_{t+1})$ in a larger table.

   The aim is to increase the sampling efficiency and to update the parameters using saved and stored information by breaking the correlation between the successive samples. The removal of the correlation leads to more stability. Deep-Q learning helps in speeding up the process.

3. **Loss Function:** The loss function is the difference between the predicted Q-values (Predictor network) and the target (Target network). The loss function is mostly mean square error or the difference.

4. **ε-greedy:** The algorithm used to select action is epsilon-greedy. If the ε value is less, the algorithm tries new actions, which is called exploration. If the ε value is 1, only the known action is taken, which is called exploitation. The scenario of exploration and exploitation is given in Box 18.5.

5. The hyperparameters used are – the reward discount factor (γ) that balances the short and long-term benefits and the other parameter is the learning rate α.

Box 18.5 Exploration and Exploitation Tradeoff

Exploration is trying out different combinations of actions to get more knowledge. This knowledge is about actions and associated rewards and thus helps agents evolve an optimal strategy. The negative side of the exploration is inefficient learning, as it may lead to suboptimal actions.

Exploitation is the leveraging of knowledge to maximize the rewards. The highest rewarding strategies are chosen that help to enhance efficiency. However, the disadvantage is that much useful knowledge is missed because of a lack of exploration. This tradeoff is important.

ε-greedy algorithm is used as a tradeoff between exploration and exploitation. The ε-greedy algorithm uses a small probability ε to choose a random function and with the probability 1-ε to take greedy action. Mathematically, this algorithm can be shown as

$$a = \begin{cases} \text{argmax}_a\, Q(a) & \text{with probability } 1-\varepsilon \\ \text{random actions} & \text{with probability } \varepsilon \end{cases}$$

The final algorithm is given as follows:

1. Input states and observe Q. This is for all actions.
2. Use ε-greedy strategy and select a random action. The algorithm ε-greedy can choose a random action with $\varepsilon < 1$. The algorithm exploits the best action when ε is 1.

$$a = \arg\max(Q(s,a))$$

3. Perform the action in state s to state s' to get the reward. Form a tuple $\langle s,a,r,s' \rangle$. For many episodes, the tuples would be formed.
4. Create a replay buffer and store all $\langle s,a,r,s' \rangle$ in this buffer.
5. Use the random k-mini batches to sample and compute the loss function. The loss is the squared difference between the target Q and predicted Q.
6. Perform the gradient descent with respect to network parameters to minimize the loss and update the network parameters θ.
7. Freeze the target neural network parameters for some time. Then, after "C" iterations, update the target network parameters with the actual network parameters.
8. Repeat the steps for the predefined number of episodes.

18.8 Policy Gradient Methods

The focus of the policy gradient algorithm is to encourage good policies and discourage bad policies. The initial policy is taken, and the game is played using the policy. Then, some random actions are carried out. The actions are evaluated to see whether it is effective. If the policy is good, then the policy is encouraged; otherwise, the policy corrections are carried out, hoping for policy improvement.

Thus, the play, action evaluation, and network parameter update are done repeatedly until the policy is improved over time. The working of a policy gradient algorithm is as follows, as shown in Figure 18.12.

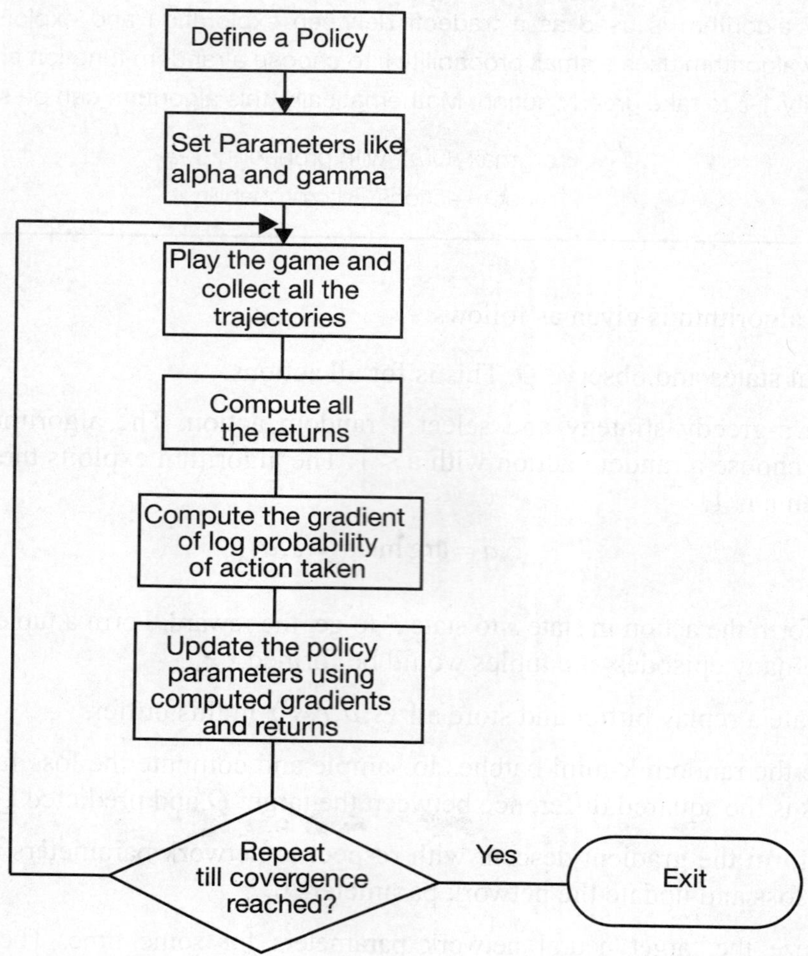

Figure 18.12 Flowchart for Policy Gradient Algorithms

The first step is to define a policy. The neural network defines the policy.

The agent interacts with the environment. The interaction is in the form of state-action-reward. This sequence is called a trajectory. The collection of the trajectories is called experience. This collection is based on the current policy.

The return is calculated from the Trajectory. The return is the sum of the rewards marked by the current time to the end of the Trajectory. The return indicates how good or bad the actions are in the Trajectory. The gradient of the expected return with respect to the policy parameters is computed. For each action, multiply the gradient of the log probability of the action and return. The gradient indicates how many adjustments need to be made based on the return.

The policy parameters are adjusted based on the gradients and trajectory returns to maximize the expected return. This adjustment ensures that actions that carry the rewards are encouraged. This process is repeated till the agent's performance improves over time.

18.8.1 REINFORCE Algorithm

Reinforce is an algorithm that stands for Reward Increment = Non=negative factor X Offset Reinforcement X Characteristic Eligibility. This algorithm improves the policy by adjusting the probability of actions based on the rewards.

Ronald J Williams designed the REINFORCE algorithm. The focus of this algorithm is to maximize the cumulative reward. This maximization is done by adjusting the policy parameters.

Initially, a neural network employs a policy. Then, to enhance the likelihood of actions towards higher cumulative rewards, the policy parameters are updated. This algorithm is an iterative process to evolve a better policy.

1. The first step is to set up an initial policy. This initialization can be done using a neural network or using parametric representation.
2. Collect the trajectories.
3. Determine the returns.
4. Compute the log-likelihood gradient to determine the gradient of the anticipated returns about the policy parameters.
5. Update the parameters so that the returns are higher.
6. Repeat Steps 2-5 till convergence.

Summary

1. Reinforcement learning is a kind of machine learning where the agent learns from the interactions with the environment.
2. Deep Reinforcement learning combines deep neural networks with the concept of reinforcement learning.
3. The environment is the framework that specifies the input, output, and rewards. The input of a reinforcement algorithm is states, and outputs are actions.
4. A specific configuration or situation of the environment is called a state.
5. The actions are outcomes or decisions or decision choices. The algorithm takes the input states, processes them, and outputs an action. The equivalent of an algorithm is called a policy.
6. The reward is a measure of agent performance given by the environment. It can be an immediate reward or a delayed reward.
7. The accumulation of all rewards collected over an action is called total reward.
8. The discount factor is the factor that controls the delaying of rewards.
9. Markov decision process is a mathematical model for specifying the system dynamics.
10. In model-free methods, there is no complete knowledge of the environment. The knowledge is gained. Directly by the agent by interacting with the environment.
11. Temporal differencing is the alternative method to the Monte Carlo method.
12. Temporal differencing measures the difference between expected and actual gain and uses it to update the estimates.
13. Q-learning is an off-policy method and used to update Q-values.
14. The deep Q algorithm combines deep neural networks and a Q-learning algorithm.
15. REINFORCE is a policy gradient algorithm that modifies the policy directly.

Glossary

1. **Environment** – The environment is the framework where the input, output, and reward are specified, and the agent interactions.
2. **State** – A specific configuration of the environment that the agent can observe is called a state.
3. **Agent** – An agent is an entity that interacts with the environment. It can be a human, a robot, or an autonomous program.
4. **State space** – A set of all possible states that an agent encounters.
5. **Action** – An action is a decision or move by the agent to influence the environment.
6. **Action space** – A set of all actions is called an action space.
7. **Output** – The resultant outcome of an RL algorithm is called an action. Actions are decisions or choices.
8. **Dynamics** – The rules and mechanisms that govern how the system can change in response to the agents' actions are called dynamics.
9. Transition – The state change in response to an action is called transition. The transition probability matrix can capture the environment dynamics.
10. **Policy** – Policy is the algorithm equivalent that maps states to actions.
11. **Learning algorithm** – The method used to improve its policy or value over time based on the rewards.
12. **Model** – The mathematical representation of a system dynamics that helps to determine the future states and rewards.
13. **Reward** – The reward is the outcome of an action. The reward measures the quality of the action.
14. **Immediate reward** – The reward that comes after the execution of an action is called immediate reward.
15. **Total future reward** - The sum of immediate reward for a current move and all other future rewards is called total future reward.
16. **Discount factor** – A factor that diminishes the returns.

17. **Markov decision process** – MDP is a mathematical framework representing the environment, agent, and their interactions.
18. **Markov assumption** – Markovian assumption is that the future state/reward depends only on the current state/action.
19. **Model-free methods** – Model-free methods are those without a model.
20. **TD error** – The difference between the estimated gain and the actual gain is called TD Error.
21. **Q-learning** is an off-policy method that computes Q-values to find an optimal policy.
22. **Q** – Q refers to quality or quality of action
23. **Trajectory** – The sequence of state-action-reward is called a trajectory.
24. **Experience** – The collection of trajectories is called an experience.
25. **Experience replay** – The act of storing and replaying games is called experience replay.

Short Questions

1. What is deep reinforcement learning?
2. What are the components of reinforcement learning?
3. Define the terms – discount factor, total reward, total future reward, and returns.
4. Why Markovian assumption is important?
5. What is temporal difference error?
6. What is the role of temporal differencing in Q-learning?
7. Why are Deep Q networks needed?
8. Why are two networks required?
9. What is a policy gradient method?

Long Questions

1. Explain the Q-Learning algorithm in detail.
2. Explain the Deep Q algorithm in detail.
3. Explain the REINFORCE algorithm.

Crossword

Across

3. A statespace is a __________ of all possible states.
6. The difference between estimated and actual gain is called TD error, (true/false)
7. The reward that comes after the execution of the action is called __________ reward.
9. The act of storing and replaying games is called __________ replay.
11. The specific configuration of the environment is called a __________
13. The __________ is the sum of all rewards.
15. The environment is a framework where the input, output, and reward are specified. (true/false)
19. The outcome of a reinforcement algorithm is an __________
20. The purpose of reinforcement learning is to maximize the cumulative rewards, (true/false)
21. An episodic task is one where there is a __________ state.
22. The sum of all immediate rewards from the current move to all future rewards is called __________ future reward.
23. The future depends on the current state and not the past states is called __________ assumption.
24. Markov __________ process is a mathematical framework that represents the states, actions, and interactions.

Down

1. Q in Q-learning refers to__________.
2. The formulation of the problem without the model is called model __________ methods.
4. The focus of the policy gradient algorithm is to encourage good policies and discourage bad policies, (true/false)
5. The discount reward factor is a __________ (hyperparameter/ parameter)
8. The factor that diminishes the returns is called a __________ factor.
10. The collection of trajectories is called an
12. The sequence of state-action-reward is called a __________
14. In continuous tasks, there is no __________ state.
16. The transition probability represents the __________ of the environment.
17. Richard __________ proposed dynamic programming.
18. Q-learning is a __________(offline/ online) policy method to find the optimal policy.
19. A policy function maps states to __________

Jumbled Sentences

A	C	T	I	O	N	T	B	M	A	R	K	O	V	I	A	N	K	B	M	W	E	W	E	B
S	P	D	J	V	Q	B	V	P	B	R	T	T	R	U	E	V	E	I	H	M	U	Z	X	B
T	A	Y	S	Y	D	W	O	C	P	M	T	N	R	I	F	T	S	H	H	G	X	E	P	R
I	F	N	B	G	S	T	F	H	F	T	X	E	Z	A	N	F	T	Y	T	R	U	E	E	I
M	Q	A	Z	T	G	V	T	R	U	E	N	D	S	U	O	U	U	P	F	W	S	X	R	E
M	R	M	T	S	S	D	D	E	C	I	S	I	O	N	P	N	E	E	T	N	Y	N	I	A
E	E	I	N	Q	S	X	L	O	L	N	K	C	S	N	E	Y	X	R	G	Q	N	Q	E	T
D	T	C	D	A	P	A	V	F	A	K	S	L	W	L	R	I	P	P	G	O	I	O	N	Q
I	U	S	D	V	N	O	F	M	T	I	A	Y	A	O	B	A	E	A	Z	X	T	T	C	E
A	R	D	I	I	E	O	L	S	D	T	T	N	T	E	K	K	R	R	F	T	X	R	E	O
T	N	L	M	P	N	L	N	P	O	I	I	C	Q	T	N	J	I	A	T	A	I	U	N	D
E	S	R	I	N	E	O	A	T	L	M	E	Y	U	E	L	S	E	M	I	F	Y	E	U	R
P	E	B	L	B	I	L	J	A	R	J	R	Z	R	I	N	T	N	E	F	L	W	C	X	W
T	H	I	M	T	S	K	U	E	A	A	I	A	U	H	E	A	C	T	D	Z	S	T	K	Y
Y	W	K	C	X	Q	Q	T	R	N	P	C	D	J	D	O	T	E	E	M	N	E	P	R	L
O	I	A	Q	L	A	D	T	H	N	T	Z	L	P	O	Y	E	T	R	B	S	Q	M	S	U
K	R	G	W	F	N	I	D	V	E	C	S	I	P	D	W	M	F	R	E	E	N	U	C	U

true	state	action	actions	immediate
total	discount	decision	Markovian	free
true	offline	quality	trajectory	experience
experience	true	hyperparameter	set	dynamics
true	returns	terminal	terminal	Bellman

Appendix A: Installation of Keras

A.1 How to Install Anaconda on Windows?

Anaconda is an open-source software. The website of Anaconda is www.anaconda.com. It has many packages that are required for deep learning. To implement deep learning projects, one has to install Anaconda. In order to install Anaconda, proceed to the Anaconda site. Check the downloading section. One can use a free download. Find the latest version. It is version 3.12 at the time of writing this book. The initial screen is shown in Figure A.1.

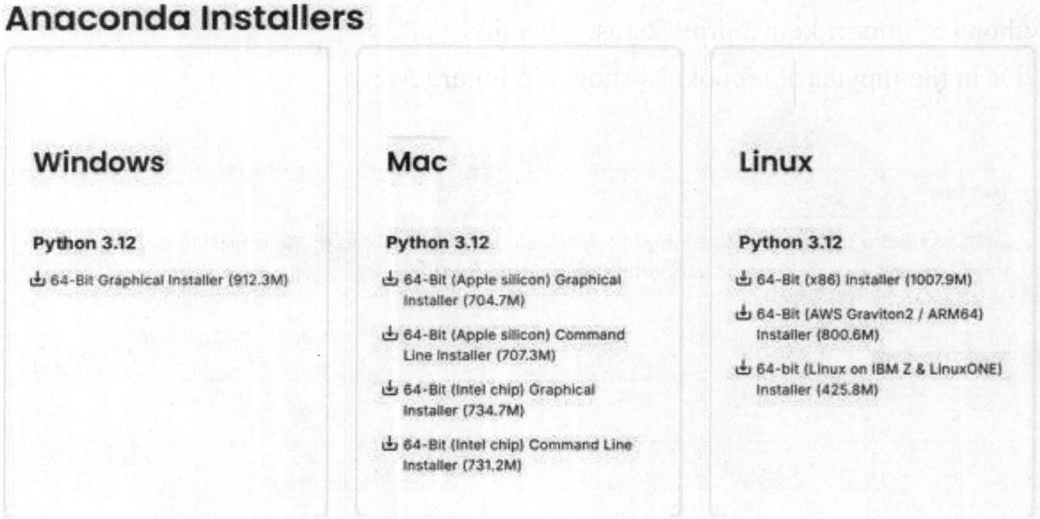

Figure A.1 Download Section

One can install Anaconda by following the instructions.

A.2 Working with Anaconda

Once the installation process is done, One can search for Anaconda Navigator from the Start Menu in Windows.

One important component of the Anaconda environment is the Jypyter Notebook. It can be used for typing programs for deep learning.

The Spyder IDE also can be used to develop deep-learning applications.

A.3 Introduction to Keras

Keras is a powerful Python library for developing deep-learning applications. It runs on the top of TensorFlow. One can easily install keras in Anaconda. The command used is called pip. One can search for anaconda navigator, and in the prompt, one can type

pip install keras

One can check the version of keras on the command line using the anaconda prompt using the following script

python -c "import keras; print(keras.__version__)."

Or in the jupyter notebook, as shown in Figure A.2.

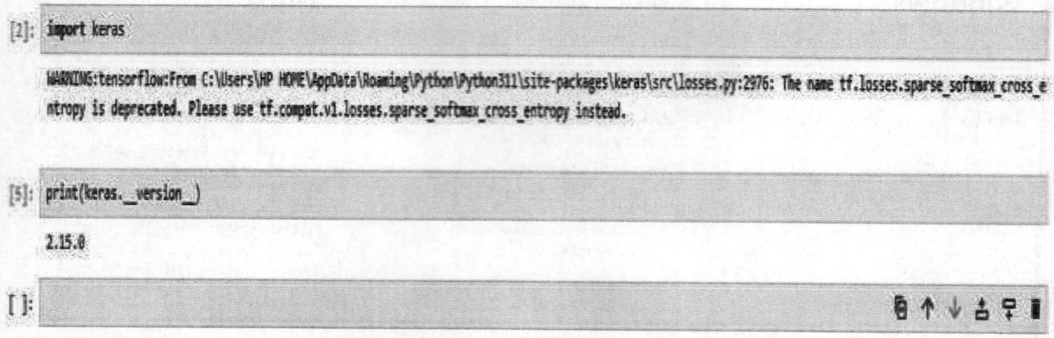

```
[2]: import keras

WARNING:tensorflow:From C:\Users\HP HOME\AppData\Roaming\Python\Python311\site-packages\keras\src\losses.py:2976: The name tf.losses.sparse_softmax_cross_e
ntropy is deprecated. Please use tf.compat.v1.losses.sparse_softmax_cross_entropy instead.

[5]: print(keras.__version__)

2.15.0

[ ]:
```

Figure A.2 Checking the Version of Keras

Credits: © Keras screenshot / © Google

The usage of keras is discussed in the next appendix.

Appendix B: Keras Programming

B.1 Build Deep Learning Models with Keras

One can create deep neural networks using Keras. The five steps of creating a model using keras are given below:

1. Define network.
2. Compile network.
3. Fit network.
4. Evaluate network.
5. Make predictions.

Step 1. Define Network

The first step is to create a neural network using Keras. The deep neural network can be created as a sequence of layers. The creation of a sequential model can be done as follows:

```
model = Sequential()
model.add(Dense(3))
```

The statement model = Sequential() creates a sequential model and model. add(Dense(3)) creates a layer of 3 neurons. Using the model.add, one can specify the activation functions also as

```
Model.add(Activation('relu'))
```

Step 2. Compile Network

One can compile the created keras network using the command as follows:

```
model.compile(optimizer='adam',loss='mean_squared_error')
```

It can be observed that it specifies the optimizer name and error.

Step 3. Fit Network

Once the network is compiled, the training data can be fitted for the model. Let X be the input, and y be the output, then the data can be fit as follows:

```
fitmodel = model.fit(X,y,batch_size=10,epoch=500)
```

It can be seen that the input data is partitioned as batch size 10 and epoch is 500. The execution returns a summary of the model.

Step 4. Evaluate Network

The evaluation of the constructed model is done after the fit of data. One small evaluation is shown below:

```
loss,accuracy = model.evaluate(X,y)
```

The above returns the loss and accuracy of the constructed model.

Step 5. Make Predictions

The following statement uses model.predict to predict the predictions of the new data. The syntax is given as follows:

```
predictions = model.predict(X)
```

The lab manual illustrates the usage of keras for developing useful programs for deep learning.

Bibliography

1. A. Géron, *Hands-On Machine Learning with Scikit-Learn, Keras, and TensorFlow*, 2nd ed. Sebastopol, CA: O'Reilly Media, 2019.
2. A. Glassner, *Deep Learning: A Visual Approach*. San Francisco, CA: No Starch Press, 2021.
3. A. Vaswani, N. Shazeer, N. Parmar, J. Uszkoreit, L. Jones, A. N. Gomez, Ł. Kaiser, and I. Polosukhin, "Attention is all you need," in *Advances in Neural Information Processing Systems*, vol. 30, pp. 5998–6008, 2017.
4. C. C. Aggarwal, *Neural Networks and Deep Learning: A Textbook*. Cham, Switzerland: Springer, 2018.
5. C. M. Bishop and H. Bishop, *Deep Learning: Foundations and Concepts*. 1st ed., New York, UK: Springer, 2023.
6. C. Szegedy, W. Liu, Y. Jia, P. Sermanet, S. Reed, D. Anguelov, D. Erhan, V. Vanhoucke, and A. Rabinovich, "Going deeper with convolutions," in *Proceedings of the IEEE Conference on Computer Vision and Pattern Recognition (CVPR)*, 2015, pp. 1–9.
7. E. Shannon, "A mathematical theory of communication," *The Bell System Technical Journal*, vol. 27, pp. 379–423, 1948.
8. F. Rosenblatt, "The perceptron: A perceiving and recognizing automaton," *Cornell Aeronautical Laboratory*, Report No. 85-460-461, 1957.
9. F. Chollet, *Deep Learning with Python*, 2nd ed. Shelter Island, NY: Manning Publications, 2021.
10. H. J. Kelley, "Gradient theory of optimal flight paths," *ARS Journal*, vol. 30, no. 10, pp. 947–954, 1960.
11. Goodfellow, Y. Bengio, and A. Courville, *Deep Learning*. Cambridge, MA: MIT Press, 2016.

12. J. Devlin, M. W. Chang, K. Lee, and K. Toutanova, "BERT: Pre-training of deep bidirectional transformers for language understanding," *arXiv preprint arXiv:1810.04805*, 2019.

13. J. Goodfellow, J. Pouget-Abadie, M. Mirza, B. Xu, D. Warde-Farley, S. Ozair, A. Courville, and Y. Bengio, "Generative adversarial nets," in Advances in Neural Information Processing Systems, vol. 27, pp. 2672–2680, 2014.

14. J. Krohn, G. Beyleveld, and A. Bassens, *Deep Learning Illustrated: A Visual, Interactive Guide to Artificial Intelligence*. Boston, MA: Addison-Wesley, 2019.

15. J. Redmon, S. Divvala, R. Girshick, and A. Farhadi, "You only look once: Unified, real-time object detection," in *Proceedings of the IEEE Conference on Computer Vision and Pattern Recognition (CVPR)*, 2016, pp. 779–788.

16. K. Simonyan and A. Zisserman, "Very deep convolutional networks for large-scale image recognition," in *Proceedings of the 2nd International Conference on Learning Representations (ICLR)*, 2015.

17. K. He, G. Gkioxari, P. Dollár, and R. Girshick, "Mask R-CNN," in *Proceedings of the IEEE International Conference on Computer Vision (ICCV)*, 2017, pp. 2980–2988.

18. L. A. Gatys, A. S. Ecker, and M. Bethge, "A neural algorithm of artistic style," in *Proceedings of the IEEE Conference on Computer Vision and Pattern Recognition (CVPR)*, 2016, pp. 2414–2423.

19. M. Ekman, *Learning Deep Learning*. 1st ed. Boston, MA: Addison-Wesley, 2022.

20. R. B. Girshick, J. Donahue, T. Darrell, and J. Malik, "Rich feature hierarchies for accurate object detection and semantic segmentation," in *Proceedings of the IEEE Conference on Computer Vision and Pattern Recognition (CVPR)*, 2014, pp. 580–587.

21. R. Girshick, "Fast R-CNN," in *Proceedings of the IEEE International Conference on Computer Vision (ICCV)*, 2015, pp. 1440–1448.

22. S. J. D. Prince, *Understanding Deep Learning*. 1st ed. New York, NY: MIT Press, 2023.

23. S. Raschka and V. Mirjalili, *Python Machine Learning: Machine Learning and Deep Learning with Python, scikit-learn, and TensorFlow 2*, 3rd ed. Birmingham, UK: Packt Publishing, 2019.

24. S. Ren, K. He, R. Girshick, and J. Sun, "Faster R-CNN: Towards real-time object detection with region proposal networks," in *Advances in Neural Information Processing Systems (NeurIPS)*, vol. 28, pp. 91–99, 2015.

25. S. Sridhar, *Design and Analysis of Algorithms*, 2nd ed., New Delhi, India: Oxford University Press, 2014.

26. S. Sridhar, *Digital Image Processing*. 2nd ed., New Delhi, India: Oxford University Press, 2016.

27. S. Sridhar, *Machine Learning., New Delhi, India: Oxford University Press, 2021.*

28. S.Sridhar et al., Python Programming, New Delhi, Pearson Education, 2023.

29. T. Hastie, R. Tibshirani, and J. Friedman, *The Elements of Statistical Learning: Data Mining, Inference, and Prediction*, 2nd ed. New York, NY: Springer, 2009.

30. T. Mikolov, K. Chen, G. Corrado, and J. Dean, "Efficient estimation of word representations in vector space," *arXiv preprint arXiv:1301.3781*, 2013.

31. M. Turing, "Computing machinery and intelligence," *Mind*, vol. 59, no. 236, pp. 433–460, 1950.

32. W. S. McCulloch and W. Pitts, "A logical calculus of the ideas immanent in nervous activity," *Bulletin of Mathematical Biophysics*, vol. 5, pp. 115–133, 1943.

33. W. Liu, D. Anguelov, D. Erhan, C. Szegedy, S. Reed, C. Y. Fu, and A. C. Berg, "SSD: Single shot multibox detector," in *Proceedings of the IEEE Conference on Computer Vision and Pattern Recognition (CVPR)*, 2016, pp. 21–37.

34. Y. LeCun, L. Bottou, Y. Bengio, and P. Haffner, "Gradient-based learning applied to document recognition," *Proceedings of the IEEE*, vol. 86, no. 11, pp. 2278–2324, 1998.

Index

D

G

H

I

M

P

Q

R

S

T

U